MW01050024

THE UNDERGROUND RAILROAD

AN ENCYCLOPEDIA OF PEOPLE, PLACES, AND OPERATIONS

Volume One

Mary Ellen Snodgrass

SHARPE REFERENCE
an imprint of M.E. Sharpe, Inc.

SHARPE REFERENCE

Sharpe Reference is an imprint of M.E. Sharpe, Inc.

M.E. Sharpe, Inc.
80 Business Park Drive
Armonk, NY 10504

Library of Congress Cataloging-in-Publication Data

Snodgrass, Mary Ellen.
The Underground Railroad: an encyclopedia of people, places, and operations / Mary Ellen Snodgrass.
p. cm.
Includes bibliographical references and index.
ISBN 978-0-7656-8093-8 (set: hardcover: alk. paper)
1. Underground railroad—Encyclopedias. 2. Antislavery movements—United States—History—Encyclopedias. 3. Abolitionists—United States—Biography—Encyclopedias. 4. Fugitive slaves—United States—History—Encyclopedias. 5. Slavery—United States—History—Encyclopedias. I. Title.

E450.S65 2007
973.7′115—dc22 2007009199

Cover images (clockwise from upper left corner) provided by: MPI/Stringer/Hulton Archive/Getty Images; Hulton Archive/Getty Images; Library of Congress; General Research & Reference Division, Schomburg Center for Research in Black Culture, The New York Public Library, Astor, Lenox, and Tilden Foundations; Time & Life Pictures/Getty Images; MPI/Stringer/Hulton Archive/Getty Images.

Printed and bound in the United States of America

The paper used in this publication meets the minimum requirements of American National Standard for Information Sciences Permanence of Paper for Printed Library Materials, ANSI Z 39.48.1984.

MV (c) 10 9 8 7 6 5 4 3 2 1

Publisher: Myron E. Sharpe
Vice President and Editorial Director: Patricia Kolb
Vice President and Production Director: Carmen Chetti
Executive Editor and Manager of Reference: Todd Hallman
Executive Development Editor: Jeff Hacker
Project Editor: Laura Brengelman
Program Coordinator: Cathleen Prisco
Editorial Assistant: Alison Morretta
Text and Cover Design: Jesse Sanchez

For Those Who Dared

I was a starving fugitive without home or friends,
and no claim upon him to whose door I went.
Had he turned me away I must have perished.
Nay, he took me in, and gave of his food,
and shared with me his own garments.

Abigail Mott
Narratives of Colored Americans, 1875

The river has its bend, and the longest road must terminate.

Peter Randolph
From Slave Cabin to the Pulpit, 1893

Quakers and Baptists and those of no denomination . . . were all busy operating the mysterious railroad that "ran from Cincinnati to Canada." It was not easy to operate. It jeopardized livelihood. It put life and limb at hazard. But it ran.

J. Saunders Redding
A Scholar's Conscience, 1992

CONTENTS

Volume 1

Volume 2

PREFACE

The Underground Railroad: An Encyclopedia of People, Places, and Operations invites the reader—whether historian, researcher, genealogist, archivist, teacher, librarian, journalist, or general reader—to explore by name and location the small links in a vast American network.

Entry titles, ordered alphabetically, include names, places, documents, themes, publications, and social organizations. Some entries provide information on such topics as the agents who sped slaves like Med Slater, Mammy Chadwick, and Henry "Box" Brown to freedom and the means by which runaways followed the North Star and escaped dog packs and punishment to build new lives. Other entries summarize the labors of individuals and households who ensured runaways safe passage over unfamiliar terrain and offered reliable guidance past bounty hunters to waystations along the Pilgrim's Pathway, the Brown Line, and sea and river routes.

Enhancing the historical data are citations from the personal writings of Louisa May Alcott; speeches by James Miller McKim and the Edmondson sisters; sermons by Henry Ward Beecher and Theodore Dwight Weld; novels by William Wells Brown and Harriet Beecher Stowe; and a host of published documents. In addition, there are court cases, such as that of Castner Hanway and of Charles Turner Torrey; anecdotes from Levi Coffin; and a variety of human-interest stories—the birth of an Underground Railroad passenger at the safehouse of Emily Jane Hunt Grover and Joel Grover and the mock auctioning of Pinky Diggs at the Plymouth Church of the Pilgrims are dramatic instances.

Additional details appear in an outline of Underground Railroad routes and in charts of anti-slavery newspapers, codes, quilt patterns, and leaders of maroon settlements. Photos, bookplates, handbills, and sketches round out this introduction to a complex social response to the enslavement of African Americans.

For ease of use, the entry titles feature the most notable figure or primary focus of the topic—such as John Rankin, the founder of Liberty Hill, a hilltop depot at a major crossing of the Ohio River. Included in the text are the names of spouses, children, and other relatives involved in acts of rescue and concealment.

In some instances, the entry title lists a woman's name first, because she played a more noteworthy role than her husband, as in the case of Priscilla Baltimore. In other instances, a woman's name precedes her husband's when the information about them is the same. Because of the domestic nature of tending and hiding runaways and supplying them with food, clothing, and medical care, an agent's wife is invariably included in the entry title, under the assumption that she played an important, if often unsung, role in maintaining the safehouse, harboring fugitives, and otherwise abetting the Underground Railroad. Entry titles with more than four names appear in family entries that identify both patriarch and matriarch—"Forten (James, Sr., and Charlotte Vandine) Family" and "Lewis (Esther Fussell and John, Jr.) Family." Less important figures are included in the text with their birth and death dates. The *See also* list at the end of many entries identifies other entries that provide further information or general background.

Within a multitude of examples of the people, actions, events, and ideas chronicled in these multifaceted entries are the publication of *Incidents in the Life of a Slave Girl* (1861) and Fanny Kemble's journals, Osborne Perry Anderson's eyewitness account of the raid on Harpers Ferry, a doctor's testimonial to the extreme torture of a Texas slave named Lavinia Bell, the lifework of orator Frederick Douglass and of martyr Elijah Parish Lovejoy, the establishment of the refugee sanctuary Pokepatch in Ohio and of the Colored Sailors' Home in lower Manhattan, rescues on the escape vessels the *Pearl* and the *City of Richmond,* John Brown's proposed subterranean pass way through the Appalachian Mountains, and the organizational skills of John Horse and Wild Cat, the Seminole chiefs who welcomed fugitive slaves as tribe members. Cross-referencing clarifies such details as the facilitators of the "Jerry" rescue and the real name of "Free Frank."

Research materials derive from a wide variety of

sources: personal diaries, coded notes, and the published letters and advertisements that appeared in the era's newspapers, as well as sculpture and painting commemorating American generosity to refugees. Supplementing the main text are the following additional study aids, which are designed to provide an historical framework for the events described and to particularize the volunteers who defied laws that dehumanized black people:

- A chronology presents a 120-year timeline of events that illustrate the humanity of victims and their saviors and the extent of the networking that ensured safe passage from bondage. The span concludes with the passing of the Thirteenth Amendment to the Constitution and with freedmen building new lives in Canadian communities.
- Appendix A offers family trees that involve grandsons and nieces, cousins and in-laws, in the secret network. Among the 72 genealogies are clans such as the Cowleses, Garrisons, Lewises, Motts, Robinsons, and Vickerses. These families passed through three or four generations their treasured ideals of democracy and human decency.
- Appendix B names by state major wayfarers, both slave and free, who escaped and fled along secret routes to communities that valued them as human beings rather than as chattel. Included are the individuals' names, geographical locations, departure dates, and destinations. As the history of some refugees is sketchy, we list together those whose departure points are unknown.
- Appendix C groups the names of conductors by state or province and lists their names, dates, and location, along with the religious affiliations of those for whom faith was the impetus to activism.
- A bibliography presents sources: For further reading, the primary source list includes eyewitness accounts of those involved with the Underground Railroad and the oral testimony of those who either donated their homes and skills to refugees or who benefited from individual kindnesses. The secondary source list recommends to the researcher or librarian other worthy books, periodicals, and Web sites that provide more detailed information.
- A comprehensive index lists people, places, beliefs, laws, titles, social movements, and historical events and milestones, along with specific dates.

I could not have gained the insight to compile this text without valuable advice from archivists, genealogists, historians, and a long list of reference librarians, the backbone of scholarly research. Historical and genealogical societies, college libraries, church and synagogue librarians, the Library of Congress, and specialists in Quaker and black church history clarified muddles and pointed out historical cul-de-sacs. Of particular help were the Latter-day Saints on-line Web site, Family History and Genealogy Records, and the electronic versions of such nineteenth-century newspapers as the *Brooklyn Eagle, The Liberator,* and the *North Star.* Finally, many thanks to my faithful publicist Joan Lail for salient comment and support.

INTRODUCTION

The history of the Underground Railroad, the nation's first civil rights movement, survives in bits and pieces. An examination of the broad outlines of policy and political maneuvering should not be overlook or belittle the humanitarianism of individuals who risked life, property, reputation, and freedom on behalf of black wayfarers in need of respite.

The Participants

An extraordinary range of people, whose motives were as varied as their backgrounds, risked everything to help strangers. Compelled by the philosophies of Abby Kelley Foster, William Lloyd Garrison, Lucretia Coffin Mott, and John Woolman, volunteers like Captain Daniel Drayton and Captain Alfred Fountain engaged in bold acts of civil disobedience to federal laws that required citizens to support slaveholders and federal agents. Perhaps the most overlooked of altruists were women and young people. For example, Anna Murray Douglass and the student body of Oberlin College served the secret network as couriers, cooks, laundresses, seamstresses, nurses, transporters, lookouts, and protectors of liberty.

Whether living in prestigious New England mansions, Vermont and Iowa farmsteads, The Wayside in Massachusetts, or sod huts on the Kansas–Missouri divide, passionate freedom lovers offered their hearths, lofts, cellars, cupboards, and lean-tos to desperate runaways. Three of the lucky, Tice Davids, Eliza Harris, and Eliza's two-year-old son, Harry, fled only steps ahead of armed posses and bloodhounds. Those defenders who came eye to eye with stalkers brandished tongs, coal shovels, corn knives, cudgels, and pots of boiling water. One agent, Sally Hudson of Brown County, Ohio, bit and clawed her attackers until a bullet to the spine felled her.

For the sake of principle, these risk takers jeopardized their families and lost homes, outbuildings, livestock, church memberships, businesses, and savings. Bankruptcy was the fate of Sherman Miller Booth in 1854 for freeing Joshua Glover from a St. Louis jail cell. Another rescuer, Mary Meachum, was sold into slavery in Vicksburg, Mississippi. Overall, freedom fighters survived church riots, front-yard shoot-outs, child snatching, tar and feathering, being burned in effigy, and arson and murder plots—notably, the offer of cash for the assassination of the Reverend John Rankin, the famed stationkeeper at Liberty Hill in Ripley, Ohio.

A few activists died along the way, among them, Seth Concklin, who drowned in the Tennessee River. Others perished in prison or in the hangman's noose, as did insurrectionist John Brown.

A Grand but Informal Network

Historians, genealogists, and archeologists have unearthed evidence corroborating over a century of clandestine slave liberation. Beginning well before the American Revolution, the establishment of safehouses by Mennonites and Quakers such as Catherine White Coffin and Levi Coffin attested to the morality of people who longed to cleanse the nation of human bondage. To choke off the flesh trade, individuals, families, and anti-slavery associations sketched out the beginnings of a relay system that eventually reached from the Canadian provinces of Quebec and Ontario east to the Atlantic seaboard, south to Florida and the Caribbean, and west to frontier enclaves in Kansas, Texas, and Mexico.

Contributing to the successful conveyance of escapees to free territory were carters and wagoneers, maroons of the Great Dismal Swamp, blacksmiths, barbers, disguise makers, roving network agents, spies, undertakers, and security guards. Actions such as fostering of the sick by the Lewis family in Sunnyside, Pennsylvania, and the boarding of the Mendian child Margru, a survivor from the slave ship *Amistad,* by the Porter family in Farmington, Connecticut, supplied interim solutions to the placement of people uprooted by the African diaspora. Through informal or spur-of-the-moment links, rescuers reached out to watermen on canals and rivers, ship captains, physicians, the clergy, gamblers, courtesans, congregations of the African Methodist Episcopal Church, and even American Presidents Millard Fillmore and James Buchanan, Lieutenant Governor John Graves Simcoe of Canada, the British Parliament, and Queen Victoria.

The demands of the Underground Railroad ranged over the whole of human society. One common need of the runaway was footwear, which cobblers and merchants provided. Horse and ox teams, curtained carriages, river steamers, trains, skiffs, and sleighs supplemented the basic mode of conveyance, the slow and dependable hay wagon.

For winter relays, homemakers offered lap robes, shawls, quilts, caps, and baby wraps to protect Southern runaways from the chill of water passage over the Detroit River and Lake Erie and from the snows of Windsor, Ontario, and Halifax, Nova Scotia. Accompanying passengers on quick shifts at waystations were hot pots, napkin-wrapped biscuits and loaves, and pillowcases of apples, potatoes, green corn, boiled eggs, and cheese.

Abigail Goodwin, Lewis Hayden, Gerrit Smith, Lewis Tappan, and other philanthropists footed much of the bill. Dollar by dollar, they collected and disbursed thousands of dollars to board and harbor runaways and to negotiate the purchase of slaves from adamant owners. From some of the beneficiaries came letters in beginner's handwriting thanking all for their gifts.

Attacking the Problem

The vision of Underground Railroad strategists reached beyond the greed of individual flesh peddlers to an unseeing nation that profited from the goods and luxuries that slavery provided. To jolt the complacent, stir controversy, and initiate a change of heart, altruistic writers, editors, and publishers such as Gamaliel Bailey, Lydia Maria Francis Child, Benjamin Lundy, and Jane Grey Cannon Swisshelm operated the presses of the anti-slavery media, a unique segment of American journalism. Start-up journals and handbills of the American Anti-Slavery Society pressed into the public eye the truth about bondage, slave breeding, concubinage, slave pens, auction blocks, and the ripping of black babies from the arms of their parents. Providing backing were the female anti-slavery societies and their annual fairs and organizers—Maria Chapman, Catharine Rugg, Helen Benson Garrison, and others—who raised funds to keep the newspapers solvent and to underwrite the daily bills of William Still, an operative of the Philadelphia Anti-Slavery Society.

Lacking a secure mail-delivery system, strategists of the Underground Railroad communicated with the great human web through the editorials of Horace Greeley, the essays of Henry David Thoreau and Ralph Waldo Emerson, the poems of John Greenleaf Whittier, Mary Ann Shadd Cary's tract "A Plea for Emigration," the sermons of Theodore Parker and Rabbi Leibman Adler, Benjamin Hanby's song "Darling Nelly Gray" and Julia Ward Howe's anthem "The Battle Hymn of the Republic," and the speeches of Cassius Marcellus Clay, Stephen Symons Foster, and Sojourner Truth.

The biography of Harriet Tubman and slave narratives by Leonard Black, Nehemiah Caulkins, Frederick Douglass, and Harriet Ann Jacobs disclosed the hardships that reduced slaves to short-lived drones. One anti-slavery hero, Harriet Beecher Stowe, poured out her loathing of bondage in the fictional melodrama *Uncle Tom's Cabin* (1852), a truth-telling novel that riveted readers throughout North America and Europe.

The Legal Aspect

An elite layer of Underground Railroad operatives consisted of the legal minds among those who wrestled with the Fugitive Slave Law of 1793, the black codes, the Fugitive Slave Law of 1850, the Missouri Compromise, the Kansas-Nebraska Act, the Webster-Ashburton Treaty, and the confiscation laws that emerged during the American Civil War. Demanding justice for black Americans, litigants matched wits with pro-South spokesmen Pierce Butler, Henry Clay, Stephen Arnold Douglas, and Daniel Webster.

Attorneys of the secret network gathered in courtrooms across the land and in Canada and England to require proof of ownership and to intervene against unscrupulous slave owners, informants, scammers, bounty hunters, and lawmen. Such *pro bono* work ennobled some of the prominent legal minds of the day, including John Quincy Adams, Salmon Portland Chase, Richard Henry Dana, Jr., Rutherford Birchard Hayes, Ellis Gray Loring, Samuel Edmund Sewall, and Passmore Williamson.

In the U.S. Congress, libertarians chastised representatives of the plantation South for a form of venality that countenanced torture, sexual bondage, and the perversion of Judeo-Christian scripture to justify a barbarous economic system. One legislator, Charles Sumner, crumpled in the Senate chamber after a Southern opponent caned him into unconsciousness.

Slavery's Last Days

When American slavery's house of cards collapsed under the weight of abolitionism, combat, and a single document—President Abraham Lincoln's Emancipation Proclamation of January 1, 1863—a sophisticated rescue operation continued to function. In the chaos of civil war, ex-slaves could not survive in the milieu of want, combat, and conniving slave owners. As black families struggled to gather information on missing members, Union General Benjamin Franklin Butler, Mary Ann Bickerdyke and Mary Ashton Rice Livermore, two nurses volunteering with the Sanitary Commission, and others like them continued to shelter the weak and oppressed in army tents and to pass over Underground Railroad routes the many individuals in danger of losing their way to liberty. Canadian communities such as the Elgin Settlement and the Refugee Home Society burgeoned with the influx of ex-slaves. Productive workers got a new start in Ontario, Quebec, and the Maritime provinces.

When the South capitulated at Appomattox Courthouse in April 1865, the need for activism shifted to a new height as wanderers from cotton, sugarcane, and tobacco fields made their way north in hopes of reuniting shattered clans. After the Underground Railroad stowed its engines, its conductors and strategists looked toward the next struggle—the equalizing of education and the rewards of citizenship for all Americans.

The Underground Railroad: Routes to Freedom

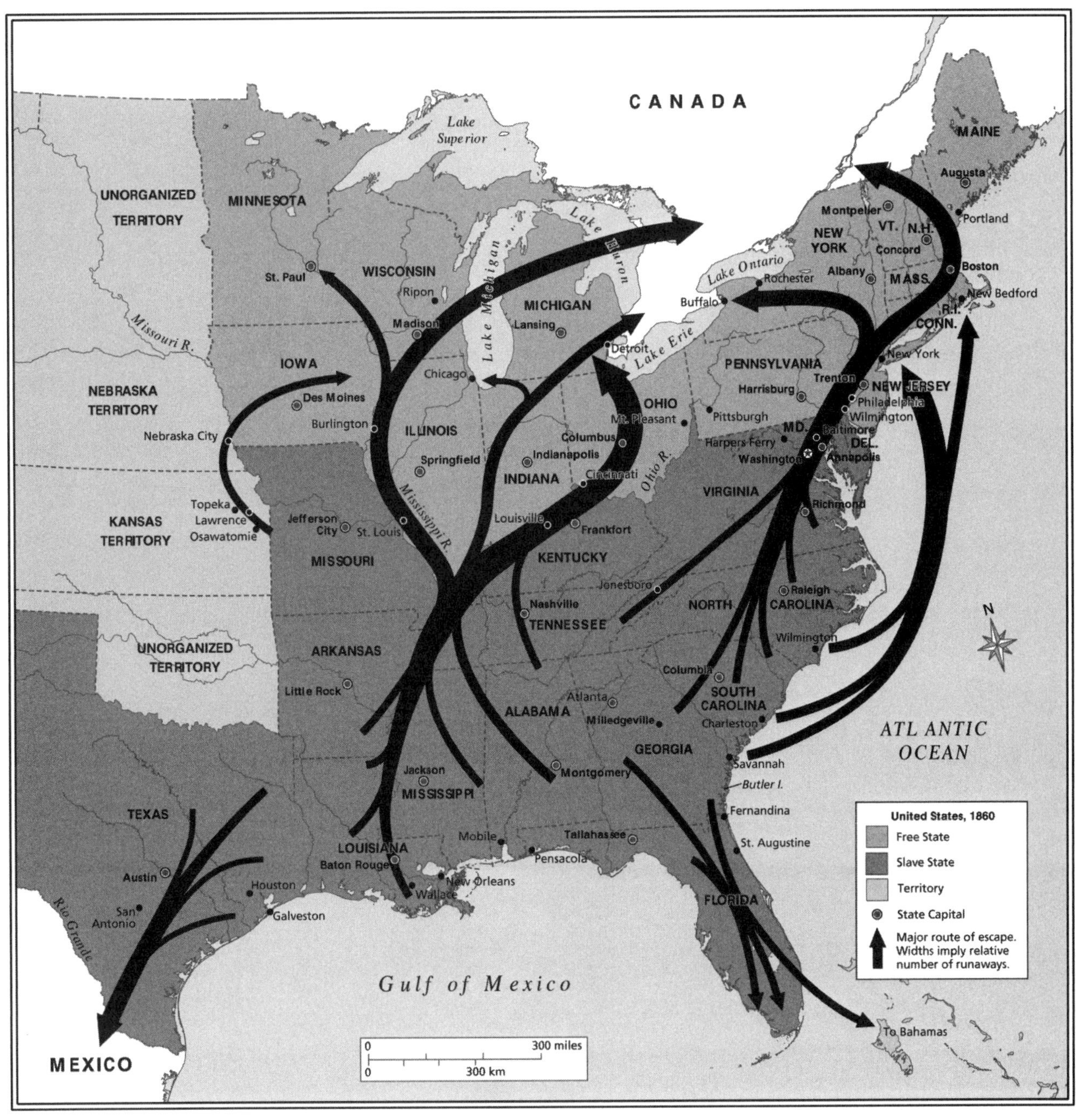

The Eastern Seaboard: Escape and Arrival Points

The Mason-Dixon Line: Notable Stops in Pennsylvania

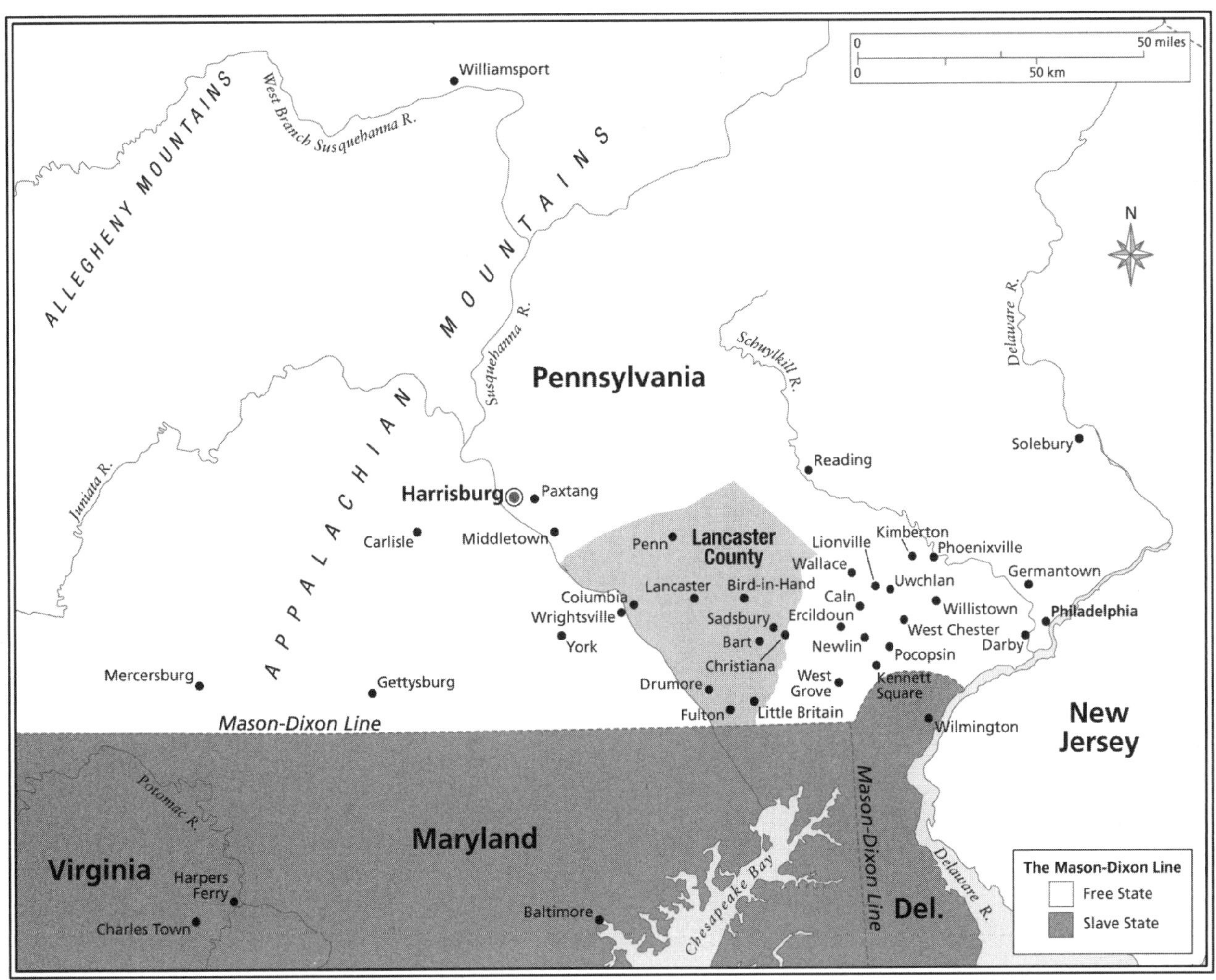

The Great Lakes Region: Crossing Points and Black Settlements in Ontario

The Ohio River Region: Stops and Crossing Points

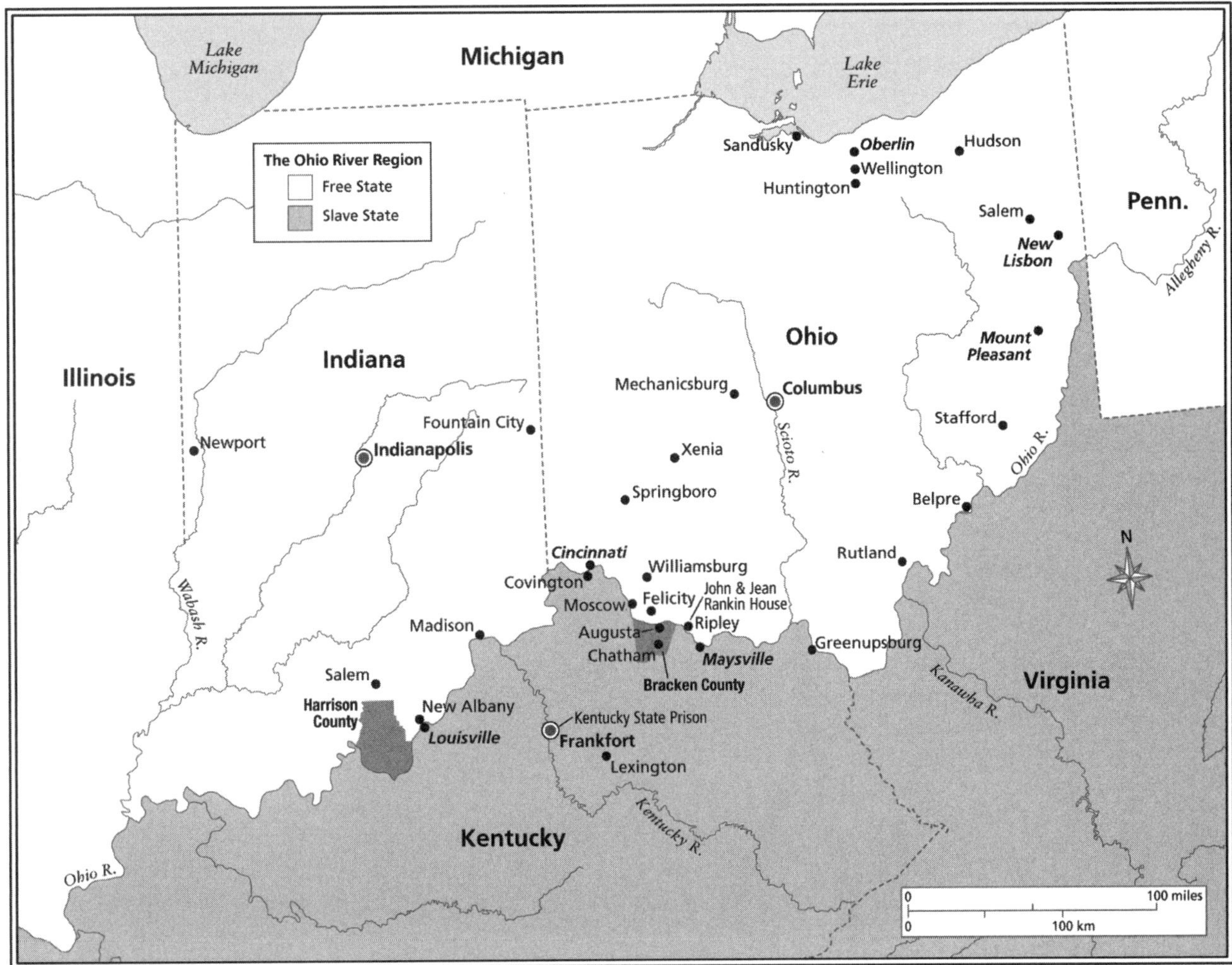

The Florida-Texas-Mexico Route

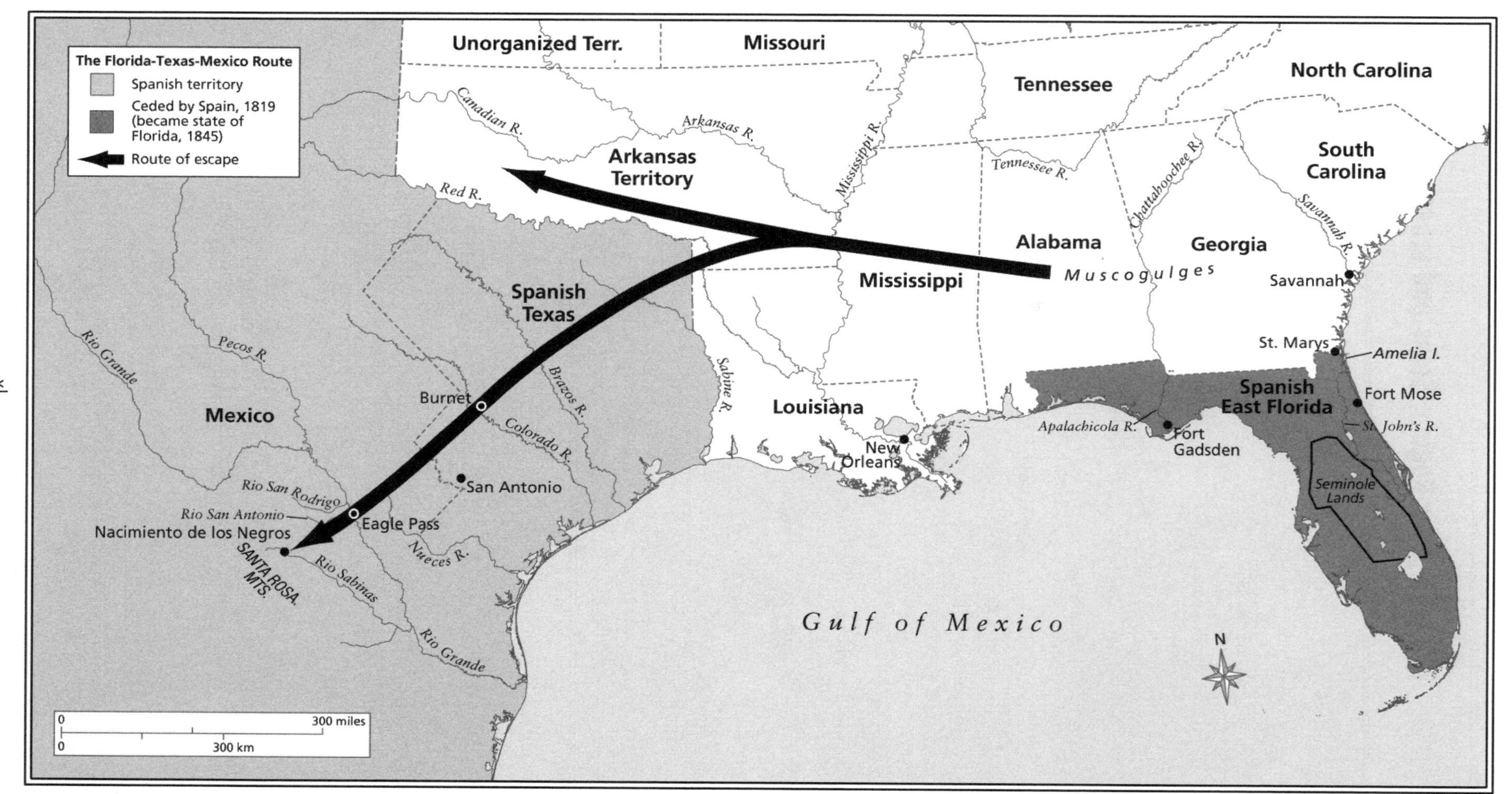

A–Z
ENTRIES

A

Abbott, George (1817–1916)
Abbott, Ruth S. Baker (1826–1916)

An Underground Railroad agent at Mannington in Salem County, New Jersey, Quaker George Abbott aided refugees on their way to Canada. In 1845, he married Ruth S. Baker. At Tide Mill Farm at 100 Tide Mill Lane, the couple earned their living as dairy farmers. They received slaves at their three-story brick house and concealed them in a hidden room before passing them on to Salem, New Jersey.

Source

Cunningham, John. *This Is New Jersey.* Piscataway, NJ: Rutgers University Press, 1953.

Abbott, James Burnett (1818–1897)
Abbott, Elizabeth Ann Watrous (1831–1920)

James Burnett Abbott of Hampton, Connecticut, aided slaves during the violent times following passage of the Kansas-Nebraska Act of 1854. His family left Rochester, New York, by emigrant wagon train for Blanton in Kansas Territory in late September 1854 and built a house on Coal Creek in southern Douglas County. James Abbott sold subscriptions to the *Kansas Herald of Freedom,* an abolitionist newspaper founded by George W. Brown of Lawrence, Kansas. He served the Wakarusa Liberty Guards as a colonel in charge of procuring Sharps rifles, muskets, and a howitzer cannon, which he purchased in Hartford, Connecticut, and St. Louis, Missouri.

In fall 1857, the Abbott home was an Underground Railroad safehouse. A black male in his early twenties arrived one day from Amasa Soule's safehouse at Lawrence and asked for help. With her husband James away on a journey to Lawrence, Elizabeth Ann Watrous Abbott took charge of the rescue. She discovered that the slave was a skilled cook who had worked on river steamers. After she sent on their way two suspicious men who arrived at the house, she armed the slave with an ax to protect him from slave catchers' bloodhounds.

The Abbotts were generous with money and assistance. In January 1857, when agent John Armstrong needed funds to complete the transfer of the fugitive Ann Clarke to Chicago, James Abbott contributed cash. He also aided John Brown's midwinter expedition from Missouri to Windsor, Ontario. On January 24, 1859, Brown's wagon train arrived at the Abbott depot. Abbott traded Brown's oxen for a fresh team of horses to pull the prairie schooners to the stone barn of agents Emily Jane Hunt Grover and Joel Grover at Lawrence. On another occasion, James Abbott received from John W. Doy at Lawrence a party of 13 black freedmen, of whom 11—including two cooks, Wilson Hayes and Charles Smith, employed in Lawrence at Eldridge House, a frontier hotel—were carrying freedom papers. Armed pursuers arrested Doy and his son, Charles Doy, and held them in the St. Joseph jail. Doy recorded the episode in *The Narrative of John Doy of Lawrence, Kansas: A Plain Unvarnished Tale* (1860), a recounting of anti-slavery work in the Midwest.

See also: bloodhounds; Kansas-Nebraska Act of 1854.

Sources

Doy, John. *The Narrative of John Doy of Lawrence, Kansas: A Plain Unvarnished Tale.* New York: T. Holman, 1860.

Morgan, Perl W. *History of Wyandotte County Kansas and Its People.* Chicago: Lewis, 1911.

abolitionism

For the daring and valor of slave conductors, couriers, depot masters, and rescuers, the abolitionist period earned a reputation as America's age of martyrdom.

The movement, a radical arm of the anti-slavery drive, began simultaneously in western Europe and the American colonies in the last quarter of the eighteenth century, at the height of the transatlantic slave trade. Humanitarians persisted in sending petitions to social agencies and government leaders; the petitions called for outright abolition of slavery or for a series of incremental measures, beginning with a halt to slave kidnap and importation. Leading the outcry were Quakers, Mennonites, Congregationalists, Unitarians, Presbyterians, Methodist Episcopalians, and evangelicals, all of whom found scriptural and philosophical grounds for denunciation of the flesh trade. The most radical abolitionists also condemned those who bought or profited from the trade of slave-made, slave-harvested goods, particularly cotton garments, tobacco, tea, indigo, molasses, rum, rice, and cane sugar.

In the United States, the break between northern manufacturers and southern planters emphasized the dependence of the 11 states of the plantation South on slave labor for cultivating and harvesting cotton, indigo, rice, sugarcane, and tobacco. By 1804, all states north of Maryland had abolished slavery. Among Northerners and some Southerners and Canadians, civil disobedience of the Fugitive Slave Law of 1793 led to the rescue and transportation of runaway slaves to safe territories northward as far as Ontario and Quebec, southeast to the Caribbean, and southwest to Mexico. Easing the virulent face-off of factions was the Missouri Compromise of 1820, which allowed for the addition of states to the Union in pairs, one slave and one free, as a means of maintaining a political balance. In 1826, black Bostonians formed the Massachusetts General Colored Association, a political pressure group demanding immediate abolition of slavery.

In *The Abolitionists: Together with Personal Memories of the Struggle for Human Rights, 1830–1864* (1905), the historian John F. Hume characterized the persecution faced by abolitionists: "In society they were tabooed; in business shunned. By the rabble they were hooted and pelted. Clowns in the circus made them the subjects of their jokes. Newspaper scribblers lampooned and libelled them. Politicians denounced them. By the Church they were regarded as very black sheep, and sometimes excluded from the fold. And this state of things lasted for years."

After the Nat Turner rebellion of August 1831 in Southampton, Virginia, resulted in the slaughter of 60 whites and more than 200 blacks, Southerners instituted restrictive Black Codes, stepped up patrols, and hired spies to divulge pockets of slave harboring in mid-Atlantic and midwestern states. In 1831, William Lloyd Garrison began publishing a weekly abolitionist paper, *The Liberator,* which featured the humanitarian writings of Lucretia Coffin Mott, Wendell Addison Phillips, and Gerrit Smith. A year later, Garrison increased the ethical squeeze on northern industrialists by co-founding the New England Anti-Slavery Society, which stressed the immorality of profiting from mills weaving slave-grown, slave-harvested cotton.

The militancy of the agrarian South met its match in the hostility of northern abolitionist ministers, editors, orators, and politicians. On December 6, 1833, Garrison formed the American Anti-Slavery Society with the concurrence of prominent Underground Railroad conductors and supporters—orator and agitator Abigail "Abby" Kelley Foster, Quaker physician Bartholomew Fussell, secret-network organizer Beriah Green, recruiter Samuel Joseph May, Quaker activist James Mott, Jr., black field manager Robert Purvis, waystation coordinator John Rankin, libertarian merchants Arthur Tappan and Lewis Tappan, and editor and essayist John Greenleaf Whittier. Simultaneously, Margaretta Forten and Quaker feminist Lucretia Coffin Mott co-founded the Philadelphia Female Anti-Slavery Society, which interjected strong support for black women fleeing domestic and sexual bondage to white masters.

High points in American abolitionism ranged from the political to the literary and personal. In 1840, Garrison's belligerent disciples split with less militant abolitionists over the issue of working within the provisions of the U.S. Constitution. The question of interfering in a state's right to take a stand on slavery compromised the soundness of the Union and foretokened the Civil War. Outrage at the passage of the Fugitive Slave Law of 1850 arose from abolitionists' belief that the U.S. Constitution guaranteed every person, slaves included, personal liberty and due process, which required a fair hearing in court. However, the stipulations of the law allowed slave catchers and federal marshals to seize and transport blacks solely on the suspicion of their being the chattel of white masters. The law flouted the concept of innocent until proven guilty. By preferring whites' civil rights over nonwhites', the law encouraged kidnap of free blacks for imprisonment in slave pens and for illicit sale on southern auction blocks. One of the goads to abolitionism was Harriet Beecher Stowe's fictional melodrama *Uncle Tom's Cabin* (1852), a best-selling novel in Europe and North America, which she based on real incidents of Underground Railroad activity in northern Kentucky and Ripley, Ohio. The personal grudge of extremist conductor John Brown against the federal government precipitated the raid on the federal armory at Harpers Ferry, Virginia (now West Virgina), on October 16, 1859. His arrest and hanging exacerbated the final clash between pro-slavery factions and a growing base of humanitarians and anti-slavery protesters, led by Garrison and Frederick Douglass. In April 1861, the diametrically opposed arguments led to the American Civil War and, on January 1, 1863, to President Abraham Lincoln's issuance of the Emancipation Proclamation. By 1865, passage of the Thirteenth Amendment to the U.S. Constitution ended the abolitionist movement by outlawing slavery.

See also: American Anti-Slavery Society; female anti-slavery societies; Fugitive Slave Law of 1793; Fugitive Slave Law of 1850; kidnap; *Liberator, The*; Missouri Compromise of 1820; Quakers; *Uncle Tom's Cabin; or, Life Among the Lowly* (1852).

Sources

Hume, John F. *The Abolitionists: Together with Personal Memories of the Struggle for Human Rights, 1830–1864.* New York: Putnam, 1905. Reprint, New York: AMS, 1973.

Lowance, Mason. *Against Slavery: An Abolitionist Reader.* New York: Penguin, 2000.

"North and South; or, The Policy of Ignorance." *United States Democratic Review* 34:4 (October 1854): 354–70.

abolitionist newspapers

The abolitionist press was an unprecedented development in North American journalism, which tended to spawn newspapers supported by political parties. As an unrelenting force for humanitarianism and liberty, the anti-slavery press fostered the rapid spread of abolitionism by giving voice to black and white journalists and to former slaves rescued by the Underground Railroad. The first abolitionist paper, Charles Worth Osborn's *Philanthropist,* first published in 1817, confronted readers with an uncompromising motto, "Emancipation, Immediate and Unconditional." The verbal challenge suited Osborn, who kept a safehouse in Mount Pleasant, Ohio. For distributors and readers, even the possession of radical abolitionist writings was dangerous. On May 22, 1839, Sherry Wilson, a 60-year-old free black in Queen Anne's County, Maryland, was sentenced to 10 years in prison for circulating inflammatory documents. With one year yet to serve, on April 22, 1848, Wilson gained his freedom through a pardon issued by Governor Phillip Francis Thomas.

Firsthand Testimony

Writers for the anti-slavery media offered eyewitness testimony to slave kidnap, flight, and rescue. One such episode, the convergence of the Salem, Ohio, anti-slavery society on a train in August 1854 to liberate a white couple's 14-year-old slave girl, concluded with a speech by the Reverend Marius R. Robinson, editor of the *Anti-Slavery Bugle.* An account in the *Tocsin of Liberty* detailed the flight of Sarah Smith and her husband and daughter from a New Orleans slave driver and the treatment of Eliza Wilson, a field hand who was lashed and soaked in brine. In 1852, the plight of Jim Phillips, a kidnap victim described in William Lloyd Garrison's weekly, *The Liberator,* caught the attention of Underground Railroad agent Mordecai McKinney of Harrisburg, Pennsylvania. As a result of McKinney's offer of cash, the kidnapper released Phillips and his wife and children. Abolitionist editors Frederick Douglass and Garrison and others presented a forthright and at times inflammatory condemnation of bondage to the reading public. Although most abolitionist papers had a small circulation, together they influenced hundreds of thousands of Americans. Among their fans were ministers, politicians, jurists, business moguls, writers, and family agents of the Underground Railroad.

Readers of the liberal press such as tanner Charles Boerstler "Boss" Huber, a route supervisor in Bethel, Ohio; sea captain Austin Bearse in New Bedford, Massachusetts; and foundryman George E. Webber of Hinkley, Ohio, learned the facts about the secret network and its humanitarian efforts. In the *National Era,* Huber read in toto the speeches of James Gillespie Birney, Salmon Portland Chase, and William Lloyd Garrison. In October 1839, editors James Caleb Jackson and Abel Brown used passages from the *Liberty Press* to upbraid a Washington, D.C., slave owner whose bondsman fled safely to Canada. Pieced together, abolitionist articles created an ongoing mon-

Leading Anti-Slavery Periodicals

Publication	Founder(s)/Editor(s)	Date	Place
Abolition Intelligencer and Missionary Magazine	John Finley Crow	1822–1823	Shelbyville, KY
Abolitionist	Luther Myrick	1841–1844	Cazenovia, NY
Advocate of Freedom	Thomas W. Newman	1838–1841	Augusta, ME
African Observer	Enoch Lewis	1827–1828	Philadelphia, PA
African Repository	Ralph Randolph Gurley	1825	Philadelphia, PA
Albany Patriot	James Nelson Tift, Edwin W. Caleb Jackson, and Abel Brown Goodwin	1845	Albany, NY
Aliened American	William Howard Day	1853–1854	Cleveland, OH
American and Foreign Anti-Slavery Reporter	Arthur Tappan and John Greenleaf Whittier	1836–1854	New York, NY
American Anti-Slavery Almanac	S.W. Benedict	1836–1847	New York, NY
American Citizen	Andrew W. Young and Jonathan A. Hadley	1836–1841	Warsaw, NY
American Freeman	Sherman Miller Booth, Ichabod Codding, and William M. Sullivan	1854–1861	Waukesha, WI
American Nonconformist	James Vincent and Mary Sheldon Vincent	1854–1861	Tabor, IA
Anti-Slavery Bugle	Abby Kelley Foster, James Barnaby, Oliver Johnson, Marius R. Robinson, and Benjamin Jones	1845–1861	Salem, OH
Anti-Slavery Record	American Anti-Slavery Society and R.G. Williams	1835–1837	New York, NY, and Boston, MA
Ashtabula Sentinel	Henry Hubbard and Matthew Hubbard	1853–1857	Ashtabula County, OH
Brooklyn Eagle	Henry C. Murphy and Walt Whitman	1841–1955	Brooklyn, NY
Castigator	David Ammen	1820s	Ripley, OH
Charter Oak	Connecticut Anti-Slavery Society and Samuel Smith Cowles	1845	Hartford, CT
Chindowan	Clarina I.H. Nichols and J.M. Waldon	1857–1858	Quindaro, KS
Christian Examiner	Orestes Augustus Brownson	1824–1869	New York, NY
Christian Freeman	William Henry Burleigh	1836	Hartford, CT
Christian Press	Charles Brandon Boynton	1854	Cincinnati, OH
Christian Recorder	Mother Bethel African Methodist Episcopal Church	1861–1902	Philadelphia, PA
Cincinnati Weekly Herald and Philanthropist	James Gillespie Birney, Gamaliel Bailey, and Achilles Pugh	1847	Cincinnati, OH, and Springboro, OH
Clarion	Henry Highland Garnet	1840s	Troy, NY
Clarion of Freedom	James Moorhead	1846	Indiana County, IN
Cleveland American	M.W. Miller and L.L. Rice	1845	Ohio City, OH
Cleveland True Democrat	William Howard Day	1851–1852	Cleveland, OH
Colonizationist and Journal of Freedom	Benjamin Bussey Thatcher	1833–1834	Boston, MA
Colored American	Philip Alexander Bell, Charles Bennett Ray, Samuel Eli Cornish, Robert Sears, and James McCune Smith	1837–1841	New York, NY
Colored Citizen	William Henry Yancy and Thomas Woodson	1845–1846	Cincinnati, OH
Commonwealth	Julia Ward Howe and Samuel Gridley Howe	1851–1853	Boston, MA
Crawford Messenger	Thomas Atkinson	1826	Meadville, PA
Daily True Democrat	E.S. Hamlin and E.L. Stevens	1846–1853	Cleveland, OH
Disenfranchised American	Alphonso M. Sumner and O.T.B. Nickens	1844	Cincinnati, OH

Leading Anti-Slavery Periodicals (*continued*)

Publication	Founder(s)/Editor(s)	Date	Place
Emancipator	Elihu Embree	1820	Jonesboro, TN
Emancipator	Arthur Tappan, Joshua Leavitt, and William Goodell	1833	New York, NY
Emancipator	Hiram Cummings, Joshua Leavitt, and Curtis C. Nichols	1845–1848	Boston, MA
Emancipator and Free American	Dexter S. King, Joshua Leavitt, and J.W. Alden	1841–1844	Boston, MA
Emancipator and Free Soil Press	Curtis C. Nichols	1848	Boston, MA
Emancipator and Public Morals	David Ruggles	1833–1842	New York, NY
Emancipator and Republican	Henry Wilson and L.E. Smith	1848–1850	Boston, MA
Emancipator and Weekly Chronicle	Joshua Leavitt and Hiram Cummings	1844–1845	Boston, MA
Examiner	Cassius Marcellus Clay	1845	Cincinnati, OH
Frederick Douglass' Paper	Frederick Douglass	1851–1860	Rochester, NY
Fredonia Censor	Willard McKinstry	1821–1865	Fredonia, NY
Free Enquirer	Fanny Wright and Robert Dale Owen	1829	New York, NY
Free Labor Advocate and Anti-Slavery Chronicle	Benjamin Stanton and Henry H. Way	1841–1848	Newport, IN
Freedman's Record	John A. Andrew	1865–1866	Boston, MA
Freedom's Journal	Samuel Eli Cornish, John Brown Russworm, and James Varick	1827–1829	New York, NY
Freeman's Advocate	Stephen Myers	1840s	Albany, NY
Freeman's Depository	Anthony Haswell and David Russell	1783	Vermont
Freemen's Press	Derick Sibley and Sereno Wright	1809–1812	Montpelier, VT
Friend of Man	William Goodell	1836–1842	Utica, NY
Genius of Liberty	George W. Litman	1805–1854	Uniontown, PA
Genius of Universal Emancipation	Benjamin Lundy and William Lloyd Garrison	1821–1837	Mount Pleasant, OH
Green Mountain Freeman	Daniel P. Thompson and Joseph Poland	1844–1878	Montpelier, VT
Harper's Weekly	James Harper	1857–1916	New York, NY
Hartford Evening Press	Joseph Hawley	1837–1861	Hartford, CT
Herald of Freedom	Parker Pillsbury, John Horace Kimball, Nathaniel Peabody Rogers, and Orson B. Ashmun	1835–1846	Concord, NH
Herald of Freedom	J.W. Chaffin	1851–1855	Wilmington, OH
Illinois Statesman	Jonathan Baldwin Turner	1843–1844	Jacksonville, IL
Independent	James Moorhead	1840s	Indiana County, IN
Independent	Henry Chandler Bowen, Henry Ward Beecher, and Theodore Tilton	1848–1861	New York, NY
Investigator and General Intelligencer	James B. Yerrington	1827	Providence, RI
Jeffersonville Republican	Dr. Nathaniel Field	late 1830s	Jeffersonville, IN
Journal of Commerce	Arthur Tappan and Lewis Tappan	1827	New York, NY
Kansas Free State	Robert G. Elliot and Josiah Miller	1855–1856	Lawrence, KS
Kansas Freeman	Edward Christie Kerr Garvey	1855–1856	Topeka, KS
Kansas Herald of Freedom	George W. Brown	1855	Lawrence, KS
Kansas Pioneer	John Speer	1854	Lawrence, KS
Kansas Post	Moritz Pinner	1859–1861	Kansas City, KS
Latimer Journal and North Star	Henry Ingersoll Bowditch, Frederick Cabot, and William Francis Channing	1842–1843	Boston, MA

Leading Anti-Slavery Periodicals (*continued*)

Publication	Founder(s)/Editor(s)	Date	Place
Liberalist	Milo Mower	1828	New Orleans, LA
Liberator, The	William Lloyd Garrison and Isaac Knapp	1831–1865	Boston, MA
Liberty Party Paper	Gerrit Smith and John Thomas	1849–1851	Syracuse, NY
Liberty Press	James Caleb Jackson and Abel Brown	1843–1848	Albany, NY
Liberty Standard	Austin Willey	1841–1848	Hallowell, ME
Lorain County News	J.F. Harmon and V.A. Shankland	1860–1865	Lorain County, OH
Madison & Onondaga County Abolitionist	Luther Myrick	1824	Greenville, TN
Manumission Intelligencer	Elihu Embree	1819	Jonesboro, TN
Manumission Journal	Benjamin Lundy	1825	Tennessee
Markesan Journal	James Burton Pond and John P. Parker	1859–1862	Markesan, WI
Mercer County Whig	Thomas Jeff Nickum, Sr.	1851–1866	Mercer, PA
Michigan Freeman	Seymour Boughton Treadwell	1836–1841	Jackson, MI
Michigan Liberty Press	Sylvanus Erastus Fuller Hussey	1847	Battle Creek, MI
Mirror of Liberty	David Ruggles	1838	New York, NY
Mirror of the Times	Mifflin Wistar Gibbs	1855–1858	San Francisco, CA
Morning Star	Oren Burbank Cheney	1826	Limerick, ME
Morning Star	William Burr	1865	Dover, NH
Mystery, The	Martin Robinson Delaney	1843–1848	Pittsburgh, PA
National Anti-Slavery Standard	David Lee Child, Lydia Maria Francis Child, Sydney Howard Gay, Aaron Powell, and Nathaniel P. Rogers	1840–1871	Boston, MA
National Enquirer	John Greenleaf Whittier	1834	Philadelphia, PA
National Era	John Greenleaf Whittier, Gamaliel Bailey, and Amos A. Phelps	1847–1859	Washington, DC
National Philanthropist	William Lloyd Garrison	1827	Boston, MA
National Reformer	William J. Whipper	1838	Philadelphia, PA
National Watchman	Henry Highland Garnet and William G. Allen	1842	Troy, NY
New England Anti-Slavery Almanac	Isaac Knapp	1838	Boston, MA
New England Weekly Review	George D. Prentice	1828	Hartford, CT
New Jersey Freeman	Dr. John Grimes	1844–1850	Boonton, NJ
New York American & Foreign Anti-Slavery Reporter	John Greenleaf Whittier	1840–1847	New York, NY
New York Daily Tribune	Horace Greeley and Sydney Howard Gay	1841–1924	New York, NY
New York Human Rights		1835–1838	New York, NY
New York Independent	Joshua Leavitt	1830	New York, NY
Non-Resistant	Maria Weston Chapman	1839–1842	Boston, MA
North Star	Frederick Douglass	1847–1851	Rochester, NY
Northern Independent	William Hosmer	1856–1867	Auburn, NY
Northern Star & Freeman's Advocate	Stephen Myers, John G. Stewart, and Charles Morton	1842–1849	Albany, NY
Oasis, The	Lydia Maria Francis Child	1834	Boston, MA
Ohio American	R.B. Dennis	1844–1845	Ohio City, OH
Palladium of Liberty	David Jenkins and Charles Henry Langston	1842–1844	Columbus, OH
Pennsylvania Freeman	John Greenleaf Whittier, Cyrus Moses Burleigh, Charles Callistus Burleigh, and James Miller McKim	1854	Philadelphia, PA

Leading Anti-Slavery Periodicals (*continued*)

Publication	Founder(s)/Editor(s)	Date	Place
Philanthropist	Charles Worth Osborn, Elisha Bates, and Benjamin Lundy	1817–1822	Mount Pleasant, OH
Pittsburgh Saturday Visitor	Jane Grey Cannon Swisshelm	1848	Pittsburgh, PA
Principia	William Goodell, Lavinia Goodell, and George B. Cheever	1852–1864	New York, NY
Protectionist	Arnold Buffum	1841	New Garden, IN
Provincial Freeman, The	Mary Ann Shadd Cary, William P. Newman, and Samuel Ringgold Ward	1853–1857	Chatham, Ontario
Ram's Horn	Thomas Van Rensselaer and Willis Augustus Hodges	1846–1848	New York, NY
Religious Herald	David B. Moseley	1846–1858	Hartford, CT
Rights of Man	William Clough Bloss	1834	Rochester, NY
Signal of Liberty	Guy Beckley and Theodore Foster	1836–1848	Ann Arbor, MI
Slave's Cry	New London Anti-Slavery Society	1838–1848	New London, CT
Spirit of Liberty	Edward Smith	1841–1847	Pittsburgh, PA
Spirit of the Times	David Morris	1826–1829	Batavia, OH
St. Cloud Democrat	Jane Grey Cannon Swisshelm	1858	St. Cloud, MN
St. Louis Observer	Elijah Parish Lovejoy	1833–1836	St. Louis, MO, and Alton, IL
Syracuse Evening Chronicle	George Barnes	1853–1856	Syracuse, NY
Tennessee Emancipator		1820	Jonesboro, TN
Tocsin of Liberty	Charles Turner Torrey, William Lawrence Chaplin, Abel Brown, and Edwin W. Goodwin	1842–1844	Albany, NY
True American	Cassius Marcellus Clay and T.B. Stevenson	1845–1846	Lexington, KY, and Cincinnati, OH
True American	James Catlin, Henry Catlin, Jr., and Martha Van Rensselaer Catlin	1853–1861	Erie, PA
True Wesleyan	Luther Lee and Orange Scott	1844–1852	Syracuse, NY
Voice of Freedom	Chauncey L. Knapp, Joseph Poland, and Jedediah Holcomb	1839–1842	Montpelier, VT
Voice of the Fugitive	Henry W. Bibb and Mary E. Miles Bibb	1851	Sandwich, Ontario
Weekly AfroAmerican	Robert Hamilton and Thomas Hamilton	1859	New York, NY
Western Citizen	Zebina Eastman and Hooper W. Warren	1842–1853	Chicago, IL

tage of Underground Railroad history: Cassius Marcellus Clay's call for a war between smallholders and slaveholders in the *True American,* Horace Greeley's thought-provoking editorial challenge to President Abraham Lincoln in the *New York Tribune,* and Mary Ann Shadd Cary's encouragement in *The Provincial Freeman* to runaways to settle in Ontario. Illustrations were a convincing form of protest—the pen-and-ink drawings by Thomas Nast dramatizing refugees in flight, a cartoon from an 1839 edition of the *New England Anti-Slavery Almanac* picturing Canadian symbol John Bull warding off an American slave catcher in pursuit of a black runaway on the safe side of the border, and David Hunter Strother's sketches for *Harper's Weekly* revealing the enclaves of maroons who hid from their owners in the Great Dismal Swamp.

Editors of abolitionist papers promoted the secret network by lauding its heroes and by recruiting conductors and donors. William Goodell's *Friend of Man* in Utica, New York, rejoiced over the safe passage of Harriet Powell in 1839 from Syracuse, New York, to Canada. In Chicago, from 1842 to 1853, Zebina Eastman, editor of the *Western Citizen,* collaborated with Dr. Charles Volney Dyer and Philo R. Carpenter to strengthen local routes. Strong affirmation of abolitionism came from Isaac Tatem Hopper's biweekly column "Tales of the Oppression" and from the editorials of a husband-wife team, David Lee and Lydia Maria Francis Child, owners of the *National Anti-Slavery Standard,* whose motto was "Without Concealment—Without Compromise." Another female writer, Maria Weston Chapman, edited annual reports for the Massachusetts Anti-Slavery Society called *Right and Wrong* before joining the staffs of the *Non-Resistant* and of Garrison's *The Liberator.* At the office of the *Daily Democrat* in Rochester, New York, printer William S. Falls played a dual role—he published news of the secret network and received runaways for concealment in his own pressroom.

Some spokespersons for the anti-slavery movement, including Mary Ann Shadd Cary, Elizabeth Buffum Chace, Abigail Kelley Foster, and Sallie Holley, educated themselves on Underground Railroad philosophy and strategies by reading several potent periodicals from different parts of the country.

The Whole Story

The libertarian media aired bad news as well as good, including the frauds seeking handouts from vigilance committees. The November 7, 1828, issue of *Freedom's Journal* warned the softhearted of Nathan Gooms and Moses Smith, two confidence men seeking free board. Most anti-slavery papers featured the fallout from the Fugitive Slave Law of 1850 and the fates of passengers Henry "Box" Brown, Anthony Burns, and Ellen and William Craft, and William "Jerry" McHenry. Papers also reported on violence in Bleeding Kansas and the terrorism of William Clarke Quantrill, who sacked Lawrence, Kansas, on August 21, 1863. The imprisonment of Philadelphia lawyer Passmore Williamson on July 18, 1855, for aiding in the flight of Jane Johnson and her sons, Daniel and Isaiah Johnson, received full coverage in the abolitionist press. Attesting to the violation of human rights by the Fugitive Slave Law of 1850 were Frederick Douglass's newspaper the *North Star,* Garrison's *The Liberator,* Parker Pillsbury's editorials for the *National Anti-Slavery Standard,* Horace Greeley's *New York Daily Tribune,* and outraged writers at the *Hartford Religious Herald,* all of whom applauded the actions of Passmore Williamson. Challenging the pro-slavery screed *The Pennsylvanian* and corroborating Jane Johnson's testimony was a liberal southern gazette, the *Fayetteville (NC) Observer.*

The adversarial give-and-take between editor and letter writer raised reader consciousness and built consensus, particularly descriptions of opportunity in Canada in letters from Henry Walton Bibb to the *Emancipator, Signal of Liberty,* and *National Anti-Slavery Standard.* During spirited exchanges between Benjamin Lundy and anonymous writers in 1825, the *Genius of Universal Emancipation* of December 24 satirized slave advertisements by offering cash for white boys and girls to be sold in Algiers. In March 1841, a notice in the *Free Labor Advocate and Anti-Slavery Chronicle* in Newport, Indiana, rejoiced at the 800 passengers per year crossing Lake Erie into Ontario. In 1847, an abolitionist pamphlet, the *Legion of Liberty,* published a pen-and-ink drawing of a shackled black woman kneeling with hands folded in prayer under the rhetorical question, "Have we not all one Father?" After the seizure of Captain Daniel Drayton for transporting 76 slaves from Georgetown, in the District of Columbia, in spring 1848, a mob of 1,000 blamed Gamaliel Bailey, editor of the *National Era,* for the mass flight. On threat of lynching the editor, the protesters launched the Washington Riot of 1848 and stoned the newspaper office until police and extra deputies cordoned off the area. The *National Era* survived and in 1852 serialized Harriet Beecher Stowe's *Uncle Tom's Cabin,* a fictionalized account of the rescue work of Jean Lowry Rankin and John Rankin, Underground Railroad conductors in Ripley, Ohio. Another victimized commentator, Marius R. Robinson, editor of the Salem, Ohio, *Anti-Slavery Bugle,* praised the abolitionist oratory of Sojourner Truth. For his adamant opposition to the flesh trade, he suffered tarring and feathering.

The abolitionist press offered a window on doctrinal differences within religious denominations over the issues of slavery and civil disobedience of the Fugitive Slave Law of 1850. To refute claims of altruistic slaveholding among southern Methodists, historian Hiram Mattison, author of *The Impending Crisis of 1860* (1859), wrote, "*Three Fourths* of all the fugitives who pass over the eastern branch of the underground railroad, run away from Methodists masters in Maryland and Virginia—from the Gorsuches and Harpers and Pattisons and Traverses of Border Methodism." Proving Mattison's contention was a paid advertisement from October 28, 1857, in the *Cambridge (MD) Democrat* naming Levi D. Travers as the owner of a runaway, Aaron Cornish. In the November 4, 1857, issue of the *Cambridge Democrat*, an ad signed by

Samuel Pattison offered a $2,000 reward for the return of "fourteen head of Negroes." The historian described Pattison as a respected member of Dorchester County's Methodist Episcopal Church and muttered, "Shame on him, and upon all other such hypocrites and apostates from God and from original Methodism! It is enough to make the body of Wesley turn over in its grave to call such men Methodists." Mattison further spiced his diatribe by citing a paragraph from the Reverend William Hosmer's paper, the *Northern Independent,* dated May 1857. The text accuses a black minister, the Reverend Henry Hutt, of slave ownership. After the slave escaped on the Underground Railroad, Hutt recovered him and sold him South. By embarrassing the clergy, Hosmer and other publishers and editors exerted pressure on slave owners and encouraged the efforts of Underground Railroad agents.

In addition to polemical coverage, anti-slavery papers suggested courses of action. A military periodical, *The Provincial Freeman,* served black history as a source of information on black abolitionism, Underground Railroad activity, and church growth. Edited by Samuel Ringgold Ward, it featured writing by Mary Ann Shadd Cary and covered the concerns of 40,000 runaway slaves who settled in Canada. The *New England Anti-Slavery Almanac* and the *National Anti-Slavery Standard* offered practical advice, such as arguments to convert pro-slave individuals and warnings of bogus offers of rescue by frauds who took money from fugitives and then left them to fend for themselves. The *National Anti-Slavery Standard* remained at the forefront of Underground Railroad news by dispatching a journalist in March 1856 to write "A Visit to the Slave Mother Who Killed Her Child," the tragic story of Margaret Garner's murder of her daughter Mary to save the child from sexual bondage to white males. On November 8, 1856, the *National Anti-Slavery Standard* declared that the Underground Railroad was flourishing. In testimony, the writer exulted that, in a 10-month period, 287 escapees had passed through Albany, New York, to freedom in Ontario. Such news gladdened operatives in rural areas and on the frontier where there was little camaraderie to sustain their efforts.

See also: civil disobedience; Dismal Swamp; Fugitive Slave Law of 1850; *Liberator, The*; maroon settlements; Missouri Compromise of 1820; *North Star*; vigilance committees.

Sources

Blassingame, John W., and Mae G. Henderson, eds. *Antislavery Newspapers and Periodicals, 1817–1845.* Boston: G.K. Hall, 1980.

Danky, James P., ed. *African-American Newspapers and Periodicals: A National Bibliography.* Cambridge, MA: Harvard University Press, 1998.

Hildreth, Richard. *Atrocious Judges.* New York: Miller, Orton & Mulligan, 1856.

Mattison, Hiram. *The Impending Crisis of 1860.* New York: Mason Brothers, 1859.

Abraham (ca. 1787–?)

A maroon leader, Abraham (also referred to as Suwanee Warrior) helped to shelter runaways from Georgia and the Carolinas in Prospect Bluff, Florida. Born in Pensacola, Florida, as the chattel of Dr. Sierra, he escaped bondage during the War of 1812. In 1815, he took charge of the fort at Prospect Bluff, southeast of Panama City on the Gulf of Mexico. After the destruction of the settlement three years later, Abraham allied with Chief Micanopy as interpreter, adviser, and legate to Washington, D.C. He led several hundred followers to Indian Territory in Oklahoma. In 2000, archaeologists studied Pelikłakaha, Abraham's slave haven on the Florida frontier.

See also: maroon settlements.

Source

Blassingame, John W. *The Slave Community: Plantation Life in the Antebellum South.* New York: Oxford University Press, 1972.

Adams, David (1826–1913)

The first black barber in Hancock County, Ohio, David Adams relayed runaway slaves along the secret network. After leaving Urbana, Ohio, and settling at Findlay, Ohio, in 1848, he married Elizabeth Conaway, became a member of the Methodist Episcopal Church, and joined the Masons, a benevolent brotherhood that aided slaves. Adams traveled regularly from his residence at 604 Lawn Avenue to Urbana to transport refugees on their way to Canada. He chose the cover of night, especially during storms, as the best strategy for circumventing recapture of his passengers by bounty hunters or posses. After the Civil War, he herded horses to California and remained there for three years before returning to the Findlay barbershop.

Sources

Martin, Asa Earl. "Pioneer Anti-Slavery Press." *Mississippi Valley Historical Review* 2 (March 1916): 510–28.

Siebert, Wilbur H. *The Mysteries of Ohio's Underground Railroad.* Columbus, OH: Long's College, 1951.

Adams, Elias Smith (1799–1863)
Adams, Susan Merritt (1801–1866)

The mayor of St. Catharines, Ontario, in the tense decade preceding the American Civil War, Elias Smith Adams supported the secret network. He joined operatives William Hamilton Merritt and Harriet Ross Tubman in aiding refugees on the last leg of the Underground Railroad passage. A native of Queenston, Ontario, he married Merritt's sister, Susan Merritt, of Grantham, Ontario, in 1823. In addition to completing rescues and protecting refugees, the couple supported the interracial Refugee Slaves' Friends Society, which William Merritt and Harriet Tubman organized in 1852 to help newcomers establish themselves in free territory.

Source

Winks, Robin W. *The Blacks in Canada.* Montreal, Quebec: McGill-Queen's University Press, 2005.

Adams, George Willison (1799–1879)
Adams, Clarissa Hopkins Shaff (ca. 1805–1850)

Abolitionist merchant and grain transporter George Willison Adams supported the Underground Railroad route through Dresden in Muskingum County, Ohio. After inheriting land in Fauquier County, Virginia, and slaves from his father, he freed the slaves and moved west to live in a free section of the frontier. With his brother Edward, George Adams invested in dry goods and, in 1828, in a large water-powered flour mill. In 1856, he chose Trinway (now Zanesville), Ohio, in the Salt Fork region north of Wakatomica Creek as the site for Prospect Place, the family's two-story, 29-room brick mansion.

Basing their altruism on staunch Presbyterianism, Adams and his first wife, Clarissa Hopkins Shaff (or Choff) Adams, turned their residence into one of the state's largest Underground Railroad depots. It featured a cellar that continued to accommodate refugees until the abolition of slavery on January 1, 1863. The Adams family provided food, blankets, and lamps to ease the travels of passengers to the north. Adams's home is listed on the National Register of Historic Places.

Source

Everhart, J.F. *History of Muskingum County, Ohio.* Cincinnati, OH: self-published, 1882.

Adams, James (fl. 1820s)

In late summer 1824, Virginian James Adams made his way out of bondage with the aid of a stationmaster on the Ohio River. The mulatto son of a slave woman and a plantation overseer, Adams fled from a plantation at the Great Kanawha River with a cousin, Benjamin Harris, a female slave, and four children. At Marietta, Ohio, the seven refugees took shelter with a conductor who harbored runaways on a nearby hill. As a signal, the rescuer raised a white cloth on a pole when passage was safe. He provisioned the party with cake and dried venison. A notched compass directed the seven refugees through woods, mountains, and wheat fields to Mount Vernon and then on to Cleveland, Ohio, where a cobbler negotiated free passage by lake schooner via Buffalo, New York, to Black Rock Ferry and, on September 13, 1824, to St. Catharines, Ontario.

Source

Drew, Benjamin. *The Refugee: The Narratives of Fugitive Slaves in Canada.* Boston: John P. Jewett, 1856.

Adams, John Quincy (1767–1848)

Congressman John Quincy Adams, formerly the sixth president of the United States (1825–1829), supported the work of the Underground Railroad. He had denounced the Missouri Compromise of 1820 as a mere stopgap measure that was bound to unleash civil war. Among his close friends was agent Edward Thurlow Weed, who operated a waystation in Albany, New York. The plight of Joseph Cinqué and the 42 other adult survivors aboard the Portuguese slaver *Amistad* in 1839 stirred Adams to aid the oppressed people kidnapped from Sierra Leone. At a trial commencing in January 1840 before Judge Andrew Judgson at the Old State House in Hartford, Connecticut, attorney Roger Sherman Baldwin defended the slaves on charges of piracy and murder. Josiah Gibbs, a professor at Yale College, located a translator, seaman James Covey, who spoke the Mende dialect and mediated between the defendants and the court.

New charges pressed by the Spanish government declared the Africans to be cargo, rather than victims.

Former President John Quincy Adams, while not a radical abolitionist, argued before the U.S. Supreme Court on behalf of the slave rebels in the *Amistad* case and helped overturn the Gag Rule against slavery-related petitions in Congress. *(Hulton Archive/Stringer/Getty Images)*

Adams, then aged 74, based his arguments on the human right to liberty. During lengthy litigation, the West Africans lodged at a safehouse that Underground Railroad agent Austin Franklin Williams and Jennet Cowles Williams constructed at 127 Main Street in Farmington, Connecticut. Following a series of appeals, the U.S. Supreme Court ruled that the Africans acted in self-defense. On March 9, 1841, the court freed them for return to their Mende homeland in Sierra Leone.

See also: *Amistad*; Missouri Compromise of 1820.

Sources

Adams, John Quincy. *Memoirs of John Quincy Adams.* Philadelphia: J.B. Lippincott, 1876.

Favors, John S. *John Quincy Adams and the* Amistad. Bergambacht, The Netherlands: Jonka, 1974.

Adams, Robert S. (fl. 1830s–1840s)

An Underground Railroad conductor and concealer of runaway slaves, Robert S. Adams used his carpentry skills to create a temporary haven at Fall River, Massachusetts. He owned the Adams Bookstore at 19 South Main Street and, out of Quaker benevolence, engaged in clandestine rescues. In 1843 on Columbia Street, the home of Andrew Robeson, Adams constructed a bookcase that hid a trapdoor that accessed the basement. With the aid of Quaker operative William Hill, Robeson managed the depot and collaborated with Adams, who led passengers by closed carriage to Worcester, Massachusetts, and Providence, Rhode Island. The first runaway to use Adams's service was James Curry, a quadroon who fled his owner, Moses Chambers, in Person County, North Carolina, in 1837. Over a period of two years, Curry fled from New Bedford to Fall River and, with Adams's help, on to the waystation of Elizabeth Buffum Chace and Samuel Buffington Chace at Valley Hills, Rhode Island, before reaching Canada.

Source

Phillips, Arthur. *The Phillips History of Fall River.* Fall River, MA: Dover, 1944.

Adler, Leibman (1818–1892)

An advocate of civil disobedience on behalf of the Underground Railroad, Rabbi Leibman Adler openly called for slave rescues. He was born in Saxe-Weimar, in what is now central Germany, and, at age 36, immigrated to the United States. He compared the plight of black fugitives to that of the Hebrews in Exodus. After the formation of Temple Beth El in Detroit, Michigan, from 1854 to 1861, he urged his reformed worshipers to aid the many slaves who crossed the Detroit River to Windsor, Ontario. Among the temple's members were transporter Mark Sloman and Emil S. Heineman and Fanny Butzel Heineman, who disguised refugees to help them escape surveillance by slave hunters.

See also: civil disobedience; disguise.

Source

Wiernik, Peter. *History of the Jews in America.* New York: Jewish Press, 1912.

African Methodist Episcopal Church

Crucial to the success of the Underground Railroad were black congregations of the African Methodist Episcopal Church. The denomination began in Philadelphia, Pennsylvania, in 1787 with the activism of the Reverend Richard Allen, who denounced whites at St. George's Methodist Episcopal Church for forcing black members to sit in a separate balcony. Allen envisioned fully integrated churches as sources of social and educational uplift for poor and disenfranchised blacks. To actualize his dream, he founded the Mother Bethel African Methodist Episcopal congregation; with the aid of James Forten and the Reverend Absalom Jones, Allen established the Free African Society. By 1846, the number of assemblies reached 300 and spread from Philadelphia to Indiana.

Wherever African Methodist Episcopal churches served black communities, ministers and congregations took seriously biblical commands in Matthew 25:36 to aid the oppressed as though they were Christ himself. Sanctuaries did double duty as worship centers and as waystations and literacy training centers for refugees. In 1795, at Providence, Rhode Island, Ichabod Northrup, a Revolutionary War veteran, co-initiated the Bethel African Methodist Episcopal congregation along with the African Freedmen's Society. At Springtown, New Jersey, pressure from Methodist slave owners forced blacks from another Bethel African Methodist Episcopal congregation. In the early 1800s, the disgruntled members left the church, assembled at Greenwich, New Jersey, and established the African Society of Methodists. In 1817, the congregants allied their small assembly and its Underground Railroad activities with the African Methodist Episcopal denomination. At Lancaster, Pennsylvania, a crucial nexus of the secret rail line, the Bethel African Methodist Episcopal Church began receiving fugitives in 1817. At the African Methodist Episcopal Church of Madison, Indiana, another key border entry, heavy traffic made the sanctuary a first stop in a free state. From 1834, the Mount Zion African Methodist Episcopal Church on Garwin Road at Woolwich, New Jersey, collaborated with Quaker conductors to shelter runaways. Long-term leaders included Pompey Lewis and Jubilee Sharper, who hid members from posses in a crawl space under the sanctuary. In 1837 on the midwestern frontier, Bishop William Paul Quinn formed the Allen Chapel African Methodist Episcopal Church in Terre Haute, Indiana. In the cellar, congregants harbored slaves arriving over the Wabash River. In 1836, the Reverend Elisha Weaver established a safehouse at Bethel Church in Indianapolis, Indiana. The catastrophic fire in 1862 that destroyed the sanctuary appears to have been revenge by pro-slavery, pro-Confederacy arsonists.

Upon reaching Canada, former slaves erected American Methodist Episcopal churches in emerging black settlements. From the 1830s, African Methodist Episcopal worship centers sprang up along the U.S.-Canada border, including a Toronto congregation in 1845 and, six years later, the Reverend Thanas Miller's start-up church at Owen Sound, Ontario. In the 1840s, Amherstburg became Ontario's African American center. Located at the narrows of the Detroit River, the town was the primary terminus of the Underground Railroad accessed by the *Mayflower,* a steamer from Sandusky, Ohio. Newcomers quarried fieldstone in 1848 to build the American Methodist Episcopal Nazrey Church, named for Bishop Willis Nazrey. He initiated a new, self-governing denomination, the British Methodist Episcopal Church. By 1856, the Canadian branch was independent of U.S. churches.

See also: British Methodist Episcopal Church; Quakers.

Sources

Chase, Henry, and Charles Blockson. "Greene County and Wilberforce." *American Visions* 10:2 (April–May 1995): 2–6.

Salvatore, Nick. *We All Got History: The Memory Books of Amos Webber.* New York: Random House, 1996.

Africanus, Edward C. (1821–1850)

The Reverend Edward C. Africanus sparked teamwork among Underground Railroad agents in Flushing, New York. He pastored the Bethel Tabernacle African Methodist Episcopal Church in Weeksville, New York and in 1848 preached in Newark, New Jersey. In collaboration with Arthur Tappan and Lewis Tappan in New York City, Africanus supported a link from waystations in Jersey City, New Jersey, up the Hudson Valley to Canada. In the decade preceding the Civil War, he fostered the use of the Macedonia African Methodist Episcopal Church at Flushing as a station of the secret network.

See also: African Methodist Episcopal Church.

Source

Tilmon, Levin. *A Brief Miscellaneous Narrative of the More Early Part of the Life of L. Tilmon, Pastor of a Colored Methodist Congregational Church in the City of New York.* Jersey City, NJ: W.W. & L.A. Pratt, 1853.

agents, Underground Railroad

Agents of the Underground Railroad were a tight-lipped lot who tended not to ask questions of their passengers nor to reveal their own identities and business. Some secret operatives chose not to speak to each other or to their passengers where others could observe them in acts of civil disobedience. According to Colonel William Monroe Cockrum's *History of the Underground Railroad As It Was Conducted by the Anti-Slavery League* (1915), the professions of volunteers included teachers, cartographers, naturalists, geologists, lawyers, ministers, surveyors, gamblers, tinkers, peddlers, carters and shippers, bargemen, and blacksmiths. Those serving as spies voiced pro-slavery opinions and curried favor with slave buyers and owners as a means of deflecting suspicion and gaining inside information. Managing routes and transfers through Illinois, Indiana, Ohio, and Pennsylvania was a single superintendent, John T. Hanover, a shadowy figure who went by the alias John Hansen.

In Cincinnati, Ohio, a loosely structured team of freedmen dock laborers and boatmen met at a stable to plot escape routes. For backup, they networked with black travelers and businessmen from cities farther north and east. Among the rescues the team completed was the retrieval from bondage of Jim Saunders and Sam Saunders, manumitted slaves of John Saunders of North Carolina. The two travelers risked capture by a kidnapper claiming to be a preacher. The wharfmen passed the two escapees to Michigan and began using them as spies and sources of information.

Laying the Groundwork

On the home scene, agents prepared for emergencies. Women canned extra vegetables, fruits, pork, beef, and sausage and dried their garden produce and wild berries over woodstoves and in attics. They kept on hand wicker baskets and hot pots for groups who had to flee at a moment's notice by carriage or wagon before they could finish a meal. Knitted shawls and mittens, horse blankets, tarps, lap robes, and baby clothes filled closets for the warming of passengers endangered by severe winter weather. The most difficult of items to stockpile were waterproof coverings and shoes and boots to replace the handmade slave goods that wore out quickly on lengthy trudges over rough ground or disintegrated from wading in creeks and swamps.

Agents had to be quick-witted and clever. Among their tricks were disguises—gloves, veils, hair dye, and face powder—and slave concealment in feather ticks, in loads of produce or manure, and in false-bottomed hay wagons. Operatives also employed decoy vehicles, dummies, lookouts, spies, and counterspies and piloted passengers south or zigzagged over unlikely routes. Henry Teller of Girard, Pennsylvania, kept runaways in a bog near his pigs. He supplied fugitives easily by concealing meals in a bucket and pretending to feed his stock. Other agents used their children and other relatives as lookouts, messengers, food distributors, and transporters. In Guilford County, North Carolina, Alfred V. Coffin, the manager of the state branch of the secret network from 1836 to 1852, coached slaves to fake loathsome diseases or lunacy to reduce their value to bounty hunters.

Operatives coded messages, including brass anti-slavery tokens, and they employed "humanity" as a password and "William Penn" and "Paul" as aliases. Like conductor Benajah Guernsey Roots of Tamaroa, Illinois, freedman George L. Burroughs of Cairo

> In a tribute to the conductors of southern Pennsylvania entitled *History of the Underground Railroad in Chester and the Neighboring Counties of Pennsylvania* (1883), its author, Robert C. Smedley, stated, "People may assume goodness when it costs nothing, or in a business point of view when a money-making object is the underlying motive, or give to a public charity, however, grudgingly, for reputation's sake; but these people, in the secret of their homes, without a thought or hope of compensation, gave of their time, labor and money, to the oppressed of a down-trodden race who sought their aid, while the public reviled them, society ostracized them, and the spirit of denunciation was manifested toward them by individuals of all ranks from a scavenger to a President."

turned his job as porter on the Illinois Central Railroad into a smuggling operation that sped runaways to Chicago in baggage cars. Merina, a black laborer in Waukegan, Illinois, escorted passengers while working for grain dealer James Cory. Onlookers assumed that Merina's companions were also in Cory's employ. In his autobiography, the Reverend Thomas James, an operative in Rochester, New York, reported on female agents who filled sacks with cayenne pepper to throw at police interfering in the rescue of a girl from a courtroom. In Cincinnati, Ohio, John Hatfield, a deacon of Zion Baptist Church, faked a funeral procession that allowed 28 refugees to exit the city undetected. At a waystation in Bloomfield, New Jersey, agents Abigail E. Holmes Rusby and John B. Rusby depended on assistance from their young son, Henry Hurd Rusby, who served as a transporter of escapees. At Marengo, on Alum Creek in Morrow County, Ohio, the Reverend Aaron Lancaster Benedict used his six-year-old cousins, Livius Benedict and Mordecai Benedict, as wagon drivers. In adulthood, Mordecai remained a part of the Underground Railroad team.

Unsung Women

A number of agents who history shortchanges were brave female stationkeepers and conductors, both adults and young girls. They included disguise artists, seamstresses and clothiers, hair cutters and beard trimmers, cooks, guides, couriers, and nurses such as Elizabeth Wickes Bradford, Catherine White Coffin, Abigail "Abby" Kelley Foster, Fanny Butzel Heineman, Lucretia Coffin Mott, Jean Lowry Rankin, and Cynthia Dunbar Thoreau. In the 1820s, laundress Vina Curry in Guilford County, North Carolina, recycled the manumission papers of her deceased husband by passing them to black males needing written proof of liberation. Elizabeth Buffum Chace, an operative at Valley Falls, Rhode Island, forged freedom documents for refugees to present on railway cars on their way to Worcester, Massachusetts. Around 1828, a slave residing with Elizabeth Cooper and Truman Cooper fled recapture and gained the support of two female agents as he passed through the Underground Railroad stations of Lancaster County, Pennsylvania, to Quiggs Tavern in Georgetown, Pennsylvania. After Hannah Quiggs freed the man from captors, he lodged at the safehouse of Jeremiah Cooper. For a week, Jeremiah Cooper's wife carried food to the slave's hideout in the woods. Clad in Jeremiah's clothing, the slave escaped to Chester County, Pennsylvania.

> A scathing denigration of Underground Railroad agents came from Samuel Seabury, a clergyman: "That these persons violate the law of the land, is, in my judgment, the last part of their guilt. I believe them to be not only *legally* but *morally* delinquent, instigators and abettors, directly, of fraud, and theft, and indirectly, and by consequence, of rapine and murder; fomenters of discontent and sedition; and I consider the credit accorded to them for philanthropy and manhood, to be the evidence of a perverted moral sentiment, and diseased state of the public mind."

At Sunnyside Home, a safehouse outside Kimberton, Pennsylvania, from the 1820s to the 1850s, Esther Fussell Lewis along with her four daughters—Elizabeth R. Lewis, Graceanna Lewis, Mariann Lewis, and Rebecca Lewis—provided comfort, nutrition, and healing for the exhausted traveler needing lengthy recuperation. Another volunteer, Elizabeth Hodgson "Eliza" Cooper at Williamson in Wayne County, New York, taught Frederick Douglass how to read and write. At Salem, New Jersey, Quaker conductors Abigail "Abbie" Goodwin and her older sister, Elizabeth "Betsy" Goodwin, managed a depot from 1838 until Betsy's death in 1860. Abbie Goodwin operated the stop alone until 1861. With the aid of local women, the Goodwins stocked a clothing closet with cloaks, sweaters, baby buntings, knitted caps, shawls, and mittens suited to the cold winters that southern slaves would encounter farther north. In 1850 in Cincinnati, Ohio, an activist and leader of a women's support system, Mrs. Andrew H. Ernst, organized a sewing circle to aid fugitives and remarked on the hundreds of runaways who found sanctuary in the area. As feminist historian Elizabeth Cady Stanton explained, these female volunteers identified with the slave's plight because of their own social, economic, religious, and political shackles. Female agents had particular compassion for girls and women who fled sexual bondage or forced prostitution.

Solving Problems

On water, operatives created their own solutions to rescues, particularly the readying of skiffs for quick crossing of creeks and rivers. Because of the large number of black bargemen, stevedores, stewards, cooks, barbers, leadsmen, and firemen on river steamers, the successful merging of another black male face in a clutch of African American laborers required little more than timing and luck. The crewmen of the brig *Casket* and other seagoing agents provided less exhaustive passage than overland treks from Alabama, the Carolinas, Florida, Georgia, Louisiana, Maryland, Mississippi, and Virginia. In 1818, men on the *Casket* concealed William Grimes in a hollowed-out cotton bale for a voyage out of Savannah, Georgia, to New York harbor. On a longer voyage, in 1858, sailors aboard the cotton sloop *Metropolis* successfully hid Tom Wilson among cotton bales until the ship exited the port of New Orleans and made its way to Liverpool, England. The risk was considerable. One sailor, James D. Lane of Albany, New York, netted a 12-year prison sentence in 1843 for allowing runaways to board a vessel in the harbor at Norfolk. For breaking laws against aiding runaways, captains could be hanged and their cargo and vessels confiscated.

Freedman William H. Robinson, author of *From Log Cabin to the Pulpit; or, Fifteen Years in Slavery* (1913), recalled the work of his father, Peter Robinson, a drayman and pilot who hid runaways for escape down the Cape Fear River in Wilmington, North Carolina, to the Atlantic Ocean. Two Quaker oystermen, Sam Fuller and a Mr. Elliot, contributed to strategies for smuggling slaves out of the South past fumigators of cargo holds and for searches led by bounty hunters and their dog packs. The success of the operation was the subject of an article in the October 29, 1849, issue of the *Wilmington Journal* about the daily departures of fugitives. Pro-slavery factions attributed the success of Underground Railroad rescues to abolitionist captains from New England, who risked hanging if caught while still in the harbor's jurisdiction.

Avoiding Capture

On water and land, Underground Railroad volunteers, both black and white, remained alert to the dangers of recapture and arrest. At Girard, Pennsylvania, the Reverend Charles Shipman armed both himself and his passenger with sticks. Some transporters removed their horses' shoes and muffled their feet with burlap and twine. They relied on sounds and sights—a dinner bell, a mourning dove's coo or whippoorwill's call, a display of a coded quilt pattern, or a pair of blue and yellow lanterns on an approaching boat—to signal that sanctuary was near. Another indicator involved the whistling or humming of a familiar tune, such as "Old Dan Tucker," the signal in Lydia Maria Francis Child's allegorical play *The Stars and Stripes* (1853). The Reverend Samuel Dutton, an agent in New Haven, Connecticut, instructed his family to listen for a coded knock at the kitchen door. In Farmington, Connecticut, a young girl, Mary Ann Cowles, studied strangers on Main Street and sang a children's song that agents recognized as a coded alert that slave nabbers were in the area. At safehouses, owners used lawn statues of black lackeys to hold signal lanterns—tied with a bright strip of cloth if passage was safe or left unlit if danger lurked. Another lawn jockey signal was the pointing of the figure's hat toward the north, the symbol for safety. At Farmington, Illinois, an operative named Deacon Birges drugged slave catchers with soporifics and relayed runways during the hunters' lengthy naps. Agents shouldered a burden of criticism from the pulpit, ostracism by family, being spied on by neighbors, and ridicule of their children by schoolmates. Many ignored threats on their lives and handbills offering rewards and the gratitude of pro-slavers for their capture or execution. One of the operatives maligned for slaving was Noadiah Moore of Champlain, New York, whose benevolent work was denounced in an 1844 issue of the *Herald of Freedom.*

Particularly offensive were allegations that agents engaged in illegal operations to acquire slaves solely as a source of free labor. The scam was the brainchild of unscrupulous individuals who hired runaways and then scared them away without paying wages for their work. In 1852, one purported slave rescuer, H.F. Painter of Clarksville, Tennessee, offered passage north in exchange for $20. After his rapid departure to Nashville in December 1852, the *Clarksville Jeffersonian* revealed his double-dealing among the slaves of Robertson County.

Costs and Risks

The price of being an agent could prove daunting. In 1857, Eliza Sly, a Missouri operative, served time in the state penitentiary at Jefferson City, Missouri, for her activism. In Louisiana, free blacks who sheltered runaways faced a fine of 30 livres per day, roughly one-half the price of a house. The Philadelphia Anti-Slavery Society provided the Reverend Arthur Bollus Bradford with a sword cane to wield against pro-slavery stalkers in Darlington, Ohio. In the case of agent Isaac Griffen in Easton, New York, the death of two of his children resulted from the concealment of a slave carrying smallpox.

It was not uncommon for agents to be injured or to be victims of stalking, stoning, arson, ruinous lawsuits, and even kidnap, torture, and murder. In 1856, Missouri ruffians swooped down on a trading post at Osawatomie, Kansas, owned by Jacob Benjamin, August Bondi, and Theodore Wiener. The three Jewish traders lost the building, goods, and livestock. Violence plagued operatives in Columbia, Pennsylvania. According to an article in the *Columbia Spy,* a pro-slavery faction fomented a riot on August 23, 1834, in protest of miscegenation. Angry whites stoned the houses of black activists and forced some families from town. Nonetheless, black agents of the Underground Railroad gathered to halt the reenslavement of William Baker and his wife from Baltimore County Plantation, whose white owner secured them in the Columbia jail. In the uproar, whites arrested a black named Cole and accused him of shooting a deputy.

Assaults and harassment took bizarre forms. In Salem, Iowa, slave owner Ruel Daggs sued 19 local rescuers of slaves. A teenage operative, Harriet Overton, saved her father in Bernadotte, Illinois, by mounting her horse and swinging a lead bar at his attackers. In August 1858, the *United States Democratic Review* reported that a Maryland agent named Bowers was tarred and feathered for his aiding a black fugitive. In mid-February 1854, Norris Day escaped a charge of luring slaves from bondage but faced a mob of angry Kentuckians who threatened lynching. Harriet Martineau, the author of *Society in America: Observations Made During a Stay in 1837* (1837), reported that those liberators found in the South risked a worse fate—flogging and torture for abetting slave insurrections. One transporter, Milton Huggins of Highland County, Ohio, died from injuries sustained during a rescue when a horse fell on him. For Willis Lago, a free black from Cincinnati, Ohio, an 1859 court case in Woodford County, Kentucky, found him guilty of assisting the flight of Charlotte Nichols, the chattel of Claiborne W. Nichols of Versailles, Kentucky. Because Lago accepted $50 to finance Nichols's escape, a famous court battle ensued in 1860 that pitted two governors—William Dennison of Ohio against Beriah Magoffin of Kentucky—in a federal case heard by the Supreme Court. No legal repercussions resulted for either Lago or Charlotte Nichols.

The memoir *A Woman's Life-Work: Labors and Experiences of Laura S. Haviland* (1882) reports the rescue of the Beach family in Michigan and the cost to agent Luther Donald. Because the slave owner sued Donald for harboring runaways and for conspiring to aid their escape, Donald lost his farm. Supporters offered funds to make up part of his loss and to keep him in service to the Underground Railroad. Farther south, an agent named Amason was arrested in Memphis, Tennessee, on his way to Cincinnati, Ohio, with two Georgia escapees. When Amason arrived in Albany, Georgia, he faced a mob angry enough to throttle him. After he escaped death, the editor of the *Macon Daily Telegraph* sided with the would-be hangmen, whom he exonerated for their murderous rage. The mysterious death of operative Elijah Anderson in the Kentucky state penitentiary on the last day of his sentence for slave theft led historians to believe that he was murdered.

To prepare for such dangers, agent John P. Parker of Ripley, Ohio, and others like him armed themselves and faced challengers head-on. At Green Township in Indiana County, Pennsylvania, George Atcheson maintained a force of armed security guards to patrol the property and shoot the bloodhounds of slave hunters and posses. In Boston, gambler John P. Coburn used his profits to hire a black regiment, the Massasoit Guards, who patrolled Beacon Hill to protect runaways from recapture.

See also: anti-slavery fairs; bloodhounds; bounty hunters; civil disobedience; code, Underground Railroad; disguise; quilts; safehouses; slave tokens; spies.

Sources

Chesney, Pharaoh Jackson, and John Coram Webster. *Last of the Pioneers: or, Old Times in East Tennessee.* Knoxville, TN: S.B. Newman, 1902.

Cockrum, Colonel William. *History of the Underground Railroad As It Was Conducted by the Anti-Slavery League.* Oakland City, IN: J.W. Cockrum, 1915.

Haviland, Laura S. *A Woman's Life-Work: Labors and Experiences of Laura S. Haviland.* Cincinnati, OH: Walden & Stowe, 1882.

Mohr, Clarence L. *On the Threshold of Freedom: Masters and Slaves in Civil War Georgia.* Baton Rouge: Louisiana State University Press, 2001.

Robinson, William H. *From Log Cabin to the Pulpit; or, Fifteen Years in Slavery.* Eau Clair, WI: James H. Tifft, 1913.

"Runaway Slaves in Maryland." *United States Democratic Review* 42:2 (August 1858): 164–76.

Seabury, Samuel. *American Slavery Distinguished from the Slavery of English Theorists, and Justified by the Law of Nature.* New York: Mason Brothers, 1861.

Agler, Margaret Van Gundy (1770–1843)

Margaret Van Gundy Agler, the widow of Frederick Agler of Cumberland County, Pennsylvania, operated a safehouse for runaway slaves. The Aglers, pioneers of Mifflin Township, Ohio, settled in Franklin County around 1806. Two years later, they purchased 908 acres of prime farmland from the U.S. military. When Frederick Agler died in 1824, his wife reared their 12 children unaided. New arrivals on the Underground Railroad identified Margaret's two-story residence at 2828 Sunbury Road at Columbus, Ohio, as a white frame house on the bend of Alum Creek. Margaret used a concealed chamber in the upstairs bathroom for hiding slaves.

Source

History of Franklin and Pickaway Counties, Ohio. Cleveland, OH: Williams Brothers, 1880.

Agnew, Allen (1796–1869)
Agnew, Maria Pierson (1810–1870)

A collaborator with Thomas Garrett and Harriet Tubman, Allen Agnew of New Garden in Chester County, Pennsylvania, superintended transfers along the Pennsylvania–Canada route. After marrying Maria Pierson of Pennsbury, Pennsylvania, in 1828, he resettled on a farm at Kennett Square and joined the Presbyterian church. In December 1854, Thomas Garrett reported to James Miller McKim that the Agnews were forwarding six men and one woman. One of the men had worn through his shoes. Some passengers traveled directly from the Agnew safehouse to neighbors Dr. Bartholomew Fussell and Lydia Morris Fussell or Dinah Hannum Mendenhall and Isaac Mendenhall or to the anti-slavery office of William Still in Philadelphia.

Source

Futhey, J. Smith, and Gilbert Cope. *History of Chester County, Pennsylvania.* Philadelphia: Louis H. Everts, 1881.

Alcott, Louisa May (1832–1888)

A gentle feminist author and defender of civil rights, Louisa May "Lu" Alcott supported the Underground Railroad. Born in Germantown, Pennsylvania, she spent her early teens at The Wayside, a safehouse in Concord, Massachusetts, where she, her mother and father, educators Abigail May Alcott and Amos Bronson Alcott, and three sisters lived from April 1845 to November 1848. A tunnel connected the main dwelling to a wine house. The Alcotts mingled with the Boston-Concord abolitionist elite—Lydia Jackson Emerson and Ralph Waldo Emerson, Margaret Fuller, James Russell Lowell, Henry David Thoreau, and Julia Ward Howe. Louisa May Alcott's maternal uncle, the Reverend Samuel Joseph May, co-founded the American Anti-Slavery Society.

After moving to Boston in 1849, Alcott supported her family with novels, essays, and short fiction that expressed her liberal leanings toward the abolition of slavery and the boycott of slave-raised or slave-made goods. Her family supported the lengthy journeys of Harriet Tubman by welcoming her to their home. At the beginning of the Civil War, Louisa May Alcott volunteered to nurse the Union wounded at the Union Hospital in Washington, D.C.

Source

Alcott, Louisa May. *Louisa May Alcott, Her Life, Letters and Journals.* Boston: Little, Brown, 1928.

Alexander, John (1813–?)

A former slave, 44-year-old John Alexander fled from Maryland to Pennsylvania aboard the Underground Railroad. In 1857, he left Kent County in company with 26-year-old Sam Benton, James Henry, and Samuel Turner. The four men received aid from secret agents of the Philadelphia Vigilance Committee.

Source

Still, William. *The Underground Railroad.* Philadelphia: Porter & Coates, 1871.

Allen, Abraham (1798–1867)
Allen, Cata Howland (1800–1866)

A conductor of the Underground Railroad, farmer Abraham "Abram" Allen, an immigrant from Armagh, Ireland, advanced the cause of liberty in Clinton County, Ohio. In 1818, he married Cata "Katy" Howland Allen of Dutchess County, New York. At their home in Wilmington, Ohio, the Allens collaborated with Elihu Oren and Jane Newcomb Oren, residents of Liberty, Ohio. In addition to feeding and housing refugees, the Allens promoted black people's right to liberty and justice.

The Wayside in Concord, Massachusetts, was home to novelist Louisa May Alcott in the late 1840s and a busy stop on the Underground Railroad. A tunnel connected the main dwelling to a wine house. *(Library of Congress)*

Abraham and Cata bundled passengers into their specially designed curtained carriage, dubbed the "Liberator," and passed them on after dark to network supervisors Elihu Oren and Jane Newcomb Oren or to Abel Beven, Joseph Coat, or Dr. Watson at Paintersville, Ohio. Among the Allens' fellow abolitionists were Dr. Abraham Brooke and Elizabeth Lukens Brooke, Amos Davis, John Hollin, Seth Linton, and John L. Thompson. Dr. Brooke, a transporter of the secret network, supported the Allens' sanctuary.

The Allens were disciples of major spokespersons for abolition—Lydia Maria Francis Child, Levi Coffin, William Lloyd Garrison, and Isaac Tatem Hopper. From 1843 to 1852, Abram Allen was a manager of the American Anti-Slavery Society. Despite the ridicule of local pro-slavery factions, the Allens maintained their principles and supported the election of Abraham Lincoln in 1860. Supporting the family's relays over the secret network were Jonathan A. Hadley, Thomas Hibben, Eli McGregor, John Work, and Thomas Wraith. In 1843, the fervor of anti-slavery activism caused a schism in the Methodist Episcopal Church and the formation of Wesleyan Methodism, a bulwark of Christian abolitionism. In subsequent years, supporters of abolition gained more converts, in part because of the fervor of the Allens.

See also: American Anti-Slavery Society.

Sources

Beers, W.H. *The History of Clinton County, Ohio.* Chicago: privately published, 1882.

Bentley, Anna Briggs. *American Grit: A Woman's Letters from the Ohio Frontier.* Lexington: University Press of Kentucky, 2002.

Allen, Nathaniel Topliff (1832–1903) Allen, Caroline Swift Bassett (1831–1913)

An educator and abolitionist in Middlesex County, Massachusetts, Nathaniel Topliff Allen and his wife,

Caroline Swift Bassett Allen of Nantucket, were friends to the runaway slave. Nathaniel corresponded with Underground Railroad organizers and philanthropists Frederick Douglass, William Lloyd Garrison, Theodore Parker, Wendell Addison Phillips, and Charles Sumner. In accordance with the family's Unitarian beliefs, the Allens maintained a depot at their home at 35 Webster Street in West Newton. Their activism resulted in threats of arson. The Allen home is listed among Registered Historic Places.

Source

Stern, Madeleine G. *We the Women: Career Firsts of Nineteenth-Century America.* Lincoln: University of Nebraska Press, 1994.

Allen, Richard (1760–1831)

At the beginning of the nineteenth century, the Reverend Richard Allen became one of the most influential black males in America. In the custody of a Delaware farmer named Stokeley, at age 17, Allen began earning the $2,000 needed to purchase his freedom by sawing firewood. His escape is one of the valuable slave narratives published in Isaac Tatem Hopper's biweekly column "Tales of the Oppression" in the *National Anti-Slavery Standard.* In flight from Maryland to Philadelphia, Allen set up a shoe repair shop in the 1790s, where he served the congregation of St. George's Methodist Church. He and the Reverend Absalom Jones, another former slave, offered heroic service to citizens during Philadelphia's yellow fever epidemic of July 1793 by going house to house to determine who survived. They buried corpses that others feared to touch and collected orphaned children. The two men issued a monograph entitled *Narrative of the Proceedings of the Black People, During the Late Awful Calamity in Philadelphia* (1793).

A fearless black man living in a white society, Allen co-founded the Free African Society of Philadelphia and in 1816 established the African Methodist Episcopal Church, a depot of the Underground Railroad. He endured unfounded suspicions that his home harbored runaways for the secret network. Following one unlawful search of his residence, he pressed a successful lawsuit requiring the bounty hunters to apologize. Isaac Hopper defended Allen in another case involving the search for a black man named Dick. The planter who owned Dick went to jail because he lacked the funds to pay the fine. Hopper paid Allen's legal bills. Allen continued rescuing slaves until his death, after which Bethel Church took over his responsibilities until blacks received national emancipation on January 1, 1863.

See also: African Methodist Episcopal Church; bounty hunters.

Sources

Meaders, Daniel. "Kidnapping Blacks in Philadelphia: Isaac Hopper's Tales of Oppression." *Journal of Negro History* 80:2 (Spring 1995): 47–65.
Wesley, Charles H. *Richard Allen, Apostle of Freedom.* New York: Associated Publishers, 1969.

Allen, Robert (1793–?)

One of numerous free black conductors in Maryland, 50-year-old Robert Allen was convicted of abetting runaways. In 1843, Queen Annes County police arrested him for harboring George Emory, a child enslaved by planter William Emory. Three witnesses helped convict Allen, who entered the state penitentiary on May 6, 1845, to serve a five-year sentence.

Source

Prison records, Maryland State Archives.

Allen, Samuel (1825–1910)
Allen, Mary Gilmore (1829–1874)

An immigrant from Ireland, Samuel Allen served the Springfield route of the Underground Railroad through Mercer County, Pennsylvania. After immigrating to the United States at age 10 with his father, Robert Allen, Samuel grew up on a farm and in 1847 married Mary Gilmore. The two supported abolition; Samuel promoted the principles and aims of the secret network in debates and public addresses.

Source

White, J.G. *Twentieth Century History of Mercer County.* Chicago: Lewis, 1909.

Allinson, William James (1810–1874)

At 301 High Street in Burlington City, New Jersey, Quaker pharmacist William J. Allinson aided fugitives at his shop. Under the influence of an abolitionist grandfather and a personal friend, journalist and poet John Greenleaf Whittier, Allinson opened the cellar of his pharmacy to runaways and used the upstairs for discussions of Underground Railroad work. In 1851, the druggist published a slave biography, *Memoir of Quamino Buccau, a Pious Methodist.*

On August 13, 1836, Allinson rescued Severn Martin, a refugee from a Virginia plantation who had lived free since 1820. When Martin's owner, Colonel Christian, seized and chained Martin and tried to pay passage on a steamboat, the captain refused to transport the former slave. Allinson intervened, sped Martin to safety, and raised $800 to pay for his manumission. A melodramatic broadside title proclaimed, *Pennsylvania and New Jersey Slave Trade!! The Case of Severn Martin* (1836).

Source

Allinson, William J. *Memoir of Quamino Buccau, a Pious Methodist.* Philadelphia: Henry Longstreth, 1851.

Alston, John (1794–1874)

A collaborator with Samuel D. Burris and a cousin and neighbor of John Hunn, Sr., the Quaker stationmaster John Alston of Middletown in New Castle County, Delaware, made a personal contribution to liberty. In addition to farming and to teaching Hunn about agriculture, Alston supported abolitionism through his church, the Appoquinimink Friends Meeting House at Odessa, where he served as treasurer and custodian. Aiding him on relays of runaways were Daniel Corbet and William Still, who maintained an anti-slavery office in Philadelphia. In 1841, Alston wrote in his diary a prayer asking God to allow him to maintain a sanctuary for slaves according to Christian dictates.

Source

Conrad, Henry Clay. *History of the State of Delaware.* Wilmington, DE: privately published, 1908.

American Anti-Slavery Society

Convened in Philadelphia between December 4 and 6, 1833, the American Anti-Slavery Society established its mission with pure ideals. Inspired by William Lloyd Garrison, founder of *The Liberator,* and nurtured by the Reverend James Miller McKim, orator Arnold Buffum, and philanthropist brothers Arthur Tappan and Lewis Tappan, the new effort attempted to supplant local abolitionist societies in New England and the Middle Atlantic states with a more vigorous, broader-based effort. As Colonel William Monroe Cockrum explains in *History of the Underground Railroad As It Was Conducted by the Anti-Slavery League* (1915), the formalized society replaced the haphazard rescues by a few unorganized abolitionist cells with teams of volunteers and a sophisticated detection and spy system. Those members who joined the society willingly accepted the possibility of fines and imprisonment for opposing federal law.

The opening session at Philadelphia faced opposition in the form of armed mobs. Nonetheless, 60 members from a total of 10 states signed the society's constitution. Members affirmed that they intended no breach of law but that they would not condemn anyone for helping a runaway escape recapture or torture and punishment.

Signers of the Constitution of the American Anti-Slavery Society

Connecticut
Robert B. Hall
Simeon S. Jocelyn
Alpheus Kingsley
Samuel Joseph May
Edwin A. Stillman

Maine
James Frederick Otis
Joseph Southwick
David Thurston
Isaac Winslow
Nathan Winslow

Massachusetts
James G. Barbadoes
Arnold Buffum
John R. Campbell
Effingham L. Capron
Joshua Coffin
William Lloyd Garrison
Daniel E. Jewett
David T. Kimball, Jr.
Amos A. Phelps
Nathaniel Southard
Daniel S. Southmayd
Horace P. Wakefield
John Greenleaf Whittier

New Hampshire
David Campbell

New Jersey
Chalkey Gillingham
John McCullough
Jonathan Parkhurst
James White

New York
Abraham L. Cox
Charles W. Denison
John Frost
William Goodell
Beriah Green, Jr.
William Greene, Jr.
John Rankin
Lewis Tappan
Elizur Wright, Jr.

Ohio
John M. Sterling
Levi Sutliff
Milton Sutliff

Pennsylvania
Edwin A. Atlee
Edwin P. Atlee
Bartholomew Fussell
David Jones
Evan Lewis
James Loughhead
Enoch Mack
Jason McCrummill
James Miller McKim
James Mott, Jr.
Robert Purvis
John Sharp, Jr.
Thomas Shipley
John R. Sleeper
Aaron Vickers
Thomas Whitson

Rhode Island
George W. Benson
Ray Potter
John Prentice

Vermont
Orson S. Murray

AMERICAN
ANTI-SLAVERY
ALMANAC,
FOR
1840,

BEING BISSEXTILE OR LEAP-YEAR, AND THE 64TH OF AMERICAN INDEPENDENCE. CALCULATED FOR NEW YORK; ADAPTED TO THE NORTHERN AND MIDDLE STATES.

NORTHERN HOSPITALITY—NEW YORK NINE MONTHS' LAW.
The slave steps out of the slave-state, and his chains fall. A free state, with another chain, stands ready to re-enslave him.

Thus saith the Lord, Deliver him that is spoiled out of the hands of the oppressor.

NEW YORK:
PUBLISHED BY THE AMERICAN ANTI-SLAVERY SOCIETY,
NO. 143 NASSAU STREET.

Among the core objectives of the American Anti-Slavery Society from its creation in 1833 were to distribute abolitionist literature and to encourage slave rescue operations. *(MPI/Stringer/Hulton Archive/Getty Images)*

Society Aims

Members bound themselves by a constitution whose aims contrasted with those of the Declaration of Independence. A series of seven resolves set the society to a number of crucial tasks: to organize satellite societies, to dispatch abolitionist agents, to circulate anti-slavery journals and pamphlets, to enlist the help of ministers and journalists, to purify churches of support for human bondage, to encourage the participation of freedmen in rescue operations, and to end slavery as soon as possible throughout the nation. By 1837, the effort had fostered 161 branches in New York State alone. Society agents, working as spies, infiltrated slave territory in the guise of cartographers, geologists, itinerant traders, lumbermen, naturalists, surveyors, and teachers. Territories were code-named after trees: beech, dogwood, hickory, linden, maple, oak, sassafras, and walnut. In addition, the society published a stream of broadsides and pamphlets clarifying issues and building consensus among citizens. At its height in 1835, the American Anti-Slavery Society Press mailed out more than 50,000 free publications per week.

Among the women who supported the effort was orator Abby Kelley Foster, whom Garrison nominated in 1840 to a standing committee. After the election of Maria Weston Chapman, Lydia Maria Francis Child, and Lucretia Coffin Mott to society offices, an antifeminist backlash led to the resignation of James Gillespie Birney, Gerrit Smith, Arthur Tappan, and Lewis Tappan. Opposing the exclusion of women were Jonathan Peckham Miller, James Mott, Jr., and Abraham Liddon Pennock, Sr. The misogyny among male abolitionists resulted in the formation of female anti-slavery societies and sewing circles, women's benevolent agencies that raised cash, held abolitionist fairs, and stockpiled clothing, blankets, and linens for the assistance of refugees. After passage of the Kansas-Nebraska Act of 1854, Lydia Jackson Emerson and her husband, orator Ralph Waldo Emerson, enlisted volunteer rescuers for the American Anti-Slavery Society.

See also: black soldiers; female anti-slavery societies; punishments; spies.

Source

Cockrum, Colonel William. *History of the Underground Railroad As It Was Conducted by the Anti-Slavery League.* Oakland City, IN: J.W. Cockrum, 1915.

American Revolution

The anticipation of liberty overwhelmed American colonists in the early months of 1776, preceding the Revolutionary War. However, free colonials and slaves held different perspectives on the establishment of an independent republic. During the colonial war for freedom from the British king George III, General George Washington debated the feasibility of enlisting black soldiers. Meanwhile, black slaves received their first offer of freedom from the British army. For those 20,000 blacks who served the British military, liberty required a victory for England.

Only 5,000 blacks found welcome in the colonial army, which began enlisting nonwhite soldiers when Congress approved the shift to an integrated force in late March 1779. Pressing the issue was John Laurens, an abolitionist from South Carolina who pledged his patrimony of 40 slaves to the colonial cause. After the colonies ousted the British in 1783 under the Treaty of Paris, 5,000 blacks established residence in Canada, a majority in the Maritime Provinces. Of those remaining in the United States, 90 percent lived in bondage in a new nation built on the concepts of liberty and human equality. From this era until emancipation on January 1, 1863, slaves escaping the plantation South looked toward Canada as a haven of freedom.

See also: black soldiers.

Source

Massey, Gregory D. *John Laurens and the American Revolution.* Columbia: University of South Carolina Press, 2000.

Ames, Orson (1799–1867)
Ames, Harlow (ca. 1804–1880)
Ames, Leonard, Jr. (1818–ca. 1893)

Three Underground Railroad agents in Mexico, New York, Orson Ames and his brothers, Harlow Ames and Leonard Ames, Jr., took part in slave rescues. A native of Litchfield, Connecticut, Orson grew up in the town of Mexico from the age of five, when his family traveled west by ox-drawn wagon to farm the New York frontier. The Ames family brought with them their Methodist Episcopal beliefs as well as concern for refugees. Orson's rise to wealth and prestige began with sheepherding, marriage to Amy Perkins (1800–1851) in 1824, and his operation of a sawmill. In 1826, he opened a tannery at Black Creek. By 1833, his investments extended to a shoe shop on South Jefferson Street and a trip-hammer mill for the manufacture of axes and scythes.

The Ames brothers established a reputation for kindness to fugitives. Leonard appears to have been an organizer and conductor. Harlow built a barn on Colosse Road above a secret chamber, where he and his wife, Adaline Mitchell Ames (1812–ca. 1880), appear to have sheltered runaways. Orson served as Superintendent of the Poor, a local outreach to the needy. On June 21, 1838, Orson Ames, James M. Barrows, and Starr Clark accepted appointment by the Oswego County Anti-Slavery Society to the vigilance committee, an agency that offered food, clothing, directions, and legal advice to slaves fleeing bounty hunters and posses.

After eight agents broke William "Jerry" McHenry (or Henry), a mulatto cooper, out of the Clinton Square jail in Syracuse, New York, on October 1, 1851, he spent two nights in Mexico, New York. The first night, he stayed at the safehouse of Amy and Orson Ames at 3339 Main Street, and then he moved on to a barn at the rural depot of Asa Beebe and Mary Whipple Beebe. Orson appears to have conspired with his younger brother, Leonard, to convey McHenry by boat to Kingston, Ontario. The blatant violation of the Fugitive Slave Law of 1850 established the dedication of Oswego County's secret network to civil disobedience.

See also: bounty hunters; Fugitive Slave Law of 1850; vigilance committees.

Sources

Churchill, John. *Landmarks of Oswego County, New York.* Syracuse, NY: D. Mason, 1895.

McAndrew, Mike, "Bold Raid Freed a Man," *Syracuse Post-Standard,* February 14, 2005.

Amistad

A unique black revolt in North American history, on July 2, 1839, a mutiny aboard the Portuguese slaver *Amistad* jolted the American public with headlines about the plight of kidnapped Africans. After the ship sailed from Sierra Leone toward the Caribbean, the slaver slipped into Havana, Cuba, by night to avoid shore patrols and advanced to Puerto Príncipe. Joseph Cinqué, a Mandingo nobleman in his mid-twenties, used a nail to liberate the human cargo from foot and neck shackles. He and a slave named Grabeau distributed machetes, and the mutineers seized the vessel for return to West Africa. The ship's white pilot deceived the slaves and sailed north to New England. On August 2, in sight of Culloden Point at Montauk, New York, the U.S.S. *Washington,* a Coast Guard surveying brig, captured the *Amistad* and anchored it at New London, Connecticut, on August 26.

At New Haven, Connecticut, Cinqué and his collaborators faced charges of murder and piracy. Against the pro-slavery views of President Martin Van Buren, Lewis Tappan, a Calvinist from Northampton, Massachusetts, led abolitionists in formal protest of the treatment of the Africans, whom officials classified as "salvage." Providing defense was attorney Ellis

In July 1839, African slaves aboard the schooner *Amistad* seized the ship en route from the Caribbean, killed the captain and cook, and sailed unwittingly to the Connecticut shore. The incident and subsequent trial put the issue of slavery in the headlines. *(Library of Congress)*

Gray Loring; financial backing came from the Reverend Simeon Smith Jocelyn of New Haven, Connecticut, and from the Reverend James William Charles Pennington, an Underground Railroad agent in New York City. Congressman John Quincy Adams, a former U.S. president, headed the defense team that carried the case through appeals. His presentation lasted over eight hours. As a result, the U.S. Supreme Court acquitted the 35 surviving Africans of the charges.

Before and after the extensive litigation, the mutineers sheltered with Underground Railroad operatives. In September 1839, the Horace Cowles family welcomed Teme (also Tamie), a young Mende girl, to their residence in Farmington, Connecticut. The male contingent of Africans lodged at a safehouse that Austin Franklin Williams, Jennet Cowles Williams, and other abolitionists built at 127 Main Street in Farmington, Connecticut, on May 4, 1841. Local abolitionists provided clothing, linens, church membership, and a 10-acre field for cultivation. During the lengthy court battle in summer 1841, one African, a teenage farmer named Foone, drowned in an estuary, perhaps in a deliberate act of self-destruction. He was buried in Riverside Cemetery. Philanthropists and mission societies funded the return of 32 of the former slaves to West Africa. Departing on November 25, 1841, aboard the *Gentleman,* they arrived at Freetown harbor in mid-January 1842.

Sources

Jones, Howard. *Mutiny on the* Amistad. Oxford, UK: Oxford University Press, 1987.

Osagie, Iyunolu Folayan. *The* Amistad *Revolt: Memory, Slavery, and the Politics of Identity in the United States and Sierra Leone.* Athens: University of Georgia Press, 2000.

Owens, William A. *Black Mutiny: The Revolt on the Schooner* Amistad. New York: Plume, 1997.

Spielberg, Steven, Maya Angelou, and Debbie Allen. Amistad: *"Give Us Free."* New York: Newmarket, 1998.

Amos, James Ralston (1824–1864)
Amos, Thomas Henry (1826–1869)

The Reverend James Ralston Amos and his younger brother, the Reverend Thomas Henry Amos, both Presbyterian ministers, promoted slave rescues via the Pennsylvania–Canada route of the Underground Railroad. The sons of farmer George Amos of Oxford, Pennsylvania, James and Thomas graduated in 1859 from Ashmun Institute, later named Lincoln University, which specialized in training black ministers to colonize West Africa. They accepted missions to Liberia, where both died.

Source

Carr, George B. "Lincoln University Origins." *Lincoln University Herald* 18:1 (January 1914): 9–11.

Anderson, Elijah (1808–1861)

An active Underground Railroad agent in Madison, Indiana, blacksmith Elijah Anderson of Fluvanna, Virginia, managed the Ohio River crossing at Carrollton, in sight of the northern border of Kentucky. A free black, he arrived in Indiana from Lynchburg, Virginia, in 1837 and settled at a cabin in the Georgetown section on Walnut Street, where he collaborated with other conductors, including the Reverend Chapman Harris and Dr. Samuel Tibbets, Jr. Around age 30, Anderson operated a smithy in Madison, Indiana. He joined the African Methodist Episcopal Church, an Underground Railroad depot at 309 East Fifth Street, and built a brick residence that served as a waystation. An intrepid stationmaster, Anderson and two collaborators, Griffin Booth and Chapman Harris, led fleeing slaves from Kentucky to freedom. After townspeople drove Anderson out of town, in the 1850s, he moved to Cleveland, Ohio, and superintended a heavily traveled route. By 1855, he had escorted more than 1,000 refugees. He earned the admiration of attorney Rush Richard Sloane, a fellow conductor at Sandusky, Ohio.

Traveling far into the South, Anderson enlisted slaves from Kentucky to flee north into free territory. Because of his notoriety and the danger of retaliation, he left the region and resumed work in Lawrenceburg, Indiana. By 1855, he had assisted hundreds of fugitives from Carroll and Trimble counties in Kentucky. In 1856, a black traitor arranged for Anderson's seizure by Trimble County slavers. On the basis of incriminating documents contained in his carpetbag, authorities charged him with grand theft. He began serving an eight-year sentence for slave theft in mid-June 1857 in the Kentucky state penitentiary at Frankfort. During his incarceration, he established a reputation as a fine penitentiary blacksmith. After his mysterious demise in prison on March 4, 1861, the last day of his sentence, his rescue work passed to a brother, William J. Anderson.

See also: African Methodist Episcopal Church.

Sources

Anderson, William J. *Life and Narrative of William J. Anderson.* Chicago: *Daily Tribune,* 1857.

Hudson, J. Blaine. *Fugitive Slaves and the Underground Railroad in the Kentucky Borderland.* Jefferson, NC: McFarland, 2002.

Anderson, George (fl. 1850s)

The leader of a party of seven runaways, George Anderson succeeded in escaping bondage. In 1856, he fled Elkton in Cecil County, Maryland. Accompanying him were three North Carolinians—Matthew Bodams of Plymouth, Peter Heines of Eatontown, and James Morris of South End—and four Virginians from Portsmouth—Nathaniel Bowser, Thomas Cooper, Charity Thompson, and Charles Thompson. The eight runaways sought aid from agents of the Philadelphia Underground Railroad before continuing on their way.

Source

Still, William. *The Underground Railroad.* Philadelphia: Porter & Coates, 1871.

Anderson, John (ca. 1831–?)

The case of John "Jackey" Anderson, the son of a black runaway, caused a stir in the United States, Canada, and England. The slave of tobacco farmer Moses Burton of Howard County, Missouri, Anderson seethed with resentment at the sale of his mother in 1838. While engaged in supervising field hands, Anderson married Maria Tomlin, a widow; he visited her and their baby at the nearby farm where she was enslaved. After Burton sold Anderson to Colonel Reuben McDaniel of Saline County, the slave bid farewell to his wife and child before he escaped bondage in late September 1853.

On his way, Anderson stabbed Seneca T.P. Diggs, a Missouri farmer who tried to capture him. Anderson crossed Missouri and continued by boat upriver to Illinois. After Diggs died of his wound, the offer of a $1,000 reward sent slave catchers in search of Anderson. With the aid of Underground Railroad agents in Chicago and Detroit, Anderson reached Windsor, Ontario, where he remained until 1860. Quaker Underground Railroad agent Laura Smith Haviland failed in an attempt to smuggle Maria Anderson from Missouri in spring 1854.

Meanwhile, detectives traced Anderson to Haviland's home in Raisin, Michigan. Laura telegraphed Anderson to move farther inland to Chatham and Caledonia near Brantford, Ontario. In spring 1860, a Detroit slave owner named Brown obtained a court judgment allowing the return of Anderson to slavery in Missouri. Complicating the case was the murder charge against Anderson, which caught the attention of pro-slavery President James Buchanan. Under the 1842 Webster-Ashburton Treaty, which Daniel Webster and Lord Ashburton had forged between Canada and the United States, Anderson was slated to return South. Because the court ruled against Anderson on December 15, 1860, he expected to die in bondage. Proponents of the Underground Railroad feared that the Anderson case spelled the end of the secret network; pro-slavery factions in Tennessee rejoiced at the prospect. Intervention by the British and Foreign Anti-Slavery Society called for a new trial in a Toronto court, which found in Anderson's favor on February 9, 1861, on a technicality.

Lest a new trial find him guilty, Anderson resolved to leave for England, where a committee was collecting funds to buy Maria Anderson and her child from Brown. After a Toronto court exonerated him on February 16, 1861, Anderson's thanks for his humane treatment appeared in the *Montreal Gazette* of March 6. Before he could book passage to England, the Civil War began. The death of Maria's owner resulted in her sale. Anderson embarked for Liberia on December 24, 1862, and disappeared from history. A year later, editor Harper Twelvetrees published *The Story of the Life of John Anderson, the Fugitive Slave* (1863).

Sources

Anderson, John. *The Story of the Life of John Anderson, the Fugitive Slave.* London: W. Tweedie, 1863.
Fradin, Dennis Brindell. *Bound for the North Star: True Stories of Fugitive Slaves.* New York: Clarion, 2000.

Anderson, Matthew (1845–1928)
Anderson, Caroline Virginia Still Wiley (1848–1919)

The Reverend Matthew Anderson applied a number of methods to help black Americans obtain freedom. A native Pennsylvanian, he became a devout Christian in childhood and aided black refugees at the family farm, a waystation of the Underground Railroad. As pastor of Berean Presbyterian Church in Philadelphia, he heartened his black congregation with uplifting sermons on character and instructed children at the city's first black kindergarten. To aid former slaves with establishing homes, he taught vocational skills at Berean Institute and founded the Berean Building and Loan Association to help with finances. Anderson married the daughter of William Still. Dr. Caroline Virginia Still Wiley Anderson, a physician educated at Oberlin College and Women's Medical College in Philadelphia, founded and ran a clinic and dispensary in Philadelphia.

Source

Donnelly, Matt, "Let Freedom Reign," *Christian History,* February 2, 2001.

Anderson, Osborne Perry (1830–1872)

The only African Canadian to leave Chatham, Ontario, to fight at Harpers Ferry, Osborne Perry Anderson also served in the Union army during the Civil War. A native of West Fallowfield, Pennsylvania, he moved to Ontario in his early twenties and settled at Chatham, where he printed Mary Ann Shadd Cary's newspaper *The Provincial Freeman.* In spring 1858, he conspired with Martin Robinson Delany and John Brown on ways to free more slaves. Following the failed assault on the federal arsenal at Harpers Ferry on October 16, 1859, Anderson fled over Underground Railroad routes to Henry Watson's waystation at Chambersburg, Pennsylvania, and then to William C. Goodridge's photography studio at Centre Square in York, Pennsylvania, where he hid in the third story. Anderson continued to William Still's anti-slavery office in Philadelphia. To honor the slaves who supported Brown's insurrection, Anderson published *A Voice from Harpers Ferry* (1861), the only eyewitness account. At the beginning of the Civil War, he enlisted soldiers for black regiments in Arkansas and Indiana. Associates of the Underground Railroad were pallbearers at Anderson's funeral at the Fifteenth Street Presbyterian Church in Washington, D.C.

See also: black soldiers.

Source

Bordewich, Fergus M. *Bound for Canaan: The Underground Railroad and the War for the Soul of America.* New York: Amistad, 2005.

After the failed assault led by John Brown at Harpers Ferry, Virginia (now West Virginia), in 1859, Osborne P. Anderson—who had come from Canada to take part—fled via the Underground Railroad. In York, Pennsylvania, he hid in the home and photography studio of William C. Goodridge. *(Library of Congress)*

Anderson, William J. (1811–?)

The Reverend William J. Anderson, a former slave, aided the passage of fugitives on the Indiana–Canada route of the Underground Railroad. He was a freeborn native of Hanover County, Virginia; in 1816, his mother found work for him with a slave owner named Vance, who sold him for $375 to a trader leading a coffle to Tennessee. His last master owned property outside St. Michaels in Talbot County, Maryland. During his long servitude, Anderson concealed from a series of abusive owners his ability to read and write.

On July 4, 1836, at age 25, Anderson wrote his own pass with the intent of journeying to New Orleans and taking a ship to Boston or New York. He fled along the Ohio River to Madison, Indiana, where he flourished in agriculture and business. He managed his own waystation of the secret network at 713 Walnut Street and co-founded Madison's African Methodist Episcopal Church, which was next door to his home. In 1857, he published a slave autobiography, *Life and Narrative of William J. Anderson: Twenty-Four Years a Slave; Sold Eight Times! In Jail Sixty Times! Whipped Three Hundred Times!*

See also: African Methodist Episcopal Church; bloodhounds.

Sources

Anderson, William J. *Life and Narrative of William J. Anderson . . .* Chicago: *Daily Tribune,* 1857.

Sobel, Mechal. *Teach Me Dreams: The Search for Self in the Revolutionary Age.* Princeton, NJ: Princeton University Press, 2000.

Andrew, John Albion (1818–1867)

John Albion Andrew spearheaded two famous test cases against the onerous Fugitive Slave Law of 1850. Born to a wealthy merchant in Windham, Maine, he studied law after graduating from Gorham Academy and Bowdoin College. In the 1850s, he led the Underground Railroad legal teams defending Thomas M. Sims, a runaway from bondage in Georgia who federal marshals seized on April 3, 1851. Sims received support from the Boston Vigilance Committee, notably from William Lloyd Garrison and Lewis Hayden, the chief conductor of the city's Underground Railroad link. Andrew's second defense of a fugitive slave involved Anthony Burns after his arrest on March 9, 1855, for escaping bondage to Colonel Charles F. Suttle in Richmond, Virginia.

Following the failed raid on the federal arsenal at Harpers Ferry, Virginia (now West Virginia), Andrew championed insurrectionist John Brown as a visionary libertarian. Andrew's strong abolitionist position netted him the largest popular vote of any candidate for the governorship of Massachusetts. In support of Abraham Lincoln, on April 15, 1861, Andrew sent five regiments to defend Washington, D.C.

See also: Fugitive Slave Law of 1850.

Source

Pearson, Henry Greenleaf. *The Life of John A. Andrew, Governor of Massachusetts, 1861–1865.* Boston: Houghton Mifflin, 1904.

Andrews, John H. (fl. 1860s)

John H. Andrews faced prison time for rescuing slaves. He was arrested in St. Charles County, Missouri, near the Illinois border. In September 1860, he confessed to enticing two slaves from their masters, an act for which he was sentenced to two consecutive terms of three years. Having left a family of three in Ohio, on January 16, 1865, he petitioned Governor Thomas C. Fletcher for clemency. The governor granted the petition the next month.

Source

Frazier, Harriet C. *Runaway and Freed Missouri Slaves and Those Who Helped Them, 1763–1865.* Jefferson, NC: McFarland, 2004.

Anthony, Abial F. (1840–ca. 1936)

At a busy nexus of the Underground Railroad, Abial F. (or Abial B.) Anthony used his knowledge of river craft to aid slaves in flight. He worked as a barber at his shop at 11 Allen Street in Burlington, Vermont. He recalled from childhood that his father, Tony Anthony, sheltered slaves from Virginia. While employed as a cook in local hotels and steamers on Lake Champlain, Anthony conspired with Underground Railroad agents John Kendrick Converse and Sarah Allen Converse to conceal passengers on vessels bound from St. Albans Bay for St. John's, Quebec.

Source

Seaver, Frederick J. *Historical Sketches of Franklin County and Its Several Towns.* Albany, NY: J.B. Lyon, 1918.

Anthony, Mason (1803–1873)
Anthony, Elihu (1768–1863)

A native of Greenfield, New York, Quaker temperance orator and slave conductor Mason Anthony guided fugitives along the Saratoga line of the Underground Railroad. Aiding him was his father, Elihu Anthony, a Quaker preacher. Mason Anthony's contribution to rescue operations began in Saratoga County in 1838. Among his innovations was the distribution of female dress to black male passengers. He then relayed the fugitives incognito through Hadley and Luzerne in Warren County and on to safety at the waystation of Rachel Gilpin Robinson and Rowland Thomas Robinson at Rokeby Farm in Ferrisburg, Vermont. The Anthonys also collaborated with Chauncey Langdon Knapp, Vermont's secretary of state, who received runaways at his office at the State House.

Source

Calarco, Tom. *The Underground Railroad in the Adirondack Region.* Jefferson, NC: McFarland, 2004.

Anthony, Susan Brownell (1820–1906)

A member of a conscientious Quaker abolitionist family, Susan Brownell Anthony was a quiet hero of the secret network. Born in Adams, Massachusetts, she grew up amid protest of the slave trade by her father, Daniel Anthony, and the slave rescues of her uncle Asa Anthony at his safehouse outside Syracuse in Onondaga County, New York. In addition to her dedication to woman's suffrage, Susan Anthony campaigned for abolitionism and personally conducted slaves to waystations. She supported the activism of William Clough Bloss, Frederick Douglass, Sarah Parker Remond, and Harriet Tubman and promoted the secret work of conductors Chandler Darlington and Hannah M. Darlington at Kennett Square, Pennsylvania, and of Harriet Forten Purvis and Robert Purvis in Philadelphia.

In addition to moral support, Anthony lent her residence at 17 Madison Street in Rochester, New York, for harboring slaves on their way to Canada. Her brother, Merritt Anthony, was a conspirator of insurrectionist John Brown. Following the execution of Brown on December 2, 1859, for the raid on the federal arsenal at Harpers Ferry, Virginia (now West Virginia) Susan Anthony, accompanied by local agent Samuel Drummond Porter, distributed tickets to a memorial service at Lake Placid, New York. Her experience aiding female slaves sparked the activist's concern for women and initiated collaboration with other feminists to demand woman's suffrage.

Source

Stanton, Elizabeth Cady, and Susan B. Anthony. *Elizabeth Cady Stanton/Susan B. Anthony: Correspondence, Writings, Speeches.* New York: Schocken, 1981.

Anti-Slavery Convention of American Women

Female supporters of the Underground Railroad staked their place in civil disobedience at a convention held in New York City (May 9–12, 1837). The assembly was the nation's first public political meeting of women and the nation's first interracial convention. In defiance of white males who rejected their membership in the American Anti-Slavery Society in 1833, female delegates, led by Quaker minister Lucretia Coffin Mott and supported by editor Lydia Maria Francis Child, began organizing routes and coordinating political pressure groups.

At the second convention, held at Pennsylvania Hall in Philadelphia (May 15–18, 1838), orator Abigail "Abby" Kelley Foster made her first public oration to a mixed audience. Addressing the 3,000 white and black women were activists Maria Weston Chapman and Angelina Emily Grimké Weld, who projected their voices above a clutch of rock-hurling protesters. Pro-slavery factions were so incensed that on May 16 they burned the building and surged toward Mott's residence. Sarah Pugh joined other delegates in marching from the structure arm in arm with a black activist. The following day, Pugh offered her classroom as an assembly hall in which to continue the convention's discussions. A strong showing at a subsequent convention in Rochester, New York, in 1842 resulted in the enlistment of Mary Ann M'Clintock and Thomas M'Clintock as waystation operators and co-founders of the Western New York Anti-Slavery Society. The coordination of slave rescues and enlistment campaigns honed women's organizational skills, which reached their zenith in the drive for woman's suffrage.

See also: civil disobedience; female anti-slavery societies.

Source

Sterling, Dorothy, ed. *Turning the World Upside Down: The Anti-Slavery Convention of American Women Held in New York City, May 9–12.* New York: Feminist Press, 1987.

anti-slavery fairs

Among the fund-raising innovations of female activism on behalf of the Underground Railroad were anti-slavery fairs. Beginning in Boston in 1834 and spreading across New York State near the end of the 1830s following the first Anti-Slavery Convention of American Women, supporters began hosting craft fairs and bake sales to raise money and solicit donations for the rescue, clothing, feeding, and medical treatment of runaway slaves. Broadsides advertised watercolor paintings, gift books and songbooks, toys and teething rings, abolitionist periodicals, purses, and handmade armlets, collars, gloves, handkerchiefs, aprons, quilts, pressed-flower pictures, and table linens. Setting the pace for subsequent fund-raisers were fairs in Junius, Rochester, Seneca Falls, Victoria, and Waterloo, New York. In Waterloo, Elizabeth M'Clintock, an Underground Railroad agent, organized fund-raising activities over a seven-year period. In New York City, avid support came from Underground Railroad agent Abigail Hopper Gibbons. The African American women at the Broadway Tabernacle held an annual fair and charged an entry fee of 12.5¢ to raise money for the vigilance committee. In Lowell, Massachusetts, Catharine Rugg Rugg, an operative of the secret network, conducted a fair in 1839 to provide funds for runaways passing through Boston.

In Boston, the fair committee combined the talents of orator Maria Weston Chapman, organizer

Abigail "Abby" Kelley Foster, printer Oliver Johnson, and Ann Terry Greene Phillips, wife of orator Wendell Addison Phillips. Anna Murray Douglass provided refreshments; Mercy O. Haskins Powell and William Peter Powell supplied British-made goods. Chapman published the *Liberty Bell,* a bound-leather keepsake volume with gilt stamping, which anthologized the writing of Elizabeth Barrett Browning, Lydia Maria Francis Child, Henry Wadsworth Longfellow, James Russell Lowell, Harriet Martineau, and Wendell Addison Phillips. In the 1840 edition appeared "The Anniversary of Lovejoy's Martyrdom" (1838), Chapman's sonnet to Elijah Parish Lovejoy, a murdered agent. Sophia Louisa Robbins Little, a writer in Newport, Rhode Island, provided similar gift books stressing the sacrifice and patriotism displayed by volunteers of the Underground Railroad.

In December 1852, Lucretia Coffin Mott tried in vain to get agent Ralph Waldo Emerson to deliver a speech at the Pennsylvania Anti-Slavery Fair denouncing the Fugitive Slave Law of 1850. Another organizer, Helen Eliza Benson Garrison, prevailed on her husband, William Lloyd Garrison, to advertise the Massachusetts Anti-Slavery Fair in the February 26, 1841, issue of *The Liberator.* The bazaar offered cakes made with free-labor sugar rather than slave-made staples. In Philadelphia, Mary Grew, Anna Mott Hopper, and Harriet Forten Purvis organized the annual Christmas bazaars, which were a tradition from 1836 to 1861. In 1851, the women's group donated $50 to the city's vigilance committee.

In Rochester, New York, Underground Railroad agent Rhoda Rogers DeGarmo superintended abolitionist bazaars. Fair organizers published a child's reader, *The Anti-Slavery Alphabet* (1847), which introduced young abolitionists to such savage concepts as cotton-field labor, lashings, slave kidnap, and bloodhounds bred to track fugitives on their way along secret routes to Canada. In 1869, Samuel Joseph May acknowledged the contributions of female fair organizers in *Some Recollections of Our Antislavery Conflict.*

See also: Anti-Slavery Convention of American Women; bloodhounds; kidnap; *Liberator, The*; quilts; *Some Recollections of Our Antislavery Conflict* (1869); vigilance committees.

Sources

The Anti-Slavery Alphabet. Philadelphia: Merrihew & Thompson, 1847.

Bacon, Margaret Hope. *Abby Hopper Gibbons: Prison Reformer and Social Activist.* Albany: State University of New York Press, 2000.

Garrison, William Lloyd. "Massachusetts Anti-Slavery Fair." *The Liberator,* February 26, 1841, 39.

Anti-Slavery Society of Canada

White and black Canadians reacted to the flood of refugees along the Underground Railroad to Canadian border communities by forming an anti-slavery society. In February 1851, founders met in Toronto to coordinate efforts to acclimate slaves to freedom outside the United States and to provide legal counsel and education for the illiterate. Aided by George Brown, editor of the *Toronto Globe,* the members established a social relief agency in collaboration with notable American abolitionists, including Frederick Douglass in Rochester, New York, and the Reverend Samuel Joseph May, a conductor in Syracuse, New York. Through the assistance of Lewis Tappan, in March 1852, the Canadian society coordinated efforts with societies in Great Britain and the United States. In 1853, the Reverend Samuel Ringgold Ward, author of *Autobiography of a Fugitive Negro: His Anti-Slavery Labours in the United States, Canada, and England* (1855), raised funds for the society during a tour of England. One of the fugitives profiting from Canadian aid was a laundress, Ann Maria Jackson, who escaped from Maryland with seven children and arrived in Toronto in 1857 via the Underground Railroad.

Sources

Landon, Fred. "The Anti-Slavery Society of Canada." *Journal of Negro History* 4 (January 1919): 33–40.

Ward, Samuel R. *Autobiography of a Fugitive Negro: His Anti-Slavery Labours in the United States, Canada, and England.* London: John Snow, 1855.

Archer, Thomas (1833–1913)

An attorney and operative of the Underground Railroad in Kansas Territory, Thomas Archer of Jefferson County, Kentucky, participated in the armed resistance against posses from Missouri. He received runaway slaves at his home on Harrison Street in Topeka. When U.S. marshals menaced John Brown's party of 11 Missouri slaves at the Albert Fuller log cabin at Straight Creek northwest of Holton, Archer joined the band of Colonel John Ritchie that gathered at the First Congregational Church. The armed posse enabled Brown to continue north to Tabor, Iowa. In 1861, Archer joined the Fifth

Kansas Volunteer Cavalry and sustained a combat wound in 1863 at Pine Bluff, Arkansas.

Source

Kiene, L.L. "The Battle of the Spurs and John Brown's Exit from Kansas." *Kansas Historical Collections* 8 (1903–1904): 443–9.

Armstead, Rosetta (fl. 1850s)

While still a minor, Rosetta Armstead fled slavery with the assistance of an unidentified Underground Railroad agent. She was the chattel of an Episcopal minister, the Reverend Henry M. Dennison of Louisville, Kentucky. In March 1855, a Dr. Miller was transporting her by train to Richmond, Virginia, to work as a nursemaid. On the approach to Cincinnati, Ohio, a black worker of the Little Miami Railroad encouraged Armstead to liberate herself. During a layover at Columbus, Ohio, the Reverend William B. Ferguson protested the girl's enslavement in a free state. In spring 1855, despite public uproar over Armstead's predicament, Judge John McLean returned her to the custody of her owner.

Source

Campbell, Stanley W. *The Slave Catchers: Enforcement of the Fugitive Slave Law, 1850–1860.* Chapel Hill: University of North Carolina Press, 1970.

Arnold, Joseph (1832–1904)
Arnold, Tacy Smith (1834–1870)

A Quaker agent of the Underground Railroad, Joseph Arnold was a pioneer and postmaster of Lynnville in Jasper County, Iowa. He was born at Arba, Indiana, in 1832, and in 1853 he married Tacy Smith of Palmyra, Iowa. While operating a flour mill and lumberyard, he studied law and collaborated with agents Josiah Bushnell Grinnell, Jarvis Johnson, and Matthew Sparks. After establishing a log safehouse, the Arnolds relayed passengers via covered wagon.

On November 4, 1857, Joseph Arnold and Matthew Sparks rescued runaways James F. Miller, Henry May, and John Ross at Newton outside Lynnville. Within weeks, the Arnolds received a black couple and their infant. The Arnolds housed the passengers and then took them over the North Skunk River to the waystation of Jarvis Johnson. In 1861, Joseph Arnold, under the pen name Old Shady, wrote an eyewitness account of his activism that was later issued in the 1912 Jasper County annals.

Source

Stocum, Susan. "Rediscovering the Road to Freedom." *Black Issues in Higher Education* 16:11 (August 1999): 30–1.

Ashley, James Mitchell (1823–1896)

A discreet operative, James Mitchell Ashley conducted slave rescues in the slave state of Kentucky. While in his twenties and living outside Greenupsburg in Greenup County, he conspired with a black operative in piloting escapees across the Ohio River to an agent named Goodrich near Portsmouth, Ohio. Local abolitionists quietly contributed cash to Ashley's efforts. In 1851, after passage of the Fugitive Slave Law of 1850, he left his waystation and moved to Toledo, Ohio.

See also: Fugitive Slave Law of 1850.

Source

Hudson, J. Blaine. *Fugitive Slaves and the Underground Railroad in the Kentucky Borderland.* Jefferson, NC: McFarland, 2002.

Atcheson, George (1793–1877)
Atcheson, Margaret McClellan (1801–?)

An Irish immigrant to Green Township in Indiana County, Pennsylvania, George Atcheson had firm notions about the human right to liberty. Born at Drumcree in County Leitrim, he settled on the Susquehanna River in 1820 and married Margaret McClellan in 1827. He became a lumberman and river pilot and joined the Methodist Episcopal Church. As an activist and philanthropist, he supported anti-slavery meetings and befriended William Lloyd Garrison, Joshua Reed Giddings, and Parker Pillsbury. During the Atchesons' service to the secret network in Clearfield and Indiana counties, they opened their home to refugees, who could see their waystation from the river.

With the support of Giddings at Jefferson, Ohio, the Atchesons received passengers from A.A. Barker, a cooper at Carrollton, and from route coordinator Jason Kirk. In dangerous times, the couple hid wayfarers in a chamber concealed by a portrait and passed them up Cush Creek to Bear Run. In 1845, the Atchesons added to the estate a guest house featuring a secret room for sheltering refugee slaves. One fugitive escaped stalkers at the front door by climbing to the roof and fleeing into the woods. To protect other slaves from posses and packs of bloodhounds, George

Atcheson hired marksmen to walk the perimeter of his property and shoot dogs.

Source

Egle, William Henry. *An Illustrated History of the Commonwealth of Pennsylvania: History of Indiana County, Pennsylvania.* Harrisburg, PA: W.C. Goodrich, 1876.

Atkinson, Abigail Oren (1795–1876)
Atkinson, Cephas (1790–1860)

Two Quaker pioneers who contributed to the reputation of their sect for benevolence were Abigail Oren Atkinson and her husband, Cephas Atkinson, of York County, Pennsylvania, agents of the Underground Railroad. Cephas migrated to Clinton County, Ohio, in 1811. After the couple's marriage in 1815, they built a cabin on 100 acres in Greene County, Ohio, where they raised livestock. When they moved to Mingo Valley in Champaign County, they practiced lifelong abolitionism by receiving fugitive slaves, whom they fed and clothed.

Source

Baxter, W.H. *History of Champaign County, Ohio.* Chicago: W.H. Beers, 1881.

Avery, Charles A. (1784–1858)

A philanthropist and proponent of slave rescue, the Reverend Charles A. Avery aided the Underground Railroad in several ways. He made his living as a pharmacist and wholesale drug seller. As a member of the secret network, he collaborated with barber John Baton Vashon in Pittsburgh, Pennsylvania. During trips south to buy cotton, Avery observed the horrors of human bondage. In 1840, he founded the three-story Allegheny Institute and Mission Church, the nucleus of Avery College, an academy for black students at Dutchtown in Pittsburgh. When Avery established the chapel, he equipped the pulpit with a staircase leading to a slave-hiding niche in the cellar. With his help, refugees passed north along the Pennsylvania–Canada route. He spent the last eight years of his service protesting the onerous Fugitive Slave Law of 1850.

See also: Fugitive Slave Law of 1850.

Source

Sajna, Mike. "Underground Railroad Leaves Tracks in Southwestern Pa," *Pittsburgh Tribune-Review,* February 25, 1990.

Avery, Egbert (1829–1907)
Avery, Harriet King (1832–?)

A blacksmith at Tabor, Iowa, Egbert Avery aided passengers traveling via the Underground Railroad. Born in Brownhelm, Lorain County, Ohio, a prominent crossing point of slaves fleeing bondage in Kentucky, Avery studied at Oberlin College and settled at Civil Bend in Fremont County, Iowa. After he married a New Yorker, Harriet King of Dutchess County, in 1856, the couple operated a depot relaying fugitives north to Canada.

See also: Oberlin College.

Source

Gue, Benjamin F. *History of Iowa from the Earliest Times to the Beginning of the Twentieth Century.* New York: Century History, 1903.

Avery, Frances Mehitable Stanton (1807–1870)
Avery, George A. (1803–1856)

A successful wholesale grocer and philanthropist, George A. Avery joined his wife, Frances Mehitable Stanton Avery, in rescuing fugitive slaves. In company with a surgeon, George Avery spent four years in Virginia and observed firsthand the hunger and sufferings of slave children, whom he saw naked or clad in tow-cloth shirts in dirt-floored cabins. After Frances and George married in the early 1830s, they profited from an import-export business centered in the West Indies. At their home at Rochester in Monroe County, New York, they practiced Presbyterian beliefs by receiving runaways for transfer over the international border to freedom in Ontario. George also operated a waystation at his shop at 12 Buffalo Street. Frances extended her outreach through participation in the Female Charitable Society, chaired by her sister-in-law, Elizabeth Cady Stanton. In *A Key to Uncle Tom's Cabin* (1853), Harriet Beecher Stowe quoted George Avery's anti-slavery testimony.

See also: Key to Uncle Tom's Cabin, A (1853).

Source

Czerkas, Jean. "The Averys and the Stantons, Family Ties That Bind." *Friends of Mount Hope Newsletter* 22:2 (Spring 2002): 1.

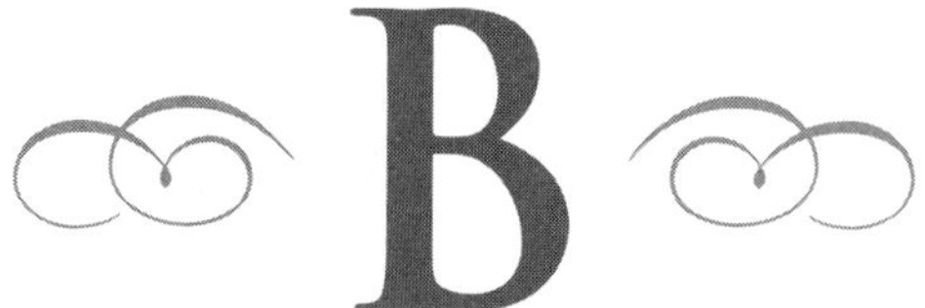

Babbitt, William D. (1823–?)
Babbitt, Elizabeth H. (1826–?)

Judge William D. "Bill" Babbitt, an agent of the Underground Railroad, defended one of the most famous runaways to pass through Minneapolis, Minnesota. Babbitt was born in New York; his wife, Elizabeth H. Babbitt, was from Maine. According to Babbitt's colleague and journalist Jane Grey Cannon Swisshelm's memoir, *Half a Century* (1880), on August 21, 1860, Judge Babbitt helped to save Eliza Winston from recapture. Eliza traveled from Memphis, Tennessee, with her owners, Colonel Richard Christmas and his wife, to Winslow House in St. Anthony in Hennepin County. Aided by an abolitionist, Emily Goodridge Grey of Pennsylvania, Winston petitioned Judge Babbitt for her freedom. He passed the case to Charles E. Vanderburgh, an unbiased judge, who declared her free since her crossing into free territory.

Threatened by mob violence from pro-slavery elements, Babbitt barricaded himself, his pregnant wife, and Eliza Winston in the family waystation at Tenth and Russell streets, which the Babbitts defended with gunfire. Supporters of the secret network arrived to aid him against showers of stones, cudgelings, and threats of arson. One neighbor ran through a cornfield to shield Elizabeth Babbitt, who was only weeks away from childbirth. Within days, secret network agents conveyed Eliza Winston to Windsor, Ontario. Attacks against the Babbitts receded to public ridicule and name-calling.

Sources

Green, William D. "Eliza Winston and the Politics of Freedom in Minnesota, 1854–1860." *Minnesota History* 57:3 (Fall 2000): 107–22.

Swisshelm, Jane Grey. *Half a Century.* Chicago: Jansen, McClurg, 1880.

Baer, William (fl. 1850s)

A bounty hunter at the time of the Christiana Riot, William Baer (or Bear) came to the conflict with a reputation already sullied from 1845 onward by raids on Underground Railroad safehouses, horse and slave stealing, and petty larceny. In September 1850, he and four others—Jack Townsend, Henderson Jouston, Perry Marsh, and Joseph White—seized Henry Williams and abducted him, bound and gagged, by wagon to parts unknown. Historians surmise that the kidnappers sold Williams to a slave dealer.

On September 11, 1851, the first significant clash over the Fugitive Slave Law of 1850 occurred at the home of Underground Railroad agents Eliza Ann Elizabeth Howard Parker and William Parker, farmers at Christiana in Lancaster County, Pennsylvania, just over the Maryland border. Long-running enmity existed between William Parker and Baer's thugs, whom black citizens combated with vigilantism. Leading the pro-slavery faction was Edward Gorsuch, a Maryland slaveholder; his son, Dickerson Gorsuch; and Federal Marshal Henry H. Kline. William Padgett, a spy for Baer's Gap Gang (also called the Gap Hill Gang or the Clemson Gang) informed the posse that Parker was sheltering runaways.

Baer's confederates intended to aid in the recovery of Noah Baley, Nelson Ford, George Hammond, and Joshua Hammond, who escaped bondage at Retreat Farm in Baltimore County, Maryland, in 1849. After Eliza Parker sounded a horn to summon help, Baer and 20 vigilantes traveled a mile and a half and assembled around Kline to serve as backup deputies. The gang came bearing a grudge against William Parker, who previously had interceded in their kidnap of a slave girl. When the Christiana shooting started, Baer and his followers fled to the woods. At the trial charging the abolitionists with treason, the defense accused Baer and his associate Perry Marsh with ransacking the home of Marsh Chamberlain at Sudsbury and assaulting John Williams, a black laborer, to obtain the whereabouts of runaways, but the allegations came to nothing.

See also: bounty hunters; Christiana Riot; kidnap; spies.

Sources

Forbes, Ella. *But We Have No Country: The 1851 Christiana, Pennsylvania Resistance.* Cherry Hill, NJ: Africana Homestead Legacy, 1998.
Hensel, W.U. *The Christiana Riot and the Treason Trials of 1851.* Lancaster, PA: New Era, 1911.

Bailey, Gamaliel (1807–1859)

Physician and journalist Dr. Gamaliel Bailey, Jr., was an active supporter of slave rescue. A native of Mount Holly, New Jersey, he studied in Philadelphia at the Jefferson Medical College. After editing the *Methodist Protestant* in Baltimore, Maryland, at age 24, he settled in Cincinnati, Ohio. From 1836 to 1847, he encouraged the activities of Underground Railroad conductors in southern Ohio by joining James Gillespie Birney in issuing the *Cincinnati Weekly Herald and Philanthropist,* a journal of the Ohio State Anti-Slavery Society. Both men and their printer, agent Achilles Pugh, faced down repeated mob violence by pro-slavery factions, who wrecked their office and dumped the press and trays of type into the Ohio River.

Aided by Washington, D.C., attorney David A. Hall, Bailey covered the trial of conductors Joseph Pettijohn and John Bennington Mahan in November 1838 for the abduction of two slaves belonging to William Greathouse of Kentucky. Abolitionists circulated excerpts of Bailey's articles, which denounced the unjust seizure of an innocent man. In the late 1840s, while publishing the influential abolitionist weekly *National Era* in Washington, D.C., Bailey encouraged Harriet Beecher Stowe to publish *Uncle Tom's Cabin* (1852), which he serialized from 1851 to 1852. His writings and those of Stowe influenced the Underground Railroad activities of Martin Conwell, Miranda Conwell, and their son, Russell Herman Conwell, in South Worthington, Massachusetts.

See also: abolitionist newspapers; *Uncle Tom's Cabin; or, Life Among the Lowly* (1852).

Sources

History of Brown County, Ohio. Chicago: W.H. Beers, 1883.
Hume, John F. *The Abolitionists: Together with Personal Memories of the Struggle for Human Rights, 1830–1864.* New York: Putnam, 1905. Reprint New York: AMS, 1973.

Bailey, Josiah (1828–?)
Bailey, William (fl. 1850s)

A valuable fugitive rescued by Harriet Tubman, 28-year-old Josiah "Joe" Bailey sought freedom from a Maryland slave owner. In November 1856, Bailey slipped away from farmer and timberman William R. Hughland of Dorchester County, whom Bailey served as manager. Rowing from Jamaica Point by night, he asked Benjamin Ross to tell his daughter, Harriet Tubman, that she could count on another passenger.

When Tubman gathered her party in Dorchester County on November 15, Josiah and his brother William "Bill" Bailey joined Eliza Noxley (also Nokey) of Talbot County and Peter Pennington on Tubman's seventh or eighth passage north. As a posse searched for the runaways, the group headed north and separated. Acting on a vision, Tubman declared a river shallow enough to ford. Assisted by the Reverend Samuel Green, Jr., a secret operative and minister of the Methodist Episcopal Church, the passengers made their way to the Christiana River in Wilmington, Delaware, and hid in safehouses until danger of recapture passed. Concealed in a wagon of bricklayers, the runaways made their way to the depot of Thomas Garrett in Wilmington, Delaware. In New York City, Tubman's party met with Oliver Johnson at the anti-slavery office before boarding a train for Canada.

Source

Bradford, Sarah H. *Harriet—The Moses of Her People.* New York: George R. Lockwood, 1886.

Baker, Thomas (1809–1863)
Baker, Eunice Harris (1814–1891)

A native of Minerva in Essex County, New York, the Reverend Thomas Baker operated a station of the Underground Railroad. While pastoring the Darrowsville Wesleyan-Methodist Church in Chestertown, in Warren County, New York, he and his wife, Eunice Harris Baker, logged for August Sherman. In collaboration with church member Myron Tripp, the Bakers used their parsonage as a safehouse until passengers could travel over Schroon Lake to the MacDougall waystation at Elizabethtown. The route continued to stations at Keene, Wilmington, or North Elba, the depot operated by insurrectionist John Brown.

Source

Calarco, Tom. *The Underground Railroad in the Adirondack Region.* Jefferson, NC: McFarland, 2004.

Baldridge, Andrew (1837–?)

A teenage slave rescuer, Andrew Baldridge was the youngest person in Missouri to serve a prison sentence. In 1855, at age 18, he entered the Missouri penitentiary in Jefferson City. Three years later, in 1858, he completed his sentence.

Source

Frazier, Harriet C. *Runaway and Freed Missouri Slaves and Those Who Helped Them, 1763–1865.* Jefferson, NC: McFarland, 2004.

Baldwin, John, Sr. (1799–1884)
Baldwin, Mary (fl. 1820s–1870s)

A pioneer of Middleburg, Ohio, and founder of Baldwin Institute, John Baldwin, Sr., operated the town's first waystation for runaways. He and his wife, Mary Baldwin, settled in the area at age 29 and founded Lyceum Village, a utopian Methodist Episcopal enclave. In 1842, John began a quarrying operation that turned native red sandstone into grinding wheels and building material. The Baldwins' two-story red house, which replaced the family's log cabin, became a familiar stop in Cuyahoga County on the Ohio–Canada route.

Source

Holzworth, W.F. *Men of Grit and Greatness: A Historical Account of Middleburg Township, Berea, Brook Park, and Middleburg Heights.* Cuyahoga, OH: self-published, 1970.

Baldwin, Roger Sherman (1793–1863)

The grandson of Connecticut patriot Roger Baldwin, a signer of the Declaration of Independence, Judge Roger Sherman Baldwin crusaded against a federal law forbidding the rescue of fugitive slaves. He was born in New Haven, Connecticut, and studied at Yale. He collaborated with the Reverend Samuel William Southmayd Dutton, Nathaniel Jocelyn, and the Reverend Simeon Smith Jocelyn, Underground Railroad agents in New Haven. After dedicating himself to the defense of fugitive slaves, in January 1840, Baldwin represented Joseph Cinqué and 34 of the other mutineers from the *Amistad,* whom slavers had abducted from the Mende nation in Sierra Leone. Underground Railroad agents Lewis Tappan and Austin Franklin Williams were responsible for hiring Baldwin and John Quincy Adams for the defense team.

The defendants faced charges of piracy and murder for seizing the ship and killing most of the crew. In state district and circuit courts and before the U.S. Supreme Court, Baldwin argued that the Africans were free at the time of their arrest and could not be treated as chattel. Contributing to his success was his location of a translator who spoke the Mende language. After the freeing of the mutineers, on November 25, 1841, donors funded the return of 32 of the survivors aboard the *Gentleman* to Freetown, Sierra Leone.

See also: Amistad; Fugitive Slave Law of 1850.

Source

Jones, Howard. *Mutiny on the* Amistad. Oxford, UK: Oxford University Press, 1987.

Baldwin, William (1825–1888)
Baldwin, Harriett Ann Hughson (1833–?)

An Underground Railroad conductor at Volney, in Oswego County, New York, tanner William Baldwin of Sandy Creek and his wife, Harriett Ann Hughson Baldwin, rescued desperate fugitives. They were members of a cohesive abolitionist neighborhood that coordinated the work of white and black agents, some of whom were members of Bristol Hill Congregational Church, a biracial congregation east of Fulton. At their residence at 323 Baldwin Road, the Baldwins sheltered and fed runaways. Their grandchildren preserved their benevolence in oral stories.

Source

History of Oswego County, New York. Philadelphia: L.H. Everts, 1877.

Baltimore, Priscilla (1801–1882)
Baltimore, John (fl. 1820–1840s)

A freedwoman, nurse, and transporter for the Underground Railroad, "Mother" Priscilla Baltimore operated a rescue service in heavy river trade along the Missouri River. She was born in Bourbon County, Kentucky, to a slave woman and her white owner, who sold Priscilla farther west in 1811. After a third master, a missionary, paid $1,100 for Priscilla, she saved for seven years and purchased her freedom papers and those of her husband, John Baltimore. The couple began aiding others in flight from slavery in

Kentucky and Missouri. In May 1841 in a log cabin on Main Street, Priscilla founded an abolitionist church, St. Paul African Methodist Episcopal Church of St. Louis, Missouri, the first American Methodist Episcopal church west of the Mississippi River. In 1857, she deeded two lots to the church campus.

Priscilla Baltimore combined religion with courageous rescues. She collaborated with the Reverend Jordan Winston Early on retrieving slaves crossing the Missouri River north of St. Louis at Alton, Illinois. She and Bishop William Paul Quinn co-founded the Campbell Chapel African Methodist Episcopal Church in Alton and directed its outreach to fugitives. Among their rescues was Daniel Alexander Payne, whom Quinn transported by buggy to the Baltimore residence in East St. Louis, Missouri. Citizens revered Baltimore as the St. Louis Harriet Tubman for rowing and rafting runaways to free territory in St. Clair County, Illinois.

Sources

Early, Sarah J.W. *Life and Labors of Rev. Jordan W. Early.* Nashville, TN: American Methodist Episcopal Church Sunday School Union, 1894.

Richardson, Marilyn. *Black Women and Religion.* Boston: G.K. Hall, 1980.

Banks, Elizabeth (1830–?)

A runaway from bondage in Easton, Maryland, 25-year-old Elizabeth Banks requested help from the Underground Railroad. In 1855, she fled Talbot County and arrived at William Still's office of the Philadelphia Vigilance Committee in Philadelphia. In 1857, slave hunters came so near that she continued to Canada.

Source

Still, William. *The Underground Railroad.* Philadelphia: Porter & Coates, 1871.

Banks, George (1835–?)

George Banks served prison time for aiding in a slave rescue. An ostler in Baltimore, Maryland, he was 19 years old when he was arrested. He entered the Maryland state penitentiary at Baltimore on May 9, 1854, to begin a seven-year sentence. After he and other inmates were involved in a suspicious prison fire, he gained his release on July 24, 1857. He resettled at Baltimore and worked as a day laborer and oyster shucker.

Source

Prison records, Maryland State Archives.

Baquaqua, Mahommah Gardo (ca. early 1820s–after 1857)

Mahommah Gardo Baquaqua was the rare South American slave transported via the Underground Railroad. He was born to Hausa Muslims in Djougou, Benin. In his youth, he was a prisoner of war until his brother paid his ransom. Captured by slavers at age 20 in north Benin in the early 1840s, Baquaqua was transported through Togo to Ouida, Dahomey, and by ship to Pernambuco, Brazil. In New York City, where David Ruggles superintended rescues for the vigilance committee, agents searched a ship from Brazil for runaway slaves from South America. At their urging, in June 1847, Baquaqua jumped ship.

Baquaqua traveled over much of the secret network before he disappeared from history in England. Conductors passed him to Boston and by sea to the free black state of Haiti. While studying at Central College in McGrawville, New York, Baquaqua feared recapture under the Fugitive Slave Law of 1850 and migrated to Chatham, Ontario. He sought the aid of Underground Railroad agent Gerrit Smith to return to Africa but never reunited with his mother's family in Katsina. Baquaqua produced the only narrative written by an American slave born in Africa.

See also: Fugitive Slave Law of 1850; vigilance committees.

Source

Farrow, Don C. *The Historical Practice in Diversity.* New York: Berghahn, 2003.

Barber, Amy Clark (fl. 1830s)
Barber, Joseph (fl. 1830s)

Amy Clark fled slavery in 1832 and reached Cincinnati, Ohio, by steamer. She found work on College Hill, an abolitionist enclave, and married Joseph Barber. The couple transported slaves by wagon to Lebanon for five years. In 1837, they relocated in Windsor, Ontario.

Source

Smiddy, Betty Ann. *A Little Piece of Paradise . . . College Hill, Ohio.* Cincinnati, OH: College Hill Historical Society, 1999.

Bardwell, John Payne (1803–1871) Bardwell, Cornelia C. Bishop (1815–1894)

The Reverend John Bardwell, a Congregationalist minister, put his abolitionist beliefs into action by rescuing runaways. A native of Edmiston, New York, in 1834, he married Cornelia C. Bishop, another New York–born abolitionist, from Gilbertville. From 1838, while the couple studied at Oberlin College, they maintained a one-story wood-frame boardinghouse and safehouse at 181 East Lorain Street in Oberlin, Ohio, a fervidly anti-slavery community. Under the eaves of the one-story dwelling, the Bardwells concealed slaves in secret niches, which fugitives accessed through sliding panels in closets. John's altruism took a new turn with his ordination at age 40, when he ministered to the Chippewa at Leech Lake, Minnesota. While traveling through Grenada, Mississippi, on behalf of the American Missionary Association, he was assaulted by a mob for organizing freedmen's schools. In September 1975, the city of Oberlin named the Bardwell house an Oberlin Historic Landmark.

See also: Oberlin College.

Source

Blodgett, David. *Oberlin Architecture, College and Town: A Guide to Its Social History.* Kent, OH: Kent State University Press, 1985.

Barker, David (1794–1886) Barker, Pennsylvania Herendeen (1796–1877)

A pair of Quaker agents for the Underground Railroad, David Barker and Pennsylvania Herendeen "Aunt Vania" Barker aided desperate refugees. Born in Charlotte, Chittenden County, Vermont, David bore the surname of the barker, the woodworker who stripped bark from beech, hemlock, and oak trees for use in tanning leather. In Barker, a village that he established in Niagara County, in northwestern New York, he homesteaded a 100-acre parcel near the shore of Lake Ontario. At age 40, he married Vania Herendeen of Massachusetts. The couple operated a safehouse south of Somerset Village on Nye and Quaker roads, a last stop along the Niagara River corridor before passengers crossed into Ontario. The Barker residence is currently a part of the New York State Freedom Trail.

Source

Porter, Ruth B. *The Story of Somerset.* Lockport, NY: Niagara County Historical Society, 1972.

Barker, Jacob (1779–1871) Barker, Elizabeth Hazard (1783–1861)

Quaker shipping magnate and financier Jacob Barker opened a waystation in the Deep South. A native of Swans Island, Maine, in 1801, he married Elizabeth Hazard of New Bedford, Massachusetts. After promoting the building of the Erie Canal and the establishment of the *New York Times,* in 1834, he invested in cotton and sugar in New Orleans, Louisiana. He gained a reputation for protecting blacks from police harassment. From their home, the Barkers supervised the New Orleans nexus of the Underground Railroad, a large territory that involved water and land relays from the Mississippi River Delta west to Texas or south to Mexico. After his wife died, shortly after the onset of the Civil War, Jacob Barker continued the rescue operation.

Source

Barker, Jacob. *Incidents in the Life of Jacob Barker of New Orleans, Louisiana.* Washington, DC: self-published, 1855.

Barnard, Alonzo (1817–1905) Barnard, Sarah Philena Babcock (1819–1853)

A Presbyterian clergyman known as Father Barnard, the Reverend Alonzo Barnard was a missionary to American Indians and a rescuer of fugitive slaves. A native of Peru, in Bennington County, Vermont, he grew up in Elyria, Ohio, and studied at Oberlin College, where he began aiding the Underground Railroad. After a period of mission work in Louisiana and Mississippi from 1837 to 1838, he dedicated himself to the welfare of slaves by teaching members of a black settlement in Chatham, Ontario. With the assistance of his wife, Sarah Philena Babcock Barnard, a fellow abolitionist at Oberlin, he also worked among the Chippewa and Sioux. The Barnards spent their most altruistic years in Pomona, Michigan.

See also: Oberlin College.

Source

Powers, Perry Francis. *A History of Northern Michigan and Its People.* Chicago: Lewis, 1912.

Barnard (Eusebius, Sarah Painter, and Sarah Marsh) Family

Among the most devoted Quaker stationmasters at Pocopsin, Pennsylvania, were the Reverend Eusebius Barnard (1802–1865), his first wife, Sarah Painter Barnard (1804–1849), and his second wife, Sarah Marsh Barnard (1819–1887), daughter of Underground Railroad agent Gravner Marsh and Hannah Marsh of Caln, Pennsylvania. The Barnards involved their sons in the transfer of slaves to safety. The family received passengers fleeing Delaware, Georgia, Maryland, and Virginia from Dr. Bartholomew Fussell at Kennett Square; Rachel Mendenhall Garrett and Thomas Garrett at Wilmington, Delaware; Daniel Gibbons and Hannah Wierman Gibbons at Bird-in-Hand; and Dinah Hannum Mendenhall and Isaac Mendenhall at Kennett Square. After a meal and rest on beds on the kitchen floor, the runaways left around 2 A.M. in the custody of Eusebius Barnard or one of his sons, Enos Barnard (1836–?) or Eusebius R. Barnard (1840–1915), or with his oldest child, Elizabeth Barnard (1830–1856). Those fugitives who stayed on the Barnard farm received wages for their service to the family.

The Barnard family worked as a team. On one occasion, Enos led a party of 17 males to the home of his uncle, William Barnard (1803–1864), who lived nearby. Another time, Eusebius drove eight refugees by curtained buggy to Dr. Jacob K. Eshleman in Strasburg. On October 27, 1855, 11 escapees from a Maryland plantation sought shelter. After rest and a meal, the runaways followed Eusebius to Downingtown to lodge with Dr. Jacob K. Eshleman, Esther Logue Hayes and Mordecai Hayes in Newlin, Benjamin Price and Jane Paxson Price in East Bradford, or Zebulon Thomas. From there the fugitives traveled by way of Abigail Paxson Vickers and John Vickers's waystation at Uwchlan to Graceanna Lewis's safehouse, Sunnyside Home, outside of Kimberton, Pennsylvania.

In mid-March 1861, six runaways—two handicapped females and four children—traveled muddy roads to the Barnard station. Eusebius undertook the journey, which resulted in a string of false starts before concluding at Dr. Eshleman's safehouse by dusk. William Barnard continued the family's work by receiving slaves in flight during the uproar following the Christiana Riot of September 11, 1851. He concealed the escapees in corn fodder for a day before directing them to safety.

See also: Christiana Riot.

Source

Cope, Gilbert. *Historic Homes and Institutions and Genealogical and Personal Memoirs of Chester and Delaware Counties, Pennsylvania.* New York: Lewis, 1904.

Barnard, Joanna Pennock (1828–1866) Barnard, Vincent S. (1825–1871)

Quaker stationmasters at Kennett Square, Pennsylvania, Joanna Pennock Barnard and her husband, Vincent S. Barnard, aided runaways on the Pennsylvania-Canada route. A native of East Marlborough, Pennsylvania, Vincent Barnard moved to 315 East Linden Street in Kennett Square to work as a botanist for his father-in-law, Samuel Pennock, and to aid desperate runaways. In addition to receiving fugitives, the Barnards established a two-acre test field of indigenous and rare flowers, shrubs, and trees. At the outbreak of the Civil War, Vincent Barnard registered as a conscientious objector.

Source

Kashatus, William C. *Just Over the Line.* West Chester, PA: Chester County Historical Society, 2002.

Barnard, Sarah Darlington (1807–1881) Barnard, Simon (1802–1886)

Quaker conductors Simon Barnard and his wife, Sarah Darlington Barnard, operated an Underground Railroad waystation in Newlin, in Chester County, Pennsylvania. The couple received hundreds of passengers from Hannah Peirce Cox and John Cox at their farm in Longwood, from Dinah Hannum Mendenhall and Isaac Mendenhall in Kennett Square, and from Chandler Darlington and Hannah M. Darlington in Kennett Square. The Barnards moved the runaways swiftly along in a covered wagon dubbed the Black Maria. By suspending a quilt over the front, they could cloak up to a dozen passengers for conveyance to the stations of Nathan Evans and Zillah Maule Evans in Williston, to Isaac Meredith and Thamosin Pennock Meredith in Newlin, to Benjamin Price and Jane Paxson Price's safehouse in East Bradford, or to John Vickers in Uwchlan. Aiding the Barnards was a neighbor, Simon's brother, Richard Barnard, a state legislator.

In addition to assisting the nameless slave, the Barnards befriended the abolitionists of their day—Cyrus M. Burleigh, William Lloyd Garrison, Isaac Tatem Hopper and Sarah Tatum Hopper, James Russell Lowell, Lucretia Coffin Mott, and Thomas Parker. Simon Barnard traveled widely to anti-slavery meetings and escorted orators to the podium. When speaker and tractarian Charles Callistus Burleigh was arrested in Oxford, Pennsylvania, Barnard bailed him out of the West Chester County jail. During the Civil War, Sarah and Simon retired to Philadelphia.

Source

Futhey, J. Smith, and Gilbert Cope. *History of Chester County, Pennsylvania.* Philadelphia: Louis H. Everts, 1881.

Barnes, Isaac O. (1798–?)

An abolitionist law officer and orator, Isaac O. Barnes possessed inside information about the flight of desperate slaves. The Bedford, New Hampshire, native studied law at Middlebury College, in Vermont, and practiced at Barnstead, New Hampshire. After he married Hannah Trask Woodbury in 1825, he monitored customs for Boston and Charlestown, Massachusetts. While living in Boston and serving the state of Massachusetts as a federal marshal and clerk of civil court, he fought against the cruel dictates of the Fugitive Slave Law of 1850. He was lax in looking for runaways. When he learned that passengers were moving through the state, he spread a warning over the Underground Railroad network and distributed to agents physical descriptions and particulars of mode of travel.

See also: Fugitive Slave Law of 1850.

Source

"The Underground Railroad and Those Who Operated It," *Springfield (OH) Republican,* March 11, 1900.

Barnes, John B. (1807–1893)
Barnes, Sophronia King (1805–ca. 1880s)

An abolitionist physician and probate judge, Dr. John B. Barnes supported the Underground Railroad route through Shiawassee County, Michigan. A native of Marlborough, Massachusetts, he trained at Williams College and opened a practice in Lockport, New York. In 1842, he moved to Owosso, Michigan, where he was elected mayor and served as deacon of the Congregational church. The family established a waystation at Oliver and Water streets. Influenced by Wendell Addison Phillips and William Lloyd Garrison, Barnes directed the secret network in his area. He and his wife, Sophronia K. Barnes, aided desperate escapees at their home at Oliver and Water streets. Slaves frequently zigzagged from Owosso to Detroit to escape detection by bounty hunters and posses. In July 1853, the Boston Vigilance Committee paid Barnes $10 for treating fugitive slaves. During the Civil War, the Barneses' son, John H. Barnes, was an infantryman in the Union army.

See also: bounty hunters; vigilance committees.

Source

History of Shiawassee and Clinton Counties, Michigan. Philadelphia: D.W. Ensign, 1880.

Barrows, Justin Spaulding (1829–1905)
Barrows, Adeline E. Newell (1831–ca. 1910)

A preacher at the Pynchon Street Church (later Trinity Methodist Church) in Springfield, Massachusetts, the Reverend Justin Spaulding Barrows and his wife, Adeline E. Newell Barrows of Vermont, agitated for an end to human bondage. During the family's service to the Underground Railroad safehouse on Pynchon Street in the early months of the Civil War, from 1861 to 1862, Justin Barrows hired security guards to ward off pro-slavery assassins. One of the passengers requiring shelter came from William Lloyd Garrison, publisher of *The Liberator.* The Barrows welcomed the man, and Adeline provided him dinner. Justin collared two parishioners to donate cash for the rest of the passage. One of the Barrows' rescues was a black orator who addressed the congregation on the miseries of enslavement.

See also: Liberator, The.

Sources

De Caro, Louis A. *"Fire from the Midst of You": A Religious Life of John Brown.* Albany: New York University Press, 2002.
"The Underground Railroad and Those Who Operated It," *Springfield (OH) Republican,* March 11, 1900.

Bartlett, George (1798–1887)
Bartlett, Ruth Bartlett (1802–?)

A native of Guilford, outside New Haven, Connecticut, George Bartlett and his wife operated a stop of the Underground Railroad. At age 23, George

Bartlett married his second cousin, Ruth Bartlett. To accommodate their nine children, in 1840, they completed the upper floor of their one-and-a-half story frame home at 111 Goose Lane. During relays, they conspired with the Reverend Zolva Whitmore, pastor of the Congregational church at North Guilford. On busy nights, the Bartletts retrieved loads of six to eight fugitives from Branford, Connecticut. Slaves passed through a trapdoor in the Bartletts' living room to the basement to rest until transporters from Old Saybrook relayed them to the next depot. The Bartlett residence survived until 2003 as the Sachem House Restaurant.

Sources

Helander, Joel E. *Guilford Long Ago.* Guilford, CT: privately published, 1970.
Talcott, Alvan. *Families of Early Guilford, Connecticut.* Baltimore: Genealogical, 1984.

Bartley, Mordecai (1783–1870)

During his service as a state legislator and governor of Ohio, Mordecai Bartley challenged prevailing notions of fair treatment for fugitive slaves. A native of Fayette County, Pennsylvania, and a scion of Virginians from Loudoun County, he married Elizabeth Welles and established a home, general mercantile, and farm in Jefferson County, in eastern Ohio. After his military duties in the War of 1812 came to an end, in 1814, he moved his family to the Ohio frontier in Richland County. Elected governor in 1844, he promoted repeal of Ohio's Black Laws, which required free blacks to post bond and excluded their testimony in court against whites.

In 1844, Governor Bartley and Governor James McDowell of Virginia clashed over the fugitive slave issue. The discord began when an armed posse of 16 Virginians seized three white members of Ohio's Underground Railroad—Daniel (or Peter) Garner, Creighton Loraine, and Mordecai Thomas—for harboring Daniel Partridge and Frederic and Hannah Gay and their three children, Burnet, Harriet, and Mary. The six runaway slaves belonged to George Harwood, who pursued them from Washington Bottom, in Wood County, Virginia (now West Virginia), across the Ohio River to Belpre, Ohio, at the confluence of the Little Kanawha River. Harwood's confederates seized all but Daniel Partridge, who escaped to the north.

The Virginia authorities lodged suspects Garner, Loraine, and Thomas in the Parkersburg jail until their trial. In response to interstate trafficking in kidnap victims, Governor Bartley, until cooler heads dissuaded him from the plan, plotted a jailbreak to be executed by 100 Ohio militiamen. Instead of taking a violent course of action, on November 3, 1844, Bartley demanded that Governor McDowell extradite the 16 Virginians for trial in Ohio. Governor McDowell allowed the prisoners' wives to visit the jail but kept the secret network agents under heavy guard. Following guilty verdicts, on January 10, 1845, the Ohioans paid $100 bail each, left on their own recognizance, and never returned to Virginia for trial. McDowell exonerated the kidnappers. The incident heightened pre–Civil War mistrust between abolitionist and proslavery factions.

See also: kidnap.

Source

Dickinson, C.E. *History of Belpre, Washington County, Ohio.* Marietta, OH: self-published, 1920.

Bassett, Bayless S. (1821–1902)
Bassett, Esther Eliza Crandall (1831–1891)

Bayless S. Bassett and a fellow agent, the Reverend Darwin Eldridge Maxson, a Baptist minister from Alfred, New York, provided refuge for runaway slaves journeying to Canada. A native of Watson in Lewis County, New York, Bayless Bassett settled in Allegany County in 1826 and married Esther Eliza Crandall in 1849. At the Bassett residence at 29 North Main Street, a garret niche under the eaves was converted into a shelter. Blacks felt secure in the Bassett home until they could continue north on the route to Canada. The Bassetts' waystation is now the property of the Union University Church.

Source

Minard, John S. *Allegany County and Its People: A Centennial Memorial History of Allegany County, New York.* Alfred, NY: W.A. Fergusson, 1896.

Batcheldor, Joseph B. (1818–1845)
Batcheldor, Louisa Ann (1818–1845)

Methodist members of an Underground Railroad team on the Illinois frontier, Joseph B. Batcheldor (or Batchelor) and his wife, Louisa Ann Batcheldor, aided their neighbors in conveying desperate slaves. Until their untimely deaths at age 27, the Batcheldors operated a safehouse at their farm in Rich Township near Western Avenue and Sauk Trail in Chicago. They collaborated with John McCoy and Sabra Clark McCoy, agents of the secret network at Thornton, west of Chicago. The Batcheldor farm is part of Park Forest, Illinois.

Source

Candeloro, Dominic, and Barbara Paul. *Chicago Heights at the Crossroads of the Nation.* Charleston, SC: Arcadia, 2005.

Bateman, Warner Mifflin (1827–1897) Bateman, Ella Louise Snowbridge (1831–?)

U.S. District Attorney Warner Mifflin Bateman operated one of the 27 secret network depots in Springboro, Ohio. He was the nephew of Underground Railroad agents Jonathan Wright and Mary Bateman Wright, Quaker founders of Springboro in Warren County, Ohio; a cousin of operative Mahlon Wright; and a colleague of Salmon Portland Chase, an attorney for the secret network. As a lawyer, Bateman had vowed to uphold the law, but he had to violate federal statutes regarding the harboring of fugitive slaves in order to maintain his allegiance to Christian principle. He constructed a two-story home at 400 South Main Street. After marriage in 1852, he and his wife, Ella Louise Snowbridge Bateman, sheltered runaway slaves arriving from Cincinnati, Ohio, until national emancipation on January 1, 1863. In 2000, the waystation was listed on the National Register of Historic Buildings.

Source

Lovelace, Janice. "Railroad Ties." *Cincinnati Magazine* 37:8 (May 2004): 38–40.

Baylis, William (ca. 1813–1881)

William "Captain B" Baylis of Wilmington, Delaware, suffered arrest and jailing for his involvement with the Underground Railroad. It was no secret that he had a covert compartment in his ship's quarters and that he spread straw over underdeck chambers to muffle the sounds of refugees. He aided a slave working in an oyster house in Richmond, Virginia, in April 1856. The rescue triggered demands by editors of the *Richmond Dispatch* for the launching of water police along the James River. The following year, Baylis's seagoing brothers, John Baylis, Jr., at Indian River Hundred, and Samuel Baylis in Wilmington, retired after successful careers as slave transporters.

On May 31, 1858, seizure of the two-masted schooner *Keziah* resulted in the arrest of Captain Baylis and his first mate, Joseph J. Simpkins, for theft of five slaves—John Bull, a valet of businessman Andrew Kevan; Gilbert and Sarah, employees of Powell's Hotel; Joe Mayo, the chattel of Laura Hare; and William, a tobacco worker owned by Oliver Hamilton. The passengers boarded at the James River on May 29 and paid $50 each for conveyance along with barrels containing 1,200 bushels of wheat. When Baylis's ship grounded below City Point, Virginia, on May 30, it held the five runaways. Authorities connected Baylis with an Underground Railroad cell at 213 Witton Street in Petersburg, Virginia, that had operated for several years. A mob of 2,000 collected at the Appomattox River to protest slave rescues. News of the event alerted Virginians to anti-slavery activism in the state and spread across the secret network to Baltimore; New York; Providence, Rhode Island; and Canada.

At the hearing on June 1 in Petersburg, so many onlookers collected that the mayor postponed the session for the next two days. Pro-slavery factions rejoiced in Baylis's 40-year sentence in the Virginia state penitentiary and at the seizure of his schooner, valued at $800; abolitionists disapproved of the captain's demand for a $50 fare from each runaway. Simpkins was acquitted. John Bull's owner sold him for $1,150; Gilbert and Sarah's owner was bankrupt. After serving six years of his sentence, Baylis gained his freedom through the efforts of his wife, Martha Baylis.

Source

Kneebone, John T. "A Break Down on the Underground Railroad: Captain B. and the Capture of the *Keziah,* 1858." *Virginia Cavalcade* 48:2 (1999): 74–83.

Bayne, Thomas (ca. 1821–1888)

A successful escapee from bondage, Dr. Thomas Bayne found welcome in the black port city of New Bedford, Massachusetts. He was born Samuel Nixon in Norfolk, Virginia, where he worked as assistant and accountant for the dentist who owned him. His professional work enabled him to aid slaves in fleeing capture in the tidewater area by placing them aboard

Atlantic steamers bound for Philadelphia, Pennsylvania. In summer 1855, at age 34, Samuel Nixon escaped and renamed himself Thomas Bayne. He arrived in free territory on the New Jersey shore and hid at the home of Abigail Goodwin and Elizabeth Goodwin in Salem. Because of the danger to runaways from the Fugitive Slave Law of 1850, William Still, an Underground Railroad agent and officer of the Philadelphia Vigilance Committee, urged Bayne to move farther north to Canada.

Bayne refused the advice and settled in New Bedford, where he opened a dental practice. He joined attorney William Henry Johnson in forming a local vigilance committee to receive runaway slaves and protect them from slave hunters. In 1860, residents elected Bayne to the town council. After serving as a quartermaster for the Union army during the Civil War, he returned to his hometown, Norfolk, and, on December 4, 1867, took part in the Virginia Constitutional Convention.

Source

Parramore, Thomas C. *Norfolk: The First Four Centuries.* Charlottesville: University of Virginia Press, 1994.

Beale, Charlotte Hoopes (1813–?)
Beale, Joseph H. (1812–1883)

Two Quakers from Chester County, Pennsylvania, Charlotte Hoopes Beale of West Bradford and her husband, Joseph H. Beale, aided slaves in flight via the secret network. After their marriage in 1832, the Beales settled in White Plains, New York, operated a free labor store at 376 Pearl Street, and supported the New York–New England route of the Underground Railroad. For relays, they allied with Vermont conductor Oliver Johnson in Peacham, Charles Marriott and Sarah White Marriott on the Hudson River in New York, and Rachel Gilpin Robinson and Rowland Thomas Robinson at Rokeby Farm in Ferrisburg, Vermont. Joseph Beale conferred with the Robinsons in 1842 and 1844 concerning the safety of a runaway, Jeremiah Snowden, who was working as a stockman for the Robinsons.

See also: free labor store.

Source

Williams-Myers, A.J. "The Underground Railroad in the Hudson River Valley: A Succinct Historical Composite." *Afro-Americans in New York Life and History* 27:1 (2003): 55–73.

Beard, David (1774–1849)
Beard, Rebecca Brown (1778–1858)

An early Underground Railroad supervisor, David Beard, and his wife, Rebecca Brown Beard, of Jamestown, North Carolina, rescued destitute slaves. Both joined the Deep River Friends Church. They collaborated with fellow Quaker agents Delphina Mendenhall and George C. Mendenhall and George's brother, Richard Mendenhall, in Guilford County. After inheriting his father's hatter's tools, in 1795, David Beard opened a tannery and a fur and hat shop one mile north of town next to the family's brick home. Beard concealed refugees under heaps of rabbit skins. When authorities arrested him for harboring fugitives, George Mendenhall represented Beard in court. Because of Beard's advanced age, the judge lectured him and let him go.

See also: Quakers.

Source

Beal, Gertrude. "The Underground Railroad in Guilford County." *Southern Friend: Journal of the North Carolina Friends Historical Society* (Spring 1980): 18–28.

Beard, William (1788–1873)
Beard, Rachel Pierson (1789–1856)

A well-connected Quaker agent, William Beard teamed with midwestern operatives of the Underground Railroad. Born in Guilford County, North Carolina, he married Rachel Pierson in 1808. The couple managed a stop in Salem, in Union County, Indiana. They received passengers from brothers David Morrison Wilson and Joseph Gardner Wilson in Cincinnati, Ohio, and advanced slaves from Lane Seminary to Billingsville, Indiana, and on to the safehouse of Catherine White Coffin and Levi Coffin in Fountain City. The members of the Henry County Female Anti-Slavery Society made a special effort to keep the Beards supplied with blankets and clothing for refugees. To assure safety and prosperity for ex-slaves, in 1844, William Beard surveyed Amherstburg, Ontario, a settlement at the end of the line. Superintendent Levi Coffin lauded Beard's steady labor in defense of the oppressed.

See also: female anti-slavery societies.

Source

Smiddy, Betty Ann. *A Little Piece of Paradise . . . College Hill, Ohio.* Cincinnati, OH: College Hill Historical Society, 1999.

Bearse, Austin (1808–1881)

Captain Austin Bearse, a native of Barnstable, Massachusetts, provided sea passage for runaways from Cape Cod. From boyhood until age 22, he served as mate on slave-trading vessels out of New Orleans and off the South Carolina coast. On southern shores, he observed the cruelties of slave pens and the auction block. He reported to Harriet Beecher Stowe, the author of *Uncle Tom's Cabin* (1852), that trade in human flesh reflected the economic principles of commerce in farm livestock. He compared American slavery to similar institutions in Algeria, France, Spain, and Turkey and found his native land as barbarous as any other on the globe.

After resettling in New Bedford, Massachusetts, in 1845, Bearse remained alert to Underground Railroad business by reading William Lloyd Garrison's newspaper, *The Liberator.* Bearse boldly searched vessels for slaves being returned south. In July 1847, he helped sisters Abigail Mott and Lydia Mott, Quaker agents in Albany, New York, in transporting runaway George Lewis to Long Island Sound and on to Boston. Bearse aided the Boston Vigilance Committee on May 16, 1851, by paying escapee Sam Ward's passage to Plymouth, Massachusetts; on June 3, he donated $14 to aid fugitive Samuel Jones. On April 16, 1851, he worked as a harbor spy for the committee. Bearse's philanthropy continued on February 1, 1854, with a donation of $21.10 to a fugitive named Mrs. Neille. In July 1854, he gave a cash gift to Julia Smith and her child.

Bearse remained active in rescue work. Members considered enlisting Bearse in the rescue of Thomas M. Sims, whom the U.S. sloop *Acorn* bore south into bondage on August 19, 1851. In *Cheerful Yesterdays* (1899), memoirist Thomas Wentworth Higginson mentions hiring Bearse to sail the *Flirt,* a vessel intended for rescuing slaves from slave ships and for separating them from dry land long enough to stymy slave hunters. Bearse accepted a request from orator Wendell Addison Phillips in 1854 to retrieve a runaway held on the *Sally Ann,* a schooner from Belfast, Maine, that was moored on the Cape Fear River in Wilmington, North Carolina. By tying hats and jackets along the railings of his sloop, Bearse convinced the captain of the *Sally Ann* that he had considerable backup. The captain turned the slave over to Bearse, who sailed to South Boston and lodged the man at his home. The slave continued on the Underground Railroad route to Worcester, Massachusetts, and Canada.

In October 1854, the Boston Vigilance Committee enlisted Bearse to reclaim a man from the *Cameo,* a brig out of Augusta, Maine. Although the captain transferred the runaway to the schooner *William,* Bearse saw through his deception and located the fugitive, whom the captain had threatened to throw overboard. Free at last, the slave passed to agent Lewis Hayden and went by carriage with William Ingersoll Bowditch along the New York–Canada line to freedom. Until 1855, Bearse collected dues from other Boston Vigilance Committee members. Shortly before Bearse's death at age 73, he published his memoirs, *Reminiscences of Fugitive Slave Law Days in Boston* (1880).

See also: Liberator, The; philanthropists; spies; *Uncle Tom's Cabin; or, Life Among the Lowly* (1852).

Sources

Bearse, Austin. *Reminiscences of Fugitive Slave Law Days in Boston.* Boston: W. Richardson, 1880.

Higginson, Thomas Wentworth. *Cheerful Yesterdays.* Boston: Houghton Mifflin, 1899.

Beasley, Alfred (1803–1868)

A Kentucky-born confederate of renowned Underground Railroad agents on the Ohio River in Ripley, Ohio, Dr. Alfred Beasley managed a medical office and waystation at 124–128 Front Street. One of his daring interventions required medical treatment of a bounty hunter and the man's quarry, whom Beasley patched up in separate rooms of his two-story home office. The two patients were unaware of each other's presence. Beasley plotted rescue strategy with his neighbors, Dr. Alexander Campbell and Thomas Collins on Front Street, and with Catherine McCague and Thomas McCague at the North Star station, foundryman John P. Parker, and Jean Lowry Rankin and John Rankin of Liberty Hill, one of the busiest safehouses in Underground Railroad history. Beasley passed groups of fugitives to the Reverend James Gilliland at Red Oak Presbyterian Church. In 1912, Dr. Beasley was an honoree listed on Ripley's Liberty Monument on Maine Street.

See also: bounty hunters.

Source

Parker, John P. *John P. Parker, His Promised Land: The Autobiography of John P. Parker, Former Slave and Conductor on the Underground Railroad.* New York: W.W. Norton, 1996.

Beck, Isaac M. (1811–1890) Beck, Cassandra Graham Lamb (1807–1901)

An innovative stationmaster at Sardinia in Brown County, Ohio, Dr. Isaac M. Beck and his wife, Cassandra Graham Lamb Beck, concentrated on conducting slaves safely to free territory. Dr. Beck, a native of Clermont County, Ohio, worked at farming and then learned printing in Georgetown. At the office of William B. Chipley in Bethel, Ohio, Beck studied medicine. In July 1829, he built one of Sardinia's first residences and opened a medical practice. Four years later, he married Cassandra Lamb, daughter of Ohio pioneers. He lectured twice at the Methodist Episcopal church on the evils of slavery. A colleague of abolitionists Dr. Alexander Campbell and Jean Lowry Rankin and John Rankin of Ripley, Isaac Beck was also well connected to other networkers, including the Reverend James Gilliland of Red Oak, John Bennington Mahan at White Oak Creek, the Reverend Jesse Lockhart and William McCoy of Russelville, Catherine McCague and Thomas McCague, John P. Parker, and the Pettijohn clan. For teamster John D. Hudson's assistance as courier, Beck paid him 25¢ per relay to the next station.

To ease the passage of Ike and other hunted men like him through the territory, Beck enlisted Quakers and Wesleyans to fill out a 40-mile stretch with waystations. Beck's recovery of Ike, a refugee from Maxon County, Kentucky, ended in a brief recapture. However, when the slave owner left Ike standing outside while the posse ate dinner, a party of blacks directed Ike to agents that John Hudson had summoned by a blast on a conch shell. A tragic confrontation occurred on April 21, 1839, when slave hunters attempted to seize agent Moses Cumberland from the Gist community. John Hudson's sister, Sally Hudson, bit, clawed, and slapped the pursuers, who shot her in the spine. Dr. Beck treated her for two weeks but could not save her.

See also: Gist Settlement; Quakers.

Sources

Bordewich, Fergus M. *Bound for Canaan: The Underground Railroad and the War for the Soul of America.* New York: Amistad, 2005.

History of Brown County, Ohio. Chicago: W.H. Beers, 1883.

Beckley, Guy (1803–1847)

A stationkeeper in Ann Arbor, Michigan, the Reverend Guy Beckley, a Methodist Episcopal preacher, served the Underground Railroad for five years. The American Anti-Slavery Society employed him to lecture in New England. In 1839, he settled in Michigan near his brother and sister-in-law, agent Josiah Beckley and Minerva Bird Beckley, who operated a waystation at 1709 Pontiac Street. Guy Beckley became an officer of the Michigan Anti-Slavery Society. With tracts and lectures, he began persuading local people to accept abolitionism. In 1842, at 1425 Pontiac Street, he opened a two-story safehouse in which he had equipped upstairs closets with lowered ceilings to create niches for hiding slaves.

In the last 11 years of his life, Guy Beckley joined Theodore Foster in rescuing runaways and in publishing a nationally distributed abolitionist weekly, the *Signal of Liberty,* formerly known as the *Michigan Freeman.* Beckley filled the pages with eyewitness accounts of bondage, including the flight of 23-year-old Robert Coxe in May 1843 to Adrian, Michigan. Beckley encouraged volunteers to join the Underground Railroad effort in Washtenaw County. During agent Lyman Goodnow's relay of Caroline Quarles to Canada, in early fall 1843, the pair stopped to rest at Beckley's station. The Beckley home is featured on the Journey to Freedom tour and the National Park Service Underground Railroad Network to Freedom.

Sources

Arndt, Leslie E. *The Bay County Story: From Footpaths to Freeways.* Port Huron, MI: Huron News Service, 1982.

Ryan, Virginia, et al. *Early Ann Arbor and Its People.* Ann Arbor, MI: Ann Arbor Instrument Works, 1974.

Beebe, Asa (ca. 1792–1878) Beebe, Mary Whipple (?–1878)

Two Underground Railroad operatives involved in the rescue of William "Jerry" McHenry, Deacon Asa Beebe and his wife, Mary Whipple Beebe, broke federal laws on behalf of runaway slaves. At age 15, Asa Beebe, a native of Bennington, Vermont, arrived in

Mexico, in Oswego County, New York, and served in the War of 1812. He made his living as a foundryman and built a reputation for tenacity and Presbyterian beliefs. In 1840, the Beebes moved to Main Street, near Black Creek. Eleven years later, they moved outside the village to Toad Hollow.

After eight secret network volunteers seized runaway William "Jerry" McHenry, a mulatto cooper, from the Clinton Square jail in Syracuse, New York, on October 1, 1851, transporters placed him at the safehouse of Amy Perkins Ames and Orson Ames for one night. For the next two weeks, McHenry hid in the Beebes' barn. Aiding the couple in the dangerous concealment was their son, Winsor Beebe (ca. 1830–?), who conveyed food to the fugitive. Winsor served as relay agent in mid-October; shielding McHenry behind burlap bags in a farm wagon, he drove the fugitive to the next waystation, which may have been that of Olive Clarke and Sidney Clarke in Fulton, the last stop before McHenry traveled by boat over Lake Erie to Kingston, Ontario.

Source

McAndrew, Mike, "Bold Raid Freed a Man," *Syracuse Post-Standard,* February 14, 2005.

Beecher, Henry Ward (1813–1887)

A legendary Congregationalist minister and supporter of the Underground Railroad, the Reverend Henry Ward Beecher drew throngs to his diatribes against slavery. A native of Litchfield, Connecticut, he was the younger brother of Harriet Beecher Stowe, author of *Uncle Tom's Cabin* (1852). In his late teens, Beecher wrote editorials and essays for abolitionist newspapers. After training for the pulpit at Amherst College, he attended Lane Theological Seminary, where he armed himself during area patrols to stop the kidnap of free blacks. While preaching in Indianapolis, Indiana, from 1839 to 1847, he served the secret network as an agent. He also supported the rescue operations of Samuel Bowne Parsons and Susan Howland Parsons at Flushing, New York.

Beecher earned a reputation for blatant civil disobedience after he settled in Brooklyn, New York, in autumn 1847. At the invitation of Henry Chandler Bowen, Beecher pastored the new Congregationalist assembly, the Plymouth Church of the Pilgrims on Hicks Street, which earned the nickname Grand Central Depot of the Underground Railroad. Beecher coordinated slave rescues from Manhattan with the

Congregationalist minister Henry Ward Beecher (the brother of novelist Harriet Beecher Stowe) argued passionately against slavery and for aid to runaways. No stranger to civil disobedience, he participated directly in the rescue of slaves. *(Hulton Archive/Stringer/Getty Images)*

Reverend Charles Bennett Ray. The congregation, including Lewis Tappan and treasurer Stephen Van Culen White, relayed slaves from underground passages to their own waystations.

Through his persuasive sermons and one-on-one encounters with volunteers, Beecher promoted an expansion of aid to runaway slaves. His raising of $2,250 and, on November 4, 1848, his mediation of a slave purchase resulted in the freedom of sisters Emily Edmondson and Mary Catherine Edmondson. He enlisted as agents journalist Theodore Tilton and, in 1851, the Reverend Amos Noah Freeman, an operative at Siloam Presbyterian Church in Brooklyn. Beecher surprised his congregation on June 1, 1856, when he presented the story of Sarah, a mulatto worth $1,200 to her owner. While she sat beside the pulpit, he dramatized the terrors of bondage. At his request for funds to buy her liberty, church members immediately collected more than enough to free Sarah and her two-year-old child.

In 1857, operative Lewis Tappan aided Beecher in extending routes of the secret network. As abolitionist fervor increased, Beecher received James Robinson, a slave fleeing bondage in Wilmington, North Carolina. That same year, Beecher purchased rifles to assist insurrectionist John Brown in the assault on the federal armory at Harpers Ferry, Virginia. On February 5, 1860, Beecher held a mock slave auction and raised $900 from his listeners and a gold ring from Rose Terry to purchase a nine-year-old slave named Sally Maria Diggs, nicknamed "Pinky" or "Pink," whom slavers had seized from her grandmother and dispatched south. In gratitude, Pinky changed her name to Rose Ward to honor both Terry and Beecher. After her education at Howard University and marriage, Rose Ward Hunt settled in Washington, D.C. She visited Plymouth Church of the Pilgrims in 1927 to thank the congregation for buying her freedom and for awarding her the gold ring as a token of liberty.

After his move to Peekskill, New York, in 1861, Beecher continued serving the Underground Railroad. He maintained a tunnel from his residence as a hideaway and escape route for slaves fleeing to Ontario. At his death from stroke in his sleep at age 74, the city of Plymouth held a day of mourning. Black veterans of the Union army led the funeral cortege.

See also: abolitionist newspapers; civil disobedience; kidnap; Plymouth Church of the Pilgrims; routes, Underground Railroad; *Uncle Tom's Cabin; or, Life Among the Lowly* (1852).

Sources

"The Friday Evening Prayer Meeting," *Brooklyn (NY) Eagle*, January 15, 1881, 2.

Shaw, Wayne. "The Plymouth Pulpit: Henry Ward Beecher's Slave Auction Block." *American Transcendental Quarterly* 14:4 (December 2000): 335.

Bell, Charles R. (1827–1912)

Former slave Charles R. Bell gained his freedom with help from the Underground Railroad. He was born a bondsman to James H. Inship in Romney, Virginia (now West Virginia). After Inship's death, Bell was auctioned for $1,050. On the advice of Inship's abolitionist son, in August 1859, Bell took his wife, Catherine Bell, and their seven-year-old son, William, and fled through the Appalachian Mountains. Because posters advertised a reward, the Bells stuck to overhanging rocks and thick forest. They traveled by night and survived on berries and raw corn. Four weeks later, they arrived in Pittsburgh, Pennsylvania. The Pennsylvania Underground Railroad supplied a covered wagon for the remainder of the journey to the American House, a reception center in St. Catharines, Ontario. In 1867, Charles Bell returned south to visit his mother. On his way back, the Reverend Justin Rolph Loomis hired him on the spot to top trees at Bucknell University in Lewisburg, Pennsylvania. For four decades, Bell served as campus custodian.

Source

Alcorn, Sam. "Backward Glance." *Bucknell World* (January 2006).

Bell, David Williamson (1794–1873)
Bell, Charles A. (1840–1864)

A father-son team of rescuers, David Williamson Bell and his son Charles A. "Charlie" Bell had ample opportunity to aid runaways at Indiana's first known Underground Railroad depot. After moving to the state in 1829, David Bell and Elizabeth Wright Bell (1795–1862) settled at Morvin's Landing, a farm in Harrison County. With the assistance of Charlie Bell, the elder Bell operated a ferry over the Ohio River from Mauckport, Indiana, to Brandenburg, Kentucky. During Charlie Bell's upbringing, he came under the influence of his mother's sister, Julia Wright "Aunt Julie" Jones, a fervid abolitionist.

On September 25, 1857, the Bells helped a Kentucky fugitive, blacksmith Charles Woodruff, to flee enslavement of Dr. Charles Henry Ditto. David Bell led Woodruff by mule to the safehouse and concealed him for several weeks, during which the party plotted the theft of Woodruff's wife, Mary Ann Woodruff. Aiding the operation was a free black transporter, Oswell (also Oswald or Oswel) Wright of Corydon, who had been the slave of David Bell's father-in-law, Jeremiah Wright. Oswell Wright completed the transfer to Brownstown, in Jackson County. Woodruff gained his freedom in Canada and settled in California before returning east to enlist in a colored regiment of the Union army.

According to an article in the November 19, 1857, issue of the *Louisville Courier*, a spy named C.E. Johnson infiltrated the Bells' operation and alerted Henry Ditto to their role in slave theft. Pursuers arrived from Kentucky. On the pretext of rescuing Mary Ann Woodruff, the posse abducted David Bell, his son Charlie, and Oswell Wright and locked them in a cell. Bond was set at $3,000 for the black agent and $5,000 each for Bell and his son. A face-off across the river pitted Colonel William C. Marsh and an armed band from Corydon, Indiana, against the Meade County Rangers and the Kentucky Legion on the proslavery side. As litigation dragged into May 1858, the Kentucky governor hired 200 minutemen—mostly volunteer merchants and lawyers—to guard the county offices.

After racing home from Nicaragua via Panama and the Mississippi and Ohio rivers, Horace Bell (1830–?) and John Bell (fl. 1850s) received the blessing of their mother Elizabeth Wright Bell, to engineer a jailbreak. On July 29, 1858, the brothers freed their father and younger brother from jail. The chaotic escape by skiff concluded with Horace firing his pistol to keep a posse from overtaking them at the pier. On October 22, 1858, a vengeful party of five Kentucky outriders seized Horace Bell on Main Street in New Albany and bore him to jail in Louisville, from which he posted a bond of $750 before departing for California.

In the late 1850s, producer Woodward Hall capitalized on the ongoing border feud by presenting a three-act play, *Horace Bell: Champion of Freedom,* which concluded with the singing of the "Marseillaise" and a bow to the audience from Horace Bell. Because the initial jailbreak did not include Wright, he served out part of a five-year sentence in the Kentucky penitentiary at Frankfort before being pardoned. Charlie and Horace Bell fought for the Union army in the Civil War. Horace attained the rank of major; Charlie, a captain in the Twentieth Indiana Infantry, died in combat at Petersburg, Virginia, in 1864.

See also: spies.

Sources

"Excitement at Brandenburg, Kentucky," *Harrison (IN) Democrat,* November 17, 1857, 2–3.

Gresham, Matilda. *Life of Walter Quintin Gresham, 1832–1895.* Chicago: Rand McNally, 1919.

Strassweg, Elsa. "The Kidnapping of Horace Bell." *Indiana History Bulletin* 25:7 (July 1948): 132–8.

Bell, James Patterson (1748–1834)

A veteran of the Revolutionary War, Colonel James Patterson Bell of West Fallowfield at Colerain in Chester County, Pennsylvania, operated Station 17 of the Pilgrim's Pathway, a 17-stop network through southern Lancaster County. He was appointed an officer of the Chester County militia on November 21, 1778. As a reward for service to the Continental army, he received 1,200 acres along Street Road from the government and built a two-story brick residence, gristmill, and sawmill. During chancy rescues, slaves could exit his home through a brick tunnel to Octorara Creek, from which they could reach Andrew's Bridge and journey on to Oxford, Pennsylvania. Bellbank Bridge, a covered crossing built in 1850, bears Colonel Bell's name.

See also: American Revolution; Pilgrim's Pathway.

Source

Spotts, Charles Dewey. *The Pilgrim's Pathway: The Underground Railroad in Lancaster County.* Lancaster, PA: Franklin & Marshall College Library, 1966.

Bell, Lavinia (fl. 1840s–1860s)

The publication of Lavinia Bell's story awakened citizens of Quebec to the plight of fugitive slaves traveling north via the Underground Railroad. Bell was born free in Washington, D.C. In childhood, she was kidnapped and sold in Texas to work as a dance hall girl. In her mid-teens, she began laboring in cotton fields. In 1861, after numerous escape attempts, she reached Montreal. On January 28, 1861, Dr. John Reddy examined her twisted spine and distorted ribs, which cruel treatment had permanently crippled. Her owner had notched her ears, branded her left hand and abdomen, lopped off her little finger, and fractured her skull. Scarring on her scalp and face and broken teeth attested to repeated assaults. When Reddy's observations appeared in the Canadian press, readers realized that Harriet Beecher Stowe had not exaggerated the desperation of runaways in her fictional slave novel *Uncle Tom's Cabin* (1852).

See also: kidnap; *Uncle Tom's Cabin; or, Life Among the Lowly* (1852).

Source

Siebert, Wilbur H. *The Underground Railroad: Slavery to Freedom.* New York: Macmillan, 1898.

Bell, Philip Alexander (1808–1889)

Editor and activist Philip Alexander Bell solicited volunteer agents for the Underground Railroad. At his birthplace, New York City, he studied at the African Free School. After his marriage to Rebecca Elizabeth Fenwick of Charleston, South Carolina, in 1832, he represented the American Anti-Slavery Society and sold subscriptions to William Lloyd Garrison's newspaper *The Liberator.* Bell aided refugees in flight from bondage. With his partners, Samuel Cornish and the

Reverend Charles Bennett Ray, Bell published the *New York City Weekly Advocate,* later named the *Colored American,* the most influential black weekly from 1839 to 1841.

Bell's newspaper informed readers of one of the most stirring moral issues of the times. On October 19, 1839, he championed Joseph Cinqué, leader of the African mutineers aboard the Portuguese slave ship *Amistad.* After Cinqué's extensive court battles, in March 1841, Bell thanked agent Robert Purvis for disseminating the African's photo and compared Cinqué with American libertarians John Adams, Samuel Adams, John Hancock, Patrick Henry, and Thomas Jefferson. Following Bell's move to San Francisco in 1855, he continued supporting efforts to rescue fugitive slaves in a successful California weekly, the *Elevator.*

See also: Amistad; Liberator, The.

Sources

"Cinqué and Heroes of the American Revolution," *Colored American,* March 27, 1841.

"On Cinqué," *Colored American,* October 19, 1839, 1.

Beloved (1987)

American author Toni Morrison jolted the reading public with stark images of the plight of blacks and Underground Railroad rescues with her best-selling historical novel *Beloved.* Like Harriet Beecher Stowe's *Uncle Tom's Cabin* (1852), Morrison's fiction put a human face on the refugees seeking a scrap of liberty to dignify their lives and hopes. The granddaughter of Kentucky slaves, Morrison grew up in Lorain, Ohio, a crucial reception point for fugitives crossing the Ohio River into free territory. Based on the crime of Margaret Garner, an escapee from Boone County, Kentucky, who murdered her infant daughter Priscilla on January 29, 1856, the novel describes the desperation of female breeders. Their lives were a cycle of rape and childbearing to satisfy the need for new laborers to replenish the southern plantation system. A tale of spiritual haunting, the fictional text employs Gothic elements to illustrate the persistence of the sin of bondage in American history.

Grounding her work in extensive research into bondage and the reclamation of humanity in dispirited slaves, Morrison depicts the activism of black agents of the Underground Railroad and the operation of a safehouse. Along the way from a Kentucky plantation called Sweet Home, Sethe, the protagonist, gives birth in a canoe and struggles to elude pursuers. Only minutes after her daughter is born, Sethe experiences the confusion and dislocation that once frustrated the uneducated runaway. Without a knowledge of geography, she looks for a signal and connects with an agent, who calls himself Stamp Paid. Sethe and a stream of refugees pass through the home of Grandma Baby Suggs, a self-proclaimed minister to the grieving, displaced blacks seeking her aid and comfort. In addition to offering food and shelter, she repairs worn shoes, a recurrent symbol of hard traveling. She preserves the disparate messages that journeyers leave for relatives and friends who have been sold and transported across the South. The yearning for reunion reprises a period of black history when the basics of family and community were fragmented by the greed of slave owners.

Sources

Daniel, Janice Barnes. "Function or Frill: The Quilt as Storyteller in Toni Morrison's Beloved." *Midwest Quarterly* 41:3 (2000): 321–9.

Hamilton, Cynthia S. "Revisions, Rememories, and Exorcisms: Toni Morrison and the Slave Narrative." *Journal of American Studies* 30:3 (1996): 30–32.

Morrison, Toni. *Beloved.* New York: Plume, 1987.

Beman, Jehiel C. (1789–1858)
Beman, Nancy Scott (fl. 1830s–1850s)
Beman, Amos Gerry (1812–1894)

An evangelical preacher and civil rights activist, the Reverend Jehiel C. Beman (or Beaman) conducted slaves to freedom via the Underground Railroad. Born in Colchester, Connecticut, Jehiel Beman was the son of Sarah, a slave, and her husband, Caesar, a bondsman who earned freedom by taking his master's place in the militia during the American Revolution. Jeheil took the surname that his father created from "be a man." Beman trained as a cobbler and preached at the Cross Street Church. He completed his education at Wesleyan University and, in 1838, began preaching at the Temple Street Congregational Church in New Haven, Connecticut, a waystation of the secret network into the 1850s.

Jehiel Beman joined the anti-slavery movement in New England and New York and founded the Middletown Anti-Slavery Society in South Glastonbury, Connecticut. He and his son, the Reverend Amos Gerry Beman, aroused passions for abolitionism and maintained a safehouse on the New England–Canada route. With the aid of his children and his second wife, Nancy Scott Beman, of New Haven, Jehiel received runaways. At age 50, he moved to Boston, where he pastored the First American Methodist Episcopal Zion Church. In 1841, he supported William Lloyd Garrison's abolitionist journal, *The Liberator.* In league with Lewis Tappan, Amos Beman co-established the American and Foreign Anti-Slavery Society.

See also: American Revolution; black soldiers; *Liberator, The.*

Sources

Houseley, Kathleen. "Yours for the Oppressed: The Life of Jehiel C. Beman." *Journal of Negro History* 77:1 (1992): 17–29.

Zitka, Amy L., "Remembering Black History Heroes," *Middletown (CT) Press,* February 20, 2005.

Benedict, Aaron Lancaster (ca. 1804–1867)
Benedict, Livius (fl. 1840s–1850s)
Benedict, Mordecai (1845–1927)

A faithful Quaker minister and member of an abolitionist clan, Aaron Lancaster Benedict opened his Ohio home to black refugees. After settling in Marengo, on Alum Creek in Morrow County, Ohio, he established an Underground Railroad stop. History records his involvement in 60 rescues in one month's work for the secret network. In 1838, Benedict wrote a poem on the evils of slavery. Because of his notoriety as a rescuer, Southerners offered a $1,000 bounty for him. His six-year-old cousins, Livius Benedict and Mordecai Benedict, served as transporters and drove refugees in wagons to Joseph Morris's waystation at Richland Township in Marion County, Ohio. In adulthood, Mordecai Benedict became a respected stationmaster of the Ohio network for maintaining a welcoming atmosphere at his home, Valley Cottage, in Peru, also on Alum Creek. His father, Daniel Benedict (1814–1899), worked as a fellow conductor.

Source

Morris, Joseph. *Reminiscences of Joseph Morris.* Columbus, OH: Friends, 1881.

Benedict, Reuben (1768–1850s)
Benedict, Anna T. Stevens (1770–1831)

A Quaker stationkeeper in Peru, in Morrow County, Ohio, Reuben Benedict received runaways at his two-story brick home on Alum Creek. After Benedict married Anna T. Stevens in 1791, the couple arrived in the area from New York in 1812 and with other pioneers established a village, where Benedict farmed and milled flour. The Benedicts operated a temperance hotel as a stage waystation. Their home at 1463 County Road welcomed refugees at a busy point on the Ohio–Canada route. In 1839, the Benedicts harbored "Black Bill" Anderson, a Virginian sought by slave catchers. Reuben Benedict and other Quaker operatives transported Anderson along the route to Canada. The Benedict residence is listed on the National Register of Historic Places.

Source

History of Morrow Township and Ohio. Chicago: O.L. Baskin, 1880.

Benjamin, Jacob (1817–1863)

A militant abolitionist, financier Jacob Benjamin defended black slaves escaping from Missouri into Kansas Territory. After immigrating from Bohemia, he settled at North Middle Creek in Lawrence, Kansas. In league with August Bondi and Theodore Wiener, Benjamin fought in the May 1855 Potawatomi skirmish against pro-slavery ruffians from Missouri. In his autobiography, insurrectionist John Brown empathized with Benjamin during his imprisonment for his role in the anti-slavery uprising.

Source

Sanborn, F.B. *The Life and Letters of John Brown: Liberator of Kansas, and Martyr of Virginia.* Boston: Roberts Brothers, 1885.

Benson, Benjamin (fl. 1810s)

Freeborn Benjamin Benson became the first black American to sue successfully for his liberty. He was one of many blacks kidnapped and sold south into bondage. Slave catchers seized him in Delaware in 1817 and transported him to Greensboro, North Carolina, where slaveholder John Thompson took possession of him. After Quaker Underground Railroad agent Vestal M. Coffin learned of the outrage, he pressed Delaware authorities to intercede.

After a sheriff's deputy warned Thompson that he might lose his investment, Thompson quickly sold Benson to a Georgia buyer. Coffin, supported by letters from Dr. George Swain and Enoch Macy, exhorted the Delaware legislature to appropriate funds to buy Benson. Thompson incurred a debt of $1,600 for repurchasing Benson and transporting him to a Delaware courtroom. After four years of litigation, the court found Thompson guilty and freed Benson.

See also: kidnap.

Source

Coffin, Addison. *Life and Travels of Addison Coffin.* Cleveland, OH: W.G. Hubbard, 1897.

Benson, Catharine K. Stetson (1809–1890)
Benson, George W. (?–1864)

Quaker peace proponents Catharine (or Catherine) K. Stetson Benson and George W. Benson of Rhode Island operated a waystation at 60 Pomfret Road near Brooklyn, Connecticut. In 1828, George Benson welcomed Benjamin Lundy, a promoter of slave rescue, who addressed fellow abolitionists. Benson joined the following of young William Lloyd Garrison in 1830, after the orator's discovery by Samuel Joseph May and his cousin, attorney Samuel Edmund Sewall. With the aid of May, the Benson home flourished as a waystation. It received the name Friendship Valley from teacher Prudence Crandall, whom the Bensons sheltered from persecution in February 1833 for opening a school for black students. In 1834, George Benson's sister, Helen Eliza Benson, married William Lloyd Garrison, publisher of *The Liberator.* In September 1836, Benson and Garrison corresponded on issues arising from a Boston riot.

George Benson managed the American Anti-Slavery Society in 1841 and in March joined J.D. Fitch and Samuel L. Hill in arranging the Eastern Connecticut Anti-Slavery Convention. Benson and his wife collaborated with Underground Railroad operative Moses Brown in Providence, Rhode Island, and aided another former slave, Sojourner Truth, who worked as the Bensons' housekeeper in 1847. Three years later, Benson ended his volunteerism for the Underground Railroad after the failure of his cotton mill. He was killed in 1864 while serving in the Union army. His safehouse is currently a bed and breakfast listed on the National Register of Historic Places.

See also: American Anti-Slavery Society; *Liberator, The.*

Sources

May, Samuel Joseph. *Some Recollections of Our Antislavery Conflict.* Boston: Fields, Osgood, 1869.
Pendleton, Leila Amos. *A Narrative of the Negro.* Washington, DC: R.L. Pendleton, 1912.

Berry, Amanda (1837–1915)
Berry, Mariam Matthews (fl. 1840s)
Berry, Samuel (fl. 1840s)

Born in slavery, holiness evangelist and missionary Amanda Berry joined her family in escorting fugitives to freedom. She grew up at Long Green Plantation in Long Green, Maryland, apart from her parents, Mariam Matthews and Samuel Berry, who were enslaved by Shadrach Green and Darby Insor, respectively. After Samuel purchased his freedom in 1841, he farmed in York County, Pennsylvania, and opened a waystation of the Underground Railroad a few miles over the Maryland state line in Shrewsburg. Amanda Berry, the eldest of 13 children, was homeschooled. She came of age in a setting that often welcomed 20 refugees at a time. From the waystation, Samuel Berry accompanied fugitive couples and individuals all night to the next stop and then returned home to sleep a few hours before going to work.

Samuel Berry tracked information about runaways in the *Baltimore Sun* and maintained a simple life that fooled the spies from New Market who watched the Berry house. On one occasion, a well-dressed runaway from New Orleans, Louisiana, knocked after midnight and asked for food. While he ate, six or seven white slave catchers interrupted and accused Berry of harboring fugitives. They beat Berry and threatened Mariam Berry with a dagger. The slave leaped from an upstairs window into the custody of Ben Crout, who returned the man to Baltimore, Maryland. The next time that whites accused Berry of harboring fugitives, Mariam Berry snatched up a cane with a blade concealed in it and brandished it in the faces of the whites on the doorstep. The next morning, she stood at the entrance to the largest tavern in the area and shamed the white slave hunters by name before the public.

Two years later, a valuable male fugitive arrived at the Berry house after shifting locations for two weeks along the secret network. While the man hid upstairs under the straw ticking of a cord bed, Mariam Berry showed the sheriff around the house and threw back the covers to reveal her sleeping son. The runaway was weak from terror but passed safely to Canada. At harvest, another man arrived footsore from a three-week trek from New Orleans. His master threatened to sell him for falling asleep and ruining hogsheads of molasses. The master's daughter unlocked the handcuffs that shackled the man in the cellar, gave him cash, and told him to follow the polestar. Mariam Berry and her children bathed the man's feet and fed him for two weeks before dispatching him to Canada.

The Berry family was familiar with bloodhounds, bounty hunters, and rapid rescues. After one of the Berrys' freeborn daughters was seized and sold during the family's visit to Maryland relatives, Amanda worked as a laundress and domestic to raise $50 to buy her sister's freedom. Amanda married Calvin Devine in 1854 and was widowed during the Civil War. She subsequently launched a career in preaching and Christian education in Monrovia, Liberia.

See also: bloodhounds; bounty hunters; spies.

Source

Smith, Amanda. *An Autobiography: The Story of the Lord's Dealings with Mrs. Amanda Smith.* Chicago: Meyer & Brother, 1893.

Beveridge, John Lowrie (1824–1910)
Beveridge, Helen Mar Judson (1829–1909)

A governor of Illinois from 1873 to 1876, John Lowrie (or Lourie) Beveridge earned renown as a humanitarian and operative of the Underground Railroad. A native of Greenwich, New York, he was the son of Scots immigrants who farmed in Washington County. He developed hatred for slavery while teaching school in Jackson, Overton, and Wilson counties in Tennessee. At age 24, he married Helen Mar Judson, daughter of a Methodist Episcopal minister in Chicago. While living at Somonauk, in De Kalb County, Illinois, Beveridge made his living as an attorney. In the Beveridges' barn, underneath a covering of straw, a circular chamber nearly eight feet deep harbored runaways. During the Civil War, John Beveridge attained the rank of colonel of the Eighth Illinois Cavalry and led his regiment at the battle of Gettysburg.

Sources

MacMilian, Thomas C. *The Scots and Their Descendants in Illinois.* Chicago: Illinois State Historical Society, 1919.

Portrait and Biographical Album of Champaign County, Illinois. Chicago: Chapman Brothers, 1887.

Bezan, Jacob (1790–?)
Bezan, Martha (1795–?)
Bezan, George (fl. 1830s–1840s)

Two Underground Railroad conductors at Mercersburg in Franklin County, Pennsylvania, Jacob Bezan (or Bissan) and his wife, Martha, collaborated with their son, George, during slave rescues. The trio hid fugitives in the loft of their log house at West California Street. George Bezan, who was large and muscular, served as security guard for his parents' operation. Escapees arrived through a nearby cornfield and departed through a brickyard.

Source

Follow the Drinking Gourd (pamphlet). Mercer, PA: Mercer County Historical Society, 2002.

Bias, James Joshua Gould (?–1860)
Bias, Eliza (fl. 1850s)

A church leader and conductor of the Underground Railroad, Dr. James Joshua Gould Bias set an example of courage. Born into slavery in Maryland, he was the carriage driver for a physician. After gaining his freedom, Bias moved to Philadelphia, joined the Philadelphia Vigilance Committee, and graduated from the Eclectic Medical College in 1852. A folk healer, he pulled teeth, practiced phrenology, and applied leeches to the sick.

James Bias and his wife, Eliza, operated a waystation in alliance with the Reverend Charles Turner Torrey of Boston and with Harriet Lee Smith Whipper and William J. Whipper of Columbia, Pennsylvania. As described in William Parker's narrative "The Freedman's Story: In Two Parts" (1866), Bias treated the ills of exhausted, sick, pregnant, feeble, and injured refugees. The Reverend Daniel Alexander Payne, a rescuer in Edenton, North Carolina, delivered the eulogy at James Bias's funeral.

Sources

Handy, James A. *Scraps of African Methodist Episcopal History.* Philadelphia: A.M.E. Book Concern, 1902.

Parker, William. "The Freedman's Story: In Two Parts." *Atlantic Monthly* 17 (February–March 1866): 152–66, 276–95.

Bibb, Henry Walton (1815–1854)
Bibb, Mary E. Miles (ca. 1828–1877)

Having a respected white father and a slave mother, orator and activist Henry Walton Bibb knew the frustration of the mulatto. Born into bondage in Shelby County, Kentucky, he was the son of Mildred Jackson and Senator James Bibb. Henry Bibb had six siblings, the slaves of planter Willard Gatewood, who sold the children to several buyers. James Bibb hired out his son for wages. Henry Bibb studied briefly at a Sabbath school operated by a Miss Davies until patrollers disbanded classes. Henry married Malinda, a slave, around 1833, and sired a daughter, Mary Frances Bibb. Bibb could not stop his wife's owner from forcing her into prostitution, a degradation that he described in a speech in August 1844 in Columbus, Ohio.

At age 22, Henry Bibb fled to Cincinnati, Ohio, with his savings of $2.50. When he returned for his wife six months later, he was enslaved again. Both Mary Frances and Henry Bibb were sold to a planter in Vicksburg, Ohio. On a second flight, Bibb was caught while fending off a wolf pack. After his sale to Cherokees on the Kansas-Oklahoma border, he again tried to free his family by posing as a freedman and demanding rooms at upscale hotels. He traveled overland to St. Louis, Missouri, booked steamer passage to Ohio, and rode horseback to Michigan. He arrived in Detroit at the Second Baptist Church, a waystation operated by the Reverend William Charles Monroe. While in hiding in winter 1842, Bibb received literacy training from Monroe. That same year, Bibb joined William Wells Brown and Frederick Douglass as an abolitionist orator and activist for the Underground Railroad and the Liberty Party of Michigan. One of Bibb's rescues, Kentucky runaway Lewis Richardson, reached Amherstburg, Ontario, in 1846 with Bibb as personal escort.

After the death of his first wife, Bibb married a freeborn Bostonian, author and activist Mary E. Miles, and began writing an autobiography, *Narrative of the Life and Adventures of Henry Bibb, an American Slave* (1849). Because the Fugitive Slave Law of 1850 made recapture a possibility, he crossed into Canada in November 1850 and settled his wife and mother at Sandwich, Ontario. Henry and Mary Bibb aided Josiah Henson in establishing the Refugee Home Society. On January 1, 1851, the couple founded the *Voice of the Fugitive,* Canada's first black newspaper, which they published in Sandwich. An upbeat article in the first issue reported on the Elgin Settlement, a last stop of the Underground Railroad where former slaves thrived. Among the cautions the newspaper issued was a warning in 1854 that rescuers demanding a high price for transport were merely imposters posing as agents of the Underground Railroad. The Bibbs dedicated themselves to organizing rescues across the Detroit River, receiving newcomers, and welcoming them to liberty through the Refugee Home Society. Along with Henson and J.T. Fisher, Henry Bibb organized the North American Convention of Colored

The Kentucky-born mulatto Henry Bibb escaped slavery on several occasions, each time returning south for family members. A lecturer, newspaper editor, and prominent autobiographer, he led a campaign to settle fugitives in Canada. *(Library of Congress)*

Freemen, held at St. Lawrence Hall on September 10, 1851.

See also: Elgin Settlement; Fugitive Slave Law of 1850; Refugee Home Society.

Sources

Bibb, Henry. *Narrative of the Life and Adventures of Henry Bibb, an American Slave, Written by Himself.* New York: privately published, 1849.

Cooper, Afua. "The Fluid Frontier: Blacks and the Detroit River Region: A Focus on Henry Bibb." *Canadian Review of American Studies* 30:2 (2000): 129–49.

Jenkins, David. "Mr. Bibb." *Palladium of Liberty* 1:27 (August 1844): 2.

Bickerdyke, Mary Ann Ball (1817–1901)

An herbalist and heroic Civil War nurse-dietitian, Mary Ann Ball Bickerdyke aided the Underground Railroad in Cairo, Illinois. A native of Mount Vernon, in Knox County, Ohio, she graduated from Oberlin College and studied nursing privately. While nursing the sick during a cholera epidemic in Cincinnati, Ohio, she became an operative of the secret network. In widowhood, she lived in Galesburg, Illinois, and came under the influence of Congregationalist minister Edward Beecher. On June 9, 1861, she traveled by train to Cairo for river passage to the Union army. After she joined the hospital corps of General William Tecumseh Sherman, she received runaways and put them to work in the Union army laundry and kitchen. Her fair treatment of slaves and tender care of wounded soldiers earned her the name Mother Bickerdyke.

Source

Snodgrass, Mary Ellen. *Historical Encyclopedia of Nursing.* Santa Barbara, CA: ABC-CLIO, 1999.

Bigelow, Ann Hagar (1813–1898)
Bigelow, Francis Edwin (1809–1873)

Two agents, blacksmith Francis Edwin Bigelow and his wife, Ann Hagar Bigelow of Weston, Massachusetts, facilitated the escape of Fredric "Shadrach" Minkins from Boston to Concord, Massachusetts. Ann Bigelow founded the Concord Women's Anti-Slavery Society. The couple maintained a two-story frame safehouse in Concord, Massachusetts, which averaged one slave rescue per week. At 3 A.M. on February 17, 1851, the Bigelows received Minkins from conductor Lewis Hayden and John J. Smith, who had transported the runaway by carriage from Cambridge. With shutters closed, Ann Bigelow cooked a hasty breakfast on a bedroom stove.

Joining the group was attorney Nathan Brooks, a family friend and fellow operative of the secret network who lived across the street with his wife, abolitionist activist Mary Merrick Brooks. Brooks found the Bigelows outfitting Minkins in more substantial clothes because his garments were tattered from hard traveling. Francis Bigelow concealed Minkins's face with Brooks's hat. After securing a rented horse and a carryall from Lowell Fay, Bigelow drove Minkins to the station of agents Frances Hills Wilder Drake and Jonathan Drake at Leominster, Massachusetts. Ironically, when Elizur Wright came to trial in 1852 for complicity in Minkins's escape, the attorneys empaneled Francis Bigelow on the jury. Later in his involvement with refugee slaves, Bigelow supported insurrectionist John Brown, who led the raid on the federal arsenal at Harpers Ferry, Virginia, on October 16, 1859. After national emancipation of slaves on January 1, 1863, Ann Bigelow reminisced on the dedication of philosopher Henry David Thoreau, a transporter of slaves from Concord.

Sources

"Cheerful Yesterdays." Part 5, "The Fugitive Slave Period." *Atlantic Monthly* 79:345 (1897).

Collison, Gary. *Shadrach Minkins: From Fugitive Slave to Citizen.* Cambridge, MA: Harvard University Press, 1997.

Bigelow, Jacob (1790–1865)

An elderly abolitionist attorney for the Washington Gas Light Company, Jacob Bigelow of Washington, D.C., played a major role in the liberation of Ann Maria Weems from slavery in Rockville, Maryland. As a volunteer for the Philadelphia Vigilance Committee, he negotiated with slave owners Caroline and Charles M. Price to pay $1,000 for Ann Maria Weems's mother and $1,600 for a sister. Aided by William Still, in November 1855, Bigelow helped 12-year-old Ann Maria, a domestic, to travel via the Underground Railroad from Maryland to Canada. To disguise her as coachboy Joe Wright, Bigelow cut her hair and dressed her in boy's clothing. Choosing for himself the alias Professor H, Bigelow transported her from Pennsylvania Avenue in front of the White House. Claiming lightheadedness, he kept "Joe" in his room as a personal servant to attend the "master" during the night. Weems arrived safely in Chatman, Ontario, on Thanksgiving Day.

Sources

Dixon, Joan M. *"National Intelligencer" Newspaper Abstracts: The Civil War Years.* Westminster, MD: Heritage Books, 2004.

Harrold, Stanley. "Freeing the Weems Family: A New Look at the Underground Railroad." *Civil War History* 42:4 (1996): 289–306.

Bigelow, Lucius (1802–ca. 1870) Bigelow, Susan Ann Moser (1814–ca. 1880)

A collaborator with agents in Burlington, Vermont, Lucius Bigelow was a dependable transporter of fugitive slaves. He was respected as the publisher of the *Burlington Daily News* and as a humanitarian. In league with the Reverend Joshua Young, Mary Elizabeth Plympton Young, and Salmon P. Wires, Bigelow received escapees from Wires's insurance agency on College Street and hustled them into the Bigelow family's three-story home, a station he managed with his wife, Susan Ann Moser Bigelow. From cellar hiding places, he ferried passengers to the local railway station and concealed them in freight or baggage cars of the Central Vermont Railroad bound for Montreal.

Lucius Bigelow's work increased dramatically after passage of the Fugitive Slave Law of 1850. When slave catchers watched the route, Bigelow relayed fugitives to the depot at St. Albans and paid fares from his own funds. He kept one exhausted slave from Tennessee for three weeks until she was able to press on to Quebec. When a waiter at the Lake House Hotel was in danger of recapture, Bigelow conveyed him to the train and then made arrangements for his wife and children to follow. Bigelow sold the family's house and sent the proceeds to the family's new home in Canada. On December 8, 1859, Bigelow accompanied Joshua Young to North Elba in Essex County, New York, where Young eulogized insurrectionist John Brown at his grave site.

See also: Fugitive Slave Law of 1850.

Source

Allen, Robert Willis. *Marching On: John Brown's Ghost from the Civil War to Civil Rights.* Northfield, VT: Northfield News and Printery, 2000.

Biggs, Basil (1819–1906) Biggs, Mary Jackson (fl. 1840s)

Basil Biggs and his wife, Mary Jackson Biggs, contributed to the Underground Railroad network in Adams County, Pennsylvania. At age 39, Basil Biggs moved from Carroll County, Maryland, to Gettysburg and obtained a tenancy on a farm south of the city. In the 1840s, he married Mary Jackson and worked as a farrier. Assisted by freedman Edward Mathews and local Quakers, the couple aided runaways fleeing north through Quaker Valley to Canada. After the battle of Gettysburg on July 3, 1863, Basil Biggs, working for local authorities, exhumed 3,360 soldiers and placed their remains in pine coffins.

See also: Quakers.

Source

Creighton, Margaret. *The Colors of Courage: Unheard Voices from the Battle of Gettysburg.* New York: Basic Books, 2005.

Bird, Harry (fl. 1830s)

An escapee from Woodstock, Virginia, Harry Bird and a slave named George profited from the throngs of New York abolitionists who engineered their jailbreak. The two settled at Utica, New York, in September 1836. In January 1837, Bird's owner, John Goyer, dispatched a slave catcher to return him. While the fugitives were lodged in jail, attorney Alvan Stewart of South Granville, represented them in court. During trial preliminaries, supporters of the Underground Railroad thronged around the building, entered the chambers of Judge Chester Hayden, and freed the two inmates.

Source

Calarco, Tom. *The Underground Railroad in the Adirondack Region.* Jefferson, NC: McFarland, 2004.

Birney, James Gillespie (1792–1857)

Philanthropist, attorney, and pamphleteer James Gillespie Birney supported the U.S. Constitution while he actively promoted the work of the Underground Railroad. A native of Danville, in Robertson County, Kentucky, he established a law practice in Huntsville, Alabama. In June 1834, he freed the slaves he received through marriage to Agatha McDowell and opposed bondage through political oratory and editorials. In October 1835, he moved to free territory in Cincinnati, Ohio. By dispatching runaways on stagecoaches to Lebanon, Ohio, he supported the escape route that channeled slaves to Sarah E. Bowen Hussey and Sylvanus Erastus Fuller Hussey's waystation in Battle Creek, Michigan. While joining Gamaliel Bailey, Jr., in publishing the *Cincinnati Weekly Herald and Philanthropist,* a journal of the Ohio State Anti-Slavery Society, Birney and his printer, agent Achilles Pugh, encountered mob violence, which destroyed the printing office on July 12, 1836, and again on July 30.

In 1837, Birney served the American Anti-Slavery Society as executive secretary. After the election of Maria Weston Chapman, Lydia Maria Francis Child, and Lucretia Coffin Mott to offices, he resigned from the organization. That same year, he acquired notoriety for a suit charging him with harboring a mulatto housekeeper, Matilda Lawrence, whom he had assumed was white. Matilda fled slavery the previous year from a boat docked at Cincinnati on the Mississippi River. After her arrest, her owner, Larkin Lawrence of St. Louis, Missouri, who was also her father, sold her at auction in New Orleans. In January 1838, Salmon Portland Chase successfully defended Birney before the Ohio Supreme Court on charges of violating an Ohio law of 1804 that forbade aiding and abetting slave escape. Birney further angered pro-slavery factions by publishing *American Churches, the Bulwarks of American Slavery* (1840). In 1845, he was handicapped after a fall from a horse. In 1890, his son, William Birney, compiled a biography, *James G. Birney and His Times.*

See also: American Anti-Slavery Society.

Sources

Birney, James Gillespie. *American Churches, the Bulwarks of American Slavery.* 1840. Concord, NH: Pillsbury, 1885.

———. *Letters of James Gillespie Birney, 1831–1857.* New York: D. Appleton-Century, 1938.

Stephenson, Wendell H. "Letters of James Gillespie Birney, 1831–1857." *Mississippi Valley Historical Review* 25:4 (March 1939): 571–72.

Black, Leonard (1814–?)

After two decades in bondage, Leonard Black profited from the kindness of a Quaker conductor of the Underground Railroad. In flight from his home on the Bradford estate in Anne Arundel County, Maryland, Black escaped an uncertain future with a cruel master. In 1837, he followed the advice of a Quaker who described the route to Boston, Massachusetts, and offered 75¢ as traveling money. Black at first feared that a road companion named Henry had informed the master. Pursued by hounds, Black sped rapidly through New Jersey, New York, Rhode Island, and Massachusetts before reaching Canada. A decade later, he published a slave narrative, *The Life and Sufferings of Leonard Black, a Fugitive from Slavery* (1847).

Source

Black, Leonard. *The Life and Sufferings of Leonard Black, a Fugitive from Slavery.* New Bedford, MA: Benjamin Lindsey, 1847.

black soldiers

The commitment to the Union cause of black runaways, freedmen transporters, nurses, informants, and Underground Railroad operatives helped to speed the end of American slavery. Their stories attest to the devotion of blacks to liberty for all, particularly the story of conductor Harriet Tubman, who served as a spy, scout, laundress, and medic for the federals. Another hero, William H. Carney, fled bondage through the assistance of agent Loum Snow and later became the first black soldier to earn a Congressional Medal of Honor. Recruitment flourished thanks to the efforts of supporters of the Underground Railroad. At South Glens Falls in Warren County, New York, John Van Pelt, husband of Lucretia Van Pelt, a passenger of the secret network, encouraged black men to enlist with the Fifty-fourth Massachusetts Volunteer Infantry, America's first all-black infantry. From Longtown, a black depot of the Underground Railroad founded by James Clemens and Sophia Sellers Clemens in Greenville, Ohio, young runaways volunteered for the Fifty-fourth. To the east, at Harrisburg, Pennsylvania, General Thomas Morris Chester, a black journalist and Underground Railroad agent, joined white operative Lewis Hayden in recruiting volunteers for the Fifty-fourth. In Franklin County, Pennsylvania, 45 blacks rushed into the fray by supporting agent Martin Robinson Delany's recruiting campaign for the same regiment. The boost to the Union army made Pennsylvania the leading state in black enlist-

> Writing later on of the eagerness of blacks to rescue their fellow African Americans from slavery, the prominent black activist and historian W.E.B. Du Bois described the transition from an all-white military force in 1862: "Thousands of black men during that year, of all ages and both sexes, clad in rags and with their bundles on their backs, gathered wherever the Union Army gained foothold—at Norfolk, Hampton, at Alexandria and Nashville and along the border towards the West."

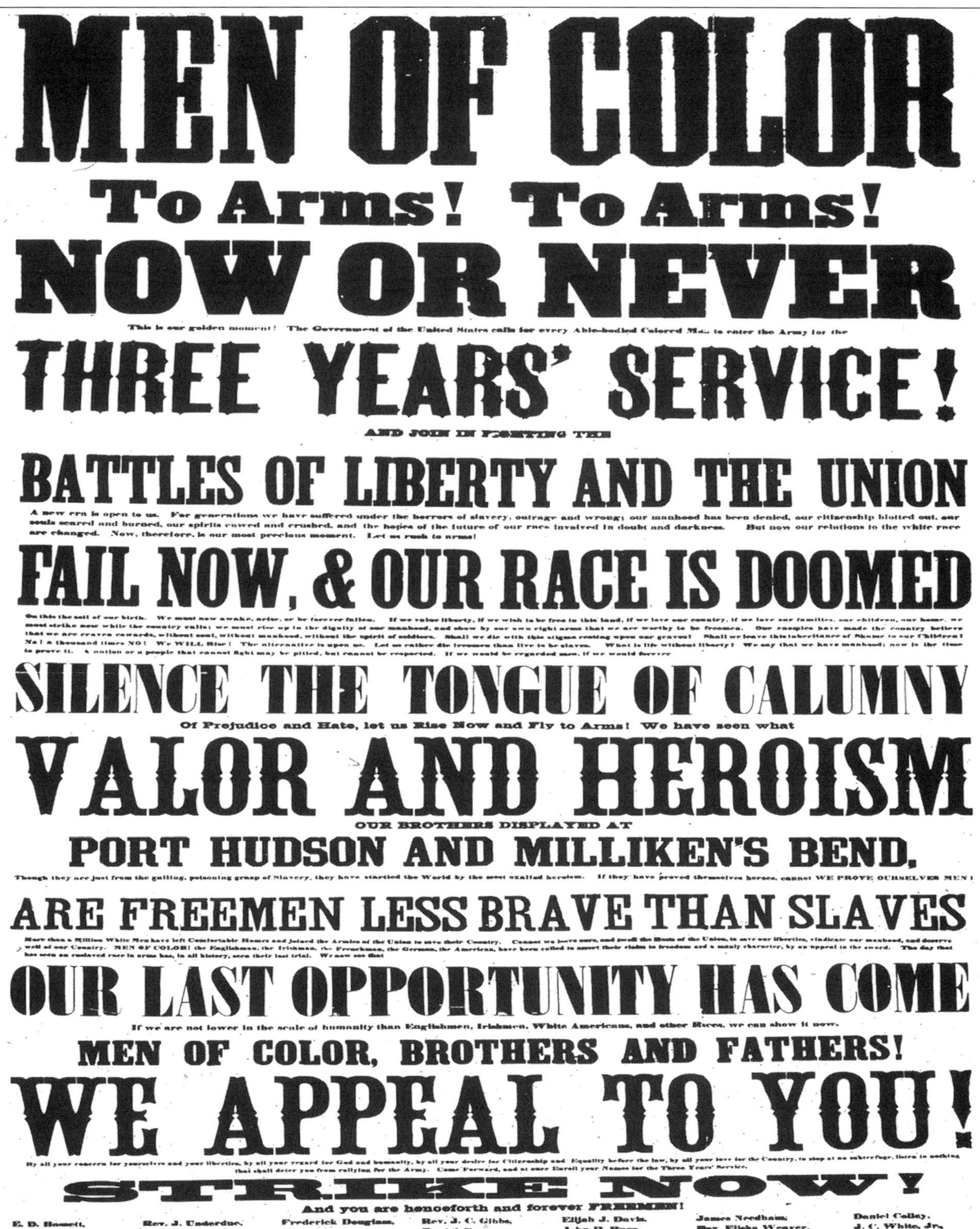

The Union began recruiting black soldiers after the Emancipation Proclamation in 1863. By the end of the Civil War, nearly 200,000 blacks had served in the army and navy. Operatives of the Underground Railroad encouraged ex-slaves to enlist. *(Kean Collection/Hulton Archive/Getty Images)*

ments. On April 18, 1861, Nicholas "Nick" Biddle became the first black Union soldier injured in the Civil War, after an anti-abolitionist hurled a brick at Biddle in the Baltimore train station during a skirmish to protect Washington, D.C., from rebel forces. Biddle's service preceded by over a year a U.S. congressional vote to arm black troops.

Among subsequent black warriors was Osborne Perry Anderson, an African Canadian who survived John Brown's raid on the federal arsenal at Harpers Ferry, Virginia. After the firing on Fort Sumter on April 12, 1861, began the Civil War, Anderson formed black regiments in Arkansas and Indiana. Freedman William Henry Johnson joined Connecticut volunteers and fought at the battle of Bull Run. Chester followed the Fifty-fourth into combat as a war correspondent for the *Philadelphia Press.* In 1863, Canadian agent Alexander Milton Ross encountered three of the first parcel of slaves he helped escape from Richmond, Virginia, six years earlier through Erie, Pennsylvania, to Ontario. He registered them in Philadelphia's colored regiment. Supporting their black comrades were white Union soldiers who refused to uphold the Fugitive Slave Law of 1850. Army nurse Mary Ashton Rice Livermore, another abolitionist committed to civil disobedience, rescued two slave children, Lizzie and Johnny, whose father died a prisoner of war at Libby Prison in Richmond, Virginia. Johnny followed his father's example and fought in the Civil War; he also did not survive. In 1864, runaway Elijah P. Marrs guided 27 followers from Simpsonville, Kentucky, to enlistment headquarters in Louisville. His heroic service included combat at Bowling Green and Elizabethtown, Kentucky.

See also: American Revolution; Civil War.

Sources

Ayers, Edward L. *In the Presence of Mine Enemies: The Civil War in the Heart of America, 1859–1863.* New York: W.W. Norton, 2003.

Du Bois, William Edward Burghardt. *The Gift of Black Folk.* Boston: Stratford, 1924.

Ross, Alexander Milton. *Recollections and Experiences of an Abolitionist: From 1855 to 1865.* Toronto, Ontario: Rowsell & Hutchison, 1875.

Blackburn, Lucie (?–1895)
Blackburn, Thornton (ca. 1814–1890)

Early escapees to Toronto, Lucie (also Ruth or Ruthie or Rutha) Blackburn and Thornton Blackburn faced arrest in Detroit until volunteers of the Underground Railroad incited a riot. On July 3, 1831, Thornton Blackburn, a native of Maysville, Kentucky, fled from his owner at Louisville. With his West Indian wife, Lucie, Thornton Blackburn took the steamer *Versailles* up the Ohio River to Cincinnati, Ohio, and boarded the stage for Sandusky, Ohio. After a 15-day journey, they arrived in Detroit. In 1833, they were captured, jailed on Fort Street, and slated for return south when local blacks intervened. Mrs. Madison Lightfoot and the wife of the Reverend George French visited Lucie Blackburn at her cell. Mrs. French and Lucie exchanged clothing, and Lucie escaped from the jail and crossed the Detroit River into Ontario.

Thornton was rescued on June 15, 1833, when a mob of 400 abolitionists incited a riot, the first race riot in the city's history. Blackburn's rescuers took him from the sheriff's custody and rushed him to the Randolph Street wharf. An agent exchanged a gold watch for Blackburn's passage. After Blackburn reunited with his wife in Toronto, the couple settled on Eastern Avenue, their home for a half century. The refusal of Robert Jameson, the attorney general of Canada, to extradite Blackburn set a precedent that stood unaltered until the Emancipation Proclamation of January 1, 1863.

In 1837, Thornton initiated the city's first four-passenger horse-drawn cab service. The following year, he chanced a visit south and returned to Toronto with his aged mother. A lawsuit initiated by the slave owner against the steamship line that transported Lucie Blackburn was still in litigation in June 1846. In 1985, a site survey by Karolyn Smardz Frost for the Archaeological Resource Centre of Toronto designated the Blackburn house as the only fugitive slave residence in the province to be excavated.

Source

McRae, Norman. "Crossing the Detroit River to Find Freedom." *Michigan History* 67:2 (1983): 35–39.

Blanchard, Ira D. (1808–1872)
Blanchard, Mary Walton (1807–1864)

Baptist missionaries at the Delaware Mission at Edwardsville, in Wyandotte County, Kansas Territory, Dr. Ira D. Blanchard and his wife, Mary Walton Blanchard, also succored fugitive slaves. In January 1857, Ira rescued a 45-year-old domestic, Ann Clarke, of

Lecompton, Kansas, and relayed her to the care of agent John Armstrong, who completed her passage to Chicago. In December 1858, the Blanchards received Eliza and another female slave owned by S.F. Nuckolls of Nebraska City, Nebraska. After agent John Williamson led the girls across the Missouri River, Nuckolls offered $200 reward for their return. Ira transported the girls to an Underground Railroad depot at Tabor, Iowa, and, on a dark night, arranged for their transfer past detectives lurking at nearby bridges. From Chicago, Illinois, the girls completed their escape to Ontario. Nuckolls sued Chicago agents, but the Civil War intervened and mooted the lawsuit.

In 1860, Blanchard sought the return of three free blacks, Henry Garner, his sister Maria, and John Williamson. As Blanchard drove them by covered carriage from Percival, Iowa, to Omaha, Nebraska, three assailants jumped the three blacks and crushed Henry Garner's jaw bone. Williamson escaped, but the kidnappers locked Henry and Maria Garner in a slave pen in St. Louis, Missouri, preparatory to auctioning them. Blanchard set out with collaborator George B. Gaston to recover the siblings. The Garners were delighted to see Blanchard, who freed them. Authorities arrested the kidnappers and put them in a jail in Council Bluffs, Iowa, from which they escaped.

See also: kidnap.

Source

Todd, John. *Early Settlement and Growth of Western Iowa.* Des Moines: Historical Department of Iowa, 1906.

Blanchard, Jonathan (1811–1892)
Blanchard, Mary Avery Bent (1819–1890)

The Reverend Jonathan Blanchard of Rockingham, Vermont, a lecturer and educator, supported the slave rescue work of abolitionists in Pennsylvania and Illinois. Blanchard became an activist for black liberty in 1837 after meeting attorney Thaddeus Stevens, an Underground Railroad agent at Lancaster, Pennsylvania. Blanchard wrote for the *Gospel Publisher* and toured the country championing abolitionism. While consulting with the black community in Gettysburg, Pennsylvania, he fled from a pro-slavery mob that threatened his life. After 15-years as president of Knox College in Galesburg, Illinois, in 1859, he established a similar liberal institution, Wheaton College, at Wheaton, Illinois, to educate women and nonwhites. With the assistance of his wife, Mary Avery Bent Blanchard of Middlebury, Vermont, he aided refugees from bondage on Missouri plantations. The Blanchards depended on the town's two main transporters, George Davis and Samuel Hitchcock.

Source

Blanchard, Jonathan, and N.L. Rice. *A Debate on Slavery.* New York: Arno, 1969.

Bliss, George Ripley (1816–1893)
Bliss, Lucy Ripley (1843–1935)
Bliss, Mary Ann Raymond (1821–1912)

At Lewisburg in Union County, Pennsylvania, Dr. George Ripley Bliss and his family operated a safehouse of the Underground Railroad. A native of Sherburne, New York, Bliss graduated from Madison University and Hamilton Theology Seminary and pastored the Baptist church of New Brunswick, New Jersey. He taught biblical literature and Greek and served as president and librarian at Bucknell University from 1856 to 1865. Aided by fellow professors Thomas F. Curtis and Howard Malcolm, both on staff at the university, Bliss and his wife, Mary Ann Raymond Bliss of Chester, Pennsylvania, received runaway slaves in their residence at 63 University Avenue. The rescuers concealed passengers in the carriage house or in a niche under the kitchen floor. Their oldest daughter, Lucy Ripley Bliss, made beds for the passengers, who arrived in loads of hay and departed by night.

Source

Commemorative Biographical Record of Central Pennsylvania. Chicago: J.H. Beers, 1898.

Blockson, Charles LeRoy (1933–)

Historian Charles LeRoy Blockson developed a passion for details of the Underground Railroad. The author's great-great-grandfather Spencer Blockson was a slave on the Delmarva Peninsula in Sussex County, Maryland, where slave catcher Patty Cannon and her gang thrived. At age 10, Blockson learned from his grandfather that his great-grandfather James Blockson left Seaford, Delaware, in his teens in 1856 and escaped to Canada by the secret network. The route north to St. Catharines, Ontario, passed through Wilmington, Philadelphia, and New York City.

Two years later, a cousin, Jacob Blockson, also followed the network from Seaford to St. Catharines. Jacob explained to agent William Still in Philadelphia that his master, Jesse W. Paten (or Layton), went bankrupt and was about to sell his slaves like livestock. On December 26, 1858, he wrote to his wife, Lear (or Leah) Blockson, that he wanted her to arrive by August 1859 with their son Alexander. He promised to meet her in Albany, New York.

Charles Blockson's dedication to family stories and black history resulted in a sizable collection of black genealogy and slave narratives. In 1984, he donated his library of 150,000 items, including reference works, photos, drawings, sheet music, posters, handbills, and broadsides, to Temple University. Three years later, he completed *The Underground Railroad: First Person Narratives of Escapes to Freedom in the North* (1987).

Source

Blockson, Charles L. "Escape from Slavery: The Underground Railroad." *National Geographic* 166:1 (July 1984): 2–39.

Blodgett, Avis Dodge (1796–1882)
Blodgett, Israel Porter (1779–1861)

Pioneers of Du Page County, Illinois, Avis (or Avice) Dodge Blodgett and Israel Porter Blodgett aided refugee slaves. Israel Blodgett was born in Amherst, Massachusetts, and settled on the frontier at 812 Randall Street in 1829 during tense animosities between the Potawatomi and the Sauk. He collaborated with abolitionist editors Elijah Parish Lovejoy and Owen Glendower Lovejoy and with neighbor conductors Pierce Downer and Henry Lyman. The Blodgetts received passengers from Carolyn Blodgett Strong and William Jagger Strong in Aurora, Illinois. From Israel Blodgett's blacksmith shop in Downers Grove, where he manufactured plows, he escorted slaves along the Underground Railroad. One beautiful mulatto, the child of a white master, appealed to the Blodgetts' anti-abolition neighbor, who not only relayed her to Chicago but also became a confederate of the secret network.

The Blodgetts' altruism influenced their sons to champion the fight for liberty. Their son Wells Howard Blodgett won a Congressional Medal of Honor for service during the Civil War with the Thirty-seventh Illinois Infantry. A second son, Judge Henry Williams Blodgett (1821–1905), and his wife, Althea Crocker Blodgett (1822–1876), operated a safehouse at 404 South Sheridan Road. The residence featured a large underground chamber that extended from the front door to the back porch.

Sources

MacMilian, Thomas C. *The Scots and Their Descendants in Illinois.* Chicago: Illinois State Historical Society, 1919.

Taylor, Glennette Tilley. *The Underground Railroad in Illinois.* Glen Ellyn, IL: Newman Educational, 2001.

bloodhounds

The pursuit of black refugees by dog packs required the owners to be skilled at wood lore and experienced in tracking. Known for their persistence and savagery, hounds were bred and trained for slave pursuit. Their peculiar baying cry carried long distances, echoing over lakes and bayous. Travel writer Frederick Law Olmsted gave particulars of the breed in *A Journey in the Seaboard Slave States* (1856). He described them as a mixed species of bloodhounds, foxhounds, staghounds, bulldogs, and even curs that were taught from puppyhood to target blacks. Trainers set the hounds after quarry by offering a shoe or shirt marked with scent. In anticipation of a reward, dog packs scampered over fields and into swamps and woodlands. Some suffered the fate intended for all pro-slavery factions—slicing with scythes and bowie knives, throttling, cudgeling, shooting, and even poisoning and hanging.

Dog packs became standard investigative equipment for slave hunters. In 1845, William Gambel advertised in the *Sumpter County (AL) Whig* his purchase of "Negro dogs" and his charge of $3 per day for hunting fugitives. For capturing a runaway, Gambel demanded $15. Another tracker, A.G. Neal of Shelby County, Tennessee, used his pack of six dogs as a lure to potential clients. The effectiveness of vicious dogs was a recurrent horror in slave narratives. In 1853, a kidnapped freeman, Solomon Northup, published *Twelve Years a Slave*, in which he described the mur-

> William J. Anderson, a fugitive from Virginia, remarked on the dangers of posses and their packs of bloodhounds: "It is no uncommon thing for slaveholders to keep . . . savage dogs, trained to hunt and follow the track of the poor colored fugitive, day and night, till they catch him. Men who do not own such hunters hire them for the purpose of running down God's unfortunate creatures, whose great sin among the whites is the darkness of their skin. I do think that the hearts of the masters must be far blacker than the negro's skin."

der of a runaway Louisiana boy named Augustus. After slave hunters removed him from a cane rick, they set 15 dogs on him, which gnawed his body to the bone in 100 places. Northup was relieved that Augustus suffered only one day before dying. In 1857, the Reverend Benjamin Franklin Crary of New Albany, Indiana, reported that slave catchers were also crossing the Ohio River into free territory with dog packs, which they set on the trail of fugitives.

Bloodhounds were so crucial to slave governance that a municipal code of 1859 in East Feliciana Parish, Louisiana, forbade slaves from owning dogs. In the slave narrative of Mary Reynolds, *Lay My Burden Down: A Folk History of Slavery* (1945), the recovery of Aunt Cheyney Kilpatrick, a wetnurse at a cotton plantation in Mississippi, involved tracking by a slave named Old Solomon, who led the master's dogs. Upon locating his concubine and the mother of four of his mulatto children, the owner ordered pursuers to set the dogs on her. An eyewitness account by Mary Reynolds describes how the pack yanked Kilpatrick down from a tree limb, ripped off her garments, and chewed both breasts from her torso. The slave owner engineered the punishment as a warning that he would not tolerate escapes.

To conceal their scent from hounds, hunted refugees used a variety of practical methods. They trooped through pigsties and kept to water routes, such as Falling Run Creek and Silver Creek in heavily traveled Clark and Floyd counties in Indiana. John Finney of Richland County, Ohio, who began a quarter century of service to the secret network around 1825, advised passengers to rub onion juice on the soles of their shoes. A pungent whiff would confuse hounds and entice them toward any food mixtures that contained onions. Other covers ranged from snuff to turpentine, a common household solvent. In Sparta in Randolph County, Illinois, agent Almond A. Burlingame rolled passengers in carpet to cover their scent and transported them among the farm pumps he delivered to customers. In Naples, New York, Emily and William Marks directed passengers over planks from the porch to the family wagon and then carried the planks during the relay to conceal human scent from dog packs. Agent Theron Trowbridge of Denmark, Iowa, took more drastic measures. He assured the flight of fugitives from his station by ordering his son to feed poisoned biscuits to a pack of hounds.

In lieu of water routes and scent concealment, wise slaves climbed branches and leaped from tree to tree to avoid contact with the ground. According to *Among the Cotton Thieves* (1867), memoirist Edward Bacon encountered bayous so loathsome that slaves chose to face pack hounds rather than risk their lives in snake- or alligator-infested muck.

One antidote to vicious dogs was shooting, a practice of conductor William Eberle Thompson in Bethel, Ohio. In 1864, Thomas Nast, an illustrator for *Harper's Weekly,* ridiculed the unsympathetic Democratic platform by encircling with politicians' words a drawing of slaves being stalked and attacked by dogs.

See also: agents, Underground Railroad; kidnap; punishments; slave recovery; *Underground Railroad, The* (sculpture, 1993).

Sources

Anderson, William J. *Life and Narrative of William J. Anderson.* Chicago: *Daily Tribune,* 1857.
Bacon, Edward. *Among the Cotton Thieves.* Detroit, MI: Free Press, 1867.
Blight, David W., ed. *Passages to Freedom.* Washington, DC: Smithsonian, 2004.
Botkin, B.A., ed. *Lay My Burden Down: A Folk History of Slavery.* Chicago: University of Chicago Press, 1945.
Eby, Henry Harrison. *Observations of an Illinois Boy in Battle, Camp and Prisons.* Mendota, IL: privately published, 1910.
Graham, A.A., comp. *History of Richland County, Ohio: Its Past and Present.* Mansfield, OH: privately published, 1880.
Northup, Solomon. *Twelve Years a Slave.* Auburn, NY: Derby & Miller, 1853.
Olmsted, Frederick Law. *A Journey in the Seaboard Slave States.* New York: Dixon & Edwards, 1856.
Rawick, George P., ed. *The American Slave: A Composite Autobiography.* Westport, CT: Greenwood, 1972–1979.

Bloss, William Clough (1795–1863)
Bloss, Mary Bangs Blossom (1799–1879)

Methodist temperance advocate and Underground Railroad operative William Clough Bloss and his wife, Mary Bangs Blossom Bloss of Lenox, Massachusetts, aided refugees fleeing from Lockport, New York, along the Erie Canal. Born to a family of agrarian patriots in Alford, in Berkshire County, Massachusetts, William Bloss built a brick tavern in Rochester, New York, in 1823, soon after his marriage. Three years later, he renounced carousing and strong drink, sold his tavern, and redirected his energies to storekeeping, real estate, and insurance—and to the aid of alcoholics and convicts.

In the 1830s, Bloss became a vocal leader of the Rochester Anti-Slavery Society and conducted secret abolition meetings behind locked doors in the session chamber of the Third Presbyterian Church. In summer 1833, he joined the Reverend Thomas James and

Underground Railroad agent Ashley S. Sampson in establishing the Rochester Anti-Slavery Society. The Blosses established a safehouse on Lower East Avenue. When a slave woman displayed weals from a lashing, Bloss had his son touch the scars to understand the savagery of the southern plantation system. With the aid of the Reverend Thomas James, William Bloss launched a biweekly abolitionist journal, the *Rights of Man,* in 1834. From 1843 to 1845, Bloss served as manager of the American Anti-Slavery Society.

Late in the 1840s, Bloss maintained close ties with Rochester operatives Susan Brownell Anthony, Dr. Lester Clinton Dolley and Dr. Sarah Adamson Dolley, Frederick Douglass, and Samuel Drummond Porter and Susan Farley Porter. At the Bloss residence in Brighton, New York, after the enactment of the Fugitive Slave Law of 1850, the couple stepped up their involvement in the Underground Railroad. On October 7, 1858, Bloss joined Douglass in protesting capital punishment. A mob threatened the lives of both men.

See also: American Anti-Slavery Society; Fugitive Slave Law of 1850.

Sources

Devoy, John. *A History of the City of Rochester.* Rochester, NY: Post Express Printing, 1895.

Merrill, Arch. *The Underground, Freedom's Road and Other Upstate Tales.* New York: American Book-Stratford Press, 1963.

Blue, Abner (1819–1894)
Blue, Harriet N. Clay (?–1859)
Blue, Eliza N. Doolittle (1838–1921)

Abner Blue's family contributed to Underground Railroad teamwork. With his widowed mother, Mehetible Garard Blue, he moved from Troy, Ohio, to Goshen, Indiana, in his late teens. After his marriage to Harriet N. Clay of Adrian, Michigan, in 1842, he farmed and worked as a cabinetmaker and realty appraiser. His family aided the flight of slaves that Levi Coffin directed from Fountain City, Indiana, north to Cass County, Michigan. Passengers moving along the Bristol Road passed from the Blue waystation to the home of Charles L. Murray, north of Goshen. Following the death of Blue's first wife, his second spouse, Eliza N. Doolittle Blue, aided the family rescue operation.

Source

Bordewich, Fergus M. *Bound for Canaan: The Underground Railroad and the War for the Soul of America.* New York: Amistad, 2005.

Bodwell, Lewis (1827–1894)

A transporter of fugitive slaves, the Reverend Lewis Bodwell, a Congregationalist preacher from New Haven, Connecticut, served the Underground Railroad on the Kansas frontier. In September 1856, he set out with a migrant wagon train for Kansas via Iowa and Nebraska. He was preparing for a Sabbath service in Topeka, Kansas, on January 30 when John Armstrong summoned help from Bodwell's congregation. Insurrectionist John Brown was in need of support. Brown arrived at Albert Fuller's safehouse at Straight Creek the previous day with 11 slaves whom he had liberated in Missouri on December 20, 1858. With the aid of a posse raised from Bodwell's congregation, the slaves forded the creek and proceeded through Iowa and Nebraska to Canada.

Sources

Hickman, Russell K. "Lewis Bodwell, Frontier Preacher: The Early Years." *Kansas Historical Quarterly* 12:3 (August 1943): 269–99.

———. "Lewis Bodwell, Frontier Preacher: The Early Years." *Kansas Historical Quarterly* 12:4 (November 1943): 349–65.

Bogue, Stephen A. (1790–1868)
Bogue, Hannah Bonine East (1798–ca. 1870s)

Stephen A. Bogue served the Ohio–Canada route of the Underground Railroad from 1840 to 1850. A devout Quaker born in Perquimans County, North Carolina, he took over his father's plantation in early youth and witnessed the competition between smallholders and planters relying on slave labor. With only $200 in cash, Stephen Bogue moved his family to a 120-acre farm in Preble County, Ohio, in 1811. Shortly after their marriage in 1831, Stephen and his second wife, Hannah Bonine East Bogue of Grayson County, Virginia, kept a waystation in Calvin Township in Young's Prairie, Michigan, which bordered Crooked Creek Road in Cass County. Acting on Christian principle, Bogue joined other Quaker abolitionists in co-founding the Friends' Anti-Slavery Society.

While serving the secret network, the Bogues received passengers from Thomas Mason at Leesburg in Kosciusko County, Indiana. With assistance from conductor Zachariah Shugart, the Bogues aided the escape of Perry Sanford, a refugee from Greenup County, Kentucky. After being sold twice, Sanford left his new master, Milt Graves, to avoid another sale to a Mississippi cotton plantation. On an Easter Monday holiday, he joined a party of 12 runaways. They made their way via an Underground Railroad route over the Ohio River to Cass County. Stationmasters in Hamilton and Cincinnati, Ohio, and in Jonesboro, Indiana, facilitated the escape and supplied clothing. In Cassopolis, Michigan, Sanford was working for Bogue when a posse of 40 slave hunters galloped up. Bogue aided Sanford's escape and raised the alarm among neighbors. Hannah hid Sanford on the second floor of their house.

On August 1, 1847, Sylvanus Erastus Fuller Hussey mailed an alert to Bogue and Shugart about a posse of 13 raiders on their way from Bourbon County, Kentucky. The kidnappers stopped first at the safehouse of Josiah Osborn and seized a family of five refugees. Bogue, Shugart, and Osborn confronted the slave nabbers, who sought court action in Cassopolis. Wright Modlin obtained a writ demanding that the insurgents free their captives. During arraignment and litigation, Shugart led nine of the runaways to the safehouse of Ishmael Lee and Miriam Marmon Lee in Williamsville, south of Cassopolis. When the group grew to 50 escapees, Shugart guided them on to Canada. Another slave disappeared from jail. In February 1848, the Kentuckians sued eight secret network agents, including Bogue and Shugart. Because of claims and counterclaims, the matter remained unresolved in January 1851. In September 1850, passage of the Fugitive Slave Law made recovery of escaping slaves easier for their owners.

See also: Fugitive Slave Law of 1850; kidnap; Quakers.

Sources

Glover, Lowell H. *A Twentieth Century History of Cass County, Michigan.* Chicago: Lewis, 1906.
Mathews, Alfred. *History of Cass County, Michigan.* Chicago: Waterman, Watkins, 1882.

Boileau, Nathaniel Brittain (1762–1850) Boileau, Hesther Leech (1767–1797) Boileau, Ann Leech (1761–1834)

The Nathaniel Brittain Boileau family welcomed fugitives fleeing the plantation South. Before the establishment of Underground Railroad routes, Nathaniel and his wife, Hesther "Hetty" Leech Boileau, operated a two-story brick shelter for refugees at 440 South York Road in Hatboro, Pennsylvania. After Hetty's death, Boileau married her sister, Ann Leech. Passengers moved north to the next stop in Newtown. Nathaniel's political career included terms in the state legislature and as Pennsylvania secretary of state. During excavations of the brick waystation in 1863, builders located an underground chamber containing artifacts from runaway slaves.

Source

Reganhard, Jack. *Hatboro.* Charleston, SC: Arcadia, 1999.

Bolding, John A. (1823–1899)

One of the early challenges to the Fugitive Slave Law of 1850, the arrest of a mulatto, John A. Bolding, in Poughkeepsie, New York, made headlines in the abolitionist press. In 1847, Bolding fled bondage under a Mrs. Dickinson in South Carolina and worked as a tailor on Main Street in Poughkeepsie. Mrs. Dickinson sold his papers to Robert C. Anderson of Columbia, South Carolina. In 1851, Bolding fell into the hands of a U.S. marshal from New York, who conducted him south by train into Anderson's custody before local agents could intervene. On August 26, a court found in favor of the slave owner. During Bolding's incarceration, Underground Railroad operatives and philanthropists raised $800 of the $2,000 price for his liberation. According to the diary of Matthew Vassar, Jr., by tapping over 150 other supporters, including brewer and philanthropist Matthew Vassar, Sr., the secret network freed Bolding once more to return to his family and home on Pine Street. In protest of Bolding's mistreatment, on October 30, 1851, agent William Peter Powell published an editorial in the *National Anti-Slavery Standard.*

See also: Fugitive Slave Law of 1850; philanthropists.

Sources

The Fugitive Slave Law and Its Victims (tract). New York: American Anti-Slavery Society, 1856.
Vassar, Matthew. *Autobiography and Letters of Matthew Vassar.* New York: Oxford University Press, 1916.

Boley, Joseph (fl. 1860s)

Joseph Boley (or Bowley) faced 12 years in prison for conducting a slave to free territory. A freedman in Anne Arundel County, Maryland, in fall 1863, Boley aided his wife, 35-year-old Elizabeth "Lizzy" Boley, and four other women—Marlena Boley, 15-year-old Mary Ann Boley, 10-year-old Nancy Ann "Nannie" Boley, and 12-year-old Susannah Boley—in escaping bondage under Joseph Benson. Upon Joseph Boley's arrest, the women were returned to slavery. On November 10, 1863, a court found him guilty. On July 29, 1865, Governor Augustus Williamson Bradford pardoned Boley for committing a crime that no longer existed.

Source

"Joseph Boley," *Annapolis (MD) Gazette,* September 10, 1863.

Bond, Emily Hockett (1811–1892)
Bond, John H. (1807–1897)

A Quaker conductor in league with a coordinated rescue team, Underground Railroad agent John H. Bond of Westfield in Surry County, North Carolina, and his wife, Emily Hockett Bond, aided refugees fleeing through the Midwest. John Bond operated a sawmill and in the 1840s established a gristmill. After passage of the Fugitive Slave Law of 1850 forced more runaways farther west into Ohio, Indiana, and Illinois, many crossed the Ohio River into Indiana. Twenty miles from the Ohio-Indiana border, the couple managed a rescue service in Windsor in Randolph County, Indiana, where local abolitionists established an anti-slavery society after 1836. For alerts to fugitives in need, the Bonds relied on William Beard in Union County and on Levi Coffin, the network superintendent; for medical emergencies, the rescuers depended on a Quaker physician, Dr. Henry H. Way. The Bonds received as many as 17 passengers at a time by wagon from Newport and relayed them to Camden or Jonesboro. During the transportation of a party of 10, Bond had to set up camp for a night to make the journey safely.

One intervention involved the flight of Margaret and Susan from Tennessee in winter 1839. Slave owner Thomas Stringfield pursued the slave women to Cabin Creek in Randolph County but cowered from the corn knife wielded by Milly Wilkerson, the girls' grandmother. After Stringfield sent a posse of 17 men to seize the girls, Milly and her husband, Tom Wilkerson, received the aid of black neighbors and armed sentries. When the tense situation ended, Stringfield discovered that the girls, disguised in boys' clothing, had gone. The Bonds received the girls at their waystation and passed them north to Ontario.

Sources

Smith, John L., and Lee L. Driver. *Past and Present of Randolph County, Indiana.* Indianapolis, IN: A.W. Bowen, 1914.
"Underground Railroad," *Brooklyn (NY) Eagle,* May 14, 1882, 4.

Bondi, August (1833–1907)
Bondi, Henrietta Einstein (1833–1900)

One of the defenders of the Underground Railroad through Lawrence, Kansas, August Bondi supported the militia of insurrectionist John Brown. A Hungarian Jew from Vienna, Austria, he was originally named Anshl (or Anschel) Bondi. At age 15, he joined his family in fleeing the war-torn region and emigrating to New Orleans, Louisiana. He apprenticed in printing in St. Louis, Missouri, and worked as a grocer and a waterman on the Mississippi River. Most repugnant to him was the condition of slaves in the plantation South.

Bondi settled at Osawatomie, Kansas, in 1856 and joined Jacob Benjamin and Theodore Wiener in opening a trading post. To protect his investment, Bondi joined the militia of insurrectionist John Brown but doing so failed to avert the burning of his cabin, destruction of his store, and theft of his livestock. On June 1, 1856, Bondi and his fellow fighters led a raid on Missouri ruffians at Potawatomi Creek. In 1860, Bondi married Henrietta Einstein, a German immigrant from St. Louis, Missouri, and opened a depot of the secret network at Leavenworth. During the Civil War, he joined the Kansas Volunteer Cavalry.

Source

Sanborn, F.B. *The Life and Letters of John Brown: Liberator of Kansas, and Martyr of Virginia.* Cambridge, MA: Harvard University Press, 1885.

Bonsall, Abraham (1764–1840)
Bonsall, Mary Andrews (1764–?)
Bonsall, Susan P. Johnson (1794–1847)
Bonsall, Thomas (1797–1882)

A sympathetic Quaker abolitionist from West Chester, Pennsylvania, farmer Abraham Bonsall and his wife, Mary Andrews Bonsall, and their son and daughter-in-law witnessed the desperation of runaways. After working black laborer John Clark in his fields, in 1805, Abraham Bonsall discovered that Clark's owner had seized the man and had him jailed. Rather than return south, Clark drew a razor from his coat and slit his own throat. Another incident, involving the violent snatching of a slave girl on the Bonsall premises, so terrified Mary Bonsall that the memory of it threatened her health. Nonetheless, the Bonsalls completed links to waystations, received slaves from Phebe Wierman Wright and William Wright on the Pilgrim's Pathway at South Mountain, and conducted their passengers up the line.

In the family tradition, the Bonsalls' son, Thomas Bonsall, a Quaker elder, pursued abolitionism and co-founded the Clarkson Anti-Slavery Society. Shepherding runaways dispatched from Deborah T. Simmons Coates and Lindley Coates in Sadsbury, Daniel Gibbons and Hannah Wierman Gibbons in Wrightsville, and Lewis Peart at Lampeter, a village in Valley Forge, Thomas and his wife, Susan P. Johnson Bonsall, received blacks at their farm in Wagontown and conducted them to Abigail Paxson Vickers and John Vickers in Wagontown and to Gravner Marsh and Hannah Marsh in Caln. Some passengers remained in Bonsall's employ and prospered from the gentle treatment and meals offered by Susan. Because the Bonsall home was watched, Thomas hid runways in the granary of his barn's top floor and sent them food via his daughter. Bonsall's service extended over 35 years. At the reading of the Emancipation Proclamation in Christiana on January 1, 1863, Thomas Bonsall led the celebration. In subsequent years, he encountered blacks who remembered his kindness and thanked him.

See also: Pilgrim's Pathway.

Source

Smedley, Robert C. *History of the Underground Railroad in Chester and the Neighboring Counties of Pennsylvania.* Lancaster, PA: Office of *The Journal,* 1883.

Bonsall, Daniel (1802–1879)
Bonsall, Martha W. Sharp (1805–1841)
Bonsall, Ann Hoopes (1801–1865)

Daniel Bonsall and his wife, Martha W. Sharp Bonsall, two Quaker volunteers for the Underground Railroad, rescued up to 13 runaway slaves at a time. Daniel learned altruism from his uncle and aunt, Daniel Gibbons and Hannah Wierman Gibbons, who operated a stop of the Pilgrim's Pathway in Lancaster County, Pennsylvania. After their marriage in 1825, the Bonsalls settled at a farm at West State Street outside Salem, Ohio, where the family concealed passengers of the Underground Railroad. On one winter rescue, Daniel Bonsall awakened farm laborer Simeon Sharp and instructed him to hitch horses to a sled for relay of six slaves to the next stop, in Canfield. Following Martha Bonsall's death, Daniel married Ann Hoopes in 1843, who contributed to the family's volunteerism. For relays, the Bonsalls depended on a nephew, William Gibbons, and on Dr. Benjamin Stanton and his pupil, Keyser Thomas, who drove the farm wagon of William Waterworth. Some relays were completed by Susanna Myers, a 10-year-old wagoneer, the daughter of agents Nancy Robinson Myers and Samuel Myers.

Source

Shaffer, Dale. *Salem: A Quaker City History.* Charleston, SC: Arcadia, 2002.

Booth, Griffin (1811–1889)

An operative of the Underground Railroad, Griffin Booth suffered the suspicions of a violent anti-abolition mob. At age nine, Booth was apprenticed to Moses Boggs in Zanesville, Ohio. After moving to Madison in Jefferson County, Indiana, he joined brothers Elijah Anderson and William J. Anderson in rescuing slaves for the secret network as they arrived across the Ohio River in Carrollton, in sight of the northern border of Kentucky. The group headquartered at the African Methodist Episcopal Church at 309 East Fifth Street in Georgetown, a section of Madison. Booth was pummeled and threatened for refusing to disclose the hiding place of passengers of the Underground Railroad.

See also: African Methodist Episcopal Church.

Source

Obituary, *Madison (IN) Courier,* July 5, 1889.

Booth, Sherman Miller (1812–1904)

Abolitionist organizer Sherman Miller Booth of Davenport, New York, led a revolt against slave catching in Wisconsin that erupted into a six-year conflict in Ripon, Wisconsin, that became known nationally as the Booth War. After graduating from Yale, Booth joined the Reverend Ichabod Codding in publishing the *American Freeman* (or *Wisconsin Freeman*) in Waukesha. On March 10, 1854, Booth conspired to raise a mob to free Joshua Glover, a slave from St. Louis, Missouri, living in Racine, Wisconsin, since January. A deputy U.S. marshal had seized Glover at gunpoint and imprisoned him in a Milwaukee jail. After an anti-slavery throng burst into the courthouse and forced the cell door open, Glover continued on his way over the last 60 miles of the Underground Railroad to Canada. When Booth was arrested for assisting a runaway slave, Wendell Addison Phillips dispatched copies of Theodore Parker's writing as an aid to attorney Byron Paine's successful appeal of the case. Advancing from the state supreme court to a federal court, the case weakened the Fugitive Slave Law of 1850.

After Booth lost his last appeal, Glover's owner, Benjamin S. Garland, sued Booth for the fixed restitution sum of $1,000 for the loss of a valuable laborer. Although court entanglement ruined Booth, the uproar stirred abolitionist agitation. Thanks to the groundswell favoring Booth, the Wisconsin legislature passed a law in 1857 preventing kidnapping and relieving abettors of slave flight of prosecution. The total cost of 19 separate trials was $35,000. In view of local protests and defiance of the U.S. Supreme Court decision, in March 1861, James Buchanan, in one of his final acts as president, pardoned Booth.

See also: Fugitive Slave Law of 1850.

Sources

"Fugitive Slave Law," *Brooklyn (NY) Eagle,* July 27, 1854, 2.
Unconstitutionality of the Fugitive Slave Act. Milwaukee, WI: Rufus King, 1855.

Borden, Nathaniel Briggs (1801–1865)
Borden, Sarah Gould Buffum (1805–1854)

Nathaniel Briggs Borden and Sarah Gould Buffum Borden offered aid to runaway slaves at their safehouse. After entering the textile trade, in February 1843, Nathaniel Borden married into a family of devoted Underground Railroad conductors, including his Quaker in-laws, Arnold Buffum and Rebecca Gould Buffum. At the Borden residence at Second Street in Fall River, Bristol County, Massachusetts, passengers remained until conveyor Robert Adams could provide a closed carriage to Valley Falls, Rhode Island, the waystation of Elizabeth Buffum Chace and Samuel Buffington Chace, the younger sister and brother-in-law of Sarah Borden. In mid-February 1854, Nathaniel Borden aided his neighbor Andrew Robeson in the concealment of a fugitive who had fled Norfolk, Virginia, by boat. Borden's involvement in public affairs included two terms as Fall River's mayor, one term in the state legislature, and two terms in the U.S. Congress.

Source

Laurie, Bruce. *Beyond Garrison: Antislavery and Social Reform.* New York: Cambridge University Press, 2005.

Boston, Peter (1770–?)

Before the establishment of a formal Underground Railroad, Peter Boston was an early victim of punishment for conductors of runaway slaves. A freeborn farmer in Anne Arundel County, Maryland, in 1820, he was arrested for abetting the flight of a slave to free territory. A jury found Boston guilty.

Source

Prison records, Maryland State Archives.

Bouchet, Susan Cooley (1818–1920)
Bouchet, William Francis (1817–?)

Susan Cooley Bouchet of Connecticut and her husband, William Francis Bouchet, supported the Underground Railroad route through New Haven, Connecticut, to Canada. In bondage in Charleston, South Carolina, William Bouchet worked as a valet to John B. Robertson, a student at Yale. When Robertson graduated in 1824, Bouchet gained his freedom and worked as a janitor at the university and as a porter at the Palladium Building. The Bouchets promoted the operation of a fugitive slave depot at the Temple Street Congregational Church, where William Bouchet was a deacon and his son, Edward Alexander Bouchet (1852–1918), was church sexton.

Source

Mickens, Ronald E., ed. *Edward Buchet: The First African-American Doctorate.* River Edge, NJ: World Scientific, 2002.

Boude, Thomas (1752–1822)
Boude, Alice Amelia Atlee (1763–1824)

A colonial hero, General Thomas Boude, and his wife, Alice Amelia Atlee Boude, set the style of slave rescue before the organization of the Underground Railroad. Both natives of Lancaster, Pennsylvania, they married in 1789. After Thomas Boude's service in the Continental army under General Anthony Wayne, he returned to civilian life and operated a lumberyard. In 1804, the Boudes bought seven-year-old Stephen Smith from bondage in Dauphin County, Pennsylvania, and received him into the Boude residence in Columbia, Pennsylvania. When Smith's mother, Nancy Smith, fled enslavement, she joined her son at the safehouse. The slave owner attempted to retrieve Nancy and Stephen, but townspeople intervened and halted the return to bondage. The citizens of Columbia, many of them abolitionist Quakers, supported the Boude family's efforts to aid fugitives. Stephen Smith became an agent of *Freedom's Journal,* a minister of the African Methodist Episcopal Church, and a leader of Columbia's black community.

Source

Shaffer, Dale. *Salem: A Quaker City History.* Vol. 1. Charleston, SC: Arcadia, 2002.

Boulware, John B. (1819–?)

An agent of the Underground Railroad on the Nebraska frontier, John B. Boulware (or Boulwar), a native of Waddy in Shelby County, Kentucky, transported slaves by water. The son of Colonel John Boulware, a Nebraska pioneer, John B. Boulware built a log home in 1847 at Fort Kearney (now called Nebraska City). By 1852, he was operating a ferry service from Commercial Street to western Iowa some 10 miles north of the Missouri border. Allen B. Mayhew, Barbara A. Kagi Mayhew, and her father, Abraham Neff Kagi, relayed passengers via Boulware's ferry to stops in Knox and Tabor, Iowa. Boulware ended his service to the Underground Railroad and moved to Corinne, Utah.

Source

Nebraska State Historical Society. Lincoln: Nebraska State Historical Society, 1885.

bounty hunters

Prior to the Civil War, adventurers found work as professional slave catchers. For each capture, the bounty hunter brandished a certificate of approval from a magistrate to attest to the legality of the seizure. To give runaways an opportunity to slip out of range, in November 1850, two months after passage of the Fugitive Slave Law of 1850, the Boston Vigilance Committee dispatched Peter Belly to post 300 handbills warning of bounty hunters, whose descriptives passed rapidly via grapevine telegraphy. On December 12, 1850, two more hirelings of the committee issued 2,000 handbills.

Such public opposition to recapture forced up the price of stalking and collaring fugitives. Henry Frank reported that, in summer 1858, one slave master paid his hireling $500 for the return of three adults and one infant slave. The sizable reward explains why bounty hunters risked the danger and discomforts on the trail of wily runaways.

> As described in Frank H. Severance's history *Old Trails on the Niagara Frontier* (1899), bounty hunters "made their living by ferreting out and recapturing fugitive slaves and returning them to their old masters; or, as was often the case, selling them into slavery again. Free black men, peaceful citizens of the Northern states, were sometimes seized, to be sold to unscrupulous men who stood ever ready to buy them. . . . There was little hope for blacks carried south of Mason and Dixon's line in the clutches of these hard men, who generally carried a detailed description of runaways from the border States, and received a large commission for capturing and returning them into bondage."

Slave catching had its down side. In 1856, Peter Heck, a tailor from Uniontown, Pennsylvania, conspired with Bob Stump, a bounty hunter from Virginia, to profit from slave recapture. The two seized a fugitive in Blairsville, Pennsylvania, with the intent of splitting the bounty. To their surprise, the man fought for his liberty. When a mob of abolitionists gathered, Heck and Stump fled up a towpath. It took the Blairsville mayor and sheriff to rescue the conspirators from committed agents of the Underground Railroad.

William H. Robinson's autobiography, *From Log Cabin to the Pulpit; or, Fifteen Years in Slavery* (1913), reported the pursuit of slaves in a swamp outside Wilmington, North Carolina. Black hunters, hired by slaver James Anderson, captured 19. Anderson's mulatto son, Frank Anderson, made a break from the posse and died of a gunshot wound. Of the slave catchers, Robinson noted that pursuers earned only $3 per recovery. At the Philadelphia home of the Reverend Richard Allen, a bounty hunter's illegal search precipitated a lawsuit. Allen was so annoyed with the suspicion that he harbored runaways that he insisted on an apology. In Columbia, Pennsylvania, a community known for its white Quaker and black abolitionists, Isaac Brooks fell among an angry anti-slave faction. The men seized him, stripped him naked in the snow, and lashed him with hickory sticks. Brooks fled the area for good.

See also: bloodhounds; Fugitive Slave Law of 1850; grapevine telegraphy; kidnap; slave recovery.

Sources

Meaders, Daniel. "Kidnapping Blacks in Philadelphia: Isaac Hopper's Tales of Oppression." *Journal of Negro History* 80:2 (Spring 1995): 47–65.

Robinson, William H. *From Log Cabin to the Pulpit; or, Fifteen Years in Slavery.* Eau Claire, WI: James H. Tifft, 1913.

Severance, Frank H. *Old Trails on the Niagara Frontier.* Buffalo, NY: n.p., 1899.

Bowditch, Henry Ingersoll (1808–1892)

An operative of the Underground Railroad, Dr. Henry Ingersoll Bowditch campaigned for the abolition of slavery. Born in Salem, Massachusetts, he was the older brother of William Ingersoll Bowditch, an attorney and operative of the secret network. Henry Bowditch studied medicine at Harvard in Boston and in Paris and specialized in diseases of the chest. During a sojourn in England, he came under the influence of anti-slavery crusader William Wilberforce. Bowditch settled in Boston, practiced medicine at Massachusetts General Hospital, and taught at Harvard. He married Olivia Yardley of London, England.

After joining the Boston Vigilance Committee, Bowditch aided a team of volunteers who intervened in the recapture of runaway slaves. In autumn 1842, he advised George W. Latimer, a runaway from James B. Gray in Norfolk, Virginia, on incarceration and on summoning aid from other volunteer agents. As an enduring memento of slavery, Bowditch had photographers make pictures of the right palm of Jonathan Walker, whose jailers branded his palm with a double *S* for slave stealing. After Ellen Smith Craft and William Craft fled Macon, Georgia, on December 21, 1848, and made their way north via the secret network, Bowditch transported them to England. On April 16, 1851, Bowditch paid the passage of A.J. Bunton to safety. Bowditch examined army recruits during the Civil War. His son, Nathaniel Bowditch, was killed in 1863 while fighting for the Union army.

Source

Bowditch, Vincent Yardley. *Life and Correspondence of Henry Ingersoll Bowditch.* Boston: Houghton Mifflin, 1902.

Bowditch, Sarah Rhea Higginson (1819–1919)
Bowditch, William Ingersoll (1819–1909)

In Brookline, outside Boston, Massachusetts, Sarah Rhea Higginson "Sally" Bowditch and attorney William Ingersoll Bowditch of Salem, Massachusetts, operated a safehouse of the Underground Railroad. William Bowditch was the younger brother of Dr. Henry Ingersoll Bowditch, an activist and member of the Boston Vigilance Committee; Sarah Bowditch was the cousin of agent Thomas Wentworth Higginson. While working in Boston as a title conveyancer, William Bowditch was an abolitionist and member of the Boston Vigilance Committee. From 1845 to the national emancipation of slaves on January 1, 1863, Sarah and William Bowditch welcomed refugees to their L-shaped two-story residence at Nine Toxteth Street and relayed them to the homes of Ellen Dorinda Jackson, Francis Jackson, and William Jackson in Newton, Massachusetts. In early January 1849, the Bowditch waystation harbored Ellen Smith Craft and William Craft, who fled Macon, Georgia, on December 21, 1848. William Bowditch drove the Crafts to their next stop, the safehouse of Ellis Gray Loring in Brookline, Massachusetts.

The Bowditch family remained active in the 1850s. On July 15, 1853, William joined others of the local vigilance committee in sailing on Captain Austin Bearse's sloop *Moby Dick* to rescue a stowaway on the brig *Florence* off Fort Independence. Bearse bullied the first mate and apprehended the runaway in a matter of minutes. Bowditch completed the mission by driving the man to Brookline. Six years later, after the arrest of insurrectionist John Brown following the failed raid on the federal arsenal at Harpers Ferry, Virginia, on October 16, 1859, the Bowditch family sheltered Brown's son.

Source

Hinton, Richard Josiah. *John Brown and His Men: With Some Account of the Roads They Travelled to Reach Harpers Ferry.* New York: Funk & Wagnalls, ca. 1894.

Bowen, Abraham (1803–1889)
Bowen, Sarah Ann Read (1804–1891)

Two members of the secret network, house painter Abraham Bowen and Sarah Ann Read Bowen, facilitated the passage of slaves over an Underground Railroad lane passing through Fall River, in Bristol County, Massachusetts. In 1827, Abraham Bowen married Sarah Ann Read, daughter of a veteran of the War of 1812. In 1841, Abraham published the *Fall River Gazette.* While editing the *All Sorts,* during the 1840s, he and his wife operated a grain shipping firm and used the proceeds to finance secret networking at their white clapboard safehouse at 175 Rock Street.

Source

Hurd, D. Hamilton. *History of Bristol County, Massachusetts.* Philadelphia: J.W. Lewis, 1883.

Bowen, Henry Chandler (1813–1896) Bowen, Lucy Maria Tappan (1825–1863)

Under the influence of New York abolitionists, Henry Chandler Bowen, a native of Woodstock, Connecticut, promoted the Underground Railroad. In 1833, while living in New York City, he clerked for silk merchants Arthur Tappan and Lewis Tappan, two radical organizers of the secret network, and fought a pro-slavery throng in 1834 that torched Arthur Tappan's store. After partnering with Theodore McNamee in Bowen & McNamee, a mercantile and silk wholesaler on Williams Street, Henry Bowen married Lucy Maria Tappan, daughter of Lewis Tappan and niece of Arthur Tappan. In fall 1847, Henry invited Henry Ward Beecher to pastor a new Congregationalist assembly, the Plymouth Church of the Pilgrims on Hicks Street in Brooklyn, New York, an urban waystation dubbed the Grand Central Depot of the Underground Railroad. From 1848 to the beginning of the Civil War, Bowen published an abolitionist weekly, the *Independent.* He issued a retort to his critics: he did not intend to abide by the Fugitive Slave Law of 1850.

See also: Fugitive Slave Law of 1850; Plymouth Church of the Pilgrims.

Source

Boulton, Alexander Ormond. "The Gothic Awakening." *American Heritage* 40:7 (November 1989).

Bowers, James L. (1815–1882) Bowers, Rebecca Lower (1807–1842)

Delaware-born conductor James L. Bowers was charged with abetting in slave flight. While farming in Kent County, Maryland, he and his wife, Rebecca Lower Bowers of Philadelphia, supported abolitionism. In 1853, James was exonerated of the charge of aiding runaways. On June 23, 1858, a band of 30 men lured Bowers to the woods and dipped him in tar and feathers. In response, fellow abolitionists ran the attackers out of town. A consortium of slave holders met to discuss the work of Bowers and others in freeing their chattel. In October 1858, Bowers tried to return home. Some 300 vigilantes drove him from the state to Middletown, Delaware. He continued by rail to Philadelphia.

Sources

Fields, Barbara Jeanne. *Slavery and Freedom on the Middle Ground: Maryland During the 19th Century.* New York: Yale University Press, 1985.

"Slaveholders Protecting Themselves," *Planters Advocate,* July 21, 1858.

Bowers, Joseph (ca. 1826–?)

Joseph Bowers of Washington County, Maryland, suffered imprisonment for rescuing a slave. On April 25, 1861, he aided Henry Stanton in an escape from slave owner Elizabeth O'Neal. On November 22, when the case reached circuit court, the Reverend John Alexander Adams of St. Paul's Protestant Episcopal Church substantiated the not guilty plea. Nonetheless, Bowers was condemned to the Maryland state penitentiary at Baltimore on December 21, 1861, to serve eight years and six months. On May 30, 1865, Governor Augustus Williamson Bradford pardoned Bowers for committing a crime that no longer existed.

Source

Prison records, Maryland State Archives.

Bowlus, Henry (1810–ca. 1896) Bowlus, Catharine Keller (1811–1848) Bowlus, Rebecca Catharine Williamson (1824–1891)

A German-American abolitionist, farmer and stockman Henry Bowlus of Frederick County, Maryland, and his wife, Catharine Keller Bowlus of Tiffin, Ohio, welcomed runaway slaves to their home. After their marriage in 1833, they settled in Sandusky County, Ohio, and supported the Methodist church. While living peaceably with the Seneca, Tawa, and Wyandotte Indians, the couple farmed and raised livestock and received slaves at their waystation on the way to Canada. After Catharine Bowlus's death at age 37, in 1848, Henry Bowlus married Rebecca Catharine Williamson, who continued the family's aid to runaway slaves.

Source

A History of Sandusky County, Ohio. Cleveland, OH: H.Z. Williams & Bros., 1882.

Boyd, Eliza E. Bennett (fl. 1830s–ca. 1898)
Boyd, Rufus, Jr. (1805–1883)

Safehouse keepers at Glens Falls, New York, Eliza E. Bennett Boyd and Rufus Boyd, Jr., insisted on discretion from their family. The couple married in 1830 and moved from North Bolton to a residence at Elm and Park streets in Glens Falls in 1847. Around 1850 at their Warren County farm, the Boyds' son, Samuel Gregory Boyd, discovered the feet of a sleeping runaway protruding from the haymow in the barn. Rufus swore his son to secrecy about the pails of food and the nighttime sleigh ride by which Boyd passed the fugitive to a Quaker stationmaster at Swanton, Vermont, for the final leg of a journey to Canada. Samuel Boyd wrote of his family's Underground Railroad activities in a memoir, *In the Days of Old Glens Falls* (1939).

Source

Boyd, Samuel. *In the Days of Old Glens Falls.* Glens Falls, NY: Glens Falls Times, 1939.

Boyer, Jacob Matthias (1835–?)

Jacob Matthias Boyer was one of the rescues of William Still, an Underground Railroad agent in Philadelphia. At age 20, in 1855, Boyer faced the prospect of the auction block after the death of his owner, bank cashier Richard Carman of Anne Arundel County, Maryland. In flight from Annapolis, Boyer ran north to Philadelphia and sheltered at Still's waystation.

Source

Still, William. *The Underground Railroad.* Philadelphia: Porter & Coates, 1871.

Boynton, Charles Brandon (1806–1883)

A minister and pamphleteer from Stockbridge, Massachusetts, the Reverend Charles Brandon Boynton labored to free runaway slaves. He resettled in Cincinnati, Ohio, in 1846. At the Sixth Presbyterian Church, he advocated abolitionism and founded an Underground Railroad station on the premises. When his liberalism offended the presbytery, he renamed his church the Vine Street Congregational Church. While editing the *Christian Press,* an abolitionist weekly, he continued rescuing slaves. From his pulpit, he issued strong denunciations of slave owners and encouraged participation in the secret network. During the Civil War, he led a regiment at the battles of Chickamauga and Missionary Ridge and attained the rank of brigadier general.

Sources

Dolbee, Cora. "The Second Book on Kansas." *Kansas Historical Quarterly* 4:2 (May 1935): 164–87.

History of Cincinnati and Hamilton County, Ohio. Cincinnati, OH: S.B. Nelson, 1894.

Bradford, Arthur Bullus (1810–1899)
Bradford, Elizabeth Wickes (1813–?)
Bradford, Oliver Bloomfield (1837–1905)
Bradford, Ruth Bullus (1841–1928)

A radical Presbyterian lecturer, the Reverend Arthur Bullus Bradford contributed leadership and vigor to the network of agents through Beaver County, Pennsylvania. A native of Reading, Pennsylvania, and graduate of Princeton, he claimed as a forebear Governor William Bradford, a passenger on the *Mayflower.* Arthur Bradford was traumatized at the sight of a woman torn from her family and sold from an auction block in Washington, D.C. He believed that Eli Whitney's invention of the cotton gin retrieved the institution of slavery from a natural demise in 1835. Without the boost to the southern economy, Bradford noted that there would have been no Civil War. To express his outrage at human bondage, he contributed commentary to William Lloyd Garrison's abolitionist weekly, *The Liberator.*

Bradford married Elizabeth Wickes of Philadelphia in 1836 and filled a pulpit at the Mount Pleasant Presbyterian Church at Darlington, Pennsylvania. In league with Quaker conductors at New Brighton, the couple received passengers from Wellsville, Ohio, and from Wellsburg, Virginia. They sheltered runaways in a nearby coal mine or at their brick residence, Buttonwood, which Arthur Bradford deeded to friends to save it from forfeiture if he were caught breaking the Fugitive Slave Law of 1850. Elizabeth Bradford and her daughter, Ruth Bullus Bradford, provided clean clothes and disguises, which they made from their own wardrobes. At night, the Bradfords' son, Oliver Bloomfield Bradford, and a hired transporter relayed slaves through Enon Valley to the next depot at Salem, Ohio. Among Bradford's contacts were Elizabeth P. Weaver Heaton and Jacob Heaton, Quaker conductors who welcomed fugitives to their home and adjacent dry goods store in Salem. The Philadelphia Anti-Slavery Society provided Arthur Bradford with a sword cane as a defense against local pro-slavery factions. Oliver Johnson praised Bradford's dedication in a biography, *William Lloyd Garrison and His Times; or, Sketches of the Anti-Slavery Movement in America, and of the Man Who Was Its Founder and Moral Leader.*

See also: disguise; Fugitive Slave Law of 1850; *Liberator, The.*

Sources

Howett, Thomas, and Mary Howett, eds. *The Salem Story, 1806–1956.* Salem, OH: Budget Press, 1956.

Johnson, Oliver. *William Lloyd Garrison and His Times; or, Sketches of the Anti-Slavery Movement in America, and of the Man Who Was Its Founder and Moral Leader.* Boston: Houghton Mifflin, 1881.

Bradford, Moses (1819–1898) Bradford, Mary Eleanor Van Horn (ca. 1828–1888)

A Quaker conductor of the Underground Railroad, Moses Bradford of Hardy County, Virginia, and his wife, Mary Eleanor (or Ellen) Van Horn Bradford of Zanesville, Ohio, acted on principles of egalitarianism and pacifism. Moses Bradford was born in Hardy County, Virginia, and settled on the Mississinewa River at North Marion in Grant County, Ohio. He married Mary Eleanor Van Horn in 1849 and earned his living as a stockman, storekeeper, and butcher. The couple received passengers from John S. Harvey and Quincy Baldwin. During a trip through Cincinnati, Moses Bradford required assistance from fellow Quaker operatives to avoid a pro-slavery mob.

Source

Centennial History of Grant County Indiana 1812–1912. Chicago: Lewis, 1914.

Bradley, James (ca. 1819–?)

A coordinator of slave rescues at Lane Theological Seminary, a Presbyterian ministerial training center in Cincinnati, Ohio, James Bradley volunteered out of empathy for the oppressed. After slavers ripped him from his mother's arms at age three and transported him from Africa, he crossed the Atlantic in relative freedom because he was too small to chain below deck. He was auctioned from a Charleston, South Carolina, slave pen and bought by a white man named Bradley from Pendleton County, Ohio. When the family resettled in Arkansas, 14-year-old Bradley performed a man's labors. At night, he wove horse collars for sale at the rate of two per week. From the proceeds of his industry and from the sale of pigs, he purchased his liberty.

Bradley educated himself by carrying a speller in his hat and by studying during free moments. He settled in Cincinnati and joined a campus anti-slavery faction. In 1834, he transferred to the Sheffield Manual Labor Institute, a branch of Oberlin College in Oberlin, Ohio, and issued a testimonial in *The Oasis,* an abolitionist annual edited by Lydia Maria Francis Child. He aided refugees on their way north from Kentucky over the Ohio River to freedom in Ontario. At Covington, Kentucky, a bronze statue of Bradley commemorates his activism.

See also: Oberlin College.

Source

Bradley, James. "Brief Account of an Emancipated Slave Written by Himself, at the Request of the Editor." *Oasis* (June 1834).

Bragdon, George Lindsay (1805–1879) Bragdon, Eliza S. Salisbury (1805–1893)

In Richland, near Port Ontario, New York, George Lindsay Bragdon was a member of a cohesive group of Underground Railroad agents. Born to Samuel Bragdon, a veteran of the Revolutionary War, in Acton in York County, Maine, George Bragdon joined five brothers in homesteading along Sandy Creek. After his marriage in 1828 to Eliza S. Salisbury of Pulaski, New York, the couple joined the Baptist church in Oswego County, New York. The Bragdons received runaways at Chestnut Hill, their home at 7943 Route Three. George Bragdon formed the nondenominational Bethel Church outside Selkirk after he and his wife were ousted from their church for their radical abolitionism. The Bragdons were friends of abolitionist orator Asa Sylvester Wing, who stayed at their safehouse during his lecture tours.

Source

Siebert, Wilbur H. *The Underground Railroad: Slavery to Freedom.* New York: Macmillan, 1898.

Brand, Joseph C. (1810–1897)

Reared in the plantation South, Joseph C. Brand underwent a fervid change of heart that committed him to the Ohio anti-slavery network. Born in Bourbon

County, Kentucky, he grew up amid the flesh trade and observed slave owners and their human chattel. After settling in the Midwest to operate a dry goods business and marrying Lavinia E. Talbot, he gained a new perspective from living in Mechanicsburg, Ohio. In late May 1857, one of his rescues, Addison "Ad" White, the slave of Daniel White in Flemingsburg in Fleming County, Kentucky, fled from federal marshals. Brand sounded an alarm that saved conductors Udney Hyde and the Reverend Charles B. Taylor from arrest. During the Civil War, Brand enlisted volunteers for the Sixty-sixth Ohio Volunteer Infantry and served as quartermaster.

Source

Baxter, W.H. *History of Champaign County, Ohio.* Chicago: W.H. Beers, 1881.

Brewster, Silas Wadsworth (1813–1882)
Brewster, Mary Ann Walden (1811–1890)

A merchant and Underground Railroad operative in Hannibal, in Oswego County, New York, Silas Wadsworth Brewster aided escapees on the New York–Ontario route. In 1836, he opened a dry goods store and apothecary shop near the post office on the village square, later known as the Brewster Block. After his marriage to Mary Ann Walden of New York City in 1837, the couple operated a safehouse at 963 Cayuga Street and hid fugitives in their barn.

Source

History of Oswego County, New York. Philadelphia: L.H. Everts, 1877.

Bridge, Bezaleel, Jr. (1808–1863)
Bridge, Emily Sophia Bagley (1818–1854)

Bezaleel Bridge, Jr., established a safehouse in West Windsor, in Windsor County, Vermont. After the death of his first wife, in 1842, he married Emily Sophia Bagley. From 1848 until the Emancipation Proclamation on January 1, 1863, the couple and their six children received refugees at their two-story home at the crest of a hill on Sheddsville Cemetery Road. The residence, a stagecoach stop, may have been the construction of Bezaleel's grandfather Abel Adams in 1803 and a gift to Adams's daughter and son-in-law, Hannah Adams and Bezaleel Bridge, Sr. After hiding in a niche on the side of a first-floor chimney, slaves passed on to Hartland or South Woodstock, Vermont.

Source

Aldrich, Lewis Cass, and Frank R. Holmes, eds. *History of Windsor County, Vermont.* Syracuse, NY: D. Mason, 1891.

Bridge, Jonathan Davis (1812–1856)
Bridge, Abigail Learnard Bullard (1811–1893)

In Springfield, Massachusetts, the Reverend Jonathan Davis Bridge, a radical abolitionist from Northfield, and his wife, Abigail Learnard (or Learned) Bullard Bridge, sheltered desperate runaways. While pastoring the Pynchon Street Methodist Episcopal Church, Jonathan Bridge condemned slavers for the damnable sin of profiting from the flesh trade. The couple's son Melville Wells Bridge (1834–1911) later attested that refugees fleeing to Canada stopped at the parsonage. The Bridges depended on their young son to find safehouses among the congregation. A younger son, Watson Wilberforce Bridge, served during the Civil War as captain of the Fifty-fourth Massachusetts Volunteers, the nation's first all-black infantry regiment. The Pynchon Street Methodist Episcopal Church is featured on the African American Heritage Trail.

Source

"The Underground Railroad and Those Who Operated It," *Springfield (OH) Republican,* March 11, 1900.

Bridgman, Edward P. (1834–1915)

Teacher and soldier Edward Bridgman of Northampton, Massachusetts, aided the cause of black refugees passing through Kansas on their way to Canada. He was the son of a Congregationalist minister. In 1856, he built a homestead at Osawatomie, Kansas. He was an eyewitness to pro-slavery destruction of Lawrence, Kansas, and to the swift retaliation of insurrectionist John Brown. Bridgman joined Brown's followers in fighting off a second attack at Osawatomie in May 1856. At the beginning of the Civil War, Bridgman fought for abolition of slavery with the Thirty-seventh Massachusetts Infantry at the battles of Fredericksburg, Chancellorsville, and Gettysburg.

Source

Hinton, Richard Josiah. *John Brown and His Men: With Some Account of the Roads They Travelled to Reach Harpers Ferry.* New York: Funk & Wagnalls, ca. 1894.

Brillinger, Jacob (1802–?)
Brillinger, Magdalena (1811–?)

A bank director in York, Pennsylvania, Jacob Brillinger, and his wife, Magdalena Brillinger, converted sections of their elegant two-story residence, Elmwood Mansion, to conceal runaways from slave catchers. Built around 1850 at 400 Elmwood Boulevard, the home was a prominent landmark of Spring Garden Township. Clever carpentry in a false attic allowed slaves to hide behind a support wall. Through trapdoors, escapees could pass to a back hallway over the kitchen or into a third-floor bedroom.

Source

Gibson, John. *History of York County, Pennsylvania.* Chicago: F.A. Battey, 1886.

Brinton, Joshua (1811–1892)
Brinton, Mary Emma Passmore (1827–1912)

In Salisbury, Pennsylvania, Joshua Brinton and his wife, Mary Emma Passmore Brinton, operated an outstation of the Underground Railroad off the standard route through Lancaster County. The beloved Quaker couple wed in 1848. Because of their Christian principles, they were known for understanding and welcoming black runaways. They helped passengers escape to the station of Mary Charles Thorne and William J. Thorne in Selma, Ohio.

Joshua Brinton offered work on his farm or found employment elsewhere for fugitives settling in the area, without questioning their past. He and his wife gained a reputation for sharing more than they could afford to give. One farmworker named Tom-up-in-the-barn disappeared one morning on his way to thresh grain for the Brintons. Agents surmised that kidnappers had seized him.

See also: kidnap.

Source

Meginness, John Franklin. *Biographical Annals of Lancaster County, Pennsylvania.* Chicago: J.H. Beers, 1903.

Brisbane, William Henry (1806–1878)

A pamphleteer, Baptist minister, and officer of the American Medical Association, Dr. William Henry Brisbane experienced a change of heart that turned him into a supporter of the Underground Railroad. Born in Beaufort, South Carolina, and educated at Furman Theological Institution, Brisbane was a Charleston aristocrat and slave owner on prime lowlands property overlooking the Ashley River. He married Gloriana "Anna" Lawton in 1825 and settled in Cincinnati, Ohio, as pastor of the First Baptist Church.

Brisbane published the pro-slavery newspaper the *Southern Baptist and General Intelligencer* until his arguments for human bondage rang hollow. In 1840, with the assistance of abolitionist attorney Salmon Portland Chase, Brisbane manumitted his slaves, the source of his wealth, and hired them as family servants. Against his wife's admonition, he returned to South Carolina to buy his field hands and liberate them in Baltimore, Maryland. To channel the principles of liberty, he published tracts, an abolitionist column in the *Saturday Visitor,* and a policy statement, *Slavery Examined in the Light of the Bible* (1847).

In partnership with Levi Coffin, Brisbane became a daring rescuer of slaves. He solicited funds for the legal defense of fugitives and accompanied recaptured runaways to court. During a visit to South Carolina relatives, he had to flee in the night from a throng threatening to tar and feather him for being an abolitionist turncoat. At age 50, he relocated to Arena, Wisconsin, and pastored the First Baptist Church of Madison. In 1861, he volunteered as chaplain of the Second Wisconsin Cavalry. On January 1, 1863, in Port Royal, South Carolina, the Reverend Thomas Wentworth Higginson, an agent of the secret network, chose Brisbane to read aloud Lincoln's Emancipation Proclamation.

Sources

Cowles, S.S. *A Former Slaveholder Explains How He Became an Abolitionist, 1840.* Hartford, CT: privately published, 1840.
Rowland, Lawrence S., Alexander Moore, and George C. Rogers, Jr. *The History of Beaufort County, South Carolina.* Columbia: University of South Carolina Press, 1996.

British Methodist Episcopal Church

A rescue center for slaves crossing from the United States into Canada, the British Methodist Episcopal Church welcomed newcomers, made them feel secure from recapture or kidnap, and helped them acclimate to a new country. The denomination took on its unique aims and organization after separation from the American Methodist Episcopal Church at Chatham, Ontario, on September 29, 1856. British Methodist Episcopal Church activities were a rallying point for dispirited southern black newcomers, who knew little about living and working in a cold climate. In addition to Christian missions, Canadian churches offered literacy training and an introduction to Canadian citizenship.

In Sydenham Village (now called Owen Sound), on Georgian Bay northwest of the crossing at Buffalo, New York, from 1843, the British Methodist Episcopal Church received migrants from the Chatham and Windsor settlements. Many former slaves found jobs as kitchen staff and stewards on lake steamers and as cooks, groundskeepers, and domestics in hotels and inns. The ministry promoted a community atmosphere and shielded former slaves from racial discrimination. At Little Zion, the log chapel on the Sydenham River, under the leadership of Father Thomas Henry Miller, the son of a slave, the congregation enjoyed a sense of belonging. Unity grew as their numbers swelled and new sanctuaries replaced the original. By 1864, the church family numbered 120 members, most of them passengers of the Underground Railroad.

See also: kidnap.

Source

Winks, Robin W. *The Blacks in Canada.* Montreal, Quebee: McGill-Queen's University Press, 2005.

Broadus, Angeline (fl. 1850s)
Broadus, Irvin (fl. 1850s)

According to an item from the June 14, 1857, issue of the *Louisville Courier,* refugees Angeline Broadus and Irvin Broadus escaped enslavement to Colonel C.A. Withers in Covington, Kentucky, on June 10 and connected with Underground Railroad agents in Cincinnati, Ohio. The chief suspect of slave rescue, William A. Conolly, an editor of the Cincinnati *Daily Commercial,* was away from his Vine Street residence when U.S. Marshal John C. Elliott and five deputies arrested the black couple. After Irvin Broadus knifed Elliott, the sheriff jailed the black couple to protect them from angry anti-abolitionists. The Cincinnati Vigilance Committee, established by Quaker mastermind Levi Coffin, apparently helped Conolly slip away from authorities.

Source

Hudson, J. Blaine. *Fugitive Slaves and the Underground Railroad in the Kentucky Borderland.* Jefferson, NC: McFarland, 2002.

Brogden, Abraham (1820–?)

Freedman Abraham "Abram" Brogden served two years in prison for abetting a slave escape. While working as a laborer for farmer James Curly in Baltimore, Maryland, on December 21, 1848, Brogden helped his 24-year-old wife, Cinderella Brogden, escape George F. Worthington, her owner in Anne Arundel County. According to the overseer, Edward H. Brown, Worthington offered $100 for her return. Abraham Brogden's arrest preceded his wife's sale out of state. Despite local respect for Brogden, in April 1849, he was sentenced to four years at the Maryland penitentiary. After Cinderella's death, on May 23, 1851, Governor Enoch Louis Lowe pardoned Abraham Brogden.

Source

"One Hundred Dollars Reward," *Baltimore Sun,* December 23, 1848.

Brooke, Abraham (1806–1867)
Brooke, Elizabeth Lukens (1806–1836)
Brooke, Samuel (1808–1889)

Quaker humanitarians, Dr. Abraham "Abram" Brooke and Elizabeth Lukens Brooke maintained a refuge for runaways in Salem, Ohio. In 1836, Dr. Brooke, a physician from Maryland, allowed Sereno W. Streeter to convert him to radical abolitionism. Joining Brooke in the effort was his brother, Samuel Brooke, also of Maryland, who published abolitionist essays in the *Anti-Slavery Bugle.* The next year, Brooke and his wife formed the Clinton County Anti-Slavery Society and welcomed men and women as members. In 1840, Abraham Brooke unsuccessfully charged a Virginia slave owner with crossing the state with his chattel on the way to Missouri. When the slaves learned that they were free, they escaped. Dr. Brooke reported in a letter that 17 local abolitionists faced charges of rioting and that the Ohio Supreme Court overturned the charges. The *Niles Weekly Register* reiterated Dr. Brooke's contention that no master could claim human property in the free state of Ohio.

Influenced by the activism of Abby Kelley Foster and Stephen Symons Foster, Samuel Brooke, who chaired and served as general agent for the Ohio Anti-Slavery Society (later called the Western Anti-Slavery Society), developed his own style of protest. He published his distaste for slave-owning Christians in a pamphlet, *Slavery, and the Slaveholder's Religion: As Opposed to Christianity* (1846), a stalwart condemnation of the flesh trade that Parker Pillsbury admired for its candor. Samuel Brooke joined Martin Robinson Delany and James Miller McKim in supporting Frederick Douglass in 1848 in the launching of his abolitionist newspaper, the *North Star.*

See also: North Star.

Sources

Bentley, Anna Briggs. *American Grit: A Woman's Letters from the Ohio Frontier.* Lexington: University Press of Kentucky, 2002.

Boles, John B., ed. *Masters and Slaves in the House of the Lord.* Lexington: University Press of Kentucky, 1988.

Brooks, Mary Merrick (1801–1868)
Brooks, Nathan (1784–1863)

Abolitionist Mary Merrick Brooks and her husband, financier Nathan Brooks, were devoted Underground Railroad conductors on the Atlantic coast escape route through Concord, Massachusetts. Attorney Nathan Brooks, a native of Lincoln, Massachusetts, worked his way through Harvard Law School in 1809 and opened an office in the Concord Bank building on Main Street. In 1824, he married Mary Merrick, a Concord native and friend of abolitionists Ralph Waldo Emerson, William Lloyd Garrison, and Henry David Thoreau and his sister, Sophia Thoreau. Mary Brooks founded and chaired the Concord Ladies Anti-Slavery Society and coordinated abolitionist lectures. At their two-story brick home at Main Street and Sudbury Road, the Brooks family sheltered fugitives. On February 16, 1851, Nathan Brooks collaborated with secret operatives Ann Hagar Bigelow and Francis Bigelow in the early morning relay of Fredric "Shadrach" Minkins from Boston to Concord.

Source

Collison, Gary. *Shadrach Minkins: From Fugitive Slave to Citizen.* Cambridge, MA: Harvard University Press, 1997.

Brooks, Susan (ca. 1814–?)

The chattel of Thomas Eckels of Norfolk, Virginia, Susan Brooks, a domestic and cook, resolved to free herself. In 1854, a year after her husband's death, she followed her son, who had fled six months earlier. With slaves William Henry Atkins and William B. White, Susan Brooks stowed away on a steamer, the *City of Richmond,* perhaps captained by agent Alfred Fountain. Dressed like a laundress, she pretended to deliver a freshly ironed shirt and put herself into the hands of an Underground Railroad agent. Her clever ruse earned mention in William Still's history *The Underground Railroad* (1871).

Source

Still, William. *The Underground Railroad.* Philadelphia: Porter & Coates, 1871.

Brosius, Mahlon (1797–1863)
Brosius, Mary Emma Kent (1800–1870)
Brosius, Daniel Kent (1823–1847)
Brosius, Edwin (1825–1885)

In assistance to family agents of the Underground Railroad, Mahlon Brosius and Mary Emma Kent Brosius conducted slaves from the waystation of Mary's brother and sister-in-law, Benjamin Kent and Hannah Simmons Kent of Penn Township in Perry County, Pennsylvania. The Brosius family attended Quaker meetings at the school of Asa Walton, an operative of the secret network in Coleraine. They received a party of 35 Maryland refugees led by Benjamin Kent and sent the group in two parties to the waystations of James Fulton, Jr., and Gideon Pierce, collaborators in Ercildoun, Pennsylvania. Leading the way were the Brosiuses' sons, Daniel Kent Brosius and Edwin Brosius, who transported women and children by farm wagon while the male slaves followed along in the woods.

Source

Smedley, Robert C. *History of the Underground Railroad in Chester and the Neighboring Counties of Pennsylvania.* Lancaster, PA: Office of *The Journal,* 1883.

Brown, Abel (1810–1844)
Brown, Mary Ann Brigham (?–1842)

Two radical abolitionists in the Hudson Valley, the Reverend Abel Brown of Springfield, Massachusetts, and his wife, Mary Ann Brigham Brown, conspired with other Underground Railroad operatives to smooth the way for refugees. After their marriage in 1835, the couple lived in Chautauqua County, New York. Abel traveled to western Pennsylvania as an agent and lecturer for the American Anti-Slavery Society. In April 1841, he pastored the Sand Lake Baptist Church, joined the Albany Vigilance Committee, and voiced his anti-slavery opinions in letters to William Lloyd Garrison's newspaper, *The Liberator.* The next year, the Browns moved to 209 Green Street in Albany, and co-established the Eastern New York Anti-Slavery Society.

In 1842, Abel Brown joined two secret network operatives, William Lawrence Chaplin and the Reverend Charles Turner Torrey, in publishing the weekly *Tocsin of Liberty.* The editor, Edwin W. Goodwin, issued the names of passengers of the Underground Railroad and exposed the cruelties of their former owners, including Cheney Hutton, slave master of Benjamin Hutton and Phillip Hutton, escapees aboard the steamer *People's Line.* For the Browns' provocation of southern planters, Baltimore slave owners offered a reward for Abel Brown's capture and arrest. At the demise of the *Tocsin of Liberty,* Brown supported Nelson Tift and James Caleb Jackson when they renamed the paper the *Albany Patriot.*

With the aid of transporter Edwin Weyburn Goodwin in Albany County, Mary Ann Brown managed the couple's waystation and directed refugees across Lake Ontario to Canada. In 1842, Abel dispatched a runaway over the Albany–New England route with a note to Charles Hicks in Bennington, Vermont, asking for a job for the fugitive or for his transportation to the next safehouse. With Eber M. Pettit in Versailles, New York, and Fanny B. Leggett and Joseph Leggett in Chestertown, New York, the Browns coordinated relays and retained distant contacts in Vermont and Canada where refugees could seek help. At Mary Ann Brown's funeral, former slaves wept out of gratitude for her help and sorrow at her passing. A devoted agent of the secret network, the Reverend Henry Highland Garnet of Troy, New York, delivered Abel Brown's eulogy. In 1846, the Eastern New York Anti-Slavery Society disbanded from lack of leadership. Five years after Abel Brown's death, his second wife, Catherine S. Brown, wrote about his benevolence to slaves in *Memoir of Rev. Abel Brown* (1849).

See also: American Anti-Slavery Society; *Liberator, The.*

Sources

Brown, Catherine S. *Memoir of Rev. Abel Brown.* Worcester, MA: C.S. Brown, 1849.

Pettit, Eber M. *Sketches in the History of the Underground Railroad.* Fredonia, NY: W. McKinstry & Son, 1879.

Brown, Charles Henry (1828–?)

A passenger aboard the Underground Railroad, 27-year-old Charles Henry Brown eluded bondage. In 1855, he escaped the ownership of Dr. Richard Dorsey. Running from Cambridge, Maryland, Brown reached Philadelphia, Pennsylvania, and received aid from agents of the secret network.

Source

Still, William. *The Underground Railroad.* Philadelphia: Porter & Coates, 1871.

Brown, Charles Oliver (1848–1941)
Brown, Celia Marriett Burrell (fl. 1823–?)
Brown, Oliver May (fl. 1826–?)

The Reverend Charles Oliver Brown grew up amid family activism on behalf of desperate runaways. His parents, teacher Celia Marriett Burrell Brown of Connecticut and blacksmith and bargeman Oliver May Brown of Wayne, New York, farmed outside Battle Creek, Michigan. Devout Congregationalists, the family relocated to Kalamazoo, Michigan, and then to the village of Utah, Ohio, where they worked as a team to receive fugitive slaves. The idealism and generosity of his parents influenced the oratory and ministry of Charles Brown, who followed his father into the Third Ohio Volunteer Cavalry as bugler for General William Tecumseh Sherman.

Source

Crofts, Thomas. *History of the Third Ohio Cavalry.* Columbus, OH: Stoneman, 1910.

Brown, Frances Jane Scroggins (1819–1914)
Brown, Thomas Arthur (?–ca. 1891)

An abolitionist sympathizer from girlhood, Frances Jane Scroggins Brown, a mulatto, joined the secret network of conductors of the Underground Railroad. Born in Winchester, Virginia, she gained her freedom from her white grandfather, an officer of the colonial militia during the Revolutionary War. She worked as an indentured servant until her employer moved to

Cincinnati, Ohio. Around 1839, she boarded with the family of freedman James Wilkerson, who operated a safehouse in Cincinnati. Infusing her fervor for liberty was a terrifying memory of seeing an overseer whip a coffle of slaves.

Before her marriage, people called Scroggins "Crazy Jane" for the mournful songs she sang by the roadside. She came close to being kidnapped when an angry slave owner chased his slave Caroline from a steamer wharf to a house near the riverfront. The rescue required racing through the streets from house to house until Scroggins had ensured Caroline's safety. The owner was incensed that Caroline passed quickly through the hands of local agents. To recoup his loss, the slave owner tried unsuccessfully to claim ownership of Scroggins. Years later, after Caroline found liberty in Canada, she and Frances reunited.

In 1841, Frances Scroggins married freedman Thomas Arthur Brown of Frederick, Maryland, who worked on the Mississippi River as a steward and express agent aboard the steamer *Pennsylvania.* They made a home in Pittsburgh, Pennsylvania, at Monongahela House, a residence on Hazel Street, where they welcomed runaways to shelter, food, and directions to Ontario. Aiding the Browns' work were two secret operatives, freedman physician Martin Robinson Delany at Chambersburg and the Reverend Lewis Woodson in Pittsburgh. For one entire winter, the Browns kept a slave woman and five children concealed from neighbors. Another family fled bondage in Texas and sheltered with the Browns, who had the slaves photographed with the American flag wrapped around them. Thomas Brown used ingenuity to release a Maryland mulatto from her white owner, who was also her half brother. Because Brown had no key to the door of her cell, he lifted her by pulley through a transom.

See also: kidnap.

Sources

Brown, Hallie Quinn. *Homespun Heroines and Other Women of Distinction.* Xenia, OH: Aldine, 1926.

Griffler, Keith P. *Front Line of Freedom: African Americans and the Forging of the Underground Railroad in the Ohio Valley.* Lexington: University Press of Kentucky, 2004.

Brown, Henry "Box" (ca. 1815–after 1875)

One of the agile heroes of the Underground Railroad, Henry "Box" Brown earned a reputation for ingenuity.

In one of the most resourceful and audacious of all slave escapes, Henry "Box" Brown had himself shipped in a wooden produce crate from Richmond, Virginia, to Philadelphia in March 1849. The trip took 26 hours. *(Library of Congress)*

He was born into bondage in Louisa County, Virginia, and trained as a houseboy and laborer in a tobacco factory. In 1848, he mourned the sale of his wife and three children. Because of the virulence of his master and of the slave catchers around Richmond, Virginia, in March 1849, Brown sought the aid of agent Samuel A. Smith of Virginia, a shoe salesman and secret network agent, and his black employee, James Caesar Anthony Smith. Samuel Smith was later imprisoned for aiding runaways. On March 23, Brown crept into a baize-lined hooped box 3 feet by 2 feet by 26 inches and sent himself to the home of William Henry Johnson at Arch Street in Philadelphia. During a portion of the 26-hour journey, Brown traveled upside down.

The Reverend James Miller McKim of Carlisle, a member of the Philadelphia Vigilance Committee, awaited Brown's transport to the express office. For safety's sake, McKim asked a merchant, E.M. Davis, to send a regular driver to claim the box. By express train, the wood box arrived "this side up" 26 hours later. With hatchet and saw, members of the antislavery office freed Brown, who sang Psalm 40:1, "I waited patiently for the Lord, and he heard my prayer." Brown lodged at the waystation of Quaker agents James Mott, Jr., and Lucretia Coffin Mott for two days before continuing to Boston. During Brown's stay in Pennsylvania, he demonstrated to Quakers at the Schuylkill Friends Meetinghouse in

Phoenixville how he contorted his body to fit in the box. He continued to Massachusetts and lodged at the safehouse of Joseph Ricketson at New Bedford.

Partnering with James Caesar Anthony Smith, Brown presented his adventures in a panorama show at abolitionist gatherings. At the height of his prominence, in 1849, he published a memoir, *Narrative of the Life of Henry Box Brown.* Because of the hostile climate for runaways following passage of the Fugitive Slave Law of 1850, he gave up touring and moved to England, where he remained for a quarter century before returning to the United States.

See also: Fugitive Slave Law of 1850; Quakers; vigilance committees.

Sources

Brown, Henry Box. *Narrative of the Life of Henry Box Brown.* Boston: Brown & Stearns, 1849.

Williams, James. *Life and Adventures of James Williams, a Fugitive Slave.* San Francisco: Women's Union Print, 1873.

Brown, Isaac Holmes (1809–1886)

A farmer and colleague of slave conductors Benjamin H. Rice and Elizabeth Swing Rice, the Reverend Isaac Holmes Brown connected Underground Railroad links between Felicity, Ohio, and his residence in Bethel, in Clermont County, Ohio. At his 400-acre farm, Brown began aiding the secret network in 1835 and supported the relays of Gerrard Policarp Riley from Tate, Ohio. From Brown's custody, slaves journeyed on to the Reverend John Bennington Mahan at White Oak Creek and to Dr. William Eberle Thompson in Bethel. Others passed to Charles Boerstler "Boss" Huber's tannery or farm in Williamsburg, Ohio, where freedman wagoneer Marcus Sims of Virginia served as transporter. In 1845, Brown donated land in Tate Township for an abolitionist Methodist congregation, the Sugar Tree Wesleyan Church, pastored by the Reverend Silas Chase, another Underground Railroad operative.

Source

Everts, Louis H. *History of Clermont County, Ohio.* Philadelphia: J.B. Lippincott, 1880.

Brown, James (1798–?)

James Brown served four years in prison for abetting a slave rescue. A free black laborer in Elk Ridge, in Montgomery County, Maryland, he was arrested and found guilty on April 25, 1836. Before his release on April 27, 1840, from the Anne Arundel County prison, he worked as a prison cook.

Source

Prison records, Maryland State Archives.

Brown, Jeremiah (1785–1858)
Brown, Ann Kirk (1788–1816)
Brown, Mary Kirk (1792–1857)
Brown, Slater (1787–1855)

In addition to serving in the Pennsylvania legislature and the U.S. Congress, Judge Jeremiah Brown of Fulton, in Lancaster County, Pennsylvania, was a bold conductor of a 17-station route of the Underground Railroad called the Pilgrim's Pathway. He depended on his brother and sister-in-law, Mary Kirk Brown and Slater (or Slayter) Brown, and on a brother-in-law, Timothy Haines of Rising Sun, Maryland, who married Jeremiah and Slater's older sister Sarah Brown and settled in Fulton, Pennsylvania. The judge and his Quaker wife, Ann Kirk Brown, operated a landmark safehouse noted for its huge pine, called the "cannon ball tree." The tree rose above a real cannon ball buried in the branches by a soldier during the Revolutionary War. Beneath the house was a tunnel that once sheltered American Indians and that accessed the bedroom from the kitchen.

After Ann's death in 1816, Jeremiah Brown continued his volunteerism, aiding as many as eight refugee parties in a week's time. In 1847, he consulted with attorney Thaddeus Stevens about the successful transportation of two young Maryland slave women, Ellen Jackson and Emaline Raines. Brown led the two runaways to Thomas Whitson's safehouse in Bart, Pennsylvania, for ferrying over Lake Erie to Canada. A letter from Stevens warned Brown that spies of the slaves' owner, William C. Naines of Baltimore, endangered the passage. The letter preserves evidence of caution within the secret network. Perry Sanford, another refugee aided by Brown, passed through the Bethel waystation in the 1850s on his way to Toronto.

See also: Pilgrim's Pathway; spies.

Source

Spotts, Charles Dewey. *The Pilgrim's Pathway: The Underground Railroad in Lancaster County.* Lancaster, PA: Franklin & Marshall College Library, 1966.

Brown, John (1800–1859)

Both Calvinist knight and martyr, John Brown is an historical enigma. His legend identifies him variously as Brown of Kansas, Captain Brown, Osawatomie Brown, the Old Man, and a self-proclaimed angel of death. A native of Torrington, Connecticut, John Brown was the son of tanner Owen Brown and Ruth Mills Brown, stationkeepers of an Underground Railroad line through Hudson, Ohio. In a letter to the Reverend Thomas Wentworth Higginson, pastor of the Free Church in Worcester, Massachusetts, Brown declared his dedication to the Underground Railroad from boyhood. He grew up in Hudson, Ohio, where he learned tanning from his father. Brown became a wool merchant and a cattle drover and nursed unfulfilled ambitions to enter the Congregationalist ministry. Forceful to the point of mania, he inspired his 20 children and his followers to champion the rights of black slaves. One of his band was Merritt Anthony, brother of Quaker abolitionist and secret operative Susan Brownell Anthony. Anthony hid escapees under a false floor in the barn at John Brown's home in Hudson.

Several Relocations

After John Brown's move to Randolph, Pennsylvania, where he stayed from 1825 to 1835, he operated a tannery near Lake Erie. Intent on ending slavery, he hid runaways in a chamber under his barn and conducted groups of refugees to a waystation in Tabor, Pennsylvania. During his work as the postmaster of Meadville, Pennsylvania, he used his connections with other towns to sound out attitudes toward runaways and to recruit stationmasters. He established secret links to Jamestown, New York, a vital depot of the secret network. He hid slaves in his wagon while hauling surveying equipment, sacks of mail, and hides for his tannery.

In 1835, Brown relocated to Franklin Mills, Ohio, and collaborated with agents Ann Ogden Street and John Street in Salem. In 1837, Brown was incensed by the murder of abolitionist editor Elijah Parish Lovejoy in November 1837 at his print shop in Alton, Illinois. Brown outraged members of the Congregational church when he invited black worshipers from the colored balcony to his seat at the front of the congregation. His militance grew to match the terrorist extreme exhibited by the Reverend Henry Highland Garnet, who exhorted blacks to rise up and murder their masters.

During Brown's travels in the 1840s, he stayed at safehouses, including the home of Jane Campbell McKeever and Matthew McKeever in Middletown, Pennsylvania. He labored sporadically at planning an engineering marvel—a subterranean passageway through which slaves could move rapidly out of bondage and into a frontier state. Passage of the Fugitive Slave Law of 1850 alarmed Brown, who feared that federal agents would return runaways to bondage and that bounty hunters would kidnap freedmen to sell into slavery. He enhanced the aims of the Underground Railroad in January 1851 by forming the United States League of Gileadites, a militia of free blacks intended to stop U.S. marshals from seizing runaways.

From Advocacy to Action

Brown's impatience with national debate fueled his instigation of a holy war. After resettling in Lawrence, Kansas, in fall 1855, Brown and five of his sons joined the fighting on the Missouri border and supplied anti-slavery factions with provisions and weapons. He complained that too many protesters relied on talk rather than action. Unlike more philosophical abolitionists, he operated by the principle that the only victory lay in liberating individuals. Following the sacking and burning of Lawrence on May 21, 1856, by Missouri insurgents, Brown plotted revenge. Three nights later, he retaliated against five opponents, whom his band, in biblical style, slew with swords.

The Lawrence raid pressed Brown to target a broader pro-slavery faction. At a January 1857 meeting in Boston, he persuaded influential easterners—the Reverend Thomas Wentworth Higginson, Dr. Samuel Gridley Howe, the Reverend Theodore Parker, and George Luther Stearns—to purchase 200 Sharps rifles and 200 revolvers to advance the war in Kansas. In addition, they pledged a contribution of $1,000. Meanwhile, Brown marched his men to Springdale, Iowa, in December 1857. His militia lodged with Underground Railroad operatives Hannah Keislar Maxson and William Maxson. Brown stayed with Quaker depot managers Edith Dean Painter and John H. Painter. In February 1858, Brown conferred with Frederick Douglass in Rochester, New York, on raising funds for an anti-slavery war. In March or April

The building known as John Brown's Fort, originally constructed as the fire engine and guardhouse of the federal armory at Harpers Ferry, Virginia (now West Virginia), was the final refuge of Brown and several followers at the end of their ill-fated raid in 1859. *(Library of Congress)*

1858, Brown met with Harriet Tubman at her home in St. Catharines, Ontario, to discuss his intention to set up a camp for fugitive slaves in the Appalachian Mountains of Virginia. He planned to capture whites and ransom each one for a slave. Brown firmed up his plans in summer 1858 in Linn County, Kansas, where he conspired with agent John Henry Kagi and James Montgomery, an Underground Railroad supervisor.

Brown raided two Missouri plantations on December 20 and 21, 1858. After killing the slave owner and seizing 11 of his chattel, he organized a wagon train to transport them to Windsor, Ontario. Identified among the group were Mr. and Mrs. Samuel Harper of Bates County; a twelfth passenger was born to the Daniels family on January 24, 1859, at the safehouse of Emily Jane Hunt Grover and Joel Grover. Brown's route took him from Mound City through Cyrus Packard's waystation north of Topeka, Kansas, to Albert Fuller's log safehouse at Straight Creek, northwest of Holton, Kansas. The slaves then moved over the Lane Trail to Nebraska City, Nebraska. After crossing the Missouri River, the wagon train proceeded to Springdale, Iowa, where Quakers welcomed Brown's passengers. More warm receptions came from Josiah Bushnell Grinnell, a stationmaster in Grinnell, Iowa, and the Reverend John Todd and George B. Gaston in Tabor, Iowa. The train succeeded in part through the aid of agents James Burnett Abbott and the Grovers in Lawrence, Kansas, and from the intervention of Henry O. Wagoner, a Chicago operative who posted a closed sign on his mill while he housed and fed the group. After seeing to the needs of the fugitives, Brown and his staff boarded with tailor John Jones. Agent Allan Pinkerton and his 13-year-old son

Willie helped the runaways from Rock Island railcars onto a border ferry in Detroit, Michigan, that crossed the Detroit River to Windsor, Ontario. After traveling 1,100 miles in 82 days, the group reached its destination on March 10, 1859. Because of the media acclaim of Brown's feat, President James Buchanan raised the alarm among federal marshals and posted a $250 reward for Brown's arrest.

Harpers Ferry

At an all-night meeting at Gerrit Smith's house in Peterboro, New York, on February 22–23, 1858, Brown conspired with Smith, Edwin Morton, Frank B. Sanborn, George Luther Stearns, the Reverend Higginson, Dr. Howe, and the Reverend Parker. To these strategists, Brown revealed his plan to attack the federal arsenal in Harpers Ferry, Virginia, though he did not identify the site by name. The purpose of the raid was to seize arms and distribute them to slaves to launch a nationwide insurrection upriver from the nation's capital. He hoped to jolt slaves and abolitionists into a national confrontation that would settle the slavery issue once and for all. Smith urged others in the cabal to support Brown's radical solution, which would link the Underground Railroad with open revolt against the federal government. Sanborn and Smith raised the cash needed for the endeavor; donating $15 was orator Ralph Waldo Emerson. Brown coordinated a field survey of waystations and conductors to determine which operatives were willing to bear arms against federal agents to free blacks from bondage.

After convening liberators at Chatham, Ontario, in April 1858, Brown moved south to Springdale, Iowa, on April 27 to assemble his "band of shepherds," or "surveyors," as he called them, and move them farther east. Before daylight on October 16, 1859, with 20 men, he attacked the U.S. arsenal, which lay on a point of land jutting between the Potomac and Shenandoah rivers northwest of Washington, D.C. The raid was an utter failure. Captured by Colonel Robert Edward Lee and a detachment of U.S. marines, the insurgents lost 10 men, among them Brown's sons, Oliver (1835–1859) and Watson (1835–1859). At Charlestown, Virginia, on November 2, 1859, a Jefferson County judge tried John Brown and his accomplices for treason and found them guilty.

Trial, Execution, and Posthumous Acclaim

Brown's trial stirred strong feelings both for and against the insurrection. During his incarceration, editor Lydia Maria Francis Child traveled from Boston to the Charlestown prison to visit him. Brown was hanged at the Jefferson County courthouse on December 2, 1859. Wendell Addison Phillips claimed the body and transported it to a churchyard in Lake Placid, New York. Two weeks later, two of Brown's men were hanged.

Brown was hailed as a martyr by his admirers, among whom were Underground Railroad agents Elizabeth Buffum Chace and Samuel Buffington Chace in Rhode Island, French author Victor Hugo in Paris, and philosopher and essayist Henry David Thoreau in Concord, Massachusetts, who tolled a bell to mark Brown's trial. During the Civil War, Union soldiers rewrote Julia Ward Howe's anthem "The Battle Hymn of the Republic" as "John Brown's Body," which became a popular marching song. Among the eyewitnesses to Brown's feats was William Lambert, a Detroit tailor and Underground Railroad operative, who reported to the *Detroit Tribune* in 1889 a lengthy account of Brown's methods.

See also: bounty hunters; civil disobedience; Quakers; subterranean pass way.

Sources

Coffman, Elesha. "Maniac or Martyr?" *Christian History,* May 5, 2000.

Hinton, Richard Josiah. *John Brown and His Men: With Some Account of the Roads They Travelled to Reach Harpers Ferry.* New York: Funk & Wagnalls, ca. 1894.

Sanborn, F.B. "The Virginia Campaign of John Brown." *Atlantic Monthly* 35:211 (May 1875): 591–601.

Wyman, Lillie B. Chace. "Harriet Tubman." *New England* 20:1 (March 1896): 110–18.

Brown, John "Fed" (ca. 1817–?)

The runaway John "Fed" Brown lived a nightmare of ownership and flight until he made his way over the Underground Railroad to Dawn, Ontario. Brown knew little about his birth. His mother was a slave named Nancy (or Nanny), and his father, Joe, was an Ibo tribesman enslaved to Benford, a planter in Northampton, Virginia; he had twin siblings, Lucy and Silas. Brown grew up in a two-room log cabin on Betty Moore's estate on Nottoway River in Southampton County, Virginia. After his mother's forced marriage to a man named Lamb, she had three more children, Cain, Curtis, and Irene Lamb. Brown tended the little children by day and picked seed from cotton at night. At the division of slaves to the owner's family, he, Curtis Lamb, and their mother, Nancy Lamb, passed to James Davis, Betty Moore's son-in-law.

Around 1827, Davis weighed and sold Brown by the pound to Starling Finney, a speculator from Georgia who auctioned the boy to Thomas Stevens at Milledgeville. At a plantation in Baldwin County, Georgia, Brown transported whiskey and meal for his often brutal master, from whom Brown endured floggings and a kick to the head that broke his nose and dislodged his right eye. Two years after witnessing the torture of John Glasgow, a British freeman whom Stevens bought at auction, Brown, then aged 24, was the subject of experiments to find a natural remedy for sunstroke. In desperation, he ran away to Buck Hurd, a member of a ring of slave thieves, who returned the unfortunate Brown to Stevens.

Following sale to De Cator Stevens, Brown worked at farming and carpentry until he could store up food and get a pass for his escape. After one failed attempt, Stevens fitted him with horns and bells. Three months later, Stevens removed the device and Brown fled west to Cassville, Georgia; living on stolen sweet potatoes, he continued to Tuscumbia, Alabama. He made a raft and poled his way to the Ohio River and then caught a steamer for New Orleans. Upon recapture by a slave trader named Theophilus Freeman, Brown passed to the custody of Jepsey James, a cotton planter. Brown moved on through the wetlands for three months to St. Louis, Missouri.

Ten months after fleeing De Cator Stevens, the runaway, having learned of the Quakers and the Underground Railroad, headed for a station 100 miles from Carthage, Illinois. A kind agent offered a room with washbasin and clothes and welcomed Brown to breakfast at the family table. The courtesy overwhelmed him. From the waystation to the next shelter, he galloped from nightfall until midnight between two conductors. Additional rapid departures preceded his arrival in Marshall, Michigan, where he met a clutch of runaways—Thomas Christopher, Elias Earle, Noel Johnson, Samuel Patterson, and Thomas Smith—who were building a chapel. On the Canadian border, Brown worked for Captain Joe Teague, a copper miner. At Dawn, Ontario, Brown labored in a sawmill for six months before booking passage to Liverpool, England, in June 1850. Around age 35 or 40, he composed *Slave Life in Georgia* (1855), a valuable slave narrative and testimonial to the organization and efficiency of the secret rail line. Brown first published his account in the April 1853 issue of Arthur Tappan's abolitionist newspaper, the *American and Foreign Anti-Slavery Reporter.*

See also: Quakers.

Source

Brown, John. *Slave Life in Georgia: A Narrative of the Life, Sufferings, and Escape of John Brown, a Fugitive Slave, Now in England.* London: W.M. Watts, 1855.

Brown, John Mifflin (1817–1893)

A strategist, recruiter, and fund-raiser for the Underground Railroad, Bishop John Mifflin Brown supported the rescue of runaway slaves. A minister of the African Methodist Episcopal Church, he was born in Delaware and educated in Philadelphia. He studied at Oberlin College and preached in Amherst, Massachusetts; Poughkeepsie, New York; and Norfolk, Virginia. Brown was partially responsible for the rescue of Lewis Hayden and his family, whom agents Calvin Fairbank and Delia Webster whisked away on September 28, 1844. In 1845, Brown joined the Boston Vigilance Committee and collaborated with Hayden on a speaking tour. On his return to Boston, on March 4, 1851, Brown paid passage for fugitive Alex Duvalls to England. In 1853, Brown established the St. James African Methodist Church in New Orleans, Louisiana. In the 1850s, authorities arrested him on five occasions for allowing slaves to attend his sermons.

See also: African Methodist Episcopal Church; Oberlin College.

Source

Runyon, Randolph Paul. *Delia Webster and the Underground Railroad.* Lexington: University Press of Kentucky, 1996.

Brown, Levi (fl. 1850s)

Levi Brown, the chattel of William Lumbudd in Frederick County, Maryland, stood trial for violating the Fugitive Slave Law of 1850 because he had conducted a slave to liberty. On October 30, 1858, he pled not guilty to charges brought by Somerset R. Waters. The case also involved three free black defendants—David Biggers, Caleb Burgess, and Abraham Lowry. On November 11, 1855, Brown and the three men were sold out of state.

Source
Court records, Maryland State Archives.

Brown, Moses (1738–1836)
Brown, Phebe Waterman (1748–1808)

After a sincere change of heart, Quaker entrepreneur Moses Brown turned from slaver to secret operative of the Underground Railroad. Born to slave trader James Brown in Providence, Rhode Island, Moses Brown made a fortune in cloth manufacture, shipping, banking, chocolate manufacture, ironworks, rum distilling, and the sale of oil and candles, by-products of the whaling industry. Unlike his brothers John, Joseph, and Nicholas and their uncle Obadiah Brown, all of whom profited from slaving, in 1765, Moses Brown abandoned the flesh trade and freed his slaves. In 1789, he co-founded the Providence Abolition Society, a forceful band that convinced slavers to abandon the kidnap of Africans.

On the east side of Providence, Brown and his wife, Phebe Waterman Brown of Warwick, Rhode Island, used their wealth to manage a waystation at Humbolt and Wayland avenues. Passengers arriving by way of the harbor in New Bedford, Massachusetts, sought shelter at his residence. The couple bought acreage for the housing of former slaves, hid runaways on Moses Brown's merchant fleet, and gave others cash to pay their passage to Canada. The naming of Brown University for Moses Brown attests to his generosity.

See also: kidnap; philanthropists.

Sources
Bayles, Richard M. *History of Providence County, Rhode Island.* New York: W.W. Preston, 1891.
Hedges, James B. *The Browns of Providence Plantations: Colonial Years.* Cambridge, MA: Harvard University Press, 1952.

Brown, Paola (1807–1852)

A former slave, Paola (also Paole, Paoli, or Peole) Brown left his home state of Pennsylvania at age 21 to aid runaway slaves passing through Niagara, New York, to Niagara, Ontario. While working as a handyman and town crier, he settled refugee families on free land at Gore and Niagara. In the 1820s, he became a leader of the Hamilton community. At age 30, he abetted the liberation of Jesse Happy, a Kentucky slave who fled north in 1837. Happy's protection by Governor Sir Francis Bond Head above the international border set a precedent in that it assured refugees security in Canada.

Source
Ripley, C. Peter, et al., eds. *The Black Abolitionist Papers.* Vol. 2, *Canada, 1830–1865.* Chapel Hill: University of North Carolina Press, 1992.

Brown, Rachel Milner (fl. 1800s–1820s)
Brown, William (fl. 1800s–1820s)

In Little Britain, in Lancaster County, Pennsylvania, Quaker conductors Rachel Milner Brown and her husband, William "Billy" Brown, operated Station 15 of the Pilgrim's Pathway, a 17-part network of the Underground Railroad. They married in 1805. At their home, at the foot of Laurel Hill along Octorara Creek, slaves found adequate hiding places in the nearby wilderness. Fugitives John and Mary and their son Charlie hid in the Browns' attic and worked for the family. During a failed flight, a Maryland slave owner reclaimed the trio from a deserted house at the creek and manacled John. An ex-slave, Neddy Johnson, raised a search party and freed the couple. Covertly, supporters of the Browns' waystation severely beat the slave owner and torched his house. Attesting to the couple's commitment to liberty is a slave narrative, *John and Mary; or, The Fugitive Slaves, a Tale of South-Eastern Pennsylvania* (1873).

See also: Pilgrim's Pathway.

Source
Griest, Ellwood. *John and Mary; or, The Fugitive Slaves, a Tale of South-Eastern Pennsylvania.* Lancaster, PA: Inquirer Printing, 1873.

Brown, Thomas (1795–?)
Brown, Mary McClanahan (fl. 1830s–1850s)

An enterprising pair of Underground Railroad agents, Irish immigrant Thomas Brown and his wife, Mary McClanahan Brown, concealed their volunteerism as a part of their work. After their marriage in 1833, they posed as an unassuming traveling peddler and a milliner. Operating in Henderson County, Kentucky, the Browns shut their runaway passengers beneath heavy curtains that also shielded wares from sun, dust, and inclement weather. Despite this ruse, the couple gained a reputation for transporting refugees, and so at a community meeting on June 7, 1854, local pro-slavers requested that Mary Brown leave the region.

In April 1855, increased surveillance of slave rescuers in Union County, Ohio, led to the capture of Thomas Brown, whom U.S. marshals jailed. On May 18, 1855, a state court sentenced him to three years in the Kentucky state penitentiary at Frankfort. After seeing a free black from Evansville, Indiana, murdered by guards, Brown was terrified during the remaining two months until his release on May 18, 1857. He published *Three Years in Kentucky Prisons* (1857), an exposé of the vindictiveness of an antiabolitionist warden, who permitted flogging and beatings as punishments to operatives of the secret network.

See also: punishments.

Source

Brown, Thomas. *Three Years in Kentucky Prisons.* Indianapolis, IN: Courier, 1857.

Brown, William Wells (1814–1884)

Commended in the Reverend Samuel Joseph May's *Some Recollections of Our Antislavery Conflict* (1869) as a diligent spokesman for freedom, William Wells Brown was a vocal advocate of abolition. Born one of seven children in 1814 outside Lexington, Kentucky, Brown, called William Young, was the son of a slave, Elizabeth Young, and a white planter, George Higgins, who was the cousin of Elizabeth's owner, Dr. John Young. During labors for his owner, Major Freeland, Brown took refuge in the woods, but pursuers returned him to his master, who soundly whipped him and lodged him near a tobacco fire in the smokehouse. When the household settled in St. Louis, Missouri, Brown hired out at an inn, on a river steamer, and in the newspaper office of Elijah Parish Lovejoy, who edited the *St. Louis Times.* While Brown's sister awaited sale to Natchez, in 1827, Brown and his mother networked their way north to Illinois. Slave catchers apprehended the pair and sold Elizabeth Young south.

Working for a tailor and a steamboatman, Brown remained in St. Louis until winter 1834, when he fled bondage. Contributing to his eagerness was a clairvoyant named Uncle Frank who foresaw Brown's liberation. Brown reached the outskirts of Dayton, Ohio, and renamed himself Wells Brown, after the aged Quaker conductor who helped to liberate him. With the aid of an Underground Railroad agent named Colonel Rice, for nine years, Brown established himself as a boatman who ferried slaves free of charge from Cleveland across Lake Erie to Ontario. One captain who manned the route from Cleveland to Buffalo, New York, hired Brown as a pilot. Brown attested that in 1842, from May to December, he conveyed 69 refugees to freedom in Canada. He also supported a waystation at the Michigan Avenue Baptist Church in Buffalo at 511 Michigan Avenue.

Under the influence of William Lloyd Garrison and orator Wendell Addison Phillips, a special correspondent for the *New York Tribune,* Brown became adept at lecturing for temperance and for the New York Anti-Slavery Society. While living in Boston, he wrote *Narrative of William W. Brown, a Fugitive Slave, Written by Himself* (1847), which contains a preface by radical Quaker abolitionist Joseph Comstock Hathaway of Farmington, New York. Five years later, Brown compiled details of his work on both sides of the Atlantic in *Three Years in Europe; or, Places I Have Seen and People I Have Met* (1852). He followed with *Clotel* (1853), a fictional disclosure of President Thomas Jefferson's sexual relationship with Sally Hemings, a slave at his home, Monticello, situated outside Charlottesville, Virginia. Brown's subsequent works include a play, *The Escape; or, A Leap for Freedom* (1858), *The Negro in the American Rebellion: His Heroism and His Fidelity* (1867), *The Negro in the American Revolution* (1873), and *My Southern Home; or, The South and Its People* (1880), issued four years before his death in Chelsea, Massachusetts.

Sources

Brown, William Wells. *My Southern Home; or, The South and Its People.* Boston: A.G. Brown, 1880.

———. *The Narrative of William W. Brown, a Fugitive Slave.* 1847. Mineola, NY: Dover, 1969.

———. *The Negro in the American Rebellion: His Heroism and His Fidelity.* Boston: Lee & Shepard, 1867.

May, Samuel Joseph. *Some Recollections of Our Antislavery Conflict.* Boston: Fields, Osgood, 1869.

Severance, Frank H. *Old Trails on the Niagara Frontier.* Buffalo, NY: n.p., 1899.

Bruce, David (fl. 1830s)

David Bruce, a mulatto conductor, spent four years in jail for rescuing a slave. On December 24, 1833, a Frederick County circuit court sentenced him to four years in the Maryland state penitentiary at Baltimore. He exited prison in December 1837.

Source

Prison records, Maryland State Archives.

Bruin, Joseph (1809–1882)

A notorious flesh merchant in Alexandria, Virginia, Joseph Bruin maintained a slave jail. Around 1840, he left his employment at the Price, Brich & Company slave auction house at 1315 Duke Street and opened a slave clearinghouse next door to his residence at a two-story brick dwelling in West End on two acres facing 1707 Duke Street. He partnered with another slaver, Alexander Grigsby at Centreville, Virginia. In December 1845, Bruin advertised his flesh market, which he operated in partnership with Henry Hill. Prices ranged from $50 for a child to $1,000 to $1,800 for an adult male and $500 to $1,500 for a female, the price depending on her value as a breeder.

After the flight of sisters Emily and Mary Catherine Edmondson from the District of Columbia on April 15, 1848, slave hunters captured them and lodged them in Bruin's holding pens. The notoriety of the Bruin-Hill warehouse influenced author Harriet Beecher Stowe, who used the setting in her melodramatic novel *Uncle Tom's Cabin* (1852) as a model of barbarity. She enlarged on the history of the slaving business in *A Key to Uncle Tom's Cabin* (1853). The Bruin-Hill warehouse is listed on the National Register of Historic Places. In 1864, U.S. marshals seized Bruin's slave pen.

See also: Key to Uncle Tom's Cabin, A (1853); *Uncle Tom's Cabin; or, Life Among the Lowly* (1852).

Source

Stowe, Harriet Beecher. *A Key to Uncle Tom's Cabin.* London: Clarke, Beeton, 1853.

Bryant, Abijah (1801–?)
Bryant, Levinia Richardson Cowdry (1803–?)

Deacon Abijah Bryant, an agent of the Underground Railroad, combined volunteerism with farming. Assisting him was his wife, Levinia (or Lavina) Richardson Cowdry Bryant of Reading, Massachusetts, whom he married in March 1834. The couple concealed escaped slaves at their three-story wood-frame residence at 307 Main Street in Stoneham, Middlesex County, Massachusetts.

Source

Blockson, Charles L. *Hippocrene Guide to the Underground Railroad.* New York: Hippocrene, 1994.

Buchanan, James (1791–1868)

The only U.S. president born in Pennsylvania, James Buchanan was native to a state that hosted major depots and routes of the Underground Railroad. He maintained animosity toward an abolitionist neighbor, attorney Thaddeus Stevens, a slave conductor in Lancaster, Pennsylvania. Backed by southern advisers, Buchanan entered the White House with the intent of appeasing southern planters by stifling anti-slavery agitators. During his term of office, his administration handed major defeats to abolitionists—the Dred Scott decision and the execution of insurrectionist John Brown for his failed raid on the federal arsenal at Harpers Ferry, Virginia, on October 16, 1859. After the rescue of John Price in Wellington, Ohio, on September 13, 1858, Buchanan orchestrated the indictment of 37 Underground Railroad agents for violation of the Fugitive Slave Law of 1850. Rising to the support of conductors, Joshua Reed Giddings held a rally in Cleveland, Ohio, on May 24, 1859, featuring the orators Salmon Portland Chase and John Mercer Langston, both of whom condemned the court action and disparaged Buchanan. In disgust at Buchanan's lack of compassion for runaway slaves, journalist Jane Grey Cannon Swisshelm labeled him the "slaveholders' tool."

In the last months of Buchanan's pro-South, pro-slavery presidency, from November 1860 to the inauguration of Abraham Lincoln in March 1861, Buchanan felt thwarted and frustrated at the declining unity of southern and northern factions and at protests of the Fugitive Slave Law of 1850. On December 1, 1860, he delivered a despairing State of the Union Address to Congress proposing a constitutional amendment confirming the right of slave owners to their human property. His inability to deal with threats of secession heightened traffic on the secret network as runaways sought safety in Canada. In one of his final official acts, in March 1861, Buchanan pardoned abolitionist organizer Sherman Miller Booth for inciting a mob to liberate Joshua Glover, a slave from St. Louis, Missouri, from jail on March 11, 1854, in Milwaukee County, Wisconsin. The pardon did little to retrieve Buchanan from the list of history's least admired national leaders.

See also: Fugitive Slave Law of 1850; routes, Underground Railroad.

Sources

Smith, Elbert B. *The Presidency of James Buchanan.* Lawrence: University Press of Kansas, 1976.

Walther, Eric H. *The Shattering of the Union: America in the 1850s.* Wilmington, DE: Scholarly Resources, 2004.

Buckout, Abram (1813–1884)

A conductor of the Underground Railroad, Abram Buckout collaborated in the smooth organization of rescues in Oswego, New York. From 1852 to national emancipation on January 1, 1863, he supported fugitive slaves while maintaining a reputation as a respectable businessman. Two of his associates, barber Charles Smith and Tudor E. Grant, concealed passengers at Buckout's barn behind his residence on West Fifth Street Road. Runaways continued on their way north over Lake Ontario to Kingston, Ontario.

Source

History of Oswego County, New York. Philadelphia: L.H. Everts, 1877.

Buffum, Arnold (1782–1859)
Buffum, Rebecca Gould (1781–1818)

Quaker hatmaker Arnold Buffum of Providence, Rhode Island, and Rebecca Gould Buffum introduced their children to concern for runaway slaves. They married in January 1804 and, in 1828, settled at Fall River, Massachusetts. The first president of the New England Anti-Slavery Society, Arnold Buffum was a collaborator with Oliver Johnson, the Reverend Samuel Joseph May, and Samuel Edmund Sewall, who enlisted Buffum as a proponent of the young William Lloyd Garrison. Arnold Buffum co-formed the American Anti-Slavery Society and served as a lecturer and anti-slavery essayist. He carried his platform oratory from the Atlantic coast to Ohio and Illinois, where he enlisted volunteers to aid the secret network. In 1834, the Buffums relocated to Philadelphia, where Arnold Buffum sold subscriptions to Garrison's weekly, *The Liberator.* The family produced two devoted workers for the Underground Railroad—Sarah Gould Buffum Borden, wife of Nathaniel Briggs Borden, a stationkeeper in Fall River, Massachusetts, and Sarah's younger sister, Elizabeth Buffum Chace, wife of Samuel Buffington Chace, both philanthropists and supporters of fugitive slaves.

See also: American Anti-Slavery Society; *Liberator, The*; philanthropists.

Source

Ripley, C. Peter, et al., eds. *The Black Abolitionist Papers.* Chapel Hill: University of North Carolina Press, 1992.

Bull, Jason (1793–1861)
Bull, Delia Matoon (1796–1843)
Bull, Sarah Sawyer (1805–1892)

A noted Methodist conductor of the Underground Railroad, the Reverend Jason Bull and his wife, Delia Matoon Bull, received runaways at their home and church. They married in 1815. As part of the Ripley–Canada line, the couple collaborated with the Reverend James Preston Poindexter, pastor of Second Baptist Church at 186 North Seventeenth Street in Columbus, Ohio. Poindexter hired teamster Louis Washington and his son, Robert Washington, to transport runaways to the Bull family's waystation at Clintonville, Ohio. Runaways hid in burrows within the church woodpile. The Bulls' children supplied food and water. During the period from 1840 to 1849, when a state law outlawed sheltering runaway slaves, Bull and his co-conspirators risked heavy fines for their activism. After Delia's death in 1843, Jason Bull married Sarah Sawyer Bull, who continued their volunteer work.

Source

Cheek, William, and Aimee Lee Cheek. *John Mercer Langston and the Fight for Black Freedom, 1829–1865.* Champaign: University of Illinois Press, 1996.

Bulla, William (1777–1862)
Hoover, Andrew (1752–1834)

In a rare case of aggressive Quaker rescue of a fugitive, William Bulla conspired in a plot to liberate a runaway slave. With his Quaker brother-in-law, Andrew Hoover, Bulla helped a fugitive, Peter Todd, the chattel of Samuel Todd of Kentucky, escape two slave catchers. The pursuers reached Wayne County, Indiana, in spring 1825—four years after Peter Todd had fled bondage—and captured him on June 18. Because Bulla and Hoover freed Peter Todd, Samuel Todd sued them for $1,500 for loss of property and costs. A relative, Judge David Hoover, counseled Bulla and Hoover to pay the owner $1,000 for Peter Todd rather than face an indictment for slave stealing.

Source

McLean, Hulda Hoover. *Genealogy of One Branch of the Hoover Family.* Rancho del Oso, CA: self-published, 1959.

Burghardt, Mary Eliza Jones (1842–1898)

Two Underground Railroad passengers passing through Warsaw in Wyoming County, New York, succeeded thanks to the good will of secret operatives. In 1849, Mary Jones (also called Anna Jones and Mary Douglas) led Mary Eliza (or Lila), her seven-year-old child, on a 20-day flight. Agent Cyrus Osborne, a greengrocer, directed them from Washington, D.C., to East Hill, New York. An abolitionist farmer concealed them in a hidden compartment of a farm wagon and covered them with vegetables for the ride to the heavily traveled depot at Warsaw. At the safehouse operated by Elizabeth Beedon Smallwood and Michael Smallwood, an Englishman from Yorkshire, Mary Jones gave birth to Charles William Jones.

At Mary's death from tuberculosis, the infant passed into the care of D.C. Martin. Merchant Allen Y. Breck and his wife, Isabella Breck, fostered Mary Eliza Jones at their home on West Buffalo Street. In 1864, Jones married a free black barber, William Burghardt, settled at the intersection of Center and Orchard streets, and operated a catering business. For Warsaw's bicentennial, the United Church of Warsaw presented three performances of Harvey Granite's play about the runaways entitled *The Woman in the Box* (2002).

Source

Phelan, Helene C. *And Why Not Every Man?* Almond, NY: privately published, 1987.

Burkett, Elizabeth (fl. 1860s)
Burkett, Henry (fl. 1860s)

A slave couple, Elizabeth Burkett and Henry Burkett, enlisted the aid of the Underground Railroad to free them from bondage. In 1860, the Burketts joined Hale Burton, John Purnell, Mary Ann Sipple, and Thomas Sipple in fleeing Kunkletown in Worcester County, Maryland. The fugitives bought a boat and, while defending themselves from bounty hunters, followed the coastline from Delaware Bay toward Philadelphia. At Cape May, New Jersey, a sea captain took them the remaining distance by oyster boat. At the office of William Still in Philadelphia, they connected with John W. Jones, an agent who relayed the group along the secret network.

See also: bounty hunters.

Source

Still, William. *The Underground Railroad.* Philadelphia: Porter & Coates, 1871.

Burkle, Jacob (1834–1874)

Legendary Underground Railroad agent Jacob Burkle, an immigrant from Germany, operated Slave Haven, a safehouse in Memphis, Tennessee. After his flight from Germany to escape required service in the army of Otto von Bismarck, Burkle made a substantial living off his bakery and stockyards. In 1859, he applied for American citizenship. His one-story white clapboard residence at 826 North Second Street harbored runaways from 1859 until the national emancipation of slaves on January 1, 1863.

Burkle's location near a thick forest three blocks from the Mississippi River enabled him to conceal passengers in a basement chamber and in adjacent tunnels until he could supply them with bogus liberty papers and passage on a river steamer. As a cover for his relay of slaves, he kept a small house staff and occasionally reported some of them missing. One grateful passenger wrote a letter thanking Burkle for his aid. Since 1983, the house has been a museum.

Source

Busbee, James. "The Persistence of Folklore." *Memphis Flier,* February 27, 1997, 1.

Burleigh, Charles Callistus (1810–1878)
Burleigh, Cyrus Moses (1820–1855)

A convert of the Reverend Theodore Dwight Weld, attorney and orator Charles Callistus Burleigh (or Burly) supported the work of the American Anti-Slavery Society. In his hometown of Plainfield, in Windham County, Connecticut, he attended college at age 11 and began teaching school three years later. In Brooklyn, New York, he edited the *Brooklyn Unionist* and lectured on behalf of temperance and abolitionism. While he wrote for the *Pennsylvania Freeman*, he received aid from his younger brother, abolitionist Cyrus Moses Burleigh, also from Plainfield. In the February 20, 1851 issue, Cyrus Burleigh reported on the dangers that free blacks faced from "land pirates," who abducted victims in the dead of night and profited by selling them into bondage.

At the residence of Elizabeth Buffum Chase and Samuel Buffington Chace, Charles Burleigh joined organizers William Wells Brown, Abby Kelley Foster and Stephen Symons Foster, Wendell Addison Phillips, Parker Pillsbury, Charles Remond, and Henry C. Wright to plan strategy and enhance routes. One of Charles Burleigh's jobs was enlisting new conductors for the Underground Railroad; one such recruit was Dr. Bartholomew Fussell, a Quaker physician from Chester County, Pennsylvania. Charles Burleigh also promoted the volunteerism of conductors Oliver Johnson in Peacham, Vermont; Daniel Howell Hise and Margaret Hise in Salem, Ohio; Elizabeth Maxwell Monroe and the Reverend James Monroe in Oberlin, Ohio; and Amelia Kirk Russell and John Neal Russell in Drumore, Pennsylvania.

In the execution of his duties, Charles Burleigh frequently stood in harm's way. In 1835, he shielded William Lloyd Garrison during mob violence in Boston, where a pro-slavery faction threatened lynching. In 1839, a human blockade prohibited Charles Burleigh from speaking at Bristol, Pennsylvania. Quakers rescued him and offered him the podium at their meeting house. When Burleigh was arrested in Oxford, Pennsylvania, Underground Railroad operative Simon Barnard bailed him out of the West Chester County jail. After passage of the Fugitive Slave Act of 1850, pro-slavery rowdies pelted the carriage of Burleigh and Lindley Coates with rotten eggs.

Working in league with Caleb C. Hood, Cyrus Burleigh was a major player in Erie County on the Pennsylvania–Canada route. No less committed than his brother Charles, in 1851, Cyrus and his wife, Margaret Jones Burleigh, served the executive committee of the Pennsylvania Anti-Slavery Society along with Mary Grew, Abby Kimber, James Miller McKim, Sarah Pugh, and Robert Purvis. Cyrus Burleigh also supported the rescue work of fellow Quaker agents James Mott, Jr., and Lucretia Coffin Mott and the rehabilitation center that the Lewis sisters, Elizabeth, Graceanna, Mariann, and Rebecca, maintained for sick or injured refugees. The Burleighs aided a slave named Maria, the mother of nine children. Maria fled alone after learning that she had been sold south. She remained at agent William Howard Hood's station until winter, when her escaped son found work in Massachusetts and sent for her. Burleigh arranged the transportation to Philadelphia, where Maria and her son reunited.

See also: American Anti-Slavery Society; Quakers; routes, Underground Railroad.

Sources

Bowen, Clarence Winthrop. *History of Woodstock Connecticut.* Norwood, MA: self-published, 1943.

Peters, Pamela R. *The Underground Railroad in Floyd County, Indiana.* Jefferson, NC: McFarland, 2001.

Burlingame, Almond A. (1812–1898) Burlingame, Jane A. Halland (1815–1881)

At Sparta in Randolph County, Illinois, manufacturer Almond A. Burlingame, a native of Adams, Massachusetts, and his wife, Jane A. Halland Burlingame, joined their neighbors in aiding fugitives fleeing along Underground Railroad routes. After their marriage in 1835, they settled in Nisbits Corners, New York. As part of his wagon, pump, and plywood business, Almond Burlingame rolled slaves in carpet and relayed them in his rig while on deliveries to customers. For convenience, he crossed the Mississippi River where the main channel narrows at Liberty (now Rockwood), Illinois.

See also: bloodhounds.

Source

Richards, Becky. "The Underground Railroad in Southwestern Illinois." *Illinois History* (February 1996): 28–29.

Burnett, Cornelius (fl. 1830s–1840s)

On June 25, 1841, Cornelius Burnett, a British subject, and his three sons supported the Cincinnati Anti-Slavery Society by harboring a refugee from Kentucky traveling the Ohio–Canada line. Burnett began service to the secret network around 1830. When a local pro-slavery faction raised an uproar and besieged the Burnett residence, authorities arrested the Burnetts for accosting a slave owner and Constable Robert Black. Burnett chose jail rather than payment of a $3,000 bond. Proof of Burnett's complicity with the Underground Railroad came from a letter that the *Cincinnati Enquirer* published in September 1841, when race riots raged in the city.

Source

Griffler, Keith P. *Front Line of Freedom: African Americans and the Forging of the Underground Railroad in the Ohio Valley.* Lexington: University Press of Kentucky, 2004.

Burns, Anthony (ca. 1824–1862)

The flight of Anthony Burns was the third in a series of tests of the Boston Underground Railroad's defiance of the Fugitive Slave Act of 1850. Burns lived in Richmond, Virginia, in the possession of Colonel Charles F. Suttle. On March 24, 1854, Burns fled to Boston to work in the clothing shop of Coffin Pitts. Suttle learned of Burns's whereabouts by intercepting a letter from the runaway to his brother in Richmond. According to Burns's side of the story, which journalist William Lloyd Garrison printed in *The Liberator* on March 9, 1855, Suttle had Boston authorities arrest Burns on a bogus charge of breaking into a silversmith's shop. Underground Railroad attorneys John Albion Andrew, Robert Morris, and Richard Henry Dana, Jr., made an unsuccessful attempt to defend Burns in late May 1854.

The recapture and transportation of Burns attested to the difficulty U.S. marshals had in returning runaways to their owners. According to the *Life of Rev. Thomas James, by Himself* (1886), 25 federal agents from New York, Philadelphia, Richmond, and Washington, D.C., assembled secretly for the foray. Under command of Marshal Watson Freeman and U.S. Commissioner Edward G. Loring, on May 24, 1854, the authorities seized the runaway from his workplace at the intersection of Cambridge and Hanover streets. They clapped him in manacles and informed onlookers that Burns was wanted for robbing a jewelry store. Boston attorney John Albion Andrew, later governor of Massachusetts, headed the legal defense team as he had for Thomas Sims, a previous test case of the onerous law.

Abolitionists, inspired by orator Stephen Symons Foster of Pelham, Massachusetts, immediately distributed handbills to Underground Railroad agents along the Virginia–Boston line. Assemblies studied the matter at Meionaon Hall and Faneuil Hall, where orators Wendell Addison Phillips and Theodore Parker spoke on May 26, 1854. They offered $1,300 for Burns's freedom, but the marshals rejected the deal. An angry mob led by the Reverend Thomas Wentworth Higginson converged from as far away as Lowell, Massachusetts. They distributed axes and beams and battered the courthouse door, but two artillery regiments from Fort Warren and the Charlestown Navy Yard restored order. Lewis Hayden, Boston's prominent Underground Railroad stationmaster and member of the executive board of the city's vigilance committee, attempted to steer the court case to an abolitionist judge. The foiled attempt at mob violence left one police officer, James Batchelder, dead, shot by Martin Stowell. The failure of the effort forced Hayden to press suit against the slave owner for $10,000.

THE
BOSTON SLAVE RIOT,
AND
TRIAL
OF
Anthony Burns,

CONTAINING THE
REPORT OF THE FANEUIL HALL MEETING; THE MURDER OF BACHELDER; THEODORE PARKER'S LESSON FOR THE DAY; SPEECHES OF COUNSEL ON BOTH SIDES, CORRECTED BY THEMSELVES; VERBATIM REPORT OF JUDGE LORING'S DECISION; AND, A DETAILED ACCOUNT OF THE EMBARKATION.

BOSTON:
FETRIDGE AND COMPANY.
1854.

Press of J. S. Potter & Co., 2 Spring Lane and 130 Washington Street.

The case of Anthony Burns, formerly of Virginia, became an abolitionist cause célèbre after slave hunters captured him in Boston and, under the Fugitive Slave Law, forced him back to bondage. *(MPI/Stringer/Hulton Archive/Getty Images)*

Burns relied on an illiterate accomplice to deliver letters to attorney Richard Henry Dana. The uproar over the prisoner's exit stirred Bostonians to amass in the streets while church bells tolled and shopkeepers draped their doors in black crepe. One protester suspended a black coffin from a third-story window. In mid-June 1854, a flimsy charge of inciting a riot with abolitionist speeches and interfering with the duties of a U.S. marshal failed to get an indictment against Higginson, Phillips, and Parker. After Burns's return to Virginia, abolitionists raised funds to purchase his freedom, including a donation of $1,300 from the Twelfth Baptist Church in Boston, pastored by agent Leonard Andrew Grimes, who kept watch on Burns

According to the historian George Lunt, proponents of the Underground Railroad met at Faneuil Hall and stirred up crowds to protest the arrest of Anthony Burns: "In the condition of popular sentiment in Boston at the period in question, a dozen or two resolute officers might have taken the slave to the vessel which was to convey him to Georgia, at noonday, without the least danger of serious tumult. But word was given out previously of the day chosen for the purpose; the militia, to the number of probably a thousand men, were turned out, together with the marines in considerable force, from the neighboring navy yard, with their cannon, and lined the streets through which the procession was to pass. Rural people thronged into the city, and, doubtless, more than a hundred thousand persons witnessed the demonstration. Burns himself, who had been treated with great kindness during his detention, and who had been provided with a new and shining black suit for the occasion, by the bounty, it was understood, of the pro-slavery supporters of the law, looked like any thing but a victim; he marched with an air, and was said to have felt highly flattered by the novel distinction conferred upon him" (*The Origin of the Late War* [1866]). The military overreaction indicates a nervousness at popular reaction and a respect for the ability of abolitionists to mount a sizeable revolt in short order.

through grapevine telegraphy. The minister volunteered to negotiate directly with Colonel Suttle to obtain freedom papers. Meanwhile, Suttle shoved Burns behind a trapdoor for six months of imprisonment before selling him to a slave dealer to work as a coachman. The whole episode cost Suttle and the state and federal government over $20,000. Afterward, Burns described his experiences on the abolitionist lecture circuit until his death in Canada from tuberculosis. In November 1855, his battle with the Reverend John Clark, Baptist pastor of the Church of Jesus Christ in Union, Virginia, denounced Baptists for excommunicating Burns the previous October for running away from his master. In 1856, Charles Emery Stevens, an eyewitness and strategist of the jailbreak, published a biography, *Anthony Burns: A History,* which dramatizes cries of "Kidnappers!" as officers hauled Burns to the dockyard.

See also: Liberator, The.

Sources

Barnes, Joseph W., ed. "The Autobiography of Rev. Thomas James." *Rochester History* 37:4 (October 1975).

Pearson, Henry Greenleaf. *The Life of John A. Andrew, Governor of Massachusetts, 1861–1865.* Boston: Houghton Mifflin, 1904.

Roth, Ronica. "The Trial of Anthony Burns." *Humanities* 24:3 (May–June 2003).

Burr, James E. (fl. 1840s)
Thompson, George (fl. 1840s)
Work, Alanson (fl. 1840s)

James E. Burr and two fellow ministerial students, George Thompson and carpenter Alanson Work, accepted an assignment from abolitionist David Nelson's Mission Institute in Quincy, Illinois, to rescue slaves on the opposite shore of the Mississippi River. On July 12, 1841, the three abolitionists were arrested for traveling to Palmyra in Marion County, Missouri, in search of slaves belonging to R. N. Woolfolk to conduct them to freedom in Canada. According to a report in the *Illinois Republican* on July 23, 1841, the slaves, working near the Fabius River, betrayed the white agents, whom local slave owners held at gunpoint and threatened to lynch. Sentenced by a circuit court to a 12-year term on September 15, 1841, the trio began cell time at hard labor in the Missouri state penitentiary in Jefferson City for grand larceny.

Editorials in William Lloyd Garrison's *The Liberator* and the Reverend Edward R. Tyler's *Connecticut Observor* in Hartford opposed the harsh sentences. A lengthy letter and petition campaign from Underground Railroad agents to Governor John Cummins Edwards collected the signatures of 200 people, including Phebe Work, Alanson Work's sister, who offered to take his place in prison. Work was released after 43 months. Burr, whose arm was crushed up to the elbow in a bagging machine, remained another 11 months. Thompson served five years.

As a result of Thompson's risky slave rescues, Missourians formed vigilance committees to question outsiders about their business. Because Mark Twain's father, John Marshall Clemens, served on the jury, the author, then age six, attended the trial, which he referred to in *A Scrap of Curious History* (1903).

See also: vigilance committees.

Sources

Smith, E.H. "Squire Clemens, Father of 'Mark Twain,' Insisted on Keeping Peace." *Chicago Daily Tribune,* November 21, 1909, J22.

Thompson, George. *Prison Life and Reflections: or, A Narrative of the Arrest, Trial, Conviction, Imprisonment, Treatment, Observations, Reflections, and Deliverance of Work, Burr, and Thompson.* Hartford, CT: Alanson Work, 1849.
Trexler, Harrison Anthony. *Slavery in Missouri, 1804–1865.* Baltimore: Johns Hopkins Press, 1914.

Burrell, Robbins (1799–1887)
Burrell, Eliza Brigham (1801–1870)
Burrell, Jabez Lyman, Jr. (1806–1900)

Farmer Robbins Burrell networked with agents in Oberlin, Ohio, to direct runaways to Canada. After leaving his birthplace in Sheffield, in Berkshire County, Massachusetts, he settled with his parents in Sheffield Village, Ohio, in 1815. On 740 acres at 2792 East River Road, the elder Jabez Burrell erected a two-story residence of split oak beams and bricks hand made at Sugar Creek. Under the management of his sons, the property was known as Station 100. From the 1840s, Robbins Burrell and his wife, Eliza Brigham Burrell, concealed refugees in their barn and cheese house before relaying them two miles to the next stop in the hidden chamber in his produce wagon. During layovers, runaways slept in upstairs halls or sheltered in a dry water tank, accessed through a trapdoor in the dining room.

Aiding the couple after 1851 was Robbins's younger brother, Jabez (also Jaybez or Jaybezz) Lyman Burrell, Jr., who lived at 315 East College Street. Jabez superintended hiding places in the barn and grain house. He also shuttled passengers into a water tank through a trapdoor in the dining room of his home at 315 East College Street in Oberlin. Jabez Burrell cofounded Oberlin College, an active station of the secret railway. State historians speculate that the Burrell brothers, along with Oberlin students, may have aided John Price, the runaway freed by the Oberlin-Wellington rescue on September 13, 1858.

For water transport, Robbins Burrell depended on a cousin, Captain Aaron (or Arron) Root, who operated a boatworks on Lake Erie. Root placed passengers on ships at Big Bottom, on the Black River, bound for Charleston (now called Lorain), Ohio. The last leg of the journey was only 20 miles across the lake to Ontario. Because of Robbins Burrell's activity, federal marshals watched his home and raided it several times. Both Jabez and Robbins Burrell fought on the Union side during the Civil War. The Burrell homestead, now a museum, is listed on the National Register of Historic Places.

See also: Oberlin College.

Source

Robinson, Alice. "Underground Railroad Connections." *Lisbon (OH) Morning Journal,* February 18, 2001.

Burris, Samuel D. (1808–1868)

A freedman agent of the Underground Railroad, Samuel D. Burris led refugees to the station of Rachel Mendenhall Garrett and Thomas Garrett in Wilmington, Delaware. Burris was born free in Willow Grove, in Kent County, Delaware, and affiliated with the Appoquinimink Friends Meeting House in Odessa, where associate John Hunn hid runaways in 1844. While living in Philadelphia, Burris began

A free black from Delaware, Samuel Burris made repeated rescue trips across the Mason-Dixon line beginning in 1845. After his capture and sentencing to the auction block, abolitionists posing as slave traders purchased him and set him free. *(Schomburg Center for Research in Black Culture/Manuscripts, Archives and Rare Books Division/New York Public Library/ Astor, Lenox, and Tilden Foundations)*

traveling across the Mason-Dixon line in 1845 to aid blacks in Delaware and Maryland. Risking the loss of his own freedom if caught, he collaborated with operatives Harriet Forten Purvis, Robert Purvis, and William Still. In December 1845, one transfer required trudging through snow some 25 miles north with four runaway slaves. A larger party—Emeline and Sam Hawkins and their four children and two other children from Queen Anne County, Maryland—required transfer by Burris's wagon team to Camden, Delaware.

While escorting Maria Mathews from Dover Hundred in June 1847, Burris was arrested and jailed for 14 months. After his conviction for theft, he faced the auction block. While impersonating a slaver, Isaac A. Flint, a member of the Pennsylvania Anti-Slavery Society, carried funds raised by Thomas Garrett, John Hunn, and the Reverend James Miller McKim of Carlisle, Pennsylvania. Flint examined Burris thoroughly and then purchased him for $500 and returned him north. Although Burris curtailed his ventures south, he remained active in the cause of liberty until he resettled in Strawberry, California, in 1852. After 1865, he solicited donations to clothe and educate ex-slaves.

Sources

Newton, James E. "The Underground Railroad in Delaware." *Negro History Bulletin* 40:3 (1977): 702–3.

Simmons, William J. *Men of Mark: Eminent, Progressive, and Rising.* Cleveland, OH: George M. Rewell, 1887.

Burroughs, George L. (fl. 1840s–1850s)

A courageous black pilot of runaway slaves, George L. Burroughs relayed passengers of the Underground Railroad to safety. At Cairo, Illinois, he used his job as a Pullman porter aboard the Illinois Central Railroad as an opportunity to transport runaways. The depot, located at the confluence of the Mississippi and Ohio rivers, was constantly under surveillance by U.S. marshals and bounty hunters. When the train reached Chicago, detective Allan Pinkerton took charge of the fugitives and boarded some at his residence under the care of his wife, Joan Carfrae Pinkerton.

See also: bounty hunters.

Sources

Mackay, James. *Allan Pinkerton, the First Private Eye.* New York: Wiley, 1996.

"The Underground Railroad: A Stop in Tamaroa," *Southern Illinoisan,* 2004.

Burt, Elijah (1742–1820)
Burt, Deborah Colton (1745–1792)

Elijah Burt maintained the only secret waystation at East Longmeadow, in Hampden County, Massachusetts. Located at 201 Chestnut Street, the two-story wood frame house was a stagecoach stop built in 1702. Elijah married Deborah Colton in 1767. When the Burts bought the house, the dwelling featured a secret stair to the basement, where the couple hid runaways. In 1976, it was listed on the National Register of Historic Places.

Source

Hess, John Y. *East Longmeadow.* Charleston, SC: Arcadia, 2000.

Bush, William (1798–1866)
Bush, Lucinda Clark (1805–?)

A grocer and rescuer of slaves on the Atlantic coast, Deacon William Bush, a mulatto, knew from experience the difficulties confronting a fugitive. Born free in Loudoun County, Virginia, he came from a family of libertarians, notably, his uncle, the Reverend Leonard Andrew Grimes of Boston. In 1849, Bush married and left Washington, D.C. He settled in New Bedford, Massachusetts, an active slave rescue center and the home of his wife, Lucinda "Lucy" Clark Bush, a former slave of James Pumphry in Maryland. Lucy may have abetted the flight of 77 runaways aboard the *Pearl* on April 15, 1848.

While operating a chain of three coastal inns—at Six Coffin Street, and at 36 and 69 South Water Street—Lucinda and William Bush received parties of runaways, who sheltered at their residence on 128 Third Street. The couple supported Captain Daniel Drayton, who was imprisoned for his role in the unprecedented flight from bondage.

In 1853, the couple welcomed George Teamoh, a homeless fugitive who remained with them through the winter until he found work in the shipyard. In his autobiography, *God Made Man, Man Made the Slave* (1990), he commended the couple for their mercy and dedication to slave rescue.

Source

Teamoh, George. *God Made Man, Man Made the Slave.* Macon, GA: Mercer University Press, 1990.

Bush, William (fl. 1820s–1840s)

A runaway from the South, William Bush reached the waystation of Catherine and Levi Coffin in Newport, Indiana. Bush wore wooden clogs that he had carved for the journey. After his arrival, he established a blacksmith shop and helped other fugitives over the secret network. Local people lauded his courage for burying victims of an epidemic.

Source

Blockson, Charles L. "Escape from Slavery: The Underground Railroad." *National Geographic* 166:1 (July 1984): 2–39.

Bushong, Henry (1783–1870)

At Quarryville, Quaker activist Henry Bushong (also Beauchamp), a Franco-American Underground Railroad agent, maintained Station 10, a busy terminal at a pivotal point on the Pilgrim's Pathway, the 17-stage route through Lancaster County in southern Pennsylvania. His passengers arrived from John Neal Russell, Thomas Pownall, Oliver Furniss, Tacy Shoemaker Smith, and Joseph Smith in Drumore. Before conveying refugees by hay wagon to the next depot, Bushong concealed them behind a half door in an attic closet or in a stone outbuilding constructed by freedman Moses Johnson.

One local man, Hamilton Moore, who bore a Caucasian appearance, faced reclamation by his slave owner father. Neighbors repulsed the pursuers and ferried Moore to Bushong, who piloted him to a safehouse. After Bushong settled in Bart, in summer 1835, with his second wife, Esther Valentine Gilbert Bushong (1799–1867), he aided William "Snow" Wallace in his flight from the Carolinas through Joshua Gilbert's depot. In spring 1836, Bushong received Moses Johnson, a runaway slave from Frederick, Maryland. A more pressing case was the rescue of an injured woman and her daughter in 1832; the woman's lashed back had become infected from 500 strokes of the cat-o'-nine-tails. Her owner had brutalized her for refusing to reveal the location of one of her escaped children. Bushong escorted both mother and daughter east to the next station.

See also: Pilgrim's Pathway.

Source

Smedley, Robert C. *History of the Underground Railroad in Chester and the Neighboring Counties of Pennsylvania.* Lancaster, PA: Office of *The Journal,* 1883.

Bushong, Jacob (1813–1880)
Bushong, Margaret Hobson (1818–?)

The son of abolitionist Henry Bushong and a member of the Lancaster County, Pennsylvania, stationmasters, Jacob Bushong and his wife, Margaret Hobson Bushong, lived in Bart, a crucial stop on the Underground Railroad. In summer 1835, they helped William "Snow" Wallace to hide from six slave catchers, who bound and transported Wallace's wife and oldest child to the county jail. Lodging the woman in jail with the wife of John Urick, the pursuers departed to search for other runaways. Aiding Jacob and Margaret Bushong's rescue operations were Edith Kinsey Paxson Bushong (1837–?) and her husband, Jacob's half-brother, Gilbert Bushong (1836–1911).

Source

Smedley, Robert C. *History of the Underground Railroad in Chester and the Neighboring Counties of Pennsylvania.* Lancaster, PA: Office of *The Journal,* 1883.

Bustill, Joseph Cassey (1822–1895)

One of a covey of activists at the Longwood Meeting in Kennett Square, Pennsylvania, Joseph Cassey Bustill supported the efforts of some of the most outspoken abolitionists of antebellum America. Born to prominent black Philadelphians, he began his activism in 1839. He taught school in Harrisburg, Pennsylvania, and co-founded the First Colored Presbyterian Church. He collaborated with agents Thomas Morris Chester and Mary and William Jones in Harrisburg and with Underground Railroad supervisor William Still, chairman of the Vigilance Committee of the Pennsylvania Anti-Slavery Society. Bustill's daughter, Anna Bustill Smith, credits her father with safeguarding over 1,000 runaways, some of whom he hid at the Wesley Union American Methodist Episcopal Zion Church.

Bustill co-formed the Harrisburg Fugitive Slave Society. In spring 1856, he began routing escapees through a black community at Cranberry Street in Harrisburg, Pennsylvania, known as Tanner's Alley. On March 28, he corresponded with John S. Fiery of Washington County, Maryland, concerning negotiations for liberating the Taylor family—Mary Ann and Owen Taylor and their son Edward, who had fled north to freedom in a stolen carriage and horses.

Aided by Judge John James Pearson, a justice of the peace, Bustill juggled placements in residences, American Methodist Episcopal and Presbyterian churches, halls, and lodges. In the mid-1850s, he hid slaves at his safehouse on Cranberry Street, only a block from the sanctuary of Mary Jones and Dr. William "Pap" Jones. Bustill used the Reading & Pennsylvania rail line for transporting groups of fugitives to safety.

See also: African Methodist Episcopal Church.

Source

Smith, Anna Bustill. "The Bustill Family." *Journal of Negro History* 10:4 (October 1925): 641.

Butler, Benjamin Franklin (1818–1893)

A hero of the Civil War, General Benjamin Franklin "Beast" Butler aided runaways fleeing the collapsing southern economy. A native of Deerfield, New Hampshire, he studied law and served in the Massachusetts state legislature. During the Civil War, he conspired with Elizabeth Van Lew, an informant and Underground Railroad depot manager in Richmond, Virginia. Upon the occupation of Baltimore, Maryland, on May 13, 1861, he began receiving slaves eager for liberty. On the night of May 23, 1861, Frank Baker, Shepherd Mallory, and James Townsend, field hands of Colonel Charles Mallory, approached Fort Monroe outside Hampton Roads, Virginia, near the mouth of the Chesapeake Bay. To avoid being pressed into service in the rebel army in South Carolina, the trio volunteered to aid General Benjamin Franklin Butler.

Butler sheltered the three escapees from recapture and gave them work building a military bakery. He ridiculed Shepherd Mallory, a citizen of a state no longer in the Union, for citing as authority the Fugitive Slave Law of 1850. News of Butler's welcome to black contraband encouraged hundreds of escapees to shelter in Fort Monroe. In August 1861, the U.S. Congress legitimized Butler's assistance to runaways by passing the Confiscation Act, which sanctioned the receipt of escaping slaves into military encampments. To further the Union cause, Butler organized black soldiers into the First Louisiana Native Guards.

See also: black soldiers; Civil War; Fugitive Slave Law of 1850.

Source

Casstevens, Frances H. *Edward A. Wild and the African Brigade in the Civil War.* Jefferson, NC: McFarland, 2003.

Butler, Morris (1804–1875)

Morris Butler maintained the final stop on the underground route from Buffalo, New York, to Canada. His house at Linwood Avenue and West Utica Street was built in 1857. His involvement as a railway conductor remained hidden until the late 1890s, when the structure was razed. Historians discovered that the carpenter who constructed the residence provided hiding places flanking the front entrance. The niches were accessible from the basement.

Sources

"Butler," *Buffalo (NY) Daily Courier,* January 13, 1875, 2.

Severance, Frank H. *Old Trails on the Niagara Frontier.* Buffalo, NY: n.p., 1899.

Butterworth, Henry Thomas (1809–1893) Butterworth, Nancy Irvin Wales (1810–1909)

Henry Thomas Butterworth and his wife, Nancy Irvin (or Irwin) Wales Butterworth, a North Carolina cousin of Levi Coffin, labored in Ohio as conductors of the Underground Railroad. Henry Butterworth was the Quaker son of a Lynchburg, Virginia, planter who liberated his slaves. The family safehouse was a two-story stone structure built into a hill on the Little Miami River at Foster in Warren County north of Lebanon. Slaves hid among sweet potatoes in the root cellar. Henry Butterworth delivered passengers to Nancy's sister and brother-in-law, Jane Finley Wales Nicholson and Valentine Nicholson, in Harveysburg. As a cover for the relays, he took along his daughter, Jane Wales Butterworth (1831–?). After passage of the Fugitive Slave Law of 1850, the Butterworths ceased their operation. At Henry Butterworth's funeral, the casket was borne by black and white pallbearers.

See also: Fugitive Slave Law of 1850.

Source

Bogan, Dallas. *Warren County, Ohio, and Beyond.* Bowie, MD: Heritage Press, 1979.

Byrd, John Huntington (1816–1897)
Byrd, Elizabeth Adelaide Lowe (1821–1912)

A farmer, circuit rider, and missionary, the Reverend John Huntington Byrd of Vergennes, Vermont, joined an Underground Railroad team passing runaways through Lawrence, Kansas. After training at Oberlin College, in 1847, he married Elizabeth Adelaide Lowe of Vienna, New York, and began a ministry on the frontier. He conducted a mission in Sicily, Ohio, and, in 1854, pastored a Congregational church in Atchison, Kansas. In April 1857, he directed a female slave to Tabor, where she passed to the care of agent George B. Hitchcock and donned a cloak, gloves, and veil for the route from Lewis, Iowa. In 1860, Byrd supported others of the Territorial Executive Committee seeking relief for Kansas settlers beset by race wars and drought.

See also: Oberlin College.

Source

Todd, John. *Early Settlement and Growth of Western Iowa; or, Reminiscences.* Des Moines: Historical Department of Iowa, 1906.

Cable, Jonathan R.W. (1799–1884) Cable, Sarah Booth (1809–1887)

The Reverend Jonathan R.W. Cable, an abolitionist Presbyterian at Farmer's College, offered his services to slaves crossing the Ohio River into Indiana. A native of Harford, New York, he established an Underground Railroad depot with his wife, Sarah Booth Cable of Long Meadow, Massachusetts. When Levi Coffin rescued a party of 28 Kentucky runaways from Lawrenceburg, Indiana, Jonathan Cable welcomed one buggy load and coordinated the fitting of shoes to ease the rest of the journey. He advised Coffin on a safe route through Hamilton, West Elkton, Eaton, Paris, and Newport, Indiana.

See also: routes, Underground Railroad.

Source

Coffin, Levi. *Reminiscences of Levi Coffin, the Reputed President of the Underground Railroad.* Cincinnati, OH: Western Tract Society, 1876.

Cain, Augustus Way (1809–1887) Cain, Lydia Ann Dickinson (1819–1867)

A Mennonite agent in league with Moses Whitson, Christian Frantz, and Samuel Brinton, Dr. Augustus Way Cain, a physician in West Sadsbury, Chester County, Pennsylvania, and his wife, Lydia Ann Dickinson Cain, saw spirited action on behalf of passengers of the Underground Railroad. In collaboration with Joseph Moore, Cain assisted in relaying passengers from Christiana to Ercildoun. After pro-slavery agents burned the barns of Deborah T. Simmons Coates and Lindley Coates and of Samuel Whitson in Sadsbury around 1850, Cain hired security guards to patrol his barn over the next two months. The morning of the Christiana Riot at the tenant house of Eliza Ann Elizabeth Howard Parker and William Parker on September 11, 1851, Cain extracted a bullet from the forearm of Henry C. Hopkins and another bullet from John Long's thigh. To maintain his innocence of civil disobedience, Cain refused to hear details of the riot.

See also: Christiana Riot; civil disobedience.

Source

Smedley, Robert C. *History of the Underground Railroad in Chester and the Neighboring Counties of Pennsylvania.* Lancaster, PA: Office of *The Journal,* 1883.

Campbell, Alexander (1779–1857)

A public servant and valuable conspirator and strategist of slave rescues, Dr. Alexander Campbell coengineered the Ohio–Canada network of Underground Railroad agents and depots. A native of Frederick County, Virginia, he settled on the Ohio River in Ripley, in Brown County, Ohio, in his late twenties. His home was the town's first courthouse. In 1809, Ohio citizens elected Campbell to the U.S. Senate.

At a crucial point along the northern border of the plantation South, Campbell opened a medical practice at his two-story home and office at 114 Front Street and continued his political career as speaker of the Ohio legislature. In 1835, he served as president of the Ripley Anti-Slavery Society with the Reverend James Gilliland as vice president. Campbell's assistance with rescues involved him with operatives Dr. Alfred Beasley at 124 Front Street, Rhoda Jones in the Africa Hill community, Nancy Wilson Collins and Nathaniel Collins and their sons in Ripley, and Catherine McCague and Thomas McCague at the North Star station. In Ripley, Campbell conspired with foundryman John P. Parker and with Jean Lowry Rankin and John Rankin at Liberty Hill. Dr. Campbell's sister, Jane Campbell McKeever, joined her husband, Matthew McKeever, and their two sons, the Reverend Thomas Campbell McKeever and the younger Matthew McKeever, in operating a waystation in Middletown, in Greene County, Pennsylvania. In 1912, Dr. Campbell was an honoree depicted on Ripley's Liberty Monument.

Source

Parker, John P. *John P. Parker, His Promised Land: The Autobiography of John P. Parker, Former Slave and Conductor on the Underground Railroad.* New York: W.W. Norton, 1996.

Campbell, John (1808–1891) Campbell, Elizabeth Caldwell Clarke (1815–1893)

An abolitionist foundryman and entrepreneur, John Campbell founded the iron industry in Lawrence County, Ohio, and channeled his earnings into the Underground Railroad. He was born in Georgetown, Ohio, and grew up in Ripley. Along the Ohio River, he began managing stores and investing in the river steamer *Banner.* In 1837, he married Elizabeth Caldwell Clarke, who was born to Scotch-Irish immigrants in Manchester, Ohio. The Campbells espoused Presbyterian beliefs that encouraged civil disobedience to an unjust federal law.

Under the influence of Jean Lowry Rankin and John Rankin, agents of the secret network at Liberty Hill in Ripley, Ohio, the Campbells joined the effort to save runaway slaves by concealing them in their residence in Ironton. In the early 1840s, John Campbell developed the iron business by building blast furnaces. With the profits from ironworks in Gallia, Mt. Vernon, and Ironton, the Campbells financed slave rescues in Pokepatch, Ohio, a settlement operated on behalf of escaping slaves. In the first week of the Civil War, Elizabeth Campbell sewed battle flags for the Union army.

See also: civil disobedience; Pokepatch, Ohio.

Source

Hudson, J. Blaine. *Fugitive Slaves and the Underground Railroad in the Kentucky Borderland.* Jefferson, NC: McFarland, 2002.

Camper, James (1833–?)

An escapee aboard the Underground Railroad, 24-year-old James Camper fled Maryland with four companions. In 1857, he joined 19-year-old Noah Ennells, 34-year-old William Griffen, 30-year-old Henry Moor, and 22-year-old Levin Parker. Camper initiated the flight from the ownership of Henry Hooper of Cambridge in Dorchester County, Maryland. The five runaways reached Philadelphia, Pennsylvania, and sought assistance from agents of the secret network.

Source

Still, William. *The Underground Railroad.* Philadelphia: Porter & Coates, 1871.

Canada

Variously called Freedom Land and Canaan, Canada held out hope and promise to runaway slaves, 80 percent of whom were healthy, productive males. After the American Revolution, Nova Scotia welcomed the first sizable community of former slaves. In 1783, the Black Pioneers Regiment, a Tory company of engineers and laborers led by Thomas Peters and Murphy Still, received free land and built the communities of Shelburne and Birchtown, home to 3,000 former slaves. Runaways to Nova Scotia settled black communities in Boylston, Guysborough, Hammond Plains, Lincolnville, Milford Haven, Preston, and Tracadie. These beginnings preceded Lieutenant Governor John Graves Simcoe's formal abolition of slavery throughout the provinces on July 9, 1793.

News of the haven in the north spread as soldiers returned from the War of 1812. Those tough enough and devoted to liberty provided Canada with an enduring strain of black and mulatto citizens. Receiving runaway children in Niagara, Ontario, were rescuers Richard Bury and the Reverend Francis Lacy, a blacksmith and Baptist preacher. In the July 22, 1826, issue of Benjamin Lundy and William Lloyd Garrison's anti-slavery newspaper, *Genius of Universal Emancipation,* Henry Clay, secretary of state under President John Quincy Adams, noted with displeasure that the escape of slaves to refuge in foreign countries had reached such proportions that the president was studying the matter. Despite objections of the Canadian government to mass immigration, white settlers welcomed blacks to the area north of

> Newcomers to Canada from the American South confronted winter conditions of a ferocity they could never have imagined. Yet, trading bondage in a warm climate for freedom in the North was an easy choice; as one passenger of the Underground Railroad remarked, "I prefer snow and frost to de crack of the slave whip."

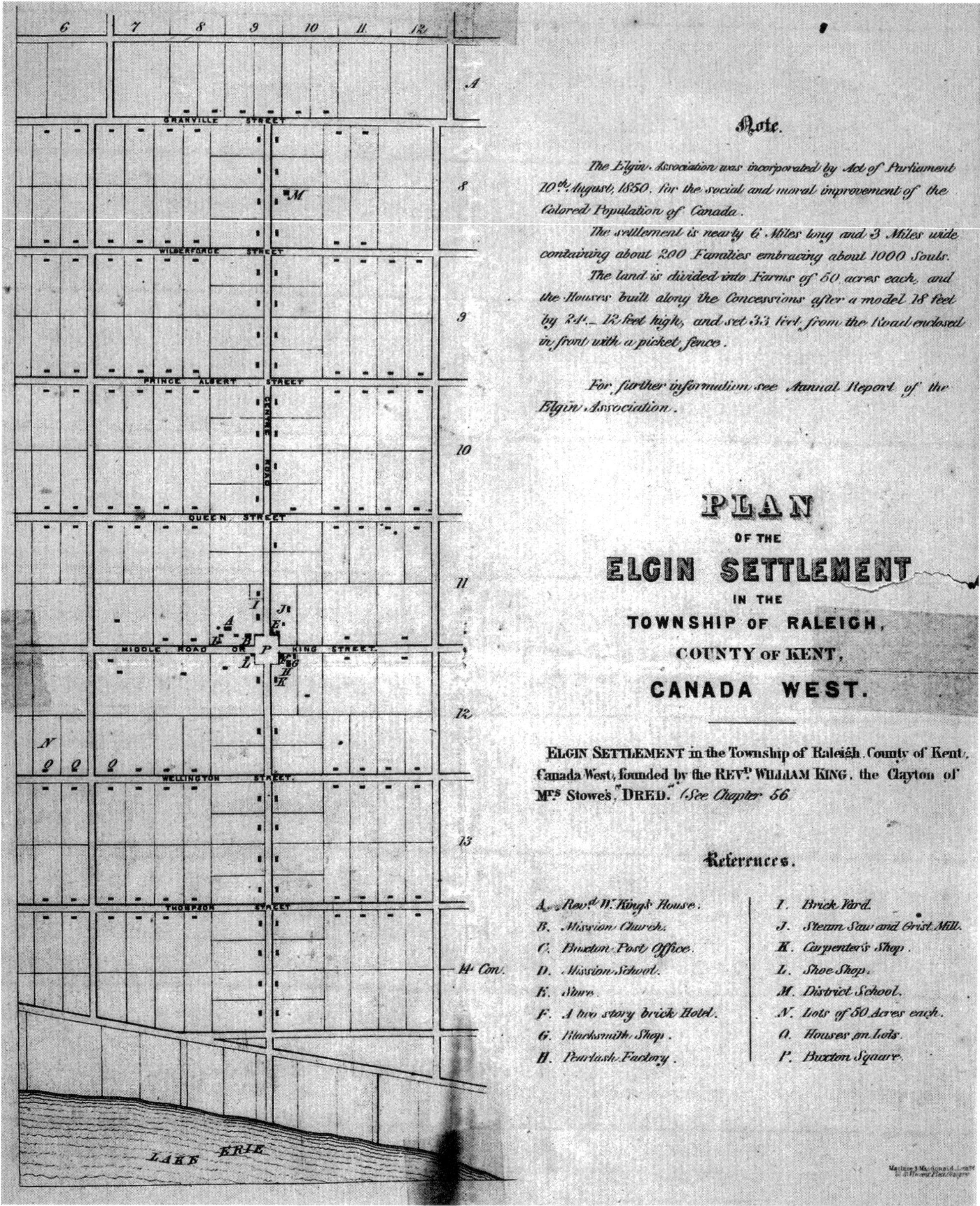

The Elgin Settlement in Buxton, Ontario, was a planned settlement for black refugees founded in 1849. Antislavery advocates extolled it as the model of a self-sufficient black community. *(Library and Archives Canada/ William King Collection/R4402-5-0-E/C-114548)*

the Great Lakes, where the addition of black citizens became a deterrent against a U.S. invasion

A More Welcoming Land

The first major emigration over the divide began in 1829 with the passing of an ordinance in Cincinnati, Ohio, calling for a $500 bond for any free black to reside within the city limits. The unreasonable fee caused Thomas Cressup and Israel Lewis to investigate land costs and to gauge pro-black sentiment in upper Canada. The mayor of Cincinnati rescinded the statute out of fear of losing the area's pool of cheap labor, but his action came too late to stop Cressup and Lewis from guiding 1,000 blacks north to a friendlier environment. Contributing to the mass exodus of American blacks was the encouragement of Underground Railroad agents Levi Coffin, Harriet Tubman, and Dr. Alexander Milton Ross.

The resultant black network strengthened the Underground Railroad. In Ontario, Abraham H. Galloway of Wilmington, Delaware, and others like him formed political action groups, aid societies, and militias and published newspapers to help newcomers acclimate to freedom and to help prevent kidnappers from returning them to bondage. Nonetheless, the Zulu-Mohawk family of John "Daddy" Hall of Amherstburg suffered capture and enslavement, from which Hall fled when he gained adulthood. Other free blacks had to contend with economic, legal, and social bias among some Canadian provincials. Nelson Moss, a settler in London, Canada, remarked that prejudice existed in his new homeland but that it did not approach the sufferings he endured as a slave in Virginia or as a fugitive in Pennsylvania. Aiding the adaptation of former slaves to a new environment was the Anti-Slavery Society of Canada, established in 1851 and based in Toronto, which had the support of orators Elihu Burritt and Frederick Douglass. Agent Hiram Wilson opened a depot in St. Catharines, Ontario, and convinced border patrols to ease customs fees to allow blacks free entrance.

America's Response

The expanded exodus to Canada outraged Kentucky-born Senator Henry Clay, who, in 1828, denounced the Canadian government for encouraging black flight. Southerners demanded extradition of fugitives by the British, who rejected border negotiations requiring the return of former slaves to bondage. In 1842, Alfred Wallace, an Arkansas businessman, demanded that authorities in Chatham, Ontario, return his slave, Nelson Hacket, whom Wallace charged with thievery. To support his claim, Wallace cited the Webster-Ashburton Treaty, which Secretary of State Daniel Webster negotiated in August 1842 with the British Foreign Minister, Alexander Baring. Although the accord did not mandate unlimited extradition of escapees, it did allow for the return to the United States of anyone accused of murder, piracy, arson, robbery, or forgery. The uprising of anti-slavery factions defeated Wallace's efforts and substantiated Canada's intent to remain neutral in matters of slave recapture. Fanning the flames of abolition were slave narratives in the *Quebec Gazette,* published in English and French. Complete abolition occurred with the Emancipation Act of 1833, which ended slavery throughout the British Empire.

Opportunities and Support

Despite outbreaks of bigotry, the lot of refugees embracing liberty in Canada was primarily positive. The newcomers found jobs cutting stone, whitewashing walls, keeping stores, cooking and serving at hotels and restaurants, driving delivery wagons, making dresses and doing fine hand laundering, tending the sick, and crewing river barges and sloops. Contributing to the contentment of runaways in Canada were the African Methodist Episcopal Church, founded in 1840, and the Common Schools Act of 1850, which established literacy centers for all black children in the province of Ontario.

Runaways found a haven at St. Catharines, which received Jacob Blockson and his cousin, James Blockson, both antecedents of historian Charles LeRoy Blockson. At the first prosperous black community in upper Canada, the Reverend Hiram Wilson accommodated fugitives dispatched by Frederick Douglass and Joseph P. Morris (1820–?), a Rochester barber. Abolitionist William H. Merritt, a member of Parliament, encouraged black settlement by building safehouses and offering lots for houses in Coloured Town. Aiding refugees on the last leg of their flight from bondage was the Refugee Slaves' Friends Society, which Mayor Elias Smith Adams formed in 1852. By 1855, 123 former slaves had established families in the area. Coordinating activities with the Underground Railroad was the Fugitive Aid Society, established in 1861. Historian Benjamin Drew, author of *Refugee: The Narratives of Fugitive*

Estimated Black Population of Notable Fugitive Sites in Canada (mid-1850s)

Town	Estimated Black Population
Amherstburg	ca. 500
Chatham	800
Colchester	450
Galt	40
Gosfield	78
Hamilton	274
London	350
Sandwich	100
St. Catharines	800
Toronto	1,000
Windsor	250
Total	4,642

Slaves in Canada (1856), reported that, in mid-century, nearly all adult black citizens were former slaves.

Blacks found employment as barbers, cobblers, servants, chimney sweeps, joiners and masons, dressmakers, beauticians, launderers, and hotel cooks and maids. Daniel Williams repaired watches; David T. Williamson opened a jewelry shop. Renix Jonston, Francis Scott, and Nelson Williams started a shoemaking business; Charles Burns, George Page, and Robert Young managed a saloon. In 1838, black citizens formed the Methodist Society of the American Methodist Episcopal Church. Some of the newcomers to St. Catharines arrived under the guidance of Harriet Tubman; a famed Underground Railroad conductor, she occupied a house in Coloured Town behind St. Catharines British Methodist Episcopal Church at Geneva and North streets in spring 1858, when she met with insurrectionist John Brown.

Pluses and Minuses

Life in African Canadian communities was a mixed blessing. Despite religious and educational advantages, African Americans reared in the rural South found adaptation to long, cold Canadian winters difficult and sometimes deadly. Frederick S. Cozzens reported in his book *Acadia; or, A Month with the Blue Noses* (1859) on the misery of blacks settling in the Atlantic shores of Nova Scotia. Nonetheless, the riders of the secret railway poured north in a steady stream. The success of most African Canadians influenced novelist Harriet Beecher Stowe to describe a runaway family in her 1852 melodrama, *Uncle Tom's Cabin.* She depicted Eliza and George Harris and their young son Harry arriving at a reception center in Amherstberg and settling into secure jobs in Montreal, Quebec.

On June 16, 1860, the *Brooklyn Eagle* reported a census showing 45,000 refugees living in southern Ontario and still arriving at the rate of 10,000 per year. The newcomers passing through Underground Railroad stations in Detroit, Michigan, slipped over water routes at the western end of Lake Erie to Amherstburg, Buxton, Chatham, Colchester, Dresden, Sandwich, and Windsor, Ontario. To the northeast, additional settlements sprang up at Port Stanley, Lucan, London, and Port Burwell. At the eastern end of Lake Erie, slaves fleeing through Niagara Falls, New York, sheltered at Fort Erie, Buffalo, and the Canadian side of Niagara Falls. At the juncture with Lake Ontario, blacks built communities in St. Catharines, Toronto, and Hamilton. Additional communities included Kingston, at the eastern end of Lake Ontario; Oro, on Lake Simcoe; and Collingwood and Owen Sound on Georgian Bay, an offshoot of Lake Huron. The pioneering movement of former slaves into promising territory took hundreds west by ship to the Pacific coast to Victoria, on Vancouver Island. Others settled the prairies of Alberta, Manitoba, and Saskatchewan.

See also: abolitionism; African Methodist Episcopal Church; American Revolution; Canadian Anti-Slavery Baptist Association; Chatham Convention; routes, Underground Railroad; slave recovery; *Uncle Tom's Cabin; or, Life Among the Lowly* (1852).

Sources

Cecelski, David S., and Timothy B. Tyson. *Democracy Betrayed: The Wilmington Race Riot of 1898 and Its Legacy.* Chapel Hill: University of North Carolina Press, 1998.

Cozzens, Frederick S. *Acadia; or, A Month with the Blue Noses.* New York: Derby & Jackson, 1859.

Hurley, Philomena, "Many Found Refuge Here When City Was Terminal of 'Underground Railway,'" *Owen Sound (Ontario) Sun Times,* November 16, 1966, 10.

Loguen, Jermain Wesley. *The Rev. J.W. Loguen, as a Slave and as a Freeman: A Narrative of Real Life.* Syracuse, NY: J.C.K. Truair, 1859.

"A Recent Census," *Brooklyn (NY) Eagle,* June 16, 1860, 2.

Stuart, Reginald C. *United States Expansionism and British North America, 1775–1871.* Chapel Hill: University of North Carolina Press, 1988.

Ward, Samuel R. *Autobiography of a Fugitive Negro: His Anti-Slavery Labours in the United States, Canada, and England.* London: John Snow, 1855.

Canadian Anti-Slavery Baptist Association

A pre–Civil War bolstering of the Michigan–Canada route of the Underground Railroad resulted in 1856 from the union of the Amherstburg Baptist Association and the Canadian Anti-Slavery Baptist Association. Leading the coalition movement was grocer Albert Beckford Jones, a Kentucky-born freedman and director of the London (Ontario) Anti-Slavery Society, who stood as a model of the success an ambitious former slave in free territory could achieve. As a result of the merger, churches in Buxton, Chatham, Colchester, Dawn, Detroit, London, and Mount Pleasant collaborated on rescuing runaway slaves on the American side of the border and on securing their safety in Canada. In addition to hands-on aid to the desperate fugitive, pastors and religious publishing houses stepped up pressure on churches that either supported slavery or took no action to defend blacks against the greed and inhumanity of the plantation South. Contributing to the fervor of abolitionist Baptists was the detrimental effect of the Fugitive Slave Law of 1850, which endangered the liberty of freeborn blacks as well as settled fugitives by allowing kidnappers and bounty hunters to seize suspects at will.

See also: bounty hunters; Fugitive Slave Law of 1850; kidnap.

Sources

Finkenbine, Roy E. *The Black Abolitionist Papers.* Vol. 2, *Canada, 1830–1865.* Chapel Hill: University of North Carolina Press, 1986.

Lewis, James K. "Religious Nature of the Early Negro Migration to Canada and the Amherstburg Baptist Association." *Ontario History* 58:2 (June 1966): 117–32.

Cannon, Ansal (1832–?)

In flight from bondage in Dorchester County, Maryland, 24-year-old Ansal Cannon reached free territory. In company with John Pinket, the slave of Mary Brown, Cannon eluded his owner, Kitty Cannon, in 1857. The two runaways arrived in Philadelphia, Pennsylvania, and received help from agents of the secret network.

Source

Still, William. *The Underground Railroad.* Philadelphia: Porter & Coates, 1871.

Cannon, Patty (1783–1829)

Lucretia Patricia "Patty" Hanly Cannon led a gang of slave catchers near the Nanticoke River in Sussex County, Maryland. Her clutch of turncoat blacks headquartered in Johnson's Tavern, an alehouse managed by her son-in-law, Joe Johnson, in Reliance, Maryland, on the Delaware state line. The gang lured fugitives to their homes by passing them off as waystations of the Underground Railroad. In 1826, a written complaint mailed to Joseph Watson, mayor of Philadelphia, charged that the Cannon gang kidnapped blacks from Pennsylvania and sold them in the South. Patty Cannon's crimes extended from abduction to torture and murder. After her apprehension for slaying two adult fugitives and two children, she swallowed a lethal dose of arsenic on May 11, 1829, in the Georgetown, Delaware, jail. Her legend was known to the great-great-grandfather of black historian Charles L. Blockson.

Sources

Cannon, Lucretia P. *Narrative and Confessions of Lucretia P. Cannon.* New York: privately published, 1841.

Lynch, Nancy E., "Infamous Delmarva Woman Returns to Print," *Delaware News Journal,* November 3, 2005.

Carleton, Edmund (1797–1882)
Carleton, Mary Kilburn Coffin (1812–1880)

Attorney and lumberman Edmund Carleton and his wife, Mary Kilburn Coffin Carleton, maintained a safehouse on the Underground Railroad in Littleton, in Grafton County, New Hampshire. In 1837, shortly after their marriage, Mary Carleton established the Littleton Anti-Slavery Society. Influenced by the editorials of William Lloyd Garrison, publisher of *The Liberator,* Edmund donated his time and professional services to runaways. He defended Allen Brown and Erastus Brown, whom authorities charged with interrupting a church service to make abolitionist speeches. At the Carleton home, husband and wife partnered in the duties of boarding refugees and transporting them by wagon to the next stop.

See also: Liberator, The.

Source

Jackson, James R. *History of Littleton, New Hampshire.* Cambridge, MA: Harvard University Press, 1905.

Carlisle, Lucretia E. Lucas (1811—ca. 1880)
Carlisle, Samuel B. (1804–1880)

A Highland County, Ohio, family, Lucretia E. Lucas Carlisle and Samuel B. Carlisle and their 12 children, maintained a waystation of the Underground Railroad in northern Washington Township. Samuel Carlisle was born in Virginia and, after settling in Ohio, married Lucretia Lucas in 1830. Reared as Altruists, the Carlisles' two daughters—Jenny Carlisle Hyer (1846–?), wife of Jacob Hyer (1841–1895), and Mary Carlisle Kerns (1834–?), wife of Charles Kerns (1838–?)—married into abolitionist families in Marshall Township.

Source

Ayres, Elsie Johnson. *Highland Pioneer Sketches and Family Genealogies.* Springfield, OH: H.K. Skinner & Son, 1971.

Carnahan, William McFarland (1818–1879)

An Underground Railroad operative of the Iowa–Illinois route, William McFarland Carnahan recorded detailed information about waystations. A native of Lawrence County, Pennsylvania, in 1839, he settled in Mercer County, Illinois, and married Sarah Ann Nevius (or Nevins) of Greene County, Ohio. Because his abolitionism put him at odds with the Presbyterian assembly, he co-founded Free Presbyterianism. In early July 1854, he took part in a difficult transfer of George and Sam, Missouri runaways passing through Iowa to Keighsburg in southern Illinois. The slaves arrived at his residence from Sunbeam, Illinois, and journeyed on to James Oxford's safehouse in Henry County. William Carnahan celebrated the escape as a Fourth of July victory.

Source

Taylor, Glennette Tilley. *The Underground Railroad in Illinois.* Glen Ellyn, IL: Newman Educational, 2001.

Carneal, Sarah Howell Stanley (1782–1847)
Carneal, Thomas David (1786–1860)

Oral tradition supports claims that Sarah "Sally" (or Sallie) Howell Stanley Carneal and her husband, Thomas David Carneal of Alexandria, Virginia, operated a waystation of the Underground Railroad. The Carneals, settlers of Covington in Kenton County, Kentucky, married in 1815 and built Elmwood Hall. In 1828, they built Carneal House at 405 East Second Street. The imposing mansion harbored fugitives until agents of the secret network could pilot them up the Licking River and across the Ohio River to Cincinnati, Ohio.

Source

Simon, F. Kevin. *The WPA Guide to Kentucky.* Lexington: University Press of Kentucky, 1939.

Carnes, Martha B. Carnes (1809–1865)
Carnes, William (1809–ca. 1880)

A husband-and-wife team of Underground Railroad agents, Martha B. (Carnes) Carnes and William Carnes used their social prominence and wealth to aid the oppressed. Born of Scots ancestry in Boston, Massachusetts, William Carnes owned two homes. At the family's primary residence, a brownstone mansion at 558 Massachusetts Avenue in the Roxbury district, the couple offered rooms to passengers of the secret network. When slave catchers canvassed the neighborhood, the Carnes family moved their household to their second home, also a slave waystation, which stood dark and deserted when the family was not in residence. In the mid-twentieth century, the original mansion sheltered a struggling music student, Coretta Scott, who worked as a domestic until her marriage to Martin Luther King, Jr., in 1953. The house currently headquarters the Dieppa Studio for the arts and the League of Women for Community Service.

Source

Chadwick, Bruce. *Traveling the Underground Railroad: A Visitor's Guide to More Than 300 Sites.* Secaucus, NJ: Citadel, 1999.

Carney, William H. (1840–1908)

One of many fugitives aided by abolitionist mariners, William H. Carney escaped bondage in Norfolk, Virginia. He worked at oystering for Major Carney, a slave owner who promised to manumit him. Like other recalcitrant and duplicitous owners, the man failed to note Carney's liberation in his will. In 1857, Carney joined Andrew Allen and fled his new owner, Sarah Twyne. Allen and Carney arrived in Philadelphia. Carney settled in New Bedford, Massachusetts, and engaged abolitionist shipper Loum Snow to negotiate for the freedom of his wife, Ann "Nancy" Dean Carney. In September 1859, Snow completed the deal. After Nancy Carney's arrival, the couple purchased one of their two sons and their three daughters. William Carney joined the Fifty-fourth Massachusetts Regiment as color bearer. During the

Civil War, Sergeant Carney retrieved the American flag and incurred bullet wounds to the legs, chest, head, and arm. Eight years before his death, he became the nation's first black recipient of the Congressional Medal of Honor, conferred for heroism on July 18, 1863, at the assault of Fort Wagner, South Carolina, the central episode of the film *Glory* (1989).

See also: black soldiers.

Source

Grover, Kathryn. *The Fugitive's Gibraltar: Escaping Slaves and Abolitionism in New Bedford, Massachusetts.* Amherst: University of Massachusetts Press, 2001.

Carpenter, Joseph (1793–1873)
Carpenter, Margaret W. Cornell (1793–1874)

A Quaker farmer and abolitionist in New Rochelle, New York, Joseph Carpenter and his wife, Margaret W. Cornell Carpenter, took pride in aiding orphans and in helping refugees escape slavery. At the Carpenter safehouse near Weaver Street in Westchester County, the couple sheltered slaves before passing them to Joseph Pierce in Pleasantville, New York, and on to Bedford to Pierce's brother-in-law Judge John Jay in Katonah or to David Irish and Martha Titus Irish in Quaker Hill, outside Pawling in Dutchess County. The Carpenters traveled to Boston, where they received the thanks of Lydia Maria Francis Child for 30 years of activism. The Carpenters are buried on Stratton Road in a cemetery that they donated for the interment of freed slaves from Eastchester, New Rochelle, and Scarsdale, New York.

Source

Powell, Aaron M. *Personal Reminiscences of the Anti-Slavery and Other Reforms and Reformers.* New York: Colored Press, 1899.

Carpenter, Philo R. (1805–1886)
Carpenter, Sarah Forbes Bridges (1806–1830)
Carpenter, Anne Thompson (1806–1866)

Chicago's first pharmacist, Deacon Philo R. Carpenter, a wealthy philanthropist from Savoy, Massachusetts, involved himself in slave rescues and in establishing routes for the Underground Railroad. After his arrival in Chicago from Troy, New York, at age 27, he opened a drugstore on Lake Street and married Sarah Forbes Bridges of Savoy. After her death, he married Anne Thompson in 1834. Philo Carpenter took responsibility for civic improvement by serving on the boards of education and health and by co-founding the Chicago Relief and Aid Society and the First Presbyterian Church. His collaboration with route planners Ichabod Codding, Zebina Eastman, and Allan Pinkerton extended transportation routes to the west. In addition to the Carpenters' two-story safehouse at Morgan and West Randolph streets in Chicago, the couple also concealed slaves in the First Baptist Congregational Church.

Many refugees came from Missouri by way of Avis Blodgett and Israel Porter Blodgett's waystation in Downers Grove, from Thomas Filer in Glen Ellyn, and from John Coe in Hinsdale, Illinois. Philo sent these fugitives on to their final destination by paying boat passage to Ontario. During one transfer, Anne Carpenter accepted passengers through the back door and hid them in an overhead service hole to the stovepipe. Because of the Carpenters' ready service to destitute escapees, their house was frequently the target of spies and slave nabbers. In 1842, Philo joined operatives Calvin DeWolf and Dr. Charles Volney Dyer in launching an abolitionist newspaper in Chicago, the *Western Citizen*, edited by Zebina Eastman.

See also: abolitionist newspapers; routes, Underground Railroad; spies.

Source

Trexler, Harrison Anthony. *Slavery in Missouri, 1804–1865.* Baltimore: Johns Hopkins Press, 1914.

Carpenter, Stephen Decatur (1819–1906)

Abolitionist Stephen Decatur "Pump" Carpenter of Pittstown, New York, became one of the unofficial historians of the Underground Railroad. As the official state printer and senior editor of the *Madison (WI) Patriot,* he contributed to the history of the Underground Railroad by collecting news clippings in scrapbooks. He settled in Madison in 1850 and, in partnership with John T. Martin, bought the *Daily Patriot,* a newspaper famous for muckraking until it ceased publication in 1864.

After Carpenter published a first edition of his *Logic of History* in 1863, he sold 6,000 subscriptions to abolitionists in Illinois, Iowa, Indiana, Minnesota, New York, Pennsylvania, and Wisconsin. In November 1863, he compiled a second edition and received orders for two-thirds of his press run before it was completed. Chronicling bondage from ancient times in Greece and Rome, he advanced to articles on slavery in the Caribbean and to insurrectionist John Brown's raid on the federal arsenal in Harpers Ferry on October 16, 1859, a harbinger of the Civil War soon to come. Among the cases involving the secret network that Carpenter published were the rescues of Joshua Glover from the Milwaukee County jail on March 11, 1854, and of Anthony Burns from a Boston lockup on May 24, 1854.

Source

Carpenter, S.D. *Logic of History.* Madison, WI: self-published, 1864.

Carrier, Richard (1811–?)

Richard Carrier faced a seven-year sentence for aiding escaping slaves. In December 1838, at age 27, he entered the Missouri state penitentiary at Jefferson City. Nearly five years later, on September 2, 1843, he escaped confinement.

Source

Frazier, Harriet C. *Runaway and Freed Missouri Slaves and Those Who Helped Them, 1763–1865.* Jefferson, NC: McFarland, 2004.

Carter, George Washington (1801–1878)

A black barber, tobacconist, and Underground Railroad operative, George Washington Carter was a respected citizen and a daring rescuer of the oppressed. He escaped from a Virginia plantation and came to reside in New Albany, Indiana, around 1825, where he bought a home four years later on Upper High Street. While relaying fugitive slaves, he continued to invest in small businesses. Opening a barbershop near the *New Albany Daily Ledger* enabled him to stay informed of abolitionist activities.

Source

Peters, Pamela R. *The Underground Railroad in Floyd County, Indiana.* Jefferson, NC: McFarland, 2001.

Carter, Jacob (fl. 1850s)
Carter, Joseph (fl. 1850s)
Carter, Richard (fl. 1850s)

The Carter brothers of Leesburg, Virginia, had no time to plan their escape from bondage. In fall 1856, the sale of Jacob and Joseph Carter and their transport to Richmond concluded with lodging in a slave pen and temporary employment. The two slipped away, retrieved Richard Carter, and fled north. An overseer tracked them to a stream, where the brothers challenged him to cross and take his chances. The tracker raised a pursuit party, but they lost the Carters at a thicket. Aiding the trio were Underground Railroad agents Dr. Joseph Gibbons, Lindley Coates, and the conductors from Ercildoun, Pennsylvania. Joseph Carter and Richard Carter found work in the southern part of the state. Jacob Carter purchased land and established a ministry in Ercildoun.

Source

Smedley, Robert C. *History of the Underground Railroad in Chester and the Neighboring Counties of Pennsylvania.* Lancaster, PA: Office of *The Journal,* 1883.

Carter, Luke (1775–ca. 1850s)
Carter, Sarah (1794–ca. 1850s)

Black assistants to agent William Lawrence Chaplin's network in Washington, D.C., Luke Carter and his wife, Sarah Carter, received runaways for the Underground Railroad. Both were born in Maryland. After Chaplin located passengers in the South, he relayed them north to the Carters' waystation.

Source

Case of William L. Chaplin. Boston: Chaplin Committee, 1851.

Carver, Frances Almira Porter (1817–1897)
Carver, Lewis E. (1806–1890)

A husband-and-wife team, Frances Almira Porter Carver and Dr. Lewis E. Carver operated a frontier slave rescue depot. Lewis Carver, a native of Hebron, Connecticut, practiced medicine after studying privately in Bolton, Connecticut. The couple married in 1838 and, in 1844, resided in Orland, in Steuben County, Indiana. In token of their Presbyterian faith, they served as stationmasters of the Underground Railroad.

Source

Illustrated Historical Atlas of Indiana. Chicago: Baskin, Forster, 1876.

Cary, Mary Ann Shadd (1823–1893)

Author and lecturer Mary Ann Camberton Shadd Cary established a reputation for bold defense of slaves. Born to Abraham Doras Shadd and Harriet Parnell Shadd, both black agents of the Wilmington, Delaware, secret network, Mary Ann was the first of their 13 children. She learned about abolitionism from reading William Lloyd Garrison's abolitionist newspaper, *The Liberator,* which her father distributed. Despite laws forbidding the education of blacks, she studied at the Quaker boarding academy of slave rescuer Phoche Darlington (1810–1896) in West Chester, Pennsylvania. At age 16, Cary began teaching in Wilmington, Pennsylvania, and continued her career in New York City and Norristown, Pennsylvania.

After passage of the Fugitive Slave Law of 1850, Cary was no longer safe in the United States. She and her younger brother, Isaac Shadd, relocated in Windsor, Ontario, where she established a career as writer and editor. To aid others escaping bondage, she issued a popular tract, *A Plea for Emigration: Notes on Canada West* (1852). It summarized opportunities for black refugees in free territory beyond the reach of the Fugitive Slave Law of 1850, which allowed federal marshals to recover runaways from free territory. The text explained the workings of the Refugees' Home, a settlement open only to escaped slaves.

Passage of the Fugitive Slave Law of 1850 prompted Mary Ann Shadd Cary to move from Delaware to Canada, where she became a leader and spokesperson for former slaves. In Windsor, Ontario, she published a weekly newspaper called *The Provincial Freeman. (Library and Archives Canada/Mary Ann Shadd Cary Collection/C-029977)*

To inform newcomers of political events, Cary published a weekly, *The Provincial Freeman,* which she printed with the aid of Underground Railroad agent John Henry Hill. Assisting the pair was a fellow African Canadian, Osborne Perry Anderson, one of insurrectionist John Brown's men who attacked the federal arsenal in Harpers Ferry, Virginia, on October 16, 1859. Cary used her influence to oppose the binational black settlement in Essex County, Ontario, administered by the Refugee Home Society, headed by Henry Walton Bibb and Mary E. Miles Bibb. Cary encouraged Anderson to publish a pamphlet, *A Voice from Harpers Ferry* (1861), the only eyewitness account. During the Civil War, she enlisted volunteers for the Union army. After the war, she completed a law degree from Howard University.

See also: abolitionism; abolitionist newspapers; Fugitive Slave Law of 1850; *Notes on Canada West* (1852); Refugee Home Society.

Sources

Olbey, Christian. "Unfolded Hands: Class Suicide and the Insurgent Intellectual Praxis of Mary Ann Shadd." *Canadian Review of American Studies* 30:2 (2000): 151–74.

Shadd, Mary Ann. *A Plea for Emigration: Notes on Canada West.* Detroit, MI: George W. Pattison, 1852.

Case, Charles G. (1800–1875)
Case, Mary Ann (fl. 1840s–1850s)

Banker Charles G. Case and his wife, Mary Ann Case, supported the Underground Railroad in Fulton, in Oswego County, New York, near Lake Ontario. The Cases were charter members of the Wesleyan Methodist Church of Fulton. At their waystation on Second Street, they welcomed runaways from the South. In July 1845, they received nine Maryland escapees from the slave pens of dealer Hope Slatter, who intended to sell them in New Orleans. In 1850, the Case family moved operations to 133 South First Street near the Otsego River and continued their work, despite the disapproval of neighbors.

Sources

"Charles G. Case," *Fulton (NY) Daily Palladium,* December 10, 1875.

Drought, Cliff, "Area Beginning to Track Its Roots Through the Underground Railroad," *Oswego (NY) Valley News,* January 20, 2001.

Catlin, Henry, Jr. (fl. 1830s–1860s)
Catlin, James (1824–1890)
Catlin, Martha Van Rensselaer (1823–1892)

The Catlin brothers, Henry and James, used their print shop as a hiding place for refugees. James Catlin, a physician, began aiding runaways in 1845 at Allegheny College in Meadville, Pennsylvania, where he hid a slave in his room. He and his wife, Dr. Martha Van Rensselaer Catlin, also a physician, acted upon their beliefs that slavery was wrong. At their home and safehouse at East Mill Street in Sugar Grove, Pennsylvania, Martha Catlin treated the sick and exhausted. After the Catlin brothers began publishing the *True American,* an abolitionist newspaper printed in Erie, Pennsylvania, from 1853 to 1861, they hid fugitives in bins of paper until Hamilton E. Waters and other local agents could arrange passage over Lake Erie. In 1858, Henry Catlin, Jr., received death threats for inviting Frederick Douglass to speak on April 24 at Park Hall.

Source

Catlin, Henry, "The Visit of Frederick Douglass," *True American,* April 29, 1858.

Cattell, Jonas (ca. 1813–1895)

Jonas Cattell was a resourceful Quaker conductor of the Underground Railroad. Around 1810, he erected a two-story brick residence at 999 Jennings Avenue in Salem, Ohio. Into the planning went a recessed platform in the chimney of the cellar butchering room. Slaves could also hide under his porch, in a secret niche in an upstairs closet, and behind metal shields in a first-floor fireplace. For quick getaways, passengers could exit through a tunnel that led north into high brush.

Source

Shaffer, Dale. *Salem: A Quaker City History.* Charleston, SC: Arcadia, 2002.

Caulkins, Nehemiah (1824–?)

Nehemiah Caulkins, a slave carpenter, fled from an atmosphere of cruelty to New England via the Underground Railroad. At a plantation outside Wilmington, North Carolina, his owner, John Swan, allotted him seven quarts of meal and two gallons of rice per week. Caulkins observed the overseer punishing a runaway by shooting him in the back with duck shot. The overseer locked a slave named Harry in stocks for a week before fastening him to a logging chain. An unfortunate slave called Old Ben had the wretched task of flogging male and female slaves at the direction of his master and mistress. Caulkins escaped the menacing environment and bondage and arrived in Waterford, in New London County, Connecticut. For the American Anti-Slavery Society, in 1839, he compiled memories of enslavement for publication in the *Anti-Slavery Examiner.* His reports of the inhumanity of North Carolina slave owners appeared in orator Theodore Dwight Weld's *American Slavery As It Is: Testimony of a Thousand Witnesses* (1839) and in William Goodell's *The American Slave Code in Theory and Practice* (1853).

See also: American Anti-Slavery Society.

Sources

Goodell, William. *The American Slave Code in Theory and Practice: Its Distinctive Features Shown by Its Statutes, Judicial Decisions, and Illustrative Facts.* New York: American and Foreign Anti-Slavery Society, 1853.

Pettit, Eber M. *Sketches in the History of the Underground Railroad.* Fredonia, NY: W. McKinstry & Son, 1879.

Weld, Theodore. *American Slavery As It Is: Testimony of a Thousand Witnesses.* New York: American Anti-Slavery Society, 1839.

Chace, Elizabeth Buffum (1806–1899)
Chace, Samuel Buffington (1800–1870)

A Quaker human rights reformer and suffragist from Providence, Rhode Island, Elizabeth Buffum Chace, dubbed the Conscience of Rhode Island, was an operative of the Underground Railroad. Like her parents, agent Arnold Buffum and Rebecca Gould Buffum, Elizabeth Chace fought slavery openly. After her marriage to Quaker cotton textile manufacturer Samuel Buffington Chace in 1828, she gave up teaching. In her fight for justice, she became an agent of the New England Anti-Slavery Society and a vice president of the Fall River (Massachusetts) Female Anti-Slavery Society. Her diary, *My Anti-Slavery Reminiscences* (ca. 1831–1891), names as the first successful relay that of James Curry, who made his way from Person County, North Carolina, in 1837 and passed through Fall River to Canada in 1839.

Influenced by the abolitionism of William Lloyd Garrison, publisher of *The Liberator*, the Chaces managed a waystation at Hunt and Broad streets in Valley Falls (now Central Falls), Rhode Island.

The home of Quakers Elizabeth Buffum Chace and her husband, Samuel Chace, in Valley Falls (now Central Falls), Rhode Island, was a waystation in the clandestine network and a meeting place for organizers of the American Anti-Slavery Society. *(Schomburg Center for Research in Black Culture/General Research and Reference Division/New York Public Library/Astor, Lenox, and Tilden Foundations)*

In 1851, Elizabeth Chace began a two-year term as a manager of the American Anti-Slavery Society. Organizers William Wells Brown, Charles Callistus Burleigh, Cyrus Burleigh, Abby Kelley Foster and Stephen Symons Foster, Wendell Addison Phillips, Parker Pillsbury, Charles Remond, and Henry C. Wright used the Chace home as a meeting place to plan strategy. When Wright came to Valley Falls to deliver an abolitionist address, the Chace family joined a phalanx around him to shield him from proslavery hooligans. Elizabeth Chace considered interaction with abolitionists an educational experience for her children, as were readings from Benjamin Stanton's *Anti-Slavery Standard,* Garrison's *The Liberator,* and Harriet Beecher Stowe's melodrama *Uncle Tom's Cabin* (1852).

The Chaces relied on the discretion of their children and Irish servants and maintained ties with other local safehouse keepers, including Quaker agent Robert S. Adams and Elizabeth Chace's brother-in-law and sister, Nathaniel Briggs Borden and Sarah Gould Buffum Borden at Fall River. The two women shared the labor and dangers of concealing in their cellars the individuals and families who arrived from the Carolinas, Virginia, and Maryland. Elizabeth Chace threw together warm raiment to protect runaways from cold transport to Canada and provided forged liberation papers to ease relays by railcar. During one relay, the Bordens costumed a male blacksmith in the veil and simple garb of a Quaker woman. With the aid of transporters Israel Buffington and his son, Benjamin Buffington, slaves reaching the Chace home at the Fall River nexus could depart by land on the Worcester, Massachusetts–Canada route or by sea in small trading vessels to New Bedford. For the New En-

Elizabeth Buffum Chace described her family's method of transporting runaways in her diary, *My Anti-Slavery Reminiscences* (ca. 1831–1891): "We received them, and, after preparing them for the journey, my husband would accompany them a short distance, on the Providence and Worcester railroad, acquaint the conductor with the facts, enlist his interest in their behalf, and then leave them in his care. . . . I used to give them an envelope, directed to us, to be mailed in Toronto, which, when it reached us, was sufficient by its postmark to announce their safe arrival, beyond the baleful influence of the Stars and Stripes, and the anti-protection of the Fugitive Slave Law."

gland route, the Chaces relied on the planning and teamwork of the Reverend Joshua Young and Mary Elizabeth Plympton Young in Burlington, Vermont.

In the years preceding the Civil War, the Chace family remained involved in anti-slavery issues. They hung black crepe on their door to mourn the hanging of insurrectionist John Brown at the Jefferson County courthouse on December 2, 1859. Elizabeth Chace groomed the next generation of female anti-slavery speakers by fostering the platform career of Anna Elizabeth Dickinson, a Quaker who began addressing abolitionist gatherings in her teens. Annoyed with the Society of Friends for its refusal to denounce slavery, after the Civil War, Elizabeth Chace resigned her membership and poured her energies into equal rights for blacks and women.

On March 12, 2002, Rhode Island officials dedicated a bronze statue of Elizabeth Buffum Chace, making her the first woman to be so honored at the state capitol.

See also: American Anti-Slavery Society; philanthropists; *Uncle Tom's Cabin; or, Life Among the Lowly* (1852).

Sources

Allen, Sephi. "Abolitionist, Suffragist, Philanthropist: The Life and Work of Reformer Elizabeth Buffum Chace." *Journal of Women's History* 16:4 (2004): 183–90.

Lovell, Malcolm R., ed. *Two Quaker Sisters: From the Original Diaries of Elizabeth Buffum Chace and Lucy Buffum Lovell.* Introduction by Malcolm R. Lovell. New York: Liveright, 1937.

Chadwick, Abel (1802–1885)
Chadwick, Elizabeth Starrett (1807–1900)

An Underground Railroad operative on the New England–Canada route, banker Abel Chadwick aided runaways on their way to freedom. Assisted by his wife, Elizabeth Starrett Chadwick, he operated a safehouse in an isolated part of Kennebec, Maine. At the north end of China Lake in China, Maine, the couple received slaves on the final leg of the route across the St. Lawrence River to Quebec Province.

Source

Grow, M.M. *China, Maine: Bicentennial History.* Weeks Mills, ME: Marion T. Van Strien, 1975.

Chadwick, Mammy (1799–1899)

Mammy Chadwick, a resident of Chatham, Ontario, was born into bondage in Virginia. After being auctioned in New Orleans, Louisiana, and transported to Kentucky, in her late thirties in 1837, she fled north via the secret railway. She remembered the date of her arrival at Fort Erie as contemporaneous with the crowning of Queen Victoria. Following her settlement in Chatham, Chadwick lived the rest of her century-long life there and died at age 100 at the Kent County House of Refuge.

Source

Severance, Frank H. *Old Trails on the Niagara Frontier.* Buffalo, NY: n.p., 1899.

Chamberlain, John Abbot (1794–1853)
Chamberlain, Mary Rogers Clough (1798–1856)

Aided by his nephews, John Abbot Chamberlain and his wife, Mary Rogers "Polly" Clough Chamberlain, rescued runaway slaves. John Chamberlain was born in Loudon, in Merrimack County, New Hampshire, and married in December 1817. In the late 1830s, the Chamberlains received refugees at their two-story brick farmhouse outside Canterbury, New Hampshire. They directed passengers from Salem and Concord, Massachusetts, along West Road to a safehouse on Meredith Ridge in Belnap, New Hampshire.

Source

Stearns, Ezra S. *Genealogy and Family History of the State of New Hampshire.* New York: Lewis, 1908.

Chambers, Henry (1832–?)
Chambers, John (fl. 1850s)

Two brothers from Cecil County, Maryland, Henry Chambers and John Chambers sought the help of operatives of the Philadelphia–New York route of the Underground Railroad. In 1856, the two joined 21-year-old Samuel Fall and 18-year-old Jonathan Fisher in escaping their owners, farmer William Rybold and A. Rybold of Sassafras Neck, Pennsylvania.

Source

Still, William. *The Underground Railroad.* Philadelphia: Porter & Coates, 1871.

Chambers, Stephen (1836–?)

A black teenage laborer in Baltimore, Maryland, Stephen Chambers paid a high price for rescuing a slave. On September 29, 1854, he began serving a six-year sentence in the state penitentiary in Baltimore. After his release six years later, he remained in Baltimore, married, and established a family.

Source

Prison records, Maryland State Archives.

Chandler, Elizabeth Margaret (1807–1834)

Abolitionist pioneer and author Elizabeth Margaret Chandler extended the outreach from Quakers to Presbyterians and other denominations. A cradle Quaker, she was born in Wilmington, Delaware, and lived with her grandmother in Philadelphia, Pennsylvania. Chandler began writing at age 18 for Benjamin Lundy's abolitionist newspaper *Genius of Universal Emancipation* and eventually edited the Ladies' Repository section. In 1830, she settled on a farm outside Tecumseh in Lenawee County, Michigan, and organized the Logan Female Anti-Slavery Society. Among her volunteers was Underground Railroad agent Laura Smith Haviland.

See also: abolitionist newspapers; Quakers.

Source

Haviland, Laura S. *A Woman's Life-Work: Labors and Experiences of Laura S. Haviland.* Cincinnati, OH: Walden & Stowe, 1882.

Chandler, Zachariah (1813–1879)
Chandler, Letitia Grace Douglas (1820–?)

Zachariah Chandler served his country as U.S. senator, secretary of the interior, and a conductor of runaway slaves. Born in Bedford, New Hampshire, on December 10, 1813, he managed the family farm, taught school, and devoted himself to Presbyterianism. He grew wealthy after setting up a wholesale dry goods business in Detroit at age 20. After establishing a safehouse in Bedford on Fort Street, in December 1844, he married Letitia Grace Douglas from New York. The couple aided the city's Underground Railroad terminus before Zachariah's election as mayor of Detroit and, in 1857, to the U.S. Senate.

Zachariah Chandler preferred to keep his abolitionist opinions to himself. Nonetheless, he directed his philanthropy toward the activities of the secret network. When Charles T. Gorham incurred a $2,000 fine for aiding the network, Chandler, Isaac Davis, and neighbors in Climax, Michigan, donated the money. Chandler supported Abraham Lincoln, opposed the admission of Kansas as a slave state, and predicted that a civil war was inevitable. He stated in a letter to Governor Austin Blair of Michigan that the nation would have to experience bloodshed to survive. At Chandler's sudden death in Chicago on October 31, 1879, he was a frontrunner for the Republican candidacy for president.

See also: philanthropists.

Sources

Burton, Clarence Monroe. *The City of Detroit, Michigan, 1701–1922.* Detroit, MI: S.J. Clarke, 1922.

Wilson, James Grant, and John Fiske, eds. *Appleton's Cyclopaedia of American Biography.* New York: D. Appleton, 1888.

Chapin, Titus (1801–1865)
Chapin, Emily McKinstry (1806–1842)

Abolitionist Titus Chapin, a corn and potato farmer, used his job as village constable to rescue slaves from bounty hunters. He married Emily McKinstry in 1830. At their home in Chicopee, in Hampden County, Massachusetts, the Chapins hid runaways in an inner chamber. While Titus Chapin marketed his produce at Cabotville, he relayed slaves in his farm wagon to Holyoke by way of the South Holyoke Ferry and by Smith's Ferry across the Connecticut River to the next stop. He packed cheese and bread for passengers' travel food, provided 50¢ each in coin, and directed the refugees to walk through woods and pasture to the waystation of Cecilia Lyman Williston and John Payson Williston on King Street in Northampton, Massachusetts.

See also: bounty hunters.

Source

"The Underground Railroad and Those Who Operated It," *Springfield (OH) Republican,* March 11, 1900.

Chaplin, William Lawrence (1796–1871)

A conductor and radical lecturer and journalist, General William Lawrence "Will" Chaplin arranged a famous failed rescue, the escape of the Edmondson family from slavery in Washington, D.C. The last of a family of nine, Chaplin was born in Groton, Massachusetts. An editor and writer for the *Albany Patriot,* he lived in Albany, New York, and supported the New York Anti-Slavery Society by serving as secretary and by publishing biographies of fugitive slaves. In 1839, he attended an anti-slavery convention with activists Gerrit Smith, Joshua Leavitt, and Henry Brewer Stanton. Chaplin replaced a martyred roving agent, the Reverend Charles Turner Torrey, who died in prison in May 1846. Chaplin began traveling below the Mason-Dixon Line to aid slaves. Local operatives Luke and Sarah Carter, John Eaton, and Eber M. Pettit in Versailles, Indiana, assisted Chaplin's work by harboring runaways after they crossed into free territory.

While furthering the aims of his Bureau of Humanity, on April 15, 1848, Chaplin arranged the flight of five siblings—Emily, Ephraim, Mary Catherine, Richard, and Samuel Edmondson—in a party of 77 slaves aboard the schooner *Pearl.* After the ship was halted on its way southeast from Chesapeake Bay, federal marshals recaptured its human cargo. Slave dealers marked the girls for sale as concubines. Officers arrested Chaplin in Rockville, Maryland, for participating in a gunfight and for resisting arrest during the escape of two Georgia slaves belonging to members of the U.S. Congress, Alexander H. Stephens and Robert Toombs. To hire a defense team and pay bail, organizers of the Chaplin Fund Committee raised cash from philanthropists Salmon Portland Chase, Joshua Reed Giddings, David A. Hall, Joseph Comstock Hathaway, Francis Jackson, Gerrit Smith, Lewis Tappan, and John Greenleaf Whittier.

Chaplin remained in the Rockville jail until December 1850, under indictment for three counts of assault with intent to kill, two counts of abetting slave flight, and two counts for grand larceny. Following his marriage to Theodosia Gilbert, he jumped a bail bond of $25,000 and, to the disappointment of his supporters, narrowed his labors for abolitionism to the lecture circuit. A treatise, *The Case of William L. Chaplin* (1851), bore the subtitle *Being an Appeal to All respecters of Law and Justice, Against the Cruel and Oppressive Treatment to Which, Under Color of Legal Proceedings, He Has Been Subject, in the District of Columbia and the State of Maryland.*

See also: philanthropists.

Sources

Case of William L. Chaplin. Boston: Chaplin Committee, 1851.

Ricks, Mary Kay, "Escape on the Pearl," *Washington Post,* August 12, 1998, H1.

Chapman, Maria Weston (1806–1885)

A feminist and abolitionist, Maria Weston Chapman of Weymouth, Massachusetts, raised funds and enlisted volunteers for the Underground Railroad. With her sisters, Anne, Caroline, and Debora, Maria Chapman grew up in an anti-slavery household and associated with a strong abolitionist cousin, Ann Terry Green Phillips, wife of orator Wendell Addison Phillips. In 1830, Maria married Henry Grafton Chapman, a member of a family that boycotted cotton, indigo, rice, sugar, and tobacco because they were produced by slave labor. The Chapmans invited Wendell Addison Phillips to their home to meet William Lloyd Garrison, a young orator just discovered by the Reverend Samuel Joseph May and his cousin, attorney Samuel Edmund Sewall. In 1832, Maria and her sisters co-founded the Boston Anti-Slavery Society; two years later, they organized fund-raising fairs in Boston, Abington, and Weymouth. In 1839, Maria Chapman joined Lydia Maria Francis Child and Lucretia Coffin Mott as the first female officers of the American Anti-Slavery Society. An antifeminist backlash caused the resignation of James Gillespie Birney, Gerrit Smith, Arthur Tappan, and Lewis Tappan from the society.

Chapman used her talents in a broad span of projects. In 1842, she opposed the raising of funds to redeem George W. Latimer, a 22-year-old runaway from Norfolk, Virginia. She declared reimbursement of slave owner James B. Gray an insult to humanity. With Sydney Howard Gay and Edmund Quincy, in 1844, she began editing the *National Anti-Slavery Standard.* For the annual anti-slavery fairs in Boston, she published a gift book, the *Liberty Bell,* which featured a poem by English poet Elizabeth Barrett Browning. Chapman served the Massachusetts Anti-Slavery Society as treasurer and edited its annual report, *Right and Wrong in Massachusetts.* She also wrote for the *Non-Resistant* and William Lloyd Garrison's *The Liberator.* In 1855, she published *How Can I Help to Abolish Slavery; or, Counsels to the Newly Converted,* a practical handbook encouraging anti-slavery fairs and the boycotting of all slave-made products.

See also: American Anti-Slavery Society; anti-slavery fairs; free labor store; *Liberator, The.*

Sources

Emerson, Dorothy May. *Boston Women Who Worked for Racial Justice.* Boston: Unitarian Universalist Women's Heritage Society, 1993.
Venet, Wendy Hammond. *Neither Ballots nor Bullets: Women Abolitionists and the Civil War.* Charlottesville: University Press of Virginia, 1991.

Chase, Isaac, Jr. (1801–1872)
Chase, Lucy Sheldon (1801–1872)

In Parma, in Monroe County, New York, Quaker storekeeper Isaac Chase, Jr., aided in the rescue of slaves via the Underground Railroad. He followed the humanitarian traditions of his parents, Isaac Chase, Sr. (1761–1833), and Sarah Bond Chase (1769–1842) of Worcester, Massachusetts, who settled their family at Greece, New York. In 1834, Isaac Chase and his first wife, Lucy Sheldon Chase, moved to Parma and built a two-story cobblestone safehouse at 1191 Manitou Road. The residence featured a concealed chamber in the cellar accessed by a trapdoor. Isaac Chase, Jr., piloted passengers in a hay wagon seven miles to Lake Ontario for the final journey to Canada.

Source

Husted, Shirley C. *Parma and Hilton.* Charleston, SC: Arcadia, 2000.

Chase, Leonard (1810–?)
Chase, Susanna Shattuck (1807–?)

Merchant and furniture manufacturer Leonard Chase of Millbury, Massachusetts, and his wife, Susanna Shattuck Chase of Groton, Massachusetts, operated an Underground Railroad station in Milford, New Hampshire. After their marriage in March 1844, they hid slaves at their residence at 15 High Street. The couple shared responsibilities for the stop with their next-door neighbor, Daniel Putnam, who was also Leonard's partner, and with newspaper publisher Tom Beach.

Source

Shattuck, Lemuel. *Memorials of the Descendants of William Shattuck.* Boston: Dutton and Wentworth, 1855.

Chase, Salmon Portland (1808–1873)

Salmon Portland Chase supported the Underground Railroad in the roles of recruiter of stationmasters and defender of slaves and their rescuers. A native of Cornish, New Hampshire, he studied law at Dartmouth before establishing a practice in Cincinnati, Ohio. As a member of the Cincinnati Anti-Slavery Society, he influenced the abolitionism of John Finney, a safehouse keeper in Richland County, Ohio, and supported the volunteerism of Warner Mifflin Bateman in Springboro, Ohio. Chase offered free legal counsel to fugitive slaves. He defended David Putnam, Jr., an agent in Marietta, Ohio, from a lawsuit pressed by Virginia planter George Washington Henderson charging Putnam with seducing nine slaves from bondage. The suit ended in dismissal in U.S. district court in Columbus.

Chase was the lead counsel in a number of significant cases involving slave rescue. In spring 1855, he joined Cincinnati attorney Rutherford Birchard Hayes in protecting Rosetta Armstead from repossession by her owner, the Reverend Henry M. Denison of Louisville, Kentucky. In an Ohio Supreme Court of January 1838, Chase defended James Gillespie Birney for aiding and abetting slave escape. Two years later, Chase helped Dr. William Henry Brisbane of Charleston, South Carolina, manumit his slaves. With Thomas Morris, Chase pursued the case of conductor John Van Zandt of Glendale, Ohio, for a decade after the defendant's death in 1847. In 1848, Chase partnered with Francis Jackson, Samuel Gridley Howe, Horace Mann, Robert Morris, and Samuel Edmund Sewall in defending Captain Daniel Drayton, who attempted the rescue of 77 runaways on the sloop *Pearl* from Georgetown, in the District of Columbia, to New Jersey. The guilty verdict placed the captain under a 20-year sentence for violating the Fugitive Slave Law of 1850.

Chase was elected to the U.S. Senate in 1849 and joined Joshua Reed Giddings in fighting the flesh trade in Congress. After passage of the Fugitive Slave Law of 1850, Chase and colleagues John P. Hale, Charles Sumner, and Benjamin Franklin Wade publicly denounced a statute that forced abolitionists to aid in slave recapture. In December 1853, Chase joined forces with William Henry Seward to cleanse the record of Richard Eells of Quincy, Illinois, for aiding a fugitive slave named Charley. The two lawyers failed in their appeal to the U.S. Supreme Court.

On May 24, 1859, Giddings invited Chase and John Mercer Langston to speak in Cleveland, Ohio, against the pro-South leanings of President James Buchanan. Chase's anti-slavery speeches influenced a number of Underground Railroad agents, such as Charles Boerstler Huber of Williamsburg, Ohio, who read platform orations in Gamaliel Bailey's newspaper, the *National Era.* During the Civil War, Chase supported aggression in the name of abolition of slavery and quarreled with President Abraham Lincoln over the enlistment of black males in the Union army.

See also: black soldiers; Fugitive Slave Law of 1850.

Source

Buckmaster, Henrietta. *Let My People Go: The Story of the Underground Railroad and the Growth of the Abolition Movement.* New York: Harper & Brothers, 1941.

Chase, Silas (1813–1864)

An abolitionist Methodist, the Reverend Silas Chase, also a physician, supported the Bethel, Ohio, Underground Railroad network. In 1845, he founded and pastored the Sugar Tree Wesleyan Church in Felicity, in Clermont County, Ohio. The congregation included conductors Isaac Holmes Brown, Richard Mace, Lewis Pettijohn, Benjamin H. Rice, Elizabeth Swing Rice, and William Eberle Thompson. Chase conveyed refugees to colleagues Brown or Thompson in Bethel, Ohio, or to Charles Boerstler "Boss" Huber's tannery or farm in Williamsburg, Ohio. After Chase left his post, the Reverend Gerrard P. Riley continued the church's commitment to desperate runaways.

Source

Everts, Louis H. *History of Clermont County, Ohio.* Philadelphia: J.B. Lippincott, 1880.

Chatham Convention

Before insurrectionist John Brown's attack on the federal arsenal in Harpers Ferry, Virginia, on October 16, 1859, he gathered forces and studied the fervor and loyalty of his backers. At the time of his survey of Underground Railroad arrivals to Chatham, Canada West claimed some 75,000 fugitive settlers. Among the newcomers was physician Martin Robinson Delany, a recruiter of agents for the secret network and Brown's most trusted adviser.

Louisianian Isaac Holden, a Canadian resident for a quarter century, invited Brown to his home in April 1858 for a preconvention assembly of route organizers to enlarge the operation to a Subterranean Pass Way. Held on May 8 and 10, 1858, the Chatham Convention mustered the life's blood of the Underground Railroad for suggestions of ways to streamline operations and to reshape the U.S. government to reflect a multiracial citizenry. The enclave, chaired by the Reverend William Charles Munroe and recorded by secretary John Henry Kagi, included dedicated rescuers—Delany, Kagi, William Lambert, Charles Smith, James Lawrence Smith, and John A. Thomas. The men studied the operation of secret routes and plotted a bloodier but more immediate method of ending slavery. The plans looked beyond national emancipation by mapping a constitutional government for a nation of ex-slaves.

See also: civil disobedience; subterranean pass way.

Source

Hinton, Richard Josiah. *John Brown and His Men: With Some Account of the Roads They Travelled to Reach Harpers Ferry.* New York: Funk & Wagnalls, ca. 1894.

Cheney, Ednah Dow Littlehale (1824–1904)

Abolitionist, reformer, and philanthropist Ednah Dow Littlehale Cheney of Boston, Massachusetts, supported runaway slaves through the New England Freeman's Aid Society. In 1856, her outreach expanded after the death of her husband, Seth Wells Cheney, who left her a substantial fortune. Two years before her death, she published *Reminiscences of Ednah Dow Cheney* (1902), in which she expressed her sympathy for human chattel. Among her closest associates of the Underground Railroad were Louisa May Alcott, Lydia Maria Francis

Child, Julia Ward Howe, and Harriet Beecher Stowe, the author of *Uncle Tom's Cabin* (1852).

See also: philanthropists; *Uncle Tom's Cabin; or, Life Among the Lowly* (1852).

Source

Cheney, Ednah Dow Littlehale. *Reminiscences of Ednah Dow Cheney.* Boston: Lee & Shepard, 1902.

Cheney, Moses (1793–1875)
Cheney, Abigail Morrison (1796–1881)
Cheney, Elias Hutchins (1832–ca. 1924)
Cheney, Oren Burbank (1816–1903)

A paper manufacturer, Deacon Moses Cheney, harbored slaves passing through Peterborough, New Hampshire, on their way to Canada. The son of English Puritans, he was born in Thornton, New Hampshire, where he developed a strong religious faith. After his marriage to Abigail Morrison, a fervid abolitionist from Thornton, in June 1816, the couple settled at Upper Union Street. They began work for the Underground Railroad in 1835 and continued for a decade. The Cheneys' sons, Elias Hutchins and Oren Burbank, completed slave transfers along Windy Row to Hancock, the next stop. Frederick Douglass stayed with the Cheney family in 1840 when he addressed the New England Anti-Slavery Society. In adulthood, the Reverend Oren Cheney, the founder of Bates College in Lewiston, Maine, maintained the family's Freewill Baptist beliefs. In Dover, New Hampshire, at Locust and Washington streets, he fostered abolitionism with his newspaper, the *Morning Star.*

Source

Stearns, Ezra S. *Genealogy and Family History of the State of New Hampshire.* New York: Lewis, 1908.

Cheny, Charles (1803–1874)
Cheny, Frank Woodbridge (1832–1909)

A native of Manchester, Connecticut, Charles Cheny (or Cheney) rescued runaways on the frontier route of the Underground Railroad. After marrying Waitsell Dexter Shaw in 1829, he opened a general store in Providence, Rhode Island. During an unpromising financial period, he settled his family on 87 acres at Mount Healthy, near Cincinnati, Ohio. After the death of his wife in 1841, Charles and his son, Frank Woodbridge Cheny, maintained a safehouse on their property. The two used a farm wagon for relays to the next stop.

Source

Smiddy, Betty Ann. *A Little Piece of Paradise . . . College Hill, Ohio.* Cincinnati, OH: College Hill Historical Society, 1999.

Chester, George (?–1859)
Chester, Jane Marie (?–1884)
Chester, Thomas Morris (1834–1892)

Restaurateurs George Chester and his wife, Jane Marie "Auntie Jane" Chester, received runaways traveling via the Underground Railroad. Jane, an escaped slave from Baltimore, freed herself and married George Chester, the owner of an oyster and ale house and catering service at Market and North Third streets in Harrisburg, in Philadelphia County, Pennsylvania. The site housed abolitionist gatherings and featured copies of William Lloyd Garrison's weekly, *The Liberator,* and Frederick Douglass's *North Star.* The Chesters harbored slaves at their business and at their home and published letters in *The Liberator* promoting slave rescue. In widowhood in 1859, Jane Chester appears to have given up her volunteerism for the secret network.

Her son, journalist and attorney Thomas Morris Chester, assisted his parents' volunteerism in boyhood and remained faithful to the abolitionist cause. He collaborated with other abolitionists to create more Underground Railroad routes. At his safehouse at Market Square and Third Street, he coordinated transfers with Joseph Cassey Bustill, a co-founder of the Harrisburg Fugitive Slave Society, in concealing fugitives on freight cars of the Reading & Pennsylvania railway. During the Civil War, Thomas recruited blacks for the Fifty-fourth Massachusetts Regiment and, as the first black war correspondent from a major newspaper, covered combat for the *Philadelphia Press.*

See also: Liberator, The; *North Star*; routes, Underground Railroad.

Sources

"Borne to Lincoln Cemetery," *Harrisburg (PA) Patriot,* October 4, 1892.

Osler & Irvin's Harrisburg Directory for 1856. Harrisburg, PA: Osler & Irvin, 1856.

Child, Lydia Maria Francis (1802–1880)
Child, David Lee (1794–1874)

Propagandist and publisher Lydia Maria Francis Child and her husband, David Lee Child, assisted black

Writer and journalist Lydia Maria Francis Child worked alongside other women in the abolitionist movement, helped write and edit anti-slavery publications, and, with husband David Lee Child, assisted passengers in the network outside Boston. *(Hulton Archive/Stringer/Getty Images)*

passengers of the Underground Railroad. Lydia Child grew up in Medford, Massachusetts, until age 12, when she went to live with her sister in Norridgewock, Maine. While residing in Watertown, Massachusetts, in 1822, she became a friend of conductor Abigail Goodwin and met poet and essayist Ralph Waldo Emerson, the Reverend Theodore Parker, and editor and poet John Greenleaf Whittier, abolitionists who influenced her to support slave rescues. Lydia was also close to her niece, Mary Elizabeth Preston Stearns, the wife of abolitionist and secret network proponent George Luther Stearns of Medford.

After publishing *Hobomok* (1824), a novel about a white woman's marriage to a Pequot man, Lydia made a niche for herself among the Boston intelligentsia. In 1828, she married a fellow abolitionist, attorney David Lee Child of West Boylston, Massachusetts, who supported her membership in the Boston Female Anti-Slavery Society and her essays for *The Liberator.* After he published *The Despotism of Freedom; or, The Tyranny and Cruelty of American Republican Slave-Masters, Shown to Be the Worst in the World* (1833), she issued *An Appeal in Favor of That Class of Americans Called Africans* (1833), a text favored by the American Anti-Slavery Society for its conversion of new supporters.

In August 1836, Lydia Child and other female abolitionists helped to free the child Med Slater, a slave from New Orleans, Louisiana, and to set a precedent for other slaves transported to free states. Lydia gained the respect of agents Abraham and Katy Allen, William Ellery Channing, the Reverend Thomas Wentworth Higginson, Elihu Oren, and Wendell Addison Phillips and of female abolitionists Maria Weston Chapman, and Lucretia Coffin Mott. After the election of Chapman, Child, and Mott to offices in the American Anti-Slavery Society, an antifeminist backlash caused the resignation of James Gillespie Birney, Gerrit Smith, and Arthur and Lewis Tappan.

While David Child raised sugar beets as a protest against slave-harvested cane sugar, Lydia joined in the farm chores and supported the family by writing. From 1841 to 1854, the couple edited the *National Anti-Slavery Standard,* a respected abolitionist newspaper that influenced the Underground Railroad rescues of Jonathan Paxson Magill and his sons, Edward Hicks and Watson Magill, in Bucks County, Pennsylvania. Lydia published in the *Oasis* (1834) the testimonial of a kidnapped slave, James Bradley, whom slavers brought from Africa to Charleston, South Carolina. In 1841, she wrote the story of Wagelma, an apprenticed 10-year-old rescued from abduction by Isaac Tatem Hopper.

In 1853, Lydia Child serialized an allegorical play, *The Stars and Stripes,* which fictionalized an historical ruse—the use of an icehouse as a Detroit waystation. The signal for slaves to hide was the singing of "Old Dan Tucker." In the story, an historical couple, Ellen Smith Craft and William Craft, make their way to the steamer *Henry Clay,* which bears them to Canada in 1850. Child's abolitionist activity included a trip to the prison at Charlestown, Virginia, to visit insurrectionist John Brown, who was condemned on November 2, 1859, to hanging for treason. In 1860, she issued "The Duty of Disobedience to the Fugitive Slave Act," a directive to fence sitters on the subject of aiding escapees. A more poignant contribution to slave literature was Harriet Ann Jacobs's autobiography, *Incidents in the Life of a Slave Girl* (1861), which Lydia Child edited and published.

See also: abolitionist newspapers; American Anti-Slavery Society; civil disobedience; *Incidents in the Life of a Slave Girl* (1861); kidnap.

Sources

Child, Lydia Maria, "*The Stars and Stripes:* A Melodrama," *National Antislavery Standard,* January 23 and 30, 1853, 4.
Porter, Dorothy B. "Anti-Slavery Movement in Northampton." *Negro History Bulletin* 24:2 (1960): 33–34, 41.

Chion, Emma (1833–?)
Chion, William (1833–?)

In flight from Bushong Blake, 27-year-old Emma Chion and her husband, William Chion, escaped from Dorchester County, Maryland. In 1860, they arrived safely in Philadelphia, Pennsylvania, and requested help from Underground Railroad agents. To conceal their identity from their masters, Emma and William changed their surname to Williams.

Source

Still, William. *The Underground Railroad.* Philadelphia: Porter & Coates, 1871.

Christian, Washington (ca. 1776–1850)

The Reverend Washington Christian assisted in the settlement of runaway slaves in Toronto, Ontario. After ordination in the Abyssinian Baptist Church in New York, he became a New England circuit rider. At age 51, he settled in York, Ontario, and became the first black preacher to minister to blacks arriving in the Toronto area via the Underground Railroad. Unsettled conditions in Ohio in 1829 increased the flow of passengers over the secret network. In 1834, Christian's followers built a church on March Street. Within two years, his parishioners numbered 66, most of whom were former slaves or their descendents. He formed other congregations in Hamilton and St. Catharines, Ontario, and superintended black settlement from Chatham to Sandwich.

See also: Canada.

Source

Landon, Fred. "The Negro Migration to Canada after the Passing of the Fugitive Slave Act." *Journal of Negro History* 5 (January 1920): 22–36.

Christiana Riot

At Christiana, Pennsylvania, just over the Maryland border, the virulence of public outcry against slave catching impacted the nation a decade before the outbreak of the Civil War. The face-off of September 11, 1851, was the first armed bloodshed in response to the Fugitive Slave Law of 1850. Trouble began in August when farmer Edward Gorsuch, a Maryland slaveholder; his son, Dickerson Gorsuch; and Federal Marshal Henry H. Kline advanced to Pennsylvania. Gorsuch carried with him directions to the home of Underground Railroad agent William Parker outside Columbia, Pennsylvania. The slave owner intended to recover four young runaways—Noah Baley, Nelson Ford, George Hammond, and Joshua Hammond—who fled Retreat Farm in Baltimore County, Maryland, in 1849.

Underground Railroad agents in Philadelphia tipped off local conductors. On September 10, 1851, Samuel Williams recognized the posse on the train and, exiting the car at Penningtonville, spread the alarm among abolitionists. At dawn the next day, Edward Gorsuch arrived at Parker's residence and demanded the escaped slaves, who threw heavy objects at the posse from the upstairs windows and hurled an ax and fishing spear when Gorsuch approached the stairs. Under gunfire, Parker's wife, Eliza Ann Elizabeth Howard Parker, blew a horn out the attic window to summon help. A Quaker miller, abolitionist Castner Hanway, joined Henry C. Hopkins, Elijah Lewis, Joseph P. Scarlett, and other neighbors in a show of nonviolent support for Parker. By the time the riot concluded, Edward Gorsuch had been shot to death by black women, Dickerson Gorsuch had been wounded, two other members of the party had suffered buckshot wounds, Henry C. Hopkins had a bullet in the arm, and the freedmen who joined the fight had been arrested. Three other slaves—James Dawsey, William Howard, and Charles Long—escaped the uproar and sheltered at the safehouse of brothers Caleb C. Hood and Joseph Hood in Bart, Pennsylvania.

Afterward, William Parker fled to Levi Pownall's house. Pownall's wife, Sarah, dressed Parker and his brothers-in-law, Alexander Pinkney and Abraham Johnson, in suits and hats and escorted them through the front door past guards as though they were honored guests. Parker reached Frederick Douglass's waystation in Rochester, New York. Upon presentation of warrants, Sarah Pownall rebuked the authorities for naming Parker, Pinkney, and Johnson as current runaways. Angered by flagrant disregard for federal law, President Millard Fillmore activated a marine unit to respond. U.S. marines arrived from Philadelphia, Pennsylvania, to secure order.

Eighty local officers searched the county for anyone suspected of fomenting the riot. One man hid in a cave to avoid arrest. The sheriff apprehended Eliza Parker and her sister-in-law but let them go as a gesture to assuage the public outrage that arose at the jailing of women for protecting their homes. A roundup of blacks in Christiana resulted in the return of Parker's mother-in-law and five others to slavery. Quaker agent Levi Pownall burned Parker's records to conceal letters from runaways and conductors. Authorities charged Hanway with refusing to aid the marshal in the standoff, which involved seven white males, five black males, and two black women.

In all, Castner Hanway, Elijah Lewis, Joseph P. Scarlett, and 35 blacks faced treason charges, a number that set a precedent in American law. The 38 men remained in Moyamensing Prison in Philadelphia for 97 days, until November 1851. Hanway was the only participant to come to trial. He appeared in the court of Judge Elisha Kent Kane at Independence Hall in Philadelphia, with Thaddeus Stevens, a Lancaster attorney, defending him. Lucretia Coffin Mott showed her support by sitting in the audience knitting strands of red, white, and blue yarn. Black demonstrators wore red-white-and-blue bandanas as evidence of patriotism.

The jury required only 20 minutes to exonerate Hanway. After the acquittal, Judge Robert C. Grier lambasted rescue agents as "infuriated fanatics and unprincipled demagogues . . . teaching that theft is meritorious, murder excusable, and treason a virtue." The incident, a high point of Underground Railroad fervor, was an antecedent of the Civil War. In 1866, William Parker published "The Freedman's Story," an account of the riot in the February and March issues of *Atlantic Monthly.*

See also: Quakers.

Sources

Bacon, Margaret Hope. *I Speak for My Slave Sister—The Life of Abby Kelley Foster.* New York: Thomas Y. Crowell, 1974.

———. *Rebellion at Christiana.* New York: Thomas Y. Crowell, 1975.

Hensel, W.U. *The Christiana Riot and the Treason Trials of 1851.* Lancaster, PA: New Era, 1911.

Smedley, Robert C. *History of the Underground Railroad in Chester and the Neighboring Counties of Pennsylvania.* Lancaster, PA: Office of *The Journal,* 1883.

Church, Jefferson (1802–1885)

Dr. Jefferson Church, a friend of insurrectionist John Brown, aided the work of the Underground Railroad in Springfield, Massachusetts. Church studied medicine privately in Castleton, Vermont, and earned a degree from Pittsfield Medical College. In May 1826, Church married Betsey Little of Middlefield in Peru, Massachusetts; the following year, he opened a homeopathic practice. Fugitives usually traveled up the Connecticut River to his safehouse. In 1851, he began a two-year term as a manager of the American Anti-Slavery Society.

See also: American Anti-Slavery Society.

Source

DeCaro, Louis A. *Fire from the Midst of You: A Religious Life of John Brown.* New York: New York University Press, 2002.

Cinqué, Joseph (ca. 1811–ca. 1879)

On July 2, 1839, Joseph Cinqué (originally Sengbe Pieh), a Mandingo nobleman from Sierra Leone, led a mutiny aboard the Portuguese slaver *Amistad.* Dubbed the Black Prince, Cinque was a chief's son and rice farmer in the village of Mani. In April 1839, Spanish slaver Pedro Blanco seized Cinqué and penned him with other slaves in a barracoon on Lomboko Island at the Galinas River delta on the Sierra Leone–Liberia border. The *Amistad,* bound for a market in Guanaja, Honduras, contained 53 Mende kidnap victims, whom Cinqué freed from their manacles with a nail. Armed with machetes, the Africans followed Cinqué's command. However, the Spanish pilot ordered to navigate, instead of steering east for Africa, moved north, and along the way, eight captives died. After two months at sea, the *Amistad* arrived in Long Island Sound off New London, Connecticut.

Cinqué and his fellow mutineers were arrested on charges of murder and piracy. Authorities jailed them in New Haven, Connecticut. In collaboration with the Reverend Simeon Jocelyn of New Haven and the Reverend Joshua Leavitt, editor of the *Emancipator,* Underground Railroad agent Lewis Tappan led a protest of the jailing of Cinqué and the 42 other adult Africans. When the trial began, Leavitt stirred emotions by publishing "A Poem for Cinqué," by William Cullen Bryant. Because of cogent arguments by lawyer Roger Sherman Baldwin, on March 9, 1841, the U.S. Supreme Court declared that the African kidnap victims had mutinied in self-defense. The black press provided full coverage of the unfolding moral dilemma, with Philip Alexander Bell's popular New York weekly, the *Colored American,* offering regular commentary.

Underground Railroad operatives provided lodging, clothing, and moral support during the lengthy litigation. Cinqué developed a close friendship with abolitionist John Treadwell Norton and his son Charles. On March 19, 1841, Cinqué and his fellow Africans traveled through a spring snowstorm to the First Church of Christ in Farmington, Connecticut, to address abolitionists and raise money for the return voyage to Sierra Leone. Cinqué was the frequent spokesmen for the kidnap victims. His passionate cry for liberty infused New England's abolitionists with new fervor. Philanthropists Samuel Deming, John Hooker, and John Norton contributed to the fund, which netted $1,200 in cash to ease the mutineers' plight. On May 4, 1841, Austin Franklin Williams and local supporters built a barracks at 127 Main Street in Farmington, Connecticut, to house the Africans until they could return home. In summer 1841, Cinqué reported the drowning of Foone, a teenage farmer who despaired of ever seeing Sierra Leone again.

See also: Amistad; kidnap.

Sources

Jones, Howard. *Mutiny on the* Amistad. Oxford, UK: Oxford University Press, 1987.

Osagie, Iyunolu Folayan. *The* Amistad *Revolt: Memory, Slavery, and the Politics of Identity in the United States and Sierra Leone.* Athens: University of Georgia Press, 2000.

Owens, William A. *Black Mutiny: The Revolt on the Schooner* Amistad. New York: Plume, 1997.

Spielberg, Steven, Maya Angelou, and Debbie Allen. Amistad: *"Give Us Free."* New York: Newmarket, 1998.

civil disobedience

The history of the Underground Railroad demonstrates large-scale defiance of unconscionable and barbaric laws. Nonetheless, the dedication of abolitionists to their cause varied in intensity and scope. At the heart of dissension was the question of civil disobedience to federal and state law concerning the purchase, breeding, and selling of slaves and the return of runaways to slave owners. For some defiers, the goad that pricked the conscience was evidence from eyewitnesses and from the abolitionist press of amputations and torture, sexual enslavement, and the breeding of children like livestock for sale on auction blocks. On the side of the law-abiding citizen were nonviolent dissidents, many of whom were pacifist Quakers. They posed Bible-based arguments for buying slaves from bondage and for offering sanctuary and sustenance to the desperate and hungry, but they abstained from outright slave theft and transportation of individuals from their owners.

> A mild-mannered libertarian and conductor of the secret network, Henry David Thoreau promoted social justice and passive resistance by refusing to pay poll tax to a government that condoned human bondage. In his 1859 essay, "A Plea for Captain John Brown," he described the explosive nature of civil disobedience among agents of the secret network: "The only free road, the Underground Railroad, is owned and managed by the Vigilant Committee. They have tunnelled under the whole breadth of the land. Such a government is losing its power and respectability as surely as water runs out of a leaky vessel."

As anti-slavery voices began dominating the public forum, the emerging campaign threatened to destabilize or sever the Union. At the Anti-Slavery Convention of American Women held in New York City on May 9 through 12, 1837, publisher Lydia Maria Francis Child and Quaker orator Lucretia Coffin Mott set the tone of informed law breaking. A decade later at the Plymouth Church of the Pilgrims in Brooklyn, New York, the Reverend Henry Ward Beecher directed Congregationalists to join the crusade to free slaves. Opponents of bondage chose President Millard Fillmore as a symbol of oppression after he signed the Fugitive Slave Law of 1850, the breaking point of civilian patience with the southern plantation system. In response, anti-slavery activists such as the Reverend Henry Highland Garnet in Troy, New York, felt such outrage at the flesh trade that they condoned any method of release for the slave, including sabotage, theft, piracy, and violence against slave owners, kidnappers, bounty hunters, and U.S. marshals. As the situation worsened for libertarians with the election of President Franklin Pierce in 1853, Esther Fussell Lewis of Kimberton, Pennsylvania, and other parents passed family traditions of abolitionism to their children and grandchildren. For these extended clans, civil disobedience became a treasured spiritual heirloom.

The concerted violators of the law sided with William Lloyd Garrison, the radical publisher of *The Liberator,* who believed that slavery should end at once rather than piecemeal, as the laws of New York state decreed. Some Quakers followed the example of Catherine White Coffin and Levi Coffin, who relied on networking as a means of passing slaves from danger to safety. Many conductors were so moved to action that they split assemblies of the Society of Friends over issues of deliberate and planned intervention rather than passive disapproval of bondage. Among them were Isaac Tatem Hopper, his wife, Sarah Tatum Hopper, and their daughter and son-in-law, Abigail Hopper Gibbons and James Sloan Gibbons. For their uncompromising charity to runaways, Isaac Hopper and James Gibbons were disowned by their fellow Quakers. Out of religious fervor, moral warriors of many faiths turned churches and parsonages into waystations and organized social committees into outfitters of runaway families for the long road ahead. The most adamant rebels armed themselves and posted lookouts along Underground Railroad lanes and at safehouses. In Jeffersonville, Indiana, Cassius Marcellus Clay called for all-out war between federal agents and abolitionists.

The Midwest produced a unique strand of civil disobedience. At Temple Beth El in Detroit, Michigan, Rabbi Leibman Adler denounced human bondage by comparing it with the plight of the Hebrews in Exodus. His congregants Mark Sloman, Emil S. Heineman, and Fanny Butzel Heineman responded by joining the effort to whisk escapees across the Detroit River to Windsor, Canada. The most extreme form of Garrisonian abolitionism erupted in the midwestern heartland from the predations of insurrectionist John Brown. At the Chatham Convention held May 8 and 10, 1858, in Chatham, Ontario, Brown assembled a fighting force and plotted the overthrow of the U.S. government. To begin the violent end of slavery, he proposed the seizing of the federal arsenal in Harpers Ferry, Virginia, and the distribution of arms among militant blacks as an impetus to a race war. Although his plot failed, repercussions of his revolt were a major factor precipitating the Civil War.

See also: Anti-Slavery Convention of American Women; bounty hunters; Chatham Convention; Fugitive Slave Law of 1850; kidnap; *Liberator, The*; Plymouth Church of the Pilgrims; Quakers.

Sources

Dreese, Michael A. *The Hospital on Seminary Ridge at the Battle of Gettysburg.* Jefferson, NC: McFarland, 2002.

Thoreau, Henry David. *Civil Disobedience and Other Essays.* Mineola, NY: Dover, 1993.

Civil War

The outbreak of war on April 12, 1861, at Fort Sumter, South Carolina, brought a host of new agents to the Underground Railroad. In Girard, Pennsylvania, the Reverend Charles Shipman increased his civil disobedience to federal law by enlisting the congregation of the Universalist church as rescuers and emancipators of refugees. The groundswell of aid and sanctuary to the oppressed continued until national emancipation on January 1, 1863. In the last years of the war, humanitarianism took the form of assistance to ex-slaves, separated families, orphans, the elderly and infirm, and displaced persons.

As blacks began fleeing the South, Union soldiers and nurses such as Mary Ann Bickerdyke and Mary Ashton Rice Livermore claimed orphaned youngsters and concealed adult runaways in tents and bivouacs until agents could lead them to safety in the North. In spring 1861, Fort Monroe, Virginia, was overrun by escapees, after General Benjamin Franklin Butler refused to return fugitive slaves to their former owners. A similar situation occurred at Camp Nelson, Kentucky, where recruitment of black soldiers strengthened the Union presence below the Mason-Dixon line. To the north, Camp Warren Levis in Godfrey, Illinois, maintained a reputation for rescue of fugitives from Missouri. In early June 1864, after the battle of Cold Harbor, Virginia, Aaron Martin Landis, a 16-year-old enlistee in the 187th Pennsylvania Volunteers, received three runaways from Richmond, Virginia, and directed them along the Underground Railroad.

In Tennessee, a plantation domestic, Virginia Washington, fled bondage with the aid of Union infantrymen and settled in Cincinnati, Ohio, where she found work as a cook. In Brush Creek, in Ralls County, Missouri, one mother, Martha Jane Tolton of Kentucky, saw her husband, Peter Paul Tolton, off to war and then made a break for freedom. She carried a toddler, Anna, and led nine-year-old Cordella and two sons, Augustus and Charles, through wilderness to Hannibal, Missouri,

The latter stages of fighting in the Civil War brought a surge of uprooted slaves seeking refuge behind Union lines. Humanitarians came to the aid of former slaves, separated families, orphans, the elderly and infirm, and other displaced persons. *(Time & Life Pictures/Stringer/Getty Images)*

where soldiers smuggled her across the Mississippi River to Quincy, Illinois. Augustus Tolton became the first African American Catholic priest.

See also: black soldiers; civil disobedience.

Sources

Hemesath, Mary, "The Crossing," *Ave Maria,* May 21, 1966, 14–15.

Scott, John Welden. *African Americans of Harrisburg.* Charleston, SC: Arcadia, 2005.

Simmons, William J. *Men of Mark: Eminent, Progressive, and Rising.* Cleveland, OH: George M. Rewell, 1887.

Clark, Harriet Loomis (1794–1873)
Clark, Starr (1793–1866)

For three decades, Underground Railroad agents Harriet Loomis Clark of Torrington, Connecticut, and Starr Clark, a fugitive slave from Lee, Massachusetts, harbored refugees at the family hardware store and tinshop. The Clarks were pioneers to the New York frontier in 1816, when they arrived from New England by oxcart. In 1832, they settled at 3250 Main Street in Mexico, Oswego County, New York, and joined the First Presbyterian Church. Beginning in 1837, they maintained interlinking waystations at their business and residence, which they connected by a tunnel. In collaboration with their neighbor, banker James Chandler, the couple directed passengers to Cape Vincents, Port Ontario, or to Sackett's Harbor, New York.

On December 5, 1837, Starr Clark offered aid to George, a black patron of the local tavern who had arrived from the coast. Within days, local conductors sped George across Lake Ontario to Canada. On June 21, 1838, Starr joined Orson Ames and Joseph M. Barrows in serving on the town vigilance committee. In 1841, the Clarks' activities included joining Charlotte Ambler Clarke and Edwin W. Clarke, secret network coordinator Gerrit Smith, and New York Governor William Henry Seward in pressuring Governor Andre Bienvenu Roman of Louisiana to liberate a kidnap victim, James Watkins Seward, from a New Orleans jail.

In 2001, the Clark tinshop was listed on the National Register of Historic Places.

See also: kidnap; safehouses; vigilance committees.

Source

McAndrew, Mike, "Shop Hid Slaves and Found Place in History," *Syracuse Post-Standard,* February 1, 2005.

Clarke, Ann (ca. 1812–?)

A middle-aged domestic, Ann Clarke required two attempts before succeeding in freeing herself. The chattel of two federal agents, George W. Clarke and Colonel H.T. Titus, she lived in Lecompton, Kansas Territory, during the turmoil following the Kansas-Nebraska Act of 1854. In January 1857, she fled captivity and was apprehended by slave catchers from Deer Creek. While the men celebrated with liquor, she escaped again before the two could claim their reward. Assisting her was Dr. Ira D. Blanchard, a Baptist missionary at the Delaware Mission in Edwardsville, in Wyandotte County, Kansas.

Ann Clarke passed through a series of safehouses before reaching Mrs. Scales, a boardinghouse keeper at Topeka. After six weeks of hiding in a straw-filled sugar barrel, Clarke moved on through the secret network with the aid of Dr. Ira D. Blanchard and Mary Walton Blanchard to Civil Bend, Iowa. Transferred by John Armstrong in a mule-drawn carriage, Clarke traveled three weeks before settling in Chicago, Illinois. Armstrong raised $70 to pay the expenses, part of which came from donations by agent James Burnett Abbott and Governor Charles Robinson.

See also: safehouses.

Source

Sheridan, Richard B., ed. and comp. *Freedom's Crucible: The Underground Railroad in Lawrence and Douglas County Kansas, 1854–1865.* Lawrence: University of Kansas, 1998.

Clarke, Charlotte Ambler (1809–ca. 1860)
Clarke, Edwin W. (1801–1884)

Two Underground Railroad agents in Oswego, New York, educator Charlotte Ambler Clarke and her husband, attorney Edwin W. Clarke, operated a safehouse. Edwin Clarke came of age in Manlius, New York, and studied law. After their marriage in 1833, the Clarkes bought a 250-acre farm and involved themselves in letters to abolitionist newspapers, anti-slavery societies, abolitionist petitions, and the dissemination of tracts. They collaborated with Edwin Clarke's brother and sister-in-law, Sidney Clarke and Olive Jackson Clarke, who harbored slaves at their farm outside of Oswego before conducting them to the next depot in Sackett's Harbor or to sailboats on Lake Erie. Edwin Clarke also chaired the Oswego County Anti-Slavery Society and served as fund-raiser and political activist.

In 1841, Edwin failed to save a young slave woman fleeing via the Oswego Canal. That same year, the Clarkes joined Harriet Loomis Clark and Starr Clark, secret network coordinator Gerrit Smith, and New York Governor William Henry Seward in petitioning for the freeing of a kidnap victim, James Watkins Seward, from a New Orleans jail. Edwin Clarke's role in the campaign was a letter to the *Oswego Palladium* dated April 13, 1840, testifying to Seward's residence in Oswego County from 1826. The Clarke home harbored William "Jerry" McHenry, a mulatto cooper on the run through New York on his way to Canada in October 1851. In 1857, the Clarkes built a brick dwelling at 80 East Seventh and Mohawk streets featuring a concealed chamber in the cellar behind the furnace. Ventilating the room was an air vent under the front steps.

See also: abolitionist newspapers; kidnap; safehouses.

Sources

Clarke, Edwin W, "Re: James Watkins Seward," *Oswego Palladium,* April 29, 1840.

Henderson, Madison. *Trials and Confessions of Madison Henderson.* St. Louis, MO: Chambers & Knapp, 1841.

McAndrew, Mike, "When Being Black Was Called a Crime," *Syracuse Post-Standard,* February 24, 2005.

Clarke, Lewis Garrard (1812–1897)

Lewis Garrard Clarke of Madison County, Kentucky, lectured and wrote about his experiences as a runaway fleeing via the Underground Railroad. The son of a Scots weaver, a veteran of the battle of Bunker Hill, Clarke was a slave like his mother, Letitia Campbell Clarke, the mulatto daughter of William Campbell; Letitia was also William Campbell's servant until his death around 1822. After joining his brother Milton Clarke (ca. 1817–1901) in fleeing the cruelties of their mistress, Betsey Banton, in August 1841, Lewis rode on horseback all night toward the Ohio River.

The slave memoir *Narrative of the Sufferings of Lewis Clarke* (1845) reveals how the runaway followed the advice of conductors in Cincinnati, Ohio. He traveled upriver to Portsmouth, took the canal toward

Cleveland, and then crossed Lake Erie into Ontario. He returned to Kentucky to free his brother Cyrus and settled in New York City. Lewis and Milton Clarke teamed as lecturers and advisers to other runaways and cowrote an expanded version of Lewis Clarke's narrative. In 1860, Lewis married Catherine Storum (?–ca. 1875), daughter of secret network agents Sarah Storum and William Storum of Busti, New York. Lewis Clarke lived for a time with the sister-in-law of Harriet Beecher Stowe. The novelist used him as a model for the fictional George Harris in *Uncle Tom's Cabin* (1852).

See also: Uncle Tom's Cabin; or, Life Among the Lowly (1852).

Sources

Clarke, Lewis Garrard. *Narrative of the Sufferings of Lewis Clark.* Boston: Bela Marsh, 1845.

Stowe, Harriet Beecher. *A Key to Uncle Tom's Cabin.* London: Clarke, Beeton, 1853.

Clarke, Olive Jackson (1819–?)
Clarke, Sidney (1803–1869)
Clarke, John Jackson (1858–ca. 1940)

A diligent family of rescuers, Olive Jackson Clarke and her husband, Sidney Clarke, displayed compassion for the oppressed. After their marriage in 1844, they established a safehouse west of City Line Road in Fulton, in Oswego County, New York. The couple collaborated with Sidney's brother and sister-in-law, Edwin W. Clarke and Charlotte Ambler Clarke, who owned a 250-acre farm in Oswego. Aiding them was an extended family of Underground Railroad activists. Their transporter was a young nephew, John Jackson Clarke, who relayed passengers to Sackett's Harbor, New York, or to schooners or sailboats crossing Lake Erie.

Source

McAndrew, Mike, "Bold Raid Freed a Man," *Syracuse Post-Standard,* February 14, 2005.

Clarke, William Penn (1817–1903)

A civil servant and abolitionist, William Penn Clarke supported the work of the Underground Railroad. He was born in Baltimore, Maryland, learned the printer's trade in Gettysburg, Pennsylvania, and settled at age 21 in Cincinnati, Ohio, a major thoroughfare for escaped slaves. In addition to practicing law and editing the *Logan (OH) Gazette,* Clarke joined the abolitionist volunteerism in Iowa City, Iowa. His anti-slavery letters appeared in the *National Standard.* He managed a safehouse and claimed as a confederate insurrectionist John Brown, whom Clarke met during the border fighting preceding the statehood of Kansas. During the Civil War until 1866, Clarke served as army paymaster.

Source

"Clarke, William Penn," *Annals of Iowa* 3:11 (April 1893–1923): 458.

Clarkson, James C. (1842–1918)

A politician, civil servant, and journalist, James C. Clarkson of Brookville, Indiana, was devoted to the harboring of runaway slaves. He learned printing in his father's shop in Grundy County, Iowa. In his teens, James began operating a 28-mile route of the Underground Railroad that funneled passengers from Arkansas, Missouri, and Texas, toward Ontario. Among his associates was insurrectionist John Brown. Following the Civil War, Clarkson edited the *Iowa State Register.*

Source

Gue, Benjamin F. *History of Iowa from the Earliest Times to the Beginning of the Twentieth Century.* New York: Century History, 1903.

Clay, Cassius Marcellus (1810–1903)

A journalist and prisoner of war during the Mexican-American War, Cassius Marcellus Clay recruited volunteers for the Underground Railroad. Born near Richmond in Madison County, Kentucky, he married Mary Jane Warfield and prepared for a career in law and politics. He came under the influence of orator William Lloyd Garrison, who enlisted Clay in the fight to end slavery. Clay called for a class war between smallholders and slaveholders in the *True American,* the newspaper he published in Lexington, Kentucky. In 1845, a proponent of slavery engaged Clay in a duel. Clay attacked the man with a Bowie knife, sliced off an ear, gouged out an eye, and split his face. On June 15, 1849, during a speech at Foxtown, Kentucky, Clay faced a would-be assassin, Cyrus Turner, who stabbed Clay in the lung. The injury required a lengthy recuperation. During the Civil War, Clay commanded the Union battalion defending Washington, D.C. For his devotion to the abolitionist cause, black settlers in Jeffersonville, Indiana, named their community Claysburg.

Source

Peters, Pamela R. *The Underground Railroad in Floyd County, Indiana.* Jefferson, NC: McFarland, 2001.

Clemens, James (1781–1870) Clemens, Sophia Sellers (fl. 1800–1820s)

Former slaves James Clemens and his mulatto wife, Sophia (or Sofia) Sellers Clemens of Rockingham County, Virginia, operated a safehouse of the Underground Railroad. The pioneer couple left Virginia in 1818 and established a farm in Darke County, Ohio. They built a Methodist church and founded Longtown, a black agricultural and crafts commune in Greenville, Ohio, which harbored runaways until they could arrange passage to safe territory. At 467 Stingley Road, the Clemens' two-story brick home was an inviting waystation. At the outbreak of the Civil War, their grandson, James R. Clemens, joined other blacks from Longtown in enlisting in the Union army. The Clemens farmstead is listed on the National Register of Historic Places.

See also: black soldiers.

Source

Hannah, James, "Helping Preserve Black History," *Cincinnati Post,* January 7, 2003.

Clements, Marian (1821–?) Clements, Samuel (1816–?)

Activists Marian Clements and her husband, Samuel Clements, went to jail for aiding runaway slaves. In September 1852, the couple entered the Missouri penitentiary in Jefferson City to begin concurrent two-year sentences. Because she conceived during incarceration, Marian Clements served only 14 months and received a pardon from Governor Austin A. King on December 27, 1853. Samuel Clements completed his sentence and exited prison in 1854.

Source

Frazier, Harriet C. *Runaway and Freed Missouri Slaves and Those Who Helped Them, 1763–1865.* Jefferson, NC: McFarland, 2004.

Clemmer, John S. (1825–1875) Clemmer, Maria Miller (1825–?)

Rescuers of slaves in the Ohio Valley, Major John S. Clemmer and his wife, Maria Miller Clemmer, put their sympathy for runaways into action. Born in Stark County, Ohio, John Clemmer came of age in Summit County and apprenticed as a potter and maker of stoneware. The Clemmers supported the Underground Railroad by operating a safehouse. In 1861, John joined the Ninth Ohio Volunteers and, on June 9, 1862, survived a serious wound at the battle of Port Republic, Virginia.

Source

History of the Upper Ohio Valley. Madison, WI: Brant & Fuller, 1891.

Coates (Deborah T. and Lindley) Family

Quaker abolitionists Deborah T. Simmons Coates (1801–after 1856) of Pennsgrove, Pennsylvania, and her husband, Lindley Coates (1794–1856) of Caln, in Chester County, operated Station 5 on the Pilgrim's Pathway, a 17-stage network of the Underground Railroad. The Coates were connected to depots on the Pennsylvania–Ontario route. From their home in Sadsbury, in Lancaster County, Pennsylvania, they promoted the American Anti-Slavery Association, which elected Lindley Coates a manager in 1840. After January 1843, they shared their home with their son and daughter-in-law, school board superintendent Simmons Coates (1821–1862) and Emmeline Jackson Coates (1822–1894). The foursome provided transportation for slaves who arrived by way of Robert Loney's ferry crossing of the Susquehanna River in Wrightsville and from the stations of brothers Caleb C. Hood and Joseph Hood in Caln, Lewis Peart in Lampeter, and Joseph Smith and Tacy Shoemaker Smith in Drumore. Deborah Coates made a quilt with representations of the coded visual messages that directed slaves along the way to freedom. She hid runaways under corn shocks until it was safe to pass them on in safety.

In league with agents James Fulton, Jr., Joseph Fulton, Gideon Pierce, William Parker, and Robert Purvis, the Coates family transferred their passengers to Gravner Marsh and Hannah Marsh in Caln, to Micajah Speakman and William Allibone Speakman in Wallace, and to Mary Charles Thorne and Williams J. Thorne in Selma, Ohio. The Coates grew so bold at the task of freeing slaves that they recruited future escapees and transported them from New Bern, North Carolina, by ship up the Atlantic coast to Philadelphia, Pennsylvania. Slaves passing from the southern Pennsylvania stations of Daniel Gibbons and Hannah Wierman Gibbons in Bird-in-Hand through the Coates' depot zigzagged from Susan P. Johnson Bonsall and Thomas Bonsall's farm in West Chester or Martha Holison Whitson and Thomas Whitson's home in Bart to the residence of farmer Jeremiah Moore and Elizabeth W. Ely Moore in Christiana and into Canada using fake certificates of freedom. Other transfers involved secret operatives Mordecai Hayes, Emmor Kimber, and James Williams. With the declining use of Daniel Gibbons as a transporter from Bird-in-Hand, Lindley Coates accepted responsibility for the family's relays. After passage of the Fugitive Slave Law of 1850, proslavery rowdies pelted the carriages of Lindley Coates and Charles Callistus Burleigh with rotten eggs. Around 1850, the same gang burned the Coates' barn as a suspected shelter of runaways. In Lindley Coates's last years, ill health prevented his active piloting of slaves. His son Major Kersey Coates (1823–1887) pursued abolitionism in Kansas City, Missouri, in 1854 and served in the Missouri militia during the Civil War.

See also: abolitionism; American Anti-Slavery Society; code, Underground Railroad; Fugitive Slave Law of 1850; Pilgrim's Pathway; quilts.

Source

Smedley, Robert C. *History of the Underground Railroad in Chester and the Neighboring Counties of Pennsylvania.* Lancaster, PA: Office of *The Journal,* 1883.

Coates, Edwin Howard (1813–1883)
Coates, Sarah Dull (ca. 1818–1848)

A Philadelphia stationmaster of the Underground Railroad, Edwin H. Coates operated a tailoring business while supporting abolitionism and temperance. A promoter of the Philadelphia Anti-Slavery Society, he was one of the founding members of the secret network, which then involved Robert Purvis and Jacob C. White, Sr. Edwin Coates married Sarah Dull in October 1834. They kept a safehouse at Cherry and Sixth streets, where they readied fugitives for the last leg of the journey to Ontario. The Coates family was in league with Joseph Fulton and his daughter, Mary Ann Fulton, both intrepid conductors at Sadsbury. When John Greenleaf Whittier joined the local association, Edwin Coates explained the system of routes and waystations to him.

See also: routes, Underground Railroad.

Source

Whittier, John Greenleaf. *The Works of John Greenleaf Whittier.* New York: Samuel T. Pickard, 1894.

Coates, Mary Ann (1804–?)

In early 1862, a female slave fled to the residence of Mary Ann Coates, a freeborn black resident of Baltimore, Maryland. Coates was conducting the girl to a reunion with the girl's grandmother in Pennsylvania when they were arrested in Baltimore County. Coates went to jail; the girl returned to bondage. In May 1862, Coates was sentenced to a six-year term in the Maryland state penitentiary in Baltimore. In 1863, abolitionists petitioned Governor Augustus Williamson Bradford to pardon her. Because the crime she committed no longer existed, the governor granted her release on May 30, 1865.

Source

Prison records, Maryland State Archives.

Coburn, John P. (ca. 1811–1873)

John P. Coburn, a Massachusetts native, was a worthy addition to the Boston nexus of the Underground Railroad. A building contractor, tailor and clothier, and dedicated abolitionist, he joined the Boston Vigilance Committee to aid wayfarers on their way through the city. He managed two clothing stores, at 20 Brattle Street and at 59 Cornhill Street. After the construction of his home at Two Phillips Street in 1844, Coburn supervised gaming tables for aristocratic black gentlemen. The discreet venture made his fortune at the same time that it added another safehouse to the Boston network.

With the proceeds, Coburn financed slave rescues, notably that of Fredric "Shadrach" Minkins, whom a mob freed from the Boston courthouse at noon on February 15, 1851. Authorities arrested Coburn, but the court exonerated him of all charges in the jailbreak. To police Beacon Hill, in 1854, he formed the Massasoit Guards, a black security force that warded off kidnappers, posses, and bounty hunters. When insurrectionist John Brown plotted an overthrow of the federal government, Coburn helped him recruit volunteers.

See also: black soldiers; kidnap.

Source

Ware, Vron, and Les Back. *Out of Whiteness: Color, Politics, and Culture.* Chicago: University of Chicago Press, 2002.

Cockrum, James Washington (1799–1875) Cockrum, William Monroe (1837–1924)

A respected team, Colonel James Washington Cockrum and his son, Colonel William Monroe Cockrum, managed a major portion of the fugitive slave escape route through Gibson County in southwestern Indiana. James Cockrum emigrated west from North Carolina to a farm outside Oakland City in 1818. In addition to serving as a militia officer, he invested in pork packing and tobacco transport aboard his two steamers and a fleet of flatboats. Because he campaigned against public saloons, enemies burned the Cockrum residence. He conspired with other conductors, particularly local agent Andrew Adkins, Ben Swain in Rockport, and Dr. John Wesley Posey, a physician and coal mine owner, in Petersburg, Indiana.

Around 1849, James Cockrum networked with Ira Caswell in Hart, Indiana. Caswell sent him Jefferson "Jeff" Lewis and Lewis's wife from northwestern Kentucky about midnight on a hurried transfer from the Ohio River. Cockrum used the root cellar in his hickory log barn to hide runaways before leading them to Quaker agents Isaac and Rachel Street or to Basil (or Bazil) Simpson's sanctuary west of the Dongola covered bridge over the Patoka River. The slave party then moved north through Terre Haute and Vincennes, Indiana, and on to Chicago or Detroit.

William Cockrum shared his father's compassion and in boyhood helped to operate the family Underground Railroad station. William served as messenger boy for an agent of the Indiana Anti-Slavery Society, John T. Hanover, a shadowy figure posing as a real estate agent, John Hansen. After passage of the Fugitive Slave Law of 1850, William joined 11 agents in apprehending and pummeling a 10-man posse of slave kidnappers. During the Civil War, he earned admiration for his service at the battles of Stone River, Murfreesboro, and Chickamauga, Tennessee, and for surviving Libby Prison in Richmond, Virginia, a confinement that left him handicapped. In Nashville, Tennessee, in fall 1864, he encountered Jeff Lewis, a black cavalryman whom James Cockrum had rescued. William Cockrum compiled two valuable works, *A Pioneer History of Indiana* (1907) and *History of the Underground Railroad As It Was Conducted by the Anti-Slavery League* (1915), which pinpoints 12 rescue sites along the Ohio River. In 2002, restoration of Cockrum Hall, the family waystation, honored local service to refugees.

See also: kidnap.

Sources

Cockrum, William. *History of the Underground Railroad As It Was Conducted by the Anti-Slavery League.* Oakland City, IN: J.W. Cockrum, 1915.

Paff, Sarah, "Onetime Underground Railroader's Home to Be Restored," *Evansville Courier and Press,* July 15, 2002.

Stormont, Gil R. *History of Gibson County, Her People, Industries and Institutions.* Indianapolis, IN: B.F. Bowen, 1915.

Codding, Ichabod (1810–1866)

One of the planners of Underground Railroad networking in the Midwest, the Reverend Ichabod Codding joined a team of organizers to enhance routes and add waystations. A native of Bristol, in Oneida County, New York, he joined the abolitionist movement during his enrollment at Middlebury College. A colleague of editor Elijah Parish Lovejoy, Codding was recruited for the American Anti-Slavery Society by the Reverend Theodore Dwight Weld. Codding became a convincing platform speaker across New England. Because of his radical defense of the runaway slave, he often had to defend himself against catcalls and threats.

In 1842, Codding was ordained a Congregational minister in Joliet and Waukesha, Wisconsin. He helped slaves passing through Illinois by relaying them to John Hossack in Ottawa, Illinois. Codding joined Philo Carpenter, Zebina Eastman, and Allan Pinkerton in extending transportation routes to Illinois and the midwestern frontier. In 1854, Codding partnered with Sherman Miller Booth in publishing an abolitionist newspaper, the *American Freeman.*

See also: abolitionist newspapers; American Anti-Slavery Society; routes, Underground Railroad.

Source

History of Sauk County Wisconsin. Chicago: Western Historical Society, 1880.

code, Underground Railroad

The private signals, gestures, and Underground Railroad codes enabled runaways to identify authentic rescuers and safehouses. These codes and signs thread in and out of Underground Railroad lore in letters, memoirs, media articles, and carefully worded conversations. For example, in Sand Lake, New York, the Reverend Nickolas Van Alstyne incorporated messages into his sermons at the Second Evangelical Lutheran Church. The code name he adopted for himself was Paul. A fellow minister, Charles Shipman of Girard, Pennsylvania, created signs and ended each message with a triple *X*. Another agent, Captain Shepard, one of the pilots on the dangerous last leg of the Underground Railroad to Ontario, rescued slaves from stops in Sandusky, Ohio, and Detroit, Michigan. On one mission, he pretended to aid a slave catcher during a three-day hunt. He transported the slave owner aboard the *Walk-in-the-Water*, the first steamer on the Great Lakes, which entered service on May 18, 1818, in Buffalo, New York. Ironically the ship's name refers to "Wade in the Water," a spiritual that served as a verbal invitation to fugitives.

The code list varies from place to place, with some words indigenous to a particular route, for example, the Ohio–Canada line. In Salem, Ohio, one transporter referred to two refugees as "two volumes of 'The Irrepressible Conflict' bound in black."

Underground Railroad Code: Terms and Designations

abolitionist: a person who opposes slavery
across the line: across the U.S.-Canadian border
agent: coordinator of routes and maker of contacts for escapees
apples: passengers
baggage: a group of fugitives
bales of black wool: fugitives
band of shepherds: John Brown's army
beech, dogwood, hickory, linden, maple, oak, sassafras, and walnut: code names for territories of American Anti-Slavery Society agents
birds have flown: slaves have escaped their pursuers
bundles of wood: fugitives
Canaan: Canada
Canada road: route from Corning, New York, to St. Catharines, Ontario
cargo: party of runaways
chariot: transportation on the secret network
citadel of liberty: Harriet Bell Hayden and Lewis Hayden's home in Boston
coach: a wagon, sleigh, or buggy
collision: capture by posse
commission: clothing, medicines, and food for refugee slaves
conductor: relayer of slaves from one station to the next
convoy: runaways transported as a group
the cove: Gerrit Smith's harbor in Oswego, New York
crew: outriders who scouted the way and fought off posses
dead trees point the way: follow moss on the side of dead trees when the North Star is not visible
dispatcher's office: Levi Coffin's store in Cincinnati, Ohio
dress goods: female passengers
drinking gourd: the Big Dipper or Ursa Major
dry goods: female runaways
Egypt: the South
employees: route assistants who provided money, clothing, medical care, blankets, and food
Ethiopia: rescue from bondage
father of the Underground Railroad: Charles Turner Torrey
foreman: a harborer of slaves during transit
forwarding: passing a party of fugitives to the next station
freedom baggage car: the 4 A.M. Northern Central Railway train from Philadelphia, Pennsylvania, to Niagara Falls, New York
freedom line: Underground Railroad
Freedom Road: an 80-mile stretch of the Allegheny River
Freedom Stairway: the 100 stone steps leading from the Ohio River to the home of Jean Lowry Rankin and John Rankin at Liberty Hill in Ripley, Ohio
freedom train: Underground Railroad
Free Haven: Lawnside, New Jersey
freight: fugitive slaves
a friend of a friend sent me: a password for unescorted escapees to identify themselves to Underground Railroad agents
friends of liberty: Underground Railroad officials
a friend with friends: password identifying a conductor and passengers to an unknown stationkeeper
game abroad and hunters close: fugitive slaves pursued by slave catchers
give leg-bail: run away
Glory to God: Windsor, Ontario
God be praised: Port Stanley, Ontario
goods: passenger or passengers
gospel train: Underground Railroad
grand central depot: Plymouth, New York
grand central station: the home of Catherine White Coffin and Levi Coffin in Newport, Indiana; also, Farmington, Connecticut

the great emporium: Ashtabula, Ohio
handle freight: rescue or pilot fugitive slaves
hardware: male runaways
heaven: Canada
hen: slave mother with children
hope: Cleveland, Ohio
human cattle: slaves
humanity: a code word legitimizing letters from conductor Jacob Haines of Wolf Run near Muncy, Pennsylvania
Indianapolis Station: Bethel African Methodist Episcopal Church on Georgia Street in Indianapolis, Indiana
in transit: between waystations
Jordan: the Canadian border
land of freedom or land of promise: Canada
land pirates: kidnappers
last great river to cross: Christina River in northern Delaware
left foot, peg foot: identity of a conductor with a wooden leg
leg-bail: flight from the authorities
leg-victory: successful escape
Libertyville: Canada
library meeting: a planning session of route superintendents in Indiana
Lightning Train: route through Harrisburg, Pennsylvania, to Niagara Falls, New York
line: overland route
load of goods: party of runaways
load of potatoes: slaves hidden in a wagon under hay or produce
lookout: watchers for the safe arrival of a convoy or for spies and kidnappers
merchandise: passenger or passengers
midnight: Detroit, Michigan
Moses: Harriet Tubman
mother: a common reference runaways applied to aged black women who aided them
Mother Hubbard's Cupboard: Ashtabula, Ohio
mother of the Underground Railroad: Harriet Tubman
Mr. T: Charles Turner Torrey, an abolitionist spy and organizer
the Old Man: John Brown
mysterious tracks: Underground Railroad
other side of Jordan: across the U.S.–Canadian border
package or parcel: party of escapees
partridge under the hill: a runaway
Paul: password
pharaoh: slave owner
Pilgrim's Pathway: a route from the Susquehanna River north to Lancaster County, Pennsylvania
pilot: a conductor by water
president of the Illinois Underground Railroad: Charles Volney Dyer
president of the Underground Railroad: Levi Coffin
Promised Land: Canada
Queen Victoria's pasture: Canada
railroad fever: yearning for liberty
Red Fox: James Ditcher, a wily conductor in the Ohio Valley
river bank makes a mighty good road: walk in water to throw trackers' dogs off the scent
river ends between two hills: description of the southern approach to the Ohio River
River Jordan: Mississippi River or Ohio River
rolling stock: wagons
shepherd: conductor
ship cargoes: transport runaways
ship of Zion: transportation aboard the secret network
Signal House: a two-story home on Front Street in Ripley, Ohio
Slave Haven: the Jacob Burkle residence in Memphis, Tennessee
Sons of Liberty: conductors in southwestern Indiana
soul drivers: slave traders
southern friends: fugitive slaves
station: safehouse or refuge, such as a cave, sheltering cliff, or hollow tree
Station A: Macedonia African Methodist Episcopal Church at 265 Spruce Street in Camden, New Jersey
stationkeeper or stationmaster: owner of a safehouse
steal away to Jesus: warning from one slave to others to prepare for an escape
stock: passengers
stockholder: donor of transport, food, clothing, or cash to the secret network
sunrise: Sandusky, Ohio
superintendent of the Underground Railway from Wilmington down the Delmarva Peninsula: agent John Hunn, Jr.
switch turner of the Underground Railroad: agent Joseph Smith in Drumore, Pennsylvania

tavern of strength: Lewis Hayden, an agent in Detroit, Michigan
temples of refuge: Harriet Bell Hayden and Lewis Hayden's network of Boston safehouses
ten: Pennsylvania
terminal: main station
there are people on the hill: runaways are approaching a waystation
third basement: a subcellar dug out as a hiding place
throne of Jesus: freedom
ticket: connection with a conductor for future transfer north
track: route
track walker: Underground Railroad scout or reconnaissance agent
trackless train: Underground Railroad
twenty: Seville, Ohio
twenty-seven: Medina, Ohio
Uncle Johnny: the Reverend John Rankin, a conductor in Ripley, Ohio
Uncle Sam: the United States
Uncle Tom's Cabin: the safehouse of Clarina Irene Howard Nichols in Quindaro, Kansas
when the first quail calls: early spring
when the sun comes back: early spring
William Penn: password
wind blowing from the South: alert to conductor that fugitives fleeing slave hunters are approaching

See also: African Methodist Episcopal Church; agents, Underground Railroad; American Anti-Slavery Society; bloodhounds; kidnap; Pilgrim's Pathway; quilts; safehouses; slave tokens; spies; spirituals.

Source

Shaffer, Dale. *Salem: A Quaker City History.* Charleston, SC: Arcadia, 2002.

Coffin, Alethea Flukes (1798–1891)
Coffin, Vestal M. (1792–1826)
Coffin, Addison (1822–1897)
Coffin, Alfred V. (1819–?)

Cousins of Underground Railroad founder Levi Coffin, Quaker conductors Alethea Flukes (also Aletha or Alethe Flook) and Vestal M. Coffin and their sons and daughter-in-law freed slaves from bondage. From 1813, when Vestal and Levi Coffin set up Sunday school classes for blacks, Vestal devoted himself to the cause of liberty and human rights. He and Alethea Coffin managed a depot at Guilford College, outside Greensboro, North Carolina, near the home of conductors George Mendenhall and Richard C. Mendenhall in Jamestown. The Coffins's first rescue was John Dimery (or Dimrey), a freedman seized by kidnappers in 1819 in New Garden, North Carolina. Aided by Isaac White and Saul (also Sol or Solomon) Hamilton, Vestal confronted the lawbreakers while Dimery leaped from a window and raced away. Underground Railroad operatives guided Dimery to Richmond, Indiana, where he earned enough money to send for his family.

In widowhood in 1826, Alethea Coffin acted as matron at the New Garden Boarding School and operated the family safehouse and farm with the aid of her young sons, Addison and Alfred. Among her collaborators was the school laundress, freedwoman Vina Curry. In 1833, Alethea settled with family in Hendricks County, Indiana, and continued harboring refugees. Addison, a respected abolitionist orator and writer, joined other Quaker families in migrating to Hendricks. In his autobiography, *Life and Travels of Addison Coffin* (1897), he reported on escape routes leading out of the South and on his celebrity among other Underground Railroad supporters in Newport and Richmond, Indiana. In summer 1844, he found the rescues along the Wabash line running smoothly, with depots no more than 30 miles apart.

Addison Coffin's texts included rather detailed instructions—for example, on how to make a raft for a

> In an unpublished manuscript, "Early Settlement of Friends in North Carolina" (1894), Addison Coffin revealed how nails were used to direct runaways fleeing via the Underground Railroad: "From the starting point in North Carolina to the great turnpike in Virginia the Underground Railroad was built, constructed, or marked, as we may call it, by driving nails in trees, fences, and stumps. When there was a fork in the road there was a nail driven in a tree three and a half feet from the ground half way round from front to back, if the right hand road was to be taken the nail was driven on the right hand side, if the left was the road the nail was to the left. If there were fences and no tree, the nail was driven in the middle of the second rail from the top, over on the inside of the fence, to the right, or left as in the trees, if neither tree, nor fence was near then a stake, or a stone was so set as to be unseen by day, but found at night."

water crossing by roping together four to six fence rails, followed by instructions to then dismantle the evidence by cutting the rails apart. He describes his older brother, Alfred Coffin, a physician as well as the manager of the North Carolina branch of the secret network from 1836 to 1852. Unlike Addison, who made bold rescues, Alfred preferred cunning, such as teaching slaves to fake loathsome diseases or lunacy to reduce their value on the auction block. To create symptoms of erysipelas, slaves rubbed their bodies with hot burdock root. During the winter of 1851/1852, Alfred helped 32 runaways reach Canada. He fled a pro-slavery mob in North Carolina in 1852 and settled with his wife, Mary E. Johnson Coffin, and children with the Coffin clan in Hendricks County.

See also: kidnap; routes, Underground Railroad.

Sources

Beal, Gertrude. "The Underground Railroad in Guilford County." *Southern Friend: Journal of the North Carolina Friends Historical Society* (Spring 1980): 18–28.
Coffin, Addison. *Life and Travels of Addison Coffin.* Cleveland, OH: W.G. Hubbard, 1897.
Hamm, Thomas D. "Addison Coffin: Quaker Visionary." *Southern Friend* 18:1 (1996): 51–66.

Coffin, Catherine White (1803–1881)
Coffin, Levi (1798–1877)

Renowned Quaker philanthropists Catherine White "Aunt Katy" Coffin and Levi Coffin kept a station of the Underground Railroad at their homes in Indiana and Ohio. Levi Coffin was a native of Greensboro, North Carolina, the only son of seven children born to Quaker farmers. By 1805, he knew that bondage inflicted harm on innocent people, whom he saw chained and hustled along the road to Alabama, Georgia, and Louisiana. At age 15, he joined his cousin, 22-year-old Vestal M. Coffin, in opening a slave Sunday school in New Garden, in Guilford County, North Carolina. In addition, Levi managed a rescue at the family farm in New Garden after witnessing the suffering of Stephen, a Philadelphian kidnapped and enslaved in Georgia. Coffin enlisted other rescuers to the secret network, including farmer Andrew Caldwell Murrow, a wagoneer who drove slaves from North Carolina to Indiana.

In 1826, Coffin and his wife transferred their rescue work to their two-story brick home at 115 Main Street in Newport (now Fountain City), Indiana. They prospered as millers of linseed oil and as pork merchants and shared their wealth with refugees. At their rambling Indiana residence, the Coffin family concealed slaves in the upper story without revealing their presence to relatives and houseguests. Beds covered a small door opening into the attic; an indoor well provided water for a large influx of passengers. Levi conspired with Vina Curry, a laundress in Guilford County, North Carolina, to reuse the freedom papers of her husband, Arch Curry. In 15 rescues, the papers arrived with runaways and were passed back to Vina Curry for additional use.

The Coffins were placid but canny conductors who received some 300 passengers annually. Usually arriving at night, the refugees passed from the safehouse of the Reverend Andrew Coombs, Jr., in New Richmond, Ohio; from Dr. Henry W. Way and Rachel Manlove Way in Newport; from Thomas Hicklin in southern Jennings County, Indiana; and from depots in Ripley, Ohio, operated by the Reverend John Bennington Mahan and his younger brother, William Jacob Mahan, and by Jean Lowry Rankin and John Rankin at Liberty Hill overlooking the Ohio River. The Anti-Slavery Sewing Society maintained a clothes closet for refugees at the Coffin farm to provide shoes and warm wraps for winter journeys. Katy Coffin hid food baskets under stacks of freshly ironed garments.

Among the groups the Coffins received was a party of 28 from Kentucky, whom relayer John Fairfield guided over 20 miles from Lawrenceburg, Indiana. John Hatfield alerted the Coffins to the group's plight after Fairfield pulled a sinking skiff to safety on the shoals of the Ohio River. To complete the transfer, Coffin hired carriages to form a phony funeral cortege to the station at Cumminsville in West Creek. The passage required coffee and food from Mrs. Hatfield's kitchen and shoes, clothes, and blankets from the Reverend Jonathan Cable, a Presbyterian abolitionist at Farmer's College in Springdale, Ohio. Along the way, a black infant died from exposure to cold. The slaves passed through Hamilton, West Elkton, Eaton, and Paris, Indiana, in three straw-filled wagons. From there, they entered Michigan and crossed the Detroit River to Windsor, Canada.

The rollcall of fugitives aided by the Coffins lists unusual passengers, including William Bush, who carved wooden shoes for his journey. In 1829, when throngs of blacks fled Cincinnati, Ohio, after the passage of an ordinance calling for a $500 bond for free blacks living in the city limits, the Coffins,

Called the "president of the Underground Railroad," Quaker abolitionist Levi Coffin, along with wife Catherine, ushered more than 2,000 ex-slaves through their home in Newport (now Fountain City), Indiana, and their store—which stocked goods made by free labor—in Cincinnati. *(Library of Congress)*

along with Dr. Alexander Ross and Harriet Tubman, provided safe travel to Canada. In February 1839, the Coffins rehabilitated Eliza Harris and her infant son, Harry, after their escape the previous December over ice floes on the Ohio River from planter Thomas Davis, outside Dover, Kentucky. Eliza and the boy arrived safely in Chatham, Ontario. After the Coffins' move to Cincinnati in 1847, their outreach continued with proceeds from their cotton, spice, and sugar warehouses. Their store at Elm and Sixth streets earned the name "the dispatcher's office of the Underground Railroad." In 1851, one of their rescues, Thomas Harrison, from Kentucky, established a new life with his wife, Isabella Benton Harrison, in London, Ontario. In October 1853, a slave named Louis slipped out of a Cincinnati federal court and lodged a few doors down the street from Coffin's store. On February 11, 1856, Levi Coffin joined women's rights leader Lucy Stone in the audience for the trial of Margaret Garner in Cincinnati, Ohio. Coffin and Stone offered silent support for Garner, who faced a charge of murdering her infant Mary rather than return the child to bondage in Kentucky.

Catherine and Levi Coffin influenced others to aid the Underground Railroad and supported their efforts, especially those of martyr Richard Dillingham of Peru, Ohio, and of Abraham and Cata Howland Allen and Elihu and Jane Newcomb Oren in Clinton County, Ohio. Among the Coffins' other converts to civil disobedience were the Reverend John Gregg Fee and Matilda Hamilton Fee in Bracken County, Kentucky; Virginia planter John Butterworth, who freed his workers and joined the anti-slavery effort; and Seth Concklin, who drowned in mid-March 1851 while in the custody of authorities for his aid to runaways. For a colleague, the Reverend Calvin Fairbank, who lost his eyesight during a harsh prison term, Levi Coffin joined Cincinnati operative Catherine "Kittie" Doram in raising funds to hasten Fairbank's release. On June 10, 1857, a local vigilance committee founded by the Coffins helped agent William A. Conolly, an editor of the *Daily Commercial,* escape authorities for his role in aiding Angeline and Irvin Broadus flee bondage in Covington, Kentucky.

While attending a free-labor convention in Salem, Indiana, at age 48, Levi Coffin undertook the supervision of network business. In April 1847, he founded a mercantile store at Elm and Sixth streets to sell goods made by former slaves. The building featured tunnels in the cellar and an attic connected to other buildings to allow refugees quick getaways. In his sixties and seventies, he raised funds in England for the Western Freedmen's Aid Society and participated in the International Anti-Slavery Conference in Paris, France. In his final months, he compiled a memoir, *Reminiscences of Levi Coffin, the Reputed President of the Underground Railroad* (1876). Harriet Beecher Stowe honored Levi Coffin by making him the model for Simeon Halliday in her novel *Uncle Tom's Cabin* (1852). The next year, landscape artist Charles T. Webber painted *Fugitives Arriving at Levi Coffin's Indiana Farm, a Busy Station of the Underground Railroad* (1853) for the World's Columbia Exposition. The Coffins' Indiana waystation is listed as a National Historic Landmark.

See also: kidnap; philanthropists; Quakers; vigilance committees.

Sources

Coffin, Addison. *Life and Travels of Addison Coffin.* Cleveland, OH: W.G. Hubbard, 1897.

Coffin, Levi. *Reminiscences of Levi Coffin, the Reputed President of the Underground Railroad.* Cincinnati, OH: Western Tract Society, 1876.

Coffin, Joshua (1792–1864)

A founder of the New England Anti-Slavery Society and the American Anti-Slavery Society, historian and teacher Joshua Coffin of Newburyport, Massachusetts, took seriously the threat that slavery posed to independence and civil rights. He observed the rise of abolitionist sentiment in churches, schools, and courtrooms. In his classroom lectures at Dartmouth College, he warned that enslavement of blacks was a danger to the nation's security. Among his pupils was poet and editor John Greenleaf Whittier, who joined the campaign to end bondage.

Underground Railroad business became so demanding in 1842 that Coffin had to request extra agents and funds from the Boston Vigilance Committee. He lost his job with the Philadelphia post office for aiding desperate refugees. In 1842, he urged editor Lydia Maria Francis Child to meet the famed runaway Harriet Jacobs, who compiled *Incidents in the Life of a Slave Girl* (1861) with Child's assistance. In 1860, Coffin published a pamphlet, *An Account of Some of the Principal Slave Insurrections.* The text called for an investigation into the handling of insurrectionist John Brown's attack on Harpers Ferry, Virginia, and the execution of Brown and his conspirators.

See also: American Anti-Slavery Society; *Incidents in the Life of a Slave Girl* (1861).

Sources

Coffin, Joshua. *An Account of Some of the Principal Slave Insurrections.* New York: American Anti-Slavery Society, 1860.

Hume, John F. *The Abolitionists: Together with Personal Memories of the Struggle for Human Rights, 1830–1864.* New York: Putnam, 1905. Reprint New York: AMS, 1973.

Coffin, Lorenzo Swett (1823–1915) Coffin, Mary Chase (1825–?)

Missionary and educator Lorenzo Swett Coffin offered his services to the Underground Railroad. A scion of Puritan founders of the Massachusetts Bay Colony, he was born in Alton, in Stafford County, New Hampshire, and married Mary Chase of Fabius, New York. After the Coffins settled at Wolfboro, New Hampshire, Lorenzo attended school briefly. He farmed and educated himself until he was ready to teach at the Geauga Seminary. When his wife's health faltered, in 1854, he moved to Fort Dodge in Webster County, Iowa, and farmed a 720-acre tract. After his years of helping refugees at his safehouse, during the Civil War, he served the Thirty-second Iowa Infantry as chaplain.

Source

Biographical Record and Portrait Album of Webster and Hamilton Counties, Iowa. Chicago: Lewis, 1888.

Cohen, Anthony (1963–)

A devotee of black history, Anthony "Tony" Cohen retraced the footsteps of slaves escaping over the Underground Railroad. Born in Silver Spring, Maryland, he worked for Montgomery County, Maryland, as a freelance historian. At age 33, he set out on an 800-mile trek from May 4 to July 6, 1996, to understand the whys of slave flight and to encourage curiosity about black accomplishments. Beginning at Montgomery County, he made the nine-week journey to Ontario alone with support from the National Parks and Conservation Association. He based his route and transportation methods on research he had done at the Library of Congress. His passage moved along in ten 25-mile increments, the distance covered by the typical black runaway from depot to depot. Along the way, well-wishers e-mailed their prayers and support. His only pursuers were mean dogs and mosquitoes.

Cohen's backpack contained clothes and food for one day, maps, and a first-aid kit. He carried an Ethiopian walking stick, an antique token dating before the 1790s. On May 17, he surveyed Wilmington Prison, a Maryland slave pen that displays manacles and chains. In Waterloo, Maryland, he investigated the caves on Deep Run Stream where Harriet Tubman hid slaves before pressing on to the Patapsco River. His modes of transport included boats, buggies, horseback, and even freight. In imitation of the escape of Henry "Box" Brown, on May 20, Cohen traveled from Richmond to Philadelphia by Amtrak in a crate 24 inches by 28 inches by 30 inches marked "books." In Harlem, he visited a lectern used by Frederick Douglass and Sojourner Truth. Through New York, from Spencerport to Medina, Cohen entertained himself by singing spirituals, some of which bore the verbal directional coding essential to preliterate fugitives.

Cohen's stopping places bore historical significance to the anti-slavery movement—a Quaker settlement in Sandy Spring, Maryland; Plymouth, Pennsylvania; and along a towpath of the Erie Canal in Middleport, New York. In Pittsford, New York, he examined a niche in the attic of the Hargous-Briggs Mansion, where Judge Ashley S. Sampson harbored refugees; in Burt, he mused over a trapdoor in a barn that may have led to an authentic slave hiding-place. From Buffalo and Niagara Falls, New York, he completed the last leg by skiff to Amherstburg, Ontario, a black community established by fugitives. Five days after Cohen's arrival, a town crier preceded him toward the Amherstburg museum and welcomed the newcomer as a free man. Three years later, he repeated the journey with the aid of a cameraman, who photographed the waystations.

See also: spirituals.

Sources

Cohen, Anthony. *The Underground Railroad in Montgomery County, Maryland: A History and Driving Guide.* Montgomery County Historical Society, 1997.

Newsome, Melba. "Linked to the Past—and the Present: Computers and Technology." *American Visions* 11:5 (October–November 1996): 36–37.

Collins (Nancy Wilson and Nathaniel) Family

Aids to the Ripley line of the Underground Railroad through southern Ohio, Nancy Wilson Collins (1783–1856) and her husband, Nathaniel Collins (1776–1831), were pioneers of Ripley. They joined their sons—James (1808–1880), Theodore (1801–1894), and Thomas Wilson Collins (1809–?)—in assisting Jean Lowry Rankin and John Rankin, stationmasters at Liberty Hill, on the Ohio River. Nancy and Nathaniel Collins began hiding runaways in their cornfields in 1815 and dispatched passengers on horseback in care of their sons. On November 25, 1835, Theodore and Thomas co-founded the Ripley Anti-Slavery Society. Theodore, who maintained an auxiliary stop behind the Rankins' property, protested the unlawful search of his property by slave hunters in March 1852. In the *Ripley Bee*, he posted a challenge to the traitor who set up the invasion of his privacy. A pro-slavery neighbor, Ira Shaw, replied in the same newspaper and attested to fugitive comings and goings from the Collins house.

In league with foundryman John P. Parker, Dr. Alexander Campbell, transporter Rhoda Jones, and the Reverend James Gilliland, Thomas Collins, a cabinetmaker by trade, operated a two-story brick safehouse built in 1812 at 200 Front Street. Refugees hid in coffins displayed at his shop before following Collins to stations in Red Oak or Russellville. In addition to establishing a library of abolitionist reading material for the use of the Ripley Anti-Slavery Society, he involved himself in daring exploits involving refugees crossing the Ohio River from Kentucky to Brown County, Ohio. In February 1838, he used a skiff to rescue Eliza Harris, a slave who served as a model for the main character in Harriet Beecher Stowe's *Uncle Tom's Cabin* (1852). In 1912, Theodore and Thomas Collins were honorees on Ripley's Liberty Monument.

See also: Uncle Tom's Cabin; or, Life Among the Lowly (1852).

Source

Hagedorn, Ann. *Beyond the River: The Untold Story of the Heroes of the Underground Railroad.* New York: Simon & Schuster, 2002.

Collins, Nathan (1832–?)

Nathan Collins, a 25-year-old slave, left his wife behind when he escaped from the bondage of Josiah Wilson. In company with 26-year-old Thomas Henry, Collins departed New Market, Maryland, in 1857. The two runaways received guidance from Underground Railroad agents in Philadelphia, Pennsylvania.

Source

Still, William. *The Underground Railroad.* Philadelphia: Porter & Coates, 1871.

Colman, Ezekiel Andrus (1814–1898) Colman, Mary Jane Wendell (1817–1905)

An abolitionist and idealistic pioneer of Kansas Territory, Ezekiel Andrus Colman of Ashby in Middlesex County, Massachusetts, served the Underground Railroad as an agent. In 1838, he married Mary Jane Wendell of Salem, Massachusetts. In 1854, he abandoned his wallpaper factory and joined the New England Emigrant Aid Society. The Colmans occupied a dugout on their farm in Kanwaka, south of Lawrence, Kansas, a nexus of the secret network. A door in the kitchen admitted runaways to shelter under the house. One of the fugitives harbored by the Colmans was a man named Neeley, who passed from John Brown's waystation to the Colmans' stop. Slave catchers seized Neeley in the fields and tried to return him to Missouri, but Neeley escaped and remained free. After operating a general store, in 1858, the Colmans invested in a fruit and nut orchard on their 168-acre parcel.

Source

Sheridan, Richard B., ed. and comp. *Freedom's Crucible: The Underground Railroad in Lawrence and Douglas County Kansas, 1854–1865.* Lawrence: University of Kansas, 1998.

Colver, Nathaniel (1794–1870)

An organizer and rescuer of the New York–Canada line, the Reverend Nathaniel Colver of Champlain, New York, dedicated his career to transporting passengers via the Underground Railroad. In addition to preaching at the Bottskill Baptist Church in Union Village (now Greenwich), in October 1836, he served the American Anti-Slavery Society as spokesman in New England and enlister of volunteer conductors. He conspired with Dr. Hiram Corliss on the concealment of slaves passing through Union Village and on the defiance of slave hunters.

In 1839, Colver accepted a call to the Tremont Street Church in Boston, Massachusetts. In May 1846, he conducted the funeral of the Reverend Charles Turner Torrey, an Underground Railroad martyr who died in prison from tuberculosis while serving a six-year sentence of hard labor for slave rescue. On October 20, 1850, Colver delivered a sermon on civil disobedience, "The Fugitive Slave Bill; or, God's Laws Paramount to the Laws of Men." The text defines the Christian's responsibility to aid the oppressed as a sacred rather than a patriotic duty.

See also: American Anti-Slavery Society; civil disobedience.

Source

Rosenberger, Jesse Leonard. *Through Three Centuries: Colver and Rosenberger, Lives and Times 1620 to 1922.* Chicago: University of Chicago, 1922.

Comfort, Ezra (1777–1847) Comfort, Margaret Shoemaker (1782–1873)

Two influential Quakers in Plymouth, Pennsylvania, Ezra Comfort and his wife, Margaret Shoemaker Comfort, contributed to the successful flight of runaways through Montgomery County. The couple wed in October 1800. The Comforts and fellow abolitionists at the Plymouth Meeting aided slaves escaping via the Underground Railroad. On January 9, 1826, Ezra Comfort joined Peter Dager in an attempted rescue of sibling runaways, John Lewis and Westley Lewis, from their owner who apprehended them in Dager's stable. After the owner tied the men and relayed them by wagon to a magistrate in Norristown, the two Quakers proffered $900 for the slaves—$600 for John and $300 for Westley—and set them free.

See also: Quakers.

Source

Contosta, David R., and Gail C. Momjian. *Plymouth and Whitemarsh Townships, Pennsylvania.* Charleston, SC: Arcadia, 2003.

Comstock, Elizabeth Leslie Rous Wright (1815–1891)

An Anglo-American reformer, feminist, and operative of the Underground Railroad, Elizabeth Leslie Rous Wright Comstock involved herself in humanitarian causes. She was a cradle Quaker born in Maidenhead, England. After emigrating from Belleville, Ontario, to Rollin, Michigan, in 1858, she became a pulpit minister. Elizabeth and her husband, John T. Comstock, received fugitive slaves at their home. According to her memoirs, Elizabeth was involved in the rescue of a female escapee suffering from bloody bare feet. Agent James Green completed the relay to Canada. During pursuit by a posse, a Quaker farmer concealed the slave in his barn to prevent her recapture.

Elizabeth Comstock reported on the plight of Lucy, a quadroon bearing an infant, who arrived in Rollin in 1858. After completing a passage to Sandusky, Lucy saw a reward poster in the train station offering $1,200 for her and her child's apprehension. The train conductor stowed mother and child in the baggage car of a train bound for Detroit. Another agent transformed Lucy by cutting her hair and dressing her in the guise of a male porter. The agent's wife carried Lucy's baby onto a lake steamer, where Lucy passed by her owner without being recognized. During the Civil War, Elizabeth Comstock increased the number of refugees she received and volunteered at prison camps and military hospitals. Her vivid memories of the secret network appear in a collection, *Life and Letters of Elizabeth L. Comstock* (1895), which her sister, Marian Andrews, published under the pen name Caroline Hare.

Source

Hare, Caroline, comp. *Life and Letters of Elizabeth L. Comstock.* Philadelphia: J.C. Winston, 1895.

Concklin, Seth (ca. 1800–1851)

Seth Concklin was a Quaker martyred during action on behalf of runaway slaves. A native of Sandy Hill, New York, he supported his mother and four siblings after his father's death in 1817. While surveying Kentucky and Tennessee, he traveled unarmed and established hideouts and recruited secret operatives. He also noted the gathering spots of bounty hunters and spies throughout Illinois and Indiana. In addition to reconnaissance work for the Underground Railroad, he and an accomplice, agent David Stormont of Princeton, Indiana, liberated ex-slave Peter Friedman Still's wife, Lavinia "Vina" Friedman, and their sons, Levin and Peter. Concklin (or Conklin) created an elaborate plan for rescuing the family from a plantation in the deep South.

In winter 1851, Concklin received $100 in expense money from Still for the long journey from Florence, Alabama, to freedom. Concklin, on advice from Quaker agent Levi Coffin, established a safehouse in southern Indiana to receive the refugees. He purchased a six-oar boat to ferry his passengers from the Bernard McKiernan plantation in the Muscle Shoals area on the Tennessee River. Aided by cobbler William Handy, Concklin plotted a 400-mile escape route up the Tennessee, Ohio, and Wabash rivers to New Harmony, Indiana, and by land to Ontario. To gain Vina Friedman's confidence, Concklin identified himself by producing Peter's gingham cape.

In mid-March 1851, the party began a seven-day water passage to New Harmony. From the banks of the Wabash River, Concklin conducted the family to the stations of freedman Charles Grier and David Stormont. Slave hunter John Emison apprehended the Stills and had them jailed at Vincennes in hopes of gaining the owner's $1,000 reward—$400 for the slaves and $600 for the agent. McKiernan returned the group south via stagecoach and the boat *Paul Anderson* to Paducah, Kentucky. Upon the party's return from Smithland, Kentucky, Concklin, bound in chains, leaped toward a passing barge, fell into the river, and drowned. Other accounts allege that the slave hunters murdered Concklin.

See also: bounty hunters; spies.

Sources

Pickard, Kate. *The Kidnapped and the Ransomed: The Narrative of Peter and Vina Still After Forty Years of Slavery.* Syracuse, NY: William T. Hamilton, 1856.

Stormont, Gil R. *History of Gibson County, Indiana: Her People, Industries, and Institutions.* Indianapolis, IN: B.F. Bowen, 1914.

Connelly, William M. (fl. 1850s)

A journalist for the Cincinnati, Ohio, *Daily Commercial,* William M. Connelly suffered imprisonment for an Underground Railroad rescue. In 1858, he was tried in federal court in southern Ohio for helping two slaves escape on June 13, 1857. The couple, who hid for a week in an upper story at a building on Vine Street, faced a raid by U.S. marshals. Rather than be returned to Covington, Kentucky, the male slave fatally stabbed one officer and survived severe wounds. Connelly fled town and began work for the New York *Sun.* Months later, officers arrested Connelly and extradited him to Ohio.

Philanthropist and slave conductor Levi Coffin negotiated bail for Connelly. On May 5, 1858, the court sentenced Connelly to three weeks in jail and a $10 fine. Unitarian supporters visited him daily and provided him with rich desserts. A bribe to the jailer produced comfortable cell furniture. Sentiment favored the defendant for civil disobedience to the Fugitive Slave Law of 1850. The notoriety of the case stained the legal career of Judge Thomas Stanley Matthews, an appointee of James Buchanan, a U.S. president already discredited for favoring southern slave owners. Connelly's release was celebrated with a torchlit parade, and he was exonerated in the July 2, 1858, issue of *The Liberator.* He became a star of the anti-slavery lecture circuit.

See also: civil disobedience; Fugitive Slave Law of 1850.

Source

Gara, Larry. *The Liberty Line: The Legend of the Underground Railroad.* Lexington: University of Kentucky Press, 1961.

Conrey, Anna Layman (?–1848)
Conrey, James D. (1799–1860)

Residents of Butler County, Ohio, from 1827, Anna Layman Conrey and the Reverend James D. Conrey, a Methodist Episcopal circuit rider, operated a noteworthy safehouse at Spread Eagle Tavern. A former stop for stagecoaches traveling in 1840 from Cincinnati to Lebanon, Ohio, the building lay near the top of Mount Pisgah two miles north of Sharonville, a major intersection of routes for runaways. In league with John Van Zandt and Nancy Van Zandt in

Mount Pierpont, Ohio, the Conreys could dispatch passengers out the back entrance through open fields or conceal them behind a false foundation that extended six feet around the building. Another clever niche was a pair of attics, reached by separate stairs. Spread Eagle is listed on the National Register of Historic Places.

See also: routes, Underground Railroad.

Source

Shewalter, Virginia. *History of Union Township, Butler County, Ohio.* West Chester, OH: self-published, 1979.

Converse, John Kendrick (1801–1880) Converse, Sarah Allen (1810–1873)

A Congregationalist minister, the Reverend John Kendrick Converse of Lyme, New Hampshire, supported an Underground Railroad team at Burlington, Vermont. A Princeton graduate, from 1832 to 1844, he pastored the First Congregational Church. In 1834, he married Sarah Allen. The Converses' home on Winooski Avenue was their first safehouse. In league with transporter Abial F. Anthony, a barber and cook who knew the water routes, the couple passed fugitives to steamers bound from St. Albans Bay across Lake Champlain to St. John's, Quebec. John and Sarah Converse continued serving the secret network after they moved to Griswold Place, where John was principal of the Burlington Female Seminary.

See also: routes, Underground Railroad.

Source

Seaver, Frederick J. *Historical Sketches of Franklin County and Its Several Towns.* Albany, NY: J.B. Lyon, 1918.

Conway, Moncure Daniel (1832–1907) Conway, Ellen Davis Dana (?–1897)

The Reverend Moncure Daniel Conway, a pacifist minister and author, promoted abolitionism and guided slaves to free territory. An aristocrat from Falmouth in Stafford County, Virginia, he was born at Middleton Plantation and grew up among apologists for slavery. After studying at Dickinson College and Harvard Divinity School, in 1855, he found himself unwelcome in his home state because of his defense of oppressed slaves. The Unitarian Church in Washington, D.C., ousted him for his anti-slavery preaching. Although his two brothers' service in the Confederate army reignited old animosities, he made peace with his humanistic philosophy in Ohio, where he pastored the First Unitarian Congregational Church of Cincinnati.

With his wife, Ellen Davis Dana Conway, in summer 1862, Moncure led his family's 31 slaves from war-ravaged Virginia by train to Yellow Springs, Ohio. He sought the assistance of Salmon P. Chase and Abraham Lincoln but discovered that no agency could guarantee safe passage through pro-slavery territory. The most dangerous impasse occurred during a three-hour layover in Baltimore, Maryland, where jubilant black supporters faced a knot of bitter whites. When the train crossed into free territory, the former slaves cheered and celebrated. Among the group were Dunmore Gwinn and Eliza Gwinn, who settled the trekkers temporarily in a barn. The Gwinns formed a settlement called Conway Colony along the Little Miami River and prospered as domestics and truck farmers. Local whites marveled at the Gwinns' polished southern manners and their knowledge of the Bible. At the urging of William Lloyd Garrison, editor of *The Liberator,* and of orator Wendell Addison Phillips, Moncure Conway promoted the work of the Underground Railroad and toured England to champion the cause of liberty.

See also: abolitionism; *Liberator, The.*

Sources

Conway, Moncure. *Autobiography, Memories and Experiences of Moncure Conway.* Boston: Houghton Mifflin, 1904.
Freehling, William W. *The Road to Disunion: Secessionists at Bay, 1776–1854.* Oxford, UK: Oxford University Press, 1990.

Conwell, Martin (1811–?) Conwell, Miranda Wickham (1817–1877) Conwell, Russell Herman (1843–1925)

A farmer and stonemason in the Berkshire hills, Martin Conwell, and his wife, Miranda Wickham Conwell of New York, operated a safehouse in South Worthington, Massachusetts. To prepare their sons, Charles and Russell Herman, for the struggles of the era, Miranda read them Bible stories, Harriet Beecher Stowe's *Uncle Tom's Cabin* (1852), and the Reverend Henry Ward Beecher's anti-slavery sermons. Supplementing their studies were current events articles from two abolitionist newspapers, John Greenleaf Whittier's *New York Tribune* and Gamaliel Bailey's

National Era. The readings attested to the moral good of civil disobedience on behalf of the Underground Railroad.

The Conwells welcomed insurrectionist John Brown as their friend. They received fugitives at their home and barn until they could arrange passage by farm wagon to Cummington. One escapee, J.G. Ramage of Atlanta, Georgia, wrote a thank-you note concerning his rescue in 1856. These influences shaped the ministry of Russell Conwell, who became a famous abolitionist minister and orator in the Connecticut Valley. During the Civil War, he attained the rank of captain of the Forty-sixth Massachusetts Infantry.

See also: abolitionist newspapers; civil disobedience; *Uncle Tom's Cabin; or, Life Among the Lowly* (1852).

Source

Burr, Agnes Rush. *Russell H. Conwell.* Philadelphia: John C. Wilson, 1917.

Conyne, Abraham (1791–1874)
Conyne, Matilda Parker (fl. 1830s–1840s)

An abolitionist and collaborator with farmer Hiram B. Miller, Abraham "Abram" Conyne was an early supporter of the Underground Railroad in Strongsville, in Medina County, Ohio. A native of Scharie County, New York, Conyne relocated to Ohio at age 29 with his wife, Matilda Parker Conyne, and joined the brotherhood of Masons. He built and operated Albion's first gristmill. In 1834, he organized the region's first antislavery society and promoted abolitionism with Ahijah Haynes, Alijah Lyman, and Philander Pope, agents of the secret network.

Ten years later on a stormy summer night, Hiram B. Miller drove up to the Conyne residence with a woman and her two daughters, who were fleeing a mob. Miller intended to relay the trio to Cleveland. Abraham supplied his own team and continued on horseback down Wooster Pike when 30 outriders approached him and demanded that he show the contents of the wagon. Abraham revealed the woman, a toddler, and a suckling babe and stared down the pursuers. In 1845, Conyne received a thank-you letter from the woman he rescued.

Source

Holzworth, W.F. *Men of Grit and Greatness: A Historical Account of Middleburg Township, Berea, Brook Park, and Middleburg Heights.* Cuyahoga, OH: self-published, 1970.

Cook, Eli (1814–1865)

A defender of runaway slaves, attorney Eli Cook aided fugitives along the Underground Railroad route from Buffalo, New York, to Canada. Born in the town of Palatine Bridge, in Montgomery County, New York, he grew up in Manilus and, at age 16, began studying law. He opened offices in Tennessee and Mississippi before settling at 170 Franklin Street in Buffalo in 1838. One of his successful defenses of runaways was a case involving Sneedon, a refugee accused of murder. In 1853, Cook was elected mayor of Buffalo.

Source

Rizzo, Michael F. *Through the Mayors' Eyes: Buffalo, New York, 1832–2005.* Morrisville, NC: Lulu, 2005.

Cook, Harmon (1841–1922)
Cook, Dianah Cox (1820–1909)
Cook, Robert (1818–1852)

Pioneer and farmer Harmon Cook of Plainfield, Indiana, learned the task of the conductor in boyhood. His parents, Dianah Cox Cook and Robert Cook, fed runaways who hid in the woods before crossing from Middle River to Summit Grove, Indiana. After relocating to Dallas County, Iowa, in 1857, Harmon educated himself in the winter months while farming to support his widowed mother. Like his father, he aided the Underground Railroad by transporting slaves over the Iowa prairie by moonlight to Des Moines. After studying printing in Indianapolis, Indiana, Harmon married Lucinda Mills in 1861 and began editing the *Western Journal.* In the Civil War, he patrolled the Mississippi River with the Forty-sixth Iowa Infantry. In the field, he encountered a black lieutenant who had been one of his passengers on the secret network.

Source

Compendium of History Reminiscence and Biography of Lyon County, Iowa. Chicago: George A. Ogle, 1974.

Coombs, Andrew, Jr. (1805–1864)
Coombs, Kitty Ann Shannon (1811–1906)

The Reverend Andrew Coombs, Jr., of New Richmond in Clermont County, Ohio, transported slaves along the secret network. In 1832, he married Kitty

Ann Shannon. While pastoring Lindale Baptist Church, Andrew Coombs became a founding officer of the Gilead (Ohio) Anti-Slavery Society along with James Gillespie Birney. At their farm, the Coombs received runaways who crossed the Ohio River from Pendleton County, Kentucky. They linked the relays of Jean Lowry Rankin and John Rankin at Liberty Hill in Ripley, Brown County, Ohio, with the main station of Catherine White Coffin and Levi Coffin in Newport, Indiana.

Source

Hagedorn, Ann. *Beyond the River: The Untold Story of the Heroes of the Underground Railroad.* New York: Simon & Schuster, 2002.

Cooper, Caroline (fl. 1850s)

A triumph of the Pittsburgh Vigilance Committee was the rescue of a freedwoman, Caroline Cooper. However, in March 1855, network agents learned of her recapture by a slave hunter named Slaymaker. While Slaymaker was eating breakfast at the City Hotel, abolitionist agents freed Caroline and hustled her out a back way to a barbershop and on to a sanctuary at Cherry Alley. Slaymaker went to the mayor with a complaint and lied and said that Cooper came to the hotel of her own free will. Dr. Martin Robinson Delany, a journalist and a member of the Pittsburgh Philanthropic Society, an adjunct of the Underground Railroad, mediated the complaint and believed Slaymaker's story. Cooper was returned to bondage.

See also: slave recovery; vigilance committees.

Source

Blight, David W., ed. *Passages to Freedom.* Washington, DC: Smithsonian, 2004.

Cooper, Griffith Morgan (1791–1864) Cooper, Elizabeth Hodgson (1790–1873)

A Quaker conductor and former naval officer, Griffith Morgan Cooper superintended a link on the New York–Canada route of the Underground Railroad. He was a reformer, a mediator with the Onondaga and Seneca nations, and in 1836, a missionary to a reservation school outside Buffalo, New York. His wife, Elizabeth Hodgson "Eliza" Cooper, taught Frederick Douglass to read and write. At a three-story fieldstone farmhome in Williamson, in Wayne County, New York, the Coopers received passengers from Pliny Sexton and his son, Pliny Titus Sexton, Jr., in Palmyra. Accessed by a trapdoor in the roof, a three-sided ell under the left eave led to a room over the kitchen that provided concealment for 10 people.

The Coopers once hid escapees in a haystack. Slave hunters plunged swords into the mass and pierced one man, who had been shielding his family with his body. The man made no outcry despite being seriously hurt. The Coopers summoned a doctor, who cauterized the wound to halt bleeding. From the Cooper home, the slaves journeyed five miles to conductor Samuel C. Cuyler, a customhouse officer and New York state senator in Pultneyville. Cuyler and courier Horatio Nelson Throop completed the steamer run over Lake Ontario to Peterboro. In addition to maintaining a waystation, Griffith Cooper managed the American Anti-Slavery Society from 1852 to 1853.

See also: American Anti-Slavery Society.

Source

Fairbanks, Eleanor. "Griffith M. Cooper (1791–1864)." *Pultneyville Historical Society Newsletter* 3:7 (August 1986): 1–2.

Copeland, John Anthony, Jr. (1834–1859)

A carpenter and abolitionist, John Anthony Copeland, Jr., developed into a rescuer of slaves. He was born in Raleigh, North Carolina, to Delilah Evans, a free mulatto domestic, and a white slave owner. At age nine, he followed his family to Oberlin, Ohio, and studied at Oberlin Academy. In September 1858, he joined community action against slave hunters stalking John Price, an escapee from Mason County, Kentucky. Copeland was among the Oberlin-Wellington rescue mob that wrested Price from his captors.

Copeland took a more dangerous course of action when he joined insurrectionist John Brown in fall 1859 to plan the seizure of the federal arsenal in Harpers Ferry, Virginia. During the attack, on October 16, federal authorities arrested Copeland while he was guarding the rifle works. Two months later, a firing squad executed him at Charlestown, Virginia, along with the other conspirators.

See also: Oberlin College.

Source

Hinton, Richard Josiah. *John Brown and His Men: With Some Account of the Roads They Travelled to Reach Harpers Ferry.* New York: Funk & Wagnalls, ca. 1894.

Copeland, Samuel (1823–1893)
Copeland, Alice Welch (1823–?)

A Virginia-born clothier, Samuel Copeland operated a safehouse in Boston, Massachusetts. After arriving in Boston in the 1840s and marrying an Irishwoman, Alice Welch, Copeland settled on Chestnut Street in Chelsea. He opened a successful clothing shop at 95 Blackstone and another on Merrimack Street. Despite the Fugitive Slave Law of 1850, which increased the danger of apprehension, fining, and imprisonment, the Copelands continued to welcome refugees to their residence and passed them off as visiting relatives. When danger of recapture ended, the Copelands relayed the slaves over northeastern Underground Railroad routes to Portland, Maine, or Nova Scotia.

See also: Fugitive Slave Law of 1850.

Source

Collison, Gary L. "The Boston Vigilance Committee: A Reconsideration." *Historical Journal of Massachusetts* 12:2 (1984): 104–16.

Corbet, Daniel (1705–1774)
Corbet, Mary Brinton (1708–1774)

An early slave rescuer, Daniel Corbet (also Corbit or Corbett) turned Clearfield Farm in Smyrna, in New Castle County, Delaware, into a reception center for the Underground Railroad. In November 1739, he married Mary Brinton. At Blackbird Hundred, an isolated spot on Paddock Road near the Delaware River, fugitives found safety and welcome. In 1755, the Corbets equipped their two-story brick residence with a concealed entrance behind a fireplace and installed a hidden basement, crawl spaces, and false panels and niches to protect passengers from recapture. They relayed refugees to safety with the help of three state agents, Rachel Mendenhall Garrett and Thomas Garrett in Wilmington and John Hunn in Middletown.

Source

McCarter, J.M., and B.F. Jackson, eds. *Historical and Biographical Encyclopedia of Delaware.* Wilmington, DE: Aldine, 1882.

Cordley, Richard (1829–1904)
Cordley, Mary Minta Cox (1820–?)

An English pioneer to the Midwest, the Reverend Richard Cordley recorded an eyewitness account of Underground Railroad activity in Kansas. Born in Nottingham, Michigan, he grew up in Livingston County from age four. After graduation from the University of Michigan and Andover Theological Seminary in Massachusetts, he pastored the Plymouth Congregational Church. Richard and his wife, Mary Minta Cox Cordley of Nottingham, also a pioneer to Livingston County, settled at 2023 Vermont Street in Lawrence, in Douglas County, Kansas, in November 1857. In *Pioneer Days in Kansas* (1903), Richard Cordley reported the largesse of a Scots agent, W.R. Monteith, who boarded a 22-year-old mulatto named Lizzie at his home in Wakarusa, Kansas, for several months. Lizzie had been a slave in Missouri.

The transfer of Lizzie to the Cordley household in summer 1859 introduced the newcomers to rescue work and to Lizzie's skills at cooking and housework. In the fall, Lizzie returned to the Monteiths. When a posse and a U.S. marshal tracked Lizzie to the area, Mary Cordley and a visiting woman posed in the Monteiths' front room as nurse and patient. Lizzie hid in the feather ticking. Monteith returned after midnight and relayed Lizzie by covered wagon to the next safehouse and on to Canada. On August 21, 1863, the raid by William Clarke Quantrill and his 450 men forced the Cordleys to flee for their lives. The raiders torched the family home.

Source

Cordley, Richard. *Pioneer Days in Kansas.* New York: Pilgrim, 1903.

Corliss, Hiram (1793–1877)
Corliss, Susan Sheldon (1794–1843)

A surgeon and intrepid safehouse keeper at Union Village (now Greenwich), New York, Dr. Hiram Corliss and his first wife, Susan Sheldon Corliss, were part of a coordinated rescue effort along the New York–Vermont border. Hiram completed his medical training in 1816 and opened a practice in Easton, New York. In earshot of an angry mob, he collaborated with other abolitionists at the Dutch Reformed church at Argyle to establish an anti-slavery society in Washington County, which elected him president. In 1842, he chaired the Eastern New York Anti-Slavery Society, which aided Joseph Rogers in 1843 on his escape from Charles Bryant in Baltimore, Maryland. That same year, the society rescued a 22-year-old sailor named Evans from Baltimore; Isaac Hinson and

Jane Hinson and their son Charles from Elkton, Maryland; 20-year-old Fester Dixon; Elizabeth Judah, a seamstress who journeyed by steamer from Baltimore; and William Johnson, the bondsman of Richard White, who took over two months to reach Albany. Other pathos-filled stories of slave recoveries during Hiram Corliss's presidency include those of Jeremiah Boggs, a wounded bondsman from Richmond, Virginia, and Henry Terry, a field hand from Madisonville, Louisiana, who had suffered a broken nose and amputation of his toes in a cottin gin.

In league with the Reverend Nathaniel Colver, Leonard Gibbs, Angelina Gifford Mowry and William H. Mowry, and Quaker volunteers Esther Wilbur and Job Wilbur, Corliss shielded slaves in flight from stalkers. He hid runaways in a basement chamber in his two-story frame house at 331 Main Street. Slaves could proceed through a tunnel to the Batten Kill River. In 1846, the flight of Charles Salter and his brother, John, from bondage in Maryland ended when Corliss welcomed them to Union Village. The Salters established themselves as citizens, joined the Union Village Free Church, and courted sisters. Charles wed Susan Weeks, and John married Priscilla Weeks. In 1848, five years after the death of Susan Sheldon Corliss, Hiram married abolitionist Almy Howland Sampson, a member of the Old Saratoga District (New York) Anti-Slavery Society.

Source

Rosenberger, Jesse Leonard. *Through Three Centuries: Colver and Rosenberger, Lives and Times 1620 to 1922.* Chicago: University of Chicago, 1922.

Cornish (Aaron and Daffney) Family

Aaron Cornish (1822–?) freed himself from bondage in Cambridge, Maryland. In a party of 29, on October 24, 1857, he and his wife, Daffney Cornish (fl. 1850s), fled after the death of his owner, William D. Travers of Town Point in Dorchester County. Preceding the Cambridge party was son Joseph Cornish, who left two years earlier with the aid of Underground Railroad conductor Harriet Tubman. Her advice appears to have served the Cornish, Anthony, and Viney families. The Cornishes and the remaining four of their five sons—Edward, George Anthony, Perry Lake, and Solomon—were accompanied by 35-year-old Kit Anthony and his wife and family, George Light, 23-year-old Solomon Light, 27-year-old Silas Long, Caroline Stanley and 35-year-old Daniel Stanley and their four children, and 40-year-old Joseph Viney and Susan Viney and their four sons, Henry, Joe, Lloyd, and Tom. The *Easton Star* listed 40 slave escapes within a span of three weeks.

Source

Still, William. *The Underground Railroad.* Philadelphia: Porter & Coates, 1871.

Corse, Barney (1799–1878)
Corse, Mary Elizabeth Leggett (1805–1899)

A New York activist and director of the Manumission Society, Barney Corse masterminded the forerunner of the Quaker-run Underground Railroad in North Carolina. He was born in Camden, Delaware. In November 1823, he married Mary Elizabeth Leggett of Bayside, Long Island, and went into partnership with Mary's father, a leather merchant at Jacob and Ferry streets in New York City.

The Corses received refugees at their safehouse at 85 Cliff Street in Manhattan. They networked the tasks of finding shelter and warding off kidnappers. In collaboration with agents Isaac Tatem Hopper and David Ruggles, in 1837, Barney Corse assisted in the rescue of 21-year-old Thomas Hughes from John P. Darg, a Virginia planter. Because Hughes had stolen some $8,000 from Darg, the owner charged Corse, Hopper, and Ruggles with grand theft. Corse arranged bail. His generosity to black refugees bankrupted him in 1843.

See also: kidnap.

Source

Hodges, Graham Russell. "The Hazards of Anti-Slavery Journalism." *Media Studies Journal* 14:1 (Spring/Summer 2000).

Corson, George (1803–1860)
Corson, Martha T. Maulsby (1807–1870)

A Quaker limemaker, quarrier, and agent of the Underground Railroad, George Corson of Hickorytown, Pennsylvania, was a well connected conductor. He was a founder of the Plymouth Meeting Anti-Slavery Society and a contributor to Peter Dager's slave relays for the Whitemarsh Township Underground Railroad. George was aided by his wife, orator Martha Maulsby Corson of Montgomery, Pennsylvania, whom he married in 1832. Martha was the daughter of secret network agents Susan Thomas Maulsby and Samuel Maulsby of Plymouth Meeting, Pennsylvania. The Corsons operated their own safehouse at One East Germantown Pike in Philadelphia, Pennsylvania, where slaves hid in the attic. For network information, the couple awaited couriers from Phoenixville, Pennsylvania, dispatched by agents Lewis Peart and Elijah Funk Pennypacker to the Plymouth Meeting Anti-Slavery Society.

On August 29, 1855, George Corson joined James Mott, Jr., and James Miller McKim in accompanying Jane Johnson to a Philadelphia federal courtroom to testify on behalf of Passmore Williamson, a Quaker attorney found guilty of abducting Johnson from her master, North Carolina planter John Hill Wheeler. In 1856, the Corsons turned the carriage house into Abolition Hall, an assembly place for seating 200. It became a venue for abolitionist orators Frederick Douglass, Stephen Symons Foster, William Lloyd Garrison, and Lucretia Coffin Mott. Around 1884, the Corsons' son-in-law, Thomas Hovendon, painted *The Last Moments of John Brown,* a dramatic depiction of the insurrectionist, who stops on the way to the gallows to kiss a black child.

Source

Contosta, David R., and Gail C. Momjian. *Plymouth and Whitemarsh Townships, Pennsylvania.* Charleston, SC: Arcadia, 2003.

Corwin, Thomas (1794–1865)
Corwin, Sarah Ross (1795–1878)

Frontiersman, politician, and orator Thomas "Tom" Corwin and his wife, Sarah Ross Corwin, volunteered their home and service to the Underground Railroad. Born in Bourbon County, Kentucky, Thomas Corwin moved west at age four. He grew up in Warren County, Ohio, studied law, and entered the Ohio state legislature at age 28. That same year, he wed Sarah Ross, a Lebanon, Ohio, native. They made their home in Lebanon, in Warren County. According to eyewitness accounts from Jesse Wilson, a black laborer, after 1839, the Corwins maintained a waystation in their attic. In 1840, Thomas was elected governor of Ohio.

Source

Cabot, John Stevens. *The History of the State of Ohio: From the Discovery of the Great Valley, to the Present Time.* Detroit, MI: Northwestern, 1875.

Cowgill, Daniel, Sr. (1802–1887)
Cowgill, Mary Naudain (1806–1877)

Two Quaker conductors, Daniel Cowgill, Sr., of Duck Creek, Kentucky, and his wife, Mary Naudain Cowgill, managed a large slave rescue operation at 151 Kings Highway in Dover, Delaware. From 1825, the couple concealed fugitives in Woodbury, their roomy three-story brick mansion, and directed the overflow to the barn. To facilitate a quick escape, Daniel Cowgill dug a tunnel from the basement to the St. Jones River, which flows into Delaware Bay. The Cowgills frequently seated passengers at their dining table and invited them to dance in the ballroom, actions that tended to elicit disapproving comments.

Source

Conrad, Henry C. *Papers of the Historical Society of Delaware.* Wilmington: Historical Society of Delaware, 1903.

Cowles, Betsey Mix (1810–1876)

Abolitionist educator and reformer Betsey Mix Cowles aided slaves fleeing over the secret network. Born to the Reverend Giles Hooker Cowles, a Congregational minister, and Sally White Cowles, Betsey was a native of Bristol, Connecticut. After growing up in Austinburg, Ohio, at age 24, she founded the Young Ladies Society for Intellectual Improvement. She led the Female Anti-Slavery Society of Ashtabula County in 1835 and conducted slaves on their flight north. Her courage earned the praise of Frederick Douglass. In 1838, she studied at Oberlin College. In her thirties, she taught in Portsmouth, Ohio, and at Grand River Institute in Austinburg.

Cowles's activism increased in the last half of her life. Under the influence of orator Abigail "Abby" Kelley Foster of Worcester, Massachusetts, Cowles began raising funds for runaway slaves. She wrote essays for Foster's abolitionist newspaper, the *Anti-Slavery Bugle,* in support of William Lloyd Garrison's demand for immediate abolition of slavery. At age 38, Cowles served as teacher and principal of a grammar school in Massillon, Ohio. She later campaigned for full citizenship for women at the 1850 Ohio Women's Convention.

See also: abolitionist newspapers; Oberlin College.

Source

Geary, Linda L. *Balanced in the Wind: A Biography of Betsey Mix Cowles.* Lewisburg, PA: Bucknell University Press, 1989.

Cowles (Horace and Mary Ann Steele Smith) Family

Abolitionist and town clerk of Farmington, Connecticut, Horace Cowles (1782–1841) and his wife, Mary Ann Steele Smith Cowles (1784–1837), opened their safehouse to a slave child from the Portuguese slaver *Amistad.* A reputable agent of the Underground Railroad, Horace Cowles supported the American Anti-Slavery Society after its formation in Philadelphia on December 4, 1833. In 1838, he joined Samuel Deming, John Treadwell Norton, and Austin Franklin Williams in founding the Connecticut Anti-Slavery Society. Two years later, Cowles was appointed a manager of the American Anti-Slavery Society.

Down the street from agents Mary Strong Wadsworth and Timothy Wadsworth, the front yard of the Cowles' two-story frame house at 27 Main Street and Meadow Road was a favorite retreat for their daughter, Mary Ann Cowles (1807–1824), who surveyed strangers for signs of slave kidnappers. When Mary Ann saw suspicious newcomers, she sang a familiar child's song to alert abolitionists of possible slave nabbing in the area. After the arrest of the mutineers aboard the *Amistad* in September 1839, the Cowles family fostered Teme (also Tamie), a young Mende girl from Sierra Leone.

Following Horace Cowles's death, his son, Samuel Smith Cowles (1814–1872), editor of the *Charter Oak*, the newspaper of the Connecticut Anti-Slavery Society, and his wife, Clarissa Law Brooks Cowles (1816–1861), took over the family waystation. Horace Cowles's niece, Jennet (or Jeannette) Cowles Williams, and her husband, Austin Williams, were members of the Farmington (Connecticut) Abolition Society and operatives of the Underground Railroad who boarded the male mutineers at a barracks built on the Williams' property.

See also: American Anti-Slavery Society; *Amistad*; kidnap.

Source

Cowles, Calvin Duvall. *The Cowles Families in America.* New Haven, CT: Tuttle, Morehouse & Taylor, 1929.

Cowles, Solomon (1758–1846)
Cowles, Polly Gleason (1759–1803)

A scion of Connecticut patriots, Solomon Cowles was an early supporter of the New England–Canada route of the Underground Railroad. A veteran of the American Revolution, he channeled his activism through the Connecticut Society of the Promotion of Freedom and for the Relief of Persons Unlawfully Holden in Bondage. The state's first abolitionist society, it was a brotherhood of Yale graduates that the Reverend Ezra Stiles coformed in 1790. Following his marriage to Polly Gleason in 1779, Cowles made a waystation of their two-story frame home at 154 Main Street in Farmington, in Hartford County. After 1784, the couple welcomed refugees. They were still active during the litigation involving the Portuguese slave ship *Amistad.* In a letter, accused mutineer Joseph Cinqué offered his thanks to Solomon Cowles as one of his supporters during a trial in Hartford's Old State House from January 1840 to exoneration on March 9, 1841.

See also: American Revolution; *Amistad.*

Source

Huston, James L. *Calculating the Value of the Union: Slavery, Property Rights, and the Economic Origins of the Civil War.* Chapel Hill: University of North Carolina, 2003.

Cowles, Thomas (1809–1884)
Cowles, Julia Ann Cowles (1810–?)

A deputy sheriff, lawyer, and politician, Thomas Cowles offered shelter to passengers of the Underground Railroad. A Yale Law School graduate in 1829, he served the Farmington (Connecticut) Anti-Slavery Society as secretary. In October 1833, he married Julia Ann Cowles. On the Farmington River west of Hartford, the couple opened their home at 148 Main Street to runaways. In 1864, Thomas Cowles was elected to the state senate.

Source

Cowles, Calvin Duvall. *The Cowles Families in America.* New Haven, CT: Tuttle, Morehouse & Taylor, 1929.

Cox, Hannah Peirce (1797–1876)
Cox, John (1786–1880)
Cox, John William (1835–1901)

A diligent Quaker family of anti-slavery reformers, Hannah Peirce Cox and her husband, farmer John Cox, along with their son, John William "Will" Cox, operated a waystation in Longwood, in Chester County, Pennsylvania. Convincing them of the need for radical action was the burning of Pennsylvania Hall in Philadelphia on May 17, 1838, and a subsequent friendship with abolitionist Thomas Garrett. John Cox chaired the Kennett (Pennsylvania) Anti-Slavery Society. Both he and Hannah Cox served as anti-slavery delegates to national conventions.

Receiving hundreds of runaways from the Carolinas, Delaware, and Virginia through agents Isaac Meredith and Thamosin Pennock Meredith of Newlin, the Cox family organized their relief efforts. They provided food and clothing, hid refugees in the attic, and dispatched Jackson, their employee, to escort passengers by carriage to the next station. During reaping season in summer 1843, a clever ruse involving the loading and unloading of hay wagons allowed the stationmasters to ferry eight male slaves to safety.

After passage of the Fugitive Slave Law of 1850, the Coxes received eight male refugees, whom their son, Will, led to West Chester by night to the care of Sarah Darlington Barnard and Simon Barnard. One midnight in November, Will made another run in the curtained carriage with 15 refugees from Delaware City to Isaac Meredith and Thamosin Pennock Meredith in Newlin. On October 31, 1857, a party of 18 needed rescue after Irish kidnappers attacked them in Centerville, Delaware. On another delivery, Will drove all night to reach the West Chester depot before the departure of a morning train.

See also: Fugitive Slave Law of 1850; kidnap.

Source

Smedley, Robert C. *History of the Underground Railroad in Chester and the Neighboring Counties of Pennsylvania.* Lancaster, PA: Office of *The Journal*, 1883.

Craft, Ellen Smith (1826–1891)
Craft, William (fl. 1840s–1860s)

The Crafts, Ellen Smith and William, were one of the most ingenious black slave couples to seek liberty. Sired by her white owner, Major James Smith, in Macon, Georgia, Ellen Smith was the daughter of an enslaved domestic, Maria Smith. Ellen's light complexion, a product of her racial mixture, aroused anger and jealousy in the master's wife. In 1846, Ellen, a seamstress, married William Craft, a slave carpenter.

To her benefit, Ellen's coloring allowed her to pass as white. Disguised in suit and top hat as William Johnson, a privileged white male planter, on December 21, 1848, she and her husband, William, traveled by train from Macon to Savannah, Georgia, with William posing as her body servant. To conceal her beardless lower face, Ellen wore a bandage that covered a jaw supposedly aching from a bad tooth. She wore her right arm in a sling to account for an inability to sign a hotel register. To show that she was dependent on a servant, she leaned on a cane, wore green glasses over her eyes, and pretended to be rheumatic and slightly deaf. After journeying by steamer and omnibus to Charleston, South Carolina, and lodging in a top-rated hotel, the two traveled by train from Wilmington, North Carolina, to Richmond, Virginia.

The Crafts encountered surprising turns of luck. When they arrived in Baltimore, Maryland, on Christmas Eve, they faced a demanding ticket agent who required a security bond for the servant. William insisted that his master was in delicate health and must hurry on. After completing the Underground Railroad route, on December 25, the Crafts received the greetings of well-wishers in Philadelphia, including Quaker agent Barkley Ivens and Robert Purvis. Ivens and his wife offered Crafts a place to rest and, over a three-week period, began teaching them to read.

Ellen and William Craft reached the main office in Boston, where the Reverend Theodore Parker performed a legal wedding ceremony and offered Ellen shelter at his safehouse for the night. With the aid of barber John J. Smith, secret operatives Harriet Bell Hayden and Lewis Hayden hid William at a depot at 66 Southac Street and lodged the couple briefly with George Stillman Hillard and Susan Tracy Howe Hillard at 54 Pinckney Street. When Dr. Robert Collins dispatched two deputies from Macon, Georgia, to recapture the Crafts, operatives sped Ellen away to William Ingersoll Bowditch's safehouse in Brookline, Massachusetts. Lewis Hayden threatened to set off two powder kegs if the pursuers entered his cellar in search of the Crafts, whom Bowditch passed to the Brighton Road waystation of abolitionist attorney Ellis Gray Loring.

Because of the passage of the Fugitive Slave Law in September 1850, the slave owner's pursuit received mention in William Lloyd Garrison's abolitionist paper *The Liberator.* Abolitionists threatened to tar and feather slave catchers named Hughes and John Knight. The two men legitimized their search with arrest warrants, which the Reverend Samuel Joseph

May disallowed as bogus. The 100-member Boston Vigilance Committee, made up of some 40 attorneys, distributed posters describing the pursuers, whom the Crafts charged with slander. Their lawsuit specified damages of $10,000. Contesting the arrest of the pursuers were two anti-abolitionists, Watson Freeman and John H. Pearsons. After making bail, Hughes and Knight faced additional charges of conspiracy to kidnap William Craft from the United States Hotel in Boston on October 22, 1850.

To protect Ellen Craft from such connivance, Susan Hilliard hid the slave in her Boston residence. Ellen began studying upholstery with a Miss Dean, but the threat of arrest, a fine, and scandal to the upright Hilliards forced the Crafts to shelter at the waystation of Lydia Neale Dennett and W. Oliver Dennett on Spring Street in Portland, Maine. From there, the runaways sailed for Halifax, Nova Scotia, and on to Liverpool, England. Before departing the harbor in New Bedford, Massachusetts, the Crafts received hospitality from agent Andrew Robeson.

A British abolitionist, William Farmer, proposed that such people as the Crafts and William Wells Brown be presented in a global exhibit as models of the caliber of the people Americans enslaved. The Crafts did indeed appear at the 1851 World's Fair in London as successful runaways. Ellen Craft recovered from frail health and, on Octobr 22, 1852, gave birth to her first freeborn child. William Craft compiled a best-selling slave narrative, *Running a Thousand Miles for Freedom* (1860). After two decades of writing and lecturing, the Crafts settled in Savannah, Georgia.

See also: disguise; Fugitive Slave Law of 1850; *Liberator, The.*

Sources

Bland, Sterling Lecater. *Voices of the Fugitives.* Westport, CT: Praeger, 2000.

Clarke, James Freeman. "The Rise and Fall of the Slave Power in America." *North American Review* 120:246 (January 1875): 47–84.

Craft, William. *Running a Thousand Miles for Freedom.* London: William Tweedie, 1860.

McCaskill, Barbara. "Yours Very Truly: Ellen Craft, the Fugitive as Text and Artifact." *African American Review* 28:4 (Winter 1994): 509–29.

Crandall, Henry White (1817–1900) Crandall, Elizabeth H. Lockhart (1819–1874)

In Almond on the busy northern route through Allegany County, New York, to New York City, abolitionist Henry White Crandall managed an Underground Railroad waystation. A farmer and dry goods merchant, Crandall was a family man, married to Elizabeth H. Lockhart of Almond, mother of their four children. The couple tended runaways arriving from a safehouse at Canisteo, New York. The Crandall homeplace, built at 100 Main Street in 1840 by Henry's father, David Crandall, featured a series of rooms in the cellar accessed by a trapdoor. A door behind bookshelves opened on a recessed path to the creek. From the Crandall depot, slaves moved north to Geneseo.

Source

Piña, Asia. "Alfred's Gallery a Stop on Underground Railroad." *Fiat Lux* 98:8 (February 3, 2004): 1.

Craner, Daniel (fl. 1850s)

A conductor in Harford County, Maryland, Daniel Craner was jailed for his rescue of slaves. Born in New Jersey, he operated a waystation at Havre de Grace, Maryland. In spring 1858, he was arrested for sheltering Ann Howard, an act for which a circuit court in Bel Air sentenced him to 10 years in the state penitentiary. On December 21, 1864, Governor Augustus Williamson Bradford freed Craner for committing a crime that no longer existed.

Source

"Conviction," *Southern Aegis,* December 8, 1860.

Cratty, William (1805–1897) Cratty, Candis Bennett (1806–1879)

A midwestern farmer, William Cratty was a cautious but compassionate member of a close-knit group of Underground Railroad operatives. He married Candis Bennett in 1826. Five years later, the couple began supporting passengers of the Underground Railroad on the Ohio–Canada line. At their waystation in Marysville, west of the Scioto River in Union County, Ohio, for nearly two decades, they received refugees from the safehouse of Deacon Samuel A. Cherry on West Fifth Street and from Aaron Skinner and John Cratty, a conductor living on the Delaware Road along the Scioto River. Slave owners grew so angry at William Cratty that they offered $3,000 for his apprehension.

Source

Obituary, *Marysville (OH) Tribune,* September 1, 1897, 4.

Cravath, Orin (1806–1874)
Cravath, Betsey Northway (1811–?)

A radical activist and co-founder of the Abolition Party from Homer, in Cortland County, New York, Orin (or Orrin) Cravath farmed, supported Oberlin College, and operated a waystation of the Underground Railroad. Of French descent, he was a patriot and scion of early settlers of Boston, Massachusetts. After marrying Betsey Northway in December 1830, he and his wife practiced their Congregational beliefs by receiving passengers journeying west of Ithaca toward the Lake Ontario crossing. In 1850, the family moved to Oberlin, Ohio. During the Civil War, the Cravaths' son, the Reverend Erastus Milo Cravath, served as chaplain of the 101st Ohio Volunteers.

See also: Oberlin College.

Sources

Compendium of History and Biography of Central and Northern Minnesota. Chicago: George A. Ogle, 1904.
"Personal Sketches." *American Missionary* 48:2 (February 1894): 76.

Crawford, James M. (1795–1850)
Crawford, Mary Rogers (1807–1894)

Two dedicated volunteers at a crucial Underground Railroad station 16 miles outside of Erie, Pennsylvania, James Crawford and his wife, Mary, were no strangers to conflict. On May 26, 1828, he and seven Presbyterians established a congregation in a log courthouse. At Sixteen-Mile Creek, opposite Lake Erie, they conducted refugees by night with the aid of William Cass, a wool manufacturer. The Crawfords and Cass booked passage for fugitives on boats crossing Lake Erie.

On one failed relay, the Crawfords admitted a passenger named Ned from North Carolina, led by agent Cass. After midnight, foundryman John Glass alerted the Crawfords to pursuers. Mary Crawford devised a scheme whereby Glass would hide the slave at the foundry in a wagon loaded with frames and implements. To confuse the posse, she put her son, Joseph W. Crawford (1844–1850), in the bed that Ned had occupied. An informer disclosed the plot to the sheriff, who recovered Ned while the runaway was boarding a sloop. Authorities returned Ned to bondage in the South.

Source

Switala, William J. *Underground Railroad in Pennsylvania.* Mechanicsburg, PA: Stackpole, 2001.

Crawford, John T. (?–1881)

A Union soldier during the Civil War, real estate speculator John T. Crawford sympathized with slaves. He escaped from Libby Prison in Richmond, Virginia, and walked to his home on College Hill in Cincinnati, Ohio. Because black families piloted and boarded him during the long trek, he established a waystation for refugee slaves. He equipped his house with a trapdoor leading to a niche under the floor.

Source

Smiddy, Betty Ann. *A Little Piece of Paradise . . . College Hill, Ohio.* Cincinnati, OH: College Hill Historical Society, 1999.

Crenshaw, John Hart (1797–1871)
Crenshaw, Francine Taylor (1800–1881)

A Carolina-born salt manufacturer and professional slave nabber, John Hart Crenshaw, posing as a pious Methodist, enriched himself by stealing runaways for resale. Beginning in 1825, fugitives passing through Shawneetown, Illinois, were in danger of theft by Crenshaw and his cohorts, John Forrested and Preston W. Davis, who posed as agents of the Underground Railroad. Victims would languish in caverns along the Saline River until the trio shuttled the refugees to the South for sale. In 1834, Crenshaw and his wife, Francine "Sina" (or Sanai) Taylor Crenshaw of Virginia, built Hickory Hill, a mansion outside Equality, Illinois. Locals dubbed it the Old Slave House because Crenshaw used one of its garrets to imprison blacks. In 1842, a Gallatin County court exonerated Crenshaw for seizing an indentured cook, Maria Adams, and two of her three children, 19-year-old Ellen and 13-year-old Nancy Jane. Crenshaw tied and manacled the three women and sold them to slave owner Lewis Kuykendall, who transported them to Texas.

Source

Musgrave, Jon Manning. *Slaves, Salt, Sex & Mr. Crenshaw: The Real Story of the Old Slave House and America's Reverse Underground Railroad.* Marion, IL: IllinoisHistory.com, 2004.

Crocker, Samuel Somerby (1813–1909)
Crocker, Martha Elizabeth Putnam (1818–1907)

Samuel Somerby (or Somerbie) Crocker, the owner of Crocker Manufacturing Company, joined a team of

Underground Railroad conductors in Fitchburg, in Worcester County, Massachusetts. In league with fellow paper manufacturer Benjamin Snow, Jr., and Mary Baldwin Boutolle Snow, Crocker and his wife, Martha Elizabeth Putnam Crocker, promoted the flight of refugees on the New England–Canada route of the secret network. Historian Wilbur Henry Siebert added a photo of Martha Snow to his artifacts from the Underground Railroad.

Source

Crane, Ellery Bicknell. *Historic Homes and Institutions and Genealogical and Personal Memoirs of Worcester County, Massachusetts.* Chicago: Lewis, 1907.

Cromwell, Robert (fl. 1840s)

The flight of Robert Cromwell from bondage in Arkansas resulted in a sensational court case that influenced passage of the Fugitive Slave Law of 1850. After escaping slavery in 1840, Cromwell crossed the Mississippi River and followed the Underground Railroad route through Indiana. He settled in Flint, Michigan, and opened a barber shop beside a hotel. Cromwell wrote his master, John Dunn, and offered to pay $100 for his sister's freedom. Dunn traced Cromwell to the Flint postmark.

In terror of recapture, Cromwell sought agents George DeBaptiste and William Lambert, secret network superintendents at a crucial crossing point in Detroit, Michigan. Cromwell remained under their protection and opened a restaurant at Brush and Larnet streets. In February 1840, Dunn conspired with U.S. District Attorney John Norvell and lured Cromwell to the courthouse at Jefferson and Griswold streets. Cromwell raised the alarm by yelling from a courthouse window. DeBaptiste, Lambert, and Seymour Finney freed Cromwell from a side door and hurried him to their skiff at Shelby Street. Cromwell crossed safely to Windsor, Ontario. The Reverend William Charles Monroe spearheaded a lawsuit against Dunn for plotting to kidnap Cromwell. Dunn remained in jail for nine months but won his case because Underground Railroad operatives could not prove that he intended to force Cromwell back into bondage.

See also: Fugitive Slave Law of 1850; kidnap.

Source

Chardavoyne, David G. "Michigan and the Fugitive Slave Acts." *Court Legacy* 12:3 (November 2004): 1–10.

Crooks, Abigail R. Short (1808–1900)
Crooks, Samuel (1802–1881)

The Crooks family rescued slaves traveling the Michigan–Canada route of the Underground Railroad. Samuel Crooks, a native of Richmond, in Ontario County, New York, preceded his wife, Abigail R. Short Crooks, and their children to Prairie Ronde, in Kalamazoo County, Michigan, in 1834 and built a log cabin west of Schoolcraft. He returned to New York for his wife and children, who crossed Lake Huron by steamer before struggling through wilderness to their homestead. The family initiated the region's first school, organized a Methodist church, and opened a depot for fugitive slaves.

Source

Fisher, David. *Compendium of History and Biography of Kalamazoo County, Michigan.* Chicago: A.W. Bowen, 1906.

Crosby, Uriah H. (fl. 1850s–1860s)

A conductor in Tazewell County, Illinois, Uriah H. Crosby operated a waystation at his residence in Morton Township, near Peoria. After receiving passengers from John M. Roberts in Morton or from John Albert Jones in Tremont, Crosby connected runaways with the Kern safehouse nine miles away, where slaves continued north to a Quaker settlement. One of Crosby's difficult relays involved an overweight couple, both Methodist evangelists, who together took up most of a single wagon seat. The couple passed through Kern's station on their way to Ontario.

Source

History of Tazewell County, Illinois. Chicago: Charles C. Chapman, 1879.

Cross, Gideon (1795–1849)

A victim of stiff penalties for conducting slaves to freedom, Gideon Cross died in prison. A native of Talbot County, Maryland, he worked as a day laborer in Baltimore. At age 50, he was arrested for conducting the slaves of W.P. Mills to liberty. Cross was sentenced to a seven-year term on October 27, 1845; he completed four years in prison and died of pulmonary edema on November 26, 1849.

Source

Prison records, Maryland State Archives.

Cross, John (1797–1875)
Cross, Lucinda Hulbert (1800–?)

The Reverend John Cross, a manager of the Underground Railroad, worked to end enslavement. Shortly after his birth in Massachusetts, he lived in New York. In 1818, he married Lucinda Hulbert of Pittsfield, Massachusetts. At age 42, he relocated to Amity, Illinois, and was ordained a minister of the Congregational Church. As an agent of the Illinois Anti-Slavery Society, Cross involved himself openly and aggressively in the work of the Underground Railroad and continued in 1839, after his move to Elba, in Knox County, to pastor a Presbyterian church.

In 1840, Cross recruited Sarah E. Bowen Hussey and Sylvanus Erastus Fuller Hussey, who became two devoted slave rescuers at their dry goods store in Battle Creek, Michigan. Two years later, Cross harbored Susan Borders "Aunt Sukey" Richardson, who fled her owner, Andrew Borders of Randolph County, Illinois, because he planned to sell two of her three children. Lawmen followed the party to the Cross waystation and found evidence of sheltering, a large cauldron of potatoes and corn that Lucinda Cross boiled on her stove. John Cross dispatched a scout to the magistrate's home. An assistant helped transfer the runaways to a wagon. Cross then drove a decoy wagon that temporarily absorbed the pursuers' attention while the runaways fled over Spoon River. Sheriff Peter Frans jailed Cross until abolitionists could raise bail. Upon gaining her freedom, Susan Richardson became a secret network operative at Knox College in Galesburg.

In 1843, he aided passengers of the secret network as they moved through Elba. After his arrest for harboring slaves, abolitionists at Osceola offered to retrieve him from the deputy sheriff, who was transporting Cross to Galesburg.

See also: Fugitive Slave Law of 1793; Fugitive Slave Law of 1850.

Sources

Chapman, Charles. *History of Knox County, Illinois.* Chicago: Blakely, Brown & Marsh, 1878.
Fuller, George N., ed. *Historic Michigan, Land of the Great Lakes.* Dayton, OH: National Historical Association, 1924.
"Liberty Line," *Chicago Western Citizen,* July 13, 1844.

> The Reverend John Cross issued a famous Underground Railroad advertisement in the July 18, 1844, issue of the *Western Citizen.* Under the line drawing of a train disappearing into a tunnel was the following message: "The improved and splendid Locomotives, Clarkson and Lundy, with their trains fitted up in the best style of accommodation for passengers, will run their regular trips during the present season between the borders of the Patriarchal Dominion and Libertyville, Upper Canada. Gentlemen and Ladies who may wish to improve their health or circumstances by a northern tour are respectfully invited to give us their patronage." The offer of free seats and clothing to runaways and the disdainful remark that posses would be transported as "dead freight to the 'Valley of Rascals'" warned slave hunters of the seriousness of the secret network.

Crosswhite, Adam (1799–1878)
Crosswhite, Sarah (fl. 1800–1860s)

Adam Crosswhite's flight to liberty created a stir preceding the Civil War. The son of a slave, he was sired by his owner, Francis Giltner, in Carroll County, Kentucky. In 1843, to avoid the sale of their oldest child, Crosswhite and his wife Sarah journeyed with their four children along Underground Railroad routes in Indiana to Calhoun County near Marshall, Michigan. In December 1846, attorney Henry Troutman, aided by a spy from Kalamazoo, pursued his grandfather's chattel to Marshall to identify them. On January 27, 1847, Troutman, Franklin Ford, David Giltner, and John S. Lee burst in on the Crosswhites. Alerted by the slave grapevine, Crosswhite was armed and ready for the approach of Sheriff Harvey Dixon, who arrived at 4 A.M. By a prearranged signal, Adam Crosswhite fired a pistol and summoned 300 supporters, who surrounded the house. Speaking for abolitionists was financier Charles T. Gorham, a respected citizen.

While the sheriff arrested the Kentuckians for assault and battery and for breaking and entering, agents George Ingersoll and Asa B. Cook drove the Crosswhites by cart along the safe route through Jackson, by train to Detroit, and over the Detroit River to Windsor, Ontario. Troutman paid a fine of $100 for illegal entry. In 1848, he successfully sued the town of Marshall for $2,752, the value of the Crosswhite family. Senator Henry Clay of Kentucky used the case as a basis for supporting a replacement of the Fugitive Slave Law of 1793 with the Fugitive Slave Law of 1850. The Crosswhites remained in Canada until 1865, when they relocated to Marshall, Michigan.

See also: grapevine telegraphy; routes, Underground Railroad; spies.

Sources

Gardner, Washington, ed. *History of Calhoun County, Michigan.* Chicago: Lewis, 1913.
Yzenbaard, John H. "The Crosswhite Case." *Michigan History* 53:2 (1969): 131–43.

Cuffe, Paul (1759–1817)

A Quaker merchant and abolitionist, Captain Paul Cuffe (or Cuffee) aided Underground Railroad activities from his home in Westport, Massachusetts. Born free in Buzzard's Bay, on Chuttyhunk (or Cutterhunker) Island, Massachusetts, he was the son of a Wampanoag mother, Ruth Moses, and a Ghanian father, Cuffe Slocum, the slave of Ebenzer Slocum, a Quaker from Dartmouth, Massachusetts. Paul Cuffe chose for a surname a version of Kofi, the Ashanti tribe from which his father was kidnapped and sold into slavery.

A whaler and boatbuilder, Paul Cuffe grew wealthy while running British blockades during the American Revolution and by expanding his activities into coastal trade from Labrador and Newfoundland south to Virginia. In 1783, he married Alice Piquet and built a home and gristmill in Westport on a 140-acre tract on the Acoaxet River. He reputedly conspired with his Pequot nephew, Thomas Wainer, on the transporting of slaves on the schooner *Alpha* from harbors in Norfolk, Virginia, and Savannah, Georgia, to Philadelphia, Pennsylvania, and Wilmington, Delaware. Cuffe encouraged the resettlement of American blacks to Sierra Leone, where he conveyed them on his schooner *Traveller.* In 1799, Samuel Sloane of Somerset County, Maryland, charged Thomas Wainer with transporting two slaves, Harry Sloane and his wife, Lucy Sloane, from Snowhill, Maryland, to Westport.

See also: American Revolution.

Source

Grover, Kathryn. *The Fugitive's Gibraltar: Escaping Slaves and Abolitionism in New Bedford, Massachusetts.* Amherst: University of Massachusetts, 2001.

Cuffy (fl. 1840s)

A thrilling Underground Railroad story describes the flight of Cuffy, the valet of a Georgia planter. Born near Cape Town, South Africa, to a prince, at age 11, Cuffy fell into the hands of pirates, who sold him in Georgia. While serving his master in Philadelphia, at age 24, Cuffy feared sale at some future time and questioned agents about the Underground Railroad. At the safehouse of Abigail Paxson Vickers and John Vickers in Lancaster County, Cuffy became a faithful worker and a companion to the family's children. He remained in Pennsylvania for the winter to study. The next spring, local abolitionists collected funds to pay Cuffy's way home to South Africa. He sent letters filled with his gratitude.

Source

Smedley, Robert C. *History of the Underground Railroad in Chester and the Neighboring Counties of Pennsylvania.* Lancaster, PA: Office of *The Journal*, 1883.

Culbertson, John Newton (1841–ca. 1926)
Culbertson, Hannah McVitty (1811–1887)
Culbertson, John McVitty (1809–1885)

An eyewitness to Underground Railroad activity in Franklin County, Pennsylvania, John Newton Culbertson recorded his family's dedication to conducting slaves to freedom. At the family farm in Amberson Valley, in autumn 1848, he recalled how his parents, Hannah McVitty Culbertson and Captain John McVitty Culbertson, gathered their children in the kitchen at dusk. Captain Culbertson reported finding a fugitive slave woman and four men in the orchard. The family hid the group in the barn and provided a food basket and water jug. When slave hunters arrived within minutes, Captain Culbertson refused to aid them in the flesh-trading business. After midnight, he piloted the group up the valley and directed them to the next stop. On a subsequent rescue, Hannah Culbertson kept a sick woman at the farm until the refugee could continue north. In 1861, John Culbertson walked to Fort Leavenworth, Kansas, to enlist in the Union cavalry.

Source

Culbertson, John Newton. "A Pennsylvania Boyhood." *American Heritage* 18:1 (December 1966): 80–111.

Culver, Erastus Dean (1803–1889)

Attorney and U.S. congressman Erastus Dean Culver of Champlain, New York, was a defender of runaway slaves and an aid to passengers of the Underground

Railway. He settled at One Washington Square in Union Village (now Greenwich), New York. In 1851, he opened an office in Brooklyn, in Washington County, New York, and served the local anti-slavery society as secretary. Three years later, while serving as judge of the Brooklyn civil court, he ruled in favor of fugitives rather than slaveholders. As reported in the May 29, 1854, issue of the *Philadelphia North American,* he was sympathetic to the brother and two nephews of the Reverend James William Charles Pennington but could not halt the return of the trio to slavery in Maryland. For Culver's service to the Union army, a Civil War monument at Prospect Hill Cemetery in Guilderland, New York, bears his name.

Source

Pierson, Michael D. *Free Hearts and Free Homes: Gender and American Anti-Slavery Politics.* Chapel Hill: University of North Carolina, 2003.

Cumberland, Moses (fl. 1830s)

Moses Cumberland was a member of a large family of free blacks in Gist, a settlement in Brown County, Ohio. He supported the slave rescues of Dr. Isaac M. Beck and his wife, Cassandra Graham Lamb Beck, and of Jean Lowry Rankin and her husband, the Reverend John Rankin, the prominent Underground Railroad agent at the Maysville, Kentucky, crossing of the Ohio River to free territory in Ripley, Ohio. On April 21, 1839, slave nabbers attempted to seize Cumberland from the Gist community. Coming to his aid were John D. Hudson, a wagoneer for the Underground Railroad, and his sister, Sally Hudson. In a vicious fray, Sally struck and bit her assailants. A bullet to the spine killed her. The stalkers failed to capture Cumberland, who escaped with the help of the Reverend John Bennington Mahan.

See also: Gist Settlement.

Source

Schwarz, Philip J. *Migrants Against Slavery: Virginians & the Nation.* Charlottesville: University of Virginia, 2001.

Cummings, Jacob (fl. 1830s)

The escape of the Reverend Jacob Cummings attests to the ingenuity of runaways and their African American rescuers. The property of farmer James Smith, Cummings escaped from Chattanooga, Tennessee, in July 1839, and sheltered on the Ohio River. He traveled beyond the Cumberland Mountains before being apprehended. In a second flight, he traveled on horseback and across the Ohio River in a stolen skiff before reaching New Albany, Indiana, at the end of September 1839. Assisting him were William Finney, "Uncle Zeke" Goins, and "Uncle Charley" Lacey, committed black abolitionists who gave Cummings work before he continued to Clark County, Indiana. A second recapture and trial resulted in dismissal. Agents quickly moved Cummings out of the area and to a black community at Cabin Creek, where he stayed before his venture into Canada.

Source

Hamm, Thomas, et al. "A Great and Good People: Midwestern Quakers and the Struggle Against Slavery." *Indiana Magazine of History* 100:1 (March 2004).

Curry, James (ca. 1815–?)

A quadroon who followed the Carolina–New England route of the Underground Railroad, James Curry was a successful rescue for Massachusetts and Rhode Island agents. Teacher and reformer Elizabeth Buffum Chace mentions Curry in her diary, *My Anti-Slavery Reminiscences,* which she began keeping in 1831. A native of Person County, North Carolina, Curry was the son of Lucy, a cook, whose father was a white man. Curry's father, Peter Burnet, traveled south as a valet and never returned. After he was sold at a slave sale to satisfy his master's debts, Curry passed to the ownership of Thomas Moses Chambers. By age 16, Curry was a trained domestic. The master's oldest son taught him to read and write.

When Curry fled to Petersburg, Virginia, in May 1837, he carried along borrowed reading material. His path took him to Washington, D.C., Alexandria, Virginia, and Hagerstown, Maryland. On July 19, he arrived in free territory in Pennsylvania. In Philadelphia, he worked for Quaker agents until late December, when secret operatives transported him to New York City and northeast to New England. In 1839, he became the first successful relay from Fall River, Massachusetts, to Canada. The next year, he sent his story to William Lloyd Garrison for publication in the weekly *The Liberator.*

Sources

Curry, James, "Narrative of James Curry," *The Liberator,* January 10, 1840, 1.

Lovell, Malcolm R., ed. *Two Quaker Sisters: From the Original Diaries of Elizabeth Buffum Chace and Lucy Buffum Lovell.* Introduction by Malcolm R. Lovell. New York: Liveright, 1937.

Curry, Vina (fl. 1820s–1830s)

Freedwoman Vina Curry aided blacks held in bondage in North Carolina. When her husband, Arch Curry, died around 1828, Vina was left to support herself. A laundress at the New Garden Boarding School in Guilford County, she became a co-conspirator with Alethea Flukes Coffin, the school matron, who was also a manager of an Underground Railroad waystation. Curry lent the manumission papers of Archie Curry, her deceased husband, to black males traveling west with pioneers. After each use, Quaker operatives Catherine White Coffin and Levi Coffin relayed the papers back to North Carolina for use by a total of 15 runaways.

Sources

Coffin, Addison. *Life and Travels of Addison Coffin.* Cleveland, OH: W.G. Hubbard, 1897.

Smith, Margaret Supplee, and Emily Herring Wilson. *North Carolina Women Making History.* Chapel Hill: University of North Carolina, 1999.

Curtis, Horace (1793–1871)
Curtis, Lydia Cole (1796–1863)

In Little Hocking, Ohio, on the Chillicothe Pike, merchant and postmaster Horace Curtis operated a depot of the Underground Railroad. In 1820, a year after his marriage to Lydia Cole of Monroe, New York, he and his wife began rescuing fugitives. Their two-story frame house featured a concealed chamber in the cellar. With a view of the Ohio River, they observed slaves fleeing from West Virginia plantations or arriving from Marietta, Ohio.

Source

Burke, Henry Robert, and Charles Hart Fogle. *Washington County Underground Railroad.* Charleston, SC: Arcadia, 2004.

Curtis, James (1783–?)

One of many black conductors on the Underground Railroad, James Curtis served a prison sentence for the crime of aiding in slave rescue. At age 51, he was free and working as a day laborer in his native Montgomery County, Maryland. On March 13, 1834, a circuit court judge sentenced Curtis to two years in the state penitentiary at Baltimore. Curtis gained his freedom on March 13, 1836.

Source

Prison records, Maryland State Archives.

Curtis, John (1830–1914)
Curtis, Benjamin (1833–1846)
Curtis, Harrison (1832–early 1860s)

A refugee from Rockingham County, Virginia, John "Rockingham John" Curtis operated a depot at his home outside Stafford in Monroe County, Ohio. He was born into bondage in the Shenandoah Valley, Virginia. At age 16, he and his brothers, 13-year-old Benjamin Curtis and 14-year-old Harrison Curtis, fled their owner's plantation in autumn and worked their way to Ellensboro, where an Underground Railroad operative directed them to the Ohio River. In heavy snow, the brothers halted at a cave near Duck Creek in Washington County, Ohio, and fought a hibernating bear for the right to occupancy. Cooking bear meat and sleeping under the hide, the trio managed to stay out of sight for two weeks.

In November 1846, Harrison and John buried Benjamin under creek stones after he died of exposure. The Feldner family, immigrant agents from Germany, found the cairn and followed footprints to the cave. The Feldners welcomed the two survivors to their safehouse and restored them to health. Another immigrant agent, William Steel of Biggar, Scotland, bought the brothers' freedom. Harrison and John worked at Steel's gristmill to repay the cost of manumission. From 1847 until the beginning of the Civil War, Harrison and John rescued other refugees from the South by passing them along northern routes to Guinea in Belmont County, Ohio. After serving in the Union army as a civilian scout, John joined the Third Regiment and served until 1865. Harrison died in the war.

Source

Sullivan, Erin, "Slavery Sparks Family's History," *Athens (OH) Post,* September 11, 1998.

Curtis, Thomas F. (1812–1900)
Curtis, Annie Fenner (ca. 1829–ca. 1910)

Immigrants from England, the Reverend Thomas F. Curtis and his wife, Annie Fenner Curtis, sheltered runaway slaves in Northumberland County, Pennsylvania. From 1856 to 1863, Thomas Curtis pastored the Milton Baptist Church. While teaching theology at Bucknell University in Lewisburg, he abetted the rescues of professors George Ripley Bliss and Howard

Malcolm, fellow agents of the Underground Railroad. Until the national emancipation of slaves on January 1, 1863, the Curtis family used their two-story brick home at 110 University Avenue in Lewisburg as a waystation. In 1977, the residence was listed on the National Register for Historic Sites.

Source

Snyder, Charles McCool. *Union County Pennsylvania: A Celebration of History.* Montoursville, PA: Penn State Press, 2000.

Cuyler, Samuel Cornelius (1808–1872)
Cuyler, Julia Speed (1812–?)

An agent of the New York–Canada route of the Underground Railroad, Samuel Cornelius Cuyler and his wife, Julia Speed Cuyler, teamed well with local volunteers. The Cuylers married in 1832. Their home in Pultneyville, in Wayne County, New York, was used as a safehouse. Samuel's appointment to custom house officer in July 1861 gave him access to inside knowledge on schooner and steamship movements over the Great Lakes. The couple received passengers from Quaker conductor Griffith M. Cooper in Williamson, New York, and conspired with courier Horatio Nelson Throop and his son, Ledyard Throop, to relay slaves by steamer over Lake Ontario to Peterboro, Ontario. From 1856 to 1857, Samuel Cuyler served in the New York state senate. In October 1861, he enlisted volunteers for the Union army to fight in the Civil War.

See also: American Anti-Slavery Society.

Sources

Klees, Emerson. *Underground Railroad Tales: With Routes Through the Finger Lakes Region.* Rochester, NY: Friends of the Finger Lakes, 1997.

Personal Items, *Pultneyville (NY) Commercial Press,* July 1861, 1.

Dager, Peter (fl. 1810s–1820s)

A Quaker philanthropist, Peter Dager contributed funds and activism to the Underground Railroad in Whitemarsh Township, Pennsylvania. In 1810 in Montgomery County, he built Linden Grove, a two-story frame house on Ridge Pike and Spring Mill Road in Plymouth, and began quarrying marble. He collaborated with fellow operatives George Corson and Martha Maulsby Corson. On January 9, 1826, Dager and Ezra Comfort aided sibling runaways, John Lewis and Westley Lewis, who were captured by their owner in Dager's stable and tied and transported by wagon to a magistrate for official identification as slaves. The two Quakers intervened and paid $900 for the slaves—$600 for John Lewis and $300 for Westley Lewis—and set them free.

See also: philanthropists; Quakers.

Source

Contosta, David R., and Gail C. Momjian. *Plymouth and Whitemarsh Townships, Pennsylvania.* Charleston, SC: Arcadia, 2003.

Damon, Samuel Dexter (1813–1884) Damon, Harriet Matilda Frank (1820–1918)

A merchant and politician, Samuel Dexter Damon, of Ludlow, Massachusetts, and his wife, Harriet Matilda Frank Damon of New York, found time to aid refugee slaves. The couple married in 1853. After operating a store in Kirtland, Ohio, the Damons ventured farther into the frontier and settled in Willoughby, outside of Cleveland, Ohio, where they launched a rescue system for runaway slaves.

Source

Siebert, Wilbur H. *The Mysteries of Ohio's Underground Railroad.* Columbus, OH: Long's College, 1951.

Dana, Richard Henry, Jr. (1815–1882)

An attorney and fiction writer from Cambridge, Massachusetts, Richard Henry Dana, Jr., supported the Underground Railroad with free legal service. After graduating from Harvard and Dane Law School and publishing *Two Years Before the Mast* (1840), he left the Congregational church and adopted Episcopalianism. In service to his beliefs, he became a conservative abolitionist and aided conductors and slaves at court trials of those charged with infractions of the Fugitive Slave Law of 1850. Among his noteworthy cases was the defense he undertook, with Ellis Gray Loring, of three secret operatives, Lewis Hayden, John J. Smith, and Robert Morris, charged with rescuing Fredric "Shadrach" Minkins from the Boston courthouse on February 15, 1851. In early April 1851, Dana defended Thomas M. Sims, a 17-year-old Georgia runaway whom agents tried to release from a Boston jail in April 1851. Dana failed to halt the runaway's return to Savannah, Georgia, and a vicious punishment inflicted by Sims's owner. Three years later, Dana was unsuccessful in defending Anthony Burns, who defied U.S. marshals on March 24, 1854. A runaway from Richmond, Virginia, Burns faced a phony charge of theft from a silversmith, a ruse by Charles F. Suttle to return Burns to bondage. After the Civil War, as the state attorney for Massachusetts, Dana fought for black civil rights.

Source

Lowance, Mason, ed. *House Divided: The Antebellum Slavery Debate in America, 1776–1865.* Princeton, NJ: Princeton University Press, 2003.

Dangerfield, Daniel (fl. 1850s)

Daniel Dangerfield (also called Daniel Webster) was a victim of civil rights abuses under the Fugitive Slave Law of 1850. Before his escape in 1853 from the French Simpson farm, he was a slave laborer at the Aldie Mill in Loudoun County, Virginia. While living in Harrisburg, Pennsylvania, he was the quarry of a Virginia slaveholder and U.S. marshals. On April 2, 1859, officials arrested Dangerfield at a public market on a phony charge of robbery. He faced arraignment two days later in Philadelphia, a change of venue intended to suppress local abolitionist support.

Dangerfield became a cause célèbre among Philadelphia's Underground Railroad agents and supporters. Quaker agent Lucretia Coffin Mott hired attorneys to defend the victim; she, activist Mary Grew, and diarist Charlotte Lottie Forten Grimké sat through the 14-hour court session. Mott and the Reverend James Miller McKim encouraged the U.S. commissioner to show mercy. The Philadelphia Abolition Society sent 300 members to mob the courthouse and demand justice. After witnesses testified that Dangerfield had lived free in Baltimore and Harrisburg, the judge dismissed the case. A victory parade bore Dangerfield in an open carriage up Arch Street to Thirteenth Street; well-wishers cheered Mott and snatched bits of Dangerfield's coat as souvenirs. After sheltering at John Lewton's home in Paschall's Alley, on April 6, 1859, Dangerfield continued along the secret network to the waystation of Norwood P. Hallowell in Boston, Massachusetts, and then on to Canada.

See also: Fugitive Slave Law of 1850.

Sources

Forten, Charlotte L. *The Journals of Charlotte Forten Grimké.* New York: Oxford University Press, 1988.
Salvatore, Nick. *We All Got History: The Memory Books of Amos Webber.* New York: Random House, 1996.

Daniels, Amasa (1786–1872)
Daniels, Sophia Ann Hammond (1803–1865)

A native of Tolland County, Connecticut, first-generation Scots-American Amasa Daniels was known for benevolence and civic activism. At age 21, he moved to Pennsylvania to pursue lumbering, was widowed in 1831, and married his first wife's sister in 1832. In fall 1836, he and Sophia Ann Hammond Daniels moved their nine children to a farm in St. Joseph County, Michigan. Amasa and Olivia Daniels earned respect for humanistic principles and for receiving fugitive slaves at the family residence, where they provided food and rest and relay to the next Underground Railroad station.

Source

Collin, Henry P. *A Twentieth Century History and Biographical Record of Branch County, Michigan.* Chicago: Lewis, 1906.

Dannaker, James T. (fl. 1840s)

James T. Dannaker of Chester, Pennsylvania, collaborated with tanner James Lewis of Marple in slave rescue. Dannaker led the way up the Pennsylvania–Canada line at the rate of two trips per week. One relay to Philadelphia, Pennsylvania, required the loading of 26 passengers at the Arch Street pier into the stateroom of Captain Whildon's steamer, an Underground Railroad transport vessel never completely identified. On another occasion, four siblings came from Columbia to Lewis's station and reunited with their parents in Norristown. When Dannaker escorted eight escapees from Norfolk, Virginia, to Philadelphia, he tried 13 safehouses before finding space at the residence of Hester Reckless. The reason for the refusals was that it had been an unusually busy night, with a total of 168 escapees needing shelter before continuing their travels by sea to Canada. After his marriage in 1842, Dannaker ended his partnership with Lewis and moved to Philadelphia.

See also: safehouses.

Source

Smedley, Robert C. *History of the Underground Railroad in Chester and the Neighboring Counties of Pennsylvania.* Lancaster, PA: Office of *The Journal*, 1883.

Darlington, Chandler (1800–1879)
Darlington, Hannah Monaghan (1808–1890)

Two Quaker assistants to the Pennsylvania route were poet and farmer Chandler Darlington and his wife, Hannah Monaghan Darlington, residents of Longwood near Kennett Square, in Chester County. Abolitionists Susan Brownell Anthony and Elizabeth Cady Stanton respected the Darlingtons for their benevolence and support of temperance and for Hannah's aid to the suffrage movement. Receiving refugees from Delaware, Maryland, Virginia, and Washington D.C., the Darlington safehouse, the Pines, formed a link with Rachel Mendenhall Garrett and Thomas Garrett's depot in Wilmington, Delaware. Slaves received a hot meal before Chandler Darlington ferried them on by curtained carriage to the station of Sarah Darlington Barnard and Simon Barnard in Newlin, Pennsylvania.

Source

Smedley, Robert C. *History of the Underground Railroad in Chester and the Neighboring Counties of Pennsylvania.* Lancaster, PA: Office of *The Journal,* 1883.

Daugherty, Sarah Bollinger (1799–1882)

A single mother and entrepreneur in Cape Girardeau, in Bollinger County, Missouri, Sarah Bollinger Daugherty (or Daughtery) earned respect for altruism. While rearing seven children, in widowhood, she operated a four-story brick and stone gristmill after the death of her father, pioneer George Frederick Bollinger of Lincoln County, North Carolina. At the same time, she managed an adjacent safehouse of the Underground Railroad until national emancipation on January 1, 1863. A century later, owners donated the mill to the Cape Girardeau County Historical Society.

Source

Smoot, Jack. "Bollinger Mill State Historic Site." *Missouri Resource Readings* (Fall 1998).

Davids, Tice (fl. 1830s)

In 1831, runaway slave Tice Davids exemplified the on-the-spot decision making necessary for a successful escape from bondage. Upon arriving at the Ohio River, he fled pursuers by swimming from the Kentucky side to the Ohio shore. Although his owner rowed a skiff toward the bank to follow him to Ripley, Ohio, the slave's disappearance forced the master to return home minus his chattel. The slave owner could only mutter that Davids appeared to have ridden away on an "underground railroad." In actuality, Davids had boarded a secret rail line staffed by conductors like Jean Lowry Rankin and John Rankin, a Presbyterian couple who hung a lantern in the window of their hilltop home in Ripley to indicate sanctuary to refugees. Davids settled outside Sandusky, Ohio.

Sources

Blight, David W., ed. *Passages to Freedom.* Washington, DC: Smithsonian, 2004.
The Firelands Pioneer. Norwalk, OH: Chronicle, 1888.

Davis, Clarissa (1832–?)

A slave in Portsmouth, Virginia, Clarissa Davis plotted to flee by ship to liberty. In May 1854, she eluded her owners, Mrs. Brown and Mrs. Burkley (or Berkely). Davis followed two brothers, 28-year-old Charles Armstead and 30-year-old William Armstead. With the aid of black sailors, the trio escaped by sea aboard the *Ellen Barnes* to Wareham, Massachusetts. For 10 weeks in early spring, Davis hid in an airless coop from bounty hunters anticipating an easy $1,000 reward. Dressed in men's clothes, Davis boarded a ship, the *City of Richmond,* bound for Philadelphia, Pennsylvania. En route, she cowered near the furnace in a box under the surveillance of William Bagnal, the ship's steward. She arrived safely on May 22. On the advice of Philadelphia Underground Railroad agents, Davis changed her name to Mary D. Armstead. Reunited with her family and elderly father, she lived in peace in New Bedford, Massachusetts. On August 26, 1855, she wrote of her gratitude to secret network supervisor William Still. Davis said of the Underground Railroad: "I hope it may continue to run and I hope the wheels of the car may be greased with more substantial grease so they may run ever swiftly."

See also: bounty hunters.

Source

Grover, Kathryn. *The Fugitive's Gibraltar: Escaping Slaves and Abolitionism in New Bedford, Massachusetts.* Amherst: University of Massachusetts Press, 2001.

Davis, Daniel (fl. 1850s)

The first challenge to the Fugitive Slave Law of 1850 in Buffalo, New York, the seizure of Daniel Davis created a stir among Underground Railroad agents and advocates. On August 15, 1851, a year after the slave's flight from bondage, Deputy U.S. Marshal George B. Gates and officer J.K. Tyler pursued Davis with the intent of arresting him as a fugitive slave. Valued at $700, Davis was working on the Ohio River as a cook aboard the packet steamer *Buckeye State.* Brandishing a kitchen knife in self-defense, he suffered a blow to the head from Tyler and serious facial burns from contact with the galley stove during his struggle to remain free.

The incident led to Davis's arraignment for the assault and battery of Benjamin S. Rust, a slave hunter representing George H. Moore, Davis's owner in Louisville, Kentucky. A crowd gathered at the office of a federal officer, U.S. Commissioner H.K. Smith, at Spaulding's Exchange, a complex in Buffalo, New York. When Davis came to trial on August 26, a federal judge in Auburn, New York, ordered Davis's release from the jail dungeon. The runaway fled to Canada. A bogus letter in the August 30, 1851, issue of the *Buffalo Morning Express* depicted Davis as eager to return to bondage. On September 2, the *New York Daily Tribune* ridiculed the *Express* for being taken in by obvious pro-slavery tricksters.

See also: Fugitive Slave Law of 1850.

Sources

"Daniel in the Den and Out," *New York Daily Tribune,* September 2, 1851.

"Fugitive Slave Case in Buffalo," *Buffalo (NY) Commercial Advertiser,* August 15, 1851.

Davis, Isaac (1793–1883)
Davis, Priscilla Rummery (1795–1880)

A blacksmith born and educated in Gorham, Maine, Isaac Davis committed himself to liberty. He set out for the frontier at age 21. After buying land in Climax, in Kalamazoo County, Michigan, he and his wife, the former Priscilla Rummery of Hollis, Maine, lived in an abandoned stable until they could build a log cabin. In 1840, the couple joined Heman Baker and Lorenzo Taylor in establishing a depot of the Underground Railroad. Up to 14 passengers at a time arrived from the safehouse of Dr. Nathan Muncie Thomas and Pamela Smith Brown Thomas in Schoolcraft. Isaac Pierce served as transporter. One of the families needing assistance was the Kirkwoods, a widow and her two daughters. The woman's husband led his family to the Ohio River in 1842 to prevent their sale. A posse shot him before they could cross to free territory. Davis remained faithful to his task until the Emancipation Proclamation on January 1, 1863. When agent Charles T. Gorham faced a fine for aiding the secret network, Davis, Zachariah Chandler, and neighbors in Climax collected $2,000 to retire the debt.

Source

Durant, Samuel W., comp. *History of Kalamazoo County, Michigan.* Philadelphia: Everts & Abbott, 1880.

Davis, Jane (fl. 1850s)

A passenger of the Underground Railroad, Jane Davis made the journey from Dorchester County, Maryland, to Pennsylvania. Part of her discontent with slavery lay in the sale of four of her 12 children. In 1857, she departed from her owner, Roger McZant of New Market, Maryland, and reached agents of the secret network in Philadelphia.

Source

Still, William. *The Underground Railroad.* Philadelphia: Porter & Coates, 1871.

Davis, Sam (1826–?)

Rescued by the Pennsylvania Underground Railroad, 33-year-old Sam Davis made his way north to freedom. In 1856, he escaped bondage to James Hurst, a slave owner in Kent County, Maryland. In company with 23-year-old Abe Fineer of Georgetown, Thomas Parker, Henry Saunders, and William Henry Thompson, Davis sought assistance from Philadelphia agents of the secret network.

Source

Still, William. *The Underground Railroad.* Philadelphia: Porter & Coates, 1871.

Day, Caleb (1842–?)

A conductor by water from Charles County, Maryland, 21-year-old firefighter Caleb Day failed to free his passengers. Late in 1863, Day and his confederates, freedman firefighter John Jones and Richard Coates, crept down the Potomac River in a stolen vessel presumably bound for Washington, D.C. Aboard was a slave, Jacob Coates, the chattel of George W. Carpenter, and other slaves who belonged to James F. Milsterd, Thomas L. Speak, and Peter Wheeler. Before summoning law officers, Carpenter beat the agents severely, leaving them hospitalized for months. After a circuit court judge charged the rescuers with aiding runaways, Day, Jones, and Richard Coates entered the Maryland state penitentiary in Baltimore for larceny. On September 1, 1865, the Freedmen's Bureau protested the 12-year sentence on behalf of Jones's wife, Dola Ann Jones. By November 11, 1865, Governor Augustus Williamson Bradford pardoned and released the three inmates.

Source

Prison records, Maryland State Archives.

Dean, Luther (1803–1850)
Dean, Ruth Brundage (1805–1883)

The owner of a flour and grain business at the four-story Nankin Mill in Portland, New York, Luther

Dean operated a depot of the Underground Railroad. In 1824, he married Ruth Brundage of Hopewell, New York. The Deans received refugees in the basement of their greenhouse and farm. Passengers arrived from James Wells, the conductor at Wells Hill in Leon, New York. In 1843, a suspicious fire that destroyed Dean's mill may have been the work of proslavery arsonists who also torched the nearby waystation of the Reverend Marcus Swift.

Source

Phelan, Helene C. *And Why Not Every Man?* Almond, NY: privately published, 1987.

DeBaptiste, George (1814–1875)

Underground Railroad agent George DeBaptiste strengthened the network between Cincinnati, Ohio, and Madison, Indiana. A native of Fredericksburg, Virginia, DeBaptiste was born free to Frances "Franky" DeBaptiste and businessman John DeBaptiste. After learning barbering in Richmond, Virginia, in his mid-teens, George made his first slave rescue. He married Maria Lucinda Lee, a slave, and purchased her freedom. In Madison around 1836, DeBaptiste invested in business and harbored black fugitives, some of whom he passed to Dr. Samuel Tibbets in Madison or to Quaker agent William Beard in Salem, in Union County, Indiana. From there, passengers dispersed to Dearborn, Decatur, Henry, Rush, and Wayne county depots. In Newport, Indiana, Catherine White Coffin and Levi Coffin, the network superintendent, arranged relays to Canada.

In February 1840, DeBaptiste joined Seymour Finney and William Lambert in the rescue of Robert Cromwell, a barber whose former owner attempted to kidnap him from the courthouse in Detroit. In 1846, DeBaptiste ranged farther from his safehouse and ferried Kentucky runaways over the Ohio River to Ohio, Indiana, Michigan, and Ontario. He also loaned his freedom papers to males of similar height and build. His notoriety as a conductor caused angry slavery supporters to insist on his arrest for the nonpayment of a $500 bond required of free blacks. Judge Stephen C. Stevens interceded and declared the law vague and unconstitutional.

George DeBaptiste became the valet of General William Henry Harrison and advanced to White House steward after Harrison was elected president. In 1841, DeBaptiste returned to Madison to his barbershop. At age 34, he moved to Detroit, ran another barbershop, and sold men's clothing at Robert Banks's store. In league with agent William Lambert, DeBaptiste joined The African-American Mysteries: The Order of the Men of Oppression and the Order of Emancipation, brotherhoods that fought slavery and raised funds for blacks in flight from the South.

DeBaptiste continued conducting slaves at the busiest point on the Canadian border. He purchased the *T. Whitney,* a lake steamer, but had to hire a white captain because blacks could not hold a license. At the time insurrectionist John Brown was planning a slave revolt, DeBaptiste proposed that conspirators blow up some of the South's largest churches. During the Civil War, DeBaptiste aided Detroit civil rights activist John D. Richards in recruiting Michigan's first black regiment. DeBaptiste's altruism continued in the late 1860s with service to the Freedmen's Association.

See also: black soldiers; kidnap.

Sources

Burton, Clarence Monroe. *The City of Detroit, Michigan, 1701–1922.* Detroit, MI: S.J. Clarke, 1922.
Lumpkin, Katherine DuPre. "The General Plan Was Freedom: A Negro Secret Order on the Underground Railroad." *Phylon* 28:1 (1967): 63–77.
Turner, Glennette Tilley. "The Underground Railroad in Illinois." *American Visions* 13:2 (April–May 1998): 33–35.

DeGarmo, Elias (1787–1876)
DeGarmo, Rhoda Rogers (1798–1873)

Two radical Quaker agents of the Underground Railroad, Elias DeGarmo and his wife, Rhoda Rogers DeGarmo, joined an active team of slave rescuers. The couple married in 1829. At their home in Gates, near Rochester, New York, the DeGarmos supported the secret network by receiving fugitives, some from Elias DeGarmo's nephew, Henry Quinby, and his wife, Sarah M. Browning Quinby. Rhoda DeGarmo, a neighbor of operative Susan Brownell Anthony and a friend of agents Sarah Davids Bills Fish and Amy Kirby Post, also promoted rescues through membership in the Western New York Anti-Slavery Society and, beginning in 1842, by organizing anti-slavery fairs. In 1849 at the seventh annual bazaar, Rhoda stirred controversy by inviting attendees of both races to sit down to a meal at the same table.

See also: anti-slavery fairs.

Source

Reisem, Richard O. "Women's Rights: The Mount Hope Connection." *Epitaph* 18:3 (Summer 1998): 1.

Delany, Martin Robinson (1812–1885)

Physician and journalist Martin Robinson Delany became known as "the father of black nationalism" for promoting the anti-slavery movement. The grandson of a Golah chief and a Mandingo noble named Shango, he was born into bondage in Charleston, West Virginia, to Samuel Delany, a slave, and Pati Peace Delany, a freeborn Nigerian American laundress and seamstress. Pati risked punishment when she bought her five children a copy of the *New York Primer and Spelling Book,* with which she and her mother, Graci Peace, taught the children to read and write. Upon Pati Delany's arrest, banker Randall Brown defended her in court and helped her to escape to Chambersburg, Pennsylvania.

At age 11, Martin Delany gained his freedom after his father saved the purchase price of himself and his son; the two reunited with Pati Delany in Chambersburg. Martin Delany left school in 1827 and worked at unskilled labor to help support the family. On July 29, 1831, he set out on foot for Pittsburgh. He apprenticed in medicine with Dr. Andrew M. McDowell, opened a cupping and leech practice in 1836, and became the first black graduate from Harvard Medical School.

A regular contributor to *Voice of the Fugitive,* Henry Bibb and Mary E. Miles Bibb's newspaper published in Sandwich, Ontario, Delany furthered the cause of abolitionism by publishing one of the first black-owned newspapers, *The Mystery.* In addition, in the basement of the Memorial African Methodist Episcopal Zion Church, he, William Cooper Nell, and Frederick Douglass cowrote essays for the *North Star.* These articles reached a height of passion in defense of Adam Crosswhite and Sarah Crosswhite after their flight via the Underground Railroad from Carroll County, Kentucky, to Detroit, Michigan, in 1843. Delany also serialized pro-black writings in the *Afro-American Magazine* and the *Weekly Anglo-African.*

Passage of the Fugitive Slave Law of 1850 increased Delany's fervor for recruiting volunteers for the Underground Railroad. Along with John Baton Vashon, a barber, and the Reverend Lewis Woodson, he organized the Pittsburgh Philanthropic Society, a citywide protection and transportation service for fugitive slaves relayed across Lake Erie. In 1852 Delany issued *Destiny of the Colored People in the United States* and scouted possible resettlement locations along the Niger Delta in west-central Africa. In 1853, he intervened in the sale of Alexander Hendrchkure, a Jamaican transported illegally by Thomas Adams, who intended to sell the boy in Kentucky.

Delany continued his assistance to blacks in 1856 by soliciting donations from English philanthropists for the Elgin Settlement near Buxton, Ontario, Canada's most successful African-Canadian community. During the Civil War, Delany recruited volunteers for the Union army. After the war, he extended his outreach by negotiating on behalf of free blacks with President Abraham Lincoln and by aiding the Freedmen's Bureau.

See also: abolitionism; African Methodist Episcopal Church; Elgin Settlement; *North Star.*

Sources

Hinton, Richard Josiah. *John Brown and His Men: With Some Account of the Roads They Travelled to Reach Harpers Ferry.* New York: Funk & Wagnalls, ca. 1894.

Ullman, Victor. *Martin R. Delany: The Beginnings of Black Nationalism.* Boston: Beacon, 1971.

Delavan, Edward Cornelius (1793–1871)

A wealthy abolitionist and temperance leader from Franklin, New York, Edward Cornelius Delavan furthered the work of the Underground Railroad. He grew up in Albany, New York, and was a skilled printer by age 13. Flourishing from trade in imported hardware, in 1820, he married Abigail Marvin Smith and opened a wholesale wine business in New York City, where he also operated the Delavan House Hotel. Spurring his volunteerism to the secret network was his friendship with Gerrit Smith, who superintended secret network activity along the Atlantic seaboard. As Delavan's philosophy became more radical, he abandoned Presbyterianism and joined the Episcopal Church. During the Civil War, he circulated temperance tracts among Union soldiers.

After gaining his freedom at age 11, Martin R. Delany became a Harvard-trained physician, abolitionist newspaper publisher, and pioneer of black nationalism. In the 1850s, he was active in recruiting operatives for the freedom network. *(Hulton Archive/Stringer/Getty Images)*

Source

Marsicano, Patricia Ruth. *Delavan.* Charleston, SC: Arcadia, 2004.

Deming, Samuel (1798–1871)
Deming, Catherine Matilda Lewis (1801–1884)
Deming, John (1825–1894)

An abolitionist and member of the anti-slavery society in Farmington, Connecticut, farmer and merchant Samuel Deming supported the reception of slaves from the ship *Amistad.* In 1838, he joined Horace Cowles, John Treadwell Norton, and Austin Franklin Williams in founding the Connecticut Anti-Slavery Society. At their two-story home at 66 Main Street, Catherine Matilda Lewis Deming, Samuel Deming, and their teenage son, John Deming, hid runaways. In league with Underground Railroad agents Norton and Williams, the Demings welcomed the Africans from Sierra Leone during the lengthy litigation over their mutiny on July 2, 1839. Catherine Deming canvassed neighbors for donations and circulated petitions demanding justice for the *Amistad* survivors. By remodeling the upper story of their dry goods store at Two Mill Lane, the Demings provided sleeping quarters and a school for the Africans until their departure to Africa on November 25, 1841, aboard the *Gentleman.*

See also: Amistad.

Source

Jones, Howard. *Mutiny on the* Amistad. Oxford, UK: Oxford University Press, 1987.

Demson, Samuel (fl. 1850s)

An ex-slave, Samuel Demson of Vicksburg, Mississippi, devised a signal system for summoning passengers to the Underground Railroad. In Cumberland, in Allegany County, Maryland, he lived in Shantytown, a community of canal workers, and served as sexton at the Emmanuel Episcopal Church on 16 Washington Street. For refugees arriving along the Chesapeake and Ohio Canal in the 1850s to receive the aid of the Reverend Hillhouse Buell, Demson gave two pulls on the church bell rope as an all-clear signal. On Fort Hill, a steep bluff in sight of the Potomac River and only five miles from the Mason-Dixon line, the Gothic church was once Fort Cumberland. The historic site featured passageways in the cellar that were useful as hiding places. Agents fed newcomers, outlined the next stage of the secret network, and pointed the way out the far side of the rectory.

Source

Switala, William J. *Underground Railroad in Delaware, Maryland, and West Virginia.* Mechanicsburg, PA: Stackpole, 2004.

Dennett, Lydia Louisa Neal (1798–?)
Dennett, W. Oliver (1799–1851)

At a land-and-sea nexus in Portland, Maine, Lydia Louisa Neal Dennett and her husband, W. Oliver Dennett, promoted the Underground Railroad. After their marriage in 1822, they opened a waystation to refugees at their residence at 55 Spring Street. In 1834, Lydia supported the inclusion of women in female anti-slavery societies. In 1842, she and Elizabeth Widgery Thomas acted as bodyguards for Stephen Symons Foster after a riot broke out at the First Parish Unitarian Church. The two women pushed Foster through the rear window of agent Comfort Hussey Winslow's safehouse next door. The Dennetts also received orator John Murray Spear, a Universalist minister, at their home for medical treatment of his injuries from the riot. In 1844, Oliver Dennett began a year's service as manager of the American Anti-Slavery Society. After the escape of Ellen Smith Craft and William Craft from Macon, Georgia, in late December 1848, the Dennetts received them from agent Samuel Joseph May. The Dennetts offered a night's rest at their home before the Crafts boarded a ship for Halifax, Nova Scotia, their next stop on the way to England.

See also: American Anti-Slavery Society; female anti-slavery societies.

Sources

Brown, Harrison, "Underground Railroad Once Was Busy Maine 'Device,'" *Portland (ME) Evening Express,* February 12, 1963, 11.

Sterling, Dorothy. *Black Foremothers: Three Lives.* New York: Feminist Press, 1988.

Dickinson, Anna Elizabeth (1842–1932)

While growing up among Underground Railroad activists, Quaker orator and educator Anna Elizabeth Dickinson developed an abiding humanitarianism. A native of Philadelphia, Pennsylvania, she was fatherless from age two after dry goods merchant John Dickinson (1788–1845) died of heart failure while delivering an anti-slavery diatribe. She recalled her father's courage in concealing a runaway in the nursery between his sleeping sons. After police made a cursory search and departed, Dickinson passed the slave to the cellar of another waystation and on to a carriage bound for Canada. John Dickinson's widow, Mary Edmondson (or Edmundson) Dickinson (1799–1889), operated the family safehouse with the help of Anna and her older sister Susan (1833–?).

At age 14, Anna sent an abolitionist letter to William Lloyd Garrison. He published it in the February 22, 1856, issue of *The Liberator* and lauded her career as an extemporaneous lecturer. Agent Lucretia Coffin Mott encouraged Dickinson to become a feminist speaker and promoter of rescue for runaway slaves. Elizabeth Buffum Chace, a secret network agent in Providence, Rhode Island, extended opportunities for Dickinson to address anti-slavery gatherings. From Pennsylvania came fan mail from Quaker abolitionist Amos Gilbert.

At one event in Boston's Music Hall in 1862, Dickinson shared the platform with two notable recruiters for the Underground Railroad, philosopher Ralph Waldo Emerson and orator Wendell Addison Phillips. In spring of that year, she resided at the safehouse of Joseph Ricketson and Sarah Beard Ricketson in New Bedford, Massachusetts. After the Emancipation Proclamation freed slaves on January 1, 1863, Dickinson continued to address issues of liberty for blacks and women. Following one address to a gathering that included President Abraham Lincoln, the *Washington Chronicle* compared her principles and intensity with those of Joan of Arc.

See also: Liberator, The.

Source

Chester, Giraud. *Embattled Maiden: The Life of Anna Dickinson.* New York: Putnam, 1951.

Dickson, Moses (1824–1901)

The Reverend Moses Dickson, an American Methodist Episcopal preacher and a founder of Lincoln University, earned respect for innovative methods of helping destitute slaves. Born in Cincinnati, Ohio, he was orphaned at age 16, when he apprenticed in barbering. While working on steamers, he traveled south and observed the horrors of slavery. On August 12, 1846, he met with 11 friends in St. Louis, Missouri, and formed the Knights of Liberty, a secret brotherhood sworn to help fugitive slaves. The members remained active into the Civil War, when Dickson served in the Union army. Father Moses, as Dickson was called, offered a benevolent outreach during Reconstruction by helping refugees settle, establish homes, and gain an education. In 1915, a monument at the Father Dickson Cemetery in Crestwood, Missouri, honored his volunteer labors.

See also: African Methodist Episcopal Church.

Source

Taylor, Glennette Tilley. *The Underground Railroad in Illinois.* Glen Ellyn, IL: Newman Educational, 2001.

Dillingham, Micajah (1797–1851)
Dillingham, Elizabeth Williams (1799–ca. 1880)
Dillingham, Richard (1823–1850)

A noted stationmaster in Peru, in Morrow County, Ohio, Micajah Dillingham contributed to a well-organized Underground Railroad route to Canada. A native of Saratoga County, New York, at age 25, he married Elizabeth "Eliza" Williams of New Garden, a Quaker abolitionist stronghold in Guilford County, North Carolina. At their Alum Creek waystation in Peru, the couple worked mostly at night in collaboration with secret network conductors William Hance and Phebe Narisa Nash Sanford and Sheldon Sanford in South Bloomfield, Ohio.

The Dillinghams' generosity set an example for their son. A Quaker teacher from Peru, Ohio, abolitionist martyr Richard Dillingham crusaded for the emancipation of slaves. On December 5, 1848, authorities arrested him in Tennessee for abetting the flight of three slaves to Cincinnati, Ohio, whom he sent by hired hack from Nashville. The breach in the secret network was a black traitor, who pointed out Richard Dillingham on horseback at a bridge over the Cumberland River.

A mob gathered outside the jail and threatened to lynch Dillingham, who reported the local belligerence in a letter to his fiancée. She wrote the jailer and implored him to comfort her beloved. On April 13, 1849, the *Nashville Daily Gazette* reported the sympathy of local people for the bold agent, who shared a crowded cell with six inmates. When the case came to trial the next day, the judge ignored efforts to invoke the death penalty and sentenced Dillingham to three years at hard labor sawing and polishing rocks in a quarry at the Tennessee state penitentiary in Nashville. While serving as steward and pharmacy aide in the prison infirmary, he died within hours of being infected with cholera during an epidemic. For his stoic refusal to implicate other agents, Dillingham received honors from novelist Harriet Beecher Stowe and agent Levi Coffin. Poet John Greenleaf Whittier dedicated the poem "The Cross" to Dillingham.

Sources

Coffin, Levi. *Reminiscences of Levi Coffin.* Richmond, IN: Friend United Press, 1991.

Hinshaw, William Wade. *Encyclopedia of American Quaker Genealogy.* Ann Arbor, MI: Edwards Brothers, 1936.

Dimmick, John F. (1794–1871) Dimmick, Sarah Heath (1801–1876)

A devout Congregationalist and member of the Underground Railroad, Major John F. Dimmick piloted desperate slaves to freedom. In 1819, he married Sarah Heath and joined the First Congregational Church, a depot of the secret network pastored by agent Ashbel Parmelee. John Dimmick retired from the U.S. military and went into business within miles of the New York–Quebec border. From his lumber yard and residence north of Malone, in Franklin County, New York, in 1840, he transported passengers some 10 miles to Jabez Parkhurst and Sarah Alexander Parkhurst, who operated a waystation at Fort Covington. During layovers, fugitives hid in a niche in the Dimmick family's chimney.

Source

Seaver, Frederick J. *Historical Sketches of Franklin County and Its Several Towns.* Albany, NY: J.B. Lyon, 1918.

disguise

The disguising of runaways and spies helped Underground Railroad operatives avoid the surveillance of slave catchers and federal marshals. In Deep River, Connecticut, for example, agents George Read and Sally Web Read transformed Daniel Fisher into William Winters with the application of a wig and a new name. In 1833, Mercy O. Haskins Powell and William Peter Powell established the Colored Sailors' Home at Gold and John streets in lower Manhattan. In addition to providing concealment and employment for runaways, they kept a closet of disguises to change appearances and conceal the whipping scars and lacerations inflicted on blacks during enslavement. New garments, a shave, and a haircut could protect newcomers from recapture by a posse or bounty hunters. Fanny Butzel Heineman, an operative in Detroit, Michigan, chose garments that allowed fugitives to blend in with urban blacks to ease passage over the Detroit River to Windsor, Ontario.

From Cloaks to Coffins

In the early 1850s, at the J.B. Allison safehouse in McDonough County, Illinois, the family stockpiled cloaks, gowns, veils, and hoods in readiness to fool slave catchers. An insurgent operating in the plantation South, Dr. Alexander Milton Ross of Belleville, Ontario, altered his appearance and adopted an alias and profession that lessened risk of detection in heavily pro-slavery territory. Another agent, Seth Concklin of Sandy Hill, New York, changed his social status by donning the workaday overalls of a fisherman. Quaker philanthropist Joseph Sturge, author of *A Visit to the United States in 1841* (1842), reported on the successful disguise of a refugee from Washington, D.C., who obscured his facial features with spectacles and a false beard. One dissembler covered his light skin with blacking and curled his hair; another faked an epileptic seizure to escape the auction block and made his way north. John H. Bond, a Quaker conductor in Windsor, Indiana, reported painting a black man white to secure him from a posse. On another occasion, a woman posed as a corpse in a coffin for passage from Indiana to Ontario.

Episodes marked by desperation reflect quick thinking. A slave advertised on a poster as having perfect teeth knocked out a front tooth to alter his appearance. In flight from Madison County, Kentucky, in August 1841, Afro-Scots slave Lewis Clarke stopped at a silversmith's shop in Mayslick and purchased glasses with green lenses and then safely dined at a nearby tavern. Another example of clever thinking was the veiling of Charlotte Giles and Harriet Eglin, who made their escape from the Baltimore, Maryland, depot on May 31, 1856, posing as mourners. When the master of one of the women approached their seat, Eglin and Giles wept copiously and passed themselves off as Mary and Lizzie. The ruse allowed the women to reach agents in Philadelphia, Pennsylvania.

A Quaker couple working for the Pennsylvania Anti-Slavery Society, Rachel Mendenhall Garrett and

Thomas Garrett of Wilmington, Delaware, were adept at altering the appearance of escapees. Thomas Garrett aided one woman by offering her Rachel's plain Quaker dress, neckerchief, and bonnet. He then escorted the "Quaker lady" out the front door of his safehouse under the nose of the woman's owner. At other times, the Garretts distributed hoes, rakes, and scythes to male fugitives so that they could pass for freedmen walking to jobs. The farm tools also provided handy weapons in the event of a challenge from slave catchers.

Swapping Clothes and Roles

Two successful runaways, Harriet Bell Hayden and Lewis Hayden, fled Lexington, Kentucky, in September 1844 with the aid of the Reverend Calvin Fairbank and his fiancée, Delia Webster. Veiled and cloaked, the Haydens hid their son under a carriage seat and posed as servants and later as a white couple. They reached the Ohio River and crossed to a waystation on the other shore. Another clever ruse aided two women from Virginia, one dark and the other light skinned. Isaac Tatem Hopper received them from agents James Miller McKim, James Mott, Jr., and Lucretia Coffin Mott. To complete the transfer, Mott dressed the lighter of the two in his wife's clothes and false curls. The trio traveled by water from Pennsylvania to New York as Isaac Tatem Hopper, a lady, and a servant.

For women making the journey, being disguised in men's clothes deflected the curiosity of onlookers. An extension of the ploy involved dressing a decoy in a refugee woman's plantation shift. Such a disguise saved Clarissa Davis of Virginia and Mary Milburn and 12-year-old Ann Maria Weems of Washington, D.C. Harriet Tubman bonneted one male refugee like a woman to conceal his gender from U.S. deputy marshals. As Tubman's brother, William Henry, prepared to escape, he bought a man's suit for his girlfriend, Catherine, to wear. While Catherine's owners were searching for her, she passed by them in elegant gentleman's attire without arousing suspicion. Another clever ruse was the dressing of light-skinned fugitives as white owners, with the other members of the party passing as servants. According to Pharaoh Jackson Chesney's *Last of the Pioneers; or, Old Times in East Tennessee* (1902), Ellen Smith Craft, in flight from Macon, Georgia, wore the garments of a male planter and also disguised her lower face with a wrapping as though cushioning a throbbing tooth. Her husband, William Craft, whose skin was darker, traveled as her attendent.

From the Daring to the Ingenious

In *Slave Life in Georgia* (1855), autobiographer John Brown reported on the high spirits of Oberlin abolitionists, jokesters who used disguises to taunt enslavers. In 1851, the arrival of runaways to an Underground Railroad safehouse enticed armed slave hunters, who converged on the spot and raced after a carriage as it dashed away toward the next town. The slave stalkers recognized the fugitives by their clothing and number. After overcoming the runaways, the pursuers had them locked up in the courthouse. When the magistrate summoned the captives, the carriage passengers disclosed their faces, all white. The college boys had smeared themselves with lamp black to deceive the hunters and to give the real quarry an opportunity to escape undetected to Canada. The magistrate charged the slave catchers with kidnapping and false imprisonment.

Other ingenious rescues involved haystacks, cornstalks, heaps of vegetables, and crates. Henry "Box" Brown had himself nailed into a wood crate, hooped, and dispatched by express train from Richmond to Philadelphia. An unnamed woman also traveled as cargo: in winter 1857, she left the Baltimore, Maryland, depot for Philadelphia, Pennsylvania, carrying scissors for the cutting of emergency airholes if confinement proved stifling. Two women, Mrs. Ash and Mrs. Myers, received and opened the crate and found the runaway mute and faint. She later completed her route via Underground Railroad to Canada. In 1857, another boxed traveler, Lear Green, fled James Noble, a butter dealer in Baltimore, to marry William Adams. With the aid of her mother, a free woman, Green crouched in a sailor's chest with a quilt, a pillow, and some food and water. While traveling on the deck of a steamer, Lear got whiffs of fresh air when her mother untied the chest and lifted the lid. After 18 hours, the chest arrived in Philadelphia. Green passed to the care of the vigilance committee and on to Elmira, New York, where she married Adams.

Risks

Disguises could also incriminate agents. In mid-August 1858, Dick Buckner and William Lewis faced trial in Louisville, Kentucky, for slave theft and for aiding a runaway. Contributing to suspicion against the men were carpetbags packed with outfits for fugitives and eyewitness reports of frequent comings and goings of black women at Lewis's residence at odd hours, presumably for aid in escaping to free territory. The additional discovery of photos of former escapees and a letter from a man who fled Shelby County, Kentucky, for Chatham, Ontario, convinced the court of Buckner's guilt. Buckner served two years in the Kentucky state penitentiary in Frankfort for complicity in the work of the Underground Railroad.

See also: bounty hunters; kidnap; Pennsylvania Anti-Slavery Society; spies.

Sources

Bradford, Sarah H. *Scenes in the Life of Harriet Tubman.* Auburn, NY: W.J. Moses, 1869.
Brown, John. *Slave Life in Georgia: A Narrative of the Life, Sufferings, and Escape of John Brown, a Fugitive Slave, Now in England.* London: W.M. Watts, 1855.
Chesney, Pharaoh Jackson, and John Coram Webster. *Last of the Pioneers; or, Old Times in East Tennessee.* Knoxville, TN: S.B. Newman, 1902.
Smith, John L., and Lee L. Driver. *Past and Present of Randolph County, Indiana.* Indianapolis, IN: A.W. Bowen, 1914.

Dismal Swamp

The Great Dismal Swamp in the Carolinas and Virginia was home to a permanent community of runaways. As described in Harriet Beecher Stowe's historical fiction *Dred: A Story of the Great Dismal Swamp* (1856), the expanse of wetlands was a source of cypress knees for lumber and fresh game for food and hides. Wetlands provided a slave lair, a terrifying morass that shielded black fugitives, who were frequently referred to as maroons. The haven extended over Nansemond, Norfolk, Princess Anne, and Wight counties in Virginia and south to Camden, Chowan, Currituck, Gates, Pasquotank, and Perquimans counties in North Carolina. The leadership of Tom Copper, a black general, established order at Scratch Hall, a maroon settlement west of Elizabeth City, in Pasquotank County, North Carolina. White recognition of his sanctuary for escaping slaves resulted in posters announcing a price on Copper's head. After Copper's capture in 1795, the search for his followers continued until 1802, when authorities seized four maroons and hanged them.

The white world's respite from maroon predations was short-lived. Chief Peter II, Pompey Little, Captain Mingo, Osman, and Auntie Ferebee and Bob Ferebee replaced Tom Copper and imposed order and structure on the slave societies. Persistent stalking by professional slave hunters with packs of bloodhounds required extremes of secrecy from hideaways, even to the point of excavating homes underground. For some, escape along the Atlantic coast depended on Underground Railroad operatives, such as Captain Alfred Fountain, who, in the 1850s, ferried runaways north to his schooner, the *City of Richmond.*

> In 1892, the *Brooklyn Eagle* reported on the success of fugitives in the Dismal Swamp: "That some of them gained their liberty is known for there were friendly hands everywhere to pass these oppressed people along the underground railroad to the relative safety of New England and the absolute safety of Canada; but it is quite probably that many of them lost their way in the wilderness and perished there in the awful silence of black waters and moss bannered trunks, sinking to death, perhaps, in the stagnant ooze or falling, exhausted with hunger and travel, amid entangling vegetation that shut out the sight of the sky that overhung the Northern land of liberty."

Slave activity along the Albemarle Sound and the Dismal Swamp channeled runaways to the Cape Fear River delta, a busy port that relied on cheap black labor, free and slave. The secret network of rescuers included swamp hermits, wharf laborers, and inland watermen in Wilmington, Beaufort, Elizabeth City, Little Washington, and New Bern, North Carolina. Aiding the efforts of conductors were black couriers, maroons, and the slaves working lumber and turpentine camps, rice plantations, and wetlands operations. One inland maroon settlement remained under the command of an anonymous runaway called the General until the dispersal of black residents in 1795. Curfews, badges, coast guards, and capricious arrests and sale into bondage failed to halt the stealth of blacks through the fens, quicksand, and backwaters. Rescuers took serious risks on behalf of fugitives; William Jordan, for example, found respite from the Cape Fear wilderness in 1855 aboard a seagoing vessel. Another, wharfman Bristol Smith, fled his owner, Benjamin Smith, in 1803 despite a reward of $50 for his decapitation.

In *My Diary North and South* (1863), traveler William Howard Russell described the desolation around Lake Drummond, a heavily overgrown region in eastern Virginia that served as an Underground Railroad station. Since the colonial era, hunters had tracked runaways and murdered them like animal prey. Because whites avoided the dark slough, slaves took advantage of its alligator- and snake-infested environs to hide until they could make contact with transporters and venture northward. One fugitive belonging to Augustus Holly of Bertie County, North Carolina, warded off the birdshot of slave catchers' shotguns by padding his coat with turkey feathers.

See also: bloodhounds; grapevine telegraphy; maroon settlements.

Sources

Leaming, Hugo Prosper. *Hidden Americans: Maroons of Virginia and the Carolinas.* New York: Garland, 1995.
Olmsted, Frederick Law. *A Journey in the Seaboard Slave States.* London: Samson Low, Son, 1856.
Russell, W. Howard. *My Diary North and South.* Boston: T.O.H.P. Burnham, 1863.
"Sale of the Dismal Swamp," *Brooklyn (NY) Eagle,* July 27, 1892, 10.

Ditcher, James (fl. ca. 1840–1860)

A bold black Underground Railroad supervisor in Ironton in southern Ohio, James "Jack" Ditcher (or Dicher) acquired the nickname Red Fox for his wily avoidance of slave catchers. A confederate of John Campbell and Gabriel "Gabe" Johnson, Ditcher piloted some 300 refugees north of the Ohio River from Portsmouth to Proctorville, Ohio, a segment of the Kentucky–Ontario line passing over the Ohio River. Contributing to the legend of the Red Fox was Ditcher's courage in the face of armed pursuers.

One precarious rescue involved rowing a black woman and her infant to Ohio and mounting horses at Campbell's barn for a dash to a black community. Fortunately for the runaways, while their pursuers stopped to drink at a saloon, Ditcher pressed on to the next depot. On his ride back to Ironton, Ditcher encountered the slave owner and lied when he was questioned about leading a horse with a sidesaddle. In mid-December 1860, Ditcher led a mother and two children to John J. Stewart's sanctuary in Pokepatch, Ohio. On the final leg by rail, Ditcher encountered the slaves' owner, who recognized him. To avoid arrest, Ditcher temporarily gave up his route work.

See also: Pokepatch, Ohio.

Source

Griffler, Keith P. *Front Line of Freedom: African Americans and the Forging of the Underground Railroad in the Ohio Valley.* Lexington: University Press of Kentucky, 2004.

Dix, John Porter (1819–1899)
Dix, Mary Jane Hay (1825–1850)

John Porter Dix and his wife rescued slaves on the frontier. A farmer from New York, John Dix married Mary Jane Hay, a member of an Ohio pioneer family, in 1844. The couple managed a waystation of the Underground Railroad in Westfield, near Seville in Medina County, Ohio. Their home was on a route that passed through Cleveland to Lake Erie. Their son, Adelbert Augustus Dix, died in 1864 during the Civil War while serving in the Forty-second Ohio Volunteers.

Source

Upton, Harriet Taylor, and Harry Gardner Cutler. *History of the Western Reserve.* New York: Lewis, 1910.

Dobbin, Matthew (1794–1874)

A teacher and resourceful stationkeeper, the Reverend Matthew "Matt" Dobbin of Washington County, Pennsylvania, welcomed fugitives to his home at 89 Steinwehr Avenue in Gettysburg, in Adams County, Pennsylvania. Growing up in a family that owned four female slaves, he developed a strong antipathy toward the flesh trade. In an addition to his two-story stone residence, he built a two-shelf crockery nook into a staircase wall. The shelves hid a cubbyhole between the first and second floors that could accommodate several fugitives.

Assisting Dobbin was a young free agent, Margaret Palm, also known as Mag and Maggie Bluecoat. On one suspenseful raid, Dobbin joined five other abolitionists in freeing fugitives who had been confined by slave catchers in a nearby waystation. When Dobbin retired in 1845, he passed his duties to Hiram Wertz. The Dobbin house, currently a restaurant, is an historic site recognized by the National Underground Railroad Freedom Center.

Source

Switala, William J. *Underground Railroad in Pennsylvania.* Mechanicsburg, PA: Stackpole, 2001.

Dobbins, David Porter (1817–1892)

A shipbuilder and lifeboat inventor from Erie, Pennsylvania, Captain David Porter Dobbins served refugees on their way to Canada. He aided William Mason, a black employee and former slave from

Kentucky fleeing a vengeful wife. After she reported Mason's whereabouts to his master, Dobbins gave Mason work and protected him from professional bounty hunters. When a pair of slave catchers halted Mason in the act of cutting up beef for Dobbins, the stalkers demanded that Mason display a telltale scar on his foot. Mason chased them off the property with a butcher knife. Before the pair could return with a warrant, Dobbins hid his employee at Josiah Kellogg's house.

Dobbins cleverly outwitted the bounty hunters. He paid a half-eagle coin to a black named Lemuel Gates to join him in a nighttime buggy ride to abolitionist Hamlin Russell's residence at Belle Valley. The ruse lured the trackers in the wrong direction. Days later, under cover of night, Dobbins collected Mason from Mrs. Kellogg's care. After Dobbins gave the secret signal, the call of a whippoorwill, he continued with Mason in a leaky skiff across Presque Isle Bay to rendezvous with a boatload of staves. After the steamer made its lumber delivery to the Canadian shore, Dobbins reported the departure to the bounty hunters. Years later, Mason returned to repay Dobbins.

See also: bounty hunters.

Source

Severance, Frank H. *Old Trails on the Niagara Frontier.* Buffalo, NY: n.p., 1899.

Dobbins, Lee Howard (1849–1853)

Lee Howard Dobbins, a four-year-old orphan, died during a quest for liberty. He was the son of his owner and an unidentified slave woman, who left him to a woman named Miriam, a family friend. In flight from Virginia with Miriam and her family, on March 17, 1853, Lee arrived in a weakened condition with the others at a depot in Oberlin, in Lorain County, Ohio, after weeks of hard traveling. With Miriam's owner pursuing his chattel, Underground Railroad agents urged Miriam to hurry on to Ontario, where she rejoined her brother. Lee Dobbins remained in the care of a physician for nine days and died from consumption on March 26, 1853. Some 1,000 people attended the boy's funeral at First Church, the headquarters of the Oberlin Anti-Slavery Society.

Source

Oberlin College Archives.

Donnell, Luther A. (1809–1868)

Luther Donnell of Nicholas, Kentucky, incurred a fine for his work as an agent of the Underground Railroad. On October 31, 1847, Caroline Ray, a 30-year-old slave, and her children—Amanda, Frances, Henry, and John Ray—journeyed north from Trimble County, Kentucky. Advancing her to George McCoy's safehouse in Decatur County, Indiana, was George Waggoner, an operative in Ripley County. From the waystation, she passed to the care of the Pernell family in Africa, a black community in Clarksburg, Indiana. Slave catcher Woodson Clark, a friend of slave owner George Ray, apprehended the five fugitives and locked them in a fodder shed in his stable. On November 1, Donnell, a resident of Fugit, Indiana, retrieved the passengers and relayed them north out of the reach of bounty hunters, who had anticipated a $500 reward.

In 1848, a state grand jury found Donnell guilty of abetting slave flight. In 1851, the Indiana Supreme Court, citing as precedent *Prigg v. Pennsylvania* (1842), overruled the grand jury's decision on the grounds that the issue of interstate slave escape was a federal matter. Nonetheless, Donnell lost a civil action that awarded George Ray $1,500 and court costs. Donnell's reward came in the form of a letter from Caroline Ray postmarked in Canada.

See also: bounty hunters; *Prigg v. Pennsylvania* (1842).

Source

Mitchell, Mary Elizabeth Donnell. "Luther Donnell—Decatur County, Indiana's Great Enemy of Slavery." *Afro-American Historical and Genealogical Society Journal* 22:2 (2003).

Doram, Catherine (fl. 1840s–1860s)

Among Cincinnati, Ohio, Underground Railroad agents, Catherine "Kittie" Doram earned a reputation for clever rescues. Doram fled bondage at age 12 and found work as a seamstress, self-employment that netted her an ample fortune. Her residence became a refuge for runaways. Her altruism earned the regard of the Reverend Calvin Fairbank, a martyr to the cause for whom Doram and Levi Coffin raised funds after Fairbank's incarceration on November 9, 1851, for abetting slave flight.

Source

Griffler, Keith P. *Front Line of Freedom: African Americans and the Forging of the Underground Railroad in the Ohio Valley.* Lexington: University Press of Kentucky, 2004.

Dorsey, Basil (1810–1872)
Dorsey, Louisa (fl. 1830s–1840s)

With aid from the Underground Railroad, Basil Dorsey made a new life for himself and his wife, Louisa Dorsey. In 1836, he and his three brothers—Charles, Thomas, and William Dorsey—escaped bondage in Liberty, in Frederick County, Maryland. In 1837 in Byberry, in Bucks County, Pennsylvania, Basil Dorsey's owner sued for his return. While the fugitive was in jail in Boylestown, Pennsylvania, Robert Purvis, an organizer of the secret network, hired a Philadelphia lawyer, David Paul Brown, to fight Dorsey's return to slavery. Purvis conspired with other black agents to launch a jailbreak if Judge John Fox ruled against Basil Dorsey. Fortunately, the contingency plan was unnecessary.

After Dorsey's release, Purvis coordinated a flight over the Delaware River and north to a waystation in Massachusetts. Secret network agents David Ruggles and Joshua Leavitt directed Basil and Louisa Dorsey and their sons through Almira Lucinda Merrick Starkweather and Haynes Kingsley Starkweather's waystation in Northampton to Chloe Maxwell Leavitt and Roger Leavitt's farm in Charlemont, Massachusetts. A teamster and jobber for Greenville Manufacturing in Florence, Massachusetts, Basil Dorsey lived at 191 Nonotuck Street and worked in the cotton mill.

Source

Laurie, Bruce. *Beyond Garrison: Antislavery and Social Reform.* New York: Cambridge University Press, 2005.

Douglas, Benjamin (1816–1894)

An Underground Railroad operative in central Connecticut, Benjamin Douglas managed a depot at 111 South Main Street in Middletown. Born in Northford, Connecticut, to a clan of patriots, he was the grandson of Colonel William Douglas, a veteran of the Revolutionary War, and the mayor of New York City from 1850 to 1856. After co-founding an anti-slavery society, Benjamin Douglas welcomed refugees to his two-story residence. Abolitionists plotted strategy at the pump shop that Benjamin and his older brother, William, a machinist, owned at Broad and William streets. During a business trip to New York City in July 1863, Benjamin Douglas rescued Ephraim Dixon, an escaped slave fleeing a mob in Manhattan. From Douglas's hotel room, Dixon ventured to the docks on the Hudson River, boarded a ferry to New London, and stayed at the Douglas waystation. Dixon opened a barber shop on Main Street. In the early months of the Civil War, Douglas was elected lieutenant governor of Connecticut.

Source

Beers, J.H. *Commemorative Biographical Record of Middlesex County.* Chicago: J.H. Beers, 1903.

Douglas, Hezekiah Ford (1831–1865)

A recruiter of rescuers, Hezekiah Ford Douglas aided the Underground Railroad movement in Toronto. Born to Mary Douglas, a slave, and a white father, William Douglas, he lived in bondage in Virginia until 1846. At age 15, Hezekiah eluded his owner and traveled northwest to Cleveland, Ohio. While barbering for a living, he learned to read. In 1850, the Massachusetts Anti-Slavery Society engaged him as a platform speaker on tour with secret network recruiters Frederick Douglass, Abby Kelley Foster, and Parker Pillsbury. In Ohio and Illinois, Douglas supported the work of the secret network. He made the greatest impact in Toronto, where he sold subscriptions to Mary Ann Shadd Cary's paper, the *Provincial Freeman*, and addressed church groups to rally support for black refugees.

During the Civil War, Douglas joined white soldiers in the Ninety-fifth Illinois Infantry. In St. Louis, Missouri, he passed a small slave named Ben Morris to Mary Ashton Rice Livermore, a nurse and operative of the secret network, for transport to Chicago to reunite with his mother. Douglas rose to the rank of captain of the Kansas Independent Battery and died shortly after the war from malaria. His widow, Sattira Douglas, aided refugees from slavery.

Source

Ripley, C. Peter, et al., eds. *The Black Abolitionist Papers.* Chapel Hill: University of North Carolina Press, 1992.

Douglas, Stephen Arnold (1813–1861)

A judge of the Illinois Supreme Court and U.S. senator, Stephen Arnold Douglas aggravated relations between pro-slavery and anti-slavery factions. He earned the nickname the Little Giant for his short stature and cocky political stance. While serving on the bench in Knox County, Illinois, he deliberated on a stream of cases involving slaves fleeing Missouri for the freedom of Adams and Knox counties. He took offense at the actions of abolitionists and network conductors who funneled refugees from Kentucky, Missouri, and Tennessee through Illinois. In April 1843, he charged Dr. Richard Eells and Julius A. Willard with sheltering a fugitive and fined Eells $400 for violating federal law. Radical commentary in the Chicago *Daily Journal* and the *Democratic Press* sharpened Douglas's wedge. Before the U.S. Senate on June 6, 1850, Douglas described the city of Chicago as a blatant booking station of the Underground Railroad. In a fevered outburst, he charged, "A venal press, and pulpits disgraced by crazy fanatics, joined in the work of misrepresentation, abuse, and denunciation [of slaveholders]."

Douglas took up the racist banner borne by the recently deceased senator Henry Clay. To turn the tide against slave escapes, Douglas pressed for passage of the Fugitive Slave Law of 1850, which shifted the nation's legal arm toward increased punishment of slaves and their rescuers. The unconstitutional elements of the law further alienated abolitionists. Rather than stem the flow of slaves from the plantation South, the law initiated a massive influx of runaways to Canada. Douglas pushed the nation further toward irremediable conflict by authoring the Kansas-Nebraska Act of 1854. Under the doctrine of popular sovereignty, the bill allowed frontier states to condone or refuse slave ownership within their boundaries. Championed by President Franklin Pierce, the law set up such a furor in Kansas that outlawry and vigilantism produced unprecedented racist violence and earned the state the name Bleeding Kansas. From the anguish arose the radicalism of insurrectionist John Brown. In 1858, Brown conspired to arm slaves with weapons from the federal arsenal at Harpers Ferry, Virginia, in preparation for an end-all confrontation between slave owners and abolitionists.

To increase his chance of winning the presidency, Douglas adroitly polarized issues. During a debate with attorney Abraham Lincoln on October 16, 1854, in Peoria, Illinois, Douglas maneuvered his opponent into revealing anti-slavery sympathies. Lincoln stated that bondage was a form of selfishness that warred eternally with justice. After Douglas defeated Lincoln for the Senate seat in 1858, he became an uncompromising proponent of states' rights and white supremacy. His stern rebuke of Underground Railroad supporters widened a split in the Democratic Party. In 1860 in a four-way race, a divided citizenry elected Abraham Lincoln to the presidency.

Although Douglas failed to win the election, he continued building coalitions against abolitionism. To stymy the secret network and add teeth to existing laws, he proposed to Confederate President Jefferson Davis a stringent enactment: "Why not make it a crime to form conspiracies and combinations to run off fugitive slaves, as well as to run off horses, or any other property? . . . It is these conspiracies to perpetrate crime with impunity, that keep up the irritation." The proposal was Douglas's final attempt at trouncing the Underground Railroad. Within months of the firing on Fort Sumter, he died of typhoid fever.

See also: abolitionism; Fugitive Slave Law of 1850.

Sources

Flint, Henry Martyn. *The Life of Stephen A. Douglas.* Philadelphia: John E. Potter, ca. 1863.
Sheahan, James W. *The Life of Stephen A. Douglas.* New York: Harper & Brothers, 1860.

Douglass, Anna Murray (ca. 1813–1882)

The first wife of the distinguished orator and publisher Frederick Douglass, Anna Murray Douglass had her own story to tell of the Underground Railroad. She was freeborn to former slaves Bambarra Murray and Mary Murray in Denton, in Caroline County, Maryland. Anna Murray never learned to read or write. From 1830 to 1839, she worked as maid for the Montell family in Baltimore. After joining the East Baltimore Improvement Society, she fell in love with Frederick Douglass, a Maryland runaway. On September 3, 1838, she offered her savings to pay for his flight to New York City. Two weeks later, they reunited at the home of David Ruggles. After the Reverend James William Charles Pennington, an agent of the secret network, performed the marriage ceremony, the couple made a home at a farm in Lynn, Massachusetts. Anna Douglass befriended the hierarchy of the secret network—William Lloyd Garrison, the Reverend Samuel Joseph May, and Wendell Addison Phillips. To support their children and her husband's volunteerism for the secret network, Anna Douglass took in laundry and bound shoes.

When the Underground Railroad took shape in Rochester, New York, in January 1848, Anna Douglass was drawn to Susan Brownell Anthony's activism. As a member of the Boston and Lynn anti-slavery societies,

Anna received fugitives during the long months that her husband toured anti-slavery conferences. At their two-story residence on Alexander Street, the Douglasses kept one room free for passengers. Anna gathered food, shoes, and clothes to supply the needy and saved money to cater refreshments for Boston's anti-slavery fairs. Dedication to ideals separated the couple. While Frederick Douglass moved in illustrious, intellectual company, Anna Douglass stayed home with her children to rest rheumatic joints and to conceal her lack of education and poise. Following a four-week confinement at Cedar Hill, the Douglass home in Anacostia, outside Washington, D.C., Anna died of a paralytic stroke at age 69.

See also: anti-slavery fairs.

Source

Davis, Elizabeth Lindsay. *Lifting As They Climb.* Washington, DC: National Association of Colored Women, 1933.

Douglass, Frederick (1817–1895)

A commanding presence in the abolitionist movement, orator and organizer Frederick Douglass, a mulatto, escaped slavery via the Underground Railroad. Born Frederick Washington Bailey in Tuckahoe, in Talbot County, Maryland, he was the son of Harriet Bailey, a slave, and her white owner, Captain Aaron Anthony. Frederick was separated from his mother in infancy and saw her only at night, after she returned from working the fields of a slave owner named Stewart 12 miles from her home. Douglass lived the precarious life of a plantation slave to a Colonel Edward Lloyd and resided with his maternal grandmother, Betsy Bailey. At age eight, he began working in Baltimore at the home of Hugh Auld, whose wife, Sophia Keithley Auld, taught the boy to read.

At age 16, Douglass returned to Lloyd's plantation, where he endured hunger and lashing. He reported in *My Bondage and My Freedom* (1857) on earning $9 and receiving 25¢ as his allowance, which he saved to pay his way north. After five years of misery under an overseer named Plummer and another named Covey, Douglass fled bondage in September 1838. Concealing his identity in a red shirt, tarp hat, and sailor's tie, he succeeded by carrying seaman's papers. Douglass passed through the safehouse of Isaac Rice and Sarah Ann Casey Rice in Newport, Rhode Island. He sped on to New York City and adopted the name Frederick Douglass. He lived in the boarding-house of David Ruggles at the corner of Church and Lispenard streets and reputedly studied reading and writing with Quaker conductor Elizabeth Hodgson "Eliza" Cooper in Williamson, in Wayne County, New York. Because of the danger of recapture, Ruggles found work for Douglass as a shipyard caulker for Rodney French, an abolitionist merchant in New Bedford, Massachusetts. It was the first home the runaway shared with his bride, Anna Murray Douglass.

In 1841, Douglass heard an address by abolitionist William Lloyd Garrison, who groomed Douglass as a platform speaker for the American Anti-Slavery Society. Douglass promoted two abolitionist journals, the *National Anti-Slavery Standard,* edited in Boston by David Child and Lydia Marie Francis Child, and *The Liberator,* Garrison's influential weekly. Four years later, the society issued his autobiography, *Narrative of the Life of Frederick Douglass, an American Slave* (1845). To assure safety from slave catchers, for the next year,

The most respected and influential of all black abolitionists, Frederick Douglass was also a stationmaster and conductor of the Underground Railroad in Rochester, New York. The thought of just one less slave, he wrote, "brought to my heart unspeakable joy." *(Library of Congress/Hulton Archive/Getty Images)*

Douglass toured Great Britain and lectured on American-style bondage. He returned to Rochester, New York, to serve a five-year term as manager of the American Anti-Slavery Society. With donations from Martin Robinson Delany in Pittsburgh, James Miller McKim in Philadelphia, and Samuel Brooke in Salem, Ohio, in 1848, Douglass founded an abolitionist newspaper, the *North Star,* which he printed near his home on Alexander Street in Rochester, New York. His residence and his print shop became waystations for as many as 13 fugitives at any one time, whom Anna Douglass often fed, boarded, and clothed without help during her husband's many absences from home. In August 1848, a scathing letter to the *Brooklyn Eagle* denounced Douglass as a freeloader on whites because he chose to remain in the United States rather than live in Canada.

The Douglasses courted danger by operating an Underground Railroad waystation on the trunk line from Baltimore to Wilmington, Philadelphia, New York, Albany, Syracuse, and Rochester and concluding in St. Catharines, Ontario. The couple's network began with Thomas Garrett in Wilmington, Delaware; Edward M. Davis, Melloe McKim, Robert Purvis, William Still, and Lucretia Coffin Mott and James Mott, Jr., in Philadelphia; Isaac Tatem Hopper, Sarah Tatum Hopper, and David Ruggles in New York City; Harriet Myers and Stephen Myers in Albany; and the Reverend Samuel Joseph May and the Reverend Jermaine Wesley Loguen in Syracuse. J.P. Morris and Douglass superintended the last link from Rochester across Lake Ontario to Canada, where the Reverend Hiram Wilson completed resettlement. Among Douglass's passengers was William Parker, who fled the Christiana Riot in September 1851. During one rescue, Douglass hosted 11 runaways in his residence and barn loft until he could collect funds for the final flight out of the United States. Discovery of his operation could have led to imprisonment and fining for feeding, harboring, and aiding escapees. Douglass declared that his participation in the secret network was one of the most rewarding tasks of his life.

In long service to ideals of humanity and racial equality, Douglass enlisted supporters for the secret network, including John Mercer Langston, an operative in Oberlin, Ohio. In June 1850, Douglass, George Downing, Jr., Samuel Ward, and Lewis Woodson coformed the American League of Colored Laborers, an outreach to former slaves who supported themselves by day labor. Douglass campaigned against Stephen Arnold Douglas and for the election of Abraham Lincoln in 1860 and encouraged President Lincoln to recruit ex-slaves for the Union army.

While living in Washington, D.C., in the 1870s, Douglass chaired the Freemen's Bank. At age 54, he was appointed assistant secretary of the Santo Domingo Commission. In 1877 he advanced to marshal of the District of Columbia and, in 1889, at age 72, to U.S. minister to Haiti. He continued refining his autobiography with his third, *Life and Times of Frederick Douglass* (1881). Douglass supported temperance, antilynching efforts, and women's rights. He collapsed on the dais at a women's suffrage rally on February 20, 1895, and died of heart failure at age 78. In 1898, the city of Rochester erected a monument to Douglass, which Governor Theodore Roosevelt dedicated.

See also: abolitionist newspapers; American Anti-Slavery Society; black soldiers; Christiana Riot; *Liberator, The.*

Sources

"Benj. F. Butler and Frederick Douglass," *Brooklyn (NY) Eagle,* August 4, 1848, 2.

Douglass, Frederick. *Life and Times of Frederick Douglass.* Boston: De Wolfe & Fiske, 1892.

———. *My Bondage and My Freedom.* Auburn, NY: Miller, Orton, 1857.

Dow, Neal (1804–1897)
Dow, Maria Cornelia Durant Maynard (1808–1883)

A two-term mayor of Portland, in Cumberland County, Maine, Neal Dow, a Quaker soldier and prohibitionist, and his wife, Maria Cornelia Durant Maynard Dow, rescued slaves for the Underground Railroad. The kitchen in their two-story brick residence at 714 Congress Street became a gathering spot for refugees arriving by sea. Collaborating with the Dows was the Reverend Amos Noah Freeman, pastor of the Abyssinian Meetinghouse, a waystation at 73 Newbury Street. In 1858, Neal Dow served in the Maine legislature; at age 61, he led the Thirteenth Maine Regiment of the Union army in the Civil War and spent nine months in Libby Prison in Virginia until his exchange for General William Henry Fitzhugh Lee. Some 3,000 well-wishers marched Dow up the street to his home in appreciation for his service. A memoir, *The Reminiscences of Neal Dow* (1898), was published a year after his death. The Dows' safehouse is a National Historic Landmark.

Source

Dow, Neal. *The Reminiscences of Neal Dow: Recollections of Eighty Years.* Portland, ME: *Evening Express,* 1898.

Downer, Lucy Ann Wilson (1784–1863) Downer, Pierce (1782–1863)

The founders of Downers Grove, Illinois, Lucy Ann Wilson Downer of Windsor, Vermont, and Pierce Downer of Plainfield, Vermont, contributed to peaceful coexistence with nonwhites and to the Illinois–Ontario route of the Underground Railroad. After traveling from Rutland, New York, and completing a three-day wagon ride from Chicago, Illinois, in May 1832, the pioneer couple arrived at what would become Downers Grove. At their 150-acre farm, the Downers resided in a log cabin at what is now an historic site at 4524 Linscott Street. While living in peace with the Potawatomi Indians, the couple learned the art of tapping maple trees for their sap. The Downers joined their neighbors, Avis Dodge Blodgett and Israel Porter Blodgett, in conducting slaves to free territory. Lucy Ann Downer died on March 25, 1863, some eight weeks after the Emancipation Proclamation; Pierce died the next day. The Downers' burial place is currently a park.

Source

Downer, David Robinson. *The Downers of America, with Genealogical Record.* Newark, NJ: Baker, 1900.

Downing, George T. (1819–1903)

A civil rights leader in two states, George T. Downing, a restaurateur, promoted the freeing of slaves. His father, Thomas Downing, co-founded free schools for fugitive slaves throughout Manhattan. In 1829, George Downing attended the African Free School in New York City on Mulberry Street with Henry Highland Garnet, James McCune Smith, and Samuel Ringgold Ward, who later became operatives of the secret network. At his resort, the Sea Girt Hotel in Newport, Rhode Island, Downing agitated for desegregation on the state level. His oyster restaurant on Broad and Wall streets in New York was part of an Underground Railroad network that extended over lower Manhattan. In the 1830s, he circulated petitions urging state legislators to enfranchise black citizens.

In the years preceding the Civil War, George Downing's activism increased. In June 1850, he and secret network organizers Frederick Douglass, Samuel Ward, and Lewis Woodson coformed the American League of Colored Laborers, an outreach to former slaves who supported themselves by day labor. Another group, the Committee of Thirteen, offered legal advice and defense to fugitive slaves apprehended in New York. In May 1862, Downing joined Henry Garnet at the Cooper Institute to celebrate the abolition of slavery in Washington, D.C. Downing's problack activism continued into the 1880s.

Source

Harris, Leslie M. *In the Shadow of Slavery: African Americans in New York City, 1626–1863.* Chicago: University of Chicago Press, 2003.

Doy, John W. (?–1861) Doy, Charles (?–1869)

A bold Underground Railroad operative during violent times in Missouri and Kansas, Dr. John W. Doy, a homeopath, and his son, Charles Doy, escorted slaves from Missouri to the free states of Iowa and Kansas. In August 1854, Jane Dunn Doy, John Doy, and their son, Charles, immigrated to North America from Hull, England. By way of Canada, they pushed on to the Kansas frontier with the New England Emigrant Aid Company and built a log cabin at Deer Creek on a 160-acre parcel in Douglas County, Kansas. With a Sharps rifle inscribed "Successful Agent of the Irrepressible Conflict," John Doy engaged in border wars at Fort Titus and in Franklin County, Kansas.

On January 25, 1859, Charles and John Doy relayed 12 blacks, some free and some slaves, from Lawrence, Kansas. One of the passengers was an infant born the previous day at the safehouse of Emily Jane Hunt Grover and Joel Grover in Lawrence. The party included Wilson Hayes and Charles Smith, two cooks on staff at the Eldridge House. As the Doys ferried the men in two wagons across the Missouri River to freedom, spies reported the rescue to authorities. The slaves fled, but authorities arrested them and the Doys 12 miles from Kansas on the way to Oskaloosa, in southeastern Iowa. In mid-February 1858 in Weston, Missouri, the Doys faced arraignment. Authorities shipped the runaways to New Orleans for auction. During the Doys' trial in St. Joseph, Missouri, on charges of aiding in slave escapes, father and son were jailed in Platte City. A Unitarian agent, the Reverend Ephraim Nute, raised funds for the Doys' defense; Samuel Forster Tappan and the Reverend Thomas Wentworth Higginson lent moral support.

After the verdict, the court exonerated Charles Doy; but John Doy earned a five-year sentence in the Missouri state penitentiary. John Doy's defense team achieved a two-month suspension while they appealed to the Missouri Supreme Court. On September 23, 1859, Silas Stillman Soule, an operative in Lawrence, Kansas, masterminded a jailbreak involving James Burnett Abbott, Joseph Gardner, Captain John E. Stewart, and six other confederates, known as the Immortal Ten. They tricked a jailer by claiming that they had captured a horse thief. The plot returned Doy to freedom in Kansas by skiff over the Missouri River and by wagon to the emigrant settlement established by Soule's father, Amasa Soule. The Immortal Ten earned a three-gun salute. John Doy published *The Narrative of John Doy of Lawrence, Kansas: A Plain Unvarnished Tale* (1860), a recounting of anti-slavery work on the midwestern frontier.

See also: spies.

Sources

Doy, John. *The Narrative of John Doy of Lawrence, Kansas: A Plain Unvarnished Tale.* New York: T. Holman, 1860.
Morgan, Perl Wilber. *History of Wyandotte County Kansas and Its People.* Chicago: Lewis, 1911.

Doyle, Edward James (ca. 1828–ca. 1850s)

An immigrant from Ireland, Edward James "Patrick" Doyle attempted a mass slave rescue. He was enrolled at Centre College in Danville, Kentucky, where he aided the secret network. After his arrest for slave stealing, he escaped from a jail cell in Louisville, Kentucky, in July 1848. On August 5 of that year, he piloted some 70 armed runaways from Lexington, Kentucky, toward the Ohio River. His charge for the service was $10 per slave. One hundred white slaveholders raised a $5,000 reward and pursued the noisy group to a hemp field at Reed's Mill on the Lickings River in Bracken County. Authorities arrested 40 of the escapees and clapped Doyle in irons. A court sentenced three fugitives to death for slave insurrection. They were hanged in Brooksville, Kentucky on October 28, 1848. Doyle began a 20-year prison term at hard labor in the Kentucky penitentiary in Frankfort but did not live to finish his term.

Source

Slade, George D. "Underground Railroad in Harrison County, Kentucky." *Harrison Heritage News* 6:2 (February 2005): 1, 3.

Drake, Frances Hills Wilder (1814–1900)
Drake, Jonathan (1804–1897)

Abolitionist agitator Frances Hills Wilder and her husband, Jonathan Drake, a shoemaker, conducted anti-slavery meetings and provided shelter for slaves. After their marriage in 1837, their home at 21 Franklin Street in Leominster, Massachusetts, served the Underground Railroad as a safehouse. Although the town of Leominster lacked the number of abolitionists needed to form a local vigilance committee, Frances Drake insisted that her residence be used as a waystation for runaways. Among the family's supporters was Wendell Addison Phillips, a firebrand orator and friend of the secret network. Jonathan Drake developed his own platform speaking style at nearby Stearns schoolhouse. On February 15, 1851, the Drakes joined Lewis Hayden in helping the slave Fredric "Shadrach" Minkins escape from a Boston courthouse. From Concord, Massachusetts, Francis Edwin Bigelow passed Minkins along the line to the Drakes for conveyance to agents Benjamin Snow, Jr., and Mary Baldwin Boutolle Snow's depot in West Fitchburg and then by train to Montreal, Quebec.

Sources

Collison, Gary. *Shadrach Minkins: From Fugitive Slave to Citizen.* Cambridge, MA: Harvard University Press, 1997.
Obituary of Jonathan Drake, *Leominster (MA) Weekly Enterprise,* January 22, 1897.

Drayton, Daniel (1802–1857)

One of the seagoing conductors of the Underground Railroad, Captain Daniel Drayton of Downs, in Cumberland County, New Jersey, carried refugees from Virginia to the Delaware Bay in his 54-ton sloop *Pearl.* Aiding these passages were innkeepers Lucinda Clark Bush and her husband, freedman William Bush, of New Bedford, Massachusetts. On April 15, 1848, Drayton attempted one of the largest mass slave escapes in U.S. history. Lucinda Bush, Daniel Bell, Thomas Ducket, and Paul Jennings, a former White House valet of the James Madison family, directed 77 runaways from Georgetown, in the District of Columbia, to Drayton's sloop at the Seventh Street Wharf for a four-day journey to freedom on the New Jersey shore.

Among the passengers on the *Pearl* were 38 men, 26 women, and 13 (or possibly 12) children of

Passengers on the *Pearl*

Name/Occupation	Age	Owner
Andrew Bell	29	Susannah Armistead, widow
Caroline Bell (Eleanora Bell's daughter)		Susannah Armistead, widow
Caroline Bell (Mary Bell's daughter)	19	Susannah Armistead, widow
Catherine Bell		Susannah Armistead, widow
Daniel Bell, Jr.	18	Susannah Armistead, widow
Eleanora Bell	21	Susannah Armistead, widow
George W. Bell	17	Susannah Armistead, widow
Harriet Bell	13	Susannah Armistead, widow
John Bell		Susannah Armistead, widow
Mary Bell		Susannah Armistead, widow
Mary Ellen Bell		Susannah Armistead, widow
Thomas Bell		Susannah Armistead, widow
Jane Brent		Nathaniel Pope Causin, physician, judge
John B. Brooke		Joseph Downing
John Calvert		Obadiah Brown, minister
Gabriel Campbell (?)		Letitia Lenham
Charles		John J. Stull
Augustus Chase	23	Vincent King
George Craig		Elizabeth Lewis
Philip Crowley	24	Rachel Harrison
Jemima "Mima" Davis		Mary Waters
Mary Day		Charles Fletcher
Minney Day		Charles Fletcher
Mary Dodson		Jonathan Y. Young
Emily Edmondson, domestic	13	Rebecca Culver, heiress
Ephraim Edmondson	30	Rebecca Culver, heiress
John Edmondson	26	Rebecca Culver, heiress
Mary Catherine Edmondson, domestic	15	Rebecca Culver, heiress
Richard Edmondson, coachman	24	Rebecca Culver, heiress
Samuel Edmondson, butler	21	Rebecca Culver, heiress
Ellen		Emily Corcoran, heiress
Joseph Forest		Jonathan Y. Young
Frank, house servant		Andrew Hoover, shoe manufacturer
Henry Graham		Samuel Brereton, grocer
Perry Gross	23	Sarah Crane
Joe, house servant		Andrew Hoover, shoe manufacturer
John		John J. Stull, bank director
Clarisa King		Francis Dodge, Jr., shipper
Edward King		William Kirkwood, lumberman
Leonard King		Jonathan Y. Young
Mary King		Jonathan Y. Young
Priscilla King (daughter)		Francis Dodge, Jr., shipper
Priscilla King (mother)		Francis Dodge, Jr., shipper
Jane Kitty		Elizabeth Dick; Margaret Laird, heiress
Elizabeth Marshall		Ignatius Francis Mudd, customs agent
Madison Marshall	24	Ignatius Francis Mudd, customs agent
Mathias Marshall	24	Ignatius Francis Mudd, customs agent
Matthew Marshall		Ignatius Francis Mudd, customs agent
Mary Ann		John J. Stull, bank director
Newman (or Truman)		L. Storm

Passengers on the *Pearl* (continued)

Name/Occupation	Age	Owner
Daphne Paine		Alexander Hunter, U.S. marshal
Paine (child)		Alexander Hunter, U.S. marshal
Madison Pitts	22	
Alfred Pope, butler	24	John Carter, politician
Harriet Queen	15	William H. Upperman, grocer
Priscilla Queen (daughter)	9	William H. Upperman, grocer
Priscilla Queen (mother)		William H. Upperman, grocer
John Ricks (or Rix)		Benjamin Franklin Middleton, grocer
Peter Ricks (or Rixx)	20	Thomas Connelly
August Rosier		Ariana Lyles, heiress
Hannibal Rosier		Ariana Lyles, heiress
Nat Rosier		Ariana Lyles, heiress
Grace Russell, domestic	18	Dr. Thomas Triplett
Sam		Elizabeth Dick; Margaret Laird, heiress
George Shanklin	23	W. Frozel
Henry Smallwood		W. Jackson
Mary Ellen Stewart, domestic	15	Dolley Madison
Isaac Turner	21	Ann McDaniel
Samuel Turner	24	Charles Lyons, investor
unnamed fugitive		Henry Moncure, slave dealer
Louisa Washington		John H. Smith
Maria Washington		John H. Smith
Melvina Washington		John H. Smith
Minerva Washington (mother)		John H. Smith
William		Matilda Ann Beall
William		Elizabeth Dick; Margaret Laird, heiress
Madison Young		James Irwin

varied ages, family connections, and circumstances. Most of the fugitives were waiters, domestics, houseboys, seamstresses, and cooks from local hotels, inns, and residences. Information on the party is scanty and inconsistent, including the identities of the fugitives.

Before reaching the Chesapeake Bay, the sloop's three-man crew encountered a squall near Point Lookout in St. Mary's County, Maryland. Thomas Orme, captain of the Georgetown police, acted on a tip from a spy named Judson Diggs, a black hackman who had recognized the Edmondsons. (Blacks later stoned Diggs and shunned him for the rest of his life.) Orme chartered the steamer *Salem* from slave owner Francis Dodge, Jr., to pursue the *Pearl* and search it for missing slaves. Drayton persuaded armed passengers to avoid bloodshed when faced by a posse armed with bowie knives and carbines.

After the *Salem* towed the sloop up the Potomac River, police arrested Drayton, sailor Chester English, and the sloop's owner, Captain Edward Sayres, for stealing and transporting runaways. On their return to Fourth Street and Pennsylvania Avenue on February 18, 1848, Drayton and his party faced a drunken lynch mob brandishing pistols and dirks. A slave trader named Joseph Gannon lurched out of the crowd and knifed Drayton in the ear. Many of the manacled slaves, including the Edmondsons, were bought for auction in New Orleans and transported south on the brig *Union*.

Drayton was incarcerated with Chester English and Edward Sayres at Judiciary Square in a stucco jail dubbed the Blue Jug. Members of the black community consoled Drayton with visits and gifts of food and a bible. At the request of Dr. Samuel Gridley Howe, a team of attorneys—Salmon Portland Chase, Francis Jackson, Horace Mann, Robert Morris, and Samuel Edmund Sewall—defended Drayton at his trial. Mann established that Drayton was merely transporting passengers without knowing they were slaves. Mann lost the first hearing, in which Drayton was sentenced to 20 years in prison, 10 years each for the theft of manufacturer Andrew Hoover's two slaves, Frank and Joe. On appeal, Mann got the judgment lowered to confinement until Drayton and Sayres could pay $10,000 each in fines. During litigation, Drayton refused to accept a $1,000 bribe from a pro-slavery faction to implicate other members of the Underground Railroad team in the rescue attempt. After he spent over four years in a stone-floored cell with no furnishing but two blankets, a can of water, and a night bucket, Drayton and his accomplices were pardoned by President Millard Fillmore.

Drayton published *Personal Memoir of Daniel Drayton, for Four Years and Four Months a Prisoner in Washington Jail* in 1854 and went on the lecture circuit to recoup his losses. During his tours, he stayed with Abigail and Elizabeth Goodwin, Quaker conductors in Salem, New Jersey. After living in Cape May, New Jersey; Philadelphia; Boston; and Staten Island, New York, he settled in New Bedford, Massachusetts, near his secret network collaborators Lucinda and William Bush. On June 24, 1857, Drayton, alienated and despondent, committed suicide at the Mansion House Hotel in New Bedford. After the mayor conducted a martyr's farewell at city hall, Drayton was buried in Rural Cemetery, where freedmen tended the plot.

See also: spies.

Sources

Drayton, Daniel. *Personal Memoir of Daniel Drayton, for Four Years and Four Months a Prisoner in Washington Jail.* New York: American and Foreign Anti-Slavery Society, 1854.

Ricks, Mary Kay. *Escape on the* Pearl: *The Heroic Bid for Freedom on the Underground Railroad.* New York: William Morrow, 2007.

Dred Scott v. Sandford (1857)

See Scott, Dred

Dresser, Amos (1812–1904)

An evangelist and vocal abolitionist, the Reverend Amos Dresser of Peru, Massachusetts, was a respected martyr to the cause of human rights. Forced out of Lane Seminary in Cincinnati, Ohio, in 1834, he and fellow supporters of the Underground Railroad, called the Lane Rebels, enrolled at Oberlin College in Oberlin, Ohio. During his four years of study, Dresser conducted slaves to Ontario. While distributing temperance tracts, the anti-slavery letters of the Reverend John Rankin, and the *Cottage Bible* in Nashville, Tennessee, on July 18, 1835, he angered a pro-slavery faction that publicly cowhided him for possessing a copy of the American Anti-Slavery Society periodical the *Anti-Slavery Record* and George Bourne's *Picture of Slavery in the United States* (1834). Dresser resettled near safehouses in Nebraska City and Brownsville, Nebraska.

See also: American Anti-Slavery Society; Oberlin College; punishments; safehouses.

Sources

Hume, John F. *The Abolitionists: Together with Personal Memories of the Struggle for Human Rights, 1830–1864.* New York: Putnam, 1905. Reprint New York: AMS, 1973.

Talty, Stephan. "Spooked: The White Slave Narratives." *Transition 85* 10:1 (2000): 48–75.

Drew, Benjamin (1812–1903)

The journalist and historian Benjamin Drew, a Bostonian, conducted a census of blacks in Canada in an era when metropolitan census takers excluded black residents. He surveyed the settlement of Canada by fugitives fleeing the United States aboard the Underground Railroad. Drew joined the Canadian Anti-Slavery Society in gathering facts and memoirs from mostly male runaways living in Ontario. He estimated the growth of the black population at a number of sites in the mid-1850s.

Supporting Drew's project were agents William Lloyd Garrison, William King, the Reverend Theodore Parker, Hiram K. Wilson, and John P. Jewett, the publisher of Harriet Beecher Stowe's melodrama *Uncle Tom's Cabin* (1852). Jewett issued the anthology of slave narratives as *The Refugee: The Narratives of Fugitive Slaves in Canada* (1856). At its completion, Drew returned to Boston and taught school.

See also: Canada; *Uncle Tom's Cabin; or, Life Among the Lowly* (1852).

Source

Drew, Benjamin. *The Refugee: The Narratives of Fugitive Slaves in Canada.* Boston: John P. Jewett, 1856.

Driver, Blackstone (1801–1858)
Driver, Margaret P. (fl. 1840s)

Blackstone Driver, a day laborer and vigorous abolitionist, and his wife, Margaret P. Driver, promoted slave rescue in Portland, in Cumberland County, Maine. Blackstone joined the Portland Union Anti-

Slavery Society and served as treasurer. The Drivers received refugees at their home near the Abyssinian church at 73 Newbury Street on Munjoy Hill, another waystation of the Underground Railroad, operated from 1841 to 1851 by its pastor, Amos Noah Freeman. At age 54, Blackstone served in Portland's Black Mariners, a brotherhood of seamen, stevedores, shipwrights, caulkers, stewards, and cooks.

Source

Obituary of Blackstone Driver, *Santa Rosa (CA) Sonoma Democrat*, December 9, 1858.

Drury, Elijah (?–1860s)

A tenant of the Reverend Charles Shipman and a circuit rider and route superintendent in Girard, Pennsylvania, Elijah Drury supported a complex series of Underground Railroad routes for three decades. He reacted emotionally to scarred backs and other evidence of cruelty to slaves. In collaboration with Henry Teller and Rosalinda Porter Teller, Drury hid passengers in his barn and made the final relay to Canada. For extra security, he dug a tunnel from the barn to a hideaway in a ravine along Elk Creek.

See also: routes, Underground Railroad.

Sources

Domowicz, Geoff. *Girard.* Charleston, SC: Arcadia, 2003.
Eiler, Linda Lee Hessong. *Girard, Pa.* Charleston, SC: Arcadia, 2005.

Duckett, Benjamin (1831–?)

Benjamin Duckett was one of many slaves receiving the aid of Pennsylvania Underground Railroad agents. He came of age at his birthplace, Darnall's Grove, Maryland, the estate of Judge Gabriel Duval. In his twenties, Duckett passed into bondage to Zachariah Berry, a major slaveholder at Bellmont plantation in Washington, D.C. Duckett escaped on September 16, 1856, possibly by sloop on the Chesapeake Bay. In early October, he sought assistance from William Still, an agent of the Philadelphia Vigilance Committee, who provided him cash for the journey to Ontario.

Source

Still, William. *Underground Railroad Records.* Philadelphia: Porter & Coates, 1883.

Dunbar, Joshua (ca. 1818–1885)

A Kentucky slave from Garrard County, Joshua Dunbar fled bondage with the aid of the Underground Railroad. He met a secret agent in the woods and, traveling by hay and produce wagons, passed through waystations on his way north. He crossed the Ohio River on a ferry. From Detroit, Michigan, he took a boat over Lake Erie. After reaching Canada, he worked as a plasterer and joined the African Methodist Episcopal Church. He fought for the Union army as a sergeant with the Fifty-fifth Massachusetts Infantry and with the Fifth Massachusetts Volunteer Cavalry. In 1871, he married a widow, Matilda Jane Murphy, a former domestic owned by Squire David Glass of Shelby County, Kentucky. The Dunbars were the parents of poet Paul Lawrence Dunbar. Joshua Dunbar died in the Old Soldier's Home in Dayton, Ohio.

See also: black soldiers.

Source

Alexander, Eleanor. *Lyrics of Sunshine and Shadow.* New York: New York University Press, 2001.

Dunmore, Henry (1825–?)

A runaway from a cruel Methodist slave owner, Henry Dunmore fled hunger and cold. Under the ownership of John Maldon of Cecil County, Maryland, Dunmore suffered near starvation and lost toes to frostbite. Fear of being sold at age 35 forced him to devise an escape plan. In 1860, he made his way north to Pennsylvania and sought aid from operatives of the Philadelphia Underground Railroad.

Source

Still, William. *The Underground Railroad.* Philadelphia: Porter & Coates, 1871.

Dutton, Achas Perry (1822–1887)

One of many sympathetic boat captains, Achas Perry Dutton of Racine, Wisconsin, labored for two decades coordinating Underground Railroad flights by schooner on the Great Lakes. At age 19, he settled at Racine before the town acquired piers and witnessed the growth of the harbor industry. He made his living in grain storage and transport. To complete some 100 land-and-water transfers of refugees, he coordinated efforts with a network of operatives—George Barrows, J.O. Bartlett, Charley

Bunce, W.L. Sitley, W.H. Waterman, George S. Wright, and Dr. Secor.

Source

Davidson, John Nelson. *Negro Slavery in Wisconsin and the Underground Railroad.* Milwaukee: Parkman Club, 1897.

Dutton, Samuel William Southmayd (1814–1866)
Dutton, Harriet Newell Waters (1814–1864)

Two of a team of rescuers, the Reverend Samuel William Southmayd Dutton and his wife, Harriet Newell Waters Dutton, received passengers of the Underground Railroad. Born in Guilford, Connecticut, Samuel Dutton trained at Yale and became a Congregationalist minister of North Church at 323 Temple Street in New Haven. After their marriage in 1838, the Duttons dedicated themselves to abolitionism. At the Dutton home at 113 College Street, they listened for a coded knock at the door. Escapees bathed and ate and then slept in the attic until dark, when it was safe to continue to Chester, Deep River, or Southington on the New England–Canada route of the secret network. Dutton and his collaborators—Judge Roger Sherman Baldwin, Nathaniel Jocelyn, and the Reverend Simeon Smith Jocelyn—provided legal defense and moral support to 35 surviving mutineers from the slave ship *Amistad.* In 1863, Dutton delivered the funeral eulogy of Roger Baldwin

See also: Amistad; code, Underground Railroad.

Source

Sweeney, Douglas A. *Nathaniel Taylor, New Haven Theology, and the Legacy of Jonathan Edwards.* New York: Oxford University Press, 2002.

Dyer, Charles Volney (1808–1878)
Dyer, Louisa Maria Gifford (1812–1875)

Charles Volney Dyer, an affable surgeon and abolitionist, and his wife, Louisa Maria Gifford Dyer of Sherburne, Vermont, lent their skills to refugees at the Underground Railroad terminus in Chicago, Illinois. A native of Clarendon Spring, a town near Rutland, Vermont, Charles Dyer completed medical training at Middlebury College and opened a medical office in Newark, New Jersey. While practicing surgery at Fort Dearborn, Illinois, he and his co-conspirators—detective Allan Pinkerton, conductors John Jones and Mary Jane Richardson Jones and Henry O. Wagoner—aided runaways passing through Chicago.

The Giffords married in 1837 and received passengers at their home at 47 State Street from Thomas Filer of Glen Ellyn, Illinois. In 1846, Charles Dyer led a daylight raid to recover a slave from Kentucky who had been bound by slave catchers and was being held under false arrest at the Mansion House Hotel on Lake Street in Chicago. With a cane, Dyer fought off a pursuer brandishing a bowie knife. Supporters of the secret group awarded the doctor a gold-headed hickory cane, which the Chicago Historical Society currently displays. That same year, Dyer chaired a subcommittee of the Abolition Party.

In Washington, D.C., Charles Dyer was instrumental in founding the *National Era*, an abolitionist newspaper edited by Gamaliel Bailey and John Greenleaf Whittier for the promotion of the Abolition Party. As president of the Chicago, Burlington, & Quincy Railroad, Dyer used his railcars to transport fugitives. For his generosity, he was nicknamed President of the Illinois Underground Railroad. Following passage of the Fugitive Slave Law of 1850, Dyer concealed refugees in storage rooms at the Tremont Hotel and filled train cars with those runaways who needed immediate transportation to Canada to avoid recapture. In 1863, his friend, President Abraham Lincoln, appointed Dyer a judge of anti-slavery proceedings held in Sierra Leone.

See also: abolitionist newspapers; Fugitive Slave Law of 1850; slave recovery.

Source

Bernstein, Arnie. *The Hoofs and Guns of the Storm: Chicago's Civil War Connections.* Chicago: Lake Claremont, 2003.

Dyer, Edward Galusha (1806–1888)

A Wisconsin pioneer, Dr. Edward Galusha Dyer managed a medical office and a depot of the Underground Railroad. He completed a medical degree at age 24 from the College of Physicians and Surgeons in New York. After his emigration from Rhode Island to Racine County in the Territory of Wisconsin in 1839, he earned local regard for donating funds to the secret network, for giving abolitionist speeches, and for aiding a well-documented rescue in summer 1843. At his home in Gardener's Prairie, near Burlington, he offered $20 in cash and a horse, a wagon, and a pillowcase stuffed with food to help 18-year-old Missouri runaway Caroline Quarrels of St. Louis, Missouri, reach Detroit, Michigan. With network assistance, she crossed the Detroit River to liberty in Windsor, Ontario. In honor of the fugitives passing through his home, Dyer named his street Liberty Avenue. In late June 1935, citizens erected a monument and sundial commemorating Dyer's humanitarian service to slaves.

Sources

"Burlington Is Starting Centennial Celebration." *Milwaukee Journal* June 16, 1935.

Golub, Rob. "Underground Railroad Remembered." *Racine (WI) Journal Times*, February 18, 2001.

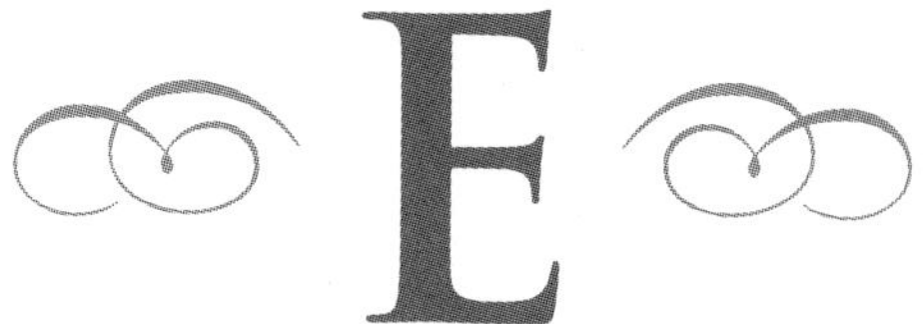

Early, Jordan Winston (1814–1903)

The Reverend Jordan Winston Early was part of an active trans–Missouri River route of the Underground Railroad. Born in slavery in Franklin County, Virginia, from age three Jordan was the foster child of Aunt Milly, a plantation nanny. He developed a love of religion at camp meetings. At age 12, his owners transported him to St. Louis, Missouri, where he settled on a religious calling. In his late teens, he was a crewman of a Mississippi riverboat serving New Orleans. Around age 20, he bought his freedom. As a minister of the African Methodist Episcopal Church, the Reverend Early established an outreach from a small log cabin in St. Louis and spread the denomination to Iowa, Illinois, and Louisiana.

Early's rescue of slaves relied on help from colleague Priscilla Baltimore, a founder of the St. Paul African Methodist Episcopal Church and a conductor of the secret network in Alton, Illinois. In 1846, a federal court charged Early with conducting runaways for the Underground Railroad. He eluded prosecution by clever courtroom testimony. During the Civil War, a posse seized him as a fugitive worth $500 but released him after he proved his liberation. He devoted the remainder of his life to church work and missions. His wife, Sarah J. Woodson Early, published a definitive biography, *Life and Labors of Rev. Jordan W. Early* (1894).

See also: African Methodist Episcopal Church.

Source

Early, Sarah J.W. *Life and Labors of Rev. Jordan W. Early.* Nashville: A.M.E. Church Sunday School Union, 1894.

Eastman, Charles Frederick (1821–1880) Eastman, Harriet E. Stephenson (1824–1913)

A black New England couple, Charles Frederick Eastman and Harriet E. Stephenson Eastman, provided sanctuary for slaves arriving by sea to the Maine coast. They received and cared for runaways at their shore home at Seven Hampshire Street in Portland. Charles Eastman, a taxidermist, clothier, sailor, and hack driver, owned a barbershop in Hancock Court and another at 129 Congress Street. He was the clerk of the Abyssinian Baptist Church at 73–75 Sumner Street (now Newbury Street), an Underground Railroad depot. He donated to the church treasury and brought in abolitionist speakers to increase awareness of the sufferings of slaves. Thanks to the secret compartment in his cab, he was able to make one rescue by transporting a man from the Portland Club to the church meetinghouse, where the Reverend Amos Noah Freeman provided sanctuary for runaways during his tenure from 1841 to 1851. The transfer concluded at the border of Quebec Province. Other late-night relays required Eastman to drive fugitives to the Portland wharves, where they boarded ships traveling to free territory.

Source

Kennedy, Kate. *More Than Petticoats: Remarkable Maine Women.* Guilford, CT: Globe Pequot, 2005.

Eastman, Zebina (1815–1883)

The first conductor to escort a runaway through Chicago to Ontario, Zebina Eastman of North Amherst, Massachusetts, supported and promoted the extension of the Underground Railroad into the Midwest. After learning the printer's trade in his late teens while working on the *Peoria Register,* he became interested in activism from aiding the Quaker editor Benjamin Lundy on the staff of the anti-slavery gazette the *Genius of Universal Emancipation* in Mount Pleasant, Ohio. Eastman developed transfer strategies with the Reverend Ichabod Codding and with Allan Pinkerton, fellow Chicago operatives and planners of slave relay routes. Eastman received refugees from Kentucky and Missouri conducted to his safehouse in Owen Glendower Lovejoy's hay wagon.

With the encouragement of Dr. Charles Volney Dyer, Henry O. Wagoner, Hooper W. Warren, and Philo R. Carpenter, in 1842, Eastman began Chicago's first abolitionist newspaper, the *Western Citizen,* the most influential liberal paper in the Midwest. He remained in charge for 11 years, during which he chided slave owners and bounty hunters for their lack of humanity. He published Lovejoy's open invitation to slaves to steal their masters' horses and follow the secret route to Canada. In March 1846, Eastman encouraged women to follow the example of the Daughters of Liberty during the Revolutionary War by getting involved in aiding fugitive slaves. To the benefit of Underground Railroad history, he kept a scrapbook of secret-network activity and abolitionist rallies.

See also: abolitionist newspapers; routes, Underground Railroad.

Sources

Blue, Frederick J. *No Taint of Compromise: Crusaders in Antislavery Politics.* Baton Rouge: Louisiana State University Press, 2005.
Eastman, Zebina. *Northwestern Liberty Almanac for 1846.* Chicago: Eastman & Davidson, 1845.

Easton, Hosea (1799–1837)

An intellectual activist and pamphleteer, the Reverend Hosea Easton promoted the freeing of slaves via the Underground Railroad until they could be emancipated by federal law. A freeman, a patriot of Afro-Wampanoag descent, and the son of a Revolutionary War veteran, he based his philosophy on the U.S. Constitution, which declared all citizens free. He began preaching in Providence, Rhode Island, in 1828 and worked as a distributor of an abolitionist newspaper, *Freedom's Journal.* His sermons remarked on his conversations with refugees, who narrated the misery of their bondage.

In June 1831, he met with other black abolitionists in Philadelphia at the Convention of Colored People. He compared the acts of slave dealers and buyers with the crimes of assassins and highway robbers. In 1833, he left Boston, Massachusetts, to pastor the Colored Methodist Episcopal Zion Church on Talcott Street in Hartford, Connecticut. After his *Treatise on the Intellectual Character and the Civil and Political Condition of the Colored People of the United States* (1836) was published, he advertised it in William Lloyd Garrison's newspaper *The Liberator.* Easton died shortly after a mob torched the sanctuary.

See also: abolitionist newspapers; *Liberator, The.*

Source

Price, George. *To Heal the Scourge of Prejudice: The Life and Writings of Hosea Easton.* Amherst: University of Massachusetts Press, 1999.

Eaton, Anna Ruth Webster (1823–?)
Eaton, Horace (1810–1883)

Agents of the Underground Railroad in Palmyra, in Wayne County, New York, Anna Eaton of Merrimack, New Hampshire, and her husband, the Reverend Horace Eaton of Warner, New Hampshire, assisted fugitive slaves approaching a crossing point at Lake Ontario. The couple married in August 1845. Horace Eaton, the pastor of the Western Presbyterian Church on East Main Street, collaborated with safehouse keepers Pliny Sexton and his son, Pliny Titus Sexton, Jr. Additional help came from parishioners, who concealed passengers in the church bell tower. Runaways could ease through a tunnel to the Erie Canal.

Source

Pettit, Eber M. *Sketches in the History of the Underground Railroad.* Fredonia, NY: W. McKinstry & Son, 1879.

Ebersole, Jacob (1812–1861)

A founder of Underground Railroad sanctuaries in Clermont County, Ohio, Jacob Ebersole laid out routes to safehouses. In addition to his first wife, Lydia Ann Rogers Ebersole (1822–1847) of California, Ohio, and his second wife, Elizabeth Rachell Hall Ebersole (1829–?) of Richmond, Kentucky, Ebersole depended on his sister, Catherine Ebersole Fee, and her husband, Robert E. Fee, a member of a family of secret network activists, and on Charles Boerstler "Boss" Huber, a tanner in Williamsburg, Ohio. The Ebersoles' 500-acre farm in Felicity overlooked the Ohio Valley. The family surveyed escape attempts below on the Ohio River, where conveyors awaited signals from runaways crossing by skiff. For backup, Huber relied on hired freedman Marcus Sims, neighbor Leavitt Thaxter Pease, and Isaac Holmes Brown in Bethel, in Brown County, to lead the way over the northern route. On the last leg, Samuel Peterson, a stonemason, supplied food and completed the transfer to Brown's farm sanctuary.

See also: routes, Underground Railroad.

Source

Williams, Byron. *History of Clermont and Brown Counties, Ohio.* Baltimore: Gateway, 1987.

Edmondson, Emily (1835–1895)
Edmondson, Mary Catherine (1833–1853)

Sisters Emily and Mary Catherine Edmondson (or Edmonson) fled the District of Columbia to find freedom in the North. The girls were among 14 children born in slavery in Montgomery County, Maryland, to seamstress Amelia "Milly" Edmondson and freeman Paul Edmondson, who farmed 40 acres in Norbeck, Maryland. In childhood, the sisters worked as domestics in upscale residences.

On April 15, 1848, 15-year-old Mary Catherine and 13-year-old Emily, along with their brothers Ephraim, John, Richard, and Samuel, received the help of conductor William Lawrence Chaplin in escaping aboard the schooner *Pearl.* In the nation's largest slave flight, the 54-ton sloop, captained by Daniel Drayton of Downs, in Cumberland County, New Jersey, carried a total of 77 runaways hidden in boxed cargo. The four-day voyage took them from Georgetown, in the District of Columbia, and the Seventh Street Wharf on the Potomac River, to the Chesapeake Bay for a sea voyage to New Jersey on Delaware Bay. A storm slowed the vessel. The escape was betrayed by a drayman, Judson Diggs, Emily Edmondson's spurned suitor, who divulged the purpose of the voyage to slave hunters.

After authorities captured all 77 escaping slaves, the Edmondson sisters survived a month in an Alexandria, Virginia, slave pen. Joseph Bruin and Henry Hill, slave-trading partners, purchased the girls and confined them in a two-story brick jail on Duke Street. Against the pleadings of Bruin's daughter, Bruin and Hill transported the Edmondson sisters to New Orleans aboard the *Union* for sale in a public market. During an outbreak of yellow fever, the sisters' new owners returned them to Alexandria to work as laundresses and seamstresses. Through the activism of their father, the New York Anti-Slavery Society, and the Reverend Henry Ward Beecher, pastor of the Brooklyn Congregationalist Church, negotiators raised $2,250 overnight to fund the girls' liberation. On November 4, 1848, Beecher completed the transaction in Washington, D.C. Hamilton Edmondson, Emily and Mary's older sibling, bought their brother Samuel out of bondage.

The sisters gained notoriety for their courage and ambition. Mary Catherine and Emily shared the platform at the Cazenovia, New York, Anti-Fugitive Slave Act Convention on August 22, 1850, with respected conductors Frederick Douglass, Abby Kelley Foster, and Gerrit Smith, all protesters of the Fugitive Slave Law of 1850. In 1852, with a $50 gift from Harriet Beecher Stowe, the author of *Uncle Tom's Cabin* (1852), the sisters enrolled at the Young Ladies Preparatory School of Oberlin College to ready themselves for the Canadian mission field. One of their classmates was Grace Russell, another former slave and survivor of the *Pearl* fiasco. After Mary Catherine's death from tuberculosis at age 20, Emily completed her education at the Normal School for Colored Girls in Washington, D.C. She taught, supported abolitionism, and bought another brother out of bondage.

See also: Oberlin College; *Uncle Tom's Cabin; or, Life Among the Lowly* (1852).

Sources

Drayton, Daniel. *Personal Memoir of Daniel Drayton, for Four Years and Four Months a Prisoner in Washington Jail.* New York: American and Foreign Anti-Slavery Society, 1854.

Paynter, John H. "The Fugitives of the *Pearl.*" *Journal of Negro History* 1:3 (June 1916).

Ricks, Mary Kay. *Escape on the* Pearl: *The Heroic Bid for Freedom on the Underground Railroad.* New York: William Morrow, 2007.

Edwards, John B. (1802–1895)
Edwards, Lydia M. Hall (1806–1856)

Colleagues of agents Hamilton B. Littlefield and Rhoda Littlefield and of organizer Gerrit Smith, John B. Edwards and his wife, Lydia M. Hall Edwards, contributed to the Underground Railroad effort in Oswego, New York. John Edwards, a native of Monmouth County, New Jersey, grew up in Lyons, New York, where he developed strong Methodist beliefs. He worked as a day laborer and superintendent during the construction of the Erie Canal. In 1826, he wed Lydia M. Hall in Norway, New York. Their two-story depot at 144 East Third Street in Oswego was a refuge for slaves fleeing pursuers. On April 29, 1852, John Edwards gave a dollar to a slave named Dorsey before a steamer ferried the man across Lake Ontario. The Edwards house is listed on the National Register of Historic Places.

Source

History of Oswego County, New York. Philadelphia: L.H. Everts, 1877.

Eells, Erastus (1808–1892)

An Ohio settler, Erastus Eells, assisted the Underground Railroad in Lisbon, in Mahoning County. A native of Clapboard Hill, Connecticut, at age nine, he moved west with his family and apprenticed with a carpenter. In 1828, he began his career as a mortician and coffin maker. In the three decades preceding the Civil War, he was a devout Presbyterian and an avid conductor of the secret network. One ailing passenger died on Eells's back porch. Lacking a way to bury the man without stirring controversey, Eells boiled the flesh from the man's skeleton and gave the bones to Dr. George McCook to use as medical reference.

Source

Cranmer, Gibson Lamb. *History of the Upper Ohio Valley.* Madison, WI: Brant & Fuller, 1890.

Eells, Richard (1800–1846)
Eells, Jane Bestor (1802–1880)

Dr. Richard Eells of Barkhamsted, Connecticut, was one of many agents of the secret network who was convicted of violating federal laws against rescuing runaway slaves. He married Jane Bestor of Simsbury, Connecticut, in 1826, and the couple settled in Quincy, Illinois, in 1833. Eells opened a medical office and taught aspiring doctors. He promoted the state and county anti-slavery societies. The Eells aided runaways on the route to Ontario at their two-story brick home at 415 Jersey Street, which they built in 1835. On August 21, 1842, Richard Eells rescued a fugitive named Charley, who had fled a farm in Monticello, Missouri. Charley swam the Mississippi River to free territory and, with the aid of freedman Barryman Barnett, arrived at Eells's safehouse three blocks away. Eells relayed his passenger by buggy to the Mission Institute waystation. After pursuers caught Charley the next day and returned him south, they found evidence of his wet clothes in Eells's buggy.

At their two-story brick house in Quincy, Illinois, close to the Mississippi River, Dr. Richard Eells and Jane Bestor Eells took in slaves who had swum or paddled to freedom from Missouri. The couple then led the runaways to safehouses across town. *(Courtesy of Con McNay, Friends of the Dr. Richard Eells House)*

Guided by conductor Samuel Guild Wright of Stark County, Illinois, Eells followed Underground Railroad routes through Galesburg to Chicago and remained there until January 1843, when he returned home to stand trial. In April, Circuit Court Judge Stephen Arnold Douglas found Eells and a confederate, Julius Alphonso Willard, guilty of harboring a fugitive and fined Eells $400 for violating federal law. The conductor appealed to the state supreme court, but lost the case in February 1844. Seven years after Eells's death, abolitionist attorneys Salmon Portland Chase and William Henry Seward failed to clear Eells's name by appealing to the U.S. Supreme Court. In 1990, restorers began refurbishing the Eells' waystation, which is listed on the National Register of Historic Places.

Sources

Moseley-Braun, Carol. "Singularity of Purpose." *American Visions* 14:2 (April 1999): 38.

Muelder, Hermann R. *Fighters for Freedom: The History of Anti-Slavery Activities of Men and Women Associated with Knox College.* New York: Columbia University Press, 1959.

Eleutherian College

A three-story stone school, Eleutherian College in Lancaster, in Jefferson County, Indiana, encouraged volunteerism to the Underground Railroad. The college, which grew out of the Eleutherian Institute, got its start in 1854 and registered some 300 students. The staff was dedicated to educating any student, regardless of race, social class, or gender. Drawing on the fervor of the Neil's Creek (Indiana) Anti-Slavery Society, the Reverend Thomas Craven of Oxford, Ohio, formed a band of abolitionists, including student agents. Local Underground Railroad conductors

Eleutherian College, founded by Baptists in southeastern Indiana for students of any race or gender, was a strategic resting place for runaway slaves crossing the Ohio River from Kentucky. Students, faculty, and administrators lent assistance. *(Indiana Department of Natural Resoures—Division of Historic Preservation and Archaeology)*

Lyman Hoyt, Samuel Tibbets, and James Nelson aided fugitives after they crossed the Ohio River and reached the hilltop campus. A sheriff arrested Nelson for conducting slaves to freedom, but an anti-slavery judge dismissed the case. In 1997, the main classroom building of Eleutherian College was named a National Historic Landmark.

Source

Savage, Beth L. *African American Historic Places.* New York: Preservation Press, 1994.

Elgin Settlement

With the aid of James Bruce, Lord Elgin, governor of British North America, the Reverend William King, a Presbyterian minister, established the Elgin settlement, the most successful African Canadian community in Canada. Also called the Buxton Mission or King's Settlement, the project took shape in Raleigh Township, north of Buxton in Kent County, Ontario, as a homeland for slaves who reached the last stop on the Underground Railroad. Parliament incorporated the town in August 1850. In the first issue of *Voice of the Fugitive,* publishers Henry Bibb and Mary E. Miles Bibb reported on the success of former slaves. In 1855, the settlers installed a liberty bell, a gift from black supporters in Pittsburgh, Pennsylvania. The bell ringer pulled the cord in celebration of each new arrival from slavery, each wedding, and each baby born in free territory.

Stock owners of some 9,000 acres offered 50-acre plots that began receiving families in December 1849. By 1866, newcomers formed a community of 190 log houses overlooking Lake Erie. Elginites flourished at growing oats, wheat, and tobacco, raising livestock, lumbering, operating gristmills, potash and pearl ash production, brick making, ironwork, coopering, running hotels, and selling dry goods. To provide seed money for expansion, in 1856, the Reverend King, along with William Day, Dr. Martin Robinson Delany, and Archibald McKellar, canvassed English philanthropists for donations.

See also: philanthropists.

Sources

Bristow, Peggy, et al. *We're Rooted Here and They Can't Pull Us Up.* Toronto, Ontario: University of Toronto Press, 1994.
"Colored Settlement," *Voice of the Fugitive,* January 1, 1851.

Ellis, William (1770–1806)
Ellis, Mercy Cox (1772–1848)

A Quaker slave conductor in Lycoming County, Pennsylvania, William Ellis championed black refugees. After marrying Mercy Cox of Philadelphia, in 1786, William Ellis sold real estate and surveyed land for Samuel Wallis. The Ellises turned Wolf Run House, their stone residence in Muncy, into a safehouse of the Underground Railroad. From 1792, the couple relayed passengers up the Genesee Road to Elklands and over the New York–Canada route. Admirers referred to the waystation as Saints' Rest. After passing to the Ellis's son-in-law and daughter, Jacob A. Haines and Rachel Ellis Haines, the property remained in service to fugitive slaves through two generations of the Haines family.

Source

Haines, Mary Rhoads. *Clovercroft Chronicles, 1314–1893.* Philadelphia: J.B. Lippincott, 1893.

Ellyson, Zachariah (1793–1867)
Ellyson, Esther Chaffin Talbot (1812–1871)

Quaker agent Zachariah Ellyson of Loudoun County, Virginia, and his Methodist wife, Esther Chaffin Talbot

Ellyson of Cass County, Michigan, combined pioneering with rescuing slaves for the Underound Railroad. Zachariah left the South out of disgust with slavery and sought a more amicable life in the Midwest. After relocating to the Michigan frontier in 1848, he worked as a mechanic and millwright. In 1859, the Ellysons moved farther west to Iowa and operated an Underground Railroad safehouse in Pleasant Plain, in Jefferson County.

Source

Portraits and Biographical Album of Jefferson and Van Buren Counties, Iowa. Chicago: Lake City, 1890.

Ely, Enoch Selden (1801–1890)
Ely, Ezra Sterling (1804–1897)

From 1850 to emancipation, Enoch Selden (also Sheldon) Ely and his older brother, Ezra Sterling Ely, operated a safehouse for fugitives. Born to Eunice Mindwell Noyes and Presbyterian missionary Israel Noyes Ely, known as the Bishop, the brothers were natives of Connecticut. They emigrated to New York in 1819 and settled on 1,500 acres. At Bellevue, Sterling Ely's home near Cayuga Creek, on Danforth Avenue in Cheektowaga, a village near Erie, New York, the brothers hid refugees under a false floor in the stone barn. Guarded by armed outriders, the Ely brothers transported runaways in a hay wagon along the secret line to the Bakers or to John N. McNeal at Amherst. In 1864, Selden Ely began a decade of service as Cheektowaga town supervisor.

Source

White, Truman C., ed. *History of Cheektowaga, New York.* Boston: Boston History, 1898.

Emerson, Ralph Waldo (1803–1882)
Emerson, Lydia Jackson (1802–1892)

Ralph Waldo Emerson, the leading liberal philosopher of his day, and his wife, Lydia Jackson "Lidian"

At their home in Concord, Massachusetts, Ralph Waldo Emerson and Lydia Jackson Emerson—with the Alcotts, the Thoreaus, and other abolitionist friends—sheltered slaves in flight on the route to Quebec. *(Library and Archives Canada)*

Emerson, sheltered runaway slaves fleeing via the Underground Railroad. After abandoning a pulpit career as a Unitarian minister, Ralph Waldo Emerson became a noted essayist and orator on the Lyceum lecture circuit. From 1834, the Emersons' home in Concord, Massachusetts, was a respite for refugees heading north on the New England–Canada route of the Underground Railroad. Among the couple's fellow stationkeepers were Amos Bronson Alcott and Louisa May Alcott at The Wayside and Cynthia Dunbar Thoreau and her son, Henry David Thoreau, and daughters, Helen Thoreau and Sophia Thoreau, members of the Concord Female Charitable Society. Emerson supported Cynthia Dunbar Thoreau's safehouse with donations of cash.

Passage of the Fugitive Slave Law of 1850 incited Ralph Waldo Emerson's anger and inspired an abolitionist speech delivered on May 3, 1851. The Emerson family's mood worsened after Congress passed the Kansas-Nebraska Act of 1854. Emerson's activism involved welcome to Harriet Tubman and her passengers and enlistment of volunteers to aid the American Anti-Slavery Society. He lauded the activism of agents Theodore Parker in Boston and Martha Malvina Snow Taylor and Oscar Taylor in Freeport, Illinois. Emerson denounced the assailants who struck abolitionist legislator Charles Sumner unconscious on May 22, 1856, in the U.S. Senate chamber. In 1858, Emerson donated $15 to support insurrectionist John Brown's mission on the Kansas-Missouri frontier. A few weeks before the Civil War began, Emerson addressed a heated assembly of the Massachusetts Anti-Slavery Society at Tremont Temple in Boston.

See also: American Anti-Slavery Society; Fugitive Slave Law of 1850; Kansas-Nebraska Act of 1854.

Sources

Richardson, Robert D. *Emerson.* Berkeley: University of California Press, 1995.

Rusk, Ralph L. *The Life of Ralph Waldo Emerson.* New York: Scribner, 1949.

Ennets, Maria (fl. 1850s–1860s)
Ennets, Stephen (fl. 1850s–1860s)

The Ennets family trusted their flight from bondage to Underground Railroad conductor Harriet Tubman. In 1860, Maria and Stephen Ennets escaped from slave owners John Kaiger and Algier Pearcy in Dorchester County, Maryland. According to secret operative Thomas Garrett of Wilmington, Delaware, the rescue of the Ennets and their three children—four-year-old Amanda, six-year-old Harriet, and a three-month-old baby—was Tubman's nineteenth and last rescue.

Source

Still, William. *Underground Railroad Records.* Philadelphia: Porter & Coates, 1883.

Ennis, Mary (ca. 1821–?)

Mary Ennis (also called Licia Hemmin) served 33 years as a field, barn, and kitchen slave to farmer John Ennis in Georgetown, in Sussex County, Delaware. In winter 1854, to save her daughters—seven-year-old Lydia and three-year-old Louisa Caroline—from the auction block, Mary fled with them to West Chester, Pennsylvania. The trek north in the wintry weather endangered the family. They passed through several waystations before reaching Philadelphia in spring 1854 and receiving care from the local vigilance committee.

Source

Still, William. *The Underground Railroad.* Philadelphia: Porter & Coates, 1871.

Eshleman, Jacob K. (1810–?)

In Lancaster County in southern Pennsylvania, Dr. Jacob K. Eshleman operated Station 3 of the Pilgrim's Pathway, a 17-part network of Underground Railroad safehouses. While maintaining a medical practice in Strasburg, he began aiding runaways in 1840 and became the link to the safehouse of Daniel Gibbons and Hannah Wierman Gibbons, only five miles away in Wrightsville. Eshleman also collaborated with Esther Logue Hayes and Mordecai Hayes and their son Jacob Hayes and Isaac Meredith and Thamosin Pennock Meredith in Newlin, with the Reverend Eusebius Barnard and Sarah Painter Barnard in Pocopsin, and with Martha Hobson Whitson and Thomas Whitson in Bart.

In 1848, Eshleman gave up medicine and settled outside Downingtown near the Ship Inn in Chester County, where he continued his service to the Underground Railroad by passing fugitives to John Vickers within 24 hours of their arrival. Black men tended to arrive on foot and women and children in closed carriages, by which Eshleman moved them to the next station under cover of night. Part of Eshleman's success was derived from the well-kept secrecy concerning where a runaway came from and how he or she arrived at the location. After the Christiana Riot of September 11,

1851, he hid three fugitives in his barn for the night. On one occasion, he kept mum while giving a ride to a slave owner from Belle Ayer, Maryland, whose runaways Eshleman had piloted on their way to Ontario.

See also: Christiana Riot; Pilgrim's Pathway.

Source

Smedley, Robert C. *History of the Underground Railroad in Chester and the Neighboring Counties of Pennsylvania.* Lancaster, PA: Office of *The Journal,* 1883.

Estabrook, Henry (1815–1907)

One unusual rescue by the Virginia secret network was the freeing of a white man, Lieutenant Henry Estabrook. A native of Wayne County, New York, Estabrook was a Union soldier and a prisoner of war of Confederate forces. On a train ride from Libby Prison in Richmond to Danville, Virginia, in 1864, he escaped and connected with black Underground Railroad agents. Through their contacts, he rejoined Union troops at Petersburg.

Source

Baker, Eric. "A Yankee Lieutenant Rides the Underground Railroad." *Military Images* 15:4 (1994): 12–15.

Evans, Nathan (1782–1852)
Evans, Zillah Maule (1786–1843)
Evans, David (1818–1898)

Isolated among pro-slavery farmers, Nathan Evans originally of Greenwich, New Jersey, and his wife, Zillah Maule Evans, boldly supported the temperance campaign and operated a busy Underground Railroad station at their Willistown farm in Chester County, Pennsylvania. Their son, David Evans, who aided their mission to runaways, kept an unusually detailed diary from 1835 to 1898 that included the comings and goings of slaves and conductors and lectures delivered by abolitionists Frederick Douglass and Lucretia Coffin Mott. In Quaker style, the Evans family welcomed all refugees and shared meals with them at the dinner table. They received runaways from Simon Barnard, Dr. Bartholomew Fussell, Esther Logue Hayes and Mordecai Hayes and their son Jacob Hayes, and Isaac and Thamosin Pennock Meredith in Newlin; from Joseph Painter in West Chester; and from Margaretta A. O'Daniel Woodward and Maris D. Woodward of Marshalltown in West Bradford. Assisting at the Evans station were Joshua Clendenon, Davis Garrett, Jr., and John Wright, who transported passengers in the family's curtained carriage. In 1839, Evans increased the capacity of the secret system by enlisting James T. Dannaker and James Lewis in Marple to conduct refugees.

The Evans family's dedication was apparent in their reception of large parties of refugees. One group of 26 drained family resources by remaining with the Evans for two weeks. In August 1842, David Evans left at 2 A.M. to deliver four runaways from Henry Lee, the transporter for the station of James Fulton, Jr., in Ercildoun, to Philadelphia's anti-slavery headquarters. That same year on September 27 and again on October 27, Zillah Evans completed a similar mission with two slave women and later with three men. From the Evans home, refugees continued to the station of James Lewis, Joseph Painter, or Elijah Funk Pennypacker. One traveled to Philadelphia on a hay wagon. On September 22, 1842, the Evans family welcomed a party of 25 slaves from James Fulton, Jr., under the charge of transporter Lukens Pierce. The agents separated the party into more manageable groups for delivery to Philadelphia that night. The deluge continued in late fall, with 11 coming on November 5, 1842, for transfer by Davis Garrett and William Hibbard in two carriages. For flagrant violation of fugitive slave laws, Nathan Evans suffered expulsion from the Society of Friends, but he continued regular meeting attendance and preaching.

See also: Quakers.

Source

Futhey, J. Smith, and Gilbert Cope. *History of Chester County, Pennsylvania.* Philadelphia: Louis H. Evers, 1881.

Evans, Thomas (?–1849)
Evans, Josiah Bispham (1811–1869)

A noted site on the Pennsylvania–New Jersey line, the home of Quaker abolitionist farmers Thomas Evans and his son, Josiah Bispham Evans, of Camden, New Jersey, received refugees. Thomas Evans bought property off Brace Road in Cherry Hill, New Jersey, in 1816. In 1840, the land, known as Croft Farm, passed to Josiah Evans, who welcomed slaves from the Woodbury stop and concealed them indoors in a garret or outdoors in haystacks. If slave stalkers lurked, Evans drove the newcomers to Mount Holly by covered farm wagon. When authorities stopped him during the relay of Jefferson Fisher and Joshua Sadler to the Mount Holly depot, Josiah Evans bought the men's freedom. The former slaves worked at Evans's gristmill and sawmill to reimburse his expenses. Sadler founded Sadlertown, a district in Haddon Township. In 1995, local officials dedicated the Evans waystation as the Cherry Hill Arts Center.

Sources

Haines, George. *Ancestry of the Haines, Sharp, Collins Families.* Camden, NJ: Sinnickson, Chew & Sons, 1902.

Hinshaw, William Wade. *Encyclopedia of American Quaker Genealogy.* Ann Arbor, MI: Edwards Brothers, 1936.

Evans, Wilson Bruce (1824–1898)
Evans, Henry (1817–ca. 1890)

A respected abolitionist, Wilson Bruce Evans operated a funeral parlor and a station of the Underground Railroad in Oberlin, Ohio. A native of Fayetteville, in Orange County, North Carolina, he earned his living at carpentry and cabinetmaking. He and his brother, Henry Evans, a mortician, married sisters, Sarah Jane Leary and Henrietta R. Leary, respectively. The two families settled in Ohio near the men's sister, Delilah Evans Copeland, the mother of John Anthony Copeland, Jr., who superintended refugee assistance in Lorain County, Ohio.

At a two-story brick safehouse at 33 East Vine Street, Wilson Evans collaborated on slave rescues with his brother-in-law, Lewis Sheridan Leary, who died during John Brown's failed raid on the federal arsenal at Harpers Ferry, Virginia, on October 16, 1859. Both Henry Evans and Wilson Evans took part in the Oberlin-Wellington rescue of John Price on September 13, 1858. Wilson Evans's next-door neighbor, Chauncey Wack, opposed abolitionism and aided the prosecution at the trial of Price's rescuers. The brothers served 84 days in jail before a judge dropped all charges. Wilson Evans fought in the Civil War on the Union side. His house is a National Historic Landmark.

Sources

Blodgett, David. *Oberlin Architecture, College and Town: A Guide to Its Social History.* Kent, OH: Kent State University Press, 1985.

Fairchild, James H. *Oberlin: The Colony and the College 1833–1883.* Oberlin, OH: E.J. Goodrich, 1883.

Fairbank, Calvin (1816–1898)

A Methodist minister, the Reverend Calvin Fairbank, risked imprisonment, torture, and martyrdom to aid black fugitives. He came of age in Wyoming County, New York, and learned about slave flight at Methodist meetings. At age 21, he conducted his first rescue via lumber raft on the Ohio River. Fairbank collaborated with Quaker leader Levi Coffin but concealed from authorities the human links in the secret rescue chain that guided a total of 47 refugees from Kentucky and Virginia to freedom. One of Fairbank's rescues, a light-skinned woman named Eliza, signaled him from the upstairs window of Megowan's Hotel, a Lexington slave pen. With the $2,000 that he had solicited from philanthropists Salmon Portland Chase, Levi Coffin, and Nicholas Longworth, Fairbank led the bidding for Eliza against a French slave buyer from New Orleans. The lurid auction involved the baring of Eliza's breast and thighs to raise the price. After Fairbank obtained ownership, he conducted Eliza to Cincinnati, Ohio, where she passed into white society and married well.

While studying at Oberlin College, on September 28, 1844, Fairbank accepted a challenge from Bishop John Mifflin Brown to free the Kentucky family of Gilson Berry from enslavement. Fairbank traveled to Lexington and joined his fiancée, Delia Ann Webster, a teacher at Lexington Female Academy. Together they attempted to retrieve the family but gave up after Berry's wife failed to arrive at the appointed place and time. That same day, they piloted Harriet Bell Hayden and Lewis Hayden and their son, Jo, who had fled from town in a carriage driven by a slave named Israel during the bustling horse-racing season. The escape began late in the afternoon; a sprinkling of flour concealed their black hands and faces. Driving all night with the child crouching under the carriage seat, the group reached Washington, Kentucky, three miles from the state border, before sunrise. Agent James Helm rowed the Haydens across the Ohio River to the free side and left the runaways in the care of stationmasters Jean Lowry Rankin and John Rankin of Liberty Hill, in Ripley, Ohio. From there, passengers moved north immediately to a Quaker depot at Sandusky, Ohio.

Both Webster and Fairbank were arrested before they could return to Lexington. An angry pro-slavery mob roiled outside the jail. After a flogging, Israel, the drayman, confessed to the plot. The authorities locked Webster in an upstairs cell at Megowan's Hotel and placed Fairbank in irons. A court found Fairbanks and Webster guilty of complicity in a slave escape. Delia Webster began a two-year sentence at the Kentucky state penitentiary in Frankfort in December 1844 but gained her freedom on February 24, 1845, with a pardon from Governor John J. Crittenden.

A veteran conductor, Fairbank admitted guilt but pretended to disavow abolitionism. He began a 15-year sentence—five years for each of the three Haydens—at hard labor cutting stone. Owing to his attempted jailbreaks, his cell block required high security. He relied on his father, Chester Fairbank, to mediate with authorities. Calvin Fairbank's incarceration ended with Governor Crittenden's pardon on August 23, 1849. Fairbank followed the Underground Railroad route to Madison, Indiana, and on to Detroit, Michigan. After arriving home in New York, he traveled to Kentucky to retrieve the body of his father, who had died on July 7, 1849, during a cholera outbreak.

Fairbank continued corresponding with abolitionist editors and agitating for emancipation of slaves. Freemason James R. Cunningham of Louisville helped Fairbank rescue Tamar Shotwell, a 22-year-old refugee from Louisville, Kentucky, owned by merchant Alfred Lawrence Shotwell. Authorities arrested Fairbank in Jeffersonville, Indiana; a court returned him to prison on November 9, 1851. The event was the lead story in the December 4, 1851, issue of the *Arkansas Whig*, which referred to Fairbank as a "notorious reverend." Flogged and beaten, he suffered solitary confinement, a persecution reported in the autobiography of the Reverend John Gregg Fee, a fellow conductor who visited Fairbank in prison. Secret network agents Levi Coffin and Catherine "Kittie" Doram raised funds to secure Fairbank's release.

Despite his sufferings, Fairbank led chapel services for fellow inmates. He received Lieutenant Governor Richard T. Jacob's pardon from the Kentucky state penitentiary on April 15, 1864. More than 17 years of brutal prison treatment blinded and weakened Fairbank, who had aided 47 fugitive blacks to escape to freedom. Eight years before his death, he published *Rev. Calvin Fairbank During Slavery Times: How He "Fought the Good Fight" to Prepare "the Way"* (1890). He moved to Florence, Massachusetts, married, and, at age 82, died a pauper in Angelica, New York.

See also: abolitionism; Oberlin College.

Sources

Fairbank, Calvin. *Rev. Calvin Fairbank During Slavery Times: How He "Fought the Good Fight" to Prepare "the Way."* Chicago: R.R. McCabe, 1890.

Fee, John Gregg. *Autobiography of John G. Fee: Berea, Kentucky.* Chicago: National Christian Association, 1891.

Fairfield, John (?–1861)

A shadowy transporter of runaways, Virginian John Fairfield supervised an Underground Railroad route in western Virginia linking to Ohio and Indiana. Fairfield was born to slaveholders but disavowed his family's southern heritage. In the guise of a poultry buyer with pro-slavery sentiments, he conducted runaways across the Appalachian Mountains to liberty. To ensure a safe passage, he stocked makeup and horsehair wigs to disguise the passengers he relayed from Harpers Ferry, Virginia, to Pittsburgh, Pennsylvania.

At a high point in his volunteerism, in the 1840s, Fairfield received a party of 28 and conducted them in three skiffs over the Ohio River at its juncture with the Miami River. The final yards of the rescue forced Fairfield out of a boat into quicksand at the shoals, where black refugees pulled him to safety. In a cold drizzle, the passengers continued on to Cincinnati, Ohio. Some walked barefoot because they had lost their shoes in the passage. Fairfield sought the assistance of conductor John Hatfield, who summoned Catherine White Coffin and Levi Coffin. The relay continued in a procession of buggies and carriages that simulated a funeral cortege. Fairfield's courtship of danger concluded shortly before the Civil War, when he was reported killed during a slave rescue in Tennessee.

See also: disguise.

Sources

Coffin, Levi. *Reminiscences of Levi Coffin, the Reputed President of the Underground Railroad.* Cincinnati, OH: Western Tract Society, 1876.

Griffler, Keith P. *Front Line of Freedom: African Americans and the Forging of the Underground Railroad in the Ohio Valley.* Lexington: University Press of Kentucky, 2004.

Fairies, Robert (1834–?)

Conductor Robert Fairies of Williamsport, Pennsylvania, passed Underground Railroad passengers to railcars. He worked in collaboration with agents of the Haines family at Wolf Run House in Lycoming County. As president of the Williamsport-Elmira Railroad, Fairies had the authority and the means to conceal refugees in baggage cars.

Source

Wolny, Philip. *The Underground Railroad: A Primary Resource History of the Journey to Freedom.* New York: Rosen, 2004.

Falls, William S. (?–1884)

William S. Falls of Monroe County, New York, used his workplace as a sanctuary for refugees. While living at 63 Chestnut Street with his wife, Anne E. Falls, in 1844, he went into the printing business and advanced to publication of the *Advertiser* in 1849. While producing the *Daily Democrat* at his print shop at Nine Elmwood Block in Rochester, he concealed slaves in the pressroom, which shared space with Frederick Douglass's newspaper, the *North Star.* In 1857, Falls was promoted to foreman of the *Daily Democrat.* In 1865, he published the annual report of the Rochester Ladies' Anti-Slavery Society.

See also: North Star.

Source

Ripley, C. Peter, et al., eds. *The Black Abolitionist Papers.* Chapel Hill: University of North Carolina Press, 1992.

Farmer, Hannah Shapleigh Tobey (1823–1891)
Farmer, Moses Gerrish (1820–1893)

Abolitionist Hannah Shapleigh Tobey Farmer of Berwick, Maine, and her husband, inventor Moses Gerrish Farmer of Boscawen, New Hampshire, promoted social reform with cash donations and activism. The couple married at Christmas in 1844. At their residence on the Piscataqua River in Eliot, in York County, Maine, they aided fugitives fleeing along the New England–Quebec route of the Underground Railroad. The couple collaborated with Harriet Beecher Stowe, Sojourner Truth, and John Greenleaf Whittier, publisher of the *New York Tribune.* A year after Hannah Farmer's death, a Boston company published her memoirs, *The Rich Legacy: Memories of Hannah Tobey Farmer* (1892).

Sources

Elliott, Margaret A. *Eliot.* Charleston, SC: Arcadia, 2005.
Farmer, Hannah Shapleigh Tobey. *The Rich Legacy: Memories of Hannah Tobey Farmer.* Boston: G.H. Ellis, 1892.

Farnham, Elisha (1806–1875)
Farnham, Mary Ring (1817–1849)

Elisha Farnham and his wife, Mary Ring Farnham, aided fugitive slaves journeying the Ohio–Canada route of the Underground Railroad. The son and grandson of veterans of the American Revolution, Elisha Farnham migrated to Ohio at age 19 and operated a carding mill, a gristmill, and a lumberyard on Conneaut Creek. While living in Conneaut, he was a justice of the peace and a supporter of fugitive slaves. Influencing his service were friendships with attorneys Benjamin Franklin Wade and Joshua Reed Giddings, both agents of the secret network. During the Civil War, the Farnhams' son, Don Alphonzo Farnham, died of tuberculosis in 1862 after serving the Second Ohio Battery.

Source

Upton, Harriet Taylor, and Harry Gardner Cutler. *History of the Western Reserve.* New York: Lewis, 1910.

Fatal, John J. (1816–1904)

An Afro-Caribbean laborer and supporter of the Underground Railroad, John J. Fatal joined dedicated agents in transporting slaves through Boston, Massachusetts. He managed the conveyance of refugees to Canada or over the New England route to Vermont. As a member of the Boston Vigilance Committee, in 1842, he supported the rescue of George W. Latimer and Rebecca Latimer, who eluded their owner, merchant James B. Gray in Norfolk, Virginia, on October 4, 1842. The public outrage at the stalking of runaways won public support for the secret network. In league with Joshua Bowen Smith and William Cooper Nell, Fatal crusaded for the education of the children of runaway slaves. Angered that integration efforts failed, he moved to 49 Lincoln Street in Cambridge and earned his living as a porter at a furniture store. After the Civil War, he opened his own home furnishings store.

Source

Obituary of John J. Fatal, *Boston Transcript,* March 19, 1904.

Fayerweather, George, III (ca. 1803–1869)
Fayerweather, Sarah Ann Harris (1812–1878)

One of the laboring-class black couples who supported the Underground Railroad, West Indian blacksmith George Fayerweather and his wife, Sarah Ann Harris Fayerweather of Norwich, Connecticut, set aside funds to help black slaves. Sarah Fayerweather developed libertarian ideals while attending the integrated girls' school founded by Prudence Crandall in Canterbury, Connecticut. After moving from New Haven, Connecticut, to Mooresfield Road in South Kingston, Rhode Island, in 1855, the Fayerweathers supported the Kingston (Rhode Island) Anti-Slavery Society. They considered rescues a sacred mission and gained tips on the conductor's work from reading issues of the *National Anti-Slavery Standard,* the *Colored American, The Liberator,* and the *New York Tribune.* Under the influence of abolitionist William Lloyd Garrison, the Fayerweathers and their six children attended anti-slavery rallies and managed a safehouse. Whatever demands runaways made on the family budget, Sarah Fayerweather supplied the needs of the hour, whether a place to sleep, first aid, a jail visit, food, or disguises. A dormitory at the University of Rhode Island bears Sarah Fayerweather's name.

See also: disguise; *Liberator, The.*

Sources
Brown, Hallie Quinn. *Homespun Heroines and Other Women of Distinction.* Xenia, OH: Aldine, 1926.
Van Broekhoven, Deborah Bingham. *The Devotion of These Women: Rhode Island in the Antislavery Network.* Amherst: University of Massachusetts Press, 2002.

Fee, Arthur (1791–1879)
Fee, Sarah Miller (1798–1873)

A cousin of the abolitionist conductors Oliver Perry Spencer Fee, Robert E. Fee, and Nancy Fee Pease, activist Arthur Fee and his wife, Sarah Miller "Sally" Fee, contributed sanctuary to the aid of runaway slaves. The couple operated a two-story frame safehouse at One Moore's Lane in Felicity, Ohio. They hid refugees in their fruit cellar before leading them to Bethel, Ohio.

Source
Everts, Louis H. *History of Clermont County, Ohio.* Philadelphia: J.B. Lippincott, 1880.

Fee, John Gregg (1816–1901)
Fee, Matilda Hamilton (1821–1895)

A member of an Anglo-Scots abolitionist clan, the Reverend John Gregg Fee, a disciple of Levi Coffin, suffered banishment and mob violence in the name of universal brotherhood. A native of Bracken County, Kentucky, Fee developed a distaste for slavery in boyhood and actively opposed the Fugitive Slave Law of 1850. He stated his anti-slavery position in *An Anti-Slavery Manual; or, The Wrongs of American Slavery Exposed by the Light of the Bible and of Facts, with a Remedy for the Evil* (1851). The text chastised churches for refusing to aid runaways and exonerated Underground Railroad agents for breaking a federal law by assisting and succoring refugees.

After establishing a Presbyterian ministry in Bracken County, the Reverend Fee, aided by Arnold Gragston, a boatman from Mason County, Kentucky, conducted refugees in earnest. Fee began his outreach to slaves by buying Julett Miles, a bondswoman of his father. The purchase created enmity between father and son that resulted in John Fee's disinheritance. In his autobiography, John Fee described the escape of Miles and her children and grandchildren over the Ohio River. She fled shortly before her owner traded all his chattel to a slave buyer. After Miles's imprisonment for stealing her family, Matilda Fee visited her in jail before Miles's transport to the Kentucky state penitentiary at Frankfort. The Fees also consoled Calvin Fairbank, a prisoner serving a 20-year sentence at hard labor for aiding slave flight. Although the Fees were banished from Berea in December 1859 for lauding John Brown's raid on Harpers Ferry, Virginia, the couple founded the racially integrated Berea College and continued their ministry to blacks during and after the Civil War.

See also: Fugitive Slave Law of 1850.

Sources
Fee, John Gregg. *An Anti-Slavery Manual.* New York: William Harned, 1851.
———. *Autobiography of John G. Fee: Berea, Kentucky.* Chicago: National Christian Association, 1891.

Fee, Oliver Perry Spencer (1823–1873)

A scion of pioneer William Fee, abolitionist storekeeper Oliver Perry Spencer Fee was part of the activist Fee family in Felicity, in Clermont County, Ohio. From his residence on Main Street, he superintended the reception and dispersal of runaways. To allow time for safe relays to Bethel, Ohio, he misdirected posses. During the stays of fugitives at his home, he provided food and clothing from his store. In 1869, Fletcher Day, the editor of the *Felicity Times,* stated that slaves who reached the network in Felicity were safe from recapture.

Source
Schaefer, Walt, "Clermont Discovers Role on the Underground Railroad," *Cincinnati (OH) Enquirer,* December 9, 1999.

Fee, Robert E. (1796–1879)
Fee, Thomas, Sr. (1763–1816)
Fee, Thomas, Jr. (1801–1862)

A member of an activist family, Robert E. Fee conducted slaves from his home in Moscow, in Clermont County, Ohio. Also involved in the family tradition of rescues were his father, Thomas Fee, Sr., of Maryland; a brother, Thomas Fee, Jr.; and a cousin, Arthur Fee and his wife Sarah Miller Fee, in Felicity, Ohio. According to Nancy Fee Pease, the daughter of Thomas Fee, Sr., her father received a party of six refugees in the last years of his life. Nancy performed her share of the rescue work from the medical office of her husband, Dr. Leavitt Thaxter Pease in Williamsburg, Ohio. Contributing to the local effort was farmer

Jacob Ebersole in Felicity, the brother of Robert Fee's wife, Catherine Ebersole Fee (1802–1877). Thomas Fee, Jr., maintained the two-story family home in Moscow and signaled to fugitives along the Ohio River by lighting candles in the window.

Robert Fee managed operations from his residence on Water Street, where he, like his brother, kept candles lit in the windows from dusk to dawn. For protection against armed posses, each family member slept near loaded firearms. The Fees relayed passengers north to Tate Township to the waystations of Isaac Holmes Brown, Richard Mace, Benjamin Rice, and the Reverend Gerrard Policarp Riley in Bethel. Robert Fee took part in a failed rescue of Fanny Wigglesworth and her four children, who had been kidnapped from the Wigglesworth residence on Big Indian Road by two slave hunters, William Moore and William Middleton. Representing freedman Vincent Wigglesworth, on November 4, 1852, Fee collaborated with Ohio State Senator Doughty Utter and U.S. legislator David Fisher at Calvary Methodist Church. Fee scouted Missouri to locate the Wigglesworth family but never found them. During the hunt, a mob threatened his life. The kidnappers were not charged. The loss began Fee's regular service to the Underground Railroad. In 1852, a grand jury in Pendleton County, Kentucky, charged Fee with abetting slave escape. The Ohio governor refused to extradite Fee to the South to stand trial.

The son of conductor Thomas Fee, Sr., the younger Thomas Fee maintained a waystation in Moscow, Ohio. Like his siblings, Robert E. Fee and Nancy Fee Pease, Thomas Fee, Jr., was a devout abolitionist. From his two-story home on Water Street, he signaled refugees with lit candles in upstairs windows. He welcomed wanderers to his cellar and provided meals and clothing from his own dry goods store before ferrying them to his cousins in Felicity.

See also: kidnap; slave recovery.

Sources

Everts, Louis H. *History of Clermont County, Ohio.* Philadelphia: J.B. Lippincott, 1880.

Leckey, Howard L. *The Tenmile Country and Its Pioneer Families.* Knightstown, IN: Bookmark, 1977.

female anti-slavery societies

Lacking economic, professional, and political clout, U.S. and Canadian women in the first quarter of the nineteenth century began asserting their domestic, ethical, and organizational skills in service to fugitive slaves. In the September 2, 1826, issue of *Genius of Universal Emancipation,* an anonymous letter from a North Carolina reader urged the founding of more female abolition societies by both white and black women. In 1833, Philadelphians Margaretta Forten, Abigail Kimber, and platform orator Lucretia Coffin Mott formed the Pennsylvania Female Anti-Slavery Society, as the embodiment of a feminist concept that spread among women excluded from the American Anti-Slavery Society. Among the members was Hester Reckless, who operated a safehouse on Rodman Street in Philadelphia. In Boston, Maria Weston Chapman, editor of the Massachusetts Anti-Slavery Society house organ *Right and Wrong in Massachusetts,* co-founded a Massachusetts chapter; in 1835, Betsey Mix Cowles led the Female Anti-Slavery Society of Ashtabula County, Ohio. Branches of women's auxiliaries gained moral strength and practical wisdom from Underground Railroad conductors Elizabeth Buffum Chace, Abby Kelley Foster, Angelina and Sarah Grimké, Margaret Hise, and Sarah Parker Remond. Contributing the perspective of a rescued slave was Eliza Jane Johnson, a member of the female anti-slavery society in Ripley, Ohio. In addition, black members of the Union Anti-Slavery Sewing Society sold handmade crafts, pastries, and needlework to support Frederick Douglass's abolitionist newspaper, the *North Star.*

The success of female anti-slavery societies derived from women's networking. In 1834, Underground Railroad supporter Comfort Hussey Winslow opened her home in Portland, Maine, to meetings that involved agents Lydia Neal Dennett and Elizabeth Widgery Thomas. Some volunteers enlisted others to the cause, as was the case with Elizabeth Margaret Chandler and Laura Smith Haviland in New York City; Lucy Coleman and Amy Kirby Post in Rochester, New York; and Lucretia Coffin Mott and Hester Reckless in Philadelphia. In August 1836, the Boston Female Anti-Slavery Society achieved the liberation of Med Slater from bondage in New Orleans, by hiring Ellis Gray Loring and Samuel Edmund Sewall to defend her in court. In 1837, the Pennsylvania Anti-Slavery Society ended gender discrimination and received women into the hierarchy, including Underground Railroad agent Sarah Pugh from New Garden. Family teams such as Charlotte Forten and her daughter, Harriet Forten Purvis in Philadelphia; Ann Terry Greene Phillips and her husband, orator Wendell Addison Phillips, in Boston; Lemuel

Stephens and Sarah Morton Stephens and their widowed daughter, Phoebe Stephens Cotton, at Plymouth, New York; Sally Wilson and Samuel Wilson in Cincinnati, Ohio; and Rachel Gilpin Robinson and Rowland Thomas Robinson in Ferrisburg, Vermont, reflected the involvement of households as rescuers and caretakers of runaways.

Membership in abolitionist societies often involved whole families. Susan Farley Porter presided over the Rochester Ladies Anti-Slavery Sewing Society, which involved her sister, Martha Farley Peck, and sisters-in-law, Maria G. Porter and Laura G. Porter Farley. By 1840, the acceptance of women in the American Anti-Slavery Society added seasoned abolitionists to formerly all-male groups. One new member, Lydia Mott of Albany, New York, received a donation from Lucretia Coffin Mott of the Philadelphia Female Anti-Slavery Society to enlarge the treasury for buying food, clothing, and medicines. In 1847, female members in Portland, Maine, formed a bodyguard to rescue three orators, Frederick Douglass, William Lloyd Garrison, and Charles Lenox Remond, from pro-slavery rowdies at the Quaker meetinghouse.

See also: abolitionist newspapers; American Anti-Slavery Society; Anti-Slavery Convention of American Women; *North Star*; Pennsylvania Anti-Slavery Society.

Source

Hewitt, Nancy A. *Women's Activism and Social Change: Rochester, New York, 1822–1872.* Ithaca, NY: Cornell University Press, 1984.

Fessenden (Samuel and Deborah Chandler) Family

A prominent family of activists, ministers, attorneys, and patriots in Portland, in Cumberland County, Maine, General Samuel Fessenden (1784–1869), his wife, Deborah Chandler Fessenden (1792–1873), and their sons—Daniel Webster (1821–1887), Samuel Clement (1815–1882), and William Pitt (1806–1869)—maintained a safehouse for runaway slaves. At age 48, Samuel Fessenden joined the American Anti-Slavery Society and the Underground Railroad effort after hearing a speech at the First Parish Unitarian Church by William Lloyd Garrison, editor of *The Liberator.* The Fessendens welcomed refugees to the family waystation at 31 India Street. In 1840, Samuel Fessenden began a four-year term as vice president of the American Anti-Slavery Society.

One of the family's hush-hush relays involved the rescue of a black stowaway aboard the HMS *Albion Cooper,* a British cargo ship carrying lumber from Savannah, Georgia, in fall 1857. The ship docked at the Franklin Street wharf. Captain D.R. Humphrey, fearing imprisonment and the confiscation of his brig by federal marshals, called for help from Portland's secret network, led by Daniel Fessenden and including Charles H.L. Pierre, a hack driver on Middle Street, and Samuel Waterhouse, a clothier on Fore Street. The group, with the aid of B.D. Peck, the editor of the *Temperance Reporter,* staged a riot: they summoned a band of abolitionists to raid the brig by night and take custody of the slave. Through teamwork of the secret network, Daniel Fessenden passed the refugee to safety in Quebec.

See also: American Anti-Slavery Society; *Liberator, The.*

Sources

Brown, Harrison, "Underground Railroad Once Was Busy Maine 'Device,'" *Portland (ME) Evening Express,* February 12, 1963, 11.

Varney, George J. *History of Portland, Maine.* Boston: B.B. Russell, 1886.

Fidget, Isaac (1825–?)

In flight from bondage in Worcester County, Maryland, 30-year-old Isaac Fidget found freedom in Canada. In 1855, joined by Oliver Purnell, Fidget made a run north to locate his wife, who had run away in previous months. Fidget and Purnell reached Pennsylvania and sought advice and aid from William Still at the office of the Philadelphia Vigilance Committee.

Source

Still, William. *The Underground Railroad.* Philadelphia: Porter & Coates, 1871.

Fields, Henry (1841–?)

In his late teens, Henry Fields escaped a cruel taskmaster with aid from the Underground Railroad. In 1859, he fled the predations of Washington Glasby and the possibility of being sold. From Port Deposit in Cecil County, Maryland, Fields made his way north via a secret route passing through the vigilance committee office in Philadelphia, Pennsylvania.

Source

Still, William. *The Underground Railroad.* Philadelphia: Porter & Coates, 1871.

Filer, Thomas (1803–?)
Filer, Permelia Barnes (1809–?)

Pioneer farmer and laborer Thomas Filer and his wife, Permelia (or Pamelia) Barnes Filer, contributed to the Underground Railroad cause. The couple married in 1832. Around 1840, the Filers moved from upstate New York to Lombard, in Du Page County, Illinois, with their two sons and one daughter. A second daughter was born in Illinois. Colleagues of conductors at Wheaton College and of Sheldon Peck in Lombard, Filer and his wife operated a waystation built in 1840 a mile away from Lombard on Crescent Boulevard in Glen Ellyn. A cubby under the stairs and double floors provided emergency concealment. Runaways followed a shaft to the basement or slipped down a tunnel to a specially built barn and boarded produce wagons bound for Tremont House in Chicago. Aiding a safe passage were agents Anne Thompson Carpenter and Philo R. Carpenter on Lake Street and Dr. Charles Volney Dyer and Louisa Maria Dyer at 27 State Street in Chicago.

Source

Taylor, Glennette Tilley. *The Underground Railroad in Illinois.* Glen Ellyn, IL: Newman Educational, 2001.

Fillmore, Millard (1800–1874)

President Millard Fillmore's name appears on both sides of the issue of human bondage. His term of office, from 1850 to 1853, placed him in power during a sharp uptick in Underground Railroad activity. From the day he took oath, he tried to strike a balance to prevent civil war and lawbreaking. Although he supported the anti-abolition efforts of his cousin, the Reverend Glezen Fillmore of the Methodist Episcopal church in Buffalo, New York, Millard Fillmore loathed slavery and donated money to the Freedmen's Aid Society.

A critical point in Fillmore's presidency, his signing of the Fugitive Slave Law on September 18, 1850, drew a warning from his wife, Abigail Powers Fillmore, who foresaw serious consequences. Her prediction rapidly became a White House nightmare. Abolitionists scorned Fillmore and denounced his presidency. Conductors in Buffalo shunned him for his denial of trial by jury to black refugees. The Reverend Jermaine Wesley Loguen proclaimed, "I don't respect this law—I don't fear it—I won't obey it! It outlaws me and I outlaw it." Loguen dared President Fillmore to call out his bloodhounds, a satiric reference to U.S. marshals.

After network coordinator Lewis Hayden and John J. Smith, a barber, coordinated the seizure of Fredric "Shadrach" Minkins from the Boston courthouse on February 15, 1851, the collaboration of 20 black agents and supporters of the Underground Railroad earned a stern rebuke from President Fillmore. He was particularly riled at the commentary of journalist William Lloyd Garrison, who issued an article in *The Liberator* on February 21, 1851, condoning civil disobedience. In retort to scofflaws, the president called for patriots to join the search for Minkins and instructed federal marshals to arraign and prosecute all lawbreakers who interfered in the recapture. In fairness to the former president, historians note that Fillmore pardoned Captain Daniel Drayton, who served four years in prison for attempting one of the largest mass slave escapes in U.S. history on April 15, 1848, by transporting 77 runaways aboard the sloop *Pearl* from Georgetown, in the District of Columbia, to New Jersey. Fillmore's antipathy toward abolitionism advanced from simmer to boil after the Christiana Riot of September 11, 1851. Irate at the men who defied federal law, he lambasted the participants—Castner Hanway, Elijah Lewis, Joseph P. Scarlett, and 35 blacks—for their lawlessness and violence.

See also: abolitionism; Christiana Riot; civil disobedience; Fugitive Slave Law of 1850; *Liberator, The.*

Sources

Scarry, Robert J. *Millard Fillmore.* Jefferson, NC: McFarland, 2001.
Zinn, Howard. *Passionate Declarations: Essays on War and Justice.* New York: HarperCollins, 2003.

Finney, John (1801–1888)
Finney, Elenor Marshal (?–1857)

A man of strong temperance and abolitionist convictions, for a quarter century, John Finney, known as Uncle John, rescued slaves passing through Springfield, Ohio. A native of Fayette County, Pennsylvania, of Scotch-Irish ancestry, at age 19, he immigrated to Harrison County, Ohio, with his father, two brothers, and three sisters. John Finney and Elenor Marshal married in 1825 and made their home in Richland

County, Ohio, where John became a trustee of the Mansfield Presbytery. While raising wheat on a farm adjoining that of John's brother James, Elenor and John Finney came under the influence of abolitionist attorney Salmon Portland Chase. The Finneys established a waystation on Walker Lake Road at a busy point on the Underground Railroad route between Kentucky and Ontario.

Aiding the Finneys were friends and neighbors, including Mathias Day, Isaac Miller, Joseph Roe, Thomas Thaker, and James Wood. One dangerous passage involved tricking six pursuers armed with pistols. The Finneys hid six women in the upstairs of their residence; the five males of the group, armed by John with pitchforks, occupied the granary. While stalling until a warrant arrived, Finney summoned local supporters. The black men fled to the woods; Finney relocated the women to Jane Woods Roe and Joseph Roe's safehouse outside Springfield. After the women pushed on to the home of James Wood, Roe pretended to help the slave hunters scour the county for the 11 fugitives.

The Finneys usually received passengers by wagon from agents Samuel and Sarah Allen McCluer in Troy Township, from Quaker conductors in Morrow County, and from the Benjamin Gass settlement in Manners-Sutton Parish. Most arrivals stayed a few days before Finney transported them by farm wagon to Oberlin, in Lorain County, or to Savannah, in Ashland County, Ohio. One of the rescues involved the son of a Mr. Greene from Tennessee. After Greene died, his two sons quarreled over instructions in the father's will to free all chattel. The good-hearted son aided the family slaves to escape and fled from his brother, who stalked him to Ohio. Finney helped the white emancipator find safety in Ontario.

When slave hunters arrived from Kentucky early one morning at the Finney farm, John Finney urged them to come in for buckwheat cakes, maple molasses, and homemade sausage. He began the meal with a long prayer. Meanwhile, he hinted to his servant that it was a good time for the runaways hiding in the barn to make their escape. Before ending the morning worship, Finney read Psalm 119, the longest psalm in the Bible. He concluded his friendly gestures by showing the visitors about his farm and outbuildings.

See also: bloodhounds.

Sources

Graham, A.A., comp. *History of Richland County, Ohio: Its Past and Present.* Mansfield, OH: A.A. Graham, 1880.

"Uncle John Finney." *Mansfield Herald* 34, no. 16 (March 6, 1884).

Finney, Seymour (1813–1899)

As manager of the Underground Railroad route through Detroit, Michigan, to Windsor, Ontario, abolitionist Seymour Finney served one of the busiest crossing points. A tailor and taverner, he moved from New York to Detroit, in Wayne County, Michigan, and began receiving passengers in 1832 at the Temperance Hotel, his three-story inn at Gratiot and Woodward streets. To distract slave nabbers, he offered whiskey and prostitutes. According to agent William Lambert, Finney aided in the rescue of Robert Cromwell from the Detroit courthouse in February 1840. Finney built a livery stable at 46 State Street in 1846 that until national emancipation served as a waystation for fugitives before they crossed the Detroit River to freedom.

Sources

Burton, Clarence Monroe. *The City of Detroit, Michigan, 1701–1922.* Detroit, MI: S.J. Clarke, 1922.

"Successful Working of the Underground Railroad," *Detroit Daily Post,* February 7, 1870.

Fish, Benjamin (1797–1882)
Fish, Sarah Davids Bills (1798–1868)

A radical Quaker couple, Benjamin Fish of Foster, Rhode Island, and Sarah Davids Bills Fish of Bridgetown, New Jersey, reared their family to show compassion for black refugees. After their marriage in 1822, they collaborated with seasoned conductors, including Elias and Rhoda DeGarmo, Frederick Douglass, Mary H. Post Hallowell and William R. Hallowell, and Amy Kirby Post and Isaac Post. At their farm and plant nursery in Rochester, New York, with the aid of their daughters Catharine Ann Fish (1823–1875) and Mary Braithwaite Fish (1826–1873), the Fishes managed one of the city's first waystations of the Underground Railroad. For their efforts, they were evicted from the Genesee Quaker assembly. Catharine Fish began her activism for human rights at age 12, when she circulated anti-slavery petitions. By 1842, she was a contributing member of the Western New York Anti-Slavery Society.

Sources

Hewitt, Nancy A. *Women's Activism and Social Change: Rochester, New York, 1822–1872.* Ithaca, NY: Cornell University Press, 1984.

Reisem, Richard O. "Women's Rights: The Mount Hope Connection." *Epitaph* 18, no. 3 (Summer 1998): 1.

Fisher, John (1825–?)

Freedman John Fisher (also called Robert Fisher or John Roberts) of Worcester County, Maryland, served six years in prison for conducting a slave woman to liberty. After his indenture on March 8, 1829, to farmer Henry Jones, Fisher worked in Baltimore as a day laborer. At age 27, he was arrested and tried for helping Eliza Cook, the chattel of George Stewart, flee Anne Arundel County, Maryland. Fisher entered the state penitentiary on April 21, 1852, and regained his freedom in 1858.

Source

Prison records, Maryland State Archives.

Fisher, Robert (1820–?)

A runaway aided by Underground Railroad agent William Still, Robert Fisher escaped after three decades of bondage. In December 1854, he joined Nathan Harris in eluding John E. Jackson, a farmer in Anne Arundel County, Maryland. After Christmas, the two raced over a wintry landscape to Pennsylvania, where Still managed an office of the Philadelphia Anti-Slavery Society.

Source

Still, William. *The Underground Railroad.* Philadelphia: Porter & Coates, 1871.

Fitzhugh, Claggett (1834–?)

Claggett Fitzhugh earned his living capturing passengers of the Underground Railroad on the dividing line between the North and the South. In a wooded area of Mont Alto near Quincy, Pennsylvania, he joined Dan Logan in stalking John E. Cook and Albert Hazlett, two confederates of insurrectionist John Brown's foiled raid on Harpers Ferry, Virginia, on October 16, 1859. The bounty hunters arrested Cook and Hazlett on October 25 in Chambersburg, Pennsylvania.

Source

Hinton, Richard Josiah. *John Brown and His Men: With Some Account of the Roads They Travelled to Reach Harpers Ferry.* New York: Funk & Wagnalls, ca. 1894.

Flanders, Cyrus Nathan (1810–1887)
Flanders, Joanna Jones (1810–1870)

Cyrus Nathan Flanders, a native of Salisbury, Massachusetts, and his wife, Joanna Jones Flanders, received runaway slaves at their home on the Kansas frontier. The couple married in June 1834. In 1856, they left Boston and built a farmhouse at what is now Ohio and Southeast 29th streets in Shawnee County, Kansas, where they joined the Methodist church. Most of the fugitives passing through their station arrived from Missouri.

Source

Connelley, William E., comp. *A Standard History of Kansas and Kansans.* Chicago: Lewis, 1918.

Fleming, Benjamin Bass (1782–1870)

A mulatto freedman from Lewistown, Delaware, Benjamin Fleming aided refugee passengers of the Underground Railroad. Born of Afro-Scots heritage, he worked in his youth as a crewman of coasters and pilot boats. During the War of 1812, he joined the crew of the U.S. brig *Niagara* in the Great Lakes region. After retiring to Erie, Pennsylvania, he settled at Presque Isle Bay and with his Afro-Indian wife, Catherine McKinney Fleming, supported runaways on the final leg of their journey over Lake Erie to freedom.

Source

Gensheimer, Lisa, and Rich Gensheimer, prod. *Safe Harbor.* DVD. North East, PA: Main Street Media, 2003.

Flint, Samuel H. (1820–?)

Samuel H. Flint of Boston offered assistance to passengers of the Underground Railroad. While living at Nine Southac Street, he worked as a waiter, a laborer, and an operator of a boardinghouse. As a colleague of black agents Lewis Hayden, Leonard Andrew Grimes, and John Swett Rock, Flint joined the Boston Vigilance Committee, a benevolent society aiding runaway slaves. On Janaury 3, 1851, Flint boarded a runaway named Thomas along with the man's wife and two children.

Source

Ripley, C. Peter, et al., eds. *The Black Abolitionist Papers.* Chapel Hill: University of North Carolina Press, 1992.

Foote, Eliza M. Becker (fl. 1840s–1890s)
Foote, Hiram (1808–1889)

The Reverend Hiram Foote and his wife, Eliza M. Becker Foote, were activists who supported runaways fleeing via the Underground Railroad. In 1848, the couple established a station of the secret network in Janesville, Wisconsin. In 1895, during the fiftieth anniversary of the First Congregational Church, Eliza Foote revealed how she and her husband had concealed fugitive slaves. One runaway named George, recovering from a bullet wound he received from pursuers, stayed for two days with the family, who provided him with food, clothing, and a satchel to help him pose as a tourist. They also gave him a stamped envelope with the family's address, which he mailed from Canada to reassure them that he had arrived safely.

Source

Harrold, Stanley. *The Abolitionists and the South, 1831–1861.* Lexington: University Press of Kentucky, 1995.

Ford, Barney Launcelot (1822–1902)
Ford, Julia Lyons (1828–1899)

A Chicago business leader, Barney Launcelot Ford devoted private time to the rescue of runaway slaves. A native of Stafford County, Virginia, he was born the mulatto son of a slave owner named Darington and a domestic named Phoebe, who drowned while trying to contact an Underground Railroad agent to free her son. In 1837, Barney was sold to a Kentucky planter and, three years later, to a plantation owner in Georgia. He fleshed out his name and became Barney Launcelot Ford and acquired an education on his own.

As a member of the crew of a river steamer, at age 25, Ford escaped in Quincy, Illinois, and took advantage of the Underground Railroad route to Chicago. While barbering at a city hotel, he came under the influence of his wife's brother and began aiding fugitives on their way to Canada. Contributing to his success was a local conspirator, Henry O. Wagoner, brother-in-law of Ford's wife, Julia Lyons Ford. During the Gold Rush, Barney managed the United States Hotel and Restaurant in Nicaragua. He moved to Denver, Colorado, and, in 1861, opened a barbershop, a diner, two Inter-Ocean hotels, a catering service, and restaurants. During the Civil War, he aided escaping slaves with food, clothing, jobs, and cash. The Barney Ford Museum in Breckenridge, Colorado, honors his many accomplishments.

Sources

"Barney Launcelot Ford," *Twin Visions Weekly,* September 22–28, 2000, 20.

"Julia Lyons Ford," *Rocky Mountain News,* May 6, 1899, 3.

Ford, Cyrus (1790–1864)
Ford, Darius (1790–1859)

Twin Quakers Cyrus and Darius Ford of Cummington, in Hampshire County, Massachusetts, joined other pioneers of the Ohio frontier in establishing links of the Underground Railroad. They moved from New England to the Midwest in 1841. After their silkworm business failed in Cleveland, Ohio, and they recovered from malaria, they settled on a 100-acre farm on Euclid Avenue on the shore of Lake Erie and established vegetable beds and orchards. In league with a neighbor, Samuel Cozad III, the Ford brothers guided a Kentucky-born mulatto woman and her young son who had escaped from a New Orleans planter and crossed the Ohio River into free territory. Cyrus concealed the pair from the slave owner's spies by dressing the woman in elegant attire and disguising the boy as a young girl. Increasing the irony of the transfer in sight of the spies was the upscale equipage Cyrus used to drive the fugitives to the wharf. Undetected, they boarded a steamer from Cleveland bound for Port Stanley, Ontario. In 1845, Horatio Clark Ford (1825–1876), Darius's son, converted to the cause of fugitive slaves after he heard a speech by agent Abby Kelley Foster.

See also: disguise; spies.

Sources

Baxter, W.H. *History of Champaign County, Ohio.* Chicago: W.R. Beers, 1881.

Morton, Marian J. *Cleveland Heights: The Making of an Urban Suburb.* Charleston, SC: Arcadia, 2002.

Ford, Sheridan (1816–?)

In *The Underground Railroad* (1871), historian William Still presented firsthand knowledge of Sheridan Ford, a refugee from southern bondage. After 28 years of misery, in 1844, Ford fled a brutal master and entrusted his life to the Underground Railroad. Traveling four days in woods, Ford endured hunger and cold until a friend carried supplies to him. He left behind two children and his wife, Julia Ford, whom the slave master jailed on suspicion that she had aided in her husband's flight. Agents helped the fugitive board a steamer from Richmond, Virginia, to Philadelphia, Pennsylvania. Ford embraced liberty in Boston, Massachusetts.

Source

Still, William. *The Underground Railroad.* Philadelphia: Porter & Coates, 1871.

Forsyth, William, Sr. (1801–1849)
Forsyth, Isaac Brock (1819–1850)
Forsyth, Nelson (1810–1892)

A safehouse at a terminus of the Underground Railroad, Bertie Hall was the home of the Forsyth family, which profited from being on land overlooking Niagara Falls. In 1830, William Forsyth, Sr., constructed the two-story brick residence at 857 Niagara Parkway in Bertie Township, Fort Erie, Ontario, at a crucial crossing of the Niagara River. Nearby was Smuggler's Cave, a 100-by-100-foot chamber that had been dug in 1785 at Frenchman's Creek by William Forsyth's father, Colonel William Forsyth, a notorious smuggler. William Forsyth, Sr., and his two abolitionist sons, Isaac Brock Forsyth and Nelson Forsyth, hid fugitive slaves in the cave until transporters could move them farther north of the New York State boundary. The cave served refugees until 1864. Among the runaways settling near Bertie Hall were John Taylor and his family, who escaped from North Carolina on May 1, 1850; James Adams and Benjamin Harris, who took the ferry to Fort Erie in 1824; Virginians Oliver Parnall and Burr Plato, who swam across the river to Ontario; and Aunt Betsy Robinson, who, in 1837, walked most of the way from Rockingham County, Virginia, and rode the ferry from Black Rock.

Sources

Davies, Charles, "Controversy Followed William Forsyth," *Fort Erie (Ontario) Extra,* April 24, 1990.

———, "Forsyth Family Lived at Bertie Hall," *Fort Erie (Ontario) Extra,* May 1, 1990.

Forten (James, Sr., and Charlotte Vandine) Family

A wealthy freeborn black activist, James Forten, Sr. (1766–1842), of Philadelphia, Pennsylvania, was the grandson of slaves. He studied in a Quaker academy and, at age 14, sailed as powder monkey in charge of explosives on the *Royal Louis,* captain Stephen Decatur's privateer. Forten survived enslavement on the English prison hulk *Jersey* and bought a sail loft. He and his wife, Charlotte Vandine Forten (1785–1884), turned their three-story brick townhouse on Lombard Street in Philadelphia into a waystation of the Underground Railroad. They also promoted slave rescues at Mother Bethel African Methodist Episcopal Church, which they co-founded. In 1831, James Forten joined William Lloyd Garrison's abolitionist campaigns on behalf of the American Anti-Slavery Society. In 1833, Charlotte Forten and her daughters—Harriet (1810–1875), Sarah (1814–1883), and Margaretta (1815–1875)—coformed the Philadelphia Female Anti-Slavery Society. That same year, James Forten, Jr. (ca. 1817–?), co-established the American Anti-Slavery Society, which elected him vice president a decade later.

Duty to the oppressed influenced the lives of the entire Forten clan. Harriet and another brother, William Deas Forten (1823–1900), continued the family dedication to fugitives. Harriet supported rescues conducted by her husband, Underground Railroad agent Robert Purvis; William allied with secret operative Albert Vosburgh in Erie, Pennsylvania. In the last year of his life, James Forten, Sr., championed the outcome of the *Prigg v. Pennsylvania* case (1842), which relieved states of enforcing the Fugitive Slave Law of 1793. In 1836, James Forten, Jr., encouraged women of the Philadelphia Female Anti-Slavery Society to contribute their talents to the abolitionist movement.

See also: African Methodist Episcopal Church; American Anti-Slavery Society, Fugitive Slave Law of 1793; *Liberator, The*; *Prigg v. Pennsylvania* (1842).

Sources

Nash, Gary B. *Forging Freedom: The Formation of Philadelphia's Black Community, 1720–1840.* Cambridge, MA: Harvard University Press, 1988.

Winch, Julie. *A Gentleman of Color: The Life of James Forten.* New York: Oxford University Press, 2002.

Fossett, Peter Farley (1815–1901)
Fossett, Sarah Mayrant Walker (1826–1906)

A scion of the staff of Thomas Jefferson at Monticello, Virginia, the Reverend Peter Farley Fossett obtained his freedom and guided other slaves over the Ohio–Canada route of the Underground Railroad. The son of Jefferson's foreman of ironwork and his chief cook, Peter Fossett was sold at age 12 to John Jones. Against orders, Fossett learned to read and made two attempts to flee bondage. In 1850, when Jones placed Fossett for sale, agent Tucker Isaacs of Springfield, Ohio, purchased him and his sister, Elizabeth-Ann (or Anne Elizabeth) "Betsy" Fossett, whom Isaacs married. Peter Fossett wed Sarah Mayrant Walker and established a catering business in Cincinnati,

Ohio. He pastored the First Baptist Church at Cumminsville and, with his wife, operated a safehouse of the secret network.

Source

Mitchell, Henry H. *Black Church Beginnings: The Long-Hidden Realities of the First Years.* Grand Rapids, MI: Wm. B. Eerdmans, 2004.

Foster, Abigail "Abby" Kelley (1811–1887)
Foster, Stephen Symons (1809–1881)

Unflappable Quaker feminist orator and teacher Abigail "Abby" Kelley Foster of Pelham, Massachusetts, and her husband, Stephen Symons Foster, fought injustice through nonviolent activism. Abby Foster became an abolitionist through friendship with Underground Railroad agent Abigail Goodwin of Salem, New Jersey, and by reading the abolitionist media, especially the *Anti-Slavery Bugle, The Liberator,* and the *National Anti-Slavery Standard.* At age 27, she co-founded the New England Non-Resistant Society to fight for social justice and made her platform debut at the Second Anti-Slavery Convention of American Women, held in Philadelphia from May 15 to 17, 1838. She served the Lynn Female Anti-Slavery Society as secretary and held a position on the board of the American Anti-Slavery Society. In 1845, she encouraged the Underground Railroad work of abolitionist educator Betsey Mix Cowles of Austinsburg, Ohio, and of orator Sarah Parker Remond of Salem, Massachusetts.

The Fosters maintained an Underground Railroad depot at their two-story brick home, Liberty Farm, at 116 Mower Street in Worcester, Massachusetts. Their residence featured a secret vault in the cellar accessed by a trapdoor. Abby Foster was so adamant that no runaways should be recaptured that she vowed to sacrifice her life to protect refugees. Among her converts to Underground Railroad activism were the Reverend Thomas Wentworth Higginson, a local Unitarian pastor and progressive essayist, and his wife, Mary Elizabeth Channing Higginson. John Chamberlain, a farmer and relative of Stephen Symons Foster, operated a waystation at West Road in Canterbury, New Hampshire. The Foster home became a National Historic Landmark.

In company with activists Frederick Douglass and Sojourner Truth, the Fosters lectured and agitated for reform. Stephen Foster joined radical minister Parker Pillsbury in charging Congregational ministers with failing to aid runaways. Stephen met opposition in Concord, Vermont, in 1841, when a church organist drowned out his message. In 1842, he shared a podium with John Murray Spear at the First Parish Unitarian Church in Portland, Maine, where he had been invited to speak; emotions ran high during their testimonials and climaxed in a riot. Two members of the Female Anti-Slavery Society, Lydia Neal Dennett and Elizabeth Widgery Thomas, escorted Stephen Foster out of the church and through the rear window of a safehouse operated by Quaker agent Comfort Hussey Winslow.

Confusing issues of abetting flight was the Fosters' adherence to pacifism. Upon the Fosters' arrest in July 1846 for distributing anti-slavery tracts on the Sabbath, they embraced and sank to the floor. A constable and his deputies dragged the couple to a buggy and lodged them under guard at a pub for the night. Their trial ended in acquittal. From 1847, the Fosters continued slave rescues at home while they tended their handicapped daughter, Alla.

Stephen Foster faced danger without qualm. One of his most noted involvements was his harangue to protesters at the jailing of Anthony Burns in Boston on May 24, 1854. When slave abductor Asa Butman appeared in Worcester in October, anti-slavery activists watched his hotel. After a stand-off hours before sunrise, authorities arrested Butman for carrying a concealed pistol. To allay volatile local anger, Stephen Foster volunteered to escort the kidnapper to the train depot. The federal marshal arrested Foster for disturbing the peace, but he defended himself in court and won the case. In a letter that appeared in *The Liberator,* Abby Foster volunteered to serve as her husband's defense counsel. She noted that authorities did nothing to shield the refugee from a predator.

See also: American Anti-Slavery Society; Anti-Slavery Convention of American Women; female anti-slavery societies; kidnap; *Liberator, The.*

Sources

Bacon, Margaret Hope. *I Speak for My Slave Sister: The Life of Abby Kelley Foster.* New York: Thomas Y. Crowell, 1974.
Riegel, Robert E. "Abby Kelley." *New-England Galaxy* 6:4 (1965): 21–26.

Foster, Amanda (1807–1905)
Foster, Henry (1811–1865)

Freedwoman and entrepreneur Amanda Foster of Albany, New York, and her husband, Henry Foster of

White Plains, New York, supported the Underground Railroad in a variety of ways. In 1815, Amanda became the baby-sitter for Mrs. King McKarge, a job she held until her teens, when she found jobs on river steamers. While working as a nurse in Arkansas, Amanda Foster loaned her papers to a female slave. In 1837, Amanda moved to Tarrytown, New York. Following the death of her first husband, John Bowmon, a barber, at age 39, she married Henry Foster, an abolitionist who had joined the Reverend John N. Mars and the Reverend James William Charles Pennington in reporting on the National Convention of Colored People in Maryland in 1840. In 1860, the Fosters established Foster Memorial African Methodist Episcopal Zion Church, which held its first assemblies in Amanda's candy shop and catering business on Main Street. The church constructed a permanent sanctuary at 90 Wildey Street to shelter escapees traveling to Canada.

See also: African Methodist Episcopal Church.

Source

Savage, Beth L. *African American Historic Places.* New York: Preservation Press, 1994.

Foster, Theodore (1812–1865)

Editor Theodore Foster encouraged the Underground Railroad through his activism and through his articles describing slave rescues. Both he and his partner, the Reverend Guy Beckley, a stationkeeper in Ann Arbor, in Washtenaw County, Michigan, aided fugitives. They issued an abolitionist paper, the *Signal of Liberty,* formerly known as the *Michigan Freeman.* From 1841 to 1847 in Ann Arbor and in 1848 in Battle Creek, the weekly paper flourished with funds from the Michigan Anti-Slavery Society. The pages contained eyewitness accounts of flights from bondage, including the rescue of a blacksmith and steamer steward named Sylvester. On June 5, 1841, the runaway pressed on to Detroit for the crossing of the Detroit River into Ontario. On May 22, 1843, a story about the escape of 23-year-old Robert Coxe from an Irish Catholic slave owner in Frankfort, Kentucky, to Adrian, Michigan, illustrated the desperation of people in bondage to cruel masters.

Sources

Arndt, Leslie E. *The Bay County Story: From Footpaths to Freeways.* Port Huron, MI: Huron News Service, 1982.

Ryan, Virginia, et al. *Early Ann Arbor and Its People.* Ann Arbor, MI: Ann Arbor Instrument Works, 1974.

Fountain, Alfred (fl. 1850s)

A valuable seagoing trader and transporter for the Underground Railroad, Captain Alfred Fountain of Norfolk, Virginia, helped refugees elude slave hunters. From Atlantic coast docks, he welcomed runaways to his schooner, the *City of Richmond.* Among them were passengers from the depot of Rachel Mendenhall Garrett and Thomas Garrett in Wilmington, Delaware. From the early 1850s, Fountain bore goods from Norfolk, Petersburg, and Richmond, Virginia, to Philadelphia, Pennsylvania. He also traveled the Great Dismal Swamp Canal to fetch slaves from the bogs along the Albemarle Sound of North Carolina. Hidden in secret compartments, his passengers avoided the exhaustion and terrors of overland travel but did suffer extreme hunger when the schooner was icebound.

Over a four-year period beginning in 1855, Fountain carried a total of 50 slaves in six trips. One night in November 1855, he concealed 21 fugitives in a load of wheat. When an armed posse arrived led by Ezra T. Summers, the mayor of Norfolk, Fountain struck a cool pose and offered to help the men search. In March 1856, Fountain safely delivered eight women and six men—David Cole and his wife; 28-year-old Benjamin Dickinson; 28-year-old Rebecca Jones and daughters Mary, Rebecca, and Sarah Frances; 18-year-old Thomas F. Page; Daniel Robinson; Isaiah Robinson; 24-year-old Arthur Spence; and Carolina Taylor and her small daughters, Mary and Nancy—a valuable cargo that fled despite the offer of a substantial reward. A rocky outcrop near the Old Swedes Church at Fort Christina State Park in Wilmington, Delaware, preserves the landing spot where Thomas Garrett, John Hillis, Severn Johnson, and William Still took charge of Fountain's passengers.

See also: Dismal Swamp.

Sources

Grover, Kathryn. *The Fugitive's Gibraltar: Escaping Slaves and Abolitionism in New Bedford, Massachusetts.* Amherst: University of Massachusetts Press, 2001.

Tucker, George, "Norfolk Was Crucial to Underground Railroad," *Virginian-Pilot,* June 5, 1994, C3.

Fox, Isaac B. (1790–1847)
Fox, Mary Ann Gregory (1811–1869)

Isaac B. Fox, a glass manufacturer in Sand Lake, in Rensselaer County, New York, used his business to shield refugees. Historians surmise that he concealed passengers of the Underground Railroad in barrels intended to haul sand from the Rensselaer Glass Factory. At their two-story frame house, Isaac and his wife, Mary Ann Gregory Fox, received runaways on the New York–Ontario route until they could safely transport them. Their son, Albert R. Fox (1810–1892), the partner of Isaac's younger brother, Samuel H. Fox (1816–1888), appears to have continued the family tradition of rescuing desperate slaves. In 2001, the Fox mansion was listed on the National Register of Historic Places.

Source

Anderson, George Baker. *History of Sand Lake, New York.* Syracuse, NY: D. Mason, 1897.

Fox, Jeremiah (1827–1909)

A former slave, Jeremiah Fox furthered Underground Railroad work in Oberlin, Ohio. After establishing himself as a teamster, he aided refugees in their flight to Canada. On September 18, 1858, he joined Ansel W. Lyman, operatives from Oberlin College, and 500 local people in rescuing John Price. The event, known as the Oberlin-Wellington rescue, saved Price from a Kentucky slave catcher, Anderson Jennings, and sped the runaway on to freedom. During the Civil War, Fox served the Fifth Colored Artillery in Vicksburg, Mississippi.

See also: black soldiers; Oberlin College.

Sources

Brandt, Nat. *The Town That Started the Civil War.* Syracuse, NY: Syracuse University Press, 1990.

Shipherd, Jacob R. *History of the Oberlin-Wellington Rescue.* Boston: John P. Jewett, 1859.

Frazier, Anna Joy (1813–1882)
Frazier, Stephen (1811–1871)

A Quaker husband-and-wife team, Anna Joy Frazier of Indiana and Stephen Frazier of Clinton County, Ohio, conducted slaves traveling through the Midwest. In Salem, Iowa, in 1833, the Fraziers took a religious and moral stand advocating civil disobedience against oppressive federal law. For their radical views on slave rescues, conservative Quakers expelled them from the Salem Monthly Meeting of Friends. In 1843, the Fraziers formed the Salem Monthly Meeting of Anti-Slavery Friends, a group of 50 disgruntled Quaker agents.

See also: Quakers.

Sources

Garretson, O.A. "Travelling on the Underground Railroad in Iowa." *Iowa Journal of History and Politics* 22 (July 1924): 418–53.

Hawley, Charles Arthur. "For Peace and Freedom." *Palimpsest* 16 (November 1935): 337–46.

Frederick, Francis (ca. 1809–?)

Francis Frederick sought Underground Railroad assistance to free him of bondage. He was one of nine children born to slave parents in Fauquier County, Virginia. In 1821, his master relocated him to a plantation near Maysville, Kentucky. Around 1855, a conductor transported Frederick to agents of the secret network who passed him along until he crossed the Ohio River. He wintered at a large depot from November until mid-May, when he journeyed on to Sandusky, Ohio, and crossed Lake Erie by steamer to Louistown, Ontario. He later traveled to Great Britain and lectured on slavery in London, New Castle, Birmingham, Manchester, Glasgow, and Dundee.

Source

Frederick, Francis. *Autobiography of Rev. Francis Frederick, of Virginia.* Baltimore: J.W. Woods, 1869.

free labor store

After passage of the draconian Fugitive Slave Law of 1850, abolitionists enlarged their secret web of waystations and increased their efforts to conduct refugees to freedom. A more overt form of protest was the free labor store, a Quaker-initiated mercantile endeavor that procured and sold non-slave-made goods and foodstuffs. Some of these stores used proceeds to fund the purchase of new shoes and clothes so that the tow-cloth shifts and handmade shoes of runaways could be replaced with sturdy, respectable outfits. In addition to making a consumer protest against bondage, the boycott of slave-made items broadened the arena of involvement for people who were unable to host Underground Railroad waystations and for women who sought more direct involvement in abolitionism. One proponent, Quaker activist Hannah Green of Cayuga County, New York, considered the boycott a direct attack on the slave-fattened purses of southern planters and manufacturers. Supporting the initiative was author Maria Weston Chapman, who championed the boycott in the pamphlet

How Can I Abolish Slavery; or, Counsels to the Newly Converted (1855).

As substitutes for the products of slave labor, merchants such as Levi Coffin in Newport, Indiana, and Cincinnati, Ohio; James Mott, Jr., William J. Whipper, and Cyrus Whitson in Philadelphia, Pennsylvania; Joseph H. Beale in White Plains, New York; and Seth Hinshaw in Indianapolis, Indiana, stocked linen stationery, rather than rag-content paper; maple syrup, as a substitute for cane sugar and molasses; and wool, muslin, and linen, to replace cotton. In 1848, Benjamin Lundy, a Quaker abolitionist and the publisher of the *Genius of Universal Emancipation,* introduced a free labor establishment in Mount Pleasant, in Jefferson County, Ohio. Until 1857, the store sold cotton and rice raised and harvested by paid labor. Other stores offered indigo, molasses, rice, sugar, tea, and tobacco purchased from dealers outside the South. The concept of a free labor economy foundered because of the lack of goods to supply demand. Nonetheless, the Mount Pleasant store survived as a museum and is listed as a National Historic Landmark.

See also: abolitionism; Fugitive Slave Law of 1850.

Source

Khan, Lurey. *One Day, Levin . . . He Be Free: William Still and the Underground Railroad.* Lincoln, NE: iUniverse, 2002.

Freeman, Amos Noah (1809–1893)

A dedicated black conductor of the Underground Railroad, the Reverend Amos Noah (or Noë) Freeman of Rahway, New Jersey, gained respect from blacks and whites for his generosity. While pastoring the Abyssinian Meetinghouse at 73 Newbury Street on Munjoy Hill in Portland, Maine, from 1841 to 1851, he opened the church as a waystation. He increased local awareness of the secret network and developed rescue strategy with agent Neal Dow, a two-term mayor of Portland. The congregation, particularly agents Charles Frederick Eastman, Harriet E. Stephenson Eastman, and Reuben Ruby, expanded the city's outreach to runaways arriving by sea.

In 1851, Amos Freeman came to Siloam Presbyterian Church, a depot established by the Reverend James A. Gloucester on Prince Street in Brooklyn, New York. Under the influence of abolitionist ministers Beriah Green and Henry Ward Beecher, Freeman organized escape routes through the area to Ontario. He befriended the outstanding anti-slavery activists of his day—Samuel Cox, Henry Highland Garnet, Lucretia Coffin Mott, Hiram Revels, Mary Ann Shadd Cary, Harriet Beecher Stowe, and the brothers Arthur and Lewis Tappan. In November 1855, Freeman completed the relay of Ann Maria Weems, a 12-year-old refugee from Rockville, Maryland, to Chatman, Ontario. For children left parentless, he co-established the Howard Colored Orphan Asylum. Freeman also supported the work of the radical abolitionist John Brown, who visited the Brooklyn safehouse in 1859.

See also: routes, Underground Railroad.

Source

"Grand Old Colored Man," *Brooklyn (NY) Eagle,* August 1, 1893, 2.

French, Rodney (1802–1882)

A vigorous rescuer of slaves, Rodney French, a shipman and merchant, coordinated efforts with other Underground Railroad agents in New Bedford, Massachusetts. Engaged as a shipyard caulker by French in 1838, Frederick Douglass established a home in the port with his bride, Anna Murray Douglass. In March 1851, French learned that a U.S. marshal intended to raid the coastal town for fugitive slaves. After observing an unknown sloop approaching the harbor, French rang a bell in Liberty Hall to alert the black population. His swift action foiled the raiders. In 1853, French served one year as mayor of New Bedford. During the Civil War, he captained a ship in the Stone Fleet, a volunteer armada that sailed down the Atlantic coast to lay siege to Savannah, Georgia.

Source

Grover, Kathryn. *The Fugitive's Gibraltar: Escaping Slaves and Abolitionism in New Bedford, Massachusetts.* Amherst: University of Massachusetts Press, 2001.

French, William Henry (1813–1866)
French, Amelia Whitney (1814–1846)
French, Ermina Emily Byington (1828–1916)

District Judge William Henry French, in addition to his service on the bench and his two terms in the state legislature, aided escapees in Vermont passing along the New England–Canada route of the Underground Railroad. He and his first wife, Amelia Whitney French, maintained a safehouse in Williston, in

Chittendon County near the Winooski River. French and his second wife, Ermina Emily Byington French, continued the family tradition.

Source

"History of Williston, Chittendon County, Vermont." *Vermont Historical Magazine* 11 (October 1867): 902–3.

Frisbie, William (1769–1857)
Frisbie, Elizabeth Davidson (1770–1850)

A friend of refugees, Dr. William Frisbie earned a reputation for compassion. A native of Saratoga County, New York, he studied medicine in Albany and opened an office in Vienna, in Ontario County. He and his wife, Elizabeth Davidson Frisbie of Peterboro, New Hampshire, sheltered the homeless and runaways. The couple's son and daughter-in-law, Dr. Elias Willard Frisbie (1799–1860) of Rutland, Vermont, and Sophronia Boynton Frisbie (1807–1885), continued the family tradition by operating a waystation of the Underground Railroad.

Source

Caverly, Abiel Moore. *History of the Town of Pittsford, Vt.: With Biographical Sketches and Family Records.* Rutland, VT: Tuttle, 1872.

Frost, George H. (1796–1873)
Frost, Zerviah Sherman (1803–1889)

After 1845, George H. Frost of Dartmouth, in Bristol County, Massachusetts, and his wife, Zerviah Sherman Frost, turned their home in Cherry Creek, in Chautauqua County, New York, into an Underground Railroad waystation. The Frosts pioneered the Cherry Creek settlement in 1823 and opened a tavern and inn. In addition to farming, storekeeping, and operating the post office, they supported local efforts to rescue slaves and earned respect for greatheartedness.

Source

Edson, Obed. *History of Chautauqua County.* Boston: W.A. Fergusson, 1894.

Fugitive Slave Law of 1793

On February 12, 1793, in the infancy of the republic, Congress enacted a law that treated fugitive slaves as personal property and their recovery much like that of a stolen horse or rustled cattle. At the Constitutional Convention of 1787, Pierce Butler, a slaveholding aristocrat from South Carolina, worded the law to stipulate that interstate slave extradition was a federal concern. To restore civil rights to black Americans, in the 1820s, both Indiana and Connecticut passed state laws requiring jury trial to determine the status of suspected fugitives. In 1840, New York and Vermont joined in with a demand for legal counsel and courtroom protocol to aid alleged runaways from unlawful seizure. Corroborating opposition was the 1842 Supreme Court decision in the case of *Prigg v. Pennsylvania,* which freed states from mandatory arrest and jailing of black refugees. As a result, no constables, sheriffs, or public jailers could participate in the imprisoning of runaways.

The organization of vigilance committees and secret rescues in the 1830s grew out of increased protest of federal support of slavery. Fueling grassroots opposition to bondage was the abolitionist press, which voiced outrage that federal authorities criminalized the actions of Underground Railroad operatives. In early May 1848, civil repercussions in Michigan against slave recovery by Kentucky agents indicated an explosive difference of opinion between Northerners and southern planters. The outcry resulted in the Fugitive Slave Law of 1850, which required more citizen involvement in the recovery of human chattel.

See also: Fugitive Slave Law of 1850; *Prigg v. Pennsylvania* (1842); slave recovery; vigilance committees.

Sources

Griffler, Keith P. *Front Line of Freedom: African Americans and the Forging of the Underground Railroad in the Ohio Valley.* Lexington: University Press of Kentucky, 2004.
"Mr. Butler's Report on Slave Stealing," *Brooklyn (NY) Eagle,* May 8, 1848.

Fugitive Slave Law of 1850

The Fugitive Slave Law of 1850 mobilized the army, the federal court system and commissioners, and special U.S. marshals to halt the flight of slaves from the South. For precedent, lawmakers built on Article IV, Section 2 of the U.S. Constitution. As drafted by Senator James Murray Mason of Washington, D.C., the wording was clear: Escaping slaves could not free themselves from ownership by fleeing from a slave state to a free state. Claimants had full right to their chattel. To this statute, on September 18, 1850, legislators added eight more sections requiring citizen assistance in apprehending

Read and Ponder

THE

FUGITIVE SLAVE LAW!

Which disregards all the ordinary securities of PERSONAL LIBERTY, which tramples on the Constitution, by its denial of the sacred rights of Trial by Jury, *Habeas Corpus*, and Appeal, and which enacts, that the Cardinal Virtues of Christianity shall be considered, in the eye of the law, as CRIMES, punishable with the severest penalties,—*Fines and Imprisonment.*

***Freemen of Massachusetts,* R E M E M B E R, That Samuel A. Elliott of Boston, voted for this law, that Millard Filmore, our whig President *approved* it and the Whig Journals of Massachusetts sustain them in this iniquity.**

SECTION 1. That persons who have been, or may hereafter be, appointed Commissioners, in virtue of any act of Congress, by the Circuit Courts of the United States, and who in consequence of such appointments, are authorized to exercise the powers that any justice of the peace or other magistrate of any of the United States may exercise in respect to offenders for any crime or offence against the United States, by arresting, imprisoning or bailing the same under and by virtue of the thirty third section of the act of the fourth of September seventeen hundred and eighty-nine, entitled "An act to establish judicial courts of the United States," shall be and are hereby authorized and required to exercise and discharge all the powers and duties conferred by this act.

SEC. 2 And be it further enacted. That the Superior Court of each organized Territory of the United States shall have the same power to appoint commissioners to take acknowledgments of bail and affidavits and to take depositions of witnesses in civil causes which is now possessed by the circuit court of the United States; and all commissioners who shall hereafter be appointed for such purposes by the superior court of any organized Territory of the United States, shall possess all the powers and exercise all the duties conferred by law upon the commissioner appointed by the circuit courts of the United States for similar purposes, and shall moreover exercise and discharge all the powers and duties conferred by this act.

SEC. 3. And be it further enacted, That the circuit courts of the United States, and the superior courts of each organized Territory of the United States, shall, from time to time, enlarge the number of commissioners with a view to afford reasonable facilities to reclaim fugitives from labor, and to the prompt discharge of [illegible] posed by [illegible]

[illegible] And be it further enacted, That the commissioners above named shall have concurrent jurisdiction with the judges of the circuit and district courts of the United States, in their respective circuits and districts within the several States, and with the judges of the territories, severally and collectively, in term time and vacation; and shall grant certificates to such claimants, upon satisfactory proof being made with authority to take and remove such fugitives from service or labor, under the restrictions herein contained, to the State or Territory from which such persons may have escaped or fled

SEC. 5. And be it further enacted, that it shall be the duty of all marshalls and deputy marshalls to obey and execute all warrants and precepts issued under the provisions of this act, when to them directed; and should any marshall or deputy marshall refuse to receive such warrant or other process when tendered, or to use all proper means diligently to execute the same, he shall, on conviction thereof, be fined in the sum of $1,000, to the use of such claimant, on motion of the claimant, by the circuit or district court for the district of such marshall; and after arrest of such fugitive by said marshall, or his deputy, or whilst at any time in his custody under the provisions under this act, should such fugitive escape, whether with or without the assent of such marshall or his deputy, such marshall shall be liable on his official bond to be prosecuted for the benefit of such claimant for the full value of the service or labor of said fugitive, in the State, Territory or district whence he escaped; and the better to enable the said commissioners, when thus appointed, to execute their duties faithfully and efficiently; in conformity with the requirements of the Constitution of the United States and of this act, they are hereby authorized and empowered, within their counties respectively, to appoint, in writing under their hands, any one or more suitable persons, from time [illegible] execute all such warrants and [illegible] process as may be issued by [illegible] performance of their respective duties, with authority to such commissioners or the persons to be appointed by them to execute process as aforesaid, to summon and to call to their aid the bystanders or posse comitatus of the proper county, when neccessary to insure a faithful observance of the clause of the constitution referred to, in conformity with the provisions of this act; and ALL GOOD CITIZENS are hereby commanded to aid and assist in the prompt and efficient execution of this law whenever their services may be required, as aforesaid for that purpose; and said warrant shall run and be executed by said officers anywhere in the State, within which they are issued.

SEC. 6. And be it further enacted. That when a person held to service or labor in any State or Territory of the United States has heretofore or shall hereafter escape into another State or Territory of the United States, the person or persons to whom such service or labor may be due, or his, her, or their agent or attorney, duly authorized, by power of attorney, in writing, acknowledged and certified under the seal of some legal officer or court of the State or Territory in which the same may be executed, may pursue and reclaim such fugitive person, either by procuring a warrant from some one of the courts judges or commissioners aforesaid, of the proper circuit, district, or county, for the apprehension of such fugitive from service or labor, or by seizing and arresting such fugitive, where the same can be done without process, and by taking, or causing such person to be taken, forthwith before such court, judge or commissioner, whose duty it shall be to hear and determine the case of such claimant in a SUMMARY MANNER and upon satisfactory proof being made, by deposition or affidavit, in writing, to be taken and certified by such court, judge, or commissioner, or by other satisfactory testimony, duly taken and certified by some court, magistrate, justice of peace, or other legal officer authorized to administer an oath and take depositions under the laws of the State or Territory from which such persons owing a service or labor may have escaped, with a certificate of such magistracy or other authority, as aforesaid, with the seal of the proper court or officer thereto attached, which seal shall be SUFFICIENT TO ESTABLISH TEE COMPETENCY OF THE PROOF, AND WITH PIOOF, ALSO BY AFFIDAVIT, of the identity of the peson whose service or labor is claimed to be due as aforesaid that the person so arrested does in fact owe service or labor to the person, or persons claiming him or her, in the State or Territory from which such fugitive may have escaped as aforesaid, and that said person escaped to make out and deliver to such claimant, his or her agent or attorney a certificate setting forth the substantial facts as to the service or labor due from such fugitive to the claimant, and of his or her escape from the State or Territory in which such service or labor was due, to the State or Territory in which he or she was arrested with authority to such claimant or his or her agent or attorney, to use such reasonable force and restraint as may be necessary, under the circumstances of the case, to take and remove such fugitive person back to the State or Territory from whence he or she may have escaped as aforesaid. IN NO TEIAL OR HEARING UNDER THIS ACT SHALL THE TESTIMONY OF SUCH ALLEDGED FUGTIVE BE ADMITTED IN EVIDENCE; and the cetificates in this and the first section mentioned, shall be conclusive of the right of the person or persons in whose favor granted, to remove such fugitive to the State or Territory from which he escaped, and shall prevent all molestation of said person or persons by any process issued by any court, judge, magistrate, or other persons whomoever.

SEC. 7. And be it firther enacted, That any person who shall knowingly and willingly obstruct, hinder or prevent such claimant, his agent, or attorney, or any person or persons lawfully assisting him, her, or them from arresting such a fugitive from service or labor, either with or without process as aforesaid; or shall rescue, or attempt to rescue, such fugitive from service or labor, from the custody of such claimant, his or her agent or attorney, or other person or persons lawfully assisting as aforesaid when so arrsted, pursuant to the authority herein given and declared; or shall aid, abet, or assist such a person so owing service or labor as aforesaid, directly or indirectly to escape from such claimant, his agent or attorney, or other peron or persons legally authorized as aforesaid; or SHALI HARBOR or CONCEAL such fugitive, so as to prevent the discovery and arrest of such person, after notice or knowledge of the fact that such person, was a fugitive from service or labor as aforesaid, shall, for either of said offences be subject to a fine not exceeding one thousand dollars, and imprisonment not exceeding six months, by indictment and conviction before the district court of the United States for the district in which such offence may have been committed, or before the proper court of criminal jurisdiction, if committed within any one of the organized territories of the United States; and shall moreover forfeit and pay, by way of civil damages to the party injured by such illegal conduct, the sum of ONE THOUSAND DOLLARS FOR EACH FUGITIVE SO LOST, as aforesaid to be recovered by action of debt, in any of the district or territorial courts aforesaid, within whose jurisdiction the said offence may have been committed.

SEC. 8. And be it further enacted, That the marshalls, their deputies, and the clerks of said district and territorial courts, shall be paid for their services the like fees as may be allowed to them for similar services in other cases, and where such services are rendered exclusively in the arrest, custody and delivery of the fugitive to the claimant, his or her agent or attorney, or where such supposed fugitive may be discharged out of custody for the want of sufficient proof as aforesaid, then such fees are to be paid in the whole by such claimant, his agent or attorney; and in all cases where the proceedings are before a commissioner, he shall be entitled to a fee of TEN DOLLARS in full for his services in each case, upon the delivery of said certificate to the claimant, his or her agent or attorney; or a fee of FIVE DOLLARS in cases where proof shall not in the opinion of such commissioner, warrant such certificate and delivery, inclusive of all services incident to such arrest and examination, to be paid, in either case, by the claimant, his or her agent or attorney. The person or persons authorized to execute the process to be issued by such commissioners for the arrest and detention of fugitives from service or labor, aforesaid, shall also be entitled to a fee of five dollars each for each person he or they may arrest and take before any such commissioners as aforesaid, at the instance and request of such claimant, with such other fees as may be deemed reasonable by such other additional services as may be necessarily performed by him or them; such as attending at the examination, keeping the fugitive in custody, and providing him with food and lodging during his detention, and until the final determination of such commissioner; and in general for performing such other duties as may be required by such claimant, his or her attorney or agent, or commissioner in the premises, such fees to be made up in conformity with the fees usually charged by the officers of the courts of justice within the proper district or county, as near as may be practicable, and paid by such claimants, their agents or attorneys, whether such supposed fugitive from service or labor, be ordered to be delivered to such claimants by the final determination of such commissioners or not.

SEC. 9. And be it further enacted, That upon affidavit made by the claimant of such fugitive his agent or attorney, after such certificate has been issued, that he has reason to apprehend that such fugitive will be rescued by force from his or their possession before he can be taken beyond the limits of the State in which the arrest is made, it shall be the duty of the officer making the arrest, to retain such fugitive in his custody, and to remove him, to the State whence he fled, and there to deliver him to said claimant, his agent or attorney. And to this end the officer aforesaid is hereby authorized and required to employ so many persons as he may deem necessary, to overcome such force, and to retain them in his service so long as circumstances may require, The said officer and his assistants, while so employed, to receive the same compensation, and to be allowed the same expenses as are now allowed by law for transportation of criminals, to be certified by the judge of the district within which the arrest is made, and PAID OUT OF THE TREASURY OF THE UNITED STATES.

SEC. 10. And be it further enacted, That when any person held to service or labor in any State or Territory, or in the District of Columbia, shall escape therefrom, the party to whom such service or labor shall be due, his, her, or their agent or attorney may apply to any court of record therein, or judge thereof in vacation, and make satisfactory proof to such court of the escape aforesaid, and that the person escaping owed service or labor to such party. Whereupon the court shall cause a record to be made of the matters so proved, and also a general description of the person so escaping, with such convenient certainty as may be, and a transcript of such record authenticated by attestation of clerk and seal of the said court being produced in any other State, Territory or District in which the person so escaping may be found, and being exhibited to any judge, commissioner or other officer authorized by the law of the United States to cause persons escaping from service or labor to be delivered up, shall be held and taken to be full and conclusive evidence of the fact of escape, and that the service or labor of the person escaping is due to the party in such record mentioned. And upon the production by the said party of other and further evidence, if necessary, either oral or by affidavit, in addition to what is contained in the said record of the identity of the person escaping, he or she shall be delivered to the claimant. And the said court, commissioner, judge or other person authorized by this act to grant certificates to claimants of fugitives shall upon the production of the record, and other evidences aforesaid, grant to such claimant a certificate of his right to take any person identified and proved to be oweing service or labor as aforesaid, which certificate shall authorize such claimant to seize or arrest and transport such persons to the State or Territory from which he escaped, Provided,

That nothing herein contained shall be construed as requiring the production as a transcript of such record as evidence as aforesaid. But in its absence the claim shall be heard and determined upon other satisfactory proof, competent in law.

HOWELL COBB,
Speaker of the House of Representatives.
WILLIAM R. KING,
President of the Senate protempore.
Approved September 18, 1850.
MILLARD FILLMORE.

Printed and For Sale at the Spy Job Office, Worcester, Mass.

An abolitionist poster in Massachusetts denounces the Fugitive Slave Law of 1850 and the politicians who voted for it. The measure, which required citizens to assist in the return of escaped slaves between states, led to violent protests in Massachusetts and elsewhere. *(MPI/Stringer/Hulton Archive/Getty Images)*

Votes of the U.S. Congress by Geographical Section

Blocs	For	Against	Abstaining	Total
New England States	7	15	10	32
Middle Atlantic States	9	33	21	63
Interior and Pacific States	16	27	8	51
Total Free States	32	75	39	146
Border Slave States	32	0	6	38
Planter States	45	0	9	54
Total Slave States	77	0	15	92
Grand Total	109	75	54	238

fugitives. According to Marion G. McDougall's vote tally in *Fugitive Slaves (1619–1865),* published in 1891, Southerners reaffirmed their bondage-based economy. The tally indicates that 54 fence-sitting votes would have made a decisive shift in the total for either side.

An outcry from fair-minded citizens shamed legislators for violating constitutional precepts dating to the Magna Carta of 1215. Most serious violations of human rights were illegal arrests and detainments and the denial of trial by jury. With cool logic, Henry Bibb, the publisher of *Voice of the Fugitive,* in Sandwich, Ontario, commented in the July 1, 1852, issue on the rapid emigration of blacks from Indiana to Ontario, many aided with funds, advice, and guidance from the Underground Railroad. He reminded readers that such a bleed-out from the labor force cost the state both brains and money. Gradually, the impact on the economy corroborated his claim.

In Detroit, Michigan, unconstitutional strictures on fugitives inflamed local blacks, who founded vigilance committees and brotherhoods, such as The African-American Mysteries: The Order of the Men of Oppression, which met on Jefferson Avenue. George DeBaptiste, William Lambert, and other bold members called for defiance of federal intervention in slave rescue and enlisted agents to journey south to help slaves arrange escapes. By mid-October 1850, Detroit abolitionists protested the apprehension of Giles Rose, a Kentucky runaway jailed on Griswold Street. Facing three units of the Grayson and Scott Guards, protesters continued threatening a violent jailbreak and departure by the steamer *Arrow* to Canada. The size and the strength of the mob forced the mayor to negotiate the raising of funds to buy Rose's manumission.

Protests among Underground Railroad operatives and supporters focused on a number of test cases involving alleged runaways:

The trial of William Smith was so heated that a policeman named Ridgeley shot and killed Smith. One victim of civil rights violations was 21-year-old Jordan Artis, a North Carolinian from Hertford County. On May 26, 1855, Artis was jailed in Halifax County despite his claim to being a freeborn black indentured to William Beale of Murfreesboro. Artis remained in jail until a slave owner could prove his case, pay charges, and take custody of the suspected runaway. Such victims were either remanded to their real or alleged masters or were sold at public auction. From 1850 to 1860, federal agents returned 332 black runaways to slavery. Only 11 cases favored the side of defendants, including John Freeman of Indianapolis, Indiana, who sued the plaintiff, Pleasant Ellington, and won a judgment of $2,000. In 1860, another case, involving Charles Nalle of Troy, New York, resulted in rescue from federal authorities.

When the U.S. Congress completed the upgraded fugitive slave act, it gained the support of President Millard Fillmore for allowing slave owners to gather posses anywhere in the United States to seize their human chattel and return them to bondage. The brutal statute fostered capricious search and seizure in churches, on seagoing vessels, and in the homes of free blacks. The law negated civil rights by allowing authorities to arrest suspected fugitives without a warrant and to convey their quarry to any white who claimed to be the owner. Suspects had no right to a jury trial or to testify in their own defense. The denial of habeas corpus and due process encouraged unscrupulous bounty hunters to kidnap free blacks and sell them to slave owners or to slave auctioneers.

The law received the denunciation of abolitionists Salmon Portland Chase, John P. Hale, Charles Sumner, and Benjamin Wade. Their ire at the measure arose from stipulations that any federal marshal refusing to collar runaway slaves would pay a penalty of $1,000. Underground Railroad conductors faced a $2,000 fine and six months in prison for each slave they aided with food and clothing, shelter, medical care, or transportation. Even bystanders were liable for refusing to aid slave catchers. Any noncompliance could precipitate charges of treason. Still, within three months, 3,000 fugitives made their way to Canada via the Underground Railroad. By 1852, the number of ex-slaves in Canada reached 25,000.

The broad terms of the Fugitive Slave Law of 1850 alarmed even pro-slavery factions and helped to turn the citizenry against federal intervention. The marshals themselves were ambivalent about the law. One federal agent in Boston posed as a faithful government servant while reporting directly to journalist and reformer William Lloyd Garrison the name of each fugitive being sought.

The most outspoken opponents of the legislation were newspaper editors Frederick Douglass of the *North Star,* William Lloyd Garrison of *The Liberator,* Wendell Addison Phillips of the *New York Tribune,* Arthur Tappan of the *American and Foreign Anti-Slavery Reporter,* and John Greenleaf Whittier of the *National Era.* Douglass charged that the law allowed any two villains to violate a black person's liberty. One example of Douglass's warning was the seizure of Solomon Northup, a freedman from Saratoga, New York, whom James H. Burch and his cohort Radburn apprehended and confined in a small barred room for transport to New Orleans. Another freedman, Isaac Mason, working in construction in Philadelphia, fled the area after passage of the law. After he recognized his master's son, Mason rapidly relocated to Massachusetts with the aid of Mr. Gibbs, a New Yorker on the secret network who directed Mason by sailboat to Boston.

The public antipathy toward enforced slave catching was effective. After U.S. Commissioner

In a memoir, *Half a Century* (1880), journalist Jane Grey Cannon Swisshelm described the Fugitive Slave Law of 1850 as a violation of the human rights of every citizen who comes to the assistance of a runaway: "[It] authorized the slave-hunter to follow the fugitive into every home, every spot of this broad land; to tear him from any altar, and demand the services of every 'good citizen' in his hellish work. Men by thousands, once counted friends of freedom, bowed abjectly to this infamous decision."

Fugitives Captured and Tried Under the Law

Fugitive	Site of Enslavement	Site of Capture	Trial
James Hamlet	Baltimore, MD	New York, NY	September 28, 1850
Adam Gibson	Elkton, MD	Philadelphia, PA	October 18, 1850
three mulattos	New Albany, IN	Louisville, KY	November 29, 1850
Stephen Bennett	Baltimore, MD	Columbia, PA	January 1, 1851
Henry Long	Richmond, VA	New York, NY	January 8, 1851
Tamar Williams	Worcester County, MD	Philadelphia, PA	February 1851
Fredric "Shadrach" Minkins	Norfolk, VA	Boston, MA	February 15, 1851
Richard Gardner	Louisville, KY	Bridgewater, PA	March 13, 1851
Thomas M. Sims	Savannah, GA	Boston, MA	April 3, 1851
Daniel Davis	Louisville, KY	Buffalo, NY	August 26, 1851
John A. Bolding	Columbia, SC	Poughkeepsie, NY	August 26, 1851
John Price	Baltimore, MD	Christiana, PA	September 1851
James Tasker	Maryland	New York, NY	February 1852
William Smith	Baltimore, MD	Columbia, PA	March 1852
Horace Preston	Baltimore, MD	Williamsburg, NY	April 1, 1852
James Phillips	Culpeper, VA	Harrisburg, PA	May 24, 1852
Thomas Brown	Cecil County, MD	Philadelphia, PA	November 1852
Jane Trainer	Mobile, AL	New York, NY	June 1853
George Washington McQuerry	Covington, KY	Cincinnati, OH	August 1853

In *Old Trails on the Niagara Frontier* (1899), Frank H. Severance commented on the difficulty of enforcing the Fugitive Slave Law: "Special officers were appointed to execute it, but in most Northern communities they were regarded with odium, and every possible obstacle put in the way of the discharge of their offensive duties. Many tragic affairs occurred; but the organization of the Underground Railroad was too thorough, its operation was in the hands of men too discreet and determined, to be seriously disturbed by a law which found so little moral support in the community through which its devious trails ran."

George Ticknor Curtis returned Thomas M. Sims from Boston to slavery on April 3, 1851, Curtis's constituents elected his political rival, Charles Sumner, to the post of U.S. senator. In May 1854, the order of Judge of Probate Edward G. Loring to restore Anthony Burns to his owner resulted in Loring's ouster from office and his rejection from the staff of Harvard University.

At the outbreak of the Civil War, a more promising rejection took shape within the U.S. military. On May 4, 1861, *Harper's Weekly* reported that Union soldiers were obeying army regulations and therefore would not enforce the Fugitive Slave Law for the sake of southern slave catchers and their packs of hounds.

See also: kidnap; *Liberator, The*; *North Star*; slave recovery; vigilance committees.

Sources

Campbell, Stanley W. *The Slave Catchers: Enforcement of the Fugitive Slave Law, 1850–1860.* Chapel Hill: University of North Carolina Press, 1970.

Clarke, James Freeman. "The Rise and Fall of the Slave Power in America." *North American Review* 120:246 (January 1875): 47–84.

Davis, David Brion. *Inhuman Bondage: The Rise and Fall of Slavery in the New World.* New York: Oxford University Press, 2006.

McPherson, James M. *Battle Cry of Freedom: The Civil War Era.* Oxford, UK: Oxford University Press, 1988.

Robboy, Stanley J., and Anita W. Robboy. "Lewis Hayden: From Fugitive Slave to Statesman." *New England Quarterly* 46 (December 1973): 591–613.

Severance, Frank H. *Old Trails on the Niagara Frontier.* Buffalo, NY: n.p., 1899.

Swisshelm, Jane Grey. *Half a Century.* Chicago: Jansen, McClurg, & Co., 1880.

"The War," *Harper's Weekly*, May 4, 1861, 2.

Williams, James. *Life and Adventures of James Williams, a Fugitive Slave.* San Francisco: Women's Union Print, 1873.

Fuller, Albert (fl. 1850s)

One of the stationkeepers of the Underground Railroad in Kansas, Dr. Albert Fuller sheltered runaway slaves. Under the influence of route organizer James Henry Lane, in 1856, Fuller welcomed escapees to his log cabin in Straight Creek northwest of Holton. On a rainy night on January 29, 1859, insurrectionist John Brown directed 11 Missouri slaves through Fuller's safehouse, having guided them to freedom on December 20, 1858. When two U.S. marshals attempted to search the cabin, they met armed resistance. A runner, John Armstrong, summoned Colonel John Ritchie from the First Congregational Church in Topeka. Ritchie's posse reached the Fuller cabin on January 31; by that time, Brown and his party had already set out unmolested for Tabor, Iowa.

Source

Sanborn, F.B. *The Life and Letters of John Brown: Liberator of Kansas, and Martyr of Virginia.* Cambridge, MA: Harvard University Press, 1885.

Fuller, James Canning (1803–1857)
Fuller, Lydia Charleton (?–1857)
Fuller, James Canning, Jr. (1821–1861)
Fuller, Sumner (1826–1876)

English Quaker philanthropists and Underground Railroad conductors James Canning Fuller and Lydia Charleton (or Charlton) Fuller donated effort, time, and money to aid black refugees. The family emigrated from Sidcot, England, and operated a handsome federal-style safehouse at West Genesee Street on a 156-acre parcel in Skaneateles, New York. The two-story frame station, called Evergreen House, received passengers from transporters at Marcellus and Syracuse. The Fuller dwelling offered hiding places under two closets for extended concealment. The family passed the runaways on to Auburn. At age 23, James Fuller was co-founder and secretary of the Skaneateles Anti-Slavery Society, whose members guarded him during his retreat from a pro-slavery mob in mid-April 1839. The attackers flung mud and rocks to protest slave rescues. That same year, the Fullers concealed Harriet Powell, a refugee from Mississippi who passed through Skaneateles and Syracuse and found freedom in Kingston, Ontario.

In 1841, the Fullers, as agents of philanthropist Gerrit Smith, bought Harriet Russell, Samuel Russell, and their five children out of bondage in southwestern Kentucky. Smith paid the owner, Samuel Worthington of Mississippi, a total of $3,500. On October 1, Smith offered the Russells a rent-free residence and charged them only $10 per month for food, clothing, and medicine. The Fullers joined Josiah Henson and the Reverend Hiram K. Wilson in establishing the Dawn Settlement, a community of former slaves outside Dresden, Ontario. In December 1841, Fuller donated $800 to the community and served as a trustee. In January 1843, Martha Coffin Pelham Wright of Auburn, New York, relayed a black man to the Fullers' safehouse, where the runaway loaded wood in gratitude for lodging and supper.

In widowhood after 1857, Lydia Fuller continued managing the waystation while her English-born son, Dr. James Canning Fuller, Jr., operated a pharmacy in Syracuse, New York. On October 1, 1851, Dr. Fuller aided in freeing a famous refugee, William "Jerry" McHenry, from a cell in Syracuse, New York, and set him on his way to Kingston, Ontario. The family was similarly attentive to the plight of Caroline E. Storum Loguen and the Reverend Jermaine Wesley Loguen, who had to abandon their horse and carriage at the Fuller residence and flee slave catchers. The Loguens traveled under the escort of Fuller's son, Sumner Fuller. Upon the Loguens' return in 1852, they found their belongings safe and the Fullers eager to welcome them back to Syracuse. The Fullers' devotion to their task earned the respect of Frederick Douglass. Also noteworthy was the petition of Dr. James Fuller, Jr., in the September 27, 1854, issue of the *Daily Standard* for funds to help desperate slaves. After Lydia Fuller's death, James Allen Root bought the farm and maintained the waystation.

See also: philanthropists.

Sources

Clayton, W. Woodford. *History of Onondaga County.* Syracuse, NY: D. Mason, 1878.
Leslie, Edmund Norman. *History of Skaneateles.* Kellogg, NY: Andrew Kellogg, 1902.

Fulton, James, Jr. (1812–1850)

A Quaker stationmaster in Ercildoun, in Chester County, Pennsylvania, James Fulton, Jr., teamed with Gideon Pierce and Lukens Pierce to share responsibilities for runaways. Fulton's farm in East Fallowfield was a central waystation. Arrivals came from Mahlon Brosius and Mary Emma Kent Brosius, Benjamin Kent and Hannah Simmons Kent and their son Henry, and Alice Eliza Betts Hambleton and Thomas Hambleton in Penn; from Deborah T. Simmons Coates and Lindley Coates in Sadsbury; and from Daniel Gibbons and Hannah Wierman Gibbons in Bird-in-Hand. Male slaves walked and women and children rode in wagons. Others traveled with the wagoneer, freedman Henry Lee. The passengers advanced to the next stop, the safehouses of James N. Taylor in West Marlborough or to Gravner Marsh and Hannah Marsh in Caln. Fulton welcomed a party of coachmen and waiters fleeing bondage in the District of Columbia. In 1841, he mourned the death of a Maryland runaway, John Matthews, and attended a Methodist funeral in Matthews's honor. On September 22, 1842, Fulton harbored one influx of 25 refugees and housed and fed them for three days before passing them to the Reverend Nathan Evans, Zillah Maule Evans, and David Evans in Willistown.

Source

Smedley, Robert C. *History of the Underground Railroad in Chester and the Neighboring Counties of Pennsylvania.* Lancaster, PA: Office of *The Journal,* 1883.

Fulton, Joseph (1782–1852)
Fulton, Mary Ann (1825–?)

Abolitionist farmer and builder Joseph Fulton and his daughter, Mary Ann Fulton, of Sadsbury, in Chester County, Pennsylvania, were astute agents of the Underground Railroad. Influenced by a number of anti-slavery publications, particularly Benjamin Lundy's journal the *Genius of Universal Emancipation,* Fulton received runaways from Deborah T. Simmons Coates and Lindley Coates in Sadsbury, Daniel Gibbons and Hannah Wierman Gibbons in Lancaster County, and Martha Hobson Whitson and Thomas Whitson in Sadsbury and passed them along to Thomas Hopkins in Downingtown, Pennsylvania, and to Mary Charles Thorne and William J. Thorne at Christiana. When black people arrived after dark, the family made few inquiries before offering a meal and shelter in the house or barn. One runaway retreated to the attic and armed himself with an ax in readiness for his former master's pursuit. One party of seven slaves included six-year-old Julia, a child the

Fulton family reared for the next 12 years. Another mulatto escapee with four daughters departed under threat of recapture and moved on to the station of Hannah Marsh and Gravner Marsh or to that of Micajah Speakman and Phebe Smith Speakman in Wallace, Pennsylvania.

After passage of the Fugitive Slave Law of 1850, the Fulton family concealed one runaway for seven days under hay bales and provided him with baskets of food from the kitchen. Mary Ann Fulton gave the man a compass and drew a map of the route to Binghamton, New York. He later wrote his thanks. She also came to the aid of two female runaways who required a horse and carriage. Against her brother's warnings, she drove from safehouse to safehouse seeking shelter for the women, who were also traveling with a child. After the intercession of an unnamed black woman, the runaways made their way to the stations of Edwin Howard Coates and Sarah Dull Coates in Philadelphia and Thomas Hopkins in Downingtown and then on to Norristown. Benjamin Johnson conducted the women to a reunion with their husbands in Toronto, Ontario.

See also: Fugitive Slave Law of 1850.

Source

Smedley, Robert C. *History of the Underground Railroad in Chester and the Neighboring Counties of Pennsylvania.* Lancaster, PA: Office of *The Journal,* 1883.

Furber, James Adams (1803–1875)
Furber, Hannah Hough Harris (1811–1869)
Harris, James Hough (1782–1858)

From 1835 to 1845, Hannah Hough Harris Furber, with her husband, James Adams Furber, and her father, James Hough Harris, maintained a safehouse of the Underground Railroad in west-central New Hampshire. The couple, both natives of New Hampshire, married in 1827. At Back Bay and Fox Hills roads in Canaan in Grafton County, the family received fugitives fleeing over the New England–Canada route. Across the street from the Furber residence was Noyes Academy, where freed slaves studied. In 1835, an anti-abolition mob employed 95 ox teams to destroy the school and drag it to a swamp for burning.

Source

Wallace, William Allen. *The History of Canaan, New Hampshire.* Concord, NH: Rumford, 1910.

Furniss, Oliver (1794–1858)

A low-key agent in Little Britain, in Lancaster County, Pennsylvania, Oliver Furniss could not turn away people in need. The son of pioneering patriots, he was a secretive conductor who kept no record of his civil disobedience to the Fugitive Slave Law of 1850. After receiving passengers from William Brown's waystation at Laurel Hill, Pennsylvania, on Octoraro Creek on the Maryland state line, Furniss guided them directly to Chester County. In times of danger, he hid refugees in the Pine Grove caves. For his benevolence, he was called the "fugitive's friend."

See also: civil disobedience; Fugitive Slave Law of 1850.

Source

Smedley, Robert C. *History of the Underground Railroad in Chester and the Neighboring Counties of Pennsylvania.* Lancaster, PA: Office of *The Journal,* 1883.

Fussell, Bartholomew (1794–1871)
Fussell, Lydia Morris (1804–1840)
Fussell, Rebecca Churchman Hewes (1804–?)

Dr. Bartholomew Fussell, a Quaker physician from Chester County, Pennsylvania, offered both medical attention and succor to fugitive slaves. He studied medicine in Maryland and opened a Sunday school for slaves. With his friends Thomas Garrett and Charles Callistus Burleigh, Fussell determined to act on his abolitionist beliefs. He and his wife, Lydia Morris Fussell, operated a safehouse in Kennett Square, Pennsylvania, and later a station in West Vincent, near the Underground Railroad station of his sister, Esther Fussell Lewis. Passing refugees to the Fussells were stationkeepers Allen Agnew and Maria Pierson Agnew in Kennett Square, and Benjamin Price and Jane Paxson Price in East Bradford, Pennsylvania. The Fussells rescued Eliza, an 18-year-old field hand, who had ridden bareback on a stolen horse for 40 miles and walked another 30 miles to safety. Because she disliked domestic work, Eliza served the Fussells as a farm laborer and, in 1838, married James Washington, another escapee, in their home.

After his wife's death in 1840, Bartholomew Fussell wed a widow, Rebecca Churchman Hewes, in 1841 and continued harboring slaves at their home in

York, Pennsylvania. He engaged a black fish and fruit vendor named Davy (or Davey) Moore of Wilmington, Delaware, as Underground Railroad courier to the Reverend Eusebius Barnard and Sarah Painter Barnard in Pocopsin to Thomas Garrett in Upper Darby. To spare Dinah Hannum Mendenhall and Isaac Mendenhall the danger, Bartholomew Fussell involved himself in the rescue of participants of the Christiana Riot of September 11, 1851, including six males conveyed to him by Henry Kent of Jackson's Valley, in Chester County. Fussell relayed William Parker and accomplices Johnson and Pinkney from the Mendenhalls' station in Kennett Square. Fussell also passed slaves on to agents Nathan Evans and Zillah Maule Evans in Willistown and Isaac Meredith and Thamosin Pennock Meredith in Newlin.

See also: Christiana Riot.

Source

Phillips, Christopher. *Freedom's Port: The African American Community of Baltimore, 1760–1860.* Urbana: University of Illinois Press, 1997.

Fussell, Edwin (1813–1882)

A Quaker abolitionist and orator, Dr. Edwin Fussell came from a family of doughty Underground Railway agents. The nephew of Esther Fussell Lewis and husband of Esther's second daughter, Rebecca Lewis (1820–1893), Edwin Fussell offered cunning, cash, and personal guidance to fugitives. Trained at the University of Pennsylvania, at the age of 22, he set up a medical practice in Chester County. For seven years, Fussell and his wife aided slaves in Pendleton, Indiana. Fussell's letters contain a testimonial to his aunt, Esther Lewis, who tended an old man lashed 100 times from tailbone to neck for the crime of visiting his wife at another plantation.

Maternity invigorated Rebecca Fussell, who, in 1843, held her infant, Linnaeus Fussell, between fugitive Frederick Douglass and an enraged assailant to halt a fight. Amid the clash of abolitionist and proslavery forces and offers of a $5 reward for the doctor's murder, the Fussells required a night watch. An attacker successfully showered the Fussells' daughter, Emma Jane Fussell (1838–1862), with acid, which burned her face. During the Civil War, Edwin and Emma Jane Fussell treated 450 casualties in a Philadelphia hospital.

Source

Smedley, Robert C. *History of the Underground Railroad in Chester and the Neighboring Counties of Pennsylvania.* Lancaster, PA: Office of *The Journal,* 1883.

Gage, Matilda Joslyn (1826–1898)

In childhood and adulthood, historian and activist Matilda Joslyn Gage, co-author of the "Declaration of the Rights of Women" (1876) and the *History of Woman's Suffrage* (1881–1186), rescued black runaways. A first-generation Scots American born in Cicero near Syracuse, New York, she grew up in an Underground Railroad waystation on Sophia Street operated by her parents, Helen Leslie Joslyn (1792–1863) and Hezekiah Joslyn (?–1865), a physician. Contributing to the family's notoriety was the procession of abolitionist orators who visited the Joslyn home. After Matilda married in 1845, her own children witnessed the family teamwork on behalf of road-weary fugitives. Gage lived in Fayetteville, where she volunteered with Caroline E. Storum Loguen and the Reverend Jermaine Wesley Loguen in the reception of passengers of the secret network.

Source

Obituary, *Syracuse (NY) Daily Journal,* November 2, 1865, 4.

Gale, George Washington (1789–1861)

A frontier educator, Presbyterian minister, and abolitionist, the Reverend George Washington Gale possessed a humanitarian concern for refugees that set an example for his students. Born in Stanford, New York, he was educated at Union College and Princeton Theological Seminary. In 1837, he purchased a 17-acre parcel and founded Knox Manual Labor College in Knox County, Illinois, where he taught literature and ethics. That same year, he and other abolitionists at Galesburg formed an anti-slavery society, the first in the state of Illinois.

Under Gale's leadership, Galesburg became a magnet for fugitives from Missouri plantations and a nexus of the Illinois–Ontario escape route. In 1843, Gale successfully countered charges that he was harboring slaves. He and his staff promoted the education of female and nonwhite students and the rescue of runaways, who sheltered on campus. Gale also fostered volunteerism in other leaders, including agent Charles T. Finney and orator Theodore Dwight Weld, a recruiter for the American Anti-Slavery Society.

See also: American Anti-Slavery Society.

Source

Muelder, Hermann R. *Fighters for Freedom: The History of Anti-Slavery Activities of Men and Women Associated with Knox College.* New York: Columbia University Press, 1959.

Galloway, Abraham H. (1837–1870)

A North Carolinian from Southport, Abraham "Abram" H. Galloway made a successful escape from slavery by water. The son of a white sea captain, John Wesley Galloway, and a slave named Hester Hankins, Abraham was the chattel of Marsden Milton Hawkins, chief engineer on the Wilmington Railroad. Although Galloway was well treated and trained in brickmasonry, he struggled to earn enough to pay his master for upkeep. In league with 25-year-old Richard Eden, a barber in service to Mary Learen, in 1857, Galloway wheedled from the captain of a schooner information about passage on the Underground Railroad.

Hidden in the cargo hold among barrels of resin, tar, and turpentine, the escapees carried with them silk oilcloth hoods tied with drawstrings to protect themselves from being smoked out, a common method used to force runaways out of hiding. In June, William Still and members of the vigilance committee greeted the successful escapees at the wharf in Philadelphia, where they appeared ill from breathing turpentine fumes. Underground Railroad agents sent them on their way to Canada. Eden wrote of their success in Kingston, Ontario, in mid-July

1857. Galloway began lecturing on abolitionism and helped others flee bondage. In March 1862, he settled in New Bern, North Carolina, and served General Benjamin F. Butler as a Union intelligence operative. Galloway mustered a black regiment and, during Reconstruction, fought the Ku Klux Klan.

See also: abolitionism; vigilance committees.

Sources

Cecelski, David S., and Timothy B. Tyson. *Democracy Betrayed: The Wilmington Race Riot of 1898 and Its Legacy.* Chapel Hill: University of North Carolina Press, 1998.

Griffith, David. *The Estuary's Gift: An Atlantic Coast Cultural Biography.* University Park: Penn State University Press, 1999.

Gansey, Isaac (fl. 1840s)
Smith, Edward (fl. 1840s)

Isaac Gansey and Edward Smith, crewmen of the schooner *Robert Centre,* were two of many black watermen who used their right of free passage from docks and harbors as a means of helping runaway slaves. In 1840, Thomas Walker Gilmer, the governor of Virginia, accused Gansey and Smith of aiding the flight of a fugitive named Isaac from Norfolk, Virginia, to New York. As a result, Gansey and Smith bore a $3,000 price on their heads for grand larceny.

Source

Quarles, Benjamin. *Black Abolitionists.* New York: Oxford University Press, 1969.

Gant, Nelson Tolbert (1821–1905)
Gant, Anna Maria Hughes (?–1877)

An Underground Railroad success story, Nelson Tolbert Gant advanced from enslaved valet to millionaire freedman. He was born a slave in Loudoun County, Virginia, and gained his liberty at age 23 in the will of his master, John Nixon. Quaker agents at Zanesville in Muskingum County, Ohio, received Gant in 1847, when he crossed the Ohio River into free territory. Abelard A. Guthrie and other agents in Putnam, Ohio, helped Gant purchase the freedom of his wife, Anna Maria Hughes Gant, a bondswoman on the Leesburg plantation of Charlye Ann Elizabeth Jane Russell. Gant raised some of the $900 by chopping cordwood on the Potomac River.

After marrying in a Methodist ceremony, the Gants lived in a two-story frame residence at 1845 West Main Street in Zanesville. They farmed and raised vegetables, bred livestock, and mined coal. They operated a safehouse and relayed passengers in their produce wagon. Nelson Gant also supported the rescues of Underground Railroad agent Francis Julius LeMoyne in Washington, Pennsylvania. In 2003, local preservationists began raising funds to restore the Gant safehouse.

Source

Switala, William J. *Underground Railroad in Delaware, Maryland, and West Virginia.* Mechanicsburg, PA: Stackpole, 2004.

Gardner, Joseph (1820–1863)
Gardner, Eliza (1825–ca. 1925)

A Quaker pioneer and an active rescuer for the Underground Railroad, Joseph Gardner took part in the border clashes in Kansas Territory. A native of Union County, Indiana, he taught school and hired out as a field and harvest laborer in summer. After passage of the Kansas-Nebraska Act of 1854, in May 1855, he and his wife, Eliza Gardner, traveled west by covered wagon and the steamer *Silver Heels* and established a farm in Douglas County, Kansas, on Washington Creek. His one-and-a-half-story log cabin was a waystation for refugees, including Napoleon Simpson, an escapee from Jackson County, Missouri, who made his way through the Gardner safehouse to Iowa in fall 1859. Bearing a price of $1,500 on his head, Simpson returned in May 1860 to retrieve his children and his wife, who had been too ill to travel the previous fall.

On September 23, 1859, Joseph Gardner joined Silas Stillman Soule, the mastermind of a jailbreak to free an Underground Railroad agent, Dr. John W. Doy, in St. Joseph, Missouri. The plot also involved James Burnett Abbott, Captain John E. Stewart, and six other confederates. The group came to be known as the Immortal Ten. For Gardner's participation, the sheriff of Buchanan County, Missouri, offered a $500 reward for the man or his corpse. At midnight on June 9, 1860, while two blacks slept in the Gardner cabin, Gardner engaged in a front-door gun battle with two slave stealers, who attempted to burn the cabin. Gardner wounded Hard Petrican of Lecompton, Kansas. Gardner's 16-year-old son, Theodore Gardner, fired from the upstairs window. One of the blacks in the cabin, Napoleon Simpson, who was working as a quarryman, died on the doorstep from a load of buckshot that Jake Herd fired into Simpson's left side. At the onset of the Civil War, 17-year-old Theodore Gardner (1844–1929) enlisted in the First Kansas Battery. In summer 1862, Joseph Gardner recruited soldiers for the First Kansas Colored Regiment.

See also: Kansas-Nebraska Act of 1854.

Source

Gardner, Theodore. "The Last Battle of the Border War, a Tragic Incident in the Early History of Douglas County." *Collections of the Kansas State Historical Society 1919–1922* 15 (1923): 548–52.

Gardner, Ozem (1797–1880)
Gardner, Mary Ann Price (fl. 1830s)

A rescuer of slaves, Ozem Gardner, known as Uncle Ozem, networked with agents of the Underground Railroad. He learned humanitarianism from his Quaker father, agent Joseph Gardner. At age 20, Ozem left his home in Otsego County, New York, to settle on the Ohio frontier in Worthington, Ohio. He and his wife, Mary Ann Price Gardner, lived in a log house, where Ozem earned his living as a brick maker and a farmer of 65 acres. At their two-story brick safehouse at 8221 Flint Road, which they completed in 1850, the Gardners received runaways and sheltered them in a shed on the creek bank. Ozem Gardner passed them on in his produce wagon to Alfred Potter and John Potter's waystation in Westerville on the route to Lake Erie.

Source

Cormany, Rachel Bowman, and Samuel Cormany. "Diary of Rachel Bowman Cormany." In *The Cormany Diaries: A Northern Family in the Civil War,* ed. James Mohr. Pittsburgh, PA: University of Pittsburgh Press, 1982.

Garlick, Charles A. (1827–1912)

Charles A. "Charley" Garlick's experience as a refugee illustrates the haphazard nature of station-to-station travel. Originally named Abel Bogguess, he was a native of Shinnston, Virginia (now West Virginia), one of 12 children born to the slaves of Richard Bogguess on a 300-acre farm in Harrison County. Garlick determined to flee bondage at age 16. A few days after the flight of his brother, Rawley Bogguess Johnson, Garlick departed from the plantation after the heirs contested his manumission in Bogguess's will.

Traveling from the safehouse of William Hefflin, in 1843, Garlick moved from depot to depot. From the ferry in Greensburg, Pennsylvania, agents directed him to Uniontown, where he hid under a haystack. After journeying by horseback to Pittsburgh, Garlick halted at a secure station kept by Jane Campbell McKeever and Matthew McKeever and their sons, Thomas and William Campbell, in Middletown, Pennsylvania, and then moved on to the care of John Baton Vashon and his son, George Boyer Vashon, in Pittsburgh. Garlick continued to the home of Mary Gilliland Marshall and Samuel Marshall in Adams Township, in Butler County, where the runaway rested for a week. From there, he pressed on to John Rainbow, the stationkeeper at New Castle, and to Amos Chews's home in Brookfield. Garlick reached Hartford, Pennsylvania, and worked for two weeks for Seth Hayes and Ralph Plumb at their cheese warehouse. To evade his pursuers, Garlick rushed on to Stod Stevens's store in Gustavus and left the next morning with transporter Joseph Barber.

Garlick arrived at the West Andover stop in George Quick's buggy and stayed for the weekend and then walked to Anson Kirby Garlick's waystation before making the crossing from Pennsylvania across Ohio into Canada. Anson Garlick persuaded the fugitive to remain in the United States for three years to attend school and grade lawns. At this time, Abel Bogguess adopted his rescuer's surname and became Charles Garlick. In 1846, Anson Garlick accompanied Charles to Gurdy's Run near Pittsburgh to look for the runaway's brother. Suspecting that his benefactor was actually using him as a decoy to locate other slaves, Charles escaped that night and reunited with his brother at the Marshalls' depot in Butler County, Pennsylvania. After a year's work, Charles Garlick fled armed slave catchers. Samuel Marshall posted notice in the local newspaper warning pursuers that they could expect bloody deaths if they returned.

Garlick's long journey to freedom concluded in 1847 with his entry into Oberlin College at Oberlin, Ohio. He lived in Liberty Hall, the dormitory for some 70 black students. He received the welcome of Oberlin attorney Joshua Reed Giddings, who offered Garlick lodging in his law office for several years. Another ex-slave of Garlick's acquaintance, William Hunt, worked on a river steamer as a porter. Hunt moved on after the passage of the Fugitive Slave Law of 1850.

Upon the death of Anson Garlick, on April 5, 1853, Charles Garlick emigrated via Ashtabula and

Cleveland, Ohio, to Amherstburg, Ontario. He chose a Sunday for the final leg of the journey in hopes that slave catchers would be attending church. At the beginning of the Civil War, he served in the U.S. Coast Guard. On his return to Ashtabula, Ohio, he worked at a steam mill near Lake St. Claire. Upon investigation, he discovered that his family was widely dispersed. He reprised his adventures in *Life, Including His Escape and Struggle for Liberty, of Charles A. Garlick, Born a Slave in Old Virginia, Who Secured His Freedom by Running Away from His Master's Farm in 1843* (1902).

See also: Oberlin College.

Source

Garlick, Charles A. *Life, Including His Escape and Struggle for Liberty, of Charles A. Garlick, Born a Slave in Old Virginia, Who Secured His Freedom by Running Away from His Master's Farm in 1843.* Jefferson, OH: Joseph Howells, 1902.

Garner (Margaret) Family

A cook and babysitter in flight from Maplewood, a 221-acre plantation in Boone County, Kentucky, Margaret "Peggy" Garner (1834–1858) sparked controversy over the cruelties of slavery. The daughter of two slaves, Duke Garner and Priscilla "Cilla" Garner, Margaret originally belonged to Major John Pollard Gaines and his wife, slave traders and hog farmers from Oregon, who bought Maplewood on August 1, 1827, for $10,000. Margaret Garner's mother was the chief domestic and child-care provider, as well as nurse for the owner's invalid mother and for his wife, who bore 11 children. Margaret learned her mother's duties and traveled with the Gaines family to Cincinnati, Ohio, around 1840.

Gaines's brother, Colonel Archibald K. Gaines, a cotton farmer from Arkansas, bought Margaret Garner, two black males named Harry and Sam, and two females named Charlotte and Hannah on November 5, 1849, for $2,500. The new master was hardhanded and erratic. He threatened to sell his chattel and lashed them; one blow marred Margaret's face with a scar. Contributing to Margaret's unrest were Gaines's sexual demands during his wife's pregnancies. Historians surmise that he was responsible for her last four pregnancies. The family also chose Margaret as a wetnurse for the Gaines infants.

On Sunday, January 29, 1856, Simon "Robert" Garner, Jr., a hog drover, took his pregnant wife, Margaret, and their children—six-year-old Thomas, four-year-old Samuel, two-year-old Mary, and nine-month-old Priscilla—to join 11 others escaping from James Marshall at Richwood Station. In light snow, the group opted to depart from Kentucky by horse-drawn sleigh. Below Covington, they reached the frozen Ohio River early on Monday morning. They crossed on foot and separated. A group of nine connected with the Underground Railroad and pressed on to Ontario. Garner's family, along with Robert's parents, Mary and Simon Garner, sought aid from Margaret Garner's cousin, freedman Joseph (or Elijah) Kite, near Mill Creek, where they awaited a conductor to lead them to the next safehouse.

When Gaines, a U.S. marshal, and slave catchers arrived to return Margaret Garner to bondage, Robert Garner wounded a deputy with a stolen pistol. Margaret Garner seized a butcher knife and slit Mary's throat and tried to kill her other children with blows from a coal shovel. She intended to prevent their having to live in slavery. Gaines wept over the corpse of the child that he had probably fathered. The Garners went to jail to await the two-week trial for the crime of destruction of property.

On January 29, 1856, the *Cincinnati Enquirer* described the slave escape as a horror tale. At the trial on February 11, 1856, the legal question of whether to return Margaret Garner to Maplewood or to try

Margaret Garner, an escaped slave from Kentucky captured in 1856, killed a daughter rather than have her returned to captivity. The story was the inspiration for Toni Morrison's Pulitzer Prize–winning novel, *Beloved* (1987). *(Library of Congress)*

her for murder as a freewoman rankled people on both sides of the abolition question. Ohioans threatened to riot over the case. The defense attorney, a Quaker named John Jolliffe, defended slaves without charge. Attending the trial were Quaker conductor Levi Coffin and feminist abolitionist Lucy Stone, who challenged Margaret Garner's concubinage to Gaines. The slave owners prevailed.

On February 28, 1856, a troop of 500 deputies escorted Margaret and Robert Garner south. Gaines shuttled the runaways aboard the *Henry Lewis* and sped them downriver toward the plantation of his brother, Benjamin Gaines, in Gaines Landing, Arkansas. A mid-river collision with the steamer *Edward Howard* caused the drowning of Priscilla Garner. The Garners were sold in New Orleans and again in Mississippi to cotton planter De Witt Clinton Bonham. Margaret Garner died of typhoid fever at age 24.

Margaret Garner's short life aroused curiosity for nearly a century and a half and inspired poets Elizabeth Barrett Browning and Frances E.W. Harper to commemorate the family tragedy in verse. When *Harper's Weekly* presented Margaret's story on May 18, 1867, the caption over Thomas Satterwhite Noble's dramatic painting of the event read "Modern Medea," an allusion to a character from Greek mythology who slaughtered her own children. Margaret Garner's story was the source of Toni Morrison's novel *Beloved* (1987) and the 1998 movie version, starring Oprah Winfrey as the child killer. A team from the University of Kentucky Department of Anthropology, Kentucky Heritage Council, Kentucky African American Heritage Commission, Boone County Office of Historic Preservation, Kentucky State University, and Georgetown College began excavating the Maplewood kitchen and smokehouse in 1998. In 2000, the site was nominated for listing on the National Register of Historic Places. On July 12, 2005, a half-hour television documentary promoted the opera *Margaret Garner,* which premiered in Cincinnati on July 14. It featured music by Richard Danielpour and libretto by Toni Morrison.

See also: Beloved (1987).

Sources

Bassett, P.C., "A Visit to the Slave Mother Who Killed Her Child," *National Anti-Slavery Standard,* March 15, 1856, 1.
"The Fugitive Slave Case," *Cincinnati Gazette,* February 11, 1856, 3.
Weisenburger, Steven. *Modern Medea: A Family Story of Slavery and Child-Murder from the Old South.* Boston: Hill & Wang, 1998.

Garnet, Henry Highland (1815–1882)

A committed rescuer of fellow slaves, the Reverend Henry Highland Garnet (also Garnett) plotted with agent Gerrit Smith some immediate solutions to human bondage. Garnet was born of Mandingo ancestry in New Market, in Kent County, Maryland. In 1824, he fled through Bucks County, Pennsylvania, to New York City with his parents, George Garnet, a cobbler, and Henrietta "Henny" Garnet. In token of their liberation, they knelt to give thanks. George Garnet rid the family of slave names by calling his daughter and son Eliza and Henry Garnet and by giving Henrietta the name Elizabeth Garnet.

Two years after gaining his liberty, Henry Garnet befriended another escapee, Samuel Ringgold Ward, who was a fellow student at the African Free School and future activist of the Underground Railroad. At age 14, Henry found a post as a cabin boy. On his return from sea, he lost his possessions when his family was rounded up during a slave raid. While working as a farm laborer, he injured a leg, which was later amputated. Freedom and schooling for Garnet and other blacks at the Noyes Academy in Canaan, New Hampshire, generated hatred among racists, who overran a classroom in 1835. Garnet armed himself with a barlow knife and joined others who combated the throng, but the attack destroyed the school.

While pastoring the Liberty Street Presbyterian Church in Troy, New York, from 1841 to 1848, Garnet joined the American Anti-Slavery Society as an exhorter and evangelist and developed close ties with another abolitionist, Frances Ellen Watkins Harper. He studied under the Reverend Theodore Sedgwick Wright, an operative of the secret network at Shiloh Church on Prince Street in New York City. In the 1840s, Garnet evolved into a militant agitator and demanded that slaves band into an armed fighting force and murder their enslavers. In the oration "Call to Rebellion: An Address to the Slaves of the United States of America," delivered on August 21, 1843, he romanticized the nobility and glory of dying in action rather than living in harness. His belligerence met with the disapproval of Frederick Douglass, who favored nonviolence over an all-out race war.

Garnet broadened his outreach to promotion of the black press, black churches, and missions to Jamaica. He sold subscriptions to the *Colored American* and, in Troy, New York, published the *Clarion* and the *National Watchman.* His support of the Underground Railroad encompassed the revolutionary aims of the insurrectionist John Brown, who raided the federal arsenal at Harpers Ferry, Virginia, on October 16, 1859. During the Civil War, Garnet was chaplain to three black regiments, the Twentieth, the Twenty-sixth, and the Thirty-first New York infantries. He also received fugitives and displaced people at his church, the Fifteenth Street Presbyterian Church in Washington, D.C. In the aftermath of Abraham Lincoln's assassination, Garnet spearheaded a drive for a national monument to honor the author of the Emancipation Proclamation.

See also: American Anti-Slavery Society; civil disobedience.

Sources

Driscoll, James, et al. *Angels of Deliverance: The Underground Railroad in Queens, Long Island, and Beyond.* Flushing, NY: Queens Historical Society, 1999.

Swift, David E. *Black Prophets of Justice: Activist Clergy Before the Civil War.* Baton Rouge: Louisiana State University Press, 1989.

Garrett, Thomas (1789–1871)
Garrett, Rachel Mendenhall (1792–1868)

An active Quaker organizer and conductor of the Underground Railroad for four decades, Thomas Garrett was so well connected to the line that he became known as "the man who helped 1,800 slaves to their natural liberty." He was the son of Sarah Price Garrett and Thomas Garrett, who owned a farm and a mill in Upper Darby, Pennsylvania. Rather than follow the family trade, he profited from ironwork and sold coal, steel, and shoes. In his youth, when one of his parents' black servants was kidnapped, on horseback, he tracked the kidnapper's wagon by the pattern of a broken wheel. In Kensington, while the slave nabbers drank at the bar, Garrett reclaimed the woman and restored her to freedom. From that day, Garrett dedicated himself to the principles of liberty.

A member of the Pennsylvania Abolition Society, Garrett and his second wife, Rachel Mendenhall Garrett, a cousin of agent Isaac Mendenhall, chose active abolitionist roles. The couple maintained a crucial safehouse at 227 Shipley Street in Wilmington, Delaware, on the busy Atlantic coastal route of the Underground Railroad. When they began work in 1822, Rachel Garrett stockpiled garments, hats, and wigs for disguising runaways. Refugees from slave rescuer Daniel Corbet in Smyrna, Delaware, rested with the Garretts before crossing into the free state of Pennsylvania to lodge with the Reverend Eusebius and Sarah Painter Barnard, Chandler and Hannah M. Darlington, or Isaac and Thamosin Pennock Meredith in Newlin; or with Micajah and William Allibone Speakman in Wallace, Pennsylvania. For field assistance, the Garretts depended on guides Henry Craig, Severn Johnson, and George Wilmer and on Captain Alfred Fountain, who smuggled passengers to northern ports on his sloop, the *City of Richmond.* The Garretts passed some runaways to Thomas Garrett's cousin Benjamin Price and Jane Paxson Price in East Chester, Pennsylvania; others journeyed to Ann Vickers Painter and Samuel M. Painter in West Chester or to Harriet Forten Purvis and Robert Purvis in Philadelphia. For backup, Garrett depended on conductor Joseph G. Walker, a West Indian of Scots descent, who led 130 fugitives during one busy fall.

Parties traveled from the Garretts' waystation on foot or by wagon and, in winter, forded the Brandywine, the last barrier on the Delaware-Pennsylvania border. Some received aid from Garrett's cousins—Isaac, Philip, and Samuel Garrett—in Delaware County, Pennsylvania. For vigilance work in Philadelphia, Thomas Garrett enlisted black organizer William Still and sought help in Maryland from transporter David A. Hall. Garrett was a special friend to Harriet Tubman, to whom he gave new shoes when she led runaways through Wilmington. He kept no record of her deliveries but estimated that she ferried around 70 slaves to his station, from which they passed to the vigilance committee in Philadelphia. In mid-November 1856, the Garretts aided one of Harriet Tubman's parties, Josiah Bailey and William Bailey, in slipping across the Christiana River past spies and police officers at the Market Street Bridge. Relaying her passengers in a wagonload of noisy bricklayers, Tubman safely deposited

> At age 59, Thomas Garrett admitted to a federal court his complicity in freeing a slave couple and their six children from Maryland. When the court bankrupted Garrett with a $5,400 fine, he declared to Judge Roger B. Taney, "Thee hasn't left me a dollar, but I wish to say to thee, and to all in this court room, that if anyone knows of a fugitive who wants a shelter and a friend, send him to Thomas Garrett, and he will befriend him."

them at Garrett's iron and hardware store a few blocks from the bridge. In his sixties, Garrett conspired with William Still and Captain Alfred Fountain for transport of runaways from the Great Dismal Swamp of Virginia and the Carolinas to Philadelphia.

In 1848, Thomas Garrett and his partner, John Hunn, lost a lawsuit pressed by Charles W. Glanding and Elizabeth Turner for abetting slave escapes. Abolitionist colleagues raised enough money to set Garrett up in business once more. Resurfacing from financial ruin, he renewed his efforts by adding a story to his house to hold more fugitives. During civil disobedience to the Fugitive Slave Law of 1850, he openly opposed the pro-southern, anti-abolition administration of President Franklin Pierce, who supported the spread of slavery on the American frontier. On November 21, 1858, he wrote a jubilant announcement to James Miller McKim concerning the safe arrival of Ann Maria Jackson and her seven children—Ebenezer Thomas, Frances Sabrina, John Edwin, Mary Ann, Wilhelmina, William Albert, and William Henry. By the end of his volunteerism, Garrett had remained faithful to the secret escape route despite a price on his head for $10,000 offered by the Maryland legislature. Jokingly, he retorted that for twice that amount, he would turn himself in to state authorities. Harriet Beecher Stowe used the litigation as a source for her character Simeon Halliday in chapter 13 of *Uncle Tom's Cabin* (1852).

By the opening of the Civil War, the Garretts were such enemies of southern planters that the Garrett property required an armed guard to protect it from the pro-slavery faction. After national emancipation, on January 1, 1863, black friends surrounded their savior for a celebration of liberty. At the passage of the Fifteenth Amendment on February 3, 1870, granting black males the right to vote, Wilmington's black population honored Garrett by pulling his carriage through the streets under a sign reading "Our Moses." Following his death on January 25, 1871, an honor guard eulogized him at his funeral and transported the coffin to his grave at Friends' Grounds. He had helped free 2,700 slaves.

See also: disguise; Dismal Swamp; kidnap; spies; *Uncle Tom's Cabin; or, Life Among the Lowly* (1852).

Sources

Thompson, Priscilla. "Harriet Tubman, Thomas Garrett, and the Underground Railroad." *Delaware History* 22:1 (1986): 1–21.

Weiss, John. *Life and Correspondence of Theodore Parker.* New York: D. Appleton, 1864.

Wyman, Lillie B. Chace. "Harriet Tubman." *New England* 20:1 (March 1896): 110–18.

Garrison, William Lloyd (1805–1879)

William Lloyd Garrison defied nation, Constitution, and church in an all-out fight to liberate slaves. He began lambasting slave owners in Benjamin Lundy's *Genius of Universal Emancipation,* the first abolitionist paper, begun in Mount Pleasant, Ohio, in 1821. Garrison first charged slave owners as criminals in 1829, when his boyhood friend poet and editor John Greenleaf Whittier bailed him out of a Baltimore jail for libeling a sea captain. On October 16, 1830, two abolitionists, the Reverend Samuel Joseph May and his cousin, attorney Samuel Edmund Sewall, discovered Garrison's talent. With the aid of network agent Amos Bronson Alcott, May and Sewall encouraged Garrison's platform career. In 1831, Garrison thundered his condemnation of gradualists in the

A preeminent figure in the American abolitionist movement, William Lloyd Garrison became increasingly vehement in his attacks against the "peculiar institution." His fiery rhetoric inspired the efforts of Underground Railroad operatives. *(MPI/Stringer/Hulton Archive/Getty Images)*

first editorial of his weekly, *The Liberator,* the first nationally distributed abolitionist newspaper. To antislavery forces proposing a piecemeal end to slavery, he insisted on immediate liberation. His uncompromising editorials appealed to readers in every northern state and, throughout the 1840s, increased the fervor of Underground Railroad operatives.

In person and in print, Garrison's influence was enormous. He encouraged the involvement of agents far and wide, including George Atcheson in southern Pennsylvania; Edmund Carleton and Mary Kilburn Coffin Carleton in Carleton, New Hampshire; and Reuben Ruby, a hack driver in Portland, Maine. While living in Roxbury, Massachusetts, Garrison co-founded the New England Anti-Slavery Society at the African Meeting House in Boston in 1833; a year later, he influenced the formation of the American Anti-Slavery Society in Philadelphia. In 1835, a mob of pro-slavery agitators put a rope around Garrison's neck and dragged him through Boston and called for his lynching. He was so outspoken an abolitionist that, in 1841, he urged free states to secede from the Union. In 1842, he served jail time along with the Reverend Charles Turner Torrey and John Greenleaf Whittier in Baltimore, Maryland, for interrupting a pro-slavery meeting in Annapolis. In 1854, Garrison supported Underground Railroad agent Amasa R. Soule in creating a free black settlement in Lawrence, Kansas. Other of Garrison's protégés included Abraham Allen and Cata Howland Allen and Elihu Oren of Clinton County, Ohio; Jonathan Paxson Magill and his sons, Edward Hicks Magill and Watson P. Magill in Bucks County, Pennsylvania; Elizabeth Buffum Chace and Samuel Buffington Chace in Fall River, Massachusetts; the Samuel Fessenden family in Portland, Maine; and Sydney Howard Gay and the brothers Arthur and Lewis Tappan of New York City.

Garrison achieved satisfaction from a life dedicated to human welfare. On May 15, 1858, he received a thank-you letter from Mary Millburn, who fled via the Underground Railroad through Philadelphia to Garrison's safehouse in Boston. She concealed her identity under men's attire and hid in a box for a steamer passage. In Boston, she abandoned her slave name and renamed herself Louisa F. Jones. Garrison's son, Wendell Phillips Garrison, married Lucy McKim, the daughter of Presbyterian-Quaker agents James Miller McKim and Sarah Allibone Speakman McKim. Wendell Garrison and his brother, Francis Jackson Garrison, co-wrote their father's four-volume biography, *William Lloyd Garrison, 1805–1875: The Story of His Life Told by His Children* (1885–1889).

See also: American Anti-Slavery Society; civil disobedience; *Liberator, The*; punishments.

Sources

Hinton, Richard Josiah. *John Brown and His Men: With Some Account of the Roads They Travelled to Reach Harpers Ferry.* New York: Funk & Wagnalls, ca. 1894.

"Underground Railroad," *Brooklyn (NY) Eagle,* May 14, 1882, 4.

Garvey, Edward Christie Kerr (1809–?)

One of the slave rescuers on the frontier, Edward Christie Kerr Garvey received runaways from Missouri. He was born in Yonge, Ontario (some sources say Ireland), and married Nourilla (also Pamila or Ponella) Shipman in 1837. After his wife's death, he migrated to Milwaukee, Wisconsin, and then to Topeka, Kansas. In 1855, he edited the *Kansas Freeman.* The Garvey House Hotel at Fifth Street and South Kansas Avenue was a gathering place for militant abolitionists, including attorney James Henry Lane and John Brown, Jr., the son of insurrectionist John Brown.

Source

Oates, Warren, and Stephen B. Oates. *To Purge This Land with Blood: A Biography of John Brown.* Amherst: University of Massachusetts Press, 1984.

Gaskins, Jacob (1792–1873)

From his own experience with enslavement, Jacob Gaskins developed compassion for the desperate fugitive. Born into bondage in Winchester, Virginia, in 1821, he grew up among his first owner's 1,000 slaves. After gaining his freedom, in 1817, Gaskins settled in Stark County, Ohio, and became a wealthy landowner. At 1500 Roadwin Circle South West, he opened a waystation of the Underground Railroad. To honor his activism, a highway marker in North Canton, Ohio, has featured Gaskins's portrait since 2005.

Source

"Underground RR Marker Dedication Planned," *Canton (OH) Repository,* February 10, 2005.

Gass, Benjamin (1794–1879)
Gass, Elizabeth McCluer (1793–1864)

A pioneer and an Underground Railroad operative in Troy Township, in Richland County, Ohio, Benjamin

Gass worked discreetly for the freeing of runaway slaves. After service in the War of 1812, he moved west with his family from Brooke County, Virginia (now West Virginia). In January 1827, he wed Elizabeth McCluer (or McClure), the daughter of secret network operatives Samuel and Sarah McCluer of Lexington, Ohio. Benjamin Gass was elected county auditor and bishop of the Church of Christ in Mansfield, Ohio.

While operating a safehouse, the Gass family allied with transporters John Finney and Joseph Roe. The Gass waystation received fugitive slaves by wagon from the McCluers and from Quaker conductors in Morrow County and in Iberia, Ohio. During the Civil War, the Gass's youngest son, James G. Gass, served as a first lieutenant in the Fifteenth Ohio Regiment. Another son, Cicero T. Gass, was a Union army quartermaster.

Source

Graham, A.A., comp. *History of Richland County, Ohio: Its Past and Present.* Mansfield, OH: self-published, 1880.

Gaston, George B. (1814–1873)

From his founding of Tabor, Iowa, in 1848, Quaker farmer and mill owner George B. Gaston performed strenuous and often dangerous labors for the Underground Railroad. Born in Danbury, New York, he launched a Presbyterian mission to Pawnee in the Kansas Territory in May 1840. During insurrectionist John Brown's passage through Iowa on a 1,100-mile trek with 11 slaves raided from two Missouri plantations on December 20 and 21, 1858, Gaston housed some of the party at his log home in Platte County, Iowa, and others at the safehouse of the Reverend John Todd and Martha Atkins Todd. In March 1860, Gaston hosted a counsel of local operatives to study the arrest of four black fugitives who had fled to Tabor, Iowa. In addition to scouring woods for kidnappers by night, Gaston received a fugitive trapped in a snowstorm and offered him work until he could reunite with a companion and press on to the Canadian border. That same year, Gaston and a colleague, Dr. Ira D. Blanchard, retrieved free siblings, Henry Garner and Maria Garner, and John Williamson from a St. Louis, Missouri, slave pen, where they were wrongfully jailed as runaway slaves. The trio hurried north to safe homes in Omaha, Nebraska.

See also: kidnap; slave recovery.

Source

Todd, John. *Early Settlement and Growth of Western Iowa; or, Reminiscences.* Des Moines, IA: Historical Department of Iowa, 1906.

Gay, Sydney Howard (1814–1888)
Gay, Elizabeth J. Neall (1819–1907)

Journalist, orator, and biographer Sydney Howard Gay served runaway slaves as advocate and rescuer. Born to a patriotic abolitionist family in Hingham, Massachusetts, he attended Harvard University before studying law with his father, Ebenezer Gay. Distraught at the plight of slaves, at age 29, he moved to New York City, joined the American Anti-Slavery Society as a traveling speaker and recruiter, and, with Maria Weston Chapman and Edmund Quincy, began editing the *National Anti-Slavery Standard,* an occupation he pursued from 1843 to 1857. Under his leadership, the abolitionist weekly grew in readership in the North and South. For six months, Gay toured abolitionist strongholds in Massachusetts with orator Charles Lenox Remond. After the imprisonment of agent Charles Turner Torrey on December 28, 1844, Gay issued an editorial calling for discretion and caution among operatives of the secret network.

In November 1845, Gay married Elizabeth J. Neall, a Quaker abolitionist from Philadelphia. Under the influence of William Lloyd Garrison, the Gays became operatives and networkers of the Underground Railroad from their home on Haley's Lane in West New Brighton, on the shore of Staten Island. The residence became a command post for strategists. Among the couple's contacts were Angelina Emily Grimké, Sarah Moore Grimké, Lucretia Coffin Mott, Wendell Addison Phillips, Robert Purvis, and John Greenleaf Whittier. In 1857, Gay began writing and editing the *New York Tribune,* where he worked throughout the Civil War. After Harriet A. Jacobs published *Incidents in the Life of a Slave Girl* (1861), Elizabeth Gay joined agent Hannah Thompson Haydock in promoting the slave narrative.

See also: American Anti-Slavery Society; *Incidents in the Life of a Slave Girl* (1861).

Sources

Blackett, R.J.M. *Building an Antislavery Wall: Black Americans in the Atlantic Abolitionist Movement, 1830–1860.* Baton Rouge: Louisiana State University Press, 1983.

Vorenberg, Michael. *Final Freedom: The Civil War, the Abolition of Slavery, and the Thirteenth Amendment.* Cambridge, UK: Cambridge University Press, 2001.

Gibbons, Abigail Hopper (1801–1893) Gibbons, James Sloan (1810–1892)

Brought up in an Underground Railroad safehouse, Abigail Hopper "Abby" Gibbons practiced humanitarianism from girlhood. She was the daughter of two legends of the secret network, route planners Isaac Tatem Hopper and Sarah Tatum Hopper. From early girlhood, she participated in the housing, feeding, and clothing of runaway slaves. In 1833, she married banker and merchant James Sloan Gibbons of Wilmington, Delaware, a supporter of the *National Anti-Slavery Standard.* She continued her outreach to fugitives at their residence in New York City, where she opened a day school and promoted anti-slavery fairs.

Conservative Quakers disowned both James Gibbons and Isaac Hopper for their civil disobedience. During the draft riots in July 1863, the Gibbons home was ransacked. At the outbreak of the Civil War, Abby Gibbons volunteered as nurse administrator at the Washington Office Hospital. Her daughter, Sarah "Sally" Hopper Gibbons Emerson, composed a biography of Abby Gibbons in 1897.

See also: anti-slavery fairs; civil disobedience; Quakers.

Source

Bacon, Margaret Hope. *Abby Hopper Gibbons: Prison Reformer and Social Activist.* Albany: State University of New York Press, 2000.

Gibbons, Daniel (1775–1853) Gibbons, Hannah Wierman (1787–1860)

An agent at Station 2 of the Lancaster County network in southern Pennsylvania, in 1802, Daniel Gibbons mapped out the Pilgrim's Pathway, the Underground Railroad route north of the Mason-Dixon Line. The son of abolitionist James Gibbons, Daniel Gibbons was a tanner and farmer. He began his rescue of slaves in 1797 and continued for 56 years. In partnership with Elizabeth W. Moore and Jeremiah Moore, Gibbons and his wife, Hannah Wierman Gibbons, received runaways from Maryland and Virginia who entered the state after crossing the Susquehanna River in Wrightsville. The couple transported the fugitives to Lewis Peart in Lampeter, to the Reverend Eusebius Barnard and Sarah Painter Barnard in Pocopsin, to Hannah Marsh and Gravner Marsh in Caln, and to Micajah Speakman, Phebe Smith Speakman, and William Allibone Speakman in Wallace.

For a quarter century, Daniel and Hannah Gibbons were elders in the Society of Friends and mentors of a nephew, Daniel Bonsall, who became an Underground Railroad conductor in Salem, Ohio. At their stone residence on Mill Creek in the hamlet of Bird-in-Hand, they received passengers from William Wright of Columbia, who resorted to providing female attire to help male slaves elude recapture. The Gibbons sequestered slaves in their barn and under corn shocks. One close call required Daniel to keep slave hunters talking while Hannah hid a runaway under a rain barrel. A man who developed smallpox received care from Hannah, who quarantined herself during the man's six-week convalescence. From the Gibbons home, slaves moved on to Susan P. Johnson Bonsall and Thomas Bonsall in Wagontown, to Joseph and Mary Ann Fulton in Sadsbury, or to Gideon Pierce and James Fulton, Jr., in Ercildoun. Around 1818, the Gibbons welcomed Abraham Boston and boarded him until kidnappers seized him. Daniel Gibbons searched the Baltimore area for his friend but never found him.

After a chronic inflammation in his feet and legs forced Daniel Gibbons to stop conducting slaves personally from station to station, he and his wife had to depend on fellow conductors, including Thomas Bonsall and Lindley Coates. The Gibbons family remained on the alert for decoys sent to their station by spies to learn the secret route. On March 14, 1848, they rescued Nelson Hilliard, a mulatto who escaped bondage to Colonel Edward Colson in Berkeley County, Virginia (now West Virginia). The couple renamed him Levi Johnson. They cataloged this and other rescues until the passage of the Fugitive Slave Law of 1850. After 1850, to ensure secrecy, Gibbons burned the record book and identified each subsequent runaway by an alias. About 1,000 escapees gained freedom through the intervention of the Gibbons family, which included an activist son, Dr. Joseph Gibbons. When Daniel Gibbons grew too feeble to board fugitives, he passed his duties to Deborah T. Simmons Coates and Lindley Coates in Sadsbury. The Gibbons' daughter-in-law, essayist and scholar Phebe Earle Gibbons, the daughter of Philadelphia abolitionist attorney Thomas Earle, edited *History of the Underground Railroad in Chester and the Neighboring Counties of Pennsylvania* (1883), the incomplete manuscript of historian Robert Clemens Smedley.

See also: Pilgrim's Pathway; spies.

Source

Gibbons, Phebe Earle. *Pennsylvania Dutch & Other Essays.* Philadelphia: J.B. Lippincott, 1882.

Gibbons, Joseph (1818–1883)
Gibbons, Phebe Earle (1821–1893)

An English Quaker whose great-grandfather settled a tract of William Penn's colony, Dr. Joseph Gibbons was a philanthropist, temperance advocate, and third-generation defender of runaway slaves. A native of Lancaster, Pennsylvania, he was the only surviving child of renowned Underground Railroad conductors Daniel Gibbons and Hannah Wierman Gibbons, who operated a safehouse in Bird-in-Hand for over half a century. Joseph grew up aiding his parents' work when his father was too sick to conduct passengers. He and his parents rescued about 1,000 refugees.

Following a boarding school education, Joseph Gibbons trained as a family physician under Dr. Francis S. Burrowes and completed a medical degree at Jefferson Medical College. After marriage in September 1845 to Quaker essayist Phebe Earle, the daughter of abolitionist attorney Thomas Earle, Joseph and his wife continued the family tradition of aiding escapees in Lancaster. For assistance, they conspired with two families of the Pilgrim's Pathway—Deborah T. Simmons Coates and Lindley Coates in Sadsbury and Thomas Whitson in Bart. A decade after he established the *Friends' Journal,* a Quaker newsletter, Joseph Gibbons died from a paralytic stroke at age 65. The *Brooklyn Eagle* accorded him a dignified obituary and honor for his aid to black refugees.

See also: philanthropists; Pilgrim's Pathway.

Sources

"Dr. Joseph Gibbons," *Brooklyn (NY) Eagle,* December 10, 1883, 4.
Gibbons, Phebe Earle. *Pennsylvania Dutch & Other Essays.* Philadelphia: J.B. Lippincott, 1882.
Wilson, James Grant, and John Fiske, eds. *Appleton's Cyclopaedia of American Biography.* New York: D. Appleton, 1888.

Gibbs, Jonathan C. (1827–1874)

A compatriot of Frederick Douglass and a contributor to the Underground Railroad activism of Rensselaer County, New York, the Reverend Jonathan C. Gibbs used the Liberty Street Presbyterian Church as the base of his operations. A freeborn black from Philadelphia, Pennsylvania, he worked as a bootblack and a carpenter during construction of the Mother Bethel African Methodist Episcopal Church, one of the city's busy reception centers for black fugitives. At age 21, he entered Dartmouth College. With an advanced degree from Princeton, he began serving churches in Troy, in Rensselaer County, New York, and in Philadelphia.

Jonathan Gibbs, like his older brother, Mifflin Wistar Gibbs, involved himself in aiding refugee slaves. In Troy, he joined the city's vigilance committee to protect fugitives from recapture. While volunteering in Pennsylvania for the Philadelphia Anti-Slavery Society, he organized and conducted slaves for the secret network and guided some passengers directly to Canada. During the Civil War, he enlisted blacks for the Union army and aided freedmen.

See also: African Methodist Episcopal Church; vigilance committees.

Source

Foner, Philip S., and Robert James Branham, eds. *Lift Every Voice: African American Oratory 1787–1900.* Tuscaloosa: University of Alabama Press, 1998.

Gibbs, Leonard (1799–1863)
Gibbs, Mary Ann Beckwith (1813–1882)

An abolitionist orator and attorney, Leonard Gibbs of Washington County, New York, was a member of a slave rescue team in Union Village (now Greenwich) on the Batten Kill River. He espoused radical ideas about the immediate abolition of slavery. In April 1834, he married Mary Ann Beckwith of Granville, New York. From 1840 to 1845, the couple conspired with Dr. Hiram Corliss, Angelina Gifford Mowry, and William H. Mowry to help runaways. The Gibbs family aided fugitives through New York City from their home at 22 Second Street and from Leonard Gibbs's office at 18 Wall Street. In 1841, Leonard began a four-year term on the executive committee of the American and Foreign Anti-Slavery Society.

After passage of the Fugitive Slave Law of 1850, Leonard Gibbs publicly denounced the measure for its violation of the Constitution and the denial of human rights. To improve state efforts on behalf of refugees, he took the organization post of the Eastern

New York Anti-Slavery Society left vacant in 1850 by the sudden death of William Mowry. Among Gibbs's clients was William "Jerry" McHenry, whom Underground Railroad agents broke from Clinton Square jail in Syracuse, New York, on October 1, 1851. In 1854, Gibbs joined William Wells Brown, Frederick Douglass, Beriah Green, and Gerrit Smith in addressing a biennial meeting of the Syracuse Anti-Slavery Society.

See also: Fugitive Slave Law of 1850.

Source

Powell, Aaron M. *Personal Reminiscences of the Anti-Slavery and Other Reforms and Reformers.* New York: Colored Press, 1899.

Gibbs, Mifflin Wistar (1823–1915)

Attorney and politician Mifflin Wistar Gibbs, like his younger brother, Jonathan C. Gibbs, devoted himself to the rescue of black slaves. Born in Philadelphia, Pennsylvania, he was the son of free blacks—Methodist preacher Jonathan C. Gibbs and Maria Jackson Gibbs. In his late teens, he joined William Still in helping escapees along the Underground Railroad route. He learned construction and carpentry before venturing into realty and retail clothing. In 1849, he toured New York with orator and editor Frederick Douglass. After a survey of the California goldfields, Gibbs settled in San Francisco, shined shoes, and bought a hotel. In 1855, he purchased an abolitionist journal, *Mirror of the Times,* California's first black newspaper, which remained in circulation until 1858. In spring 1858, Gibbs organized an abolitionist effort in California in response to the arrest of Archy Lee, a runaway. In 1902, Gibbs published a memoir, *Shadow and Light: An Autobiography with Reminiscences of the Last and Present Century.*

Sources

Gibbs, Mifflin Wistar. *Shadow and Light: An Autobiography with Reminiscences of the Last and Present Century.* Washington, DC: M.W. Gibbs, 1902.

Washington, Booker Taliaferro. *A New Negro for a New Century.* Miami: Mnemosyne, 1969.

Gibson, John (1798–1861)

John Gibson faced seven years in prison for his aid to desperate slaves. After a court found him guilty, at age 60, he entered the Missouri state penitentiary at Jefferson City in May 1858. Three years later, he died in jail.

Source

Frazier, Harriet C. *Runaway and Freed Missouri Slaves and Those Who Helped Them, 1763–1865.* Jefferson, NC: McFarland, 2004.

Giddings, Joshua Reed (1795–1864)
Giddings, Laura Waters (1798–1864)

A respected U.S. Congressman, attorney Joshua Reed "Gid" Giddings of Bradford County, Pennsylvania, maintained a depot of the Underground Railroad. In 1819, he married Laura Waters of Trumbull, Ohio. At their home and at the two-room office Joshua Giddings shared with Benjamin Franklin Wade on 112 North Chestnut Street in Jefferson, in Ashtabula County, Ohio, for two decades the Giddings family sheltered refugees, including Charles A. "Charley" Garlick, a student at Oberlin College. Passengers advanced to the one-room log cabin depot of Elias Tetirick and Sarah Ford Tetirick in Winterset, Ohio. Simultaneously, the Giddings supported the waystations of agents Elisha Farnham and Mary Ring Farnham in Conneaut, Ohio, and George Atcheson in southern Pennsylvania and fought slavery through legislation and in the courts. The U.S. Congress censured Joshua Giddings in 1841 for defending slaves transported aboard the brig *Creole* to New Orleans from Hampton Roads, Virginia. The public humiliation forced Giddings's resignation, but his reelection impressed on the proslavery factions his popularity in the Midwest. His daughter, Laura Giddings, maintained the family's anti-slavery principles by marrying George Washington Julian, a Quaker legislator in Indiana.

Giddings's subsequent support of abolition earned him respect for his candor and humanity. He joined philanthropists Salmon Portland Chase, Francis Jackson, Gerrit Smith, Lewis Tappan, and John Greenleaf Whittier in hiring a legal team to defend agent William Lawrence Chaplin, who was arrested in 1848 for aiding in the flight of a family of six—Emily, Ephraim, Mary Catherine, John, Richard, and Samuel Edmondson. The siblings joined a party of 77 slaves that Captain Daniel Drayton tried to relay to New Jersey aboard the schooner *Pearl.* In 1849, Giddings strategized with U.S. Congressman Abraham Lincoln and attorney Salmon Portland Chase on the abolition of slavery in the District of Columbia. On December 21, 1853, Giddings delivered a speech in the U.S. Congress—some 12 years after the fact—concerning

Before and during his more than two decades in the U.S. House of Representatives (1838–1859), Joshua Reed Giddings of Ohio and his family harbored refugees, led them to the next depot north, and supported other nearby waystations. *(Library of Congress)*

the rights of Joseph Cinqué and other African mutineers aboard the slave ship *Amistad.*

After the seizure of John Price on September 18, 1858, known as the Oberlin-Wellington rescue, Giddings defended civil disobedience. He harangued 2,000 protesters in Cleveland, Ohio, on the right of citizens to protect a slave from a posse. On May 24, 1859, Giddings invited Salmon P. Chase and John Mercer Langston to warn voters in Cleveland, Ohio, of President James Buchanan's connections with the slave-holding South. In 1861, President Abraham Lincoln named Giddings the U.S. consul general of Canada. The Giddings law office is a National Historic Landmark.

See also: Amistad; civil disobedience; Oberlin College; philanthropists.

Sources

Brandt, Nat. *The Town That Started the Civil War.* Syracuse, NY: Syracuse University Press, 1990.

Shipherd, Jacob R. *History of the Oberlin-Wellington Rescue.* Boston: John P. Jewett, 1859.

Gilbert, Almira M. Reed (1825–1901)
Gilbert, Warren (1822–1899)

Two Underground Railroad operatives, Almira M. Reed Gilbert and Warren Gilbert, welcomed refugees to a safehouse in Rome Township, in Lenawee County, Michigan. A native of Richmond in Ontario County, New York, Warren Gilbert was the grandson of a Revolutionary War veteran and the son of a pioneer farmer in Grand River, in Clinton County, Michigan. The Gilberts, who married in 1845, championed temperance, woman's suffrage, and abolitionism. At their farm, they rescued slaves in conjunction with the work of Thomas Chandler, Charles Haviland, and Laura Smith Haviland in Raisin, Michigan. By invigorating the Michigan Anti-Slavery Society and sheltering runaways, the Gilberts influenced their neighbors to treat the destitute wayfarer with kindness.

Source

Knapp, John I. *Illustrated History and Biographical Record of Lenawee County, Michigan.* Adrian, MI: Times Printing, 1903.

Gilbert, Amos (1781–?)

A Quaker promoter of compassion to fugitive slaves, Amos Gilbert of Bucks County, Pennsylvania, recruited others to the fight for liberty. He enlisted Daniel Howell Hise and Martha Hise, who opened a waystation in Salem, Ohio. Only three months before the onset of the Civil War, in January 1861, Gilbert encouraged the career of 19-year-old platform orator Anna Elizabeth Dickinson with a letter of advice.

Source

Cashin, Joan E. *War Was You and Me: Civilians in the American Civil War.* Princeton, NJ: Princeton University Press, 2002.

Gilbert, Hiram (1799–1857)
Gilbert, Lucy Harrington (1798–1877)

Two Underground Railroad agents in Fulton, in Oswego County, New York, Deacon Hiram Gilbert of Paris, New York, and his wife, Lucy Harrington Gilbert of Sanquoit, New York, based their actions on staunch Congregationalist beliefs. Hiram was a pioneer to the area; after moving from Oneida County in 1830, he and his brother Andrus built a dam and gristmill. At Gilbert Mills Road on Six-Mile Creek in 1837, Hiram and Lucy Gilbert began their work for the secret network with the harboring of a slave named George. As members of the racially integrated Bristol Hill Congregational Church in Volney, the couple allied with agents Amos Mason and Hannah Seward Mason in helping a fugitive slave escape. One of the Gilberts' rescues involved one of a pair of sisters. The woman was reunited with her sibling, who lodged at the safehouse of Rhoda and Stephen Griffith on Gilbert Mills Road. The Gilberts joined other church members in coming to the aid of General William Lawrence "Will" Chaplin, who was arrested in August 1850 for helping 77 slaves escaping from the Washington, D.C., area aboard Captain Daniel Drayton's sloop, *Pearl.*

Source

"Fugitive George," *Friend of Man,* July 4, 1838.

Gilbert, Mary Wetherbee (1796–1843)
Gilbert, Timothy (1797–1865)

Two respected abolitionists, Deacon Timothy Gilbert and his wife, Mary Wetherbee Gilbert of Ashburnham, Massachusetts, fought for freedom by joining in the activities at the Tremont Street Church in Boston. A wealthy piano manufacturer, Timothy Gilbert was ousted from the Charles Street Baptist Church for inviting black worshippers to share his pew in the white section of the segregated sanctuary. He and his wife founded the First Baptist Free Church (later called Tremont Street Church), the city's first integrated congregation. The Gilberts established a safehouse at Two Beach Street that could harbor as many as six runaways at a time. Mary also channeled her activism into service to the Boston Female Anti-Slavery Society. A pious, hospitable woman, she earned regard for tending the poor, malnourished, and sick hidden in her garret.

See also: female anti-slavery societies.

Source

Fulton, Justin D., ed. *Memoir of Timothy Gilbert.* Boston: Lee & Shepard, 1866.

Gillette, Francis (1807–1879)
Gillette, Elizabeth Daggett Hooker (1813–1893)

A staunch abolitionist, U.S. Senator Francis Gillette and his wife, Elizabeth "Eliza" Daggett Hooker Gillette, maintained two safehouses. They married in 1834 and made their home in Bloomfield, in Hartford County outside Hartford, Connecticut. The family lived down the street from Francis's cousin, Harriet Beecher Stowe, the author of *Uncle Tom's Cabin* (1852), and attended Asylum Hill Congregational Church. When the Gillettes opened their two-story home at 511 Bloomfield Avenue to black fugitives, Francis Gillette became the first U.S. senator to support the Underground Railroad through illegal slave rescues.

Passengers of the Underground Railroad traveling from New York through New England to Canada found welcome with the Gillettes. In 1853, they bought 100 acres and built a second waystation in their barn. Francis Gillette expressed his sentiments on the Fugitive Slave Law of 1850 in "National Slavery and National Responsibility," a speech delivered in the U.S. Senate on February 23, 1855.

See also: Fugitive Slave Law of 1850; safehouses; *Uncle Tom's Cabin; or, Life Among the Lowly* (1852).

Sources

Bushnell, Horace. *Discourse on the Slavery Question.* Hartford, CT: S.S. Cowles, 1839.
Gillette, Francis. *National Slavery and National Responsibility.* Washington, DC: Buell & Blanchard, 1855.

Gilliland, James (1769–1845)
Gilliland, Frances Baird (1773–1837)

The pastor of Red Oak Presbyterian Church in southern Ohio from 1805 to 1841, the Reverend James Gilliland of Lincoln, North Carolina, operated an Underground Railroad depot. In 1793, he married Frances Baird. He graduated from Dickinson College and entered the ministry in 1796 but immediately created dissension among pro-slavery parishioners. In Red Oak, Ohio, among southern abolitionists from Kentucky and Virginia, he raised the consciousness of Christians about the necessity for civil disobedience. The Gillilands conspired with Jean Lowry Rankin and John Rankin, conductors in Ripley, Ohio, in assisting runaways newly arrived in free territory after crossing the Ohio River. The Gillilands raised funds for destitute refugees through rallies and special collections. In 1912, James Gilliland and a compatriot, John P. Parker, were honorees of Ripley's Liberty Monument, an obelisk overlooking the Ohio River.

See also: civil disobedience.

Sources

Hagedorn, Ann. *Beyond the River: The Untold Story of the Heroes of the Underground Railroad.* New York: Simon & Schuster, 2002.

Parker, John P. *John P. Parker, His Promised Land: The Autobiography of John P. Parker, Former Slave and Conductor on the Underground Railroad.* New York: W.W. Norton, 1996.

Gillingham, James (1768–1865) Gillingham, Sarah Wood (ca. 1772–?)

Quaker Underground Railroad operatives James Gillingham and Sarah Wood Gillingham of Bucks County, Pennsylvania, depended on neighborhood cooperation to protect their depot. The couple married in 1792. At a two-story brick residence at 622 Mahantango Street in Pottsville, Pennsylvania, the family boarded refugees, who hid in a crawl space. Contributing to the success of the operation were two black collaborators, former slave Nicholas "Nick" Biddle and John Lee. A "First Defender," one of the initial volunteers after the firing on Fort Sumter, South Carolina, on April 18, 1861, Biddle, the first Union soldier injured in the Civil War, was struck in the head with a brick at the Baltimore train station during a skirmish to protect Washington, D.C., from Confederate assault.

Source

"Answering New Call, Unit to March Again," *Schuylkill (PA) Republican & Herald,* July 6, 2002.

Gist Settlement

Among those blacks seeking a life of liberty were the chattel freed on February 10, 1818, in the will of British merchant Samuel Gist, a Virginia planter and slave-ship owner worth nearly $6 million. On proceeds of a trust fund, some of the 950 manumitted bondsmen formed the Gist settlement in Dark Town, a section of New Vienna, in Brown and Highland counties north of Ripley, Ohio. Additional Gist camps sprang up in Adams, Brown, and Erie counties. Residents received 31-acre plots on which to establish their families. As agents of the Underground Railroad, they welcomed escapees and protected them from slave catchers and kidnappers.

Active in the rescues was conductor John D. Hudson of Sardinia, Ohio. For his labors, the Reverend John Bennington Mahan and others paid Hudson 25¢ per rescue. Hudson successfully guided a runaway named Ike by blowing on a conch shell as an alert to his collaborators that slave catchers were in the area. In August 1856, the failure of a rescue aroused the Gist community. A freedman, 33-year-old George Williams, allegedly led slaves from Kentucky along the Ripley, Ohio, route when the slave hunters of Dr. James E. McDowell of Mason County, Kentucky, seized Williams and threatened him with guns and knives for violating the Fugitive Slave Law of 1850. His forced confession resulted in a term at the Kentucky state penitentiary in Frankfort beginning on October 31, 1856. Williams died in his cell on December 29, 1858, of tuberculosis.

See also: Fugitive Slave Law of 1850; kidnap; slave recovery.

Source

Hagedorn, Ann. *Beyond the River: The Untold Story of the Heroes of the Underground Railroad.* New York: Simon & Schuster, 2002.

Glass, John (fl. 1840s–1850s)

One of the discreet operatives in Erie County, Pennsylvania, iron foundryman John Glass offered shelter and transport to runaways. On one failed relay, shortly after midnight, he aided Ned, a North Carolina fugitive with an unusually large reward on his head for his recapture. To escape the sheriff, Glass roused Ned from sleep at the sanctuary operated by James Crawford on Sixteen-Mile Creek. Glass hid Ned under patterns and frames in his wagon and drove the 22 miles over his usual business route to Erie. When the sheriff rifled the waystation after dawn, he found nothing and gave up the chase. Glass encountered a pro-slavery neighbor, who spied Ned in the wagon. As the neighbor raced back for the constable, Glass hurried Ned to a boat captain, who boarded the runaway on his sloop. The sheriff arrived in time to halt the transfer over Lake Erie to Canada.

Source

Thorpe, Frances Newton. *A Constitutional History of the American People, 1776–1850.* New York: Harpers, 1898.

Gloucester, James A. (fl. 1830s–1840s)

The pastor of Siloam Presbyterian Church in Brooklyn, New York, the Reverend James A. Gloucester (also Glocester) ministered to runaways. A former slave, he knew the desperation of black Americans fleeing bondage and supported Frederick Douglass's work for the Underground Railroad. After the founding of the church in 1849 at 260 Jefferson Avenue, during his tenure, from 1849 to 1851, he harbored fugitives until they could move on to private waystations. To provide for their food, medicines, and clothing, the congregation supported the New York Vigilance Committee. Church philanthropists also donated $25 to insurrectionist John Brown to supply munitions for the raid on the federal arsenal at Harpers Ferry, Virginia.

See also: philanthropists; vigilance committees.

Sources

Douglass, Frederick. *Life and Times of Frederick Douglass.* Boston: De Wolfe & Fiske, 1892.
Mitchell, Henry H. *Black Church Beginnings: The Long-Hidden Realities of the First Years.* Grand Rapids, MI: Wm. B. Eerdmans, 2004.

Glover, Joshua (ca. 1808–?)

In spring 1852, Joshua Glover, a burly 44-year-old refugee from St. Louis, Missouri, traveled the secret network to a waystation in Racine, Wisconsin. He settled in the town and worked as a sawyer at Rice's mill. Two years later, slave owner Benammi (or Benjamin) S. Garland led U.S. Deputy Marshal Charles C. Cotton to Glover's cabin, where Glover was captured during a card game. The men transported Glover by wagon over a roundabout route to Milwaukee, where he arrived bruised and bleeding with his neck constrained by a marshal's foot. On March 11, 1854, Underground Railroad agents, aided by Sherman Miller Booth, editor of the *American Freeman,* converged in the Milwaukee County jail at 2 P.M. Outraged citizens rang bells to summon a throng; 100 men arrived by boat from Racine. Using pickaxes and a wood beam that George Bingham and James S. Angove, a carpenter from Cornwall, England, wielded like a battering ram, the mob freed Glover from his cell. John A. Messinger, the owner of a brickyard, transported Glover by buggy to Waukesha, Wisconsin. Through a Racine agent, Glover boarded a boat in Racine harbor bound across Lake Michigan for Canada.

Litigation over the Joshua Glover incident—dubbed the Booth War—dragged as activists challenged the legalities involved. Four days later, federal authorities arrested Booth for violating the Fugitive Slave Law of 1850 by abetting Glover's escape. On March 31, 1854, orator Wendell Addison Phillips dispatched two volumes of the works of scholar Theodore Parker to supply Booth with arguments for his defense. Represented by attorney Byron Paine, Booth established his innocence before Wisconsin Supreme Court Judge A.D. Smith, who sympathized with Glover's rescuers.

Glover's escape from bondage developed into a rallying cry for abolitionists. On August 8, 1854, U.S. Senator Charles Sumner urged Byron Paine to publish his defense in a pamphlet, which hawkers later sold by the thousands on the streets of Boston. Phillips wrote a second time, on November 24, to congratulate Paine on freeing Booth. After Booth and his accomplice, John Rycraft of Milwaukee, were arrested by federal marshals and tried in a U.S. district court for violating the Fugitive Slave Law of 1850, a judge fined Booth $2,451 and sentenced him to 30 days in jail. Rycraft paid a fine of $200 and spent 10 days in jail. Again, Booth appealed and won. Because of intense abolitionist fervor, Judge Andrew G. Miller of the U.S. District Court of Madison chose not to press charges against others complicit in Joshua Glover's jailbreak.

See also: Fugitive Slave Law of 1850.

Sources

Clark, James I. *Wisconsin Defies the Fugitive Slave Law.* Madison: State Historical Society of Wisconsin, 1955.
Davidson, John Nelson. *Negro Slavery in Wisconsin and the Underground Railroad.* Milwaukee, WI: Parkman Club, 1897.
"Helped Save Glover," *Milwaukee Sentinel,* June 10, 1900.
Legler, Henry E. *Leading Events of Wisconsin History.* Milwaukee, WI: *Milwaukee Sentinel,* 1898.
"Letters on the Glover Incident," *Abbotsford (WI) Clarion,* December 13, 1896.

Goodell, William (1792–1878)
Goodell, Clarissa C. Cady (?–1878)

Confederates of the Reverend Edward Corrie Pritchett and Sophia Lawson Pritchett in Union Village, New York, the Reverend William Goodell and his wife, Clarissa C. Cady Goodell of Providence, Rhode Island, served the Underground Railroad. Born in Coventry, New York, William Goodell and Clarissa Cady married in 1832 and made their home in Utica. William pursued an idealistic career in temperance lectures and journalism. In 1833, he joined William Lloyd Garrison, Arthur Tappan, and John Greenleaf Whittier in forming the American Anti-Slavery Society. Goodell exhibited his knowledge of constitutional law regarding civil rights in the essay "Slavery Tested by Its Own Code," which appeared in the October 1835 issue of the *Quarterly Anti-Slavery Magazine.*

In 1836, William Goodell became editor of the weekly *Friend of Man,* a job he held for six years on behalf of the New York State Anti-Slavery Society. The Goodells invited passengers to their home and dinner table, where the table service bore a motto from the Declaration of Independence (1776): "We hold these truths to be self-evident that all men are created equal." During abolitionist activity, William Goodell and William Morrison Tallman escaped a pro-slavery mob. In 1847, Goodell promoted formation of the Liberty League, a consortium of radical activists in New York and Canada. In 1852, he continued his abolitionist journalism as editor of the *Principia,* which he co-edited with his daughter, Lavinia Goodell (1826–1880), until 1864.

See also: American Anti-Slavery Society; Liberty League.

Sources

Frost, William Goodell. *For the Mountains, an Autobiography.* New York: Fleming H. Revell, 1937.
Goodell, William. "Slavery Tested by Its Own Code." *Quarterly Anti-Slavery Magazine* (October 1835): 29.

Goodnow, Lyman (1799–ca. 1885)

A pioneer and initiator of Underground Railroad activism in Wisconsin, Lyman Goodnow (or Goodenow) harbored slaves at his residence. A native of Rutland, Massachusetts, he established a quarry at Frame Field in Prairieville (now called Waukesha), Wisconsin, and, in 1840, dealt in lime and native stone. He is best known for orchestrating the rescue of 18-year-old Caroline Quarrels, a mulatto who escaped by steamer from St. Louis, Missouri. In August 1843, Goodnow and Deacon Ezra Mendell relayed her 30 miles by horse and buggy to the Spring Prairie waystation of Solomon Ashley Dwinnell on Bowers Road in Walworth County.

The complete 600-mile journey to Detroit, Michigan, took five weeks. Dr. Edward Galusha Dyer of Burlington, Wisconsin, provided Goodnow and his passenger with a pillowcase stuffed with cheese and pastries and offered Goodnow a letter introducing him to stationkeepers along the route. On the way, Goodnow passed through the safekeeping of the Reverend Guy Beckley of Ann Arbor, Michigan. After crossing the Detroit River, Quarrels lived free in Sandwich, Ontario. On April 18, 1880, she sent Goodnow a thank-you letter. In 1934, the Waukesha County Historical Society placed a bronze tablet on Goodnow's grave in Prairie Home Cemetery.

Sources

Davidson, John Nelson. *Negro Slavery in Wisconsin and the Underground Railroad.* Milwaukee, WI: Parkman Club, 1897.
"Historical Society to Honor Lyman Goodnow," *Waukesha (WI) Daily Freeman,* December 9, 1933.

Goodrich, Joseph (1800–1867)
Goodrich, Nancy Maxson (1796–1857)

A Seventh-Day Baptist pioneer from Hancock, Massachusetts, Joseph Goodrich earned renown as an Underground Railroad operative. At age 38, he moved to Prairie du Lac on the Michigan frontier. In 1844, he housed his wife, Nancy Maxson Goodrich, and their children, Ezra and Jane, in a two-story log hotel at the crossing of American Indian trails a few miles from Janesville, Wisconsin. He built Milton House, a hexagonal stagecoach inn and store constructed of lime and gravel, which served as the local school and Seventh-Day Baptist Church. The structure also became a depot of the Underground Railroad on the road between Walworth and Johnstown.

Will Davis, one of the transporters aiding Goodrich, drove a hay wagon to the inn, paused for dinner, and returned to find slaves unloaded and conveyed to safe quarters. A dirt-floored tunnel from 3 to 5 feet high and 40 feet long led through a trapdoor in a log cabin through the root cellar to the basement of the inn, where the slaves could warm themselves, eat, and rest without detection. One of Goodrich's guests was Sojourner Truth, who arrived around 1861 to address students at Milton Academy. Attending the refugees in 1864 was a dining room employee, Mary Schackelmann Meyer.

When Goodrich heard the alarm that slave catchers were approaching, he activated an escape plan. He had his passengers reverse their route back through the tunnel to the cabin, from which they could hurry to Storrs Lake and Lake Koshkonong. Another pair of safehouses were nearby, the academy and the church at Albion, offered alternate hideaways. The secret network route continued to Fort Atkinson. One scrap of written evidence of local activism reports the delivery of Andrew Pratt from Missouri in 1861, when agent William A. Goodrich directed him to Milton. Pratt made his home in the area and worked for David Plotts. Currently a National Historic Landmark, Milton House is a showplace of the National Park Service. Archaeologist Bob Fay excavated the tavern in 2003 and located 10,000 artifacts, including pottery, glass bottles, nails, glass, and clay pipe stems.

See also: safehouses.

Source

Bicentennial History of Milton. Milton, WI: Milton Historical Society, 1977.

Goodridge, William C. (1805–1873) Goodridge, Emily Wallace (1815–1852)

William C. Goodridge was a model of the resourceful Underground Railroad operative. The mulatto grandson of a slave woman owned by Charles Carroll, a signer of the Declaration of Independence, he was born in Baltimore, Maryland. Carroll sold Goodridge's mother to the white physician who sired Goodridge. In 1811, the boy apprenticed in the Reverend William Dunn's tannery in York, Pennsylvania. A surprise manumission in 1821 allowed Goodridge to set out on his own. He married Emily Wallace of Baltimore and learned barbering, which he practiced in York at his shop on Centre Square. He invested in jewelry, wigs, a confectionery, railroads, and a newspaper clearinghouse.

The Goodridges thrived at foiling slave hunters. Under the close watch of spies, they networked with neighbors Amos Griest and Margaret Garretson Griest and conducted runaway slaves by rail and from their residence at 123 East Philadelphia Street. For security, they concealed passengers in straw in a ditch, under an outbuilding, in a cellar chamber, and behind paneling on the third story of William's photography studio at Centre Square. For rapid transport, William Goodridge placed refugees in baggage cars on direct rail routes to Columbia or Philadelphia, Pennsylvania, where runaways sheltered at the anti-slavery office of William Still, an agent of the city vigilance committee.

Another of the Goodridge family's famous rescues was Osborne Perry Anderson, the only black Canadian to join insurrectionist John Brown's attack on the federal arsenal at Harpers Ferry, Virginia, on October 16, 1859. When rebel forces overran York in June 1863, the Goodridges sought safety in Minnesota. A daughter, Emily Goodridge Grey, continued the family tradition of rescuing slaves in St. Anthony Falls, Minnesota.

See also: routes, Underground Railroad; spies.

Source

Williams, Isaac D. *Sunshine and Shadow of Slave Life: Reminiscences as Told by Isaac D. Williams to "Tege."* East Saginaw, MI: *Evening News,* 1885.

Goodwin, Abigail (1793–1867) Goodwin, Elizabeth (1789–1860)

In Salem, on the southwestern coast of New Jersey, from 1837 to 1861, Quaker conductors Abigail "Abbie" Goodwin and her older sister, Elizabeth "Betsy" Goodwin, worked into old age for the rescue of runaway slaves. An unassuming humanitarian, Abigail Goodwin was well connected to abolitionists. She was a friend and supporter of notable female conductors Lydia Maria Francis Child, Abby Kelley Foster, Angelina Emily Grimké, Sarah Moore Grimké, Lucretia Coffin Mott, and Harriet Forten Purvis. After co-founding the Female Benevolent Society in 1814, Abigail energized a committee visiting the sick. One of the Goodwins' friends, the Reverend James Miller McKim, encountered a throng of rowdies on June 21, 1837, when he came to Salem to lecture. After the Goodwins rescheduled the event at the Salem courthouse, anti-abolitionists assailed their home, shouted crude slogans, and burned McKim in effigy.

In league with agents Esther Moore, Thomas Clement Oliver, and Harriet Tubman, the Goodwin sisters maintained a waystation at 47 Market Street for refugee runaways from Delaware, Maryland, and Washington, D.C. At the urging of Quaker activist Mary Grew, in June 1837, Abbie Goodwin began superintending slave passage through Salem County. The Goodwins received passengers from Cape May, Cumberland, Elsinboro, and Greenwich and offered benevolence and medical care before sending the slaves along to the next waystation. The job required constant fundraising and enlistment of local rescuers to complete slave transport along the Raritan River to the seaport at New Brunswick. To maintain their outreach, the Goodwins scrimped on personal needs, begged for donations of fabric and thread, and organized a sewing circle to make garments for their charity closet. They dressed ragged slaves in warm stockings and cloaks and collected small garments for infants and children, who received the Goodwins' maternal concern.

In addition to financing their own depot, the Goodwin sisters contributed to the purchase of a family of 10 slaves from bondage in North Carolina. The women gave money regularly to the Philadelphia Vigilance Committee and supported schools in Canada to raise the literacy rate among black newcomers. They supported a controversial activist, Captain Daniel

Drayton of the sloop *Pearl,* who, on April 15, 1848, attempted one of the largest mass slave escapes in U.S. history. At his release following a four-year prison sentence, the Goodwins welcomed him to their home. In summer 1855, the sisters received Thomas Bayne, a dental assistant who had fled by sea from Norfolk, Virginia. At the imprisonment in 1855 of attorney Passmore Williamson in Moyamensing Prison for three months for aiding in the escape of Jane Johnson from slavery, the Goodwins lent their moral support to him through encouraging letters.

Sources

MacLean, Alexander. "The Underground Railroad in Hudson County." Speech, Hudson County Historical Society, Hudson County, NJ, 1908.

Still, William. *The Underground Railroad.* Philadelphia: Porter & Coates, 1871.

Goodwin, Edwin Weyburn (1800–1845)

A colleague of secret network organizer Gerrit Smith and a transporter of refugees, Edwin Weyburn Goodwin assisted two conductors of the Underground Railroad. From his depot at 57 DeWitt Street in Albany, New York, where he moved in 1835, he relayed passengers across Lake Ontario from the waystations of the Reverend Abel Brown in Sand Lake and the Reverend Charles Turner Torrey in Salem, Massachusetts. Goodwin chaired a political committee of the Eastern New York Anti-Slavery Society and produced pen-and-ink miniatures for two abolitionist newspapers, the *Albany Patriot* and the *Tocsin of Liberty.* For his outbursts of radicalism, the Methodist Church expelled him.

See also: abolitionist newspapers.

Sources

Harrold, Stanley. *The Rise of Aggressive Abolitionism: Addresses to the Slaves.* Lexington: University Press of Kentucky, 2004.

Storke, Elliot G. *History of Cayuga County, New York.* Syracuse, NY: D. Mason, 1879.

Gorham, Charles T. (1812–1901)

Merchant and financier Charles T. Gorham assisted refugee slaves in Marshall, Michigan. At the seizure of Adam Crosswhite and Sarah Crosswhite, passengers of the Underground Railroad from Carroll County, Kentucky, on January 27, 1847, Gorham confronted slave owner Henry Troutman for inhumane treatment of slaves. Federal agents arrested Gorham and fined him $2,000 for conveying the Crosswhites. Although colleagues Zachariah Chandler and Isaac Davis and their neighbors in Climax, Michigan, offered to solicit funds to pay the fine, Gorham chose to send his own money. U.S. Senator Henry Clay of Kentucky used the case as justification for passage of the Fugitive Slave Law of 1850.

See also: Fugitive Slave Law of 1850.

Sources

Burton, Clarence Monroe. *The City of Detroit, Michigan, 1701–1922.* Detroit, MI: S.J. Clarke, 1922.

Gardner, Washington, ed. *History of Calhoun County, Michigan.* Chicago: Lewis, 1913.

Gragston, Arnold (1840–1938)

A freedman and agent of the Underground Railroad, Arnold Gragston transported refugees by water from northern Kentucky across the Ohio River to free territory. The native of western Mason County near Maysville, Kentucky, grew up in slavery on Jack Tabb's plantation. In 1859, while courting a girl on a distant plantation, he rowed her across the river from Dover toward a light in Ripley, Ohio. Gragston's subsequent passengers came through the depot of the Reverend John Gregg Fee, an outspoken Kentucky abolitionist who offered food, rags for cold feet, and advice on evading posses.

Gragston's four years of activism on the Kentucky–Ohio–Ontario line became a personal commitment to some 300 other slaves yearning for liberty. Until slave hunters pursued him in 1863, he transported refugees singly or in groups across the Ohio River to Liberty Hill, the waystation of Jean Lowry Rankin and John Rankin in Ripley, Ohio. From there, passengers made their way to New York City, Chicago, and Detroit, and then on to Ontario, which naive blacks identified as the outskirts of heaven. At first, Gragston chose to remain with Jack Tabb, who never discovered his slave's heroism. After marrying, Gragston directed his boat toward the Rankins' light only a few months before the national emancipation of slaves on January 1, 1863. Gragston and his wife made their home in Detroit, where they reared 10 children. At age 97, Arnold Gragston submitted his oral slave narration to the Federal Writers' Project, conducted at Eatonville, Florida.

Sources

Berlin, Ira, Marc Favreau, and Steven F. Miller. *Remembering Slavery: African Americans Talk About Their Personal Experiences of Slavery and Emancipation.* Detroit, MI: Free Press, 2001.

Goodman, Cynthia, and Spencer Crew. *Unchained Memories: Readings from the Slave Narratives.* New York: Bulfinch, 2002.

Grandy, Moses (1786–?)

Anticipating the founding of a formal underground network, ferryman Moses Grandy reported eyewitness accounts of fugitives' hardships in fleeing north to liberty. The youngest of eight children, Moses belonged to Billy Grandy of Camden County, North Carolina, a heartless slave speculator who flogged Moses's mother for weeping over the sale of her children. In 1830, Moses earned money to buy his freedom by piloting a canal boat. He settled in Boston, Massachusetts, and continued to thrive as a seaman. With his earnings, he freed his wife and some of their children. Grandy's book *Narrative of the Life of Moses Grandy, Late a Slave in the United States of America* (1843), published by the American Anti-Slavery Society, reported on the untiring labor of northern abolitionists in guiding runaway slaves to free states and then to Canada. He characterized the physical strain of running by night, hiding by day, feeding on wild fruit, swimming rivers, and studying the North Star for guidance.

See also: American Anti-Slavery Society; North Star.

Sources

Andrews, William L., with David A. Davis, Tampathia Evans, Ian Frederick Finseth, and Andreá N. Williams. *North Carolina Slave Narratives: The Lives of Moses Roper, Lunsford Lane, Moses Grandy, and Thomas H. Jones.* Chapel Hill: University of North Carolina Press, 2003.

Grandy, Moses. *Narrative of the Life of Moses Grandy, Late a Slave in the United States of America.* London: C. Gilpin, 1843.

Severance, Frank H. *Old Trails on the Niagara Frontier.* Buffalo, NY: n.p., 1899.

Grant, Marie (1805–?)
Grant, Tudor E. (ca. 1800–?)

Resourceful stationkeepers in Oswego, New York, Marie Grant and her husband, Tudor E. Grant, both from Maryland, sheltered fugitives fleeing via the Underground Railroad. Tudor Grant appears to have fled bondage in 1832. He flourished in Oswego as a barber at the Welland Hotel, as a silk dyer, and as a field representative of a popular abolitionist newspaper, the *Colored American.* The Grants maintained a three-story boardinghouse and depot on West Bridge Street and concealed passengers in the barn behind Abram Buckout's residence on West Fifth Street Road. On June 21, 1838, Sidney Clarke, Tudor Grant, and John Gridley volunteered to form a vigilance committee for the Oswego County Anti-Slavery Society. In addition, Tudor Grant protested the admission of more slave states to the Union and denounced the Fugitive Slave Law of 1850. The Tudor home is on the National Register of Historic Places and the National Underground Railroad Network to Freedom.

See also: abolitionist newspapers; Fugitive Slave Law of 1850.

Sources

History of Oswego County, New York. Philadelphia: L.H. Everts, 1877.

Wellman, Judith. "The Underground Railroad and the National Register of Historic Places: Historical Importance vs. Architectural Integrity." *Public Historian* 24:1 (Winter 2002): 11–29.

grapevine telegraphy

Slave owners, planters, and rescuers were aware that slaves in a given region communicated in many ways, both openly and in secret. In 1793, news that circulated would certainly have included the abolition of slave importation to Canada. Later, field hands in Georgia and the Carolinas began spreading the news of Negro Fort, Florida, a sanctuary on the Apalachicola River that survived the War of 1812 and offered a haven to refugees. Contributing data about the settlement of runaways in the North were black sailors, who moved freely among port cities.

The successful synergy of freedmen and slaves attests to the fact that racial ties boosted the hopes of those awaiting liberation. Among them was Lewis Hayden, the slave of a clock peddler in Lexington, Kentucky. Hayden collected snippets of information from slave owners, slave hunters, politicians, barkeeps, and gamblers. A clearinghouse for information began in lower Manhattan at the Colored Sailors' Home on Gold and John streets. Underground Railroad agents Mercy O. Haskins Powell and William Peter Powell managed the boardinghouse and received seamen and runaways, who posted messages to anxious families remaining in bondage. When the Powells moved to Liverpool, England, Albro Lyons and Mary Marshall Lyons continued their outreach to sailors.

One elderly Windsor, Ontario, resident, Henry Stevenson, hazily recalled his flight from Old Franklin, Missouri. He received bits of information along the way north and managed to arrive among friends in Quincy, Illinois. Underground Railroad operatives guided Stevenson to Chicago, where an agent offered him a ride and surprised him with the network's knowledge of his long passage. With gifts of food, clothing, and cash, Stevenson traveled by boat from New Buffalo to Detroit, Michigan, and crossed the Detroit River to Windsor, Ontario. Stevenson was amazed at the efficiency of the grapevine telegraphy that charted his route.

From 1831 to 1851, the Reverend Alick (also called Father or Uncle Alick), a black Methodist preacher and missionary, carried news to and from maroon settlements in the Great Dismal Swamp of North Carolina and Virginia. Dubbed the Swamp Postman, Alick remained current in the goings and comings at the Albemarle Sound and Chesapeake Bay. His itinerant ministry enabled maroons to keep in touch with plantation blacks and with those escaping to the North. Alick involved himself directly with the Underground Railroad after the Nat Turner revolt of 1831; that year he ferried a mother and child by mule over the secret paths of the fen and out of reach of white posses. In winter 1855/1856, Kentucky slaves learned that an unusually hard freeze had left an ice bridge over the Ohio River, the shortest route to freedom in the North. Among those taking advantage of crossing the river on foot were Margaret and Robert Garner, who fled Maplewood plantation with their children in late January 1856.

Grapevine telegraphy was one of many methods that illiterate people used to communicate with each other. In addition to coded spirituals and church message centers, they used drumming, pantomime dance, the blacksmith's rhythmic pounding, and coded raps on the door. Another form of nonverbal communication, patchwork quilts served as visual maps. Airing innocently on a clothesline or a porch rail, they pointed out landmarks, danger zones, mileage over hidden trails, and safehouses. For example, a quilt square might indicate that an agent of the Underground Railroad was near or due to arrive within days. Gathering and interpreting such information involved couriers, carriage drivers, body servants, boatmen, stevedores, blacksmiths, shop porters, and sailors, who amassed data on escape routes and calculated favorable times for running away. Among their coded messages was the identity of Joseph Smith, whom they called the Underground Railroad switch-turner for the importance of his station in Drumore, in Lancaster County, Pennsylvania.

In the memoir *Last of the Pioneers; or, Old Times in East Tennessee* (1902), author Pharaoh Jackson Chesney explained the grapevine method of broadcasting potential sources of rescue. Agents of the Underground Railroad had only to indicate their presence in a community. By such devices as the spiritual "There's a Man Going 'Round Takin' Names," slaves passed the news about the neighborhood, bolstering the will of some to make a break from the South. In *From Log Cabin to the Pulpit; or, Fifteen Years in Slavery* (1913), autobiographer William H. Robinson reported that his father was deceived by his owner during a surveying expedition to California. The news reached the Robinson family in Wilmington, North Carolina, by slave grapevine. Other news of the progress of slaves in northern cities and schools, such as Eleutherian College and Oberlin College, reached parents and grandparents still being held on southern plantations. One disseminator of information, John Hatfield, a barber on Ohio River steamers, gathered crucial descriptions of posses and slave catchers scouting the Ohio–Ontario route. Slave owners grew so wary of activist freedmen like Hatfield that they jailed black crews until their boats could leave southern harbors.

See also: bounty hunters; code, Underground Railroad; Dismal Swamp; Eleutherian College; maroon settlements; Oberlin College; quilts; routes, Underground Railroad; spirituals.

Sources

Chesney, Pharaoh Jackson, and John Coram Webster. *Last of the Pioneers; or, Old Times in East Tennessee.* Knoxville, TN: S.B. Newman, 1902.

Horton, James Oliver. *In Hope of Liberty: Culture, Community, and Protest Among Northern Free Blacks, 1700–1860.* Oxford, UK: Oxford University Press, 1998.

Leaming, Hugo Prosper. *Hidden Americans: Maroons of Virginia and the Carolinas.* New York: Garland, 1995.

Robinson, William H. *From Log Cabin to the Pulpit; or, Fifteen Years in Slavery.* Eau Claire, WI: James H. Tifft, 1913.

Taylor, Glennette Tilley. *The Underground Railroad in Illinois.* Glen Ellyn, IL: Newman Educational, 2001.

Tobin, Jacqueline L., and Raymond G. Dobard. *Hidden in Plain View: A Secret Story of Quilts and the Underground Railroad.* New York: Doubleday, 1999.

Graue, Frederick (1819–1892)

Frederick "Fred" Graue, an immigrant to Illinois from Landesbergen, in Hanover, Germany, established a waystation at his workplace, which stood next to his residence. After dismaying experiences with the powerful nobility of his homeland, he commiserated with slaves and sided with abolitionists. In 1852, on 200 acres along Salt Creek in the Hinsdale–Oak Brook area of Fullersburg, in Du Page

County, Illinois, Graue and his partner, William Asche, completed an oak and brick waterwheel gristmill at 3800 South York Road. While runaways hid in the cellar, the wooden gearing ground local buckwheat, corn, oats, and wheat. When danger passed, Graue entrusted passengers to a transporter, blacksmith John Coe. In May 1975, Graue's business, now a museum, became the only gristmill listed on the National Register of Historic Places.

Source

Chiat, Marilyn Joyce Segal. *Spiritual Traveler: A Guide to Sacred Sites and Peaceful Places.* Mahwah, NJ: Hidden Spring, 2004.

Gray, Greenburg (1809–?)

A freedman from Anne Arundel County, Maryland, Greenburg Gray used forgery as a means of helping a slave escape. On May 4, 1840, a circuit court found him guilty of violating a state law dating to 1796 involving the supplying of liberty papers to slaves. On May 4, 1847, Gray was released from the Maryland state penitentiary in Baltimore after serving his entire seven-year sentence.

Source

Prison records, Maryland State Archives.

Gray, Jim (fl. 1850s–1860s)

Jim Gray and two other fugitives fled over the Underground Railroad routes to free territory. On September 4, 1859, they left the home of their owner, Richard Phillips, in New Madrid, near Cape Girardeau, Missouri, and arrived in Jonesboro, in Union County, Illinois. After authorities captured the trio, a network agent, educator Benajah Guernsey Roots of Tamaroa, Illinois, intervened and had Gray released. Phillips and a U.S. marshal then apprehended Gray, whom four abolitionist lawyers defended free of charge. To avoid a local uprising over a verdict, the judge passed the case to the U.S. commissioner in Springfield, Illinois, who ordered the slave returned to Missouri. During the prisoner transfer, agent John Hossack, a merchant from Ottawa, Illinois, seized Gray, who jumped a fence and boarded a carriage driven by Charles Campbell. Gray passed through the Streator waystation and Chicago and arrived safely in Ontario.

Source

Ottawa: Old and New, a Complete History of Ottawa, Illinois, 1823–1914. Ottawa, IL: *Republican-Times,* 1912–1914.

Gray, William (1804–1848)

William Gray, a New York pioneer and Presbyterian elder, completed the final arrangements for slaves crossing from Pennsylvania over Lake Erie to Canada. In 1836, he served as secretary of the Erie County Anti-Slavery Society. His safehouse at Beaver Dam, in Wayne Township in Erie County, Pennsylvania, was easily accessible to steamer traffic. In acts of civil disobedience, he conspired with Julia Catlin Pratt and Linus Humprey Pratt, conductors in Sugar Hill in Warren County, and with the conductor of the next stop, Seth McDonald, at Lanning Hill in Farmington.

See also: civil disobedience.

Source

Bates, Samuel P. *History of Erie County, Pennsylvania.* Chicago: Warner, Beers, 1884.

Greeley, Horace (1811–1872)

In addition to his media support of illegal aid to fugitive blacks, moralist Horace Greeley was a slave conductor in New York City. Born in Amherst, New Hampshire, he entered the printing trade at age 20. In 1834, he established the *New Yorker.* After 1841, Greeley's coverage of Underground Railroad activities in the *New York Tribune* impressed the nation; he drew especial attention in 1850 to the draconian strictures of the Fugitive Slave Law. In a test case of the law, Greeley and members of the American Anti-Slavery Society confronted slave owner John T. Smith of Richmond, Virginia, who successfully sued for custody of the runaway Henry Long.

Greeley's contributions to abolitionism ranged from discreet donations of cash to encouragement of the anti-slavery essays of Jane Grey Cannon Swisshelm and moral support to volunteers involved in civil disobedience. He championed the safehouse of Samuel Bowne Parsons and Susan Howland Parsons in Flushing, New York; Frances Seward and William Henry Seward's rescues at Auburn, New York; and freedman agent Peter Friedman Still's volunteerism in Philadelphia, Pennsylvania. Greeley received the support of essayist Henry David Thoreau for validating the humanitarianism of the Reverend Theodore Parker and orator Wendell Addison Phillips.

Greeley fostered plans for free black communities in the Midwest similar to the emigrant community of Underground Railroad agent Amasa Soule in Lawrence,

The influential New York newspaper editor Horace Greeley championed the cause of abolition and publicized the activities of the Underground Railroad. More quietly, he supported the safehouses and rescue efforts of network volunteers. *(Hulton Archive/Stringer/Getty Images)*

Kansas. To estimate progress, Greeley hired correspondent Samuel Forster Tappan, Jr., to survey successes of the secret network that spirited slaves from Missouri after passage of the controversial Kansas-Nebraska Act of 1854. Additional information came from consultations with James Montgomery, an Underground Railroad supervisor from Linn County, Kansas, and from Greeley's friends agents Martha Malvina Snow Taylor and Oscar Taylor in Freeport, Illinois.

Greeley was one of the founders of the Republican Party, which took shape in 1856 at Lafayette Hall, in Allegheny County, Pennsylvania. Joining him in the party's formation were Underground Railroad agents Joshua Reed Giddings, George W. Jackson, Owen Glendower Lovejoy, and attorney Abraham Lincoln. On August 19, 1862, Greeley targeted President Abraham Lincoln with an editorial calling for action against the flesh trade. Three days later, Lincoln replied that his priority was national union rather than liberating slaves. Greeley continued to press for immediate abolition of slavery, which Lincoln's Emancipation Proclamation granted on January 1, 1863. Greeley's altruism received mention in *Life and Adventures of James Williams, a Fugitive Slave* (1873).

See also: abolitionism; American Anti-Slavery Society; Fugitive Slave Law of 1850; Kansas-Nebraska Act of 1854.

Sources

Quarles, Benjamin. *The Negro in the Civil War.* Boston: Da Capo, 1989.

Williams, James. *Life and Adventures of James Williams, a Fugitive Slave.* San Francisco: Women's Union Print, 1873.

Green, Ann Maria (1820–?)
Green, Christopher (fl. 1850s)
Green, Nathan (1837–?)

A runaway aboard the Underground Railroad, Ann Maria Green fled Queen Annes County, Maryland, with her husband, Christopher Green, and their 20-year-old son, Nathan Green. The trio left in 1857 after their owner, James Pipper, threatened to sell mother and son to slave buyers in Georgia. The Greens connected with agents of the secret railroad in Philadelphia, Pennsylvania, who eased the family's passage from bondage to liberty.

Source

Still, William. *The Underground Railroad.* Philadelphia: Porter & Coates, 1871.

Green, Beriah (1795–1874)

For 40 years, the Reverend Beriah Green, an evangelical abolitionist, orator, and pamphleteer, aided Gerrit Smith in organizing a secret network to free slaves. Born in Guilford, Connecticut, Green studied at Andover Seminary. After ordination, he took a position as professor of Hebrew at Western Reserve College and served as president of Oneida Institute, a biracial training center in Whitesboro, New York. He espoused radical opinions about the immediate end to slavery. In his writings and volunteerism for the anti-slavery movement, he exposed the sin of breeding slaves for sale and owners using slaves for sexual gratification.

In an abolitionist harangue in Utica, New York, in October 1835, Beriah Green condemned slavery as the rot corrupting American morals: "The plain truth is, that every man, woman, and child, on finding himself involved in evil-doing is bound by obligation as high and sacred as the authority of God, immediately to break off his sin by righteousness." The "righteousness" to which he refers is direct aid to black refugees.

On December 6, 1833, Green joined Abigail Kelley Foster, Dr. Bartholomew Fussell, William Lloyd Garrison, the Reverend Samuel Joseph May, James Mott, Jr., Robert Purvis, John Rankin, Arthur Tappan, Lewis Tappan, and John Greenleaf Whittier in forming the American Anti-Slavery Society. Green's philosophy and rhetorical style influenced the activism of the Reverend Amos Noah Freeman at Siloam Presbyterian Church in Brooklyn, New York, and of the Reverend Thomas James at the Rochester African Methodist Episcopal Zion Church, both active waystations. When radical activists grew disgruntled with their lack of progress, Green supported Gerrit Smith and other idealists in the founding of the Liberty League, a pressure group that sought immediate redress of the slavery situation.

See also: African Methodist Episcopal Church; American Anti-Slavery Society; civil disobedience; Liberty League.

Source

Ryan, Mary P. *Cradle of the Middle Class: The Family in Oneida County, New York, 1790–1865.* New York: Cambridge University Press, 1981.

Green, Lear (ca. 1839–ca. 1860)

An 18-year-old domestic, Lear Green chose an unusual form of escape from bondage in Baltimore, Maryland. Around 1857, she fled her owner, butter dealer James Noble, who had inherited her from Rachel Howard. Noble posted a $150 reward in the *Baltimore Sun* for Green's return. With the aid of Baltimore Quakers, Green hid under a quilt in a sailor's chest and traveled by sea up the Atlantic coast for a reunion in Philadelphia with William Adams, a barber and tavern worker. Adams's mother, a freewoman from Elmira, New York, watched over the chest on the deck of the steamer. During the 18-hour journey, she raised the lid occasionally to let in fresh air. Transporters carried their freight from Barley Street to the safehouse of William Still, an officer of the Philadelphia Vigilance Committee. Agents of the Underground Railroad continued the journey to Elmira, where Lear Green married William Adams.

See also: Quakers.

Sources

Fradin, Dennis Brindell. *Bound for the North Star: True Stories of Fugitive Slaves.* New York: Clarion, 2000.
Washington, Booker Taliaferro. *A New Negro for a New Century.* Miami: Mnemosyne, 1969.

Green, Samuel, Jr. (fl. 1850s)

Information about the Underground Railroad exploits of Harriet Tubman identifies the Reverend Samuel "Sam" Green, Jr., from Indian Creek, in Dorchester County, Maryland, as one of her contacts. He was the son of slaves, Catharine Green and Samuel Green. During his enslavement, he was known as Wesley Kinnard, a blacksmith. On August 28, 1854, he fled bondage to Dr. James Muse and arrived in Philadelphia, Pennsylvania, among members of the

Samuel Green, Jr., escaped slavery in Maryland and became one of Harriet Tubman's contacts on the hidden route to Delaware. He was arrested in 1857 and sentenced to 10 years in prison after a copy of *Uncle Tom's Cabin* and a map of Canada were found in his room. *(Schomburg Center for Research in Black Culture/Manuscripts, Archives and Rare Books Division/New York Public Library)*

vigilance committee. In addition to his work as a minister of the Methodist Episcopal Church, Green received runaways at his home, which lay on the route to Delaware. In mid-November 1856, he helped Tubman conceal Josiah Bailey and William Bailey from pursuers. Because of Green's aid to runaways, a county court judge in Cambridge sentenced him to 10 years in the Maryland state prison in Baltimore. The prosecutor cited as evidence a map of Canada and a copy of Harriet Beecher Stowe's *Uncle Tom's Cabin* (1852) that had been found in Green's room. Green regained his freedom during the Civil War.

See also: Uncle Tom's Cabin; or, Life Among the Lowly (1852); vigilance committees.

Source

Wyman, Lillie B. Chace. "Harriet Tubman." *New England* 20:1 (March 1896): 110–18.

Green, Shields (1836–1859)

Shields "Emperor" Green was a martyr to the cause of radical abolitionism. He began aiding fugitive slaves after escaping bondage in Charleston, South Carolina. He earned the trust of insurrectionist John Brown and of orator Frederick Douglass, who escorted Shields to the waystation of the Reverend James A. Gloucester in New York City to request funds. Douglass and Green arrived in Chambersburg, Pennsylvania for a secret planning session preceding the raid on Harpers Ferry, Virginia. Douglass chose not to involve himself, but Green remained among Brown's raiding party. On October 16, 1859, Green cut telegraph lines, captured sections of the armory, and enlisted local slaves to the cause of racial war. He was captured with Brown at the engine house, convicted of treason, and hanged two months later. A Christmas memorial service at First Church in Oberlin, Ohio, preceded the placement of a stela in Westwood Cemetery honoring Green along with John Anthony Copeland, Jr., and Lewis Sheridan Leary, two other guerrilla warriors of Brown's band.

Source

Douglass, Frederick. *Life and Times of Frederick Douglass.* Boston: De Wolfe & Fiske, 1892.

Green, Wesley (1811–1845)

Wesley Green died in prison while serving a 12-year sentence for abetting slave escape. A farmer, he lived in Anne Arundel County, Maryland, at the time of his arrest. After a state court found him guilty, he entered a cell in the state penitentiary in Baltimore on April 29, 1842. He died there on October 6, 1845, at age 34, of tuberculosis.

See also: abolitionism.

Source

Prison records, Maryland State Archives.

Greene, Jacob D. (1813–?)

The autobiography of Jacob D. Greene (or Green), *Narrative of the Life of Jacob Greene* (1864), dramatizes the desperation of slaves seeking freedom. Born in Queen Annes County, Maryland, he was originally the property of Judge Charles Earle, who used him as an errand boy. After studying the North Star, Greene attempted flights from bondage in Louisville, Kentucky, in 1839 and 1846 before succeeding in 1848. In his forays along Underground Railroad routes, he passed through a waystation in Chester, Pennsylvania, but was recaptured and imprisoned.

In 1848, Greene's last attempt, at age 35, was successful. He made his way up the Ohio River on the steamer *Pike* to Cincinnati, Ohio. With the aid of black intermediaries, he hid in a chimney until an agent, David Nickens, could supply him with female garments to disguise himself for rail travel to Cleveland, Ohio. From there, agents dispatched him on the steamer *Indiana* to Buffalo and Niagara Falls, New York. An operative named Jones completed the transfer to Toronto by providing money and a ticket and by escorting Greene aboard the steamer *Chief Justice Robinson.* In the years preceding the Civil War, Greene devoted his career to lecturing on slavery and abolitionism in public school classrooms.

See also: abolitionism; disguise; North Star.

Source

Greene, Jacob D. *Narrative of the Life of Jacob Greene.* Huddersfield, UK: Henry Fielding, 1864.

Greenebaum, Michael G. (1824–1894) Greenebaum, Sarah Spiegel (1828–1897)

An attorney from a prominent Jewish clan, Michael G. Greenebaum (or Greenbaum), chose civil disobedience rather than adherence to an unjust law. He was born in Eppelsheim, Bavaria, and arrived at age 21 in New York City. He worked as a plumber and tinware seller. In 1848, he married Sarah Spiegel, the daughter of a rabbi from Abenheim, a community in the German region of Rheinhessen. Sarah made their home a social center and involved Jewish women in sewing garments for the poor.

The Greenebaums' activism in Chicago, Illinois, increased due to their disgust with the Fugitive Slave Law of 1850, which required citizen involvement in slave recapture. To rescue a runaway, in 1853, Michael Greenebaum led a mob against slave hunters and demolished a cell door guarded by a U.S. marshal. Contributing to the freeing of the slave were four Jewish confederates, German and Hebrew teacher Leopold Mayer, (ca. 1824–after 1899) of Hesse, Adolph Loeb (?–1877), financier and attorney Julius Rosenthal (?–1905), and George Schneider (1823–1905), a newspaper publisher and president of the National Bank of Illinois. That night, the five men launched an abolition brotherhood, the Hebrew Benevolent Society.

See also: Fugitive Slave Law of 1850; philanthropists.

Sources

Adams, Maurianne, and John H. Bracey, eds. *Strangers & Neighbors: Relations Between Blacks and Jews in the United States.* Amherst: University of Massachusetts Press, 1999.

Spiegel, Marcus M. *A Jewish Colonel in the Civil War: Marcus M. Spiegel of the Ohio Volunteers.* Kent, OH: Kent State University, 1985.

Grew, Mary (1813–1896)

Quaker abolitionist and suffragist Mary Grew dedicated herself to the cause of human freedom. Born in Hartford, Connecticut, to a reformer, the Reverend Henry Grew, she lived briefly in Boston, Massachusetts, and attended the Hartford Female Seminary. At age 21, she made her home in Philadelphia. She was maligned for being a forceful member of Philadelphia's Female Anti-Slavery Society, an activist group that raised nearly $35,000 during its 36 years of service. Grew aided reformer and organizer Robert Purvis with gifts of clothing and funds to support slaves escaping from Maryland and Virginia. In 1837, she persuaded Quaker activist Abigail Goodwin to superintend the Underground Railroad activity through Salem County, New Jersey.

Mary Grew accepted risk as part of the activist's role. In June 1840, she kept a diary of her attendance with agents Abigail Kimber, Lucretia Coffin Mott, Sarah Pugh, and other female abolitionists at the World's Anti-Slavery Convention in London. Although the constable, sheriff, and mayor refused them entry to Concert Hall, the women's presence made a forceful statement on women's roles in the abolitionist movement. After the arrest in Harrisburg, Pennsylvania, of Daniel Dangerfield for robbery, on April 2, 1859, Grew sat with diarist Charlotte Lottie Forten Grimké and Lucretia Mott through a 14-hour trial.

See also: female anti-slavery societies.

Sources

Brown, Ira V. *Mary Grew, Abolitionist and Feminist, 1813–1896.* Selinsgrove, PA: Susquehanna University Press, 1991.

Hanaford, Phebe A. *Daughters of America; or Women of the Century.* Augusta, ME: True, 1882.

History of Woman Suffrage. Vol. 1, *1848–1861.* New York: Fowler and Wells, 1881.

Grey, Emily Goodridge (1833–1916)

Diarist Emily Goodridge Grey aided the Underground Railroad effort in Minnesota. A mulatto born to stationmasters Emily Wallace Goodridge and William C. Goodridge of York, Pennsylvania, she took part in family activism at their depot on Centre Street. At age 24, Emily, her husband, barber Ralph Toyer Grey, and their son, Toussaint L'Ouverture Grey, moved to St. Anthony Falls, Minnesota. On August 21, 1860, Emily helped Eliza Winston flee her owner, Colonel Richard Christmas, from Memphis, Tennessee, who was vacationing with his family. With the aid of another agent of the secret network, Judge William D. Babbitt, Winston pled her case in court and gained her freedom. That night, a mob swarmed the Grey residence and demanded Eliza Winston, who had already been relayed to another safehouse. In the hands of transporters, she escaped to Windsor, Ontario. In 1893, Emily Grey published memoirs containing details of Winston's rescue. In January 2006, educator Ericka Dennis reenacted Grey's story at the Mill City Museum in Minneapolis, Minnesota.

Sources

Cannon, Mary D., and Patricia C. Harpole. "A Day in the Life of Emily Goodridge Grey." *Minnesota History* 56:4 (Winter 1998–1999).

Green, William D. "Eliza Winston and the Politics of Freedom in Minnesota, 1854–1860" *Minnesota History* 57:3 (Fall 2000): 107–22.

Griest, Amos (1795–?)
Griest, Margaret Garretson (1796–1861)

Two secret network conductors in York, in York County, Pennsylvania, Amos Griest and Margaret Garretson Griest of New Oxford joined a community of rescuers.

Both followed the principles of radical Quakers, who broke the law to save desperate slaves. After their marriage in 1835, the couple maintained a two-story brick safehouse at 322 West Market Street on York Pike. In league with agents Emily Wallace Goodridge and William C. Goodridge at 123 East Philadelphia Street, the Griests led escapees due north from Baltimore, Maryland, to their residence. Concealed in a second-floor room or in a low-beamed attic, Underground Railroad passengers remained until Goodridge could arrange travel farther north in Goodridge's railway cars.

See also: Quakers.

Source

Switala, William J. *Underground Railroad in Pennsylvania.* Mechanicsburg, PA: Stackpole, 2001.

Griffin, Enerals (1791–1878)
Griffin, Priscilla (1795–1850)

An early refugee to Canada via the Underground railroad, Enerals Griffin grew tired of waiting for manumission. He stole a horse and escaped his bondage to Edward Lee in Virginia and settled in Niagara, Ontario, in 1829. He married a white woman named Priscilla. In 1834, the Griffins and their mulatto son, James, moved to a current landmark, the House on the Hill, a two-story four-room residence at 733 Mineral Springs Road in Dundas Valley in Ancaster, Ontario. After their deaths and burial at St. Andrews Presbyterian churchyard, the homestead sheltered their descendants for 150 years.

Source

Cook, Stephen. "Griffin Homestead Restoration Lauded by Black Activist." *Ancaster (Ontario) News Journal,* March 13, 1991.

Griffing, Josephine Sophie White (1814–1872)
Griffing, Charles Stockman Spooner (1812–1880)

A vehement reformer and freedom fighter, Josephine Sophie White Griffing welcomed runaway slaves to her home. She was born in Hebron, Connecticut, to Waldensian Presbyterians and married machinist Charles Stockman Spooner Griffing of New London. After their move to Litchfield, near Cleveland, Ohio, in 1842, the Griffings became followers of journalist and reformer William Lloyd Garrison and turned their home into a waystation of the Underground Railroad. Charles Griffing allied with insurrectionst John Brown and his son, Oliver Brown, who piloted runaways to the Griffings' stables and attic. Josephine Griffing supported the Western Anti-Slavery Society and wrote for *The Liberator* and for the *Anti-Slavery Bugle,* which Abby Kelley Foster published in Salem, Ohio. In 1851, Josephine joined Sojourner Truth of Battle Creek, Michigan, in a four-year speaking tour of frontier towns and in circulating petitions to convince the U.S. Senate to wipe out slavery and to aid ex-slaves in becoming citizens.

Josephine Griffing was adept at networking. In 1853, she and Hannah Tracy Cutler initiated the Ohio Women's Rights Association, which aided former slave women and aimed to secure full citizenship for them. Working in collaboration with Mary Ann Shadd Cary and Parker Pillsbury for the American Anti-Slavery Society, Josephine surveyed racist conditions under which runaways lived. During the Civil War, she and her three daughters moved to Washington, D.C., to receive fleeing blacks—particularly the elderly and infirm—at a camp across the Potomac River in Arlington, Virginia. In 1863, she directed a resettlement plan of the National Freedman's Relief Association in Washington, D.C.

See also: American Anti-Slavery Society; *Liberator, The.*

Sources

Sterling, Dorothy, ed. *We Are Your Sisters: Black Women in the Nineteenth Century.* New York: W.W. Norton, 1984.

Venet, Wendy Hammond. *Neither Ballots nor Bullets: Women Abolitionists and the Civil War.* Charlottesville: University Press of Virginia, 1991.

Griffith, Stephen (1797–1879)
Griffith, Rhoda (1804–1888)

Underground Railroad agents Stephen Griffith of Saratoga County, New York, and his second wife, Rhoda Griffith, welcomed refugee slaves. Stephen Griffith served in local positions of authority and as a deacon of the First Baptist Church of Gilbert's Mills. The Griffiths received one of a pair of runaway sisters at their safehouse on Gilbert Mills Road, across from Church Road, in Fulton, in Oswego County, New York. The other sister stayed at the waystation of Hiram Gilbert and Lucy Harrington Gilbert, also in Fulton, until the siblings could be reunited.

Source

Churchill, John. *Landmarks of Oswego County, New York.* Syracuse, NY: D. Mason, 1895.

Grimes, John (1802–1875)

A Quaker spokesman for abolition, Dr. John Grimes championed liberty within a divided community. He developed humanitarianism under the influence of his parents, Hulda Leonard Grimes (1777–?) and Jonathan Grimes (1773–1845), who operated a depot in Parsippany, New Jersey. After four years of medical practice in Passaic County, New Jersey, in 1832, John Grimes moved to Boonton, in Morris County, and published the *New Jersey Freeman* from 1844 to 1850. His family rescued runaway slaves, who arrived in the care of agents Baxter Sayre and Elizabeth Kitchell Sayre of Madison.

After an arrest for sheltering fugitives, John Grimes parried the snipes and accusations of southern sympathizers and continued to lead a movement to eradicate the vestiges of slavery in his home state. Upon his death in 1875, an obituary in the Morristown *Jerseyman* honored both him and his parents for piloting slaves to freedom in Canada. The Grimes Homestead is listed on the National Register of Historic Places.

Source

Lobel, Jules. *Success Without Victory: Lost Legal Battles and the Long Road to Justice in America.* New York: New York University Press, 2003.

Grimes, Leonard Andrew (1815–1873)

A devoted rescuer of runaway slaves, the Reverend Leonard Andrew Grimes was a respected mulatto conductor. Born in 1815 to free blacks, Mary "Polly" Goings (or Goins) and Andrew Grimes, Leonard grew up in Leesburg, Virginia, on the Potomac River. He witnessed the misery of bondage in remote parts of the South and, like his nephew, William Bush of New Bedford, Massachusetts, resolved to serve the Underground Railroad. After Grimes's marriage to Octavia Janet Colson (also Coliston or Colston), the couple lived in Washington, D.C., on H and Twenty-second streets. Leonard Grimes worked for the American Missionary Society and used his cab service as a cover for Underground Railroad rescues.

Carter Godwin Woodson, author of *The History of the Negro Church* (1921), commended Grimes for paying the price for conducting slaves to freedom. While living in Washington, on October 26, 1839, Grimes aided a freedman in plotting the escape to Canada of his slave wife, Patty, and their seven children from Joseph Meade of Loudoun County, Virginia. Authorities arrested Grimes and held him without bond. On March 10, 1839, the court fined him $100 and jailed him for two years in the Virginia state penitentiary in Richmond. On his release, Grimes relocated to New Bedford, Massachusetts, and opened a grocery store.

Grimes and his wife moved to Boston and allied with Samuel H. Flint, Lewis Hayden, and John Swett Rock, the medical officer of the Boston Vigilance Committee. Leonard Grimes preached at the Twelfth Baptist Church for a quarter century. For its benevolence, the congregation became known as the Fugitive's Church. Grimes continued his assistance to slaves, including James Dales and Mrs. Henderson, for whom he bought sea passage on February 28, 1851. In July 1854, Grimes gave $11 to Wesley Bishop and to Thomas Jackson and his wife to aid their flight. To assist runaway Anthony Burns, a fugitive from Richmond, Virginia, Grimes's congregation raised $1,300. In 1863, Grimes performed the second marriage of Virginia runaway George Teamoh and served as the mediator between abolitionists and Anthony Burns's owner, Colonel Charles F. Suttle. During the Civil War, Grimes recruited black males for the Fifty-fourth Massachusetts Regiment, the nation's first all-black infantry. At his death in 1873, he retained his reputation for civil disobedience on behalf of liberty.

Sources

Simmons, William J. *Men of Mark: Eminent, Progressive, and Rising.* Cleveland, OH: George M. Rewell, 1887.
Woodson, Carter Godwin. *The History of the Negro Church.* Washington, DC: Associated, 1921.

Grimes, William (1784–1865)

Coachboy William Grimes made a dangerous flight from southern slavery to freedom. Born in King George County, Virginia, he was the mulatto son of a slave owner and another man's chattel. While his father was in jail, Colonel William Thornton bought Grimes for £65. The purchase was the beginning of a series of cruelties by eight different owners that Grimes resolved to end.

Aboard the brig *Casket* from Boston, in 1818, the crew concealed Grimes in a hollowed-out cotton bale for a voyage out of Savannah, Georgia. Grimes walked from the New York City harbor toward New Haven, Connecticut. After brief stays in New Bedford, Massachusetts, and Newport, Rhode Island, he married

Clarissa Caesar and moved with her to Litchfield, Connecticut, where he became a launderer. In his slave narrative, *Life of William Grimes, the Runaway Slave* (1825), he proposed leaving his lash-scarred skin to the U.S. government as a parchment to bind the Constitution.

Source

Grimes, William. *Life of William Grimes, the Runaway Slave.* New York: self-published, 1825.

Grimké, Angelina Emily (1805–1879)
Grimké, Sarah Moore (1792–1873)

A close friend of Underground Railroad agent Abigail Goodwin in Salem, New Jersey, Angelina Emily Grimké Weld and her unmarried older sister, Sarah Moore Grimké, enlisted support for the secret network. Born in Charleston, South Carolina, they were the daughters of John Faucheraud Grimké, a state supreme court judge. Because of their father's notion that education was a male privilege, the sisters had to teach themselves in the library at their home, Belmont Plantation, in Union. Angelina defied local statutes by teaching slaves to read and write. Sarah specialized in Latin and jurisprudence but had no hopes of practicing law, which was then a male dominion.

The Grimké sisters left the South to live in Philadelphia, Pennsylvania, where they converted to Quakerism and allied with Quaker conductors of the Underground Railroad. Angelina Grimké became the first female abolitionist orator to address an assembly of men and women. On assignment from the Female Anti-Slavery Society, she joined the Reverend Theodore Dwight Weld's corps of orators. Throughout the 1830s, she toured lecture halls to expose the cruelties of slave whippings and the perversity of slave breeding. Her pro-slavery enemies dubbed her Devilina. Sarah Grimké published a tract, *Epistle to the Clergy of the Southern States* (1836), a condemnation of Christian ministers who supported the flesh trade. That same year, Angelina enlisted women's support of the Underground Railroad in a pamphlet, *An Appeal to the Christian Women of the South* (1836). She followed with *An Appeal to the Women of the Nominally Free States* (1837) and *Letters to Catharine Beecher in Reply to an Essay on Slavery and Abolitionism Addressed to A.E. Grimké* (1837), tracts that influenced orator Lucretia Coffin Mott.

Angelina wed Theodore Dwight Weld in 1838. They settled on a farm at Belleville, in Perth Amboy, New Jersey, where they shared their home with Sarah. Weld and the sisters published *American Slavery As It Is: Testimony of a Thousand Witnesses* (1839). The text drew the Reverend James Armstrong Thome to abolitionism and inspired the abolitionist writings of Harriet Beecher Stowe, author of *Uncle Tom's Cabin* (1852). In alliance with Sydney Howard Gay in New York City, the Grimké sisters managed a waystation at their boarding academy, Eaglewood School, which received refugees delivered by barge along the Raritan River. In New York in 1863, Angelina gave a speech, "The Rights of Women and Negroes," that explained the fervor of female abolitionists who commiserated with the anguish of slaves suffering under white male dominance.

After the Civil War, the Grimké sisters learned of the double life of their brother, Thomas Grimké, and his siring of a son by a slave. The Grimké sisters' mulatto nephew, the Reverend Francis Grimké, wed Charlotte Lottie Forten, a scion of the Forten clan and a renowned abolitionist and agent of the Underground Railroad.

See also: abolitionism; female anti-slavery societies; *Uncle Tom's Cabin; or, Life Among the Lowly* (1852).

Sources

Lerner, Gerda. *The Feminist Thought of Sarah Grimké.* Oxford, UK: Oxford University Press, 1998.

Schneir, Miriam, ed. *Feminism: The Essential Historical Writings.* New York: Vintage Books, 1972.

Weld, Angelina Grimké. *An Appeal to the Christian Women of the South.* Whitefish, MT: Kessinger, 2004.

Grimké, Charlotte Lottie Forten (1837–1914)

Diarist and abolitionist Charlotte Lottie Forten Grimké contributed to abolitionist volunteer efforts. Born to elite black Philadelphians, she was motherless at an early age; Grimké lived with her maternal grandfather, James Forten, a sail maker, and an uncle, Underground Railroad official Robert Purvis. Privately educated, she mastered French, German, and Latin. She became a champion of the Underground Railroad. In 1854, she lived with the family of orator Charles Lenox Remond in Salem, Massachusetts, and began supporting the secret network activities of publisher William Lloyd Garrison, orator Wendell Addison Phillips, and editor and poet John Greenleaf Whittier.

In her journals, Charlotte Grimké preserved for history episodes of mobs seizing fugitive slaves and dragging them through the streets. Her teaching experience at Epes Grammar School in Salem made her the first black Massachusetts teacher of white pupils. After the Civil War, she married Francis Grimké, a Presbyterian minister, the son of Thomas Grimké and a slave woman and the nephew of orator Angelina Emily Grimké Weld and polemicist Sarah Moore Grimké, the sisters of Thomas Grimké.

Source

Forten, Charlotte L. *The Journals of Charlotte Forten Grimké.* New York: Oxford University Press, 1988.

Grinnell, Josiah Bushnell (1821–1891) Grinnell, Julia Ann Chapin (1827–1907)

A champion of freedom and the founder of Grinnell, Iowa, the Reverend Josiah Bushnell Grinnell of New Haven, Vermont, managed a waystation and organized routes of the Underground Railroad. A poor farm boy, he was the son of Catherine Hastings Grinnell and Myron Grinnell, who taught him the value of labor and piety. After studying at the Oneida Institute and completing a degree from Auburn Theological Seminary, in 1847, he served Presbyterian and Congregationalist churches. In February 1852, he married Julia Ann Chapin, moved west, and gave up the ministry to become a wool trader.

In collaboration with agents Joseph Arnold, Jarvis Johnson, and Matthew Sparks, Grinnell instituted secret network stops in 1853 that opened an Iowa–Canada route for Missouri slaves seeking liberty. He shipped passengers by boxcar and on horseback. For his activism, Missouri bounty hunters placed a price on his head dead or alive. Nonetheless, when insurrectionist John Brown sought shelter on February 20, 1859, the Grinnells welcomed him and his followers, stashed their weapons, and hid them in his covert "liberty room" and in the wool-storage barn. After Brown's execution for attacking the federal arsenal at Harpers Ferry, Virginia, on October 16, 1859, the pro-slavery press dubbed the rescuer John Brown Grinnell. Public ridicule did not stop Grinnell's assistance to runaways. Working on his farm was 15-year-old transporter Gershem H. Hill, who relayed a wagon filled with runaways from the safehouse in June 1861 to the next stop, in Marengo, Iowa. In 1891, Josiah

The Reverend Josiah Grinnell, the founder of Grinnell, Iowa, shipped runaways by boxcar and on horseback despite the pursuit of bounty hunters who sought him dead or alive. *(Library of Congress)*

Grinnell reflected on the abolitionist era in *Men and Events of Forty Years.*

See also: routes, Underground Railroad.

Sources

De Ramus, Betty. *Forbidden Fruit: Love Stories from the Underground Railroad.* New York: Atria, 2005.

Etcheson, Nicole, "Daring Death for an Idea: J.B. Grinnell and the Underground Railroad," *Grinnell (IA) Herald Register,* November 21, 1983, 1–3.

Grinnell, Josiah B. *Men and Events of Forty Years.* Boston: Lothrop, 1891.

"J.B. Grinnell," *Grinnell (IA) Herald Register,* April 7, 1891, 1.

Gross, Albert (1840–?)

A slave on a Cecilton farm, 20-year-old Albert Gross fled from Maryland to Pennsylvania with aid from agents of the Underground Railroad. After eluding his owner, farmer William Price of Cecil County, in

1859, he required the aid and travel information from secret operatives of the Philadelphia Vigilance Committee.

Source

Still, William. *The Underground Railroad.* Philadelphia: Porter & Coates, 1871.

Grover, Emily Jane Hunt (fl. 1850s)
Grover, Joel (1825–1879)

Early volunteers for the Underground Railroad routes in Lawrence, Kansas, Emily Jane Hunt Grover and Joel Grover used their farm as a depot. Joel, a native of Springfield, New York, migrated to the Midwest in his mid-twenties after passage of the Kansas-Nebraska Act of 1854. He served as a Douglas County commissioner and a major of the first militia formed in Lawrence. Emily Hunt, the daughter of an abolitionist pioneer in Douglas, Kansas, married Joel in October 1857. After building a stone barn, the Grovers were better able to secure passengers, which they received from a neighbor, Major James Burnett Abbott.

Both the Abbott family and the Grovers donated food to destitute refugees, whom Joel relayed to agents in Topeka and Valley Falls, Kansas. To allay fears of all-out war against federal agents, on May 21, 1856, Joel and eight others sent a letter to U.S. Marshal I.B. Donelson in which they promised their obedience to federal law. From 1857 to 1858, Joel kept a diary of his activities. An episode on January 24, 1859, involved the Grover barn in housing insurrectionist John Brown's ambitious midwinter wagon train traveling from Missouri to Windsor, Ontario. An addition to the original 11 passengers was an infant born on January 24, 1859, at the Grovers' safehouse. The group moved on to the waystation of Charles and John Doy, who were arrested for harboring runaways.

Source

Sheridan, Richard B., ed. and comp. *Freedom's Crucible: The Underground Railroad in Lawrence and Douglas County, Kansas, 1854–1865.* Lawrence: University of Kansas, 1998.

Grummond, Levi (fl. 1840s–1860s)
Grummond, Elizabeth Wilson Findley (fl. 1840s–1860s)

Two Scots Presbyterians, Levi Grummond and his wife, Elizabeth Wilson Findley Grummond, supported a community effort for the Underground Railroad. After immigrating from Iowa to New Concord, in Muskingum County in eastern Ohio, they operated a depot at their farm. Levi Grummond drove his wagons along the Bloomfield Road and delivered passengers to Samuel Scott's residence, where slaves hid in a niche in an upstairs room. During the Civil War, Levi joined the 130th Illinois Volunteer Infantry.

Source

Porter, Lorle. *A People Set Apart: The Scotch-Irish in Eastern Ohio.* Zanesville, OH: New Concord, 1998.

Gue, Catherine Gurney (fl. 1830s–1840s)
Gue, John (fl. 1830s–1840s)
Gue, Benjamin F. (1828–1904)

Quaker agents in Ontario County, New York, Catherine Gurney Gue and her husband, John Gue, operated a waystation of the Underground Railroad. In 1833, the couple began farming. As education for their children, they read aloud from William Lloyd Garrison's weekly abolitionist newspaper *The Liberator.* After John Gue's death, Benjamin F. Gue, the eldest child, moved his widowed mother and siblings to Rock Creek, in Scott County, Iowa. In 1855, Benjamin married Elizabeth Parker, a public school teacher. At the beginning of the Civil War, he served in the state senate. In 1899, he reflected on the abolitionist era in a compendium, *Biographies and Portraits of the Progressive Men of Iowa.*

See also: abolitionist newspapers; *Liberator, The.*

Source

Gue, Benjamin F. *Biographies and Portraits of the Progressive Men of Iowa.* Des Moines, IA: Conaway & Shaw, 1899.

Guthrie, Abelard A. (1814–1873)
Guthrie, Quindaro Nancy Brown (1820–1886)

Beginning in January 1844, pioneer diarist Abelard A. Guthrie of Dayton, Ohio, and his Wyandotte-Shawnee bride, Quindaro Nancy Brown Guthrie of Ontario, helped runaways flee bondage. Abelard Guthrie was a veteran of the Mexican-American War. After the Wyandotte nation sold 693 acres for a town site, Abelard succeeded in having the town bear the Indian name of his wife. Across the Missouri River from the slave state of Missouri, their farm at the port town of Quindaro in the Kansas

Territory became a frontier safehouse. Passengers could move directly from the Guthries' sanctuary to waystations in Lawrence, Leavenworth, and Topeka, Kansas, and from there north to Canada.

Sources

Friskel, Bob. "Early KCK History: Great Love Story Recounted," *Kansas City Kansan,* February 12, 1967.
Sengupta, Gunja. *For God and Mammon: Evangelicals and Entrepreneurs, Masters and Slaves in Territorial Kansas.* Athens: University of Georgia Press, 1996.

Hackett, Nelson (ca. 1810–?)

A runaway from Arkansas, Nelson Hackett received assistance from New York agents of the Underground Railroad. In July 1841, Hackett stole a horse and fled bondage in Fayetteville, in Washington County, Arkansas, and reached Ontario in September. His owner, Alfred Wallace, and a confederate, George C. Grigg, trailed the fugitive as he traveled through Michigan into Chatham and Windsor, Ontario. Along the way, authorities disovered Hackett's theft of the horse and saddle, as well as a coat and a gold pocket watch. On a trumped-up charge of rape, Wallace had Hackett arrested in Sandwich, Ontario, where authorities beat the fugitive over the head to extract a confession.

Although Wallace demanded Hackett's extradition to the United States, Attorney General William Henry Draper refused. Supporting Wallace was the governor of Arkansas, Archibald Yell. In January 1842, Sir Charles Bagot, the lieutenant governor of Ontario, agreed to send Hackett back. On February 8, Wallace tied and gagged his slave for the crossing of the Detroit River. During Hackett's two-month stay in a Detroit jail on suspicion of grand theft, abolitionists campaigned for his release. In April, during Wallace's journey south with Hackett aboard a riverboat, four New York operatives helped the slave to escape. However, in June in Princeton, Illinois, Hackett was again seized and finally returned to Arkansas.

For the lengthy search, Wallace spent $1,500, a figure exceeding the slave value of Hackett. Wallace betrayed his vindictive purpose by having Hackett flogged and sold to a Texas buyer. Numerous antislavery groups attempted to buy Hackett, but he disappeared from public record. In the wake of the international litigation, in 1842, Canadian and U.S. authorities signed the Webster-Ashburton Treaty, which permitted extradition of felons. The precedent further endangered the civil rights of black refugees and jeopardized the northern extremes of the Underground Railroad.

See also: Canada; punishments; slave recovery.

Source

Zorn, R.J. "An Arkansas Fugitive Slave Incident and Its International Repercussions." *Arkansas Historical Quarterly* 16 (1957): 140–49.

Hagarty, Sir John Hawkins (1816–1888)

An Irish Canadian educator and attorney, Sir John Hawkins Hagarty circumvented international law requiring the return of fugitive slaves to bondage in the United States. After settling in Bowmanville, Ontario, at age 18, he studied law in Toronto, then partnered with John Willoughby Crawford. As a judge, he was able to influence the fate of Underground Railroad passengers with his rulings. In the case of John Anderson, a Missouri fugitive charged with murder, Hagarty pondered the demand for extradition under the Webster-Ashburton Treaty of 1842, which allowed the recovery of runaway slaves who had committed crimes in the United States. By successfully disputing the documentation of the case, the larger issue of the slave's extradition became moot. In 1887, Queen Victoria knighted Hawkins.

See also: slave recovery.

Source

Armstrong, Richard. "Hon. John Hawkins Hagarty, Chief Justice of Ontario." *Barrister* 1 (1894–1895): 252–56.

Haines, George (1798–1877)
Budd, Andrew Eckard (ca. 1820–?)

George Haines and Andrew Eckard Budd, two New Jersey physicians, sheltered fugitive slaves in

Medford. Quaker volunteer George Haines, the town's first doctor, graduated from the University of Pennsylvania College of Medicine and built a two-story brick home and office at 33 North Main Street in 1826. He hid passengers in a large space under the kitchen, which was accessed through a shaft in the kitchen floor. Dr. Andrew Eckard Budd of Woodbury, New Jersey, graduated from the same university in 1842 and set up practice in the building in 1845 and extended his own welcome to fugitives.

Sources

Haines, George. *Ancestry of the Haines, Sharp, Collins Families.* Camden, NJ: Sinnickson, Chew & Sons, 1902.

"Steal Away, Steal Away . . ." (pamphlet). Trenton: New Jersey Historical Commission, 2002.

Haines, Jacob A. (1788–1866)
Haines, Rachel Ellis (1788–1862)
Haines, Jesse (1822–1895)

Quaker conductors at Wolf Run House, near Muncy, Pennsylvania in Lycoming County, Jacob A. Haines, his wife, Rachel Ellis Haines, and their son, Jesse, rescued refugees out of Christian love and duty. Born in Delaware, Pennsylvania, Jacob married Rachel Ellis in 1815 and lived with her at Wolf Run, the waystation of her parents, Mercy Cox Ellis and William Ellis. Like their pioneering forebears, the Haines family received escapees from stationmasters Micajah Speakman, Phebe Smith Speakman, and William Allibone Speakman in Chester County, Pennsylvania. The favored hiding places were the ovens of the cellar kitchen.

According to a family history written by Jacob and Rachel's daughter, Mary Rhoads Haines, farmer and surveyor Jacob Haines passed slaves along with letters of introduction signed with the code word "humanity." He transported women and children in a suitable carriage or wagon, which carried them beyond the mountains to John Hill or to Marshall Battin in Elklands, Pennsylvania. The Genesee Trail through New York took the Haines's rescues to Joseph Jones in Penn Yan for the final relay to Ontario.

See also: code, Underground Railroad.

Source

Haines, Mary Rhoads. *Clovercroft Chronicles, 1314–1893.* Philadelphia: J.B. Lippincott, 1893.

Haines, Jonathan Ridgeway (1821–1899)
Haines, Sarah Grant (1822–1903)
Haines, John Columbus (1842–1942)

Quakers Jonathan Ridgeway Haines and his wife, Sarah Grant Haines, operated a waystation of the Underground Railroad in Alliance, in Stark County, Ohio. Jonathan Haines, a childhood friend of agent Daniel H. Hise, began aiding fugitives while growing up in Salem, Ohio. In 1853, Jonathan and Sarah began their operation on their 126-acre farm, where they hid slaves in the garret above the kitchen of their farmhouse. They relayed passengers to Limaville, Marlboro, and Salem, Ohio. Before leaving on a night mission, both Jonathan Haines and his son, John Columbus "Tump" Haines, armed themselves against slave hunters. On August 13, 1859, the Haines family sponsored a meeting attended by abolitionists Charles Henry Langston, John Mercer Langston, and William J. Whipper. The following August, a similar session welcomed the Reverend Jermaine Wesley Loguen. During the Civil War, John C. Haines served in the Nineteenth Ohio Infantry.

Source

Perrin, William H. *History of Stark County.* Cleveland, OH: Baskin & Bartley, 1881.

Haines, Timothy (1768–1846)
Haines, Sarah Brown (1772–1842)

In Lancaster County, in southern Pennsylvania, Quaker agents Timothy Haines of Rising Sun, Maryland, and his wife, Sarah Brown Haines of Little Britain, Pennsylvania, maintained the initial safehouse of the Pilgrim's Pathway, a 17-stage network of the Underground Railroad. After their marriage in 1795, their residence at Fulton became Station 16 of the Underground Railroad. Located within sight of the Susquehanna River, the 150-acre farm offered shelter under the barn bridge for slaves crossing by night from Maryland. Haines worked closely with Jeremiah and Slater Brown, brothers of Haines's wife.

See also: Pilgrim's Pathway.

Source

Spotts, Charles Dewey. *The Pilgrim's Pathway: The Underground Railroad in Lancaster County.* Lancaster, PA: Franklin & Marshall College Library, 1966.

Haines, William (1817–1846)

William Haines was a Quaker physician and an operative of the Underground Railroad route outside Muncy, Pennsylvania. He was the eldest of the children of Jacob A. Haines and Rachel Ellis Haines, who with his brother Jesse Haines were all operatives in Lycoming County, Pennsylvania. Near Pennsdale, Pennsylvania, William Haines managed a waystation at Wolf Run House, property he inherited from his grandparents, agents Mercy Cox Ellis and William Ellis. Passengers arriving at Wolf Run House from Micajah Speakman, Phebe Smith Speakman, and William Allibone Speakman in Chester County, Pennsylvania, rested up for the New York–Canada route over the Genesee Trail. Fugitives from the William Haines waystation moved on to Derek Updegraff and Maria Elizabeth Peterman Updegraff of Long Reach Plantation, on the South Reach Road outside Williamsport, Pennsylvania, who passed the wayfarers through a tunnel to packet boats on the Susquehanna River. Fugitives then moved north to the home of Joseph Jones in Penn Yan, New York. Upon William Haines's death in 1846, Wolf Run passed to his brother Jacob.

Source

Wolny, Philip. *The Underground Railroad: A Primary Source History of the Journey to Freedom.* New York: Rosen, 2004.

Haines, William (fl. 1850s)

A conductor of the Underground Railroad from Pennsylvania, William Haines, an itinerant bookseller, worked under dangerous conditions in the plantation South. He attested to a successful means of enticing blacks from bondage—by sprinkling white paper along roads as a signal that rescue was nearby. In June 1850, authorities seized him in Maysville, Kentucky, and charged him with abetting slave escape. A state court lacked enough evidence for a conviction.

Source

Harrold, Stanley. *The Abolitionists and the South, 1831–1861.* Lexington: University Press of Kentucky, 1995.

Hall, Abigail Shelton (1812–1898)
Hall, Harvey (1813–1886)

Sturdy pioneers of Brown County, Ohio, Abigail Shelton Hall and her husband, farmer Harvey (or Hervey) Hall of Kentucky, operated a safehouse for the Underground Railroad. They married in April 1835. On September 1, 1837, congregants of the Ripley Presbyterian Church reprimanded Harvey Hall for his civil disobedience in aiding runaway slaves. On November 20, a follow-up report reassured church members that Hall appeared to have ceased his station management.

Source

Phelan, Helene C. *And Why Not Every Man?* Almond, NY: privately published, 1987.

Hall, Charles (fl. 1850s)

Freedman Charles Hall was one of many Maryland blacks to serve prison time for conducting slaves to liberty. On March 16, 1850, a Frederick County court sentenced Hall to three years and two months in the state penitentiary at Baltimore. His term ended six weeks after national emancipation of slaves on January 1, 1863.

Source

Prison records, Maryland State Archives.

Hall, David A. (1795–1870)

An assistant of editor Gamaliel Bailey and Quaker conductor Thomas Garrett, attorney David A. Hall of Vermont was part of a committed team of Underground Railroad operatives. He provided free legal advice to fugitive slaves and mediated the purchase of their family members to stop their sale farther south as punishment. The purchase of slave children was a priority with agents seeking to reunite fugitive slave families in free territory. On October 3, 1847, Garrett instructed Hall to buy the children of a runaway who had fled Prince George's County, Maryland, via the secret network.

The following year, Hall, Joshua Reed Giddings, and Edward Stowe Hamlin represented the 77 escapees who fled on April 15, 1848, with Captain Daniel Drayton from Georgetown in the District of Columbia. The refugees boarded Drayton's sloop *Pearl* at the Seventh Street Wharf for transport to the New Jersey shore. Hall risked violence at the hands of a pro-slavery mob gathered outside the Washington jail. Stymying efforts to free the captives was the bail, set at $76,000 for the three defendants, an amount that brought an outcry from William Lloyd Garrison in an editorial in *The Liberator.* When William Lawrence Chaplin, an agent in Washington, D.C., was arrested in August 1850, Hall again arranged bond.

See also: Liberator, The.

Source

Pacheco, Josephine F. *The Pearl: A Failed Slave Escape on the Potomac.* Chapel Hill: University of North Carolina Press, 2005.

Hall, Henrietta (fl. 1850s)
Hall, Jacob (fl. 1850s)
Hall, Charles H. (fl. 1850s)

The Underground Railroad aided a trio of slaves escaping from Cecil County, Maryland. In December 1855, Henrietta Hall outwitted Sarah Ann McGough, a drunken slave owner at Ladies' Manor who had previously sold Henrietta's brother and sister. Henrietta was accompanied by her husband, Jacob Hall (also called Henry Thomas), who belonged to slaveholder Major William Hutchins, and their son, Charles H. Hall. The couple aimed to reach Canada to reunite with Henrietta Hall's mother.

Source

Yentsch, Anne Elizabeth. *A Chesapeake Family and Their Slaves: A Study in Historical Archaeology.* New York: Cambridge University Press, 1994.

Hall, Jim "Jimmy Bow-Legs" (fl. 1840s–1850s)

A persistent maroon runaway, Jim "Jimmy Bow-Legs" Hall of Georgia made many escapes before reaching the volunteers of Philadelphia's vigilance committee. He was the son of a black woman and an Indian and the brother of Chief Billy Bow-Legs, the last head of a Creek-Seminole tribe in the Okefenokee Swamp of Florida. During service to Dr. Thomas Stephens of Oglethorpe County, Georgia, Jim Hall was a carpenter and cobbler who survived harsh overseers and prison sentences for his flight attempts. As a young man of 180 pounds, he intimidated potential buyers and continued to annoy his master with each of his six failed attempts to flee north. During his escapes, he lived in caves, swamps, and woods and survived on berries and parched corn. Stephens attempted to sell Hall in Florida, but the slave's steely gaze warded off buyers. On November 29, 1845, the *Weekly Argus* accused Hall of being a brutal killer.

See also: maroon settlements.

Sources

"The Indian Chief's Revenge," *Weekly Argus,* November 29, 1845, 4.

Williams, James. *Life and Adventures of James Williams, a Fugitive Slave.* San Francisco: Women's Union Print, 1873.

Hall, John (1823–?)
Hall, Mary Weaver (fl. 1850s)

John Hall and his Irish wife-to-be, Mary Weaver, made their way to Canada via separate routes of the Underground Railroad. After escaping ownership by South Carolina merchant James Dunlap, on April 27, 1855, John Hall (also known as John Simpson) slipped through wetlands of the Carolinas and Virginia, where he sheltered in caves. With the aid of a sympathetic sea captain, he booked passage aboard a schooner from Richmond, Virginia. Part of his fare came from Mary Weaver. A few months later, she traveled over the secret network route and joined him in Canada.

See also: routes, Underground Railroad.

Source

Blockson, Charles L. *The Underground Railroad: First-Person Narratives of Escapes to Freedom in the North.* New York: Prentice Hall, 1987.

Hall, John "Daddy" (1807–1925)

One of the first fugitive blacks to establish a home in Sydenham Village, on Owen Sound, Ontario, freedman John "Daddy" Hall was a victim of kidnap. The son of a fugitive slave woman, transported by slave ship to North America, and a Mohawk father, he was born in Amherstburg, near Windsor across the U.S.-Canadian border from Detroit. During the War of 1812, slave nabbers from southern plantations raided Amherstburg, Ontario, and seized Hall, his mother, and his 11 siblings for sale at a Maryland auction block to Kentucky buyers. John Hall fled ownership by a Kentuckian named Catlett. With his young wife, who was also a slave, Hall escaped via the Underground Railroad route across the Ohio River and through Ripley, Ohio. He searched Amherstburg for his family but found no one. After establishing a log home on Owen Sound, in 1851, he became Toronto's town crier and security guard. His voice reassured runaways, who valued the presence of a fellow fugitive in their new homeland.

See also: kidnap.

Sources

"Former Slave's Daughter Elizabeth (Hall) Hornby, 96, Born in Owen Sound," *Owen Sound (Ontario) Sun Times,* April 2, 1949.

"Reviving a Historic Tradition," *Owen Sound (Ontario) Tribune,* July 18, 1996, 1, 7.

Hall, William A. (fl. 1850s)

A native of the outskirts of Nashville, in Davidson County, Tennessee, William A. Hall attested to the persistence of secret agents in helping him gain liberty. While traveling in Louisiana in service to his master, a doctor from Bedford County, Tennessee, Hall observed the sufferings of cane mill slaves, who worked in chained coffles of 12 on the levees loading sugar. Overseers locked recalcitrant slaves in stocks to steady them for lashing. On his fourth try, in the 1850s, he fled Nashville, Tennessee; his mother and siblings were left in the hands of Mississippi cotton planters.

Like most uneducated blacks, Hall lacked direction and travel experience for his flight to Ohio. Eventually, he made his way to Golconda, Illinois. A local pilot led him to abolitionists in Mount Vernon, Illinois. In Ottawa, Illinois, Hall connected with an Underground Railroad agent who relayed him to Chicago. In February, Hall moved on to Wisconsin and got directions for crossing Lake Superior into Ontario.

Source

Drew, Benjamin. *The Narratives of Fugitive Slaves in Canada.* Boston: John P. Jewett, 1856.

Hallam, John (1821–1896)
Hallam, Aurelia Stillman Woodruff (1825–?)

A Quaker pioneer and conductor of the Underground Railroad, John Hallam put his Christian faith into action. In 1845, he married Aurelia Stillman Woodruff of Sheldon, New York. In Tabor, in Mills County, Iowa, he joined a network of stationmasters to guide slaves to freedom. On July 4, 1854, he helped S.H. Adams and James K. Gaston transport a single man and a black couple and their two children by carriage from a Tabor hotel across the Nishnabotna River. The passage took them east to Lewis, Iowa, and through Illinois, Indiana, and Michigan to Ontario. In league with Hallam were agents John Todd and Martha Atkins Todd, who aided insurrectionist John Brown and his conspirators in late summer 1858. In March 1860, Hallam helped another party of four runaways to speed through Tabor and on to Lewis, Iowa.

Sources

Farquhar, Catherine Grace Barbour. "Tabor and Tabor College." *Iowa Journal of History and Politics* 41 (October 1943): 358.

Todd, John. *Early Settlement and Growth of Western Iowa; or, Reminiscences.* Des Moines: Historical Department of Iowa, 1906.

Hallock, Horace (1807–1892)
Hallock, Elizabeth Raymond (1814–1887)

Two New York Presbyterians, merchant Horace Hallock and his wife, Elizabeth Raymond Hallock, supported the final leg of the Underground Railroad from Detroit, Michigan, to Windsor, Ontario. While operating a dry goods and clothing store, Horace Hallock served as treasurer of the Michigan Anti-Slavery Society and facilitator of escapes from Michigan to Ontario. Because the Hallock home fronted on the Detroit River, fugitives could flee out the back door and cross to Canada. After formation of the Refugee Home Society in 1851, to aid fleeing slaves in starting new lives in Essex County, Ontario, Horace Hallock served as treasurer. He coordinated efforts begun by Laura Smith Haviland to teach reading and the Bible, to clarify credit arrangements, and to simplify business contracts for the illiterate.

See also: Refugee Home Society.

Source

Finkenbine, Roy E. *The Black Abolitionist Papers.* Vol. 2, *Canada, 1830–1865.* Chapel Hill: University of North Carolina Press, 1986.

Hallowell, Mary H. Post (1823–1913)
Hallowell, William R. (1816–1882)

Mary H. Post, the child of abolitionists from Westbury, New York, continued her family's Quaker tradition of succoring runaway slaves. At age 20, she joined the Western New York Anti-Slavery Society, an activist agency founded by her parents, Hannah Kirby Post and Isaac Post. In January 1843, Mary married manufacturer William R. Hallowell and established a family on Jones Street in Rochester, New York. The couple supported the work of Frederick Douglass and maintained ties with Underground Railroad agents Susan Brownell Anthony, Wendell Addison Phillips, and Parker Pillsbury. During an influx of runaways after passage of the Fugitive Slave Law of 1850, the Hallowells and Mary Hallowell's stepmother and father, Amy Kirby Post and Isaac Post, took in as many as 15 passengers per night. In another act of benevolence, Mary launched the United Charities of Rochester.

See also: Fugitive Slave Law of 1850.

Source

Hewitt, Nancy A. *Women's Activism and Social Change: Rochester, New York, 1822–1872.* Ithaca, NY: Cornell University Press, 1984.

Hambleton, Thomas (1798–1868) Hambleton, Alice Eliza Betts (1802–1865)

Pennsylvania agent Thomas Hambleton and his family rescued runaways who reached his station in Penn Township, in Allegheny County. A native of Solebury, Pennsylvania, Thomas married Alice Eliza Betts in June 1823 and joined Asa Walton in forming the Clarkson (Pennsylvania) Anti-Slavery Society, an extension of the Homeville Meeting. Most passengers at the Hambleton waystation came through Virginia and Maryland and entered the state after crossing the Susquehanna River at Havre de Grace. In league with James Fulton, Jr., in Ercildoun and Seymour C. Williamson in Caln, Thomas Hambleton piloted passengers to the stop of Micajah Speakman, Phebe Smith Speakman, and William Allibone Speakman in Wallace, Pennsylvania.

Source

Switala, William J. *Underground Railroad in Pennsylvania.* Mechanicsburg, PA: Stackpole, 2001.

Hamilton, Elsie (fl. 1840s) Hamilton, Willis (fl. 1840s)

Two success stories of the Underground Railroad, Elsie Hamilton and her husband, Willis Hamilton, escaped bondage in Jonesboro, Tennessee. Willis Hamilton's owner, John Bayliss, was a Baptist deacon who educated his slaves in Christian worship. One slave, Aunt Lucy, chastised Bayliss for violating the Golden Rule by buying the human property of a planter named Jones. Bayliss encouraged Willis Hamilton by offering him wages, yet Bayliss sold Elsie Hamilton to a slave merchant along with the couple's two daughters. Willis Hamilton canvassed Tennessee until he found a buyer for his wife, Dr. John P. Chester, a hotelier who hired Willis. After a house servant warned Elsie and Willis that Chester planned to sell them to a trader in 1842, the Hamiltons fled bondage.

The Hamiltons hid for five weeks at a Tennessee depot of the Underground Railroad before moving on to Indiana Quaker agents named Shugart. They remained for a year until the birth of their daughter Louisa (1843–?) before moving along the network route. They next resided at the waystation of Charles Haviland, Jr., and Laura Smith Haviland in Adrian, Michigan, where Willis farmed 20 acres for the next three years. In 1846, the sight of a southern slave agent forced the Hamiltons to shelter at farms in Ypsilanti and Monroe before they felt it safe to return to the Havilands. John Chester, Elsie Hamilton's owner and the postmaster of Jonesboro, Tennessee, intercepted a letter she sent to Bayliss and attempted to capture the Hamiltons, even though Willis was a freedman.

Source

Haviland, Laura S. *A Woman's Life-Work: Labors and Experiences of Laura S. Haviland.* Cincinnati, OH: Walden & Stowe, 1882.

Hamilton, Saul (fl. 1830s)

A stirring episode in the *Life and Travels of Addison Coffin* (1897) describes the escape of Saul (or Solomon) Hamilton from slavery. In summer 1835, Addison Coffin, a 13-year-old Quaker from a clan of Underground Railroad agents in New Garden, North Carolina, learned of Hamilton's plight. After Hamilton's owner died, Ike Weatherby, a slave dealer, purchased Saul and took him to southern Georgia for sale. For the transfer, Weatherby collared Hamilton in irons and chained him to a coffle. On the long walk southwest, Hamilton broke free and started back over the same trails and rivers. At a deep creek, he eluded three bloodhounds. He killed one dog from a stump, then fought off the other two. When the attack was over, Hamilton's left arm and legs were seriously bitten. He swam in streams for several miles and arrived in pitiable condition at the safehouse of Alethea Flukes Coffin and Vestal M. Coffin in New Garden. The wretched condition of Hamilton's clothes and the suppurating lacerations dismayed Addison Coffin and turned him into a slave rescuer for life. Coffin helped Hamilton along the secret network to freedom.

Source

Coffin, Addison. *Life and Travels of Addison Coffin.* Cleveland, OH: W.G. Hubbard, 1897.

Hamlet, James (ca. 1815–?)

The flight of James Hamlet (also called James Hamilton Williams) from bondage was the first test of the Fugitive Slave Law of 1850 in New York City. A former servant at the Baltimore Shot Company, Hamlet escaped enslavement by Mary Brown in Baltimore, Maryland, in 1848 and found sanctuary with Silas Wood in New York City. Hamlet established himself in the Williamsburg section of Brooklyn, New York, as a porter at the Tilton & Malooey store at 58 Water Street. According to Lewis Tappan's treatise *The Fugitive Slave Bill: Its History and Unconstitutionality* (1850), Hamlet's owner, Mary Brown, sent her son, Gustavus, and Gustavus's son-in-law, Thomas J. Clare, from Baltimore to New York City on September 26, 1850, to identify and retrieve her slave, whom the owner valued at $800. Two days later, kidnappers seized Hamlet at work. His wife and two children had no clue to his whereabouts.

At the courthouse entrance, Deputy Federal Marshal Benjamin H. Tallmadge clamped Hamlet in manacles for transport by steamer to Baltimore. While Hamlet awaited sale in a Baltimore slave jail, New York agents and the black community planned their strategy for his rescue. Media articles about his loss of freedom terrified other runaways, who hurried across the Canadian border to avoid Hamlet's fate. Members of the Mother Mount Zion Church on Leonard Street in Manhattan protested the extradition at a meeting on October 2, 1850. They also raised $800 to buy Hamlet's liberty. Mediators from the New York Vigilance Committee purchased his freedom and returned him to his family in New York. Upon his arrival on October 5, 1850, some 5,000 supporters cheered his liberation.

See also: Fugitive Slave Law of 1850; kidnap.

Sources

The Fugitive Slave Law and Its Victims (tract). New York: American Anti-Slavery Society, 1856.
McDougall, Marion G. *Fugitive Slaves (1619–1865).* Boston: n.p., 1891.
Tappan, Lewis. *The Fugitive Slave Bill: Its History and Unconstitutionality.* New York: William Harned, 1850.

Hammond, Caroline Berry (1844–ca. 1938)

Caroline Berry Hammond followed an Underground Railroad route from Maryland to Pennsylvania. Caroline was the daughter of George Berry, a free carpenter in Annapolis, and a cook and domestic, one of the 25 slaves owned by Thomas Davidson, an aristocratic planter in Annapolis, in Anne Arundel County, Maryland. Berry saved for the manumission of his wife and children, but Davidson's death during a duck hunt in the 1850s ended the family's hopes. Berry bribed the county sheriff to provide passage for his family to Baltimore, where they sheltered at a safehouse on Ross Street. A relayer named Coleman shuttled the family by covered wagon to Hanover, Pennsylvania. Berry and his family found work in Scranton, Pennsylvania, where they lived until 1869.

Source

Archives, Maryland State Library.

Hanby, Benjamin Russell (1833–1867)
Hanby, William (1808–1880)

Composer Benjamin Russell Hanby aided his father, William Hanby, in operating a two-story frame waystation at 160 West Main Street in Westerville in Fairfield County, Ohio. With the aid of Lewis Davis, the Reverend William Hanby, a bishop of the United Brethren Church, and his son hid newcomers in their barn and their leather goods shop. At dinner, refugees ate at the Hanby table and joined the family in evening prayer. In 1842, the family received a slave dying of pneumonia. In his delirium, the runaway spoke of his sweetheart, Nelly Gray, whom a Kentucky slave owner had sold to someone in Georgia. Benjamin Hanby retained the memory of the slave's lost love. While studying at Otterbein College, Hanby composed "Darling Nelly Gray" (1856), a popular ballad sung by soldiers on both sides of the Civil War. Although the barn and leather shop burned in 1870 during a confrontation over temperance, the Hanby farmhouse still stands. A United Methodist shrine, it is listed on the National Register of Historic Places.

Source

Randall, E.O. *Ohio History.* Columbus: Ohio State Archaeological and Historical Society, 1905.

Hance, Mark (1829–1905)
Hance, Susan Crop (1836–1909)

Mark Hance and his wife, Susan Crop Hance, aided slaves on the last leg of their journey through Detroit and across the Detroit River to Canada. Mark Hance was born in Oakland County, Michigan. After the couple's marriage in 1856, they farmed northwest of Detroit at Farmington, Michigan, where the Hances operated a waystation of the Underground Railroad.

Source

Burton, Clarence Monroe. *The City of Detroit, Michigan, 1701–1922.* Detroit, MI: S.J. Clarke, 1922.

Hanna, Mary (1802–1872)
Hanna, Robert (1802–1872)

Mary Hanna and her husband, investor and abolitionist Robert Hanna, maintained a secret nook for hiding escaped slaves. Their two-story brick home, which they built at 200 South Pitt and East Beaver streets in Mercer, Pennsylvania, in 1839, offered a tiny hideaway in the stone foundation. The Hannas collaborated with Meadville agents Richard Henderson, his first wife, Ann Henderson, and his second wife, Mary Ann Harris Henderson. Mary Hanna took an active role as a conductor when she escorted a veiled slave girl to Erie, Pennsylvania. They traveled in a stagecoach with the girl's owner, who failed to notice the runaway in disguise. A relative, Mary Ann Hanna Small, wife of agent Edward Small, kept up the family tradition of benevolence to runaways at her home in Mercer County.

See also: disguise.

Source

Follow the Drinking Gourd (pamphlet). Mercer, PA: Mercer County Historical Society, 2002.

Hanover, John T. (fl. 1850s–1860s)

Under the assumed identity of a real estate agent named John Hansen, naturalist John T. Hanover superintended the Anti-Slavery League in Indiana and the volunteer network across Illinois, Indiana, Ohio, and Pennsylvania. After suffering a snakebite, Hanover lodged for 10 weeks with agents Colonel James Washington Cockrum and his son, Colonel William Monroe Cockrum, who managed a major portion of the fugitive slave escape route through Gibson County, in southwestern Indiana. During this period of recuperation, Hanover continued meeting with spies and conductors of the Underground Railroad and encouraged the involvement of William Cockrum, who later published *History of the Underground Railroad As It Was Conducted by the Anti-Slavery League* (1915). In 1865, Hanover reported that 4,000 runaways per year received Underground Railroad assistance in the 15 years following passage of the Fugitive Slave Law of 1850.

See also: Fugitive Slave Law of 1850.

Source

Cockrum, Colonel William. *History of the Underground Railroad As It Was Conducted by the Anti-Slavery League.* Oakland City, IN: J.W. Cockrum, 1915.

Hanway, Castner (1821–1893)

A miller in Lancaster County, Pennsylvania, Castner Hanway became an Underground Railroad hero for abetting a slave rescue. Hanway was well connected to operatives along Atlantic coast routes. For New England flights, he depended on agents Elijah Lewis and Martha Lewis in Farmington, Connecticut. On September 11, 1851, Hanway rode his horse past a pitched battle at William Parker's stone waystation, where Edward Gorsuch, a Baltimore County, Maryland, slave owner, demanded return of four fugitives—Noah Baley, Nelson Ford, George Hammond, and Joshua Hammond—who had been at large for two years. In defiance of the Fugitive Slave Law of 1850, Hanway, a pacifist Quaker, joined Elijah Lewis, Joseph P. Scarlett, and other neighbors in refusing to aid U.S. Marshal Henry H. Kline in the recapture. The resulting shoot-out appeared in the national press as the Christiana Riot.

President Millard Fillmore denounced the resisters as lawless and vicious. Following apprehension by federal marshals, Hanway along with Lewis, Scarlett, and 35 blacks faced treason charges. Frederick Douglass ridiculed the sedition charge as an effort by the government to depict slaves as brutes and to turn self-respecting blacks into outlaws. The 38 men remained in Moyamensing Prison in Philadelphia for 97 days, until November 1851. Defended in Independence Hall by Underground Railroad supporter Thaddeus Stevens, Hanway was the only participant to come to trial. The *National Era* reported that onlookers thronged the building. Among them was Lucretia Coffin Mott, who knitted with red, white, and blue yarn. During the three-week proceedings, Stevens shamed the court into exonerating Hanway; the verdict required only 15 minutes of deliberation. During the litigation, Hanway's wife, Martha Lamborn Hanway, died.

See also: Christiana Riot; Fugitive Slave Law of 1850; routes, Underground Railroad.

Sources

Jackson, W. Arthur. *History of the Trial of Castner Hanway and Others for Treason at Philadelphia in November, 1851.* Philadelphia: Uriah Hunt & Sons, 1852.

Mires, Charlene. *Independence Hall: In American Memory.* Philadelphia: University of Pennsylvania Press, 2002.

Happy, Jesse (fl. 1830s)

Jesse Happy made a successful journey along the Underground Railroad route. After his flight from a Kentucky slave master on a stolen horse in 1837, he gained the support of Paola Brown, a counselor to runaways passing through the secret network in Niagara, New York, into Ontario. The Kentucky governor requested Happy's extradition from Sir Francis Bond Head, the governor of Ontario. Head retained Happy in jail in Hamilton and refused to release him to Kentucky authorities without a formal hearing. The charge of horse theft foundered after U.S. marshals learned that Happy left the horse at the U.S. border and told his master where to claim it. In 1838, a Canadian court, lacking proof of a criminal act, freed Happy. The case set a precedent on issues involving extradition of runaway slaves from Canada to the United States.

Source

Murray, David. "Hands Across the Border: The Abortive Extradition of Solomon Moseby." *Canadian Review of American Studies* 30:2 (2000).

Harding, Stephen Selwyn (1808–1891)
Harding, Avaline Spraut (fl. 1830s)

An Underground Railroad operative in Versailles, in Ripley County, Indiana, Stephen Selwyn Harding networked with other abolitionists. He arrived in the southeastern part of the state in 1820 after leaving Ontario County, New York. After the marriage of Harding and Avaline Spraut in 1830, the couple opened a depot of the secret network that featured a false ceiling. In addition to investing in business and practicing law, from 1843 to 1861, Stephen Harding delivered anti-slavery lectures to hostile gatherings.

Source

French, Etta Reeves. "Stephen S. Harding: A Hoosier Abolitionist." *Indiana Magazine of History* 27:3 (1831): 212–20.

Harding, William (fl. 1840s)

William Harding (or Harden), an operative of the Underground Railroad, used his job as a steamboat steward as a means of rescuing fugitive slaves. In New Albany, Indiana, across the Ohio River from Louisville, Kentucky, he conspired with freedman James C. Cunningham, a bandleader and dance teacher in St. Louis, Missouri, who relayed runaways to free territory. Passengers followed the main lines through Floyd County to Indianapolis and South Bend, Indiana, and continued through Michigan to Canada.

Source

Peters, Pamela R. *The Underground Railroad in Floyd County, Indiana.* Jefferson, NC: McFarland, 2001.

Harmon, David Porter (1800–1869)
Harmon, Almira Sargent (1802–1857)

David Porter Harmon was a conductor of the Underground Railroad in Haverhill, in Essex County, Massachusetts. He was born in Peterborough, New Hampshire, and married Almira Sargent of Candia, New Hampshire. They harbored refugee slaves at their home, Harmon House, a clapboard residence built in 1810 at Maple Avenue and Summer Street. The couple received passengers from poet John Greenleaf Whittier, a rural operative in Amesbury, and passed them along the New England–Canada route.

Source

Chadwick, Bruce. *Traveling the Underground Railroad: A Visitor's Guide to More Than 300 Sites.* Secaucus, NJ: Citadel, 1999.

Harper, Frances Ellen Watkins (1825–1911)

Reformer, lecturer, and journalist Frances Ellen Watkins Harper aided slaves by writing poetry for the abolitionist press and by conducting slaves to freedom. Born free in Baltimore, Maryland, Harper was orphaned in 1828 and passed to the care of a paternal uncle, Underground Railroad agent William Watkins, who educated her at his school, the William Watkins Academy for Negro Youth. She lectured for the Maine Anti-Slavery Society, published abolitionist verse in William Lloyd Garrison's weekly, *The Liberator,* and maintained close contacts with other Underground Railroad operatives, including Henry Highland Garnet and William Still. In 1854, the plight of kidnap victim Solomon Northup, the author of *Twelve Years a Slave* (1853), inspired her to greater efforts on behalf of black fugitives, particularly women. Harper dedicated the royalties from her verse anthologies to the secret

The freeborn black poet Frances Ellen Watkins Harper ran a safehouse in Philadelphia, read her verse on the anti-slavery lecture circuit, and donated publication royalties to railroad operations. *(Library of Congress)*

network. Her Philadelphia safehouse at 27 Bainbridge Street was refurbished in 1988.

See also: kidnap; *Liberator, The.*

Source

Lauter, Paul. "Is Frances Ellen Watkins Harper Good Enough to Teach?" *Legacy* 5:1 (1988): 27–32.

Harper, Mary E. Goodwin (1810–1873) Harper, William Smith (1813–1892)

A generous couple, Mary E. Goodwin Harper and William Smith Harper, aided passengers of the Underground Railroad. A native of Dorchester County, Pennsylvania, William Harper, observed slavery in his uncle's household. He came under the influence of an aunt, a Quaker minister whose abolitionist beliefs influenced him to work for the secret network. In September 1851, he married Mary E. Goodwin, who inherited a farm in Westtown, Pennsylvania. The couple used their residence as a safehouse.

Source

Bordewich, Fergus M. *Bound for Canaan: The Underground Railroad and the War for the Soul of America.* New York: Amistad, 2005.

Harris, Catherine Dickes (1809–1907)

A famous mulatto in the history of Jamestown, New York, Catherine (also Catharine) Dickes Harris operated a safehouse in the black community of Africa. Born to a Dutch mother and black father in Meadville, Pennsylvania, she settled in Buffalo, New York, in widowhood at age 22 and supported herself and her daughter, Maria, as a domestic and laundress. After marrying John Harris in 1835, Catherine opened the family home at 12 West Seventh Street to refugees. Passengers arrived from Busti and Sugar Grove, Pennsylvania. When 17 slaves arrived at one time, friends provided food for Harris to cook for them. She provided sleeping quarters in her attic. Her colleagues included Phineas Crossman, Addison Price, and Silas Shearman, a harness maker on East Fourth and Pine streets. Shearman relayed Harris's passengers from a barn on Stillers Alley to stops in Barcelona, Brockton, Ellington, and Sinclairville, New York.

Source

"Aged Citizen Dead," *Jamestown (NY) Evening Journal,* February 13, 1907, 7.

Harris, Chapman (1804–1890)

A blacksmith and leader of the anti-slavery movement in Madison, Indiana, the Reverend Chapman Harris used his large size and toughness as a deterrent to slave catchers. Upon his emigration from Virginia to Jefferson County, Indiana, at age 35, he founded the St. Paul Second Baptist Church. At his smithy in Eagle Hollow east of Madison, he joined the rescue work of Elijah Anderson and developed a reputation for aiding fugitives. When the way was clear for Ohio River crossings, Harris signaled to the Indiana Anti-Slavery Society's hired transporters by pounding his hammer against an anvil that he mounted in a sycamore tree.

At a time when a pro-slavery faction forced George DeBaptiste out of town, Harris maintained his dedication to slaves crossing the Ohio River from Kentucky into free territory. He received the destitute at his cabin. When a colleague, John Simmons, betrayed secret information to the public, Harris lashed the man so severely that authorities arraigned and fined Harris for assault. According to the *Louisville Courier,* in late November 1856, Harris traveled by steamer to Louisville, where police seized his cache of arms and ammunition and ousted him from Kentucky.

Sources

Hudson, J. Blaine. *Fugitive Slaves and the Underground Railroad in the Kentucky Borderland.* Jefferson, NC: McFarland, 2002.

"The Underground Railroad: The Madison Route—Prominent Abettors of It," *Madison (IN) Courier,* September 12, 1888.

Harris, Eliza (fl. 1830s–1850s)

A stirring example of female courage, Eliza Harris fled slavery during the dead of winter. When the possibility of a slave sale loomed in 1838, the mulatto escaped from her owner, planter Thomas Davis, outside Dover, Kentucky. To save herself and her two-year-old son, Harry, from slave catchers and packs of bloodhounds, she clung to ice chunks on the frozen Ohio River at Stony Point. After losing her shoes, she suffered cuts from the jagged edges of the ice until William Lacey pulled her to shore. With the aid of Chance Shaw, a shore patrolman, and conductor Thomas W. Collins, she reached Crosby's Point on the other side and arrived at one of the most noted Underground Railroad stops, Liberty Hill, the waystation of Jean Lowry Rankin and John Rankin in Ripley, Ohio. Elizabeth and Harry recuperated from their hard journey at the safehouse of Catherine Platter "Kitty" McCague and Thomas McCague of Ripley.

For maximum security, Eliza lopped off her long hair and dressed like a man; Harry wore girl's clothing. The lengthy hop from station to station continued, from Ripley to Cabin Creek, Pennville, Greenville, and Sandusky, Ohio. One of the stops placed Eliza under the care of stationmaster Samuel Charles near Richmond, Ohio. In February 1839, agents transported mother and son to Cincinnati and on to Catherine White Coffin and Levi Coffin's sanctuary in Newport, Indiana, for a two-week respite. On this leg of the journey, Eliza rested at a log waystation near Balbec, in Jay County, Indiana, where agent Rachel Irey Sullivan hid fugitives in a space above her kitchen. From there, Eliza and her son passed to the care of Berias, Levi, and Zimri Bond, who operated a depot in Cabin Creek, in Randolph County, Indiana, outside Georgetown. Traveling by steamer over Lake Erie, the pair ended their flight in Chatham, Ontario. In 1854, Coffin's family reunited with Eliza Harris, whom novelist Harriet Beecher Stowe immortalized in a melodramatic novel, *Uncle Tom's Cabin* (1852). Eliza Harris's escape became a favorite scenario for the novel's illustrators. Stowe corroborated the account in chapter 6 of *A Key to Uncle Tom's Cabin* (1853).

See also: Key to Uncle Tom's Cabin, A (1853); *Uncle Tom's Cabin; or, Life Among the Lowly* (1852).

Sources

Coffin, Levi. *Reminiscences of Levi Coffin, the Reputed President of the Underground Railroad.* Cincinnati, OH: Western Tract Society, 1876.

Gray, Frank. "Historic Hideaway of Slave 'Railroad' Stays Tucked Away." *Blackford-Wells Tracer* 3:2 (July 1998): 104–5.

Thomas, James B. *Down Through the Years in Elyria.* Oberlin, OH: Oberlin Printing, 1967.

Harris, Hazzard (ca. 1790–1860)

A Maryland carpenter and a conductor of the Underground Railroad for two decades, Hazzard "Had" Harris helped runaways crossing the Susquehanna River into free territory in Pennsylvania. Manumitted by Joseph Prigg in 1832, Harris conspired in code with Quaker agent William "Uncle Billy" Worthington in abetting slave flight. Newcomers arrived at the river landing off Shuresville Road. At his two-story cottage, Worthington would slaughter and cook a sheep to feed passengers, who hid in surrounding cornfields. At a canal in Harford County, Maryland, Harris rowed the refugees north to a ferry.

See also: code, Underground Railroad.

Source

Mason, Samuel. *Historical Sketches of Harford County, Maryland.* Little Pines Farm, MD: privately printed, 1955.

Harris, James L. (1807–?)

A former slave of Joseph Perry Hilleary from Virginia, James L. Harris served a prison sentence for aiding a fugitive slave. In Allegany County, Maryland, on August 13, 1863, he paid the fares of six slaves riding a stage from Cumberland. Historians surmise that two of the riders, Mary Harris and Fanny Harris, were his wife and daughter. He harbored them for a day before dispatching them to Uniontown, Pennsylvania. After his arrest, he entered the Maryland penitentiary on October 13, 1863, to serve a six-year-and-six-month sentence. Fourteen months later, on December 20, 1864, Governor Augustus Williamson Bradford pardoned Harris for a crime that no longer existed.

Source

"Sentences," *Cumberland Union and Allegany County Gazette,* November 14, 1863, 3.

Harris, Philip (1817–?)

Philip Harris suffered the prejudice of Missourians against free black citizens. At age 31, he settled in St. Louis, Missouri, and worked as a cook. In September 1850, a court wrongfully judged him guilty of rescuing the female chattel of a slave owner named Gordon while crossing the Mississippi River from Illinois. Harris's wife, Rosamond, wrote appeals that gained favor with Governor Sterling Price, who pardoned Philip in June 1853.

Source

Frazier, Harriet C. *Runaway and Freed Missouri Slaves and Those Who Helped Them, 1763–1865.* Jefferson, NC: McFarland, 2004.

Harris, Rachel (fl. 1830s)

Rachel Harris, known as "Cunningham's Rache," fled bondage in Baltimore, Maryland. While she was the chattel of Henry Waters, she answered to the name Henrietta Waters. Around 1833, Henrietta served Waters and his wife during a trip to New Orleans. On the homeward journey, she took advantage of crowds on a riverbank and fled into the dark. She reached the station of a Quaker couple, Emmor Kimber and Susannah Jackson Kimber in Kimberton, in Chester County, Pennsylvania. Henrietta cooked for the family and endeared herself to Abigail Kimber, Emmor's daughter, with her gift for drama and mimicry.

Rachel married Isaac Harris, a fugitive from Maryland, and settled on Minor Street in West Chester, Pennsylvania. In 1839, Mort Cunningham of Bush River Neck, Maryland, had her arrested, alleging that she was his property. At the home of Judge Thomas S. Bell, Rachel escaped into the backyard and scaled a seven-foot fence. After scurrying through back alleys and over a seething vat at Sammy Auge's hat shop, she ended up in a kitchen, where she begged for shelter with Mrs. John T. Worthington, who employed Harris as a laundress. She dressed in men's clothes from the Worthington attic.

With her husband, Rachel boarded the carriage of agent Benjamin Price and his son, Isaac, who operated a waystation in East Bradford, Pennsylvania. They rode all night in drizzling rain through Norristown and arrived at the home of William H. Johnson in Bucks County. (Another version claims that the station belonged to Abigail Paxson Vickers and John Vickers.) The Harrises remained out of sight at the safehouse until they could cross into Windsor, Ontario.

Source

Smedley, Robert C. *History of the Underground Railroad in Chester and the Neighboring Counties of Pennsylvania.* Lancaster, PA: Office of *The Journal,* 1883.

Harrison, Thomas (?–ca. 1880s)
Harrison, Isabella Benton (?–ca. 1870s)

In flight from enslavement, Thomas Harrison took advantage of the Underground Railroad. Harrison belonged to the Bullocks of Kentucky. After the Bullocks sold his two brothers, in 1851, Harrison ran north and crossed the Ohio River. At the shore, he encountered agents of Levi Coffin, a superintendent of the secret network in Cincinnati, Ohio. Harrison followed the Ohio–Canada route through Toledo and Detroit, where he crossed the Detroit River to Windsor, Ontario. After settling in London, Ontario, in 1854, he wed Isabella Benton, a runaway from the Chouteau family in St. Louis, Missouri. The couple journeyed to Haiti but settled on London, Ontario, as their permanent home.

Source

Coffin, Levi. *Reminiscences of Levi Coffin, the Reputed President of the Underground Railroad.* Cincinnati, OH: Western Tract Society, 1876.

Hart, Thomas (1827–?)

Thomas Hart went to prison for his activism. In April 1850, in Mississippi County, Missouri, he aided Goliah Shelby to escape his owner, Charles A. Shelby, who posted the slave's worth at $600. After a trial in Cape Girardeau, Hart entered the Missouri penitentiary in Jefferson City in June 1851. He appealed his case but remained incarcerated until 1864, a year after national emancipation on January 1, 1863.

Source

Frazier, Harriet C. *Runaway and Freed Missouri Slaves and Those Who Helped Them, 1763–1865.* Jefferson, NC: McFarland, 2004.

Harvey, John S. (1821–1850)

John S. Harvey of Marion County, Indiana, began supporting the work of the Underground Railroad in his youth. With Elias Coleman, he operated a free labor store in Jonesboro that stocked no slave-made or slave-harvested goods. While teaching in Adams Township, Harvey became a respected conductor of the secret network in Clinton and Warren counties. In partnership with Quincy Baldwin, Harvey relayed runaways to Moses Bradford, a Quaker conductor in Marion, Ohio.

See also: free labor store.

Source

Baldwin, Edgar M., ed. *The Making of a Township: Being an Account of the Early Settlement and Subsequent Development of Fairmount Township, Grant County, Indiana.* Fairmount, IN: self-published, 1917.

Hatch, Jeremiah, Jr. (1819–1862)
Hatch, Lucy Ann Rigdon (1831–ca. 1919)

A volunteer couple on the busy Underground Railroad route through New York State, Professor Jeremiah Hatch, Jr., and Lucy (or Lacy) Ann Rigdon Hatch operated a waystation in Friendship. Jeremiah, a native of Ferrisburg, in Addison County, Vermont, was educated at Middlebury College. He became an abolitionist while teaching geology in New Bern, North Carolina, in the 1840s. In New York, he and his family received runaways from the Ethan Lanphear station in Nile, where Hatch became principal of the Friendship Academy when it opened in 1848. The family residence featured barred windows on the bottom floor and a subterranean passage from the cellar to the carriage house. Hatch died of fever during the Civil War while serving as captain in the 130th New York Infantry.

Source

Minard, John S. *History of Friendship Village, New York.* Alfred, NY: W.A. Fergusson, 1896.

Hatfield, Alexander (fl. 1850s)

One of the craftier Underground Railroad conductors, Alexander "Alex" Hatfield apparently posed as a drunken roustabout to conceal important business for the secret network. Living among free blacks in Louisville, Kentucky, he worked at barbering but devoted some of his time to traveling the northern route through Cincinnati, Ohio, to Ontario. According to a court report in the *Louisville Courier,* in late September 1856, the foiled escape of Jack Kidd, the chattel of William C. Kidd, resulted in the criminal trial of James Armstrong and Samuel Cole. Testimony suggests that Hatfield and his wife pretended to conceal pursuers under a bed while the defendants plotted a rescue by boat over the Ohio River.

Source

Hudson, J. Blaine. *Fugitive Slaves and the Underground Railroad in the Kentucky Borderland.* Jefferson, NC: McFarland, 2002.

Hatfield, John (fl. 1840s)

An Underground Railroad operative in Cincinnati, Ohio, John Hatfield was a key figure on the Kentucky–Ontario route. A deacon at Zion Baptist Church, he had a reputation for integrity and for complete dedication to the liberation of slaves despite the city's frequent violent eruptions over slave harboring. He conspired with Quaker superintendents Laura Smith Haviland, Catherine White Coffin, and Levi Coffin and with the Zion Baptist Church pastor, the Reverend Wallace Shelton, an agent for over three decades. Hatfield was adept at the black grapevine. While working as a barber on riverboats and operating a barber shop in Bucktown, he gained crucial information about bounty hunters and posses and quickly relayed fugitives to the North.

One difficult transfer of passengers occurred on a rainy night late in the 1840s, when John Fairfield rowed 28 runaways over the Ohio River at the confluence of the Miami River. After a difficult landing in quicksand, the fugitives lost their shoes in the muck and continued in bare feet. Hatfield received the party and passed them on to Catherine White Coffin and Levi Coffin in Cincinnati. The group posed as a funeral cortege and traveled toward College Hill in buggies and carriages.

See also: bounty hunters; grapevine telegraphy.

Sources

Buchanan, Thomas C. *Black Life on the Mississippi: Slaves, Free Blacks, and the Western Steamboat World.* Chapel Hill: University of North Carolina Press, 2004.

Coffin, Levi. *Reminiscences of Levi Coffin, the Reputed President of the Underground Railroad.* Cincinnati, OH: Western Tract Society, 1876.

Hathaway, Joseph Comstock (1810–1876)

A radical Quaker abolitionist and women's rights advocate, Joseph Comstock Hathaway aided the New York–Ontario route of the Underground Railroad. In 1840, he served the American Anti-Slavery Society as a manager. At his acreage outside Rochester at Farmington, in Ontario County in western New York, he labored openly in service to desperate fugitives and collaborated with the Reverend Samuel Ringgold Ward, a route planner in Greenwich, New Jersey. On May 5, 1842, Lydia Maria Francis Child, editor of the *National Anti-Slavery Standard,* published Hathaway's account of a 19-year-old Virginia runaway whose owner had offered him as a wager in a cockfight. Hathaway provided a preface for *Narrative of William W. Brown, a Fugitive Slave, Written by Himself* (1847), a major addition to slave narratives. In spring 1848, Hathaway joined philanthropists Salmon Portland Chase, Joshua Reed Giddings, David A. Hall, Francis Jackson, Gerrit Smith, Lewis Tappan, and John Greenleaf Whittier in raising bail for William Lawrence Chaplin, who was jailed in Rockville, Maryland, for abetting slave flight. In August 1850, Hathaway took an active part in formal protest of the Fugitive Slave Act at a convention in Cazenovia, New York.

See also: American Anti-Slavery Society; Fugitive Slave Law of 1850.

Source

Aldridge, Lewis Cass. *History of Ontario County, New York.* Syracuse, NY: D. Mason, 1893.

Haviland, Laura Smith (1808–1898)

A Canadian Quaker lobbyist and reform organizer, Laura Smith Haviland involved herself in benevolent social activism and protest. She produced *A Woman's Life-Work: Labors and Experiences of Laura S. Haviland* (1882), an eyewitness account of Underground Railroad rescues that details the human side of succoring determined freedom seekers. The daughter of the Reverend Daniel Smith and Sene Blancher Smith, she was born in Kitley, in Leeds County, Ontario, and grew up in Cambria, New York, among members of the Society of Friends. She married a Quaker farmer, Charles Haviland, Jr. (1800–1845), and established a home in Raisin, Michigan. It became the state's first Underground Railroad safehouse, which they operated in collaboration with Almira M. Reed Gilbert and Warren Gilbert of Rome, Michigan. At age 29, the Havilands founded Raisin Institute, an integrated academy. In 1837, Laura ministered to children at her orphanage for blacks. She taught domestic skills, knitting, and sewing; her husband and her brother, Harvey Smith, taught farmwork. The combined efforts evolved into a freedman's school on the order of Oberlin College in Oberlin, Ohio.

In widowhood in 1845, "Aunt Laura" Haviland allied with conductor John Hatfield, a barber in Cincinnati, Ohio. Among the fugitives she aided were George Taylor, a harvest laborer, and farmworkers Elsie Hamilton and Willis Hamilton. When three southern slave catchers closed in on the Hamiltons at the Haviland farm in Adrian, Michigan, Laura and her son, Daniel S. Haviland (1828–1893), took a decoy, James Martin, by train to Toledo, Ohio, to allow the Hamiltons time to elude capture. At a stop in Sylvania, Ohio, Laura confronted Dr. John P. Chester, Elsie Hamilton's owner, and his son, Thomas K. Chester, and refused to give up the Hamiltons. Chester brandished six-shooters in the Havilands' faces until a train conductor threatened to have him arrested.

At the urging of Levi Coffin and Catherine White Coffin, network superintendents in Cincinnati, Ohio, Laura Haviland, with Sojourner Truth, solicited travel funds for runaway slaves. As a conductor and roving agent of the Underground Railroad, she traveled south as far as New Orleans. Her work involved mapping out routes through Ohio and Indiana. She filled her shopping basket with goods from the Coffins' secondhand store, where vigilance committee volunteers made and repaired clothing for refugees. Haviland encountered considerable danger in engineering the escapes of William Allen and of Jane White and John "Felix" White. In confrontations with slave catchers, Haviland faced bowie knives, dirks, guns, and the raised fists of southern spies who stalked her property.

At the Refugee Home Society colony outside Windsor, Ontario, Haviland's benevolence to black settlers included teaching reading and the Bible, clarifying credit arrangements, and simplifying business contracts for the illiterate. With the help of Charles C. Foote, she blessed the marriages of couples who requested a formal ceremony to replace slave union solemnized by the plantation system of "jumping the broom." She organized a nondenominational Christian Union Church. One of her failed missions in Chatham, Ontario, was the attempted reunion in 1854 of fugitive Missourian John Anderson with his wife.

Haviland remained active during the Civil War. In 1863, she tended combat casualties, inmates of Libby Prison, and slave refugees through the Freedman's Relief Association and the American Missionary Association. In her first war efforts, she gathered hospital supplies and 2,000 garments for distribution in Cairo, Illinois, and joined Sojourner Truth in visits to veterans hospitals in Georgetown, in Washington, D.C.

Haviland observed bands of plantation runaways who awaited transport to the North. She compiled dismaying stories of hundreds of slaves who were hanged by their owners. In spring 1864, she and Letitia Backus of Pittsford, Michigan, collected clothing and blankets and delivered them to homeless blacks in Louisiana and Mississippi. She summarized some of her experiences for the *Detroit Tribune.* During the Reconstruction era, she continued relief work among refugees in Kansas.

See also: Oberlin College; Refugee Home Society; routes, Underground Railroad; vigilance committees.

Sources

Glesner, Anthony Patrick. "Laura Haviland: Neglected Heroine of the Underground Railroad." *Michigan Historical Review* 21:1 (1995): 19–48.

Haviland, Laura S. *A Woman's Life-Work: Labors and Experiences of Laura S. Haviland.* Cincinnati, OH: Walden & Stowe, 1882.

Hawkins, Emeline (fl. 1840s)
Hawkins, Samuel (fl. 1840s)

With her husband, freedman Samuel "Sam" Hawkins (or Hawkings), Emeline Hawkins fled bondage to James Glanding in Queen Annes County, Maryland. In November 1845, the family made the break for free territory. Traveling with them were their children, Chester, Sally Ann, Walter, and Washington, and two unidentified children. Underground Railroad agent Samuel D. Burris relayed the eight passengers and four others by covered wagon from Camden. The Hawkins bore a letter of introduction from Quaker agent Ezekiel Jenkins to the next stationkeeper. Venturing 27 miles in a snowstorm, the passengers sheltered at the Middletown, Delaware, depot of John Hunn and Mary Ann Sharpless Hunn, who served them breakfast and treated frostbite on the refugees' extremities. At Odessa, the 12 fugitives cowered in the loft of the Appoquinimink Friends Meeting House.

Constable Richard C. Hays stalked the party; bounty hunters anticipated a reward of $1,000 for the Hawkins' capture. Tricked into surrendering, Emeline and Sam Hawkins were jailed in New Castle, Delaware. The children remained with the Hunn family. Meanwhile, on December 18, 1845, the four slaves who accompanied the Hawkins family followed Burris to Thomas Garrett's hardware store at the Market Street Bridge in Wilmington, Delaware. Garrett negotiated with Chief Justice James Booth for the release of the Hawkins family. The couple and their children rested at Garrett's waystation and continued on their way to Byberry, Pennsylvania, their new home, near the depot of Robert Purvis. Operatives John Hunn and Thomas Garrett suffered stiff fines from lawsuits filed by the slaves' owners. Harriet Beecher Stowe reprised Garrett's courage in her novel *Uncle Tom's Cabin* (1852). He supplied her with an outline of the Hawkins' escape, which Stowe published in *A Key to Uncle Tom's Cabin* (1853).

See also: bounty hunters; *Key to Uncle Tom's Cabin, A* (1853); slave recovery; *Uncle Tom's Cabin; or, Life Among the Lowly* (1852).

Source

Kelley, William T. "The Underground Railroad in the Eastern Shore of Maryland and Delaware." *Friends Intelligencer* 55 (1898): 238, 264–65, 379.

Hawkins, Walter (1809–1894)

The Reverend Walter Hawkins, a former slave living in Canada, ministered to new arrivals who arrived via the Underground Railroad. Hawkins was born into bondage in Georgetown, Maryland. After his master's death, a slave dealer named Chidley sold Hawkins to Jane Robinson, who bought him for $900 to serve as a plantation plowman. Around 1825, Hawkins took his father's advice and fled by train through Baltimore to Philadelphia, Pennsylvania. Two female abolitionists recognized his terror of their questions and shared their basket of food with him.

In Philadelphia, Hawkins received the aid of a shoemaker, Walter Proctor, and reunited with a brother. With gifts of food and clothing, Hawkins traveled north to Buffalo, New York, where he worked as a waiter. He opened a grocery store in New Bedford, Massachusetts, before pressing on to Brantford, Ontario. Settled in Chatham, he led a British Methodist Episcopal congregation at Princess and Wellington streets during the influx of blacks that resulted from passage of the Fugitive Slave Law of 1850. During a speaking tour in England, he solicited donations to help fugitives establish new lives in Ontario. In 1890, he advanced to bishop of the Methodist Episcopal Church and composed his memoirs, *From Slavery to Bishopric* (1891).

See also: Fugitive Slave Law of 1850.

Source

Edwards, S.J. *From Slavery to Bishopric; or, The Life of Bishop Walter Hawkins of the British Methodist Episcopal Church Canada.* London: John Kensit, 1891.

Hayden, Lewis (ca. 1811–1889)
Hayden, Harriet Bell (ca. 1816–1893)

Abolitionist, author, and statesman Lewis Hayden and his wife, Harriet Bell Hayden, devoted themselves and their money to the freeing of slaves. Lewis Hayden was the son of a Caucasian–Native American milkmaid and a black factory worker from Lexington, Kentucky. When her owner tried to make his mother a concubine, she refused and was jailed. She attempted suicide and went insane. Sometime around 1818, she gained release to see her son. A Presbyterian minister, the Reverend Adam Runkin, sold Lewis Hayden in 1821 and auctioned off his siblings. Runkin rationalized the act of separating black families as being no worse than selling a litter of pigs.

Goaded to Learn

Lewis Hayden passed through ownership by a clock seller and three other masters. Married at age 15 to Esther Harvey, he fathered three children. After the sale of one child and the death of another in infancy, the couple reared a son. Lashings goaded Lewis Hayden to better himself; he learned to read from newspapers and the Scriptures. After a slaveholder sold Esther and her children, Hayden married Harriet Bell and adopted her son, Jo. In 1842, angered at his sale to Thomas Grant and Lewis Baxter, Hayden plotted his flight while he waited tables at the Phoenix Hotel. He rejected any strategy that required him to abandon his second family.

Late in the afternoon on September 28, 1844, during the busy horse-racing season, the Haydens and Jo fled north via the Underground Railroad. A hasty dusting of flour to face and hands concealed their dark skin. Driving them all night by carriage through northern Kentucky to Washington was a slave named Israel, the hireling of two agents, the Reverend Calvin Fairbank of Oberlin College and his fiancée, Delia Ann Webster, a teacher at the Lexington Female Academy. Jo Hayden was small enough to hide under the carriage seat. After arriving at the Kentucky side of the Ohio River, the Haydens passed into the care of James Helm, a boatman who transferred them to Liberty Hill, the waystation of Jean Lowry Rankin and John Rankin in Ripley, Ohio. To avoid pursuers, they shifted location to Red Oak, Ohio, and then to a Quaker safehouse in Sandusky, Ohio. After taking nourishment, the Haydens moved on to Detroit,

The abolitionist lecturer Lewis Hayden, who fled slavery in Kentucky in 1844, operated critical waystations with his wife, Harriet Bell Hayden, in Detroit and Boston. They defied posses and took part in dangerous maneuvers on behalf of runaways. *(Schomburg Center for Research in Black Culture/General Research and Reference Division/New York Public Library/Astor, Lenox, and Tilden Foundations)*

Michigan, where they crossed the Detroit River to Amherstburg, Ontario. Lewis Hayden later raised $650 to buy his manumission and to free the Reverend Fairbank from prison, where he was serving a 15-year sentence for complicity in a slave rescue.

Investing in Runaways

In spring 1845, the Hayden family returned to Detroit to aid the secret network at one of its most critical crossing points over the Detroit River into Windsor, Ontario. Lewis Hayden established the Church of the Colored Methodist Society and a school, which he financed from donations he received from 1845 to 1846 on a tour of New England, New Jersey, and New York for the American Anti-Slavery Society. Relocated to the Beacon Hill section of Boston on May 25, 1846, the Haydens continued their efforts on behalf of blacks in bondage and plotted rescues with strategist John J. Smith and John Swett Rock, the medical officer of the Boston Vigilance Committee.

In 1848, Lewis Hayden opened a prosperous ready-to-wear and custom-made clothing store on Cambridge Street in Boston, which supplied the cash for outfitting runaways. The Haydens lived at 66 Phillips Street, where Harriet operated a boardinghouse. She also managed the city's main Underground Railroad waystation, complete with a secret tunnel leading from the subcellar to an unknown exit. Lewis Hayden undermined the recapture of runaways by joining operatives at the Twelfth Baptist Church and among the Masons. In addition, he served on the executive committee of the Boston Vigilance Committee, which had 250 members.

After the passage of the Fugitive Slave Law in September 1850, Lewis Hayden spearheaded Boston's defiance of the federal government. At their new home at 66 Southac Street, the Haydens welcomed hundreds of escapees and underwrote their board and clothing. In October 1850, only weeks after the law was enacted, they aided Ellen Smith Craft and William Craft, a refugee couple from Macon, Georgia. Eight days after the Crafts' passage to Halifax, Nova Scotia, English abolitionist George Thompson and the American reformer and journalist William Lloyd Garrison visited the Haydens and found them barricaded behind locked doors and windows with loaded weapons at hand. Assisting the Haydens were their son Jo and some loyal freedmen who were willing to die for the cause of liberty.

The Haydens took part in other chancy Underground Railroad maneuvers. Lewis Hayden, John J. Smith, and a few freedmen rescued Fredric "Shadrach" Minkins from the Boston federal courthouse on February 15, 1851, and transported the runaway to the Haydens' station and then on to Ann Hagar Bigelow and Francis Edwin Bigelow in Concord, Massachusetts. The Bigelows relayed Minkins to the home of Francis Hills Wilder Drake and Jonathan Drake in Leominster, Massachusetts, and from there to Benjamin Snow, Jr., and Mary Baldwin Boutolle Snow's stop in West Fitchburg. Lewis Hayden, meanwhile, faced an arrest warrant for interference in the work of federal marshals. Richard Henry Dana, Jr., defended Hayden and Smith, and James N. Buffum posted bond to set Hayden free. Several months later, a hung jury ended the matter after Francis Bigelow and another abolitionist had successfully fought votes for Hayden's conviction. A prestigious trio—President Millard Fillmore and senators Henry Clay and Daniel Webster—denounced the rescue as treasonous.

The Haydens earned renown for their many volunteer efforts, including the hiring of a carriage to speed four refugees from Boston on February 18, 1851. Lewis Hayden was also responsible for the outfitting of Sam Ward for his passage to Plymouth, Massachusetts, on May 16, 1851, and for clothing William H. Fisher, who made his way through Boston on October 31, 1851. In 1852, the Haydens boarded Mrs. Cooly and her daughter, Mrs. Dunlap and her child, William Brown and Mary Brown and their children, and William Attucks. They gave cash to James Coles and Mrs. Smith. Demands on the Hayden family increased with the passage of J.W. Fisher, Mrs. Smith, and Thomas Jackson on December 8, 1852, John Cole on January 25, 1853, Mrs. Jones and her children on April 18, 1854, and John Wright in July 1854. On October 9, 1853, the Haydens paid for the funeral of Julia Smith's child; in September 1854, they donated furniture to Jane Wilson and her children.

Failures and Losses

The Haydens failed in their attempts to save Thomas M. Sims in 1851 and Anthony Burns in 1854. On April 3, 1851, Sims entered the custody of 200 armed federal officers, who successfully buttressed the holding cell and warded off rescuers. An escort returned Sims to slavery on April 19. Five weeks later on May 24, federal agents captured Anthony Burns. Lewis Hayden tried to get the case placed before an abolitionist judge. When the ploy failed, Hayden sued Burns's owner for $10,000. According to historian George Lunt, author of *The Origin of the Late War* (1866), at noon, authorities summoned armed marines from the Boston navy yard and called in artillerymen and cannoneers to subdue throngs in the streets. The melee resulted in the death of a policeman, shot by Martin Stowell. Despite civic protest, authorities returned Burns to bondage in Georgia.

The two widely publicized failures in no way dimmed the Haydens' enthusiasm for slave conducting and rescue. In 1853, Harriet Beecher Stowe interviewed 13 runaways in the couple's care and used the details for her compilation of *A Key to Uncle Tom's Cabin* (1853). In October 1854, the Hayden family received a man rescued by Captain Austin Bearse from the sloop *Cameo.* The agents disguised the runaway in women's dress and sped him away in the carriage of William Ingersoll Bowditch of Brookline, Massachusetts. Lewis Hayden weathered arrests for civil disobedience and supported passage of a Massachusetts statute in 1855 that protected escaping slaves. The family reputedly stored gunpowder under their front porch and threatened to drop lighted candles on it to stop bounty hunters from forcing their way through the front door.

Although the Haydens suffered financial loss from the Panic of 1857 and from a fire in their clothing shop, they continued to assist the Underground Railroad, harboring 75 percent of all slaves passing through Boston. For their commitment, they earned praise from conductors Frederick Douglass, William Lloyd Garrison, and the Reverend Thomas Wentworth Higginson. John Brown stayed with the family on several occasions between 1857 and 1859 and revealed his plot to seize the federal arsenal at Harpers Ferry, Virginia, and distribute the weapons to slaves for a national insurrection against the flesh trade. Hayden performed a secret role in the plot by asking Francis Jackson Merriam for a $600 donation in gold to Brown's band, a sum that Merriam delivered in person. In addition, Hayden became the first black messenger of the Massachusetts secretary of state, a post he held for the rest of his life.

Later Years

Lewis Hayden supported the use of freedmen to end the Civil War. During a call for more Union soldiers in February 1863, he directed the mustering of the Massachusetts Fifty-fourth Volunteer Infantry. The couple's son, Jo Hayden, died on July 18, 1863, at the battle of Fort Wagner, South Carolina. The Haydens' philanthropic work continued after the war with the organization of black Masonic lodges and with contributions to the Massachusetts Historical Society and the Boston Museum of Fine Arts. Two years before Lewis Hayden's death from kidney failure, he convinced Bostonians to honor black martyr Crispus Attucks, and four others who died during the Boston Massacre of March 5, 1770. In widowhood, Harriet Lewis bequeathed $5,000 for scholarships for black premed students at Harvard University Medical School at a time when the school was segregated and blacks barred from the campus.

See also: American Anti-Slavery Society; disguise; *Key to Uncle Tom's Cabin, A* (1853); Oberlin College.

Sources

"Cheerful Yesterdays V. The Fugitive Slave Period." *Atlantic Monthly* 79 (1897): 345–46.

Robboy, Stanley J., and Anita W. Robboy. "Lewis Hayden: From Fugitive Slave to Statesman." *New England Quarterly* 46 (December 1973): 591–613.

Strangis, Joel. *Lewis Hayden and the War Against Slavery.* North Haven, CT: Linnet Books, 1999.

Haydock, Hannah Thompson (1811–1878)

An assistant to the Underground Railroad workers Catherine White Coffin and Levi Coffin, Hannah (or Hanna) Thompson Haydock (or Haddock) earned a place in history for her benevolence to runaway slaves. A native of Hillsborough, in Orange County, North Carolina, she married Zeno Haydock. They reared their family in Monrovia, in Morgan County, Indiana. After six years of widowhood, Hannah married John D. Edwards in 1856. She appears as a close friend and advocate in a February 1864 entry in Lucretia Coffin Mott's collected letters, in which Hannah pitied the plight of slaves in the Mississippi Valley. For the 1893 World's Columbia Exposition, Cincinnati, Ohio, landscape painter Charles T. Webber pictured Haydock and her son, Thomas Thompson Haydock (1847–ca. 1885), receiving cold, ragged runaways in an oil painting titled *Fugitives Arriving at Levi Coffin's Indiana Farm, a Busy Station of the Underground Railroad.* Among the slaves Haydock admired was Harriet Jacobs, author of *Incidents in the Life of a Slave Woman* (1861).

See also: Incidents in the Life of a Slave Girl (1861).

Source

Yellin, Jean Fagan. *Harriet Jacobs: A Life.* New York: Basic Civitas, 2004.

Hayes, Mordecai (1794–1837)
Hayes, Esther Logue (1788–1868)
Hayes, Jacob (1804–1877)

The first Underground Railroad agents of Newlin, in Chester County, Pennsylvania, Esther Logue Hayes, her husband Mordecai Hayes, and their son, Jacob Hayes, were diligent abolitionists. Esther and Mordecai, both natives of Brandywine Hundred, in New Castle County, Delaware, married in 1813. Slaves arrived from Sarah Painter Barnard and William Barnard in Wilmington, Delaware, and passed from their station to that of Gravner Marsh and Hannah Marsh and their daughter, Sarah Marsh, in Caln, Pennsylvania. The Hayes family received slaves at the wagon shed and hid them in their residence and barn. Jacob Hayes then sped them away in a curtained carriage to the waystation of Dr. Jacob K. Eshleman in Strasburg, Nathan Evans and Zillah Maule Evans in Willistown, Esther Fussell Lewis in Kimberton, or

Abigail Paxson Vickers and John Vickers in Lionville. Continuing his parents' work in Newlin, Jacob Hayes received fugitives from a father and son team, agents Micajah Speakman and William Allibone Speakman in Wallace, Pennsylvania. The Jacob Hayes safehouse is listed among Pennsylvania's historic places.

Source

Smedley, Robert C. *History of the Underground Railroad in Chester and the Neighboring Counties of Pennsylvania.* Lancaster, PA: Office of *The Journal,* 1883.

Hayes, Phebe Cooley (1782–1865)
Hayes, Titus (1776–1832)

Phebe Cooley Hayes and her husband, Titus Hayes, aided fugitive slaves passing through Ohio on their way north to Canada. The son of a veteran of the American Revolution, Titus Hayes migrated from Hartland, Connecticut, to Wayne, in Ashtabula County, Ohio, in 1798. After he married Phebe Cooley of Granville, Massachusetts, in 1800, they built a home on Pymatuning Creek, where they received refugees. In 1825, Titus served as an associate judge.

Source

Williams, William W. *History of Ashtabula County, Ohio.* Philadelphia: Williams Bros., 1878.

Hayes, Rutherford Birchard (1822–1893)
Hayes, Lucy Ware Webb (1831–1889)

Abolitionist attorney, Civil War soldier, and nineteenth president of the United States, Rutherford B. Hayes performed personal kindnesses on behalf of the Underground Railroad. After graduating from Harvard Law School, he opened an office in Sandusky, Ohio. In the early 1850s, while practicing law in Cincinnati, Ohio, he was moved to anger by the Fugitive Slave Law of 1850 and by the caning of John Jolliffe, a Cincinnati attorney for the Underground Railroad, for his aid to blacks. Hayes made a contract with Levi Coffin to aid the work of the secret network by defending runaways in court without charging a fee. Hayes married Lucy Ware Webb, a Methodist abolitionist from Chillicothe, Ohio, in 1852. His respect for her family's anti-slavery opinions led Hayes to take a more active role in ending slavery and in halting extradition of runaways from free territory. In one startling event in October 1854, the Hayeses found a naked black infant abandoned on their doorstep in a box. The couple found a home for the child at the Negro Orphans' Asylum.

Many of the slaves involved in litigation had arrived in Ripley, Ohio, from Kentucky after crossing the frozen Ohio River during the winters of 1850–1851, 1852–1853, and 1855–1856. Hayes collaborated with Joliffe to free blacks from jail. In October 1853, Hayes defended Louis Marshall, a Kentucky escapee whose owner, Alexander Marshall of Fleming County, wanted him returned. During the judge's summation, Louis slipped out of the courtroom and hid near Levi Coffin's store at Elm and Sixth streets before being transferred to Canada. Another of Hayes's successful court interventions involved his partnering with abolitionist attorney Salmon Portland Chase in 1855 to stop the Reverend Henry M. Dennison from capturing Rosetta Armstead, a Kentucky slave girl. At age 40, Hayes served as a brigadier general in the Twenty-third Ohio Volunteers during the Civil War and sustained wounds to the head, ankle, and left arm. From 1877 to 1881, he served as the nineteenth president of the United States In 1886, he became the first president of the Civil War Library and Museum of Philadelphia.

See also: Fugitive Slave Law of 1850.

Source

Trefousse, Hans L. *Rutherford B. Hayes.* New York: Times, 2002.

Hayes, William James (1795–1849)
Hayes, Anna Johnston (1800–1861)

William James Hayes, a farmer, was a well-connected Underground Railroad operative, admired by other agents for his quiet courage. A devout Covenanter Presbyterian from Galway, New York, Hayes married Anna Johnston in 1819. The couple began aiding the secret network in the 1820s. They moved to Fort Clark, Illinois, in September 1833 and purchased a home in Randolph County the next year. In April 1842, they rescued a local indentured slave, Susan "Sukey" Richardson, her three children—Anderson, Harrison, and Jarrot—and Hannah Morrison from Cairo, Illinois. On September 5, 1842, William Hayes relayed all five to safer territory in Farmington, Illinois, but Sheriff Peter Frans recaptured them.

After Hayes's neighbor Andrew Borders arrived at the Knox County jail to take custody of the five runaways, he received only the Richardson children. Susan Richardson had escaped or fled via the Underground Railroad, and Hannah Morrison's indenture had expired. In February 1843, Borders brought suit against Hayes for trespass and slave stealing. Among supporters during Hayes's trial in Pinckneyville, Illinois, in 1844 was Underground Railroad agent T.A. Jones, who thanked Hayes for honoring a sacred trust. Hayes lost his appeal to the Illinois Supreme Court in 1848. The forfeiture of $2,500 bankrupted him but did not hinder his involvement with the secret network.

Source

Pirtle, Carol. "A Flight to Freedom: A True Story of the Underground Railroad in Illinois." *Ohio Valley History* 3:1 (2003): 3–16.

Hazlett, Hugh (1831–?)

An Irish-born attorney and Underground Railroad conductor in Dorchester County, Maryland, Hugh Hazlett aided the flight of slaves. At age 27, he was arrested while abetting the escape of John Green, Charles Anthony Light and Mary Light, Esther and Solomon Cornish, William Henry Cornish, and Thomas Ridout. After the group's flight on July 24, 1858, a freedman, Jesse Perry, informed the authorities. A posse captured all seven runaways in Caroline County, Maryland. At a steamer wharf in Cambridge, a mob voiced hatred for Hazlett. The sheriff intervened to prevent bloodshed and off-loaded the prisoners at a less public pier. On November 12, 1858, a circuit court judge sent Hazlett to the Maryland state penitentiary in Baltimore for over 44 years. On December 19, 1864, Governor Augustus Williamson Bradford pardoned Hazlett for committing a crime that no longer existed.

Source

"The Capture of a Gang of Negroes," *Easton (MD) Star,* August 10, 1858.

Head, Sir Francis Bond (1793–1875)

Sir Francis Bond Head, the provincial governor of Ontario, was one of the central figures in settling legal issues regarding flight of slaves into Canada. He supported the publication of the influential Upper Canada daily the *Royal Standard.* A request for the extraditions of Solomon Moseby and Jesse Happy in 1838 was a crucial turning point in U.S.–Canadian relations. Head conferred with British authorities in London and subsequently ruled against slave repatriation across the Canadian-U.S. border. His challenge to slave catchers set a precedent in favor of refugees from bondage and secured the Canadian border as a safe terminus of the clandestine escape route.

Source

Head, Sir Francis Bond. *A Narrative.* London: John Murray, 1839.

Concerning the extradition of fugitive slaves from Canada, Sir Francis Bond Head's logic was both humane and legally sound. He states in a memoir, *A Narrative* (1839): "It is argued that the republican states have no right, under the pretext of any human treaty, to claim from the British Government, which does not recognize slavery, beings who by slave-law are not recognized as *men* and who actually existed as brute beasts in moral darkness, until on reaching British soil they suddenly heard for the first time in their lives, the sacred words, 'Let there be light; and there was light!' From that moment it is argued they were created *men*, and if this be true, it is said they cannot be held responsible for conduct prior to their existence."

Sir Francis Bond Head, the British governor of what is now the province of Ontario, ruled in 1838 that slaves could not be recaptured across the Canadian–U.S. border. The decision secured Ontario as a major destination of the Underground Railroad. *(Library and Archives Canada, Acc. No. R9266–3154 Peter Winkworth Collection of Canadiana)*

Heaton, Jacob (1809–1888)
Heaton, Elizabeth P. Weaver (1809–1892)

A Quaker patriot, women's rights advocate, and prominent Underground Railroad operative in the Ohio Valley, Jacob Heaton rescued slaves at his home in Salem, in Columbiana County, Ohio. Born in Hilltown, in Bucks County, Pennsylvania, he started a career as a dry goods merchant and then switched to school teaching in Salem. In 1835, he married Elizabeth P. Weaver, a fellow abolitionist. He thrived at operating the Salem Exchange, a general store next door to the couple's two-story residence at 350 East State Street. The Heatons received passengers from the Reverend Arthur B. Bradford, a radical Presbyterian minister in Darlington, Pennsylvania.

For concealing fugitives, the Heaton home earned the name the Quaker Tavern, a denominational term implying welcome to all. From his home, Jacob Heaton led his passengers to safehouses in Andover, Gustavus, Hartford, and Warren, Ohio. According to his log, the Heatons' colleagues in the secret network were Salmon Portland Chase, Abby Kelley Foster and Stephen Symons Foster, Joshua Reed Giddings, James Mott, Jr., Lucretia Coffin Mott, Oliver Johnson, Wendell Addison Phillips, Gerrit Smith, and Benjamin Franklin Wade. During the Civil War, Jacob Heaton saw action at the battles of Pittsburg Landing, Chattanooga, and Murfreesboro, Tennessee. The Heaton house and store remain historical treasures of the Ohio Underground Railroad Association.

See also: safehouses.

Sources

History of the Upper Ohio Valley. Madison, WI: Brant & Fuller, 1891.
Howett, Thomas, and Mary Howett, eds. *The Salem Story, 1806–1956.* Salem, OH: Budget Press, 1956.

Heineman, Emil S. (1824–1896)
Heineman, Fanny Butzel (1844–1911)

Two of a network of Jewish rescuers of slaves, Emil S. Heineman, a Prussian clothier, and his Bavarian wife, Fanny Butzel Heineman, aided fugitives on the last leg of their journey to Canada. As members of the newly organized Temple Beth El in Detroit, Michigan, the couple absorbed the teachings of an abolitionist rabbi, Leibman Adler, and the altruism of fellow transporter Mark Sloman. In 1852, the Heinemans purchased a store at 140 Jefferson Avenue and received refugees at their home at Adelaide Street and Woodward Avenue. Before Emil directed passengers to the Detroit River crossing to Windsor, Ontario, Fanny disguised them in unassuming outfits. In 1864, Fanny headed the Detroit Ladies' Society for the Support of Hebrew Widows and Orphans, the city's first Jewish charity.

See also: disguise.

Source

Farmer, Silas. *The History of Detroit and Michigan.* Detroit, MI: self-published, 1884.

Heise, Charles (1840–?)

Slave rescuer Charles Heise (or Heisey) of South Carolina used his job as carriage driver as a cover for Underground Railroad relays. While living in Maryland, he appears to have been a collaborator of slave conductor John Kemp. On November 17, 1863, a circuit court judge in Upper Marlboro, Maryland, pressed William A. Talburtt's suit against 23-year-old Heise for abetting five runaways the previous July 5. While Governor Augustus Williamson Bradford weighed pleas for pardon, Heise entered the state penitentiary on November 24, 1863. He gained release 20 days later.

Source

Toomey, Daniel Carroll. *The Civil War in Maryland.* Baltimore: Toomey, 1983.

Helper, Hinton Rowan (1829–1909)

An abolitionist agitator, Hinton Rowan Helper, spawned his own brand of Underground Railroad operation. Like his abolitionist brother, Hardie Hogan Helper, Hinton Helper was born on a farm in Rowan County near Mocksville, North Carolina. He apprenticed in Michael Brown's print shop in Salisbury and panned unsuccessfully for gold during the California gold rush of 1849. After moving to New York and publishing a strident best-seller, *The Impending Crisis of the South: How to Meet It* (1857), and a sequel, *Compendium of the Impending Crisis of the South* (1860), he enlisted followers called Helperites to bring a rapid end to African American bondage. Among his suggestions were a tax on slaves, the ejection of slave owners from churches, and the boycott of slave-owning merchants. As a result of his incendiary social and economic strategies, both Hardie and Hinton Helper had to flee from their homes. Helper followers, including the insurrectionist John Brown, tended to suffer the same ostracism. In Madisonville, Kentucky, Edward Sloan led a slaveholders' backlash against a Helperite named Sanders of New Albany, Indiana. Sanders allegedly suggested to Sloan's slaves that they murder their owner, burn his buildings, and escape to the North.

Sources

Helper, Hinton Rowan. *Compendium of the Impending Crisis of the South.* New York: Burdick Brothers, 1860.

———. *The Impending Crisis of the South: How to Meet It.* New York: Burdick Brothers, 1857.

Hemings, Frank (fl. 1840s)

Slave rescuer Frank Hemings served a smooth Underground Railroad operation through Erie, Pennsylvania. He received escapees from Hamilton E. Waters, a clothes presser at the barbershop of Robert Vosburgh, a freedman agent in Erie. Groups moved east by wagon to a stone farmhouse on Four Mile Creek and then crossed Lake Erie by skiff to Longwood, Ontario.

Source

Gensheimer, Lisa, and Rich Gensheimer, prod. *Safe Harbor.* DVD. North East, PA: Main Street Media, 2003.

Henderson, Benjamin (1811–1890)

From 1841 to 1858, Benjamin "Ben" Henderson, a black carpenter in Jacksonville, Illinois, took pride in aiding refugees in their flight from bondage. Benjamin was born in Bourbon County, Kentucky, a slave of Will Henderson, from whom he bought his freedom for $250. He settled in the Little Africa section of town, married, and became a deacon of Mount Emery Baptist Church. A colleague of Underground Railroad agents Ebenezer Carter, Asa Talcott, Elihu Wolcott, and William Kirby, Henderson managed around two rescues per week. Clothing and supplies came from Horace Bancroft, Joseph Bancroft, T.D. Eames, and J.W. Lathrop. Aiding in the driving were wagoneers Henry Irving and Washington Price.

In the mid-1840s, Henderson concealed passengers in his delivery wagon by covering them with hay and topping them with handmade cradles. To divert suspicion from his errand, he drove through town, chatted with friends, then departed to waystations in Farmington or Springfield, where he depended on agents William Butler and Daniel Callahan. In 1853, Henderson helped a party of seven from St. Louis, Missouri, that included women, children, and a man on crutches. Despite careful planning, the group fell into the hands of slave catchers for return to Missouri. Although she could have escaped, a woman in the group refused to be separated from her daughters. The slave owner sold the family and cheated the slave hunters of their part of the profits.

Sources

Obituary, *Jacksonville Daily Journal,* November 1, 1890.

Taylor, Glennette Tilley. *The Underground Railroad in Illinois.* Glen Ellyn, IL: Newman Educational, 2001.

Henderson, Richard (1801–1880)
Henderson, Ann (ca. 1799–1854)
Henderson, Mary Ann Harris (1827–1907)

An agent of the Underground Railroad and advocate of insurrectionist John Brown, Richard Henderson was himself a runaway slave. With his sister Jane, his brothers Robert and Thomas, and a cousin named Cook, at age 15, Richard escaped bondage in Hagerstown, Maryland. Thomas Henderson settled in Canada, and Jane Henderson in Little York, Illinois. In the 1830s, Richard and Robert made their home in Meadville, Pennsylvania, where they joined a stable community of black citizens.

At his residence on Arch Street, Richard Henderson abandoned woodchopping and established a career in barbering, a trade that offered prestige to free blacks. In 1849, he supported the Bethel African Methodist Episcopal Church. After the death of Ann Henderson, his first wife, he married Mary Ann Harris of Erie, Pennsylvania, in 1855. The Hendersons dedicated themselves to slave rescue from the 1830s to national emancipation on January 1, 1863. Their home sheltered large groups. Assisting the family were James Hanna, Mary Hanna, and Robert Hanna, who owned the livery stable adjacent to the barbershop.

Source

Warren, John A., "Richard Henderson," *Christian Recorder,* March 31, 1866.

Henning, Thomas (ca. 1816–1888)

As secretary of the Anti-Slavery Society of Canada, Irish immigrant Thomas Henning influenced the aims and accomplishments of the Underground Railroad. Within months of the society's formation in 1851, he spread abolitionist fervor to Ontario: to Grey County and to the cities of Hamilton, Kingston, and Windsor. While working with the secret network, Henning conspired with agent Samuel Ringgold Ward in New York City. In 1856, Henning co-authored a pamphlet, *Slavery in the Church, Religious Societies, &c,* a denunciation of the complicity of Baptists, Congregationalists, and Wesleyan Methodists with the flesh trade. On November 30, 1858, after the safe arrival in Niagara City, Ontario, of a family of eight from Maryland—Ann Maria Jackson and her seven children, Ebenezer Thomas, Frances Sabrina, John Edwin, Mary Ann, Wilhelmina, William Albert, and William Henry Jackson—the passengers paused at Hiram K. Wilson's home in St. Catharines, Ontario, before reuniting with Ann Jackson's older son, James Henry. The nine Jacksons moved northwest to Toronto to Henning's care.

At a pivotal point in the relationship between Canadian operatives and the American Underground Railroad, a court case involving extradition threatened Henning's Toronto haven. The escape of John "Jackey" Anderson from farmer Moses Burton of Howard County, Missouri, concluded with Anderson's murder of a pursuer, Seneca T.P. Diggs. Under the 1842 Webster-Ashburton Treaty, U.S. marshals claimed Anderson as a fugitive felon. Secret network organizer Gerrit Smith hurried from New York City to aid Henning in fighting the dangerous precedent of extradition to appease southern slave owners. On December 15, 1860, Anderson lost his court case. After the British and Foreign Anti-Slavery Society demanded a retrial in a Toronto court, Anderson won his case on February 9, 1861.

Source

Brode, Patrick. *The Odyssey of John Anderson.* Toronto, Ontario: University of Toronto Press, 1989.

Henry, Frank (1838–1889)

From Wesleyville, near Erie, Pennsylvania, Frank Henry, a first-generation Irish American, participated in underground flights of slaves along the eastern shore of Lake Erie. At Erie Harbor, he maintained the Presque Isle Beacon Range Light Station. In summer 1858, he received from conductor Jehiel Towner four passengers—Sam, Martin, Martin's quadroon wife, and their infant, all of whom arrived by wagon. Aided by Major F.L. Fitch and William P. Trimble, Henry led the four to the old Wesleyville Methodist church, a community stop on the secret network route. Henry intended to continue the journey from Four Mile Creek across Lake Erie to Long Point Lighthouse in Ontario.

Three days later in heavy rain, Henry, under the surveillance of the slave owner's hireling, enlisted a pro-slavery farmer. Henry's purpose was to beg help for Martin's wife, whom the owner intended to sell south as a prostitute. The farmer protested but gathered a basket of food, some cash, a blanket, a hood for Martin's wife, and his own coat for Sam. Upon reaching safety, Sam returned several times to the South to retrieve his wife and some friends. He paid Henry $50 and another $50 to the fisherman who conveyed them to Long Point.

Henry volunteered to accompany John Brown on his raid on the arsenal in Harpers Ferry, Virginia, but was too late to join the mission. In admiration of the famed insurrectionist, Henry named his son John Brown Henry. After the Civil War, Frank Henry supplied the *Erie Gazette* with data on the Underground Railroad for feature articles. Upon his death in October 1889, villagers bore his coffin through the streets to the church to honor his diligence and discretion.

Source

Severance, Frank H. *Old Trails on the Niagara Frontier.* Buffalo, NY: n.p., 1899.

Henry, Joseph (fl. 1860s)

A young escapee from bondage, Joseph Henry made his way from Maryland to Pennsylvania. In 1860, he ran from Greenberry Parker, his rough-handed owner in Queen Annes County. In Philadelphia, Henry gained the aid of Underground Railroad agents, who sent him on his way along the secret network to freedom.

Source

Still, William. *Underground Railroad Records.* Philadelphia: Porter & Coates, 1883.

Henson, James (1823–?)

James Henson ran toward liberty with the aid of Underground Railroad agents in Pennsylvania. In 1855, the 32-year-old slave escaped bondage to Jacob Johnson in Cecil County, Maryland. In free territory,

Henson sought the assistance of secret network operatives in Philadelphia.

Source

Still, William. *The Underground Railroad.* Philadelphia: Porter & Coates, 1871.

Henson, Josiah (1789–1883)

The Reverend Josiah Henson, the person on whom Harriet Beecher Stowe allegedly based the fictional title character of *Uncle Tom's Cabin* (1852), fled slavery at age 41. The chattel of Francis Newman, Henson was born in Charles County, Maryland, and was sold three times in his youth. An assault with a split rail by a Virginia slave owner broke Henson's shoulder and left him lame in both arms. Henson's 12 children subsisted on cornmeal, salt herring, and buttermilk; he labored in the master's fields and supplemented the family diet with vegetables from his own garden. While traveling to Ohio from the Kentucky plantation where he superintended other slaves, in 1825, he refused to betray his master by running away. Three years later, he was ordained into the Methodist Episcopal ministry.

The Reverend Josiah Henson—on whom the title character of *Uncle Tom's Cabin* is said to be based—escaped bondage at age 41 and founded a settlement for fugitives in Dresden, Ontario, Canada. He was buried there in 1883. *(Hulton Archive/Getty Images)*

Henson saved $350 to buy his freedom, but he learned that it was only one-third enough cash. Upon being sent to New Orleans to be sold, in September 1830, he fled to Canada with his wife and four children. He spoke fondly of the celestial guidance system and blessed God for placing the North Star in the heavens. His route took him through Dayton, Ohio, and by a Scotsman's two-masted boat from Venice, New York, to Buffalo, and then west to Detroit, Michigan, and Lake Erie. On October 25, 1830, the family reached freedom in Ontario. In addition to managing a vital Canadian waystation of the Underground Railroad, Henson established a business, pastored the British Methodist Episcopal Church, and continued to protest slavery. He joined Canadian forces in the 1837 rebellion.

In 1841, Henson co-founded the Dawn settlement on a 200-acre section outside Dresden, in Essex County, Ontario. At his school, the British-American Institute, he taught newcomers vocations. While traveling in Great Britain, he met Queen Victoria. In 1849, he published *The Life of Josiah Henson, Formerly a Slave, Now an Inhabitant of Canada, As Narrated by Himself,* which influenced Stowe's fictional characterization of Uncle Tom. Henson died in Dresden at age 94.

See also: British Methodist Episcopal Church; North Star; *Uncle Tom's Cabin; or, Life Among the Lowly* (1852).

Sources

"The Underground Railroad and Those Who Operated It," *Springfield (OH) Republican,* March 11, 1900.
Wittenmyer, Annie. *Under the Guns: A Woman's Reminiscences of the Civil War.* Boston: E.B. Stillings, 1895.

Hesdra, Edward D. (1811–1884)
Hesdra, Cynthia (?–1879)

A wealthy mulatto agent in the Hudson Valley on the Jersey City, New Jersey–Newburgh, New York, line, Edward D. Hesdra used his home as a waystation. He was the son of Leon Hesdra, a Jew, who had been a soldier in Napoleon's army. Historians surmise that Edward's mother was a slave and that Edward may have been a fugitive slave. While living in New York City in the 1840s, he worked as a cabinetmaker and invested in real estate and a laundry. With the proceeds, he purchased the freedom of his enslaved wife, Cynthia Hesdra.

On Main Street opposite the reservoir in Nyack, in Rockland County, New York, the Hesdras built a three-story residence with mansard roof. They sheltered runaways who remained overnight before following the west bank of the Hudson River on their escape north. Because most of Nyack was pro-slavery, Hesdra relied on only a few conspirators—including George Green in Upper Nyack and John W. Towt in Nyack. The Hesdra house was demolished after a fire in June 1977. On February 25, 2005, Hesdra was named to the Rockland Civil Rights Hall of Fame.

Source

Bedell, Cornelia F. *Now and Then and Long Ago in Rockland County, New York.* Suffern, NY: Ramapo Valley Independent, 1941.

Hiatt, Henry (1816–1900)

A Quaker conductor and women's rights advocate, Henry Hiatt wrote about his work for the Underground Railroad. He was a native of Warren County, Ohio, reared among abolitionists in Dublin, Indiana. In April 1856, he settled with his wife, Frances Elizabeth Smith Hiatt, and their five children in Twin Mound, in Douglas County, Kansas. Henry Hiatt established himself as the link between Captain William B. Kennedy's safehouse and the waystation of Edwin Smith to the west. In an unpublished memoir, "My Belief and Reasons Therefore," he described his pleasure in ferrying two slaves from Topeka, Kansas, to the station of Colonel John Ritchie. Concealed in a covered spring wagon, the runaways journeyed safely along the route to Canada.

Source

Sheridan, Richard B., ed. and comp. *Freedom's Crucible: The Underground Railroad in Lawrence and Douglas County Kansas, 1854–1865.* Lawrence: University of Kansas, 1998.

Hicklin, Thomas (1788–1845)

A teacher and an agent of the Underground Railroad, the Reverend Thomas Hicklin of southern Jennings County, Indiana, collaborated with local abolitionists on relaying fugitives from bondage. Runaways from Kentucky passed through the care of Bill Crawford in Corydon, Indiana, up Graham Creek to Hicklin, who completed the network by transporting passengers to John Vawter on Otter Creek in Campbell Township. One dangerous interception involved 17 Kentucky runaways who crossed the Ohio River near Madison, Indiana, in flight from a posse. The party sought shelter at the Hicklin farm. Concealed under tarps, they journeyed on the next morning in two farm wagons to several stations before reaching the depot of Catherine White Coffin and Levi Coffin at 115 Main Street in Fountain City, Indiana.

Source

Chadwick, Bruce. *Traveling the Underground Railroad: A Visitor's Guide to More Than 300 Sites.* Secaucus, NJ: Citadel, 1999.

Hickman, Robert Thomas (fl. 1830s–1900)

A runaway log splitter from Boone County, Missouri, the Reverend Robert Thomas Hickman joined four other slave families to form a pilgrim church. In summer 1862, he built a flatboat to carry him, his son John, and some 75 refugees from Jefferson City, Missouri, across the Mississippi River to freedom. On May 5, 1863, an abolitionist shipman, the captain of the side-wheeler packet *War Eagle* (also identified as the *Northerner*), on his way from St. Louis, provided a tow. Because Irish laborers refused to let the flatboat land at St. Paul, Minnesota, the refugees had to continue north to Fort Snelling. When they finally reached St. Paul, on April 12, 1863, Hickman united the group as the city's first black congregation, Pilgrim Baptist Church, on Morris and Sibley streets. Among the organizing members were fellow runaways Fielding (or Freeling) Combs, Giles Crenshaw, Henry Moffitt, and John Trotter, all of whom traveled on Hickman's flatboat. On October 26, 2005, a local theatrical company performed a reenactment of the voyage, titled *Adrift on the Mississippi.*

Source

Taylor, David Vassar. *African Americans in Minnesota.* St. Paul: Minnesota Historical Society Press, 2002.

Hickok, William Alonzo (1801–1852)
Hickok, Polly Butler (1804–1878)
Hickok, James Butler "Wild Bill" (1837–1876)

A pioneer and a Presbyterian deacon, William Alonzo Hickok was an Underground Railroad operative in Homer (later called Troy Grove), in LaSalle County, Illinois. He was born in North Hero, in Grand Isle County, Vermont, and married Polly Butler in 1826. At their farm on Little Vermillion Creek, the couple operated Green Mountain House, a general store as well as a safehouse for black refugees. The Hickoks were impressed by the righteous activism of Quakers and followed their example by hiding fugitives in their attic and cellar. One arrival named Hannah remained with the family until her marriage. Aiding the Hickoks in rescues were their two daughters and four sons, one of whom, James Butler Hickok, the namesake of his maternal grandfather, was later known as "Wild Bill" Hickok, a Union army scout and U.S. marshal. In his teens, he became a transporter for the secret network. On one difficult mission, he was accompanying his father on a relay when an armed posse fired at their hay wagon.

See also: Quakers.

Source

Rosa, Joseph G. *Wild Bill Hickok: Sharpshooter and U.S. Marshal of the Wild West.* New York: Rosen, 2004.

Hicks, Charles (1795–1878)
Hicks, Lamira Henry (1797–1865)

Charles Hicks piloted slaves over a major route of the Underground Railroad through Vermont. At age 27, he wed Lamira Henry. In partnership with the Reverend Abel Brown and his wife, Mary Ann Brigham Brown of Chautauqua County, New York, Charles and Lamira Hicks kept watch on slave catchers in the Bennington area and surveyed the best modes of travel, including the Champlain Canal. The couple received a note in 1842 from an escapee in need of work.

Source

Duffy, John J., Samuel B. Hand, and Ralph H. Orth, eds. *The Vermont Encyclopedia.* Lebanon, NH: University Press of New England, 2003.

Hicks, Rachel Seaman (1789–1878)

One of a network of aggressive Quaker agents, Rachel (also Rachael) Seaman Hicks championed the cause of the runaway slave. Born to cradle Quakers, she grew up among the Westbury Orthodox Friends in Westbury, New York. When Long Island's Quakers split into two factions, the more militant group followed exhorter Elias Hicks, Rachel Hicks's uncle, and took the name Hicksite Quakers. In an entry to her journal in 1808, Rachel describes overcoming diffidence to travel from Canada to the Midwest for the purpose of reinvigorating Quakers. She anticipated that the virulence of the slavery issue would result in bloodshed. Her personal credo, however, demanded quiet obedience to Christian principles rather than the outspoken liberalism of Lucretia Coffin Mott. Rachel Hicks's observations on the issues of activism and civil disobedience reached print two years after her death as *Memoirs of Rachel Hicks Written by Herself Late of Westbury, Long Island, a Minister in the Society of Friends* (1880).

See also: civil disobedience; Quakers.

Source

Driscoll, James, et al. *Angels of Deliverance: The Underground Railroad in Queens, Long Island, and Beyond.* Flushing, NY: Queens Historical Society, 1999.

Hicks, Robert (1793–1849)
Hicks, Mary Underhill Mott (1793–1862)
Hicks, Valentine (1782–1850)

A Quaker conductor of the Underground Railroad, Robert Hicks, a member by marriage of the abolitionist Mott clan, expressed his antipathy toward the flesh trade. The son of religious leader Isaac Hicks and a distant cousin of Elias Hicks, a Quaker patriarch, Robert Hicks earned his living in New York City as a trader. He became an active rescuer after joining the New York Manumission Society, founded in 1785. One female fugitive left Hicks's house clad in a dress and veil provided by his wife, Mary Underhill Mott Hicks. Taking the arm of the Reverend Richard Mott, Hick's brother-in-law and partner, the fashionably dressed slave strolled to the Motts' sloop, the *Harry Maybe,* which took her to the safehouse of Richard Mott and Mary Mott's brother, Samuel "Uncle Sammy" Mott, a shipping magnate in Cowneck, New York.

Contributing to the Hicks family's reputation for activism was Robert's uncle, Valentine Hicks, a wealthy New York City businessman. In retirement, he bought a house on Long Island, in Jericho, New York, and, in the late 1830s, began aiding fugitives arriving in Westbury. Runaways worked on the Hicks farm, climbed a stair in the closet, entered a door that resembled a cupboard, and hid in a secret room in the attic. In one rescue, Valentine Hicks waited until dark to transport a slave by wagon to a mooring on Long Island Sound for relay to Westchester, New York.

Sources

McManus, Edgar J. *A History of Negro Slavery in New York.* Syracuse, NY: Syracuse University Press, 1966.

Vahey, Mary Feeney. *A Hidden History: Slavery, Abolition, and the Underground Railroad in Cow Neck and on Long Island.* Port Washington, NY: Cow Neck Peninsula Historical Society, 1998.

Hiestand, Abraham S. (1771–1859) Hiestand, Ann Fitz (1774–1824)

Owners of two Underground Railroad stations, Abraham S. Hiestand and his wife, Ann Fitz (or Fitts) Hiestand, ensured the safety of slaves passing through York County, Pennsylvania. The Hiestands married in 1793. One of their waystations, the Buttonwood Tree House, built in Rapho Township in 1760, rises over solid rock foundations more than two feet thick. Slaves entered the property through a fireplace niche that led to the basement. The Hiestands concealed fugitives by heaping the corner with stones. Passengers could escape through the meat closet by climbing out vent holes. The Hiestands' second stop, the Old York Inn, built in 1738 and situated at a crossroads between Maryland and Lancaster, Pennsylvania, also received runaways. An arched cellar sheltered escapees. In 1865, Abraham's daughter, Sarah Hiestand Wilson (1818–?), a conductor during the Civil War, inherited the inn from her stepmother, Susan Myers Hiestand (1780–1865).

Source

Gibson, John. *History of York County, Pennsylvania.* Chicago: F.A. Battey, 1886.

Higginson, Thomas Wentworth (1823–1911) Higginson, Mary Elizabeth Channing (1820–1877)

A Union army officer and a contributor of progressive abolitionist essays to the *Atlantic Monthly,* the Reverend Thomas Wentworth Higginson devoted his skills to furthering the work of the Underground Railroad. A descendent of Massachusetts Bay colonists, he was born in Cambridge and graduated from Harvard University. His cousin, Sarah Rhea "Sally" Higginson, married William Ingersoll Bowditch, an operative of the secret network. Thomas Higginson taught school and pastored Unitarian churches in Newburyport, Massachusetts. At the urging of the abolitionist poet and editor John Greenleaf Whittier, Higginson resigned from the pulpit because his anti-slavery leanings angered conservative members of the congregation. In 1852, he assembled like-minded congregants and founded the Free Church of Worcester, Massachusetts, which he pastored until the outbreak of the Civil War. During annual commemorations of a slave rescue, Higginson delivered addresses supportive of the Underground Railroad.

Following the enactment of the Fugitive Slave Law of 1850, Higginson joined the Boston Vigilance Committee, a legal and material aid society to refugees. In league with the Reverend Samuel Joseph May and an activist couple, Quaker orators Abigail "Abby" Kelley Foster and Stephen Symons Foster of Pelham, Massachusetts, Higginson and his wife, Mary Elizabeth Channing Higginson, received refugees at their Bowdoin residence on Harvard Street. Higginson sped runaways by night to the Fosters at Liberty Farm. In 1853, one refugee spent the entire winter with the Higginsons.

On May 26, 1854, Thomas Higginson conferred with Martin Stowell on a plan to free Anthony Burns, a recaptured slave. According to a detailed account in Higginson's reflective *Cheerful Yesterdays* (1899), Higginson, the Reverend Theodore Parker, and orator Wendell Addison Phillips led a mob of protesters to the Boston courthouse to batter down the door with a beam and axes. Two artillery regiments from Fort Warren and the Charlestown Navy Yard quelled the uprising. In the clash, Higginson suffered a saber slash to the chin. Stowell shot and killed a policeman, James Batchelder. In June, a court failed to convict Higginson, Phillips, or Parker for leading the public protest in Boston Common. The Burns seizure was the last fugitive slave case tried in Massachusetts.

On June 4, 1854, Higginson delivered a sermon to the Free Church entitled "Massachusetts in Mourning," a call to action that Bostonians make their city a terminus of the Underground Railroad rather than a depot and that they defend resident fugitives against recapture.

Higginson supported the slave transfers of Charles Doy and his father, Dr. John W. Doy, from Weston, Missouri, into the free state of Kansas and solicited donations to fund Clarina Irene Howard Nichols's creation of new routes through Lawrence, Quindaro, and Topeka, Kansas. In February and March 1859, Higginson lent moral support during the Doys' jailing in

From the pulpit of Worcester Free Church, pastor Thomas Wentworth Higginson implored the congregation to take in fugitive slaves, rather than merely help transport them: "No longer conceal Fugitives and help them on, but show them and defend them. Let the Underground Railroad stop here! Say to the south that Worcester, though a part of a Republic, shall be as free as if ruled by a Queen! *Hear, O Richmond! and give ear, O Carolina! henceforth Worcester is Canada to the Slave!*"

Platte City, Missouri. He pressed supporters to advance the work of the Underground Railroad and to support insurrectionist John Brown. Goading Higgingson was his alliance with the famed rebel, who relied on Higginson and other Easterners to supply guns and ammunition for a war on the Kansas-Missouri border. At the onset of the Civil War, Higginson served as colonel of the First South Carolina Volunteers, the first black regiment in the conflict, and campaigned for full pay to nonwhite soldiers.

See also: abolitionism; black soldiers; Fugitive Slave Law of 1850; routes, Underground Railroad; Underground Railroad; vigilance committees.

Sources

Higginson, Thomas Wentworth. *Cheerful Yesterdays.* Boston: Houghton Mifflin, 1899.

———. *Out-Door Papers.* Boston: Ticknor & Fields, 1863.

———. *A Sermon Preached in Worcester, on Sunday, June 4, 1854.* Boston: James Monroe, 1854.

Hinton, Richard Josiah. *John Brown and His Men: With Some Account of the Roads They Travelled to Reach Harpers Ferry.* New York: Funk & Wagnalls, ca. 1894.

McDougall, Marion G. *Fugitive Slaves (1619–1865).* Boston: n.p., 1891.

Higley, Erastus (1772–1861)
Higley, Esther Anna Guernsey (1771–1857)
Higley, Hervey Owen (1801–1878)

Judge Erastus Higley and Hervey Owen Higley, a father-and-son team, transported slaves from the family station of the Underground Railroad. In 1798, Higley married Esther Anna Guernsey of Simsbury, Connecticut. They received runaways at Homestead, their two-story brick home built in 1811 in Castleton, in Rutland County, Vermont, despite the fact that Erastus Higley was Fairhaven's district court judge from 1814 to 1821. In 1859, Higley was elected a deacon of the First Congregational Church, a libertarian congregation. In 1991, the house passed to the Castleton Historical Society, which launched a restoration campaign.

Source

Duffy, John J., Samuel B. Hand, and Ralph H. Orth, eds. *The Vermont Encyclopedia.* Lebanon, NH: University Press of New England, 2003.

Hill, James Wesley (fl. 1840s)

Born in Maryland, James Wesley "Canada Jim" Hill was a former slave who aided fugitives on their approach to Ontario. Hill bought his liberty from his owner. As a freedman, he grew strawberries in Oakville, Ontario, and served the Underground Railroad. He gave financial stability to fugitives he piloted over the international border by offering them farm jobs.

Source

Hill, Daniel G. *The Freedom Seekers: Blacks in Early Canada.* Agincourt, Ontario: Book Society of Canada, 1981.

Hill, John Henry (ca. 1827–after 1879)

John Henry Hill, a 26-year-old slave in Richmond, Virginia, escaped via the Underground Railroad to Canada. The slave of John Mitchell of Petersburg, Virginia, Hill worked as a carpenter. He married Rose McCrae (also Rosell McCrea or McCray), a free black who bore their two children. Hill fled before Mitchell could sell him on the auction block. Beginning on January 1, 1853, Hill hid with friends—perhaps the family of Prussian American merchants Elizabeth and Jacob Bauman at Franklin and Seventh streets. He stayed in Petersburg, Virginia, for nine months until an agent could pay $125 for a private cabin for him on the 80-passenger steamer the *City of Richmond* to Philadelphia, Pennsylvania.

Armed with a brace of pistols, Hill made rapid progress across the secret network route. Within 17 days, he hurried through depots in New York City, Albany, Rochester, and Lewiston, New York, and, on September 30, 1853, crossed Lake Ontario by steamer to Hamilton, Ontario. His wife and children followed that same year, when the family settled in Toronto. Hill supported them by working as a carpenter and tobacco merchant.

John Hill remained in contact with the Philadelphia Vigilance Committee in hopes of freeing Willis

Johnson, another fugitive in Richmond. Hill also promoted Mary Ann Shadd Cary's weekly, *The Provincial Freeman.* He distributed food and clothing to newcomers and located homes and jobs for them. He also served in the militia as an officer in Queen Victoria's Rifle Guards. In 1856, Hezekiah Hill (ca. 1824–?), Hill's uncle, eluded a Petersburg slave trader, sought aid from the Philadelphia Vigilance Committee, and joined his nephew's family in Toronto. In 1861, James Hill, John's brother, escaped bondage and settled in Boston, Massachusetts. After the Civil War, John Hill returned to Richmond with his family and his uncle. John worked in Petersburg as a carpenter and became a justice of the peace.

See also: vigilance committees.

Source

Finkenbine, Roy E. *The Black Abolitionist Papers.* Vol. 2, *Canada, 1830–1865.* Chapel Hill: University of North Carolina Press, 1986.

Hillard, George Stillman (1808–1879) Hillard, Susan Tracy Howe (fl. 1830s–1850s)

Two safehouse operators, Harvard-educated attorney and editor George Stillman Hillard of Machias, Maine, and his wife, Susan Tracy Howe Hillard, daughter of Judge Samuel Howe of Northampton, Massachusetts, participated in a famous slave rescue. In 1834, George Hillard opened a law partnership with Charles Sumner, a supporter of the Underground Railroad. After the flight of Ellen Smith Craft and William Craft on December 21, 1848, from Macon, Georgia, the fugitives passed through depots in Boston, Massachusetts. The Hillards received Ellen Craft at their waystation at 54 Pinckney Street. In 1850, George Hillard was elected to the Massachusetts state senate.

Source

Professional and Industrial History of Suffolk County, Massachusetts. Boston: Boston History, 1894.

Hilles, Samuel (1788–1873) Hilles, Margaret Hill (1786–1882)

An Irish American teacher of mathematics and philosophy, Samuel Hilles contributed to the Underground Railroad network. A Quaker from Wilmington, Delaware, he and his brother, Eli Hilles, operated a girls' academy. Samuel served as secretary of the Delaware Abolition Society and superintended the state's secret network. He and his wife, Margaret Hill Hilles, lived at King and Tenth streets, where they welcomed fugitives to their barn. After the Emancipation Proclamation, on January 1, 1863, the Hilles continued their good works by collecting funds and clothing for freed slaves.

Source

History of Cincinnati and Hamilton County, Ohio. Cincinnati, OH: S.B. Nelson, 1894.

Himrod, William (1791–1870)

Philanthropist William Himrod, a white industrialist, mapped out a refugee settlement in Erie, Pennsylvania. Himrod got his start at age 19 by doing carpentry work for the poor and advanced to respected citizen and supporter of fugitive slaves. His home at French and Second streets was the area depot of the secret network. He aided passengers by opening the French Street Sabbath School and by paying the lake passage of runaways from Buffalo, New York, and Detroit to Ontario. After purchasing shorefront acreage on Lake Erie in 1828, he managed a project called New Jerusalem, a shelter for fugitive slaves. By 1845, the residential development offered home ownership to runaways. Contributing to the effort was the newly formed Wesleyan Methodist Church and the St. James African Methodist Episcopal Church, which educated slaves.

See also: African Methodist Episcopal Church.

Source

Gensheimer, Lisa, and Rich Gensheimer, prod. *Safe Harbor.* DVD. North East, PA: Main Street Media, 2003.

Hinton, Richard Josiah (1830–1901)

A British author and activist, Richard Josiah Hinton cleared up misunderstandings about the Underground Railroad by researching the era's most violent clashes. After learning stonecutting in London, at age 21, he emigrated to New York City to study printing and journalism. Dismayed at the passage of the Fugitive Slave Law of 1850, he joined the abolitionist movement and exposed the radical plots to end American slavery in a major cataclysm. With leadership and cash, he supported the Kansas route of the secret network, which directed slaves from Missouri to free territory in the North.

Hinton was well informed and well connected to Underground Railroad leadership. He corresponded with agents and involved the Reverend Thomas Wentworth Higginson in the frontier campaign for a slave-free state. At the beginning of the Civil War, Hinton recruited men for the First Kansas Colored Infantry and served as captain for two years. In 1871, Osborne Perry Anderson—the only black man in the band led by insurrectionist John Brown at the assault on the federal arsenal in Harpers Ferry, Virginia, on October 16, 1859—toured the historic site with Hinton and provided eyewitness details for Hinton's book, *John Brown and His Men* (1894).

See also: Fugitive Slave Law of 1850.

Source

Hinton, Richard Josiah. *John Brown and His Men: With Some Account of the Roads They Travelled to Reach Harpers Ferry.* New York: Funk & Wagnalls, ca. 1894.

Hise, Daniel Howell (1813–1878) Hise, Margaret (1821–?)

Quaker philanthropists and Underground Railroad conductors Daniel Howell Hise and Margaret Hise aided refugees from the plantation South. Hise, a native of New Jersey, grew up in Salem, Ohio, where he learned ironwork from his father, Aaron Hise, before becoming the engineer of a river steamer in Alabama. He opened a brickyard, lumber mill, and woodworking shop in Salem. Under the influence of abolitionists Amos Gilbert, Jonathan Haines, and Sarah Grant Haines, Daniel and Margaret Hise joined the Western Anti-Slavery Society. In the late 1850s, the Hises opened their two-story residence at 1100 Franklin Avenue to runaways. Passengers hid in the attic, basement, and barn.

The Hise family maintained connections with the Underground Railroad hierarchy. According to Daniel Hise's journal, *Pap's Diary,* which he kept from 1846 until his death, the family also welcomed Charles Callistus Burleigh, Oliver Johnson, Parker Pillsbury, and Henry C. Wright to plan strategy for extending the secret network on the frontier. When insurrectionist John Brown was hanged at the Jefferson County, Virginia, courthouse on December 2, 1859, Daniel Hise predicted that future generations would honor Brown and his raiders with a monument.

Sources

Atherton, Lewis E. "Daniel Howell Hise, Abolitionist and Reformer." *Mississippi Valley Historical Review* 26:3 (December 1939): 343–58.

Bentley, Anna Briggs. *American Grit: A Woman's Letters from the Ohio Frontier.* Lexington: University Press of Kentucky, 2002.

Hitchcock, George Beckwith (1812–1872) Hitchcock, Carolyn Grossman (1810–ca. 1880s)

The Reverend George Beckwith Hitchcock of Massachusetts, a Congregational minister, operated a waystation of the Underground Railroad in Lewis, in Scott County, Iowa. After graduating from Illinois College, in 1834, George Hitchcock married Carolyn Grossman. He began his ministry in 1844 as a circuit rider of the Iowa frontier in Eddyville and Oskaloosa. Enlisted by the Reverend John Todd of Tabor, Iowa, to extend the secret network, in 1856, the Hitchcocks aided refugees from Missouri. They housed passengers at their rural log cabin, which they replaced with a two-story sandstone residence on a 120-acre spread. Passengers arriving at the family's safehouse hid in a secret niche behind shelves of canned fruit in the basement kitchen. The Hitchcocks also supported forces fighting to make Kansas a free state. After the Civil War, George Hitchcock ministered to former slaves in Kingston, Missouri.

Source

Todd, John. *Early Settlement and Growth of Western Iowa; or, Reminiscences.* Des Moines: Historical Department of Iowa, 1906.

Hitchcock, Samuel (fl. 1840s–1850s)

A dependable refugee transporter, Samuel Hitchcock supported a team of Underground Railroad agents in Galesburg, in Knox County, Illinois. For a decade, he operated from his farm northwest of town, where he hid seven refugees in the haymow. In service to the Reverend Jonathan Blanchard and Mary Avery Bent Blanchard, Hitchcock shared responsibilities with George Davis and Nehemiah West in passing runaways through Stark County and on to Ontario Township. Hitchcock's relay method involved settling passengers on a straw bed in his wagon and topping the load with lightweight chaff-stuffed sacks. The load mimicked a normal delivery of grain to Chicago.

Source

Muelder, Hermann R. *Fighters for Freedom: The History of Anti-Slavery Activities of Men and Women Associated with Knox College.* New York: Columbia University Press, 1959.

Hoag, Abigail Robinson (1789–1855)
Hoag, Nathan Case (1785–1854)

The Quaker aunt and uncle of Rowland Evans Robinson, who was the son of agents Rachel Gilpin Robinson and Rowland Thomas Robinson of Ferrisburg, Vermont, Abigail Robinson Hoag and Nathan Case Hoag maintained a farm and aided black refugees. The Hoags operated an Underground Railroad depot in East Charlotte, Vermont, that received passengers from the waystation at Rokeby sheep farm. Fugitives could remain in the Hoags' employ to earn money for a new start in New England or Canada.

Source

Moger, Elizabeth H. "Quakers as Abolitionists: The Robinsons of Rokeby and Charles Marriott." *Quaker History* 92 (Fall 2003): 52–59.

Hockley, Benjamin (1805–?)
Hockley, Susan (1816–?)

Tennessee fugitives Benjamin "Ben" Hockley and his wife, Susan Hockley took passage over the final leg of the Underground Railroad that ended at the shores of Lake Ontario. The Hockleys purchased a house at 19 East Sixth Street in Fulton, in Oswego County, New York, in the 1840s from agent Gerrit Smith. Ben Hockley earned his living as a cook, and the Hockleys lived contentedly until passage of the Fugitive Slave Law of 1850 jeopardized their residence. On August 4, 1853, Ben Hockley fled a posse of Tennesseans by tying himself to a gate and floating it like a raft across Lake Ontario toward Canada. The crew of the steamer *Chief Justice Robinson,* traveling from Lewiston, New York, to Toronto, rescued Hockley.

See also: Fugitive Slave Law of 1850.

Source

"Remarkable Incident—Escape of a Slave," *Niagara (Ontario) Mail,* August 10, 1853.

Holley, Sallie (1818–1893)

A teacher and fellow platform orator with Abby Kelley Foster, Sallie Holley enlisted Underground Railroad agents for the American Anti-Slavery Society. Sallie gained an altruistic outlook from her father, Myron Holley, an attorney in Canandaigua, New York. She developed an abolitionist perspective on Ohio's most liberal campus, Oberlin College, where slave rescues were frequent. Influenced by anti-slavery activists, in 1850 she settled in Rochester, New York, her base of operations for extensive travels.

For abolitionist lectures, Holley took her texts from William Lloyd Garrison's newspaper *The Liberator* and from Harriet Beecher Stowe's novel *Uncle Tom's Cabin* (1852). When Holley visited the safehouse of Harriet Forten Purvis and Robert Purvis in Byberry, Pennsylvania, she dubbed it Saints' Rest for its welcome to the oppressed. After the Civil War, Holley joined educator Caroline Putnam in opening a freedman's school in Lottsburg, Virginia. In 1899, Holley summarized her ideals in an autobiography, *A Life for Liberty.*

See also: American Anti-Slavery Society; *Liberator, The*; Oberlin College; *Uncle Tom's Cabin; or, Life Among the Lowly* (1852).

Source

Holley, Sallie. *A Life for Liberty.* New York: Knickerbocker, 1899.

Holmes, David (1824–?)

In flight from bondage in Virginia, runaway David Holmes relied on Underground Railroad operatives to free him. He set out at age 28 and traveled on horseback, by wagon, and on foot to Buffalo, New York. After over a week of hiding, he received assistance and cash from agents and, in 1852, journeyed by steamer to Quebec. Without understanding the ship's destination, he continued on to Cardiff, Wales, and then to London, where he found work aboard a West Indian freighter. On February 1, 1853, the *Anti-Slavery Reporter* issued an interview with Holmes about his flight from bondage over the secret network.

Source

Schwartz, Philip. *Migrants Against Slavery: Virginians and the Nation.* Charlottesville: University of Virginia Press, 2001.

Holmes, George Young, Sr. (1820–1896)
Holmes, Elizabeth Snodgrass (1825–1884)

A Baptist immigrant from Glasgow, Scotland, the Reverend George Young Holmes, Sr., aided the New York–Canada route of the Underground Railroad. George was 10 when he and his parents and his nine siblings arrived aboard the sloop *Rodger Stewart* in New York City in May 1830. The family settled on 120 acres northwest of Claysville in Washington County, New York. In 1840, George Holmes married

Elizabeth Snodgrass, a Pennsylvania native. George preached at churches in Buffalo, Washington, and North Wheeling. The Holmeses opened their home as a waystation, where they sheltered runaways. Although neighbors suspected them of civil disobedience, they succeeded at piloting passengers by night through their orchard to the West Middletown station managed by William McKeever, a hatmaker, and his sons, Matthew and Thomas Campbell McKeever.

Source

Commemorative Biographical Record of Washington County, Pennsylvania. Chicago: J.H. Beers, 1893.

Holt, Horace (1798–1885)
Holt, Melinda Bellows (1805–1893)

In Athens County, Ohio, inventor and manufacturer Horace Holt and his family recycled packaging crates as a source of concealment for runaway slaves. Born outside Hartford, Connecticut, to Aaron Holt, Horace was an upright member of the Universalist Church. In 1857, he married Melinda Bellows and fathered a large family that joined him in aiding and transporting refugees. A canny operative of the Underground Railroad in Rutland, Ohio, in the southeastern part of the state, he manufactured weaving reeds for looms, threshers, parts for steam gristmills, parlor organs, and organ reeds. On business trips to the South, he and his sons—Columbus B. Holt (1825–?), John B. Holt (1839–1929), and Nial N. Holt (1826–?)—relayed slaves into free territory in false-bottomed wagons. The Holts' neighbors defied the Fugitive Slave Law of 1850 by feeding and clothing runaways. The oversized crates that Horace Holt shipped from his business in New Lima on the Rutland-Harrisonville Road often carried fugitives to other depots or to Canada.

See also: Fugitive Slave Law of 1850.

Sources

Harris, Charles H. *The Harris History.* Athens, OH: *Athens Messenger,* 1957.
Larkin, Stillman Carter. *The Pioneer History of Meigs County.* Columbus, OH: Berlin, 1908.

Holyoke, John, II (1773–1831)
Holyoke, Miriam Tibbetts (1779–1850)

In Brewer, Maine, near Bangor, Deacon John Holyoke II maintained a safehouse within an easy distance from freedom in Canada. In 1800, he married Miriam Tibbetts of Boothbay, Maine, and sired a large family. On a bluff along the Penobscot River, the couple's two-story frame house offered a commanding lookout for the approach of posses and slave catchers. Inside were hiding places in attic rooms and in a 49-foot subterranean tunnel that opened at the riverbank near Free Soil Wharf. The Holyokes were friends of the Passamoquoddy, whose guides knew the way north to free territory. In 1995, excavation in a niche in the attic eaves turned up a slave's crude tow-cloth shirt with drawstring collar.

Sources

Sargent, H.P. "Relating to the Early History of Brewer, Maine." *Sprague's Journal of Maine History* 7:1 (May–July 1919): 20–22.
Shaw, Richard R. *Brewer, Maine.* Charleston, SC: Arcadia, 2000.

Hood, Caleb C. (1817–1901)
Hood, Joseph (1812–1866)

On the Pilgrim's Pathway, the 17-stage route through Lancaster County, in southern Pennsylvania, Caleb C. Hood and his brother, Joseph Hood, operated Station 8 in Bart. They passed runaways from the custody of William H. Rakestraw to the barn of Thomas Pownall in Bucks. In spring 1843, the brothers received a party of eight passengers from agent Joseph Smith of Drumore. After a quick supper, Caleb transported the group to Deborah T. Simmons Coates and Lindley Coates in Caln. Another delivery involved relaying Hannah Gooseberry and her children, Judah and Stephen, on June 4, 1844, from the Reverend Charles Turner Torrey on the Susquehanna River to the Hoods and then on to James Fulton, Jr., in Ercildoun for a night's rest. The dangerous flight resulted in imprisonment and a sentence of hard labor for Torrey, who died in his cell on May 6, 1846, of tuberculosis.

After midnight on September 11, 1851, after the Christiana Riot, Caleb Hood received three participants—former slaves James Dawsey, William Howard, and Charles Long—and helped them to hide in the woods after supper. Hood solicited the back pay and belongings of the men that night and sent them on their way to a black agent, who concealed them under a false floor. Two weeks later, the trio was transferred to agent Eli Hambleton. Ten days later, the three men reached Canada. Howard's wife sold the family property and joined her husband in freedom.

See also: Christiana Riot; Pilgrim's Pathway.

Source

Smedley, Robert C. *History of the Underground Railroad in Chester and the Neighboring Counties of Pennsylvania.* Lancaster, PA: Office of *The Journal,* 1883.

Hopkins, Charles Fern (1842–1934)
Hopkins, Ann Wilson (1814–1855)
Hopkins, Nathan (1811–1889)
Hopkins, Ellen Reilly King (fl. 1850s)

Politician and abolitionist Charles Fern Hopkins of New Hope, New Jersey, began Underground Railroad work in his teens. After 1848, he came of age in Drakesville and learned the harness-making trade. In league with his parents—Ann Wilson Hopkins of Wyoming, Pennsylvania, and Nathan Hopkins of Succasunna, New Jersey, a harness maker—the proprietors of the Powerville Hotel at Boonton, the younger Hopkins did the legwork of relaying passengers between stations and along the Morris Canal. After his mother's death, the family's commitment to liberty continued after 1856 with the aid of Charles's stepmother, Ellen Reilly King Hopkins. Charles was a veteran of the Civil War, during which he survived typhoid fever and scurvy while being held in the Confederate prison in Andersonville, Georgia. He won the Congressional Medal of Honor for valor.

Source

"Steal Away, Steal Away . . ." (pamphlet). Trenton, NJ: New Jersey Historical Commission, 2002.

Hopkins, Erastus (1810–1872)
Hopkins, Charlotte Freylinghuysen Allen (1819–1899)

A prominent author, libertarian, and politician of Hadley, Massachusetts, the Reverend Erastus Hopkins was an influential advocate and lecturer. He graduated from Princeton University and was ordained a minister of the Presbyterian Church. While living in Northampton, Massachusetts, in 1848, he and his second wife, Charlotte Freylinghuysen Allen Hopkins, supported the Free-Soil Party and maintained a depot of the Underground Railroad. While a fugitive hid in the attic, the couple's children evangelized the man with stories of Jesus.

Source

Bridgman, S.E. "Northampton." *New England* 21:5 (January 1900): 589–90.

Hopkins, Henry C. (fl. 1850s)

A tenant of Dr. Augustus W. Cain in Sadsbury, west of Philadelphia, Pennsylvania, Henry C. Hopkins manned a crucial site of the Underground Railroad. He was a member of the black brotherhood that attacked a federal marshal and Edward Gorsuch, a slave owner, in the Christiana Riot. On September 11, 1851, Hopkins heard the prearranged alert blown on a horn by Eliza Ann Elizabeth Howard Parker, wife of William Parker. Hopkins armed himself with an iron rod and advanced to the Parker residence. In the fight, Hopkins sustained a bullet to the forearm. Cain extracted the bullet and urged Hopkins to flee the area.

See also: Christiana Riot.

Source

Smedley, Robert C. *History of the Underground Railroad in Chester and the Neighboring Counties of Pennsylvania.* Lancaster, PA: Office of *The Journal,* 1883.

Hopkins, Thomas (fl. 1840s–1850s)

Thomas Hopkins, a stationmaster of the Underground Railroad, was part of a smooth network of operators. He managed a safehouse outside Downingtown, in Chester County, Pennsylvania. He received runaways from Joseph Fulton and his daughter, Mary Ann Fulton, in Sadsbury and from Edwin Howard Coates, Sarah Dull Coates, and Michael Myers in Coatesville. Hopkins completed the relay to Norristown. From there, slaves boarded a train in Bridgeport and followed pilot Benjamin Johnson to Ontario.

Source

Smedley, Robert C. *History of the Underground Railroad in Chester and the Neighboring Counties of Pennsylvania.* Lancaster, PA: Office of *The Journal,* 1883.

Hopper, Isaac Tatem (1771–1852)
Hopper, Sarah Tatum (1776–1822)
Hopper, Abigail (1801–1893)

Reformer and abolitionist Isaac Tatem Hopper receives credit for inventing the concept of a secret network of safehouses. A native of Deptford, New Jersey, he was the son of a Quaker, Levi Hopper, and a Presbyterian, Rachel Hopper. In 1787, Isaac learned tailoring from his uncle in Philadelphia and set up a clothing business. Upon encountering his first runaway, a black sailor, Hopper improvised a route to a Quaker operative in Bucks Country, Pennsylvania, and drew a map to guide the man. In 1795, Hopper became a Quaker; a year later, he joined the Pennsylvania Abolition Society. He married Sarah Tatum, a Quaker minister, and sired 10 children, including abolitionist Abigail Hopper Gibbons; Hopper's second wife, Hannah Atmore (also Athmore or Attmore), bore eight children. The family maintained a waystation along the Delaware River at Dock Street.

"Friend" Hopper, as Isaac was called, defended the underdog by intervening on behalf of underage apprentices and by agitating for prison reform. He rescued debtors from homelessness. He seized a kidnapped black child from a boat traveling along the shore of the Delaware River, and he enabled Ben Jackson, a Virginia-born coachman, to escape by convincing a judge to drop the charges because of the tardiness of Jackson's owner. On one occasion, Hopper sent a black man fleeing from his home to spook a slave catcher. While the pursuer attacked the decoy, the real runaway sped in the opposite direction. Hopper then charged the slave hunter with assaulting an innocent man.

At age 29, Hopper began encouraging members of the Pennsylvania Abolition Society to promote the Underground Railroad sea routes. In 1802, he faced the guns of bounty hunters Joseph Ennells and James Frazier of Maryland near the Schuylkill River and convinced them to bring William Bachelor, the alleged fugitive slave, to court, where Hopper proved his right to freedom. Hopper again encountered Ennells, who declared the Quaker activist a menace who should be shot. Threats did nothing to deter Hopper's dedication to liberty for all races. He encouraged agents Abraham and Katy Allen and network supervisor Elihu Oren, who established secret network routes in Clinton County, Ohio. To the northeast, the Hoppers partnered with conductors Rachel Gilpin Robinson and Rowland Thomas Robinson at Rokeby farm in Ferrisburg, Vermont.

Although his generosity forced him into debt, Isaac Hopper assisted blacks as an advocate in lawsuits involving slaves and their owners. To fund the operation, his wife Sarah sold tea and groceries. Because his liberal views alienated conservative Quakers, in 1829, he settled in Manhattan on Eldridge Street and opened a bookstore at 143 Nassau Street, which pro-slavery brigands burned nine years later. Abigail raised funds for the secret network at anti-slavery fairs. Isaac served the Prison Association of New York, aided prison inmates in their return to society, and conducted runaways to Boston and Providence. In one difficuilt case dating to 1837, John P. Darg accused Hopper, his son-in-law James Sloan Gibbons, and agents Barney Corse and David Ruggles of harboring 22-year-old Thomas Hughes, the mulatto son of a Virginia planter. The trial was so long that Ruggles, held in an underground hole, nearly went blind. In November 1839, the Hughes incident concluded with trickery—Darg used Hughes's wife, Mary, as bait. When Hughes returned to slavery to unite with Mary, Darg sold her and brutalized Hughes.

For his daring, Hopper endured tribulation. He, James Gibbons, and Charles Marriott were ousted from the New York Society of Friends; in 1836, Hopper's 21-year-old son, John, faced angry pro-slavery forces in Charleston, South Carolina. At age 70, Hopper served the Anti-Slavery Society as treasurer and invited editor Lydia Maria Francis Child to board with his family. Child published the *National Anti-Slavery Standard,* for which Hopper wrote "An Interesting Case of Escape" (1840) and 79 narratives for the biweekly column Tales of the Oppression, 75 percent of which featured flights through Delaware, Maryland, New Jersey, New York, and Pennsylvania. One story described aid to a bondswoman from Anderson County, South Carolina, whose owner threatened to amputate her hand. Another story, published in April 1841, describes how Hopper pursued the kidnapper of a 10-year-old named Wagelma (or Wajelma) by ferry to the New Jersey shore to stop the boy's removal to France. In Hopper's honor, his daughter Abigail Hopper Gibbons established the Isaac Tatem Hopper home for the handicapped. In 1853, Lydia Child published a biography, *Isaac T. Hopper, a True Life.*

See also: anti-slavery fairs; kidnap; Quakers; routes, Underground Railroad; safehouses.

Sources

Bacon, Margaret Hope. *Abby Hopper Gibbons: Prison Reformer and Social Activist.* Albany: State University of New York Press, 2000.

Child, Lydia Maria. *Isaac T. Hopper, a True Life.* Boston: John P. Jewett, 1853.

Meaders, Daniel. "Kidnapping Blacks in Philadelphia: Isaac Hopper's Tales of Oppression." *Journal of Negro History* 80:2 (Spring 1995): 47–65.

Horne, Daniel H. (1828–1885)
Horne, Maria Louisa Hovey (1826–1912)

One of the pioneers of Kansas Territory, Colonel Daniel H. Horne of Dover, New Hampshire, rescued runaway slaves. He married Maria (or Marie) Louisa Hovey of Cambridge, Massachusetts, in April 1849 and arrived by a Missouri River steamer in fall 1854 to excavate a sod hut. Slaves escaping from Missouri and heading west passed through his safehouse at Southwest Second and Third streets in Topeka. For protection during the Kansas-Missouri border wars, in fall 1855, he formed a militia called the Topeka Guards. In 1865, he served as the Shawnee County land agent.

Source

Cutler, William G. *History of the State of Kansas.* Chicago: A.T. Andreas, 1883.

Horse, John (1812–1882)

A skilled guerrilla warrior, John Horse (also called Gopher John, John Caballo, John Cavallo, or Juan Caballo) superintended a Mexican branch of the Underground Railroad called the Underground South. A Georgian born in Payne's Prairie on Florida's Alachua plain, he was the son of a black slave woman and her Seminole master, Charles Cavallo. John grew up in a system of bondage similar to that of feudalism, by which black Seminoles worked for the ruling class. In 1838, he defeated General Zachary Taylor's U.S. forces when they attempted to halt the rescue of slaves by Florida Seminoles. In winter 1849, he joined Chief Wild Cat in setting up a military border guard in the free territory of Mexico at Nacimiento de los Negros, in Coahuila along the Rio Sabinas in the Santa Rosa Mountains. The community received runaway slaves from Texas and Oklahoma and protected them from recapture by bounty hunters and Texas Rangers.

See also: Seminoles.

Source

Canfield, J. Douglas. *Mavericks on the Border.* Lexington: University Press of Kentucky, 2001.

Hosea, William (fl. 1850s)

William Hosea, an operator of a cab service in New Albany, in Floyd County, Indiana, used his roamings about the city streets as a cover for Underground Railroad work. In collusion with a slave, Ralph Spalding, the property of Bishop Martin J. Spalding of Louisville, Kentucky, Hosea relayed passengers by ferry from Kentucky to southern Indiana. His depot on Sycamore Street in New Albany was surrounded by safehouses. According to articles in the *Louisville Daily Courier* and the *New Albany Daily Ledger* on January 8, 1857, Hosea was arrested in Louisville on suspicion of slave abduction. The flimsy grounds for arrest illustrate unfriendly relations between authorities in a slave state abutting a free state.

See also: safehouses.

Source

Peters, Pamela R. *The Underground Railroad in Floyd County, Indiana.* Jefferson, NC: McFarland, 2001.

Hosmer, William (1810–1889)
Hosmer, Martha Matilde Gamage (?–1878)

The publisher of the *Northern Independent,* the Reverend William Hosmer, a first-generation Welsh American, and his wife, Martha Matilde Gamage Hosmer, supported the Underground Railroad in Syracuse, New York. A native of South Brimfield, Massachusetts, William Hosmer was ordained into the Methodist Episcopal Church in 1834 and served a church near Bath, New York. In 1848, he began an eight-year stint as editor of the *Northern Christian Advocate.*

The couple lived in Auburn at 29 Washington Street, where William compiled two abolitionist treatises—*The Higher Law in Its Relations to Civil Government* (1852) and *Slavery and the Church* (1853)—denouncing Christians who supported the flesh trade. In 1856, he edited an abolitionist paper, the *Northern Independent,* which was printed at 113 Genesee Street in Auburn and remained in circulation until 1867. In February 1861, agent David Wright sent William Hosmer to warn Harriet Tubman of slave hunters in the Syracuse area.

Source

Swaney, Charles Baumer. *Episcopal Methodism and Slavery: With Sidelights on Ecclesiastical Politics.* New York: R.G. Badger, 1926.

Hossack, John (1806–1891)
Hossack, Martha Lens (1813–1899)

A Scots immigrant from Glasgow, John Hossack, a canal builder and grain and lumber merchant from Ottawa, Illinois, and his wife, Martha Lens Hossack, managed a waystation at The Columns, their two-story hilltop residence at 210 West Prospect Avenue in

LaSalle County, Illinois. The Hossacks gained fame for their abolitionist fervor in aiding Jim Gray, a runaway whom the Reverend Ichabod Codding passed to the Hossacks' care. Gray and two other slaves fled their owner, Richard Phillips, outside New Madrid, Missouri, on September 4, 1859. After authorities apprehended and jailed Gray in Union County, Illinois, he stood trial in federal court. During the prisoner transfer, Hossack grabbed Gray and shoved him through the crowd to a carriage for transport by agent Charles Campbell.

Federal marshals arrested Hossack along with E.W. Chamberlin, Claudius B. King, Hervey King, James Stout, and Dr. Joseph Stout. Two others of the eight conspirators escaped. At the Cook County jail in Chicago, the six prisoners refused bail. At Hossack's sentencing on October 3, 1860, he declared the upholding of human liberty a sacred duty. He served a 10-day jail sentence and paid a fine of $100. At a banquet held by the mayor, Chicagoans celebrated Hossack as an abolitionist hero. Hossack's *Speech of John Hossack, Convicted of Violation of the Fugitive Slave Law* was published that same year.

Sources

Hossack, John. *Speech of John Hossack, Convicted of Violation of the Fugitive Slave Law: Before Judge Drummond, of the U.S. District Court of Chicago.* Chicago: James Barnet, 1860.

Ottawa: Old and New, a Complete History of Ottawa, Illinois. Ottawa, IL: *Republican-Times,* 1912–1914.

Houghton, George Hendric (1820–1897)

An Episcopal priest, the Reverend George Hendric Houghton, received runaway slaves at his church. A native of Deerfield, Massachusetts, he lived in New York City from age 14 and supported his widowed mother. He completed a degree from the General Theological Seminary in Manhattan and married Caroline Graves Anthon. After establishing the Church of the Transfiguration in New York City in 1848, he welcomed worshippers rejected by other churches. He offered food to the homeless and unemployed. He also received fugitive slaves at a Sunday school and harbored them in the sanctuary from slave catchers. In July 1863, he stood alone against angry whites who threatened to seize Underground Railroad passengers concealed in the church. In 1870, his church became known as the Little Church Around the Corner.

Source

Holland, Jack, and Martin Dunford. *The Rough Guide to New York City.* London: Rough Guides, 2002.

Houston, Thomas Jefferson (1829–?)

A refugee from bondage in Missouri, Kentucky-born slave Thomas Jefferson Houston (or Huston) devoted himself to helping other escaping slaves. Born Thomas Jefferson Hunn, he required multiple flight plans before he reached Springfield, Illinois. He welcomed fugitives to his home and returned into slave territory to rescue his brother and sister-in-law and their children. In 1838, Houston founded the Zion Baptist Missionary Church at 1601 East Laurel Street, another of Springfield's Underground Railroad depots. At the beginning of the Civil War, he joined the Union army.

Source

Buckmaster, Henrietta. *Let My People Go: The Story of the Underground Railroad and the Growth of the Abolition Movement.* New York: Harper & Brothers, 1941.

Howe, Julia Ward (1819–1910)
Howe, Samuel Gridley (1801–1876)

An unusual couple, Julia Ward Howe, author of "The Battle Hymn of the Republic" (1861), and her husband, attorney, financier, and newspaper publisher Samuel Gridley Howe, supported the Underground Railroad. Julia Ward Howe grew up amid wealth and learned piano, voice, and modern foreign languages from tutors. She maintained ties with John Brown and the Reverend Theodore Parker and co-edited her husband's abolitionist magazine, *Commonwealth.* At their home on Chestnut Street on Boston's Beacon Hill, the Howes aided runaway slaves and protected them against recapture.

In 1846, Samuel Howe co-formed the Boston Vigilance Committee, which numbered in its members Robert Morris and William Cooper Nell. Howe was one of a team of six attorneys—the others being Salmon Portland Chase, Francis Jackson, Horace Mann, Robert Morris, and Samuel Edmund Sewall—who defended Captain Daniel Drayton for attempting to free 77 slaves on April 15, 1848. Howe excused the passage on Drayton's sloop *Pearl* as a normal sea voyage from Georgetown in the District of Columbia to New Jersey. Intervention on Drayton's behalf reduced his prison sentence from 20 to four years. The following year, Samuel Howe joined the Reverend Thomas Wentworth Higginson, Theodore Parker, and George Luther Stearns in financing John Brown's assault on the federal arsenal in Harpers Ferry, Virginia.

Source

Venet, Wendy Hammond. *Neither Ballots nor Bullets: Women Abolitionists and the Civil War.* Charlottesville: University Press of Virginia, 1991.

Howland, Emily (1827–1929)
Howland, Slocum (1794–1881)
Howland, Hannah Tallcot (1796–1867)

A family of determined abolitionists, the Howlands expressed the Christian principles of their English Quaker heritage. The granddaughter of anti-slavery pacifists, diarist Emily Howland was born and reared at the family farm outside Sherwood, in Cayuga County, New York. Her father, Slocum Howland, a wool dealer, operated Cobblestone Store in Aurora, which, from 1837, was a stop on the Underground Railroad. Her family read William Lloyd Garrison's weekly paper, *The Liberator,* and taught their children to practice humanitarianism.

According to Emily Howland's journal, a party of six—Herman and Hannah Phillips and their first four children, Martha, William, John, and Harriett Phillips—fled bondage in Maryland in 1843 and passed from the hands of agent Mathias Hutchinson to the Howlands' depot of the Underground Railroad. Others arrived from Quaker stationmasters John Mann and Mary Williams King Mann in Coudersport, Pennsylvania. The Howlands offered a tenant house, where the Phillips family remained. After Hannah Tallcot Howland's health failed in 1843, Emily maintained the home and waystation. In 1857, Emily taught black girls at the Miner School for Freedmen in Philadelphia. After national emancipation on January 1, 1863, she educated former slaves in Washington, D.C. The Howland stone store is currently a museum.

Sources

1894 Biographical Review. Boston: Biographical Review, 1894.

Rapp, Scott, "Ex-Slave's Dream Comes True in Sherwood," *Syracuse Post-Standard,* February 9, 2005.

Hoyt, Lyman (1804–1857)
Hoyt, Aseneth Whipple (1810–1897)
Hoyt, Lois L. (1844–ca. 1930)

Like other abolitionists, philanthropist Lyman Hoyt and his family fought the Fugitive Slave Law of 1850 through civil disobedience. Lyman and his wife, Aseneth Whipple Hoyt, both natives of Vermont, settled in Lancaster, in Jefferson County, Indiana, in 1834. They built a two-story stone waystation of the Underground Railroad on 60 acres in Madison. They owned a smithy, a lumberyard, and a sawmill and factories that made farm tools, cider mills, and wagons. In addition to rescuing fugitives, the family boycotted slave-made cotton, molasses, and sugar. They wore linen and wool garments and invested in a silk factory in Paris, France.

According to the writings of their daughter, Lois L. Hoyt, her family hid runaway slaves in their barn and in a cave. In addition to composing anti-slavery articles for the abolitionist newspaper the *Philanthropist,* Lyman supported the Neil's Creek Anti-Slavery Society and Eleutherian College in Lancaster. In November 15, 1850, he and Samuel Tibbets decided to offer clothing, shelter, and food to runaways. Contributing to their network were John H. Tibbets in Madison and George DeBaptiste, a route coordinator in Cincinnati, Detroit, and Madison. The Hoyt residence, now under restoration, was listed on the National Register of Historic Places in 2003.

See also: civil disobedience; Eleutherian College; Fugitive Slave Law of 1850; philanthropists.

Source

Obituary of Lyman Hoyt, *Madison Daily Evening Courier,* July 13, 1857.

Hubbard, Catherine Hulbert (1786–?)
Hubbard, William (1787–1863)

Colonel William Hubbard, a veteran of the War of 1812, and his wife, Catherine Hulbert Hubbard, fought slavery as agents of the Underground Railroad at their Ashtabula, Ohio, home on Lake Erie. Natives of Middletown, Connecticut, they married in 1810 and moved to the area from Trenton, New York, in 1834. William joined the Ashtabula County Anti-Slavery Society, as did his brothers, Henry and Matthew, who, in 1853, established an abolitionist paper, the *Ashtabula Sentinel.* Catherine and William managed the Ohio Exchange Hotel until they built a brick home in winter 1840. A runaway slave named Jake was the chief mason on the project, which became the northern terminus of the Ohio–Ontario route to freedom.

Up to 40 runaways at a time found sanctuary at 1603 Walnut Boulevard in the barn or cellar of the

At their modest home in Lancaster, Indiana, 10 miles from the Ohio River, the family of lumberman Lyman Hoyt hid fugitive slaves and guided them on their way to the next stop north. They supported the free labor movement by boycotting slave-made goods. *(Indiana Department of Natural Resoures—Division of Historic Preservation and Archaeology)*

Hubbards' two-story residence, which overlooked Ashtabula Harbor. Dubbed Mother Hubbard's Cupboard, the home was one of 30 safehouses in the community. No fugitive failed to make the lake crossing from the Hubbard waystation to Ontario. A tunnel from the barn to the shoreline aided slave concealment. In 1984, Colonel Hubbard's great-great-grandson, Thomas "Tim" Huntington Hubbard, led Underground Railroad tours that began in Wheeling, West Virginia, and concluded at Ashtabula Harbor. Listed on the National Register of Historic Places, the Hubbard residence is currently a museum displaying Underground Railroad and Civil War memorabilia.

See also: safehouses.

Sources

Makhijani, Pooja, ed. *Under Her Skin: How Girls Experience Race in America.* Emeryville, CA: Seal, 2004.

Wolny, Philip. *The Underground Railroad: A Primary Source History of the Journey to Freedom.* New York: Rosen, 2004.

Huber, Charles Boerstler (1806–1854)

Depot manager Charles Boerstler "Boss" Huber ran a farm and tannery in Williamsburg, Ohio, while supervising local Underground Railroad activities. Called Boss for his superintendency of the local network, Huber operated out of his home on Gay Street and kept up with abolitionist news by reading the speeches of James Gillespie Birney, Salmon Portland Chase, and William Lloyd Garrison in the *National Era.* Huber provided friendship as well as provisions and cash to the needy. He used his hayloft as a hiding place for refugees arriving from the waystations of the Reverend Gerrard Policarp Riley and Isaac Holmes Brown in Bethel and from the Jacob Ebersole family in Felicity, in Clermont County, Ohio. Huber hired mulatto freedman Marcus Sims to do the legwork, which involved ferrying some 500 escapees to stations throughout southern Ohio. Aiding the pair was Samuel Peterson, a stonemason, who provided meals and transportation for refugees.

Huber earned respect for assisting as many as 17 runaways in a single party. An observer, David Swing, reported in the *New York Independent* on the camaraderie between Huber and a runaway, whom Huber left with cash and a handshake in 1849 before the slave journeyed on across Ohio. Although Huber lost the 12 members of the Ball family on their arrival at the shore of Lake Erie, he remained devoted to the cause of liberty to the end of his life. Marcus Sims and Huber's neighbors and colleagues Dr. Leavitt Thaxter Pease and his wife, Nancy Fee Pease, continued Huber's work for the secret network out of the Pease home and medical office on Gay Street. Legends persist that the Huber and Pease homes were connected by a secret tunnel.

Source

Hagedorn, Ann. *Beyond the River: The Untold Story of the Heroes of the Underground Railroad.* New York: Simon & Schuster, 2002.

Hudson, David (1761–1836)
Hudson, David, Jr. (1805–1836)

A pioneer, surveyor, and philanthropist from Goshen, Connecticut, David Hudson, founder of the town of Hudson in Summit County, Ohio, also established Western Reserve College in 1826. A devout Congregationalist and one of three conductors in the area, Hudson kept a two-story waystation north of the town center at 318 North Main Street. He hid refugees in the springhouse. His son, diarist David Hudson, Jr., recorded the family's adventures in helping refugees escape capture, the first documentation of the town's involvement in the Underground Railroad. On January 5, 1826, the Hudsons connected with two Underground Railroad agents driving a sleigh and took charge of three passengers, a black woman and two children.

See also: Underground Railroad.

Source

Turzillo, Jane Ann. *Hudson, Ohio.* Charleston, SC: Arcadia, 2002.

Hudson, Jesse (1781–1844)

A conductor from Maryland, 63-year-old freedman Jesse Hudson died in prison while serving a sentence for rescuing slaves. On November 21, 1839, a Worcester County circuit court found Hudson guilty and confined him to the state penitentiary in Baltimore for six years. He died in his cell on January 8, 1844, having served four years.

Source

Prison records, Maryland State Archives.

Hudson, John D. (fl. 1830s–1860s)
Hudson, Sally (?–1839)

A courageous wagoneer for the Underground Railroad, John D. Hudson operated a waystation in Sardinia, in Brown County, Ohio. He began life in Virginia as a slave of Samuel Gift and moved to Ohio with his parents around age 10. Some 25 miles north of the Ohio River crossing from Maysville, Kentucky, into Ripley, Ohio, he and another freedman, Moses Cumberland, conspired with Jean Lowry Rankin and John Rankin at their home, Liberty Hill, and the Reverend John Bennington Mahan at his home at White Oak Creek. Hudson began rescuing blacks in the 1820s. He blew on a conch shell to alert neighbors to slave catchers. He opened his depot in 1834, six years after the Rankins began rescuing slaves, and continued relaying fugitives for three decades.

Dr. Isaac M. Beck and his wife, Cassandra Graham Lamb Beck, paid Hudson 25¢ per relay for his reliable escort service. During a difficult rescue on April 21, 1839, John received the assistance of his sister, Sally Hudson, who smacked slave owner Grant Lindsey and bit his cohort for trying to seize Moses Cumberland in the Gist community. According to a written memoir of Isaac Beck, one shot to the spine ended her life. Authorities did not convict the murderer.

See also: Gist Settlement.

Source

Hagedorn, Ann. *Beyond the River: The Untold Story of the Heroes of the Underground Railroad.* New York: Simon & Schuster, 2002.

Huggins, Robert Henderson (fl. 1830s)
Huggins, William D. (1765–1839)
Huggins, Milton (fl. 1830s)
Huggins, William (fl. 1830s–1861)

In the 1830s, the Huggins family of Clay Township, in Highland County, Ohio, supported the Ripley line of the Underground Railroad through the southern part of the state. After arriving from North Carolina in 1813 with his brother William D. Huggins, Robert

Henderson Huggins built a log cabin on his farm at Flat Run Creek for use as a safehouse. It featured a niche under the hearth for emergency shelter. Supplying the family with food and clothing were their neighbors the Van Winkles, who dug a tunnel under the Ripley turnpike tollhouse to make a subterranean hideaway.

Until the outbreak of the Civil War, Robert Huggins's sons, Milton and William, transported Kentucky refugees from the Ohio River. The brothers moved fugitives quickly by night in a covered wagon to the station of William Matthews in Flat Run. A fellow agent, Adam Lowry Rankin, delivered slaves from Ripley, Ohio, to Sardinia for concealment in the Hugginses' fodder wagon or at a log outbuilding. On one rescue, a horse fell on Milton Huggins. He died from internal injury.

See also: kidnap.

Sources

Ayres, Elsie Johnson. *Highland Pioneer Sketches and Family Genealogies.* Springfield, OH: H.K. Skinner & Son, 1971.
Hagedorn, Ann. *Beyond the River: The Untold Story of the Heroes of the Underground Railroad.* New York: Simon & Schuster, 2002.

Hughes, Denard (fl. 1850s)

Thanks to a successful relay via the Underground Railroad, Denard Hughes escaped from bondage. On March 8, 1857, Hughes left servitude to farmer Richard Meredith. With seven other fugitives—Thomas Elliot, Bill Kiah, Emily Kiah, Henry Predo, James Woolfley, Lavinia Woolfley, and one unidentified man—Hughes ran from Buckstown in Dorchester County, Maryland, to Dover, Delaware, where Thomas Otwell betrayed them to authorities to claim a $3,000 reward. The refugees extricated themselves from the sheriff's lockup by starting a fire. After the group scattered, Hughes received help from secret operatives in Philadelphia, Pennsylvania, and continued on to Canada.

Source

Still, William. *Underground Railroad Records.* Philadelphia: Porter & Coates, 1883.

Humphrey, Harvey (1796–1877)
Humphrey, Elizabeth Rogers Perkins (1793–1859)

Residents of Rochester, New York, Harvey Humphrey and his wife participated in the Monroe County Underground Railroad. A native of Goshen, Connecticut, in 1828, Harvey married Elizabeth Rogers Perkins of Norwich, Connecticut. The couple maintained a waystation at 669 Genesee Street and kept passengers until they could safely cross Lake Erie into Ontario.

Source

Ripley, C. Peter, et al., eds. *The Black Abolitionist Papers.* Chapel Hill: University of North Carolina Press, 1992.

Hunn (John, Sr.) Family

A Quaker agent of the Underground Railroad on the Delaware–Pennsylvania line, John Hunn, Sr. (1818–1894), of Middletown in Kent County, Delaware, was a member of an activist family of abolitionists. His older half brother, Ezekiel Hunn, Sr. (1810–1902), a silk merchant, and Ezekiel's wife, Lydia Jones Sharpless Hunn (1818–1911), maintained a stop of the secret network at their home, Wildcat Manor, outside Lebanon, Delaware. Discontent in his partnership with Ezekiel's Philadelphia-based business, John began studying farming with his cousin, John Alston, a fellow conductor. The two men allied with operatives Samuel D. Burris, Daniel Corbet, and William Still to relay fugitives from Great Geneva and from Wildcat Manor, both on the River Road in Camden, Delaware. John Hunn and his wife, Mary Allen Swallow Hunn (ca. 1818–1854), equipped their kitchen with a rotating pantry wall that concealed a niche. One of their frequent guests was famed agent Harriet Tubman, who used the Hunn safehouse as a rest stop on her way up the Atlantic coast.

John Hunn's service to the secret network began at sunrise on December 5, 1845. Burris rescued Emeline Hawkins and Samuel "Sam" Hawkins and their children—Chester, Sally Ann, Washington, and Walter—and four others by covered wagon from Camden in Queen Annes County, Maryland. The party traveled 27 miles in a snowstorm and stopped at the Hunns' waystation for breakfast and treatment of frostbitten hands. So large a group required concealment in the loft of the Appoquinimink Friends Meeting House in Odessa. To defuse a tense face-off with pursuers William Chestnut and Robert Hardcastle, John Hunn persuaded Sam Hawkins to surrender his knife and New Castle Sheriff Jacob Caulk to holster his gun. The negotiation resulted in the arrest of the Hawkins family and confinement in the county jail. After network coordinator Thomas

Garrett successfully negotiated with Chief Justice James Booth for the family's release, the refugees continued on their way to Byberry, Pennsylvania, their new home.

John Hunn conferred with Thomas Garrett about the lawsuit that owners Charles W. Glanding and Elizabeth Turner initiated against Hunn the next year. Setting a precedent for personal liability in slave rescue, Justice Roger B. Taney levied a fine of $2,500 against Hunn and $5,400 against Garrett. The steep settlement required the liquidation of the Hunn farm and their move to the home of relatives in Camden. Slave owners anticipated that the stiff penalty would derail the secret network. Instead, publicity brought honor to agent John Hunn, who involved himself in hundreds more rescues. He earned the titles of superintendent and chief engineer of the Underground Railway from Wilmington, Delaware, down the Delmarva Peninsula. At his death, his son, John Hunn, Jr. (1841–?), burned all correspondence and records of slave rescues. In 1973, Great Geneva was listed on the National Register of Historic Places.

Sources

Conrad, Henry Clay. *History of the State of Delaware.* Wilmington, DE: privately published, 1908.

McCarter, J.M., and B.F. Jackson, eds. *Historical and Biographical Encyclopedia of Delaware.* Wilmington, DE: Aldine, 1882.

Hunt, Jane Clothier Master (1812–1889) Hunt, Richard Pell (1797–1856)

Two Quaker supporters of abolition, Jane Clothier Master Hunt of Philadelphia and her husband, land speculator Richard Pell Hunt of Pelham, New York, operated a station of the Underground Railroad. At their 11-room mansion at Six Main Street in Waterloo, in Seneca County, New York, they converted a carriage house into a receiving center for refugees. On July 9, 1848, Jane Hunt convened a suffragist tea that included Elizabeth Cady Stanton and secret network agents Mary Ann Wilson M'Clintock, Lucretia Coffin Mott, and Martha Coffin Pelham Wright. The guests espoused their sympathy for black women forced into concubinage to their masters. In widowhood, Jane Hunt operated the Waterloo Woolen Mill as a means of boycotting slave-made cotton.

Source

Wellman, Judith. *The Road to Seneca Falls: Elizabeth Cady Stanton and the First Woman's Rights Convention.* Champaign: University of Illinois Press, 2004.

Hunt, Seth (1814–1893)

Philanthropist and radical activist Seth Hunt aided fugitive slaves from his residence in Northampton, in Hampshire County, Massachusetts. He was treasurer of the Connecticut River Railroad. In addition to maintaining friendships with Frederick Douglass, Sojourner Truth, and other agents of the Underground Railroad, he operated a waystation at 115 Bridge Street. Hunt joined other speakers in a formal protest of the Fugitive Slave Law of 1850.

See also: Fugitive Slave Law of 1850.

Source

Douglass, Frederick. *Life and Times of Frederick Douglass.* Boston: De Wolfe & Fiske, 1892.

Hunter, Charles W. (?–1860)

Merchant and real estate speculator Major Charles W. Hunter earned a reputation for dedication to Underground Railroad efforts along the Mississippi River. He started in business in St. Louis, Missouri, and then moved to Illinois, where he was nominated for an office on the Board of Corporation in March 1836. In addition to petitioning for an Illinois abolitionist society on September 27, 1837, he maintained a waystation in the 1830s and 1840s in Hunterstown, outside Alton. The location served slaves fleeing through St. Louis into free territory. Aiding Hunter was the Reverend Elijah Parish Lovejoy, an abolitionist minister and editor who was martyred in November 1837 by a pro-slavery mob. Hunter donated a plot for Lovejoy's burial.

Source

Blight, David W., ed. *Passages to Freedom.* Washington, DC: Smithsonian, 2004.

Hunter, Moses (?–1842)

A founder of the Underground Railroad route from Galesburg to Chicago, Illinois, the Reverend Moses Hunter rescued passengers en route from the Mississippi River. He allied with ministerial students James E. Burr and George Thompson, with Alanson Work, and with Dr. David Nelson, who, in 1837, established Mission Institute, a manual labor academy near Quincy. Both Hunter and Nelson were advocates of the Illinois Anti-Slavery Society and of the extension of the secret network to the west. After the capture of

Burr, Thompson, and Work in July 1841 for supporting a slave escape at Palmyra, Hunter provided moral support and legal aid. The prisoners received 12-year sentences, but they exulted that media reports caused an increase in the number of slave escapes, despite the dangers.

Source

Muelder, Hermann R. *Fighters for Freedom: The History of Anti-Slavery Activities of Men and Women Associated with Knox College.* New York: Columbia University Press, 1959.

Huntoon, Josiah Parmerley (1813–1901)

An Underground Railroad operative in Paterson, New Jersey, industrialist Josiah Parmerley Huntoon of Montpelier, Vermont, put his abolitionist philosophy to work. A pioneer in the coffee-roasting business in 1841, he ground coffee at his Paterson factory, the Excelsior Mill, which he built in 1855, and at subsidiaries in Newark and New Brunswick, New Jersey. His operation earned a comment in the November 21, 1859, issue of the *Scientific American.* The store where he made his fortune on trade in coffee, tea, and spices as far south as Mississippi also received runaways on their way to Canada. In addition, he regularly harbored the oppressed at his office near the intersection of Bridge and Broadway streets. He depended on assistance from conductor William Van Rensalier, his black engineer and partner, who apprenticed with Huntoon in 1850 at age 14. Huntoon's portrait, painted by Thomas Waterman Wood in 1874, hangs in the Paterson Library.

Source

Sharkey, Joe, "Finding a Lost Page from a Family History," *New York Times,* November 10, 1996.

Hurd, Edward B. (fl. 1840s–1850s)
Hurd, Harvey Bostwick (1828–1906)

Agent Edward B. Hurd and his brother, Judge Harvey Bostwick Hurd, operated waystations of the Underground Railroad. They were born to abolitionist parents in Huntington, in Fairfield County, Connecticut. Edward opened a tailor's shop in Chicago, Illinois. After marrying Cornelia Amanda Hillard, in 1854, Harvey built a home in Evanston and established his reputation as a juvenile court judge and professor of law. In collusion with John Brown and Allan Pinkerton, the Hurd brothers boosted the reputation of the Chicago line of the Underground Railroad for ensuring a safe passage by lake steamer to Ontario. On one relay, in sight of U.S. marshals, 13 passengers crept one by one aboard a vessel and replaced the dockworkers loading firewood in the hold.

Source

"The Underground Railroad and Those Who Operated It," *Springfield (OH) Republican,* March 11, 1900.

Hussey, Sylvanus Erastus Fuller (1800–1899)
Hussey, Sarah E. Bowen (1808–1899)
Hussey, Susan T. (1828–?)

Quaker Underground Railroad conductor Sylvanus Erastus Fuller Hussey of Scipio, New York, aided by his wife, Sarah E. Bowen Hussey, and his daughter, Susan T. Hussey, rescued some 1,000 black fugitives passing through Battle Creek, Michigan. In 1824, the family moved from New York to a frontier farm in Plymouth, in Wayne County, Michigan. The Husseys built a residence and dry goods store in Calhoun County in 1839. The next year, at the urging of organizer John Cross, they began a 20-year assault on slavery by operating a waystation in the store cellar. When the first passengers, William Coleman and Stephen Wood, arrived, system supervisor Levi Coffin came to offer advice. Refugees, as many as 45 at a time, came from Kentucky through Ohio over a central Michigan route to the Husseys and their colleagues, Theron H. Chadwick, Silas Dodge, Abel Densmore, and Henry Willis. The overland route workers coordinated efforts in Albion, Ann Arbor, Climax, Grass Lake, Marshall, and Plymouth and concluded in Detroit with passage across Lake Erie to Ontario. Hussey was the main transporter to Marshall, traveling by horse and buggy with a young assistant, Isaac Mott. Among the Hussey family's rescues was Samuel Strauther, who became a permanent citizen of Battle Creek and a network wagoneer.

On August 1, 1847, Erastus Hussey confronted spies from Kentucky posing as traveling salesmen and warned them that attempts to kidnap blacks could result in violence. He issued 500 handbills throughout the area reiterating his warning. The effort scared off armed slave hunters. Hussey also attempted to alert agents Stephen A. Bogue and Elijah Drury that a raid on Quaker depots in Cass County was imminent. The letter did not arrive in time to forestall a slave roundup by Kentuckians in Cassopolis.

At Battle Creek, in 1847, Hussey published an abolitionist paper, the *Michigan Liberty Press,* which fire destroyed that same year. In subsequent commentary, Hussey declared that he remained true to civil disobedience out of love for humanity.

See also: civil disobedience; kidnap; spies; *Underground Railroad, The* (sculpture, 1993).

Sources

"The Abolitionist Patriarch," *Battle Creek (MI) Morning Call,* May 1885.

Bingham, Stephen D. *Early History of Michigan.* Lansing, MI: Thorp & Godfrey, 1888.

Tuchalski, Yvonne. "Erastus Hussey, Battle Creek Anti-Slavery Activist." *Michigan History* 56:1 (1972): 1–18.

Hutchinson, Titus (1771–1857)

Judge Titus Hutchinson engineered a method of conducting slaves from his home upriver to safety. A local dignitary and the son of a minister in Pomfret, Vermont, he was born in Hebron, Connecticut, and graduated with honors from Princeton University in 1794. He served as president of the Vermont state bank in 1806, U.S. district attorney from 1813 to 1821, and, chief justice of the Vermont Supreme Court from 1825 to 1833. At his residence at 26 Elm Street at the corner of Central Street in Woodstock, Vermont, he dug a passage from his cellar to the Kedron River. Refugees arrived and departed by rowboat.

Source

Smith, H.P., ed. *History of Addison County, Vermont.* Syracuse, NY: D. Mason, 1886.

Hyde, Udney Hay (1808–1883)
Hyde, Amanda (1841–1913)

A revered conductor of the Underground Railroad in Mechanicsburg, in Champaign County, Ohio, Udney Hay Hyde harbored runaways in need of shelter. He lived in a log cabin and worked as a farmer and blacksmith. In 1851, he received four slaves from Jacob Pearce of South Charleston, Ohio, for transfer to Springfield, Ohio. By the next day, Hyde had three more arrivals from Urbana, Ohio. On September 20, Hyde began his relay by wagon, in which the passengers were hidden under hay. Among the passengers was Penny, a freedman who worked for a year to buy his girlfriend out of bondage in Kentucky. When the slave owner refused to honor the deal, Penny stole the woman and another couple and a single male and made his way to Mechanicsburg.

A fugitive slave, Addison "Ad" White, escaped bondage to farmer Daniel White in Flemingsburg, in Fleming County, Kentucky. En route to Canada in August 1856, White chose to reside with the Hyde family. He farmed their land for eight months while Hyde recuperated from a crushed heel. Hyde's daughter, Amanda, taught White to read from a book of speeches, Caleb Bingham and David W. Blight's *The Columbian Orator* (1797). Agent Charles Taylor aided White by sending for his enslaved wife in Flemingsburg. On April 20, 1857, a stranger arrived claiming to be transporting Mrs. Addison White. When the stranger refused to answer Taylor's queries about Mrs. White, Taylor realized that a slave hunter had been sent by the slave owner, Daniel White, to seize Ad White.

After dawn on May 15, the arrival of a posse of seven men and two deputy U.S. marshals to the Hyde farm forced Ad White to hide in the upstairs loft. White fired a pistol at Deputy Marshall Elliott of Cincinnati, Ohio, who discharged a shotgun into the overhead boards and tried to climb to the upper floor. To end the stalemate, Hyde sent Amanda to summon help. She eluded the posse by pretending to feed chickens. The gathering of 100 angry neighbors brandishing farm tools, clubs, and carpet bats forced the seven attackers from the yard. When the road cleared, Ad White continued over the secret network route to Canada. Having been identified as an Underground Railroad operative, Udney Hyde retreated to the swamp and stayed out of sight until February 1858.

When the deputies returned to Mechanicsburg with warrants, Udney Hyde was not at home. They arrested and fined the Hydes' son, Russell Hyde, pharmacist Charles Taylor, Edward Taylor, and Hiram Guthridge for violating the Fugitive Slave Law of 1850. As a result of the uproar, the Hyde rescue earned national press. Sheriff Lewis of Greene arrested and jailed the deputies because they had lied about their destination and fired on law officers, but Judge Samuel V. Baldwin freed them. Abolitionists in Mechanicsburg and Urbana, Ohio, raised $950 to buy Ad White out of bondage. After nine months in hiding, Udney Hyde returned to operating his safehouse and to rescuing parties of runaways.

During the Civil War, Ad White enlisted in the Fifty-fourth Massachusetts Regiment, the nation's first all-black infantry, and returned to Mechanicsburg in 1865. The dramatic story of slave and rescuer survived in a stage musical, *Freedom Bound,* which debuted at Mad River Theater Works in West Liberty, Ohio, in 1985.

See also: Fugitive Slave Law of 1850.

Sources

Baxter, W.H. *History of Champaign County, Ohio.* Chicago: W.R. Beers, 1881.

Howe, Henry. *Historical Collections of Ohio.* Cincinnati, OH: E. Morgan, 1851.

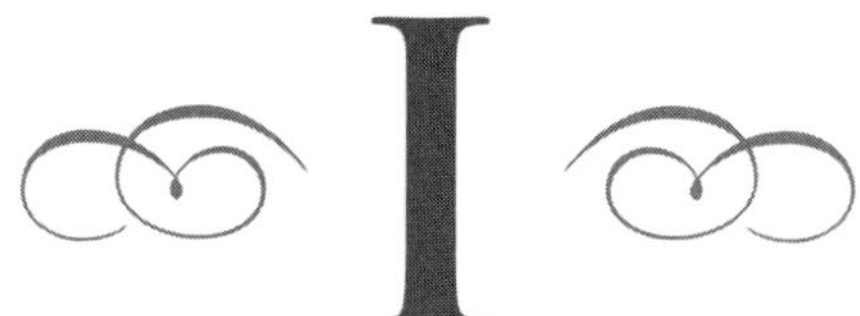

Incidents in the Life of a Slave Girl (1861)

Long misread as a novel by a white author, Harriet Ann Jacobs's autobiography *Incidents in the Life of a Slave Girl* (1861) proved to be the most intense slave narrative composed by a woman. In the 1980s, literary historian Jean Fagan Yellin collected proof that the name Linda Brent was the pseudonym of Harriet Jacobs. Yellin called the book a major contribution to female slave narrative. Initially, the book appeared in print with the aid of two Underground Railroad agents, Lydia Maria Francis Child, editor of the *National Anti-Slavery Standard,* and Amy Kirby Post, a Quaker libertarian and the founder of the Western New York Anti-Slavery Society.

Jacobs's story discloses her sexual exploitation by her owner, Dr. James Norcom, who used Jacobs's two children as bargaining tools. The text reveals the horrors of slaves on the run—the fear of bloodhounds, the uncertainty of each day, and the dangers of hiding in the snake-infested Carolina swamps. The combination of her own guile and the dedication of the secret network contributed to Jacobs's contentment in freedom and her satisfaction in relating a true story of human bondage.

See also: bloodhounds.

Sources

Blackford, Holly. "Figures of Orality: The Master, the Mistress, the Slave Mother in Harriet Jacobs's *Incidents in the Life of a Slave Girl: Written by Herself.*" *Papers on Language & Literature* 37:3 (Summer 2001): 314–36.

Jacobs, Harriet A. *Incidents in the Life of a Slave Girl: Written by Herself.* 1861. New York: Harvest, 1983.

Irish, David (1792–1884)
Irish, Martha Titus (1789–1873)

Quaker minister and farmer David Irish and his wife, Martha Titus Irish, sheltered runaway slaves at their home. The couple married in 1816 and reared three children in Quaker Hill outside Pawling, in Dutchess County, New York. The Irishes partnered with stationmaster Deborah Rodgers Willetts, a grammarian, and Jacob Willetts, a mathematics and geography teacher, in South Millbrook. Refugees fleeing through Westchester, in New York's Hudson Valley, found safety at the Irish residence on Broad Street.

Source

Driscoll, James, et al. *Angels of Deliverance: The Underground Railroad in Queens, Long Island, and Beyond.* Flushing, NY: Queens Historical Society, 1999.

Isaacs, Tucker (1809–1874)
Isaacs, Elizabeth-Ann Fossett (1812–1902)

A mulatto Jew, Tucker Isaacs took seriously the task of liberating slaves. Born free to a wealthy family in Charlottesville, Virginia, he thrived as a glazier and painter and used his resources for humanitarian purposes. After authorities investigated his forging of liberation papers for slaves, he moved to Chillicothe, in Ross County, Ohio, in 1838. In 1849, he bought freedom papers for Peter Farley Fossett, a relative of President Thomas Jefferson and Sally Hemings, from slave owner John Jones and dispatched Fossett from Monticello, Virginia, to Cincinnati, Ohio. Isaacs also liberated Fossett's sister, Elizabeth-Ann (or Anne Elizabeth) "Betsy" Fossett, whom Tucker Isaacs married. In 1856, the couple bought 158 acres in Springfield, in Ross County, Ohio, and built a two-story safehouse and barn on a knoll in sight of Scioto Valley. Legend describes a light that shone from their window to guide runaways to safety.

Source

Rothman, Joshua D. *Notorious in the Neighborhood: Sex and Families Across the Color Line in Virginia, 1787–1861.* Chapel Hill: University of North Carolina Press, 2003.

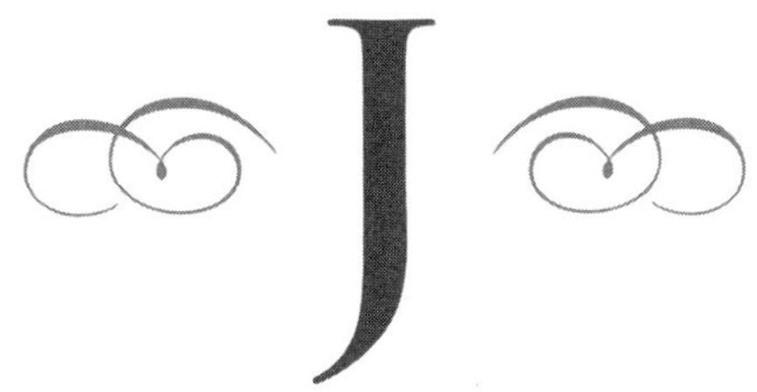

Jackson, Elizabeth Underhill (1815–?)
Jackson, George (1813–ca. 1880)

Two Underground Railroad stationmasters, Elizabeth Underhill Jackson and George Jackson, received runaways at their two-story frame dwelling in White Pot, in Newtown Township, New York. The son of Jarvis Jackson, a town manager and overseer of the poor, George Jackson learned to honor charity in childhood. After the couple's marriage, the Jacksons expressed their Quaker upbringing through hospitality to fugitives traveling along Flushing Creek. When posses threatened, passengers fled to the woods until dark, when they boarded boats for Flushing Bay. After crossing Long Island Sound, escapees continued along the route to Westchester, New York.

See also: Quakers.

Source

Driscoll, James, et al. *Angels of Deliverance: The Underground Railroad in Queens, Long Island, and Beyond.* Flushing, NY: Queens Historical Society, 1999.

Jackson, James Caleb (1811–1895)
Jackson, Lucretia Edgerton Brewster (1810–1890)

James Caleb Jackson, a physician and writer, and his wife, Lucretia Edgerton Brewster Jackson, fought slavery as conductors of the Underground Railroad in Mexico, in Oswego County, New York. James Jackson was born in Manlius, New York, to a patriotic family whose members served in the Revolutionary War and the War of 1812. Lucretia Jackson claimed a Pilgrim ancestor, William Brewster. Under the influence of secret network organizer Gerrit Smith, Dr. Jackson lectured for the Massachusetts Anti-Slavery Society and incited hundreds of listeners to aid runaway slaves. When he was away lecturing, from 1830 to 1845, Lucretia Jackson maintained their waystation.

The Jacksons settled in Peterboro, in Madison County, New York. On August 21–22, 1850, they attended the Cazenovia Fugitive Slave Law Convention, which pursued issues of slave rescue and civil rights and featured 50 black runaways. Led by Frederick Douglass, the gathering of 2,000 overflowed the Free Congregational Church, where the convention was being held, and reconvened outdoors in Grace Wilson's apple orchard on Sullivan Street to protest the eventual passage of the Fugitive Slave Law of 1850 on September 18. In partnership with Abel Brown, James Caleb Jackson edited the *Albany Patriot* and *Liberty Press.* Jackson founded the Glen Haven Water Cure, a hydrotherapy clinic, on Skaneateles Lake at Dansville, New York, and wrote extensively on cures for tuberculosis and the illnesses of women and children.

See also: Fugitive Slave Law of 1850.

Sources

Bunnell, A.O., and F.I. Quick. *History of Dansville, 1789–1902.* Dansville, NY: Instructor, 1892.

Pierson, Michael D. *Free Hearts and Free Homes: Gender and American Antislavery Politics.* Chapel Hill: University of North Carolina Press, 2003.

Jackson, Mattie Jane (ca. 1843–?)

Mattie Jane Jackson endured constant turmoil and family disruption before freeing herself from bondage. The great-granddaughter of an African captive, she learned the deceptions of slave owners from the life story of her grandfather, a freeman who was kidnapped and transported from New York to St. Charles, Missouri. Mattie's father, Westly Jackson, who married Ellen Turner, a plantation cook, never heard of the Underground Railroad. The couple was sold to a Virginia trader and before he could be resold, Westly Jackson escaped. His wife, meanwhile was left to raise three daughters, Esther J., Mattie Jane, and Sarah Ann.

At age five, Mattie accompanied her mother and siblings on a two-day flight to Illinois, where slave catchers overtook them. After a week in jail in St. Louis, Missouri, the family was again sold, this time to William Lewis, a hardhanded master. To spare her family a lashing, Ellen roasted Lewis's cowhide whip. She married George Brown, a foreman in a tobacco factory who fled to Canada, leaving his wife with her first family plus two more children. The younger boy died at age two, because the mistress required Ellen to keep him in a box so that he would not distract the slaves from their work, and his body withered from paralysis.

At the outbreak of the Civil War, 7,000 Union soldiers seized the 700 rebel soldiers of nearby Camp Jackson and imprisoned them. The Lewises became increasingly intrusive in the Jacksons' lives and beat them for no reason. Mattie escaped to the Union arsenal, where a Union general interceded with Lewis concerning the mistreatment of slaves. For subsequent abuse of Mattie, the general ordered Lewis to be flogged 100 times with a cowhide whip. In 1863, a new owner, Captain Tirrell, transported the family to Kentucky for sale. Mattie brought $900.

At her new home near Louisville, Kentucky, Mattie Jackson located operatives of the secret network of slave transporters, who set a plan in motion. With her wardrobe concealed under a hoop skirt, Mattie went to church, where an Underground Railroad agent met her and supplied a pass. Mattie proceeded to a ferry, which carried her to free territory. She settled in Indianapolis, Indiana, among Unionists who respected and educated her. Her mother escaped on her seventh try and joined Mattie in a move to St. Louis, Missouri. On the streets, the family often passed the Lewises, who resented having to wait upon themselves. In 1864, near the end of the Civil War, Mattie published an autobiography, *The Story of Mattie J. Jackson.*

See also: kidnap.

Source

Jackson, Mattie J. *The Story of Mattie J. Jackson.* Lawrence, KS: Sentinel, 1864.

Jackson, William (1783–1855) Jackson, Francis (1789–1861)

In the mid-1800s, William Jackson and his younger brother Francis maintained an Underground Railroad depot outside Boston, Massachusetts. Vocal abolitionists, they were sons of a Revolutionary War veteran and farmer, Major Timothy Jackson, one of the first settlers along the Charles River in Cambridge, Massachusetts. The brothers lived in a two-story residence at 527 Washington Street, in Newton, Massachusetts, which was also the site of William Jackson's candle and soap factory. At age 61, Francis Jackson, influenced by his friend the journalist and reformer William Lloyd Garrison, served the Boston Vigilance Committee as treasurer. Jackson published a report entitled *Treasurer's Accounts of the Boston Vigilance Committee Appointed at a Public Meeting at Faneuil Hall, October 21, 1850, to Assist Fugitive Slaves.*

The Jacksons were generous donors to the secret network. Beginning in 1809, their waystation offered shelter in a produce closet between two chimneys in the cellar. They received passengers from Sarah Rhea Higginson Bowditch and William Ingersoll Bowditch in Brookline and from Caroline Shoemaker Paxson and Dr. Jacob Longstreth Paxson, Quakers who concealed runaways in a secret compartment in their home in Norristown, Pennsylvania. William Jackson's daughter, author Ellen Dorinda Jackson (1825–1902), recorded in *Annals from the Old Homestead* (1840–1894) that Jacob Paxson tossed pebbles against their window late at night to announce an arrival. The Jackson women joined a local anti-slavery sewing circle that supplied winter clothing to adults and children on their way to cold climates. William often rode off in the night to transport refugees some 15 miles to the next safehouse on the way to Canada. The nearness of the Jackson house to the Worcester rail line facilitated hasty departures by train.

In Washington, D.C., Francis Jackson joined a secret network litigation team that included Salmon Portland Chase, Samuel Gridley Howe, Horace Mann, Robert Morris, and Samuel E. Sewall. The attorneys defended Daniel Drayton, captain of the sloop *Pearl,* who was arrested by authorities on April 15, 1848, for attempting one of the largest mass slave escapes in U.S. history. The defense achieved a reduction in prison time from 20 to 4 years. Francis Jackson's love of local history, cartography, and genealogy took shape in 1854 with publication of *History of the Early Settlement of Newton, County of Middlesex, Massachusetts, from 1639 to 1800* (1854). William's granddaughter, Louise Jackson Keith, preserved oral lore. The homestead is currently the Newton History Museum and a National Historic Site.

See also: Quakers; safehouses.

The Federal-style home of brothers William and Francis Jackson in Newton, Massachusetts, provided shelter to passengers in a basement produce closet. Today, it houses the Newton History Museum. *(Newton History Museum, Newton, Massachusetts)*

Sources

Jackson, Francis. *History of the Early Settlement of Newton, County of Middlesex, Massachusetts, from 1639 to 1800.* Boston: Stacy & Richardson, 1854.

Smedley, Robert C. *History of the Underground Railroad in Chester and the Neighboring Counties of Pennsylvania.* Lancaster, PA: Office of *The Journal,* 1883.

Jacobs, Harriet Ann (1813–1897)

Harriet Ann Jacobs fled sexual bondage and published a first-person narrative of a female slave's life on the run. A mulatto descendant of a South Carolina planter, she was born in Edenton, North Carolina, to Daniel Jacobs, a carpenter, and a breeder, Delilah Horniblow, the slave of Margaret Horniblow. An orphan at age six, Jacobs worked as a domestic six years before becoming the baby-sitter for Mary Matilda Norcom, the daughter of Dr. James Norcom and Mary Matilda Norcom. About this time, Jacobs's uncle, Benjamin Jacobs, successfully escaped to Baltimore on his second try. Womanhood brought fears to the light-skinned female in servitude to a lusty white male. At age 15, Harriet Jacobs eluded Norcom and became the kept woman of a white lawyer, U.S. Congressman Samuel Tredwell Sawyer, the father of Harriet's children, Joseph Jacobs (1829–?) and Louisa Matilda Jacobs (1833–?). To spare them from being sold at auction, Jacobs fled with them to the Carolina wetlands.

With the aid of Underground Railroad agents, Jacobs liberated herself in 1842. Her autobiography, *Incidents in the Life of a Slave Girl* (1861), published under the pseudonym Linda Brent, describes flight by water in 1835. Guided by Bishop Daniel Alexander Payne, Harriet hid with another runaway female on a ship and later took refuge in a swamp. In June, her owner took out a newspaper ad offering a reward of $100 for her return. At the house of her grandmother, Molly Horniblow, a freedwoman since 1825, Jacobs spent seven years in a rickety attic crawl space breathing stale, hot air and sleeping under an eave too low for her to sit or stand normally. After gaining passage to the Chesapeake Bay, with the aid of Cornelius Grinnell Willis, she made her way toward New York via a steamer to New Haven, Connecticut, and a train to Boston, Massachusetts. In 1844, she reunited in Boston with her children, whose father had bought their freedom. In 1849, Jacobs moved to Rochester, New York, where she made friends with William Cooper Nell, an assistant to Frederick Douglass in the publication of the *North Star.*

Passage of the Fugitive Slave Law of 1850 threatened Jacobs, who was working as a nursemaid for the Willis family in New Bedford, Massachusetts. In 1853, Willis paid $300 for Harriet's emancipation. After publishing her autobiography with the aid of two Underground Railroad agents, Lydia Maria Francis Child, editor of the *National Anti-Slavery Standard,* and Amy Kirby Post, a Quaker libertarian and the founder of the Western New York Anti-Slavery Society, Jacobs and her daughter returned to the South. At the beginning of the Civil War, they aided black soldiers and refugees in Alexandria, Virginia, and Savannah, Georgia. Jacobs's book became a classic and a favorite of Underground Railroad agents Hannah T. Haydock and Elizabeth J. Neall Gay.

See also: black soldiers; Fugitive Slave Law of 1850; *Incidents in the Life of a Slave Girl* (1861); *North Star.*

Sources

Driscoll, James, et al. *Angels of Deliverance: The Underground Railroad in Queens, Long Island, and Beyond.* Flushing, NY: Queens Historical Society, 1999.

Jacobs, Harriet A. *Incidents in the Life of a Slave Girl: Written by Herself.* New York: Harvest, 1983.

Levander, Caroline Field. *Voices of the Nation: Women and Public Speech in Nineteenth-Century American Literature and Culture.* Cambridge, UK: Cambridge University Press, 1998.

Jacobs, John (fl. 1840s–1860s)

John Jacobs, the brother of Harriet Jacobs, author of *Incidents in the Life of a Slave Girl* (1861), came from a family of runaways. After his owner took him to Washington, D.C., John began plotting an escape by sea. During a sojourn in New York City, he took a ship to Providence, Rhode Island, and made his way to New Bedford, Massachusetts. After a voyage on the whaler *Francis Henrietta,* he settled in Boston in February 1843 and became an abolitionist speaker and supporter of the Underground Railroad. His platform associate, Jonathan Walker, bore a brand on his palm for aiding seven slaves to flee Pensacola, Florida. Jacobs serialized his story in the magazine *Leisure Hour.*

See also: Incidents in the Life of a Slave Girl (1861).

Source

Jacobs, John, "A True Tale of Slavery," *Leisure Hour,* February 7–28, 1861.

James, Edwin (1791–1861)

A linguist, botanist, and geologist, Dr. Edwin James worked for abolition of slavery and the Underground Railroad. Born in Weybridge, Vermont, he earned degrees from Middlebury College and apprenticed in medicine. After assisting U.S. army surgeons on Major Stephen H. Long's expedition to the source of the Platte and Red rivers, he became the first white man to climb Pikes Peak. He studied the natural wonders of the Arkansas, Canadian, and Red rivers and edited the *Temperance Herald and Journal.* While working among the Potawatomi as an Indian subagent in Bellevue, Nebraska, he compiled grade-school spellers for use in Native American classrooms and translated the New Testament into Ojibwa. In 1836, he migrated west to Iowa, where he worked for the secret network in Burlington from age 47 until his death at the beginning of the Civil War after a fall from a stack of logs. During his association with Iowa agents Philip James in Denmark and William Maxon in Springdale, Dr. James received runaways at his home and concealed them in produce sacks, barrels, and baskets.

Source

Faux, Steven F., "Iowa's Underground Railroad Heroes," *Des Moines Register,* February 21, 1999.

James, Thomas (1804–1891)

The Reverend Thomas James, a former slave, served as an African Methodist Episcopal minister and a rescuer of runaways. James was born into bondage to Asa Kimball in Canajoharie, New York. Following the sale of his mother, brother, and sister, James passed to the ownership of a neighbor, Cromwell Bartlett and, within a few months, to farmer George H. Hess of Fort Plain in a trade involving a yoke of steers and a colt. In June 1821, James fled to Lockport, where a black agent pointed the way to Niagara and the ferry to Ontario. While working as a canal freighter, James gained an education and, in 1828, taught black children at a school on Favor Street. From his previous slave names Jim and Tom, he created his new name, Thomas James.

Influencing James's activism were Underground Railroad recruiters Frederick Douglass, Beriah Green, Gerrit Smith, and Alvan Stewart and Judge Ashley S. Sampson, an official in the African Colonization

Society. Boosting James's commitment was the story of a slave girl named Ellen who slit her throat after her recapture. After moving to Rochester in Monroe County, New York, in 1823, James joined William Clough Bloss in forming the Rochester Anti-Slavery Society and supporting Bloss's biweekly paper the *Rights of Man,* which James served as agent. After the congregation of his Favor Street Chapel dwindled, James co-founded the Rochester African Methodist Episcopal Zion Church at Ford and Spring streets and took over management of the congregation's waystation. His other network activities included aiding in the flight of Ellen Smith Craft and William Craft in December 1848 and in the jailbreak of Anthony Burns from an underground cell in the Boston courthouse on May 24, 1854. James abetted the seizure of a girl from a courtroom for immediate transport by carriage to Roxbury, Massachusetts, while three decoys departed in different directions. Complicit with James and other agents were black females armed with cayenne pepper to hurl into officers' eyes. During the rescue of a slave named Lucy in New Bedford, Massachusetts, James called on 20 supporters to protect her from recapture.

In 1861, James moved closer to the struggle for liberation when he aided Union officials in freeing slaves in the racially explosive atmosphere of Louisville, Kentucky. After locating an illicit slave pen holding 260 people, he ordered them freed and escorted them to his camp. At a hotel, he unlocked a room where a trader held nine black males. Upon gaining their liberty, the men joined the Union army. Another rescue involved the removal of a slave named Mary from the custody of a slave catcher, Bill Hurd. James dispatched Mary by train to freedom in Cincinnati, Ohio. James lost the use of his right hand while intervening between a rebel and the black women forced to cook for Confederate guerrillas. At age 82, James composed *Life of Rev. Thomas James, By Himself* (1886).

See also: African Methodist Episcopal Church; black soldiers.

Source

Barnes, Joseph W., ed. "The Autobiography of Rev. Thomas James." *Rochester History* 37:4 (October 1975).

Jamison, John (?–1863)

An Underground Railroad agent in eastern Ohio, Elder John Jamison joined fellow Scots-Irish settlers in rescuing runaway slaves. He and other pioneers established the Salt Creek Reformed Presbyterian Church. South of Norwich, Ohio, he farmed and operated a waystation of the Underground Railroad. His beliefs sanctioned civil disobedience by placing scriptural commands above federal law.

See also: civil disobedience.

Sources

Biographical and Historical Memoirs of Muskingum County, Ohio. Columbus, OH: Goodspeed, 1892.

Porter, Lorle. *A People Set Apart: The Scotch-Irish in Eastern Ohio.* Zanesville, OH: New Concord, 1998.

Jay (Allen) Family

One of many youngsters involved in Underground Railroad exploits, Allen Jay (1831–1910) began his rescue work at age 11 at the family farm in Mill Creek, in Miami County, Ohio. The son of Quaker pioneers Isaac Jay (1811–1880) and Rhoda Cooper Jay (1813–1894), Allen grew up in a family of anti-slavery activists. He took his mother's place at receiving fugitives while she recovered from illness. Allen was the lookout for Henry James, an armed escapee whom Allen guided from a peach orchard to a walnut tree in the middle of a cornfield. Rhoda Jay provided James with a meal of bacon, corn bread, and milk. That night, the boy continued the relay by concealing the slave in a wagon under a load of straw. Allen drove to the home of his grandparents Mary Macy Jay (1787–1868) and Walter Jay (1786–1865) and his uncle Levi Jay (1828–1884), the next stationmasters on the secret network. In adulthood, Allen Jay became a Quaker minister and taught in Marion, Indiana.

Source

Hinshaw, William Wade. *Encyclopedia of American Quaker Genealogy.* Ann Arbor, MI: Edwards Brothers, 1936.

Jay, John, Jr. (1817–1894)
Jay, William, Jr. (1841–1915)

Judge John Jay, Jr., and his son, William Jay, Jr., contributed to the New York–Canada route of the Underground Railroad. Judge Jay furthered the libertarian principles of his grandfather, John Jay, the first chief justice of the Supreme Court, who established the New York Manumission Society. Unlike Judge Jay's father—abolitionist pamphleteer William Jay, Sr.—the third in the dynasty chose direct action against the flesh trade by joining the American Anti-Slavery

Society. In the 1830s, David Ruggles, Isaac Tatem Hopper, and Sarah Tatum Hopper forwarded refugees from New York City to John Jay, Jr., in Katonah, in Westchester County, New York, and to Joseph Pierce in Pleasantville. When William Jay, Jr., enrolled at Columbia University, he continued the family's abolitionist tradition by harboring slaves and passing them along the secret network. During the Civil War, he rose to the rank of lieutenant colonel. The Jay homestead is a New York State Historic Site.

See also: American Anti-Slavery Society.

Source

Finkelman, Paul. *Slavery and the Founders: Race and Liberty in the Age of Jefferson.* Armonk, NY: M.E. Sharpe, 2001.

Jay, William (1789–1858)

The son of patriot John Jay, Judge William Jay, Sr., was an abolitionist pamphleteer and an activist of the Underground Railroad. He feared that the conflict over slavery might be the breaking point of constitutional law. At age 40, he inherited his parents' farm and two-story home in Bedford, in Westchester County, New York, which became a waystation. He supported the New York Manumission Society and, in 1833, coformed the New York City Anti-Slavery Society. Despite the pro-slavery sentiment of his neighbors, Jay aided runaway slaves in accordance with his Episcopalian beliefs. Assisting his efforts were Quaker conductors in Pleasantville, New York. In 1860, he noted that advertisements for mulatto fugitives stressed how many were virtually white from the interbreeding of masters with slaves.

Source

"The Underground Railroad and Those Who Operated It," *Springfield (OH) Republican,* March 11, 1900.

Jenkins, David (1811–1877)

Black journalist David Jenkins of Lynchburg, Virginia, served the Underground Railroad as an agent. At 26, he relocated to Columbus, Ohio, where he attended regular sessions of the state legislature. With the help of the free black community, in 1842, Jenkins and educator Charles Henry Langston launched an abolitionist weekly, *Palladium of Liberty.* For a motto, he chose the words "We hold these truths to be self-evident, that all men are created free and equal." Jenkins's editorial in the February 21, 1844, issue scolded people who professed to be abolitionists but who made no effort to help fugitive slaves. The following April, he rejoiced over the liberation of slaves from a Baltimore slave schooner, and he covered the death of a runaway named Mary in Plaquemines Parish, Louisiana, after she was shot by a posse led by her owner, Joseph Schlatre.

Jenkins offered advice to operatives of the secret network. On May 15 and again on June 5, 1844, he addressed the dangers of slave rescues in Columbus and warned Underground Railroad agents of slave catchers in the area. After his newspaper failed in 1844, Jenkins gave up journalism and taught school in Canton, Mississippi, where he also entered politics and was elected to the state legislature. During the Civil War, he recruited men for the 127th Ohio Infantry. After the war, he managed a Mississippi branch of the Freedmen's Bureau.

Source

Jenkins, David. "Abolitionist But." *Palladium of Liberty* 1:4 (February 1844): 3.

Jenkins, Mary Saltmarsh Farnham (1795–1891)

Jenkins, William (1795–1878)

Operatives of the Underground Railroad, Mary "Polly" Saltmarsh Farnham Jenkins and her husband, William Jenkins, conspired with transporters who completed the Boston–Canada route. A farmer and sawyer, William Jenkins built a lumber mill on his property in the cape district of Andover, Massachusetts. From the 1830s until the Emancipation Proclamation on January 1, 1863, the Jenkins family harbored slaves in their farmhouse at 89 Jenkins Road. Slaves hid from posses in a niche under the attic floor alongside the chimney. In times of danger, tunnels around the residence offered exits to the surrounding woods. One feeble refugee named Mr. Brown lived in a cottage on the Jenkins farm until his death.

Polly and William Jenkins attended anti-slavery rallies in Boston, Lynn, and Worcester, Massachusetts, and followed the principles of William Lloyd Garrison's abolitionist weekly, *The Liberator.* Frequent guests at the Jenkins home were former Virginia fugitive George W. Latimer and Harriet Beecher Stowe, author of *Uncle Tom's Cabin* (1852). When Garrison and Frederick Douglass visited the Jenkins family, the two orators shared a bed. The Jenkins farm is listed on the National Register of Historic Places.

See also: Liberator, The; Uncle Tom's Cabin; or, Life Among the Lowly (1852).

Source

Chadwick, Bruce. *Traveling the Underground Railroad: A Visitor's Guide to More Than 300 Sites.* Secaucus, NJ: Citadel, 1999.

Jewett, George Anson (1847–ca. 1930)

George Anson Jewett became an agent of the Underground Railroad in boyhood. A native of Red Rock, in Marion County, Iowa, and a member of the Church of Christ, he was the son of George Enoch Jewett and Patty Maria Matthews Jewett and the grandson of David Jewett, a pioneer who settled in Lake Prairie, Iowa, in 1843. As a wagoneer for the secret network, he conveyed runaways along the route to Canada. Contributing to the family's activism was his maternal uncle, farmer George Reynolds. George Jewett attempted unsuccessfully to enlist in the Union army at age 14. In 1862, he donated a plaque to his alma mater honoring the Civil War dead, which included his older brother, Captain Homer Harris Jewett.

Source

Iowa: Its History and Its Foremost Citizens. Des Moines: S.J. Clarke, 1916.

Jocelyn, Nathaniel (1796–1881)
Jocelyn, Simeon Smith (1799–1879)

Two Underground Railroad agents from New Haven, Connecticut, Deacon Nathaniel Jocelyn and his younger brother, the Reverend Simeon Smith Jocelyn, supported the *Amistad* mutineers during months of litigation. Simeon, a graduate of Yale University, became pastor of the Dixwell Avenue Congregational Church. In collaboration with agent Lewis Tappan, the Reverend Samuel William Southmayd Dutton, and the Reverend Joshua Leavitt, editor of the *Emancipator,* Simeon formed the Amistad Committee, which donated funds to assist the survivors of the original 54 slaves from Sierra Leone who seized the Portuguese slaver *Amistad* on July 2, 1839. The committee also hired Judge Roger Sherman Baldwin to defend the mutineers. Around 1840, Robert Purvis hired Nathaniel Jocelyn to paint an oil portrait of Joseph Cinqué, leader of the mutineers, which hangs in the New Haven Colony Historical Society headquarters.

See also: Amistad; Fugitive Slave Law of 1850.

Source

Jones, Howard. *Mutiny on the* Amistad. Oxford, UK: Oxford University Press, 1987.

Johns, Robert (fl. 1850s)
Johns, Sue Ann (1835–?)

A Maryland slave couple, Robert Johns and 23-year-old Sue Ann Johns escaped through Pennsylvania to freedom. In 1858, the two left bondage to farmer William Cassey and Susan Flinthrew in Cecil County, Maryland. In Philadelphia, Robert and Sue Ann accepted assistance from Underground Railroad agents.

Source

Still, William. *The Underground Railroad.* Philadelphia: Porter & Coates, 1871.

Johnson, Abraham (fl. 1840s–1850s)

In his youth, Abraham Johnson belonged to a slave owner named Wheeler in Cecil County, Maryland. In the mid-1840s, rumor of an impending slave sale forced Johnson to take his mother, his sister, and his sister's child to the ferry site of Robert Loney, an Underground Railroad transporter on the Susquehanna River below Columbia, Pennsylvania. The Johnson family passed to agent William Wright and on to Elizabeth W. Moore and Jeremiah Moore in Christiana, Pennsylvania. Johnson found work with the Moores, his mother with Deborah T. Simmons Coates and Lindley Coates in Caln, and his sister with Susan P. Johnson Bonsall and Thomas Bonsall in Wagontown. After unfavorable publicity following the Christiana Riot on September 11, 1851, the Johnson family sought refuge in Canada. On the way, they received aid from two Underground Railroad agents, Levi and Sarah Pownall, who packed a pillowcase with food to sustain the refugees on the way.

Source

Smedley, Robert C. *History of the Underground Railroad in Chester and the Neighboring Counties of Pennsylvania.* Lancaster, PA: Office of *The Journal,* 1883.

Johnson, Ann (ca. 1833–?)

Ann Johnson was a 24-year-old slave in Maryland when she chose to flee bondage and travel with a party of eight to Canada. In 1857, her master, Samuel Harrington of Cambridge, Maryland, sold her as punishment for her brother's escape. William Moore, a hard drinker and carouser, bought Ann Johnson at auction. With Lavina Woolfley and six other escapees, Ann Johnson walked to Dover, Delaware. After being captured, they fought their way out of the Dover jail and split up to make their way to Philadelphia, Pennsylvania. The city's vigilance committee helped both women cross the Canadian border, where Woolfley reunited with her husband, James.

See also: punishments; vigilance committees.

Source

Williams, James. *Life and Adventures of James Williams, a Fugitive Slave.* San Francisco: Women's Union Print, 1873.

Johnson, Benjamin (fl. 1850s)

Benjamin Johnson, a black transporter, conducted fugitives on the final push to Canada from a dangerous starting point on the Pennsylvania–Toronto route. He received passengers from Thomas Hopkins in Downingtown, from Edwin H. Coates and Michael Meyers in Coatesville, and from Joseph Fulton and his daughter, Mary Ann Fulton, in Sadsbury. Johnson led slaves to the railroad depot in Bridgetown and accompanied them to Toronto, Ontario.

Source

Smedley, Robert C. *History of the Underground Railroad in Chester and the Neighboring Counties of Pennsylvania.* Lancaster, PA: Office of *The Journal,* 1883.

Johnson, Eliza Jane (1805–?)

A member of the Ripley, Ohio, Anti-Slavery Society, Eliza Jane Johnson, wife of Gabriel Johnson and mother of their five children, was a victim of kidnap. Eliza was enslaved in New Orleans until around 1834, when she escaped on the *Tuscarora,* a packet plying the Mississippi River from Louisiana to Cincinnati, Ohio. On September 22, 1837, a Kentucky slave owner, James Fox, seized Eliza from her home. In close pursuit were rescuers Adam Lowry Rankin of Ripley, James Huggins of Clay, and John Bennington Mahan of nearby Sardinia, all Underground Railroad agents.

After authorities lodged Eliza in a dirt-floored cell in Mason County, Kentucky, the *Cincinnati Journal and Luminary* reported the abduction. Although the Fox family admitted that their agents had misidentified the woman, Eliza was detained in jail, and Rankin and the anti-slavery society of Ripley protested her unlawful incarceration to the governor. Judge Walker Reid refused to release her, but the Ohio Anti-Slavery Society gained her freedom on March 12, 1838.

See also: kidnap.

Source

Griffler, Keith P. *Front Line of Freedom: African Americans and the Forging of the Underground Railroad in the Ohio Valley.* Lexington: University Press of Kentucky, 2004.

Johnson, Henry (ca. 1776–1886)

Henry Johnson aided runaways passing through Oberlin, Ohio. At age 39, the chattel of Tennessee military hero Andrew Jackson, Johnson served in the artillery at the battle of New Orleans, Louisiana. After fleeing slavery in Nashville, Tennessee, around 1844, he made his way to Canada and then settled among abolitionists in Oberlin, where he found employment as a bricklayer and a groundskeeper. In old age, Johnson aided passengers of the Underground Railroad by engaging in plots to deceive slave hunters; he posed as a decoy in wagons departing the area while runaways fled by other means.

Source

Fairchild, James H. *Oberlin: The Colony and the College 1833–1883.* Oberlin, OH: E.J. Goodrich, 1883.

Johnson, Isaac (1812–?)

The last inmate incarcerated in Missouri for slave stealing, Isaac Johnson faced a decade in prison. In February 1862, at age 50, he entered the Missouri penitentiary in Jefferson City. He had served 2 years and 10 months of his term when Governor Willard Hall set him free in December 1864. Johnson had remained in a cell some 23 months after the national emancipation of slaves on January 1, 1863.

Source

Frazier, Harriet C. *Runaway and Freed Missouri Slaves and Those Who Helped Them, 1763–1865.* Jefferson, NC: McFarland, 2004.

Johnson, Jane (fl. 1850s)

The experience of slave and abolitionist lecturer Jane Johnson in Philadelphia attested to the destructive effect of the Fugitive Slave Law of 1850. On July 18, 1855, Colonel John Hill Wheeler, the U.S. ambassador to Nicaragua, conveyed three slaves, Jane Johnson and her two sons, Daniel and Isaiah, from his Hertford County, North Carolina, plantation to Philadelphia. Anguished at the sale of the children's brother, she protected her remaining family.

Before boarding the *Washington,* a passenger steamer bound for Central America, Wheeler's party left the South Broad Street train depot and visited artist Thomas Sully on Fifth Street. The group arrived at Bloodgood's Hotel on Walnut Street. While Wheeler ate lunch, he locked his slaves in a hotel room. Johnson informed a hotel domestic that she wanted to escape. Conductor William Still, a clerk at the Pennsylvania Anti-Slavery Society office, engaged attorney Passmore Williamson and other members of the Philadelphia Vigilance Committee to help in the rescue, which they completed before the boat's departure at 5 P.M. Still informed Johnson that, under Pennsylvania's Personal Liberty Law of 1847, they were no longer slaves.

The release of Daniel, Isaiah, and Jane Johnson from bondage involved a heated confrontation at the ferry landing between Wheeler and Still, Williamson, and five stevedores, John Ballard, James P. Braddock, William Curtis, James Martin, and Isaac Moore. After the trio passed through Still's Philadelphia waystation in Ronaldson's Court on the way to New York and Boston, authorities arrested Still, Williamson, and the five dockworkers for slave thievery, assault, and riot. Escorted by conductor Lucretia Coffin Mott and the Reverend James Miller McKim, Jane Johnson returned to Philadelphia on August 29 to testify that she left Wheeler of her own free will. In October 1855, black stationkeeper and historian William Cooper Nell found a job for Jane in Boston. After telling her story at abolitionist assemblies, she resided at Southack Court and married Lawrence Woodford.

See also: Pennsylvania Anti-Slavery Society; vigilance committees.

Sources

Bacon, Benjamin C. *Statistics of the Colored People of Philadelphia.* Philadelphia: T. Ellwood Chapman, 1856.

Hildreth, Richard. *Atrocious Judges.* New York: Miller, Orton & Mulligan, 1856.

Johnson, John (1821–1862)

A black agent of the Underground Railroad, John Johnson died in prison. In April 1861, at age 40, he began a five-year sentence in the Missouri state penitentiary in Jefferson City for receiving runaways. He died less than a year later, on February 10, 1862. His keepers made no notation of the cause of death.

Source

Frazier, Harriet C. *Runaway and Freed Missouri Slaves and Those Who Helped Them, 1763–1865.* Jefferson, NC: McFarland, 2004.

Johnson, John (1829–1850)

One of a number of Underground Railroad agents who died in prison, John Johnson suffered for his civil disobedience to federal law. At age 20, he began a two-year confinement in the Missouri state penitentiary in Jefferson City. Cholera killed him in August 1850.

Source

Frazier, Harriet C. *Runaway and Freed Missouri Slaves and Those Who Helped Them, 1763–1865.* Jefferson, NC: McFarland, 2004.

Johnson, John Lewis (1818–1900)

A Philadelphia-born proponent of the Underground Railroad, Dr. John Lewis Johnson served anti-slavery forces during the Civil War. He grew up in Virginia and, at age 23, settled in Forsyth County, North Carolina. After medical studies in Lexington, North Carolina, and Philadelphia, he returned to North Carolina in 1855 to sell pharmaceuticals. Johnson served the Confederate army as a field surgeon of the Forty-eighth North Carolina Regiment. After his capture at the battle of Fredericksburg, he remained in a Union prison until his parole on September 22, 1862. Upon return to civilian life in 1863, he founded the Heroes of America, a secret society supporting the Union and the abolition of slavery. With aid from its members, black refugees followed the secret network west through Wilkes County and over the Blue Ridge Mountains to Tennessee. Others moved directly north from the Carolina Quaker Belt, from mid-state west through Virginia's Shenandoah Valley to West Virginia, Kentucky, Indiana, and Ohio.

Source

Auman, William T., and David D. Scarboro. "The Heroes of America in Civil War North Carolina." *North Carolina Historical Review* 58:4 (October 1981): 327–63.

Johnson, Levi (1828–?)

A mulatto runaway aided by Underground Railroad agents, Levi Johnson found supporters in Daniel Gibbons and Hannah Wierman Gibbons. Johnson was born Nelson Hilliard, a slave to Judge W. Brokenborough in Hanover County, Virginia. At age 11, he passed to the ownership of Edward Colston and learned table service in Berkeley County, Virginia, near Martinsburg. In fall 1847, he fled to Shippensburg and found work at the farm of John Whitehill near Maytown,

Pennsylvania. On March 14, 1848, he made his way to the Gibbons' stop in Bird-in-Hand, Pennsylvania. As a safety measure, the family renamed him Levi Johnson. He worked for Daniel and his son, Joseph, outside Christiana, Pennsylvania. During the Civil War, Johnson was a wagoneer for the Union army and an infantryman in the Forty-second Colored Regiment.

Source

Gibbons, Phebe Earle. *Pennsylvania Dutch & Other Essays.* Philadelphia: J.B. Lippincott, 1882.

Johnson, Moses (?–1873)

Around 1832, Moses Johnson escaped north with Green Staunton before being apprehended by slave hunters in Frederick, Maryland. During the night, the two escapees chipped their way out of their cell with pocketknives and begged help from Staunton's father, a white planter and slave owner. Staunton sent the two via Underground Railroad to Lancaster County, Pennsylvania, to the station of Daniel Gibbons and Hannah Wierman Gibbons in Bird-in-Hand. The two runaways parted, with Johnson going to agent Allen Smith and Staunton going to George Webster and Thomas Jackson. In spring 1836, Johnson was working at Henry Bushong's farm when slave catchers seized Staunton. Abolitionists raised $400 to buy off the posse and free Staunton. Johnson reimbursed his friends and made enough money to buy a farm.

Source

Quarles, Benjamin. *Black Abolitionists.* New York: Oxford University Press, 1969.

Johnson, Nathan (ca. 1795–1880)
Johnson, Mary J. Mingo Durfree (ca. 1785–1871)

Abolitionist Nathan Johnson was a transporter of slaves through New Bedford, Massachusetts. From 1822, he and his wife, Mary J. Mingo Durfree "Polly" Johnson, maintained a reception center for runaways arriving by sea at their three-story home at 21 Seventh and Spring streets. Nathan developed strong ties to the black community and gained insight into abolitionism from a speech delivered by the Reverend Samuel Joseph May in 1835. Nathan scanned the local harbor for likely vessels for transporting fugitives to depots in Portland, Maine, and Halifax, Nova Scotia.

In September 1838, the Johnsons aided Frederick Bailey and his wife, Anna Murray Bailey, on their flight from Maryland through David Ruggles's waystation in New York City. Relaying them to the Johnson homes were Quaker transporters Joseph Ricketson and William C. Taber. The Johnsons offered the Baileys free board and the use of a saw and sawhorse during a three-year stay. At Johnson's suggestion, for the sake of safety, Frederick Bailey changed his name to Frederick Douglass after a character in Sir Walter Scott's romance *The Lady of the Lake.* In 1841, Nathan Johnson began a two-year term of office as manager of the American Anti-Slavery Society. The Johnson home, which is listed as a National Historic Landmark, houses the New Bedford Historical Society.

See also: abolitionism; American Anti-Slavery Society.

Source

Grover, Kathryn. *The Fugitive's Gibraltar: Escaping Slaves and Abolitionism in New Bedford, Massachusetts.* Amherst: University of Massachusetts Press, 2001.

Johnson, Oliver (1809–1889)
Johnson, Leonard (1797–1890)

A printer and fill-in editor for William Lloyd Garrison's weekly newspaper *The Liberator* and a volunteer at the anti-slavery office in New York City, Oliver Johnson of Peacham, Vermont, operated a safe haven for fugitive slaves. He partnered with his older brother, Leonard Johnson, a farmer and carpenter, who ran a depot at his home on Danville Road. The brothers plotted safe routes through Vermont and likely Canadian settlements in which runaways could thrive. Oliver was a founding member of the Quaker radicals from Longwood Meeting in Kennett Square, Pennsylvania, and a colleague of agent William C. Griffith.

In 1832, Oliver Johnson and 11 other abolitionists established the New England Anti-Slavery Society. He became a follower of William Lloyd Garrison, a young orator and writer discovered by the Reverend Samuel Joseph May and his cousin, attorney Samuel Edmund Sewall. Oliver edited the *Anti-Slavery Bugle,* which flourished under the motto "No Union with Slaveholders." In addition to his writings for the *National Anti-Slavery Standard,* the *New York Independent,* and the *New York Tribune* and his printed broadsides advertising the Massachusetts Anti-Slavery Fairs, Johnson aided Harriet Tubman in transporting endangered cargo.

In his twenties, Oliver Johnson, a well-connected route manager, depended on ties to station operatives Charles Callistus Burleigh, Daniel Howell Hise, Isaac Tatem Hopper and Sarah Tatum Hopper, Charles Marriott and Sarah White Marriott, James Mott, Jr., and Lucretia Coffin Mott, and William Cooper Nell. Johnson concerned himself with the safety of Joe, a 28-year-old Maryland runaway worth $2,000 to his owner. To thwart pursuers, Johnson suggested sending Joe to Ontario by train, a passage that quickly moved Joe out of the grasp of slave stalkers. On January 27, 1837, Johnson coordinated routes with Quaker agents Rachel Gilpin Robinson and Rowland Thomas Robinson at Rokeby sheep farm in Ferrisburg, Vermont, to rescue Simon, who was skilled at farming and wagoneering.

At age 32, Oliver Johnson began a two-year term on the executive committee of the American Anti-Slavery Society. In 1862, he joined agents William Barnard, Thomas Garrett, Alice Eliza Betts Hambleton, and Dinah H. Mendenhall in petitioning President Abraham Lincoln to emancipate slaves, an act that Lincoln completed on January 1, 1863. At age 80, in an address to the Congregational Club in Brooklyn, New York, Johnson acknowledged that his work for the *Anti-Slavery Standard* and the *New York Independent* helped to mold popular opinion against slavery and to chastise Protestant ministers for failing to support the Underground Railroad.

See also: American Anti-Slavery Society; anti-slavery fairs; routes, Underground Railroad.

Sources

Raffo, Steven M. *A Biography of Oliver Johnson, Abolitionist and Reformer, 1809–1889.* Lewiston, NY: Edwin Mellen, 2002.

"Rev. Dr. Storrs' Talk Before the Congregational Club," *Brooklyn (NY) Eagle*, April 23, 1889.

Johnson, Perry (1825–?)

In search of liberty, 28-year-old Perry Johnson escaped bondage and fled north from Elkton, Maryland, to Pennsylvania. In November 1853, his owner, Charles Johnson of Cecil County, flogged him for overturning a load of fodder. Johnson had already lost one eye to the mistress's lash. Crossing the Mason-Dixon line, Perry made his way to Philadelphia to seek the assistance of the Underground Railroad. Agents treated his immediate needs and sent him north.

Source

Still, William. *The Underground Railroad.* Philadelphia: Porter & Coates, 1871.

Johnson, Samuel (fl. 1850s)
Johnson, Israel (fl. 1820s–1830s)
Johnson, Jennet Rowland (fl. 1820s–1830s)
Johnson, Rowland (fl. 1820s–1830s)

Samuel Johnson, a Dutch Quaker abolitionist and friend of agent William Still, operated a stop of the Underground Railroad in Philadelphia County, Pennsylvania. His two-story stone homestead at 6306 Germantown Avenue and Washington Lane, constructed in 1768, had withstood the battle of Germantown in the Revolutionary War. In the 1850s, Johnson opened his residence as a waystation to aid fugitives in their journeys to New York and Ontario. Passengers, some conducted by Harriet Tubman, entered the residence via a rear stairway and hid in the attic. The residence is now a museum and a National Historic Landmark.

Brothers Israel and Rowland Johnson, who lived next door to the homestead, contributed to the reputation of the Johnson family through their association with agents James Mott, Jr., and Lucretia Coffin Mott. In alliance with Enoch Lewis in New Garden and with Thomas M'Clintock, in 1827, Israel chaired the Free Produce Society, which boycotted cotton, indigo, molasses, rice, rum, sugar, tea, tobacco, and other slave-harvested or slave-made goods. His wife, Jennet Rowland Johnson, superintended the feeding, clothing, and concealment of fugitives in the attic and outbuildings.

Source

Clark, Vernon, "Germantown Ave. from Top to Bottom," *Philadelphia Inquirer,* July 25, 2005.

Johnson, William Henry (1811–1896)

A fugitive from bondage, William Henry Johnson received aid from the Underground Railroad. He was born on a plantation in Richmond, Virginia, and fled to sea with his mother on the schooner *Tantovy.* Hidden by abolitionist sailors in a load of flour, William intended to reach freedom in New York harbor. When a storm crippled the ship off Sandy Hook, New Jersey, the stowaways washed overboard. Rescued by British mariners, the two made their way to Jamaica, Long Island. Under the protection of philanthropist John Jacob Astor, William remained safe until a stalker traced him to Astor House, where Johnson washed dishes. The bounty hunter returned Johnson to slavery.

On a second dash toward liberty, in 1833, Johnson sailed on the *Rodman* to New Bedford, Massachusetts. While working on the wharves as a stevedore, he taught himself to read and studied law with attorneys Timothy G. Coffin and Francis L. Porter. In May 1840, Johnson joined the American Anti-Slavery Society in New York City and toured with pamphleteer David Ruggles as an anti-slavery orator. In New Bedford, Johnson and Dr. Thomas Bayne formed a vigilant aid society to rescue runaway slaves. By age 48, Johnson was making speeches denouncing human bondage. He practiced law in Massachusetts, New Hampshire, New York, and Rhode Island. During the Civil War, he supported the formation of the Seventy-fourth Massachusetts Infantry.

See also: American Anti-Slavery Society.

Source

Smith, J. Clay. *Emancipation: The Making of the Black Lawyer, 1844–1944.* Philadelphia: University of Pennsylvania Press, 1993.

Johnson, William Henry (1833–1918)

An abolitionist journalist and an assistant to Underground Railroad superintendent Stephen Myers, William Henry Johnson supported the flight of slaves through Pennsylvania. He was born free outside Alexandria, Virginia, and departed for Philadelphia at age 12 to become a hairdresser. In his late teens, he dedicated himself to the aid of slaves seeking liberty on the secret route through Albany, New York. At age 22, he returned to Philadelphia to write and lecture for the Banneker Literary Institute. His slave rescues involved collaboration with Benjamin Price and Jane Paxson Price in East Bradford, Pennsylvania, and with Jonathan Paxson Magill and his sons, Edward Hicks Magill and Watson P. Magill, at Solebury, in Bucks County, Pennsylvania.

In 1859, to avoid arrest for sheltering slaves, Johnson fled the city and settled in Norwich, Connecticut. At the outbreak of the Civil War, he recruited volunteers for the Union army's black regiments and served the Boston newspaper the *Pine and Palm* as war correspondent. As a soldier with the Connecticut volunteers, he fought in the battle of Bull Run. After the war, he directed his activism to civil rights and to antidiscrimination legislation. In 1900, he published *Autobiography of Dr. William Henry Johnson,* which contains his speeches and letters to abolitionist journals, the names of conductors of the secret network, and his observations of former slaves fighting for the Union army.

Sources

Grover, Kathryn. *The Fugitive's Gibraltar: Escaping Slaves and Abolitionism in New Bedford, Massachusetts.* Amherst: University of Massachusetts Press, 2001.

Johnson, William Henry. *Autobiography of Dr. William Henry Johnson, Respectfully Dedicated to His Adopted Home, the Capital City of the Empire State.* Albany, NY: Argus, 1900.

Jones, Augustine (1834–1925)

An orthodox Quaker historian and stationkeeper at an undiscovered location in Maine, Augustine Jones documented Underground Railroad rescues in a journal. He attended school outside China, Maine. At age 17, he relocated to Providence, Rhode Island. He was a graduate of Bowdoin College and of Harvard Law School. While he served as principal of the Moses Brown School, a Quaker boarding academy in Providence, he received pressure from Elizabeth Buffum Chace to support libertarian ideals. Editor John Greenleaf Whittier praised Jones for summarizing the social ethics of Quakers. Jones completed his autobiography in 1911.

See also: Quakers.

Source

Fuller, Frank E., ed. *Shadows of the Elms.* Providence, RI: Moses Brown School, 1983.

Jones, Benjamin (ca. 1800–1875)

The Reverend Benjamin Jones, a former slave living near Little York, Maryland, coordinated his ministry with his rescue of runaway slaves. Called Big Ben for his large frame, Jones ran away with four others to escape the auction block. Operatives of the Underground Railroad enabled the men to reach the caves of Buckingham Mountain. Jones found work with Thomas Bye, Jonathan Fell, and William Stavely. At Mount Gilead African Methodist Episcopal Church in New Hope, in Bucks County, Pennsylvania, from 1826, Jones preached and supervised the secret route over the Delaware River to New Jersey. In 1837, five bounty hunters seized Jones at John Kitchen's farm in Solebury and returned him to his master, William Anderson, in Baltimore, Maryland. White agents Jonathan Bonham and George Chapman collected $700 to pay for Jones's manumission. Because of injuries inflicted by his master, Jones was an invalid and ward of the county for the rest of his life.

See also: African Methodist Episcopal Church.

Source

Davis, W.W.H. *The History of Bucks County, Pennsylvania.* Doylestown, PA: Democrat Book and Job Office, 1876.

Jones, John (1816–1879) Jones, Mary Jane Richardson (1819–1910)

A prosperous tailor and real estate agent in Chicago, John Jones of Greene County, North Carolina, managed a waystation of the Underground Railroad. He was the freeborn child of a black woman and a German man named Bromfield. Jones married suffragist Mary Jane Richardson, the daughter of a free blacksmith in Memphis, Tennessee. In league with abolitionists Dr. Charles Volney Dyer and Louisa Maria Gifford Dyer, attorney Lemuel Covell Paine Freer, the Reverend Byrd Parker, black activist Henry O. Wagoner, and detective Allan Pinkerton, Jones and his wife began harboring fugitives in 1845. At their Chicago residence at 119 Dearborn Street, the couple concealed runaways in the cellar and also hosted secret network operatives John Brown and Frederick Douglass. After Brown raided two Missouri plantations on December 20 and 21, 1858, he arrived in Chicago with 11 slaves and an infant who was born to the Daniels family on January 24, 1859, at the safehouse of Emily Jane Hunt Grover and Joel Grover. The Joneses received Brown and his men at their home while Henry O. Wagoner harbored and fed the group.

Self-educated in law, Jones aided abolitionists in a fight to repeal the Illinois Black Laws, which granted voting rights only to white citizens and required blacks to produce documents proving that they were free. In 1864, Jones and Joseph Medill, publisher of the *Chicago Tribune,* issued a pamphlet, *The Black Laws of Illinois and a Few Reasons Why They Could Be Repealed,* which refuted the laws issue by issue. The following year, the Illinois legislature rescinded the codes. Jones was appointed to the school board, and when he won election as a county commissioner, he became the first black elected to an office in the United States.

Sources

"Funeral of John Jones," *Chicago Tribune,* May 24, 1879.
Jones, John. *The Black Laws of Illinois and a Few Reasons Why They Could Be Repealed.* Chicago: *Chicago Tribune,* 1864.

Jones, John Albert (1806–?) Jones, Ann Marie Shipp Major (1820–?)

An attorney in Tremont, in Tazewell County, Illinois, John Albert Jones facilitated relays of passengers on the Underground Railroad. He was born in Washington, D.C., and married Ann Marie Shipp Major in 1840. From 1845, the Jones family lived at 412 East South Street in a two-story brick residence, a frequent stopping place for Abraham Lincoln when he was an itinerant attorney. Runaways hid beneath a trapdoor under a bedroom carpet. John M. Roberts, a transporter, completed the links to Uriah H. Crosby in Morton. From the Crosby safehouse, refugees hurried on to the Kern safehouse nine miles away and then north to a Quaker settlement.

Source

Staker, Joseph Peter. *Amish Mennonites in Tazewell County, Illinois.* Silverdale, WA: privately published, 2004.

Jones, John C. (1817–1893) Jones, Sarah A. (?–1887)

Two members of the Columbus, Ohio, underground network, John C. Jones of eastern Tennessee and Sarah A. Jones of Richmond, Virginia, supported an end to human bondage. Before the Civil War, the couple championed abolitionism and aided blacks seeking freedom in the North. John Jones debated issues of freedom and humanity and supported anti-slavery legislation.

See also: abolitionism.

Source

Taylor, William Alexander. *Centennial History of Columbus and Franklin County, Ohio.* Chicago: S.J. Clarke, 1909.

Jones, John Tecumseh (1808–1873)

Native American chief John Tecumseh "Ottawa" Jones contributed to the rescues of Missouri blacks from enslavement. The son of a Chippewa mother and an English father, he grew up multilingual and self-reliant in Mackinac, Canada. He studied at a Baptist mission in Carey Station, Michigan, and at Hamilton College in New York. After working as a teacher and interpreter for the Potawatomi, he joined the Ottawa nation and managed a hotel in Ottawa, Kansas. With a confederate, Baptiste Peoria, Jones guided Missouri slaves out of bondage. For Jones's humanitarianism, pro-slavers shot at him and, in 1858, burned his home and store. Jones offered his safehouse to John Brown and his militia and supported preparations for the raid on Harpers Ferry, Virginia.

Source

Hinton, Richard Josiah. *John Brown and His Men: With Some Account of the Roads They Travelled to Reach Harpers Ferry.* New York: Funk & Wagnalls, ca. 1894.

Jones, John W. (1817–1900)
Jones, Rachel Swailes (fl. 1850s)

A former fugitive, John W. Jones superintended the crucial route between Philadelphia and St. Catharines, Ontario. Born in Leesburg, in Loudoun County, Virginia, he was a houseboy and gardener on the plantation of Sally Elzy (or Ellzey), who owned his parents and grandmother. The grandmother described the flight of geese and pointed John toward liberty in the North. When Sally Elzy fell ill in May 1844, the Jones family feared for their future.

At 10 P.M. on June 3, 1844, at age 27, John Jones and his half brothers Charles and George and companions Jefferson Brown and Thomas Stewart armed themselves with pistols and knives and fled 300 miles to Chemung County, New York, leaving behind their mother and sisters. On the way, the five refugees battled mounted stalkers in Maryland. Sarah Boardman Smith found the runaways near the end of June in the haymow at South Creek Farm. She and her husband, Dr. Nathaniel Smith, sheltered the men in their barn and fed and tended them before they departed. Out of gratitude for his white rescuers, John placed flowers on Sarah Smith's grave weekly from her interment in 1884 until his death.

On July 5, 1844, the five escapees reached Elmira, New York, where John aided Seth Kelly in his candle shop and cut wood for Mrs. John Culp, a local stationmaster. Judge Arial Standish Thurston helped Jones gain an education while working as custodian at Miss Clara Thurston's girls' academy on Main Street. To aid other slaves, Jones worked closely with the Reverend Hiram K. Wilson and William Still, the network's chief organizer in Philadelphia. After returning to Virginia to retrieve two younger brothers, Jones settled with his wife, Rachel Swailes Jones, and his sons, James Edward Jones and John W. Jones, Jr., on 11 acres alongside Elmira's First Baptist Church in a one-story yellow frame house built from lumber recycled from a prison camp. In addition to farming, Jones worked as sexton of Woodlawn Cemetery and joined his wife in operating an Underground Railroad safehouse. Aiding the Joneses with clothing, food, and cash were the Reverend Thomas Kennicut Beecher; Simeon Benjamin; Jarvis Langdon, a coal and iron dealer; James M. Robinson; and William P. Yates, a jeweler. Sylvester G. Andrus, a lumberman, kept an eye to the road; Riggs Watrous, a hardware dealer on Water Street, saddled fresh mounts.

With the help of his brothers Charles and George and agents John T. Jones and Cornelius S. Croce, a fugitive from Frederick, Maryland, John W. and his family received up to 30 passengers at a time from Elijah Funk Pennypacker in Phoenixville, from Marcus F. Lucas in Bath, New York, and from agents in Harrisburg and Williamsport. In July 1845, the Jones family cared for 17 refugees in a single party. Through connections with staff of the Northern Central Railroad, after 1850, John Jones accessed a designated hideaway, the "freedom baggage car," for the 4 A.M. train from Philadelphia to Niagara Falls, New York, which passed through Watkins Glen and Canadaigua. Overland, he escorted his passengers personally to Charles G. Manley's station in Williamsport. In July 1851, the Elmira network received an alert from Jervis Langdon and saved 12 refugees from recapture in Big Flats.

By 1860, John Jones had rescued 860 slaves without losing a single passenger. In 1868, he visited the Elzy plantation and found the residence destroyed and his black family and friends departed or dead. He never located his sisters. In 1953, an Elmira housing project on Dickinson Street bore the name John W. Jones Court. At 1259 College Avenue in Elmira, the John W. Jones Museum preserves a legacy of succor to refugees.

Sources

"Death of a Prominent Colored Citizen," *Elmira Daily Gazette and Free Press,* December 17, 1900.

Mutunhu, Tendal. "John W. Jones: Underground Railroad Stationmaster." *Negro History Bulletin* 41 (March 1978): 814–18.

Ramsdell, Barbara S. "A History of John W. Jones." *Crooked Lake Review* (Fall 2002; Winter 2003).

Jones, Rhoda (1839–1933)

A passenger who followed the Underground Railroad route to Ripley, Ohio, Rhoda Jones became a rescuer of slaves. After making her way across the Ohio River to freedom, she began conducting runaways in collusion with Jean Lowry Rankin and John Rankin at Liberty Hill, in Ripley, and with Dr. Alexander Campbell,

James Collins, Theodore Collins, and Thomas Wilson Collins. Aunt Rhoda, as she was known, lived to be the oldest citizen of Africa Hill, a community of former slaves living on a knoll overlooking the city. Ripley citizens dedicated a landing monument to honor Jones and other heroes of the secret network, including Uncle Billy Marshall, a river conductor.

Source

Hagedorn, Ann. *Beyond the River: The Untold Story of the Heroes of the Underground Railroad.* New York: Simon & Schuster, 2002.

Jones, Thomas H. (1806–1890)

With the aid of Underground Railroad agents, the Reverend Thomas H. Jones retrieved his family from slavery. In August 1849, he slipped away from bondage in Wilmington, North Carolina, and stowed away on the brig *Bell.* In New York, he reunited with his wife, Mary R. Moore Jones, and her three children, whom he sent ahead to Brooklyn. In 1854, he published *The Experience of Thomas H. Jones, Who Was a Slave for Forty-Three Years.* Jones pastored a Methodist assembly in Salem, Massachusetts. While living at 191 Nonotuck Street in Florence, Massachusetts, he befriended agent Sojourner Truth.

Source

Andrews, William L., with David A. Davis, Tampathia Evans, Ian Frederick Finseth, and Andreá N. Williams. *North Carolina Slave Narratives: The Lives of Moses Roper, Lunsford Lane, Moses Grandy, and Thomas H. Jones.* Chapel Hill: University of North Carolina Press, 2003.

Jones, William M. (1791–?)
Jones, Mary (1796–?)

A clever physician and merchant, Dr. William M. "Pap" Jones concealed his activism as a transporter for the Underground Railroad. In Harrisburg, in Dauphin County, Pennsylvania, he opened a medical practice on River Avenue. Along with agents Elijah Marshall and Harriet McClintock Marshall, William and his wife, Mary Jones of New Jersey, supported the work of Wesley Union Zion African Methodist Episcopal Church, a log waystation of the secret network established in 1829 at Third and Mulberry streets. The couple partnered with Joseph Cassey Bustill in Kennett Square, Pennsylvania, and maintained contacts up the Pennsylvania–Canada line. At Tanner's Alley, a Harrisburg nexus of the secret network, the Jones family received passengers from Rudolf Frederich Kelker, a hardware dealer on Front Street, and concealed them in their barn. By employing knowledgeable transporters, Jones ensured passenger safety. In the guise of a rag dealer, he drove a covered wagon to stations in Pottsville and Wilkes-Barre, Pennsylvania.

Sources

Boyd's Business Directory. Philadelphia: William H. Boyd, 1860.

Osler & Irvin's Harrisburg Directory for 1856. Harrisburg, PA: Osler & Irvin, 1856.

Jordan, James Cunningham (1813–1891)
Jordan, Cynthia Desire Adams (1831–1908)

A pioneer and supporter of the Methodist Episcopal Church, Iowa State Senator James Cunningham Jordan operated a safehouse in West Des Moines. A native of Greenbrier County, West Virginia, he moved west to Walnut Township, in Madison County, Iowa, in September 1846. He built a log cabin along the Coon River and earned his fortune in livestock and real estate. In 1856, he married Cynthia Desire Adams of Canandaigua, New York.

On a 600-acre plot, the Jordans' two-story mansion at 2001 Fuller Road provided space for hiding runaways. James's activism earned him the title of chief conductor of Polk County. In early February 1858, the Jordans risked their reputation by hosting insurrectionist John Brown in the months preceding the attack on the federal arsenal in Harpers Ferry, Virginia. The Jordan house is a museum and repository of local history.

Source

The History of Iowa County. Des Moines: Union Historical, 1881.

Judson, Ann J. Burnham (1807–1885)
Judson, Samuel P. (1800–1849)

Ann J. Burnham Judson of Durold, New York, and her husband, Samuel P. Judson of Hallowell, Maine, were agents of the Underground Railroad in Elkhart County, Indiana. Samuel Judson was ensnared in serious litigation involving fugitive rescue. In 1847, Joseph A. Graves left his tobacco farm in Boone County, Kentucky, to recapture the slave Tom Harris, who lived at the Judson waystation. When neighbors intervened on Judson's behalf, Graves and his two cohorts broke down the door to the Judsons' residence and brandished weapons. In April 1848, authorities tried Graves for breaking and entering and inciting a riot. After losing in court, Graves appealed to the Indiana Supreme Court. On June 4, 1849, the chief justice demanded a retrial, but the issue was never reheard. Tom Harris remained free.

Source

Bordewich, Fergus M. *Bound for Canaan: The Underground Railroad and the War for the Soul of America.* New York: Amistad, 2005.

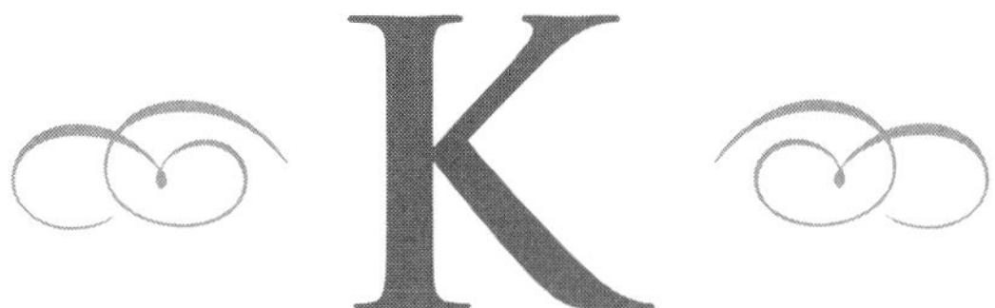

K

Kagi, John Henry (1835–1859)

A Swiss-American orator, attorney, and journalist for the *Herald of Freedom* in Lawrence, Kansas, and a disciple of the radical abolitionist John Brown, John Henry Kagi (also Henri Kagey or Kagy) of Bristolville, in Trumbell County, Ohio, engineered slave escapes across the Midwest. After his education in law in Nebraska City, Nebraska, he joined the Underground Railroad. Kagi's father, Abraham Neff Kagi (1807–1884), aided his daughter and son-in-law, Barbara A. Kagi Mayhew and Allen B. Mayhew of Nebraska City, in Otoe County, in building a one-room cabin and sleeping loft. They excavated a tunnel and the so-called Black Den, three interlinking underground chambers for hiding fugitives. In the 1850s, while living at the farm, John Kagi encouraged the Mayhews to rescue slaves. Substantiating the history of a cave as a waystation were two former couriers, Calvin Chapman and Carsten N. Karstens, and also the Mayhews' eldest son, Edward F. Mayhew, who described the cave as a storage hole for potatoes.

In 1855, when border wars in Nebraska broke out among polarized settlers, John Kagi's activism increased. In addition to his writings in the *Herald of Freedom,* Kagi published passionate letters on midwestern abolitionism in the *Chicago Tribune,* the *Cleveland Leader,* the *Kansas Tribune,* the *Lawrence (KA) Republican,* the *New York Tribune,* the *New York Evening Post,* and the *National Era.* On September 18, 1856, U.S. Marshal I.B. Donelson arrested Kagi and Colonel John Ritchie for robbery and lodged them in the jail in Lecompton, Kansas, to await trial and sentencing.

Upon Kagi's release from the Kansas state penitentiary in Tecumseh, on January 31, 1857, he was felled by shots to his chest fired by Judge Rush Elmore, a pro-slavery fanatic from Alabama, who then flailed Kagi's skull with a cane. After a difficult convalescence, Kagi returned to duty as an Underground Railroad operative. In summer 1858, he conspired with route planners Allan Pinkerton and Joan Carfrae Pinkerton in Chicago and, under the alias John Henri, plotted insurrection with John Brown and James Montgomery. John Kagi died in crossfire while trying to cross the Shenandoah River during the raid on Harpers Ferry, Virginia, on October 17, 1859.

Sources

De Witt, Robert M. *The Life, Trial and Execution of Captain John Brown.* New York: Robert M. De Witt, 1859.

Galbreath, C.B. "John Henri Kagi." *Ohio History* 34 (July 1925): 263–91.

Kane, Thomas Leiper (1822–1883) Kane, Elizabeth Dennistoun Wood (1836–1909)

Attorney and activist Thomas Leiper Kane invested money and effort in the cause of social justice. Born and educated in Philadelphia, in 1844, he studied law at the office of his father, Judge Elisha Kent Kane, and helped Mormons migrate to Deseret, Utah. To protest the Fugitive Slave Law of 1850, he resigned his job with the U.S. district commissioner. After the Christiana Riot of September 11, 1851, he clashed with his father over the jailing of Underground Railroad agents Castner Hanway, Elijah Lewis, and Joseph P. Scarlett and 35 blacks who protected four young runaways—Noah Baley, Nelson Ford, George Hammond, and Joshua Hammond—from bounty hunters. In 1853, Thomas Kane married his cousin, Elizabeth Dennistoun Wood, and committed himself to the secret network. At the beginning of the Civil War, he became the first Pennsylvanian to join the Union army and was twice wounded. After a brief imprisonment, he fought at Chancellorsville, Virginia, and Gettysburg, Pennsylvania.

See also: bounty hunters; Christiana Riot; Fugitive Slave Law of 1850.

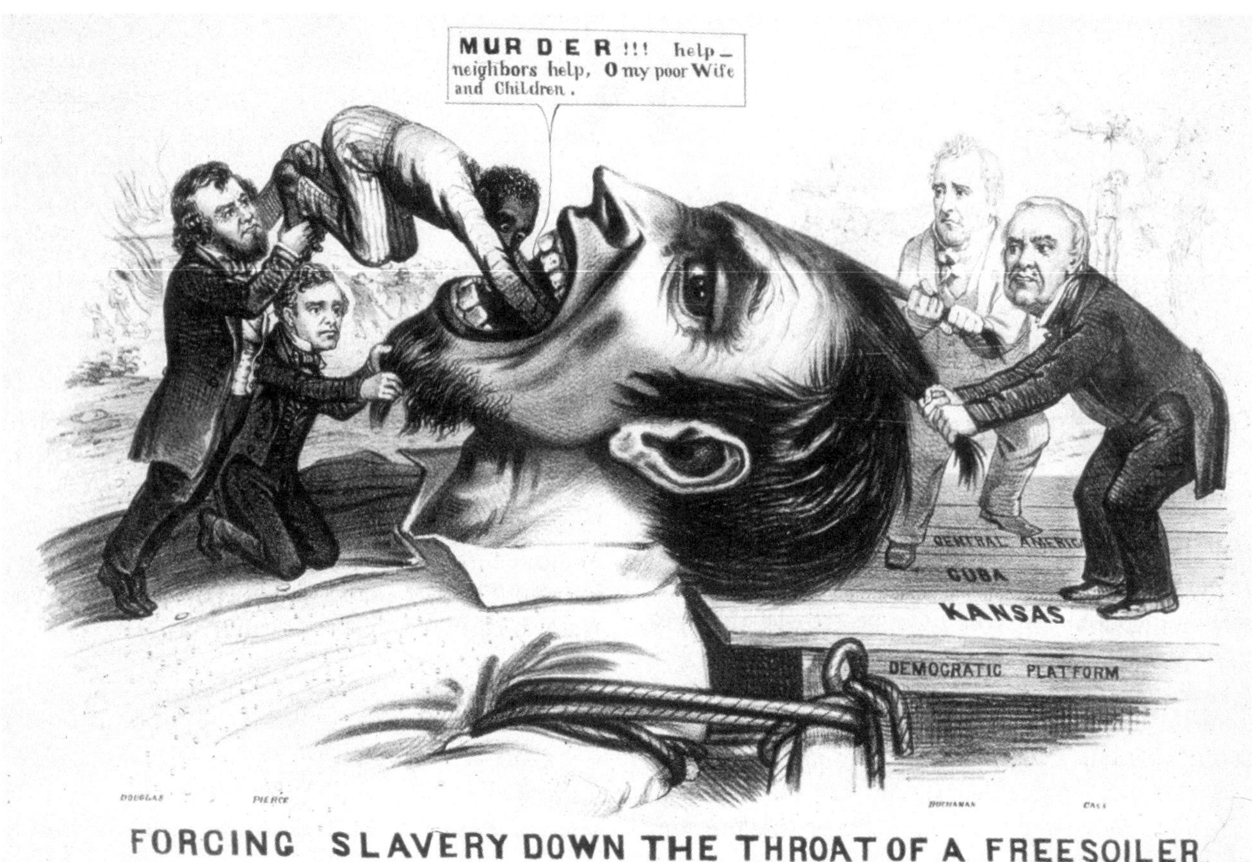

A contemporary political cartoon caricatures the response of libertarian Free-Soilers to the Kansas-Nebraska Act of 1854, which extended slavery to the western territories. The resulting frontier violence gave rise to the name "Bleeding Kansas." *(MPI/Stringer/Hulton Archive/Getty Images)*

Source

Zobell, Albert L., Jr. *Sentinel in the East: A Biography of Thomas L. Kane.* Salt Lake City, UT: N.G. Morgan, 1965.

Kansas-Nebraska Act of 1854

On May 25, 1854, the Kansas-Nebraska Act repealed the terms of the Missouri Compromise of 1820 and opened all territories to slavery. As the prospect of civil war loomed, eastern abolitionists geared up for a conflict in the Midwest more hostile and more personal than the ongoing North-South controversy. A political giant of the era, William Henry Seward—an Underground Railroad agent from Auburn, New York, who shared waystation duties with his wife, Frances Adeline Miller Seward—exhorted the United States Senate to compete with pro-slavery forces for control of Kansas and for the abolition of the flesh trade.

In April 1854, Eli Thayer, Amos A. Lawrence, and other New England operatives formed the

An editorial in the *Brooklyn Eagle* on December 1, 1855, denounced the outbreak of shooting and arson between free state advocates and pro-slavery elements: "Hordes of Abolition preachers and their disciples set out on a pilgrimage or crusade to Kansas—not invited by the fertility of soil of any of the inducements of bona fide colonization . . . Neither did they go with the peaceful implements of industry and words of hope, and fraternal amity such as would become the founders of a new sovereignty in the free wilderness, intent upon establishing benign and permanent institutions under whose protecting influence unborn generations would enjoy the blessings of freedom and civilization, but with vociferous outcries against the people of a neighboring State, and threats of underground railroads and other methods of subverting slavery in Missouri."

Massachusetts Emigrant Aid Company, a "free state" effort. They dispatched agent Charles Robinson to populate Kansas with libertarians known as Free-Soilers and to supply new communities with temporary dwellings, schools, mills, and newspapers. Similar abolitionist agencies vowed to support pioneer efforts to stop the spread of slavery along the North American frontier. In Concord, Massachusetts, one soft-spoken agent of the Underground Railroad, Lydia Jackson Emerson, refused to celebrate the Fourth of July and joined her husband, Ralph Waldo Emerson, in draping their front gate with funereal black crepe.

Heightening tensions was the juxtaposition of the Kansas Territory to Missouri, a state jubilant in its temporary triumph over anti-slavery factions. Drawn to the territory for its promise as an Underground Railroad route, northern activists engaged in open confrontation with border ruffians. The importation of firearms and resulting violence earned the territory its nickname, Bleeding Kansas.

See also: Missouri Compromise of 1820.

Sources

"Affairs in Kansas," *Brooklyn (NY) Eagle,* December 1, 1855, 2.

Cordley, Richard. *A History of Lawrence, Kansas, from Earliest Settlement to the Close of the Rebellion.* Lawrence, KS: Lawrence Journal Press, 1895.

Kaufman, Daniel (1818–1902)
Kaufman, Catharine Fortenbaugh (1824–1907)

Underground Railroad agents Daniel Kaufman (or Kauffman) and his wife, Catharine Fortenbaugh Kaufman, suffered monetary loss and annoyance from litigation pressed by an irate slave owner. At age 17, Daniel Kaufman entered service as a rescuer of slaves. After their marriage, the Kaufmans received passengers at their two-story brick residence and stable on Front and Third streets in Boiling Springs, in Cumberland County, Pennsylvania. Contributing to the Kaufmans' success was the sharing of route responsibilities with Philip Brechbill, Mode Griffith, and George Sailor. Daniel Kaufman's brother-in-law, Stephen Weakley, sped parties along routes from Chambersburg, Huntsdale, and Shippensburg and on to Dr. William Wilson Rutherford's waystation in Carlisle. On one occasion, Griffith discovered nine fugitives and hurried them to Island Grove, a wooded wetlands along Yellow Breeches Creek.

In civil court in late 1847, Maryland slave owner Mary W. Oliver charged Kaufman, Brechbill, and Weakley with harboring 13 fugitives in the Kaufmans' home. The Kaufmans concealed their passengers for 24 hours and then ferried them to the next stop the following night by farm wagon. Oliver won the first suit and received $2,800 plus $1,200 in costs from Kaufman but nothing from Brechbill and Weakley. Thaddeus Stevens, an abolitionist attorney from Danville, Vermont, represented Kaufman in a hearing before the Pennsylvania Supreme Court, which reversed the decision. During the lengthy litigation, the Kaufmans remained in service to the secret network.

Sources

Campbell, Stanley W. *The Slave Catchers: Enforcement of the Fugitive Slave Law, 1850–1860.* Chapel Hill: University of North Carolina Press, 1970.

Wing, Conway Phelps. *History of Cumberland County, Pennsylvania.* Philadelphia: James D. Scott, 1879.

Keese, Samuel (1793–1881)
Keese, Catherine Robinson (1806–1860)
Keese, John (?–1875)

A Quaker family of rescuers in Peru, in Clinton County, New York, Samuel Keese and his wife, Catherine Robinson Keese, depended on assistance from their son, John Keese. Samuel was an outspoken abolitionist who supported the work of the New York State Anti-Slavery Society and, in 1841, served as a manager of the American Anti-Slavery Society. After concealing passengers, the family relayed them through the Champlain Valley to Caroline Mattocks Moore and Noadiah Moore, who completed the final leg across the U.S.-Quebec border west of Lake Champlain. Sharing the responsibility were Samuel Keese's older sister and brother-in-law, Elizabeth Keese Smith and Benjamin Smith, and the Smiths' daughter-in-law and son, Jane Keese Smith and Stephen Keese Smith. Additional support from Keesville came from Eliza Harrington Allen Lansing and Wendell Lansing, owner and editor of the *Essex County Republican.*

See also: American Anti-Slavery Society.

Sources

Calarco, Tom. *The Underground Railroad in the Adirondack Region.* Jefferson, NC: McFarland, 2004.

Ripley, C. Peter, et al., eds. *The Black Abolitionist Papers.* Chapel Hill: University of North Carolina Press, 1992.

Kelker, Rudolf Frederich (1820–1906)

An Underground Railroad agent in Harrisburg, in Dauphin County, Pennsylvania, Rudolf Frederich Kelker aided a tight network of operatives. While operating a hardware store, he established a safehouse at Nine South Front Street in league with neighbors Mary Jones and Dr. William M. "Pap" Jones. A cave under Kelker's property accessed the banks of the Susquehanna River. Kelker concealed passengers in his barn at Barbara and River streets and waited for an opportunity to convey them to the next waystation. His neighbor, Dr. William Wilson Rutherford, assisted in the secret relays to Rutherford's brother, agent Samuel S. "Little Sam" Rutherford, who operated a stop at Paxtang. The Kelker property is now the site of the county courthouse. A Harrisburg street bears Kelker's name.

Sources

"Recall Thrills of Underground Railroad," *Harrisburg (PA) Evening News,* November 25, 1927.

Rutherford, S.S. "The Underground Railroad." *Publications of the Historical Society of Dauphin County* (1928): 3–6.

Kelley, Isaac (1825–1920)

A member of an Underground Railroad network in Upper Alton, Illinois, Isaac Kelley (also Kelly) relied on collaborators for successful relays of fugitive slaves. Kelley was born outside Macon, Georgia, on the plantation of Thomas Cooper. At age 21, he moved to Alton. He was a devoted compatriot of other networkers, in particular, journalist Elijah Parish Lovejoy, a martyr to the cause. Along the shore of the Mississippi River, Kelley and his lodge brothers of the Knights of Tabor and other free blacks offered homes and transportation to the desperate along the North Star Line. From his safehouse, a cabin on George and Sixth streets, Kelley could depend on assistance from James P. Thomas on Belle Street. The area's success also derived from the volunteerism of the Ursuline sisters, from the Campbell Chapel African Methodist Episcopal Church, and from agent Priscilla Baltimore, a founder of black churches. From 1837 until his death, Kelley tended Lovejoy's grave site in the Alton cemetery.

See also: African Methodist Episcopal Church.

Source

Taylor, Glennette Tilley. *The Underground Railroad in Illinois.* Glen Ellyn, IL: Newman Educational, 2001.

Kelley, J.W.B. (fl. 1850s)

Attorney J.W.B. Kelley (or Kelly) of Cincinnati, Ohio, pioneered slave rescue on the American frontier. A Free-Soiler and an agent of the Underground Railroad, he settled in Atchison a few miles from the Missouri state line. He worked as postmaster and volunteered with a society aiding fugitive blacks. On August 20, 1855, local officials urged Kelley to leave town. A pro-slavery faction stoned him, shaved one side of his head, and daubed him with tar. Lumped in with other border ruffians, in May 1856, he was ostracized by two anti-abolitionists, the Reverend Pardee Butler and Grafton Thomasson, and accused of maligning Missourians as outlaws.

Sources

Goodrich, Thomas. *War to the Knife: Bleeding Kansas, 1854–1861.* Lincoln: University of Nebraska Press, 2004.

Report of the Special Committee Appointed to Investigate the Troubles in Kansas. Washington, DC: Cornelius Wendell, 1856.

Kelley, John J. (1808–1866)

For over a quarter century, Father John J. Kelley contributed expertise to the busy New York–Ontario route of the Underground Railroad. After his emigration from Trillick in County Tyrone, Ireland, Kelley studied at Mount Saint Mary's College. In 1827, he joined a Jesuit community in Frederick City, Maryland, and became a circuit-riding priest to parishioners in northern New York and Vermont and across Lake Champlain in Canada. His appointment to Saint John's Church in Albany, New York, in 1831 allowed him to arrange passage for runaways through the Adirondack Mountains and over Lake Ontario. He served the Albany Vigilance Committee in creating a safe environment for the oppressed. In 1850, he issued a broadside requesting cash and clothing to aid destitute fugitives at the end of their flight from bondage. Kelley attested to the rescue of 287 slaves in the period from October 1855 to mid-July 1856.

Source

Calarco, Tom. *The Underground Railroad in the Adirondack Region.* Jefferson, NC: McFarland, 2004.

Kellogg, Josiah (1792–1884)

Josiah Kellogg was a Quaker conductor of the Underground Railroad in Erie, Pennsylvania, a main crossing point into Ontario. He received fugitives from agents in Linesville, Albion, Girard, and Eagle Village. When spies infiltrated the area, Kellogg and his associates moved passengers through Harbor Creek and Wesleyville. While operating the Dickson Tavern on Market Street from 1834 to 1841, Kellogg came to the aid of a local cook working at the United States Hotel on French Street. After a confrontation between the runaway and his former owner, a decoy led the bounty hunter out of town by the Erie and Wattsburg Road while the fugitive hid in Kellogg's basement. Agents passed the slave on to a sloop bound across Lake Erie for Ontario.

See also: bounty hunters; spies.

Source

"A Sharp Ruse," *Brooklyn (NY) Eagle,* April 25, 1886, 10.

Kelso, Lucy Sawyer (1815–1886) Kelso, William R. (1811–1860)

Lucy Sawyer Kelso and her husband, William R. Kelso, managed a safehouse in Brimfield, in Portage County, Ohio. At their two-story frame house, built in 1833, they operated both a rescue post and a town center, which served as a stage stop, post office, and meeting hall known as Union House. No details of their contributions to the secret network survive. The Kelso residence is currently a museum.

Source

History of Portage County, Ohio. Chicago: Warner, Beers, 1885.

Kelton, Fernando Cortez (1812–1866) Kelton, Sophia Langdon Stone (1819–1888)

Abolitionists Fernando Cortez Kelton and his wife, Sophia Langdon Stone Kelton, operated a two-story brick safehouse in Columbus, Ohio. Fernando Kelton, a native of Calais, Vermont, was orphaned in childhood and reared by a grandfather in Montpelier. After settling in Columbus at age 21, Kelton made a fortune in wholesale trade in pharmaceuticals and dry goods and built a house at 586 East Town Street. Beginning in 1852, the Keltons supported the local anti-slavery society and successfully sheltered runaways in their basement, servants' quarters, barn, and a 300-barrel cistern. Relay to Oberlin, Ohio, moved newcomers out of danger to a stronghold of abolitionism.

In 1864, 10-year-old Martha Hartway and her 12-year-old sister Pearl, refugees from a plantation in Powhatan County, Virginia, hid at night under a shrub at the Kelton residence. Sophia took the sisters in and obtained forged freedom papers for them. Pearl continued over the route to Canada. Martha stayed behind to recover from illness and remained for a decade. In the Kelton parlor, she married Thomas Lawrence, a free black carpenter and cabinetmaker from Cadiz, Ohio. To honor her rescuers, Martha named her son Arthur Kelton Lawrence; he distinguished himself during the Spanish-American War as a hospital steward for the Ohio Volunteer Infantry. At Fernando Kelton's death, fellow Columbus business owners closed their stores for three hours to honor his passing. In 1978, the Columbus Junior League refurbished the Kelton home into a museum and public garden. The staff performs an original drama entitled *Martha's Journey.*

See also: abolitionism.

Source

Tebben, Gerald, "Road to Freedom Ran Close to Home," *Columbus (OH) Dispatch,* February 4, 2004.

Kemble, Fanny (1809–1903)

Actor and diarist Frances Anne "Fanny" Kemble Butler published an account of the plight of slaves and their escapes from the southern plantation system. A member of the distinguished Kemble-Siddons family of actors, Fanny was born in London and studied in France. From 1832 to 1845, she lived in the United States and kept a diary, *Journal of a Residence in America* (1835), which exposed the brutality of the flesh trade. In 1834, after marrying Philadelphia attorney Pierce Mease Butler, formulator of the Fugitive Slave Law of 1793, she moved to his Georgia estate on the Altamaha River. In defiance of his political stance, she taught blacks to read, improved sanitation in the slave quarters, and secretly established a waystation of the Underground Railroad.

Kemble completed a sequel to her diary, *Journal of a Residence on a Georgian Plantation in 1838–1839* (1863), which relates the flight of slaves via the Underground Railroad and describes the physical punishment she received from her husband for promoting the flight. The Butler marriage ended in divorce in September 1849, which cost Fanny custody of their two children, Frances and Sarah Butler, and any claims to family property. History credits Kemble's diary with convincing the British Crown not to aid the Confederacy during the American Civil War. In 2000, Jane Seymour portrayed Fanny Kemble in the CBS-TV film *Enslavement: The True Story of Fanny Kemble.*

Sources

Clinton, Catherine. *Fanny Kemble's Civil Wars.* Oxford, UK: Oxford University Press, 2001.

Kemble, Fanny. *Journal of a Residence on a Georgian Plantation in 1838–1839.* Athens: University of Georgia Press, 1984.

Kemp, John (fl. 1860s)

A persistent conductor of refugees, John Kemp was twice arrested for violating the Fugitive Slave Law of 1850. While living in Prince George's County, Maryland, he appears to have conspired with a South Carolina cab driver, Charles Heise, in slave rescues. Kemp came to trial with co-conspirators Leethe Brown, William Brown, William Lee, and Henry Norton for multiple slave rescues. On May 6, 1864, a circuit court pressed formal charges, but Kemp appears to have eluded arraignment.

See also: Fugitive Slave Law of 1850.

Source

Court records, Maryland State Archives.

Kennedy, Robert (fl. 1840s–1850s)

A blacksmith in Morris, Illinois, Robert Kennedy advanced from freedman to operative of the Underground Railroad. He was the son of Kentucky slaves. While residing in Illinois southwest of Chicago on the Illinois & Michigan Canal, he observed local traffic and advised runaways of the best routes to take across Lake Michigan to Canada. He determined that the safest choices for slave concealment and transport were stables and barges.

Source

Taylor, Glennette Tilley. *The Underground Railroad in Illinois.* Glen Ellyn, IL: Newman Educational, 2001.

Kent, Benjamin (1805–1881)
Kent, Hannah Simmons (1806–1882)
Kent, Elizabeth (fl. 1830s–1840s)

Benjamin Kent and his wife, Hannah Simmons Kent, of Penn, Pennsylvania were both inspired abolitionists and unassuming rescuers of slaves for three decades. In 1831, they founded the Clarkson Anti-Slavery Society and operated a branch safehouse. Benjamin Kent's sister Elizabeth owned a mercantile business that sold goods not tainted by slave labor. She aided the secret network by clothing ragged runaways and supplying them with cash. Benjamin conducted a party of 35 armed refugees from Maryland to the station of his brother-in-law and sister, Mahlon Brosius and Mary Emma Kent Brosius, in Penn. At dusk, the slaves vacated their hiding places in the barn and left in two wagons for the 12-mile drive to Ercildoun to the stations of James Fulton, Jr., and Gideon Pierce. Leading the women and children were the family's young sons, Daniel Kent Brosius and Edwin Brosius, with the black males following in the woods. The route continued to Abigail Paxson Vickers and John Vickers's station and through Kimberton to Ontario.

After the Kents bought a wool factory in Andrew's Bridge, in Lancaster County, in 1833, they founded the Coleraine (Pennsylvania) Anti-Slavery Society and welcomed abolitionist orators but lived on too public a road to continue receiving runaways. Another move in 1845 placed the Kents in Jackson's Valley, in Chester County, a quieter spot for maintaining an Underground Railroad station. After the Christiana Riot of September 11, 1851, the couple sheltered six participants until a kinsman, Henry Kent (1835–1867), could convey them to the care of Dr. Bartholomew Fussell in Chester County.

See also: Christiana Riot.

Source

Smedley, Robert C. *History of the Underground Railroad in Chester and the Neighboring Counties of Pennsylvania.* Lancaster, PA: Office of *The Journal,* 1883.

Key to Uncle Tom's Cabin, A (1853)

In 1852, author Harriet Beecher Stowe began compiling *A Key to Uncle Tom's Cabin,* a commentary on her best-selling melodrama *Uncle Tom's Cabin* (1852). Her novel depicts barbarous treatment of slaves, incidents of torture and kidnap, and the flight of Kentucky runaways via the Underground Railroad through Ohio to freedom and prosperity in Ontario and Quebec. In *A Key to Uncle Tom's Cabin,* she justified details and incidents in the novel that readers and reviewers suspected of being overstated, biased, or false. For statistics, she interviewed an expert, Gerrit Smith, an Underground Railroad supervisor and philanthropist. She also familiarized herself with the Quaker quandary over bearing arms and firing on posses, the focus of chapter 17.

Stowe meticulously reviewed the fictional account of the escape of George Harris, his beautiful quadroon wife, Eliza Harris, and their two-year-old son, Harry, over the secret network to Amherstberg, Ontario, a frequent destination for Underground Railroad passengers. In chapter 6 of *A Key to Uncle Tom's Cabin,* the author cites a Presbyterian clergyman who corroborated the first stage of escape of the wife and mother—the Ohio River crossing of Eliza Harris and Harry. The minister quoted the agent who observed in winter 1838 as the real Eliza Harris leaped from ice block to ice block to reach a busy and well-documented depot, Liberty Hill, operated by Jean Lowry Rankin and John Rankin in Ripley, Ohio.

Stowe provided readers and critics with valuable information on the secret network. Chapter 7 of her text fleshes out the fictional Uncle Tom with details of the flight of Stowe's model, the Reverend Josiah Henson, a maimed slave who made his way to Canada from New Orleans in 1830. In chapter 13, Stowe discusses how she used Rachel Mendenhall Garrett and Thomas Garrett, agents in Wilmington, Delaware, as the models for the fictional Rachel and Simeon Halliday, Quaker humanitarians who live in a religious community that serves as a depot. The Hallidays and their fellow operatives risk fines and imprisonment for rescuing slaves. The identification of real heroes of the Underground Railroad was a triumph for Harriet Beecher Stowe. The year *A Key to Uncle Tom's Cabin* was published, she traveled to Europe to increase awareness of the civil disobedience of American abolitionists.

See also: agents, Underground Railroad; civil disobedience; kidnap; Quakers; *Uncle Tom's Cabin; or, Life Among the Lowly* (1852).

Source

Stowe, Harriet Beecher. *A Key to Uncle Tom's Cabin.* London: Clarke, Beeton, 1853.

kidnap

Because of the unconstitutional liberties granted slave catchers, unscrupulous trackers and posses could claim ownership of free blacks, transport them south, and sell them at a profit. In summer 1801, the abduction of Wagelma, a 10-year-old apprentice to a French tailor in Philadelphia, concluded with a harbor tussle between the kidnapper and Underground Railroad agent Isaac Tatem Hopper, who prevailed and retrieved the boy. Blacks had few weapons to ward off seizure beyond crude rope or wire garrotes, pocketknives, cudgels, axes and farm tools, and the rare pistol or rifle. In Calhoun County, Michigan, Nancy Stevens heated a coal shovel at her fireplace as a means of warding off would-be slave snatchers. In autumn 1823, slave nabbers from Kentucky seized Joseph Pickard, a barber in Lockport, New York. Quaker defenders Darius Comstock and his brother, Joseph Comstock, represented Pickard in court. During the hearing, Pickard leaped from a window, but the stalkers recaptured him. Because of the town's abolitionist fervor and the anti-slavery leadership of G.W. Rogers, the judge tossed out the case. The throng turned on the kidnappers and forced their hasty departure from Lockport.

> After passage of the Fugitive Slave Law of 1850, a quasi-legal form of kidnap prevailed. As Colonel William Monroe Cockrum explains in *History of the Underground Railroad As It Was Conducted by the Anti-Slavery League* (1915), "Kidnapping the negroes was accomplished by running them away from their acquaintances to a friendly commissioner, probably a partner in the business, and there the kidnapper secured his right to the negro by a judicial decision of the villainous commissioner who received from the United States ten dollars for every decision he made against the negro and but five if he made one for the negro; thus offering the Commissioner a bribe of five dollars for a favorable decision in the interest of the kidnapper. The negro was thus doomed and taken out of the south and sold into slavery."

Frequent slave apprehension brought public outcry and rapid interventions by Underground Railroad operatives and vigilance committees. According to an illustrated article in the *Anti-Slavery Almanac,* on November 20, 1836, Tobias Boudinot, John Lyon, Daniel D. Nach, and E.K. Waddy seized, gagged, and shackled Peter John Lee, a resident of Westchester County, New York. In 1852, agent Mordecai McKinney read about the kidnap of Jim Phillips in William Lloyd Garrison's anti-slavery weekly, *The Liberator.* McKinney purchased the freedom of Phillips and his family to free them from bondage in Virginia. As a result of such bold daylight crimes, activists staked out piers, inns, stables, and stage lines and scanned crowds for suspicious insurgents. An international incident that occurred south of St. Catharines, Ontario, in mid-July 1835 resulted in a riot. After a kidnapper named Tait seized a black couple and their child in Canada and took them by force to Buffalo, New York, abolitionists chased the party to the ferry in Black Rock and liberated the family. The scuffle turned vicious and resulted in serious injuries on both sides.

The kidnappers' crimes sank as low as infant and child snatching. As early as 1825, Philadelphia's slave nabbers seized young children, loaded them on sloops, and transported them along the Delaware River to southern slave markets. Reports of child stealing recurred in the abolitionist press, as with editor Benjamin Lundy's article on the seizure of two young black boys in Federalsburg, Maryland in *Genius of Universal Emancipation,* which appeared on February 25, 1826. That same year, Philadelphia Mayor Joseph Watson learned from Mississippi planters of a ring of kidnappers and resellers of blacks—in effect, a reverse Underground Railroad—led by Patty Cannon, Ebenezer Johnson, and Joseph Johnson of Sussex County, Maryland. Among the victims were Lydia Smith and Peter Hook, who reported on his rescue in Natchez, Mississippi. Hook also described the kidnap of Abraham F. Johnson, Joe Johnson, James Bayard, Benjamin Baxter, Ephraim Lawrence, and three children, Henry, Little Jack, and Little John. According to the May 1827 issue of Enoch Lewis's *African Observer,* Watson purchased some of the victims with money donated by John W. Hamilton, a planter near Rocky Springs, Mississippi, but other victims disappeared into slave pens and auction houses without a trace. Many were too small to identify themselves, their former owners, or their parents. The plight of blacks grabbed without warning and hustled across state borders is reflected in the history of Fanny Wigglesworth and her four children in Moscow, Ohio. Their kidnappers, William Moore and William Middleton, incurred no court charges for the abduction. Despite a multistate search launched by Underground Railroad conductor Robert E. Fee, the five Wigglesworths were never heard from again.

Law enforcement agencies frequently failed to enforce state and federal statutes. One incident of residential adult and child theft transpired in 1848 near Pine Grove Forge in Lancaster County, Pennsylvania. During the absence from home of a freedman, who was at his job, kidnappers overpowered the man's wife and children, tied them up, and removed them via a covered wagon already loaded with other victims. Neighbors raised the alarm. Joseph C. Taylor held the lead rider at musket point. Joseph Peirce, James Woodrow, and others apprehended the kidnappers and secured them at Lowe's tavern. Before the abolitionists could return with the sheriff, the kidnappers vanished with the wagon full of slaves.

Some kidnappers hawked their human wares from wagon beds throughout Kentucky and Tennessee. Attorney James Gillespie Birney of Huntsville, Alabama, wrote of the danger to freeborn blacks who were unaware of their value as chattel. Most were oblivious to the presence of slave nabbers or of criminals posing as Underground Railroad operatives, who could reduce their victims to bondage through guile and violence. One successful kidnapper, Colonel S.T. Bailey, left a slave woman in Hartford, Vermont, in mid-August 1844. She subsequently escaped. When Bailey managed to locate her, he and Samuel Nutt yanked her from a safehouse, tied her hands and feet, and bore her away by wagon. According to coverage in the *Green Mountain Freeman,* Bailey was found innocent of abduction the following December.

In the aftermath of the new federal law, author Harriet Beecher Stowe described slave kidnap in *Uncle Tom's Cabin* (1852) and substantiated her fictionalized accounts with actual cases, summarized in *A Key to Uncle Tom's Cabin* (1853). A dramatic confrontation between pacifist abolitionists and armed abductors occurred in October 1854 following the failure to free Anthony Burns in a contentious Boston court case. The arrival of Asa Butman in Worcester, Massachusetts, placed the bold kidnapper among sturdy slave defenders. The local vigilance committee circulated handbills warning of Butman's seedy reputation and surrounded the hotel where he lodged. When Butman drew his revolver on guards at 3 A.M., authorities arrested him for carrying a concealed weapon. A federal marshal shielded Butman in his office. To quell a potential lynch mob, orator Stephen Symons Foster of Pelham, Massachusetts, offered to accompany the kidnapper to the train depot. Although Foster won a civil suit against Butman, charging him with disturbing the peace, Butman paid a small price for his criminal plot.

See also: Key to Uncle Tom's Cabin, A (1853); *Liberator, The*; *Uncle Tom's Cabin; or, Life Among the Lowly* (1852); vigilance committees.

Sources

Bacon, Margaret Hope. *I Speak for My Slave Sister—The Life of Abby Kelley Foster.* New York: Thomas Y. Crowell, 1974.

Cockrum, Colonel William. *History of the Underground Railroad As It Was Conducted by the Anti-Slavery League.* Oakland City, IN: J.W. Cockrum, 1915.

"Fugitive Slave Case," *Buffalo (NY) Daily Commercial Advertiser,* July 13, 1835.
Winch, Julie. "Philadelphia and the Other Underground Railroad." *Pennsylvania Magazine of History and Biography* 111:1 (1987): 3–25.

Kilbourne, David (1767–1847)

David Kilbourne (also Kilborn or Kilburne) developed the conscience of an abolitionist and began rescuing runaway slaves for the Underground Railroad in New Haven, in Oswego County, New York. A native of Litchfield, Connecticut, and former resident of Canada, he was a prisoner of British forces during the War of 1812. His waystation, situated opposite the George-Hughes Road, received its first passenger in 1834. The runaway asked for shelter over the Sabbath. According to an item in the August 18, 1836, issue of the *Friend of Man,* William Goodell's newspaper in Utica, New York, at a July 21 session of the Mexico (New York) Anti-Slavery Society Kilbourne related his on-the-spot conversion to humanitarianism.

Source

"David Kilburne," *Friend of Man,* August 18, 1836.

Kilgore, Elizabeth Stewart (1808–1876)
Kilgore, James (?–1882)

Agents of the Underground Railroad in Stoneboro, in Mercer County, Pennsylvania, the Kilgores received runaways from East Lackawannock and Springfield. The couple received regular traffic over a link to Franklin in Venango County, Pennsylvania. James Kilgore, a blacksmith at Beaver and South Erie streets, maintained a link with the Travises of Liberia, a black settlement in Sandy Lake. His wife, Elizabeth Stewart Kilgore, taught passengers to read.

The Kilgores' daughter, Elizabeth Kilgore Breckinridge, corroborated the oral history of the county's role in the secret network. She attested to a secret knock by which passengers identified themselves at the basement door. She witnessed the late-night arrival of 13 refugees, whom two of her second cousins—David Young and his brother, John Young—hid in a load of hay at their stop six miles away in Indian Run. She also observed the prone figures of fugitives on heaps of straw in the basement kitchen of James Crouse's station before Joseph Sykes conducted the group to a Georgetown safehouse.

Source

History of Mercer County. Chicago: Brown, Runk, 1888.

Kimber, Emmor (1775–1850)
Kimber, Susannah Jackson (1773–1854)
Kimber, Abigail (1804–1871)
Kimber, Gertrude (1816–1869)

A Quaker minister and essayist and an early enlistee in the Underground Railroad, Emmor Kimber and his wife, Susannah Jackson Kimber, maintained a depot in Kimberton, in Chester County, Pennsylvania. The Kimbers teamed with their daughters, Gertrude and Abigail (Abbie), a teacher, an officer of the Pennsylvania Anti-Slavery Society, and a delegate to the 1840 World's Convention in London. While operating a Quaker girls' academy, French Creek Boarding School, the Kimber family received runaways from Enoch Lewis at the Westtown boarding academy, from Elizabeth Taylor Whitson and Moses Whitson in Sadsbury, and from Benjamin Price and Jane Paxson Price in East Bradford.

The Kimber family concealed refugees in the school cellar and shuttled them out a tunnel and along a well-traveled secret route. Among the many who flocked to the Kimbers for aid were Henry Franklin and Rachel Harris, a cook who remained with the Kimber family until her marriage. The academy closed around 1848, after the community learned of Abigail's work for the secret network and feared for their daughters' safety.

See also: Pennsylvania Anti-Slavery Society.

Source

Smedley, Robert C. *History of the Underground Railroad in Chester and the Neighboring Counties of Pennsylvania.* Lancaster, PA: Office of *The Journal,* 1883.

Kimberly, William (fl. 1840s)
Kimberly, Phebe Drake (fl. 1840s)

Underground Railroad operatives in Iowa, the Reverend William Kimberly and his wife, Phebe Drake Kimberly, dedicated themselves to slave rescue. In the 1840s, the family aided Missouri runaways passing over the Mississippi River and through Jefferson, Lee, and Mahaska counties. William Kimberly preached at Methodist Episcopal churches. During the Civil War, the couple's youngest son, Wesley Clark Kimberly, served with the Union army in Arkansas.

Source

Frazier, Harriet C. *Runaway and Freed Missouri Slaves and Those Who Helped Them, 1763–1865.* Jefferson, NC: McFarland, 2004.

King, Cyrus (1806–ca. 1852)

A respected black citizen of Wilmington, in Clinton County, Ohio, Cyrus King devoted work and money to the Underground Railroad cause. The son of Isaac King and Elizabeth Simons, he was born the slave of Moses Hendricks in Halifax County, Virginia. Two Quakers, the Widow Boorum and Sally Terry, transported the King family to Ohio, where they farmed land belonging to Daniel Burgess. At age 24, Cyrus King bought acreage in Greene, Ohio, and worked on a Mississippi River steamer as a cook. He risked a lashing by an angry owner when he transported two mulattos from the steamer to free territory. As King acquired land, after 1840, he operated an extensive Underground Railroad depot and hid slaves in his outbuildings. He allied with other local conductors, including Eli McGregor, a storekeeper on Main Street, and McGregor's son, John S. McGregor.

Source

Beers, W.H. *The History of Clinton County, Ohio.* Chicago: privately published, 1882.

King, Hannah Clendenon (1789–1861)
King, John (1784–1865)

Quaker immigrants Hannah Clendenon King and John King nurtured humanitarism in their children. After arrivng from England in 1795, John King's family settled first in Philadelphia and the next year in Asylum, in Bradford County, Pennsylvania. John apprenticed in land surveying and joined John Keating's mission to report on the frontier in northern Pennsylvania. In 1817, he married Hannah King, who was the daughter of Quaker missionaries on the Allegheny River in western New York. In Ceres, the couple served the Pennsylvania–Canada route of the Underground Railroad. King opened a school in his kitchen, where he taught literacy to escapees. The Kings supported the humanitarian work of their daughter and son-in-law, Mary Williams King Mann, and agent John S. Mann, a merchant in Coudersport, Pennsylvania.

Source

Switala, William J. *Underground Railroad in Pennsylvania.* Mechanicsburg, PA: Stackpole, 2001.

King, William (1812–1895)

The Reverend William King, a Scots Presbyterian minister from Newton-Limavady, in Londonderry, Ireland, led the black community of Buxton a few miles from Chatham in southern Ontario. His introduction to slave liberation came when his wife, Mary Phares King, inherited chattel in Mississippi. After her death, in 1848, King bought 9,000 acres of heavily forested government land in Canada on the northern shore of Lake Erie, which he shaped the following year into the Elgin Settlement. With the assistance of the Reverend Charles C. Foote, King settled his 15 slaves on 50 acres each. To encourage runaways to his settlement, he sold plots to those of good character at $2.50 per acre. He centered the Elgin community with a church and opened the Buxton Mission School in 1850. One of the gifts he received for valor was a coded log cabin quilt pieced by a slave woman in the 1840s.

When the Reverend Samuel Joseph May, an agent of the secret network, surveyed the Elgin settlement in 1852, he found 90 black families enjoying freedom

The Presbyterian minister William King, a leader of the anti-slavery movement in Canada, established the highly successful Elgin community for freed slaves at Buxton, in southern Ontario, in 1849. *(Photo courtesy of The J.J. Talman Regional Collection, The University of Western Ontario Archives, Jamieson Collection, B4192)*

and prosperity and flourishing without any sign of crime or alcohol abuse. By 1854, the community had 300 families who operated sawmills and grain and tobacco farms.

See also: code, Underground Railroad; Elgin Settlement; philanthropists; quilts.

Sources

Haviland, Laura S. *A Woman's Life-Work: Labors and Experiences of Laura S. Haviland.* Cincinnati, OH: Walden & Stowe, 1882.
May, Samuel Joseph. *Some Recollections of Our Antislavery Conflict.* Boston: Fields, Osgood, 1869.

Kirk, John (1805–1891)
Kirk, Susan Bingham (1808–1872)

Chicago real estate agent and merchant John Kirk and his wife, Susan Bingham Kirk, aided runaway slaves in the 1840s and 1850s. After teaching school, John Kirk abandoned education for the iron foundry business in Youngstown, in Mahoning County, Ohio. The Kirks married in 1827 and opened a waystation at their home on Front and Hazel streets. As operatives of the Underground Railroad, they manifested the principles of the Disciples of Christ Church by receiving up to 30 fugitives at a time for concealment in their basement. John Kirk became so well known for rescuing slaves that he had to travel incognito on business trips in the South.

Source

Album of Genealogy and Biography, Cook County, Illinois. Chicago: Calumet Book & Engraving, 1895.

Kirkwood, Samuel Jordan (1813–1894)

Samuel Jordan Kirkwood managed to combine abolitionism and service to fugitive slaves with a successful political career. A native of Harford County, Maryland, at age 22, he moved to Richland County, Ohio, with his parents. Before becoming a politician, he farmed, taught school, ran an inn, and studied law. In addition to aiding the Ohio–Canada route of the Underground Railroad, he served as a county prosecuting attorney. After moving to Iowa City, Iowa, in 1855, he was elected a state senator and then governor. In 1859, he aroused the ire of supporters when he denounced the raid on the federal arsenal in Harpers Ferry, Virginia, on October 16, 1859, although he expressed support for insurrectionist John Brown's abolitionism.

See also: abolitionism.

Source

Clark, Dan E. *Samuel Jordan Kirkwood.* Iowa City: State Historical Society of Iowa, 1917.

Knapp, Chauncey Langdon (1809–1898)

A multitalented operative of the Underground Railroad, Chauncey Langdon Knapp was a politician, abolitionist editor, and rescuer of slaves. A native of Berlin, Vermont, he studied printing and journalism in his youth. While serving as Vermont's secretary of state, from 1839 to 1842, he and Joseph Poland edited the *Voice of Freedom,* the newspaper of the Vermont Anti-Slavery Society. In collaboration with the Ferrisburg agents Rachel Gilpin Robinson and Rowland Thomas Robinson of Rokeby Farm, Knapp harbored runaways at his office at the Vermont State House in Montpelier. On August 20, 1838, Knapp wrote a letter to Mason Anthony, a Quaker conductor in Saratoga, New York, concerning the successful arrival of a runaway named Charles, who belonged to a slave owner in Vicksburg, Mississippi.

Source

Laurie, Bruce. *Beyond Garrison: Antislavery and Social Reform.* New York: Cambridge University Press, 2005.

Knapp, William (1825–1864)

William Knapp died in prison while serving a six-year term for rescuing slaves. In April 1861, he entered the Missouri state penitentiary in Jefferson City. He was 39 years old when he died on November 27, 1864, some 11 months after national emancipation on January 1, 1863. His sudden death was unexplained.

Source

Frazier, Harriet C. *Runaway and Freed Missouri Slaves and Those Who Helped Them, 1763–1865.* Jefferson, NC: McFarland, 2004.

Knoefel, August (1824–1894)

Pharmacist August (or Otto) Knoefel, a German immigrant, rescued runaway slaves in New Albany, in Floyd County, Indiana. Knoefel was born in Niedergrauschiortz, Saxony. At age 24, he married and immigrated to New York. On First and Market streets, he opened a drugstore near Wesley Chapel Methodist Church and kept it in operation for 38 years. After 1849, he also managed Grandview Estates, a summer hotel in a wooded area on the Old Vincennes Road. Knoefel hosted refugees who crossed the Ohio River from Kentucky and hired blacks for his staff. Passengers of the Underground Railroad could traverse a cliff leading out of the Ohio River valley and advance north to Canada.

Source

Peters, Pamela R. *The Underground Railroad in Floyd County, Indiana.* Jefferson, NC: McFarland, 2001.

Knowlton, Dexter Asa, Sr. (1812–1876)

A public-spirited citizen, Dexter Asa Knowlton, Sr., a real estate agent and the owner of a general mercantile establishment, conducted Underground Railroad passengers through Westfield, New York. Knowlton was a pack peddler from Herkimer County, New York, when he visited Westfield in 1838. While he lived in Freeport, in Stephenson County, Illinois, he welcomed orator Frederick Douglass to his home. After moving to Westfield in 1855, Knowlton built a house and joined the First Congregational Church, to which he donated a bell. At his residence, he concealed runaways behind the fireboard of his fireplace and hid others in his barn and under lap robes in his carriage. To fool slave hunters, he drove through town in a leisurely fashion before taking the main road to Dr. James Pettit's station in Fredonia for passage over Lake Erie to Ontario.

Source

Tilden, W.H. *History of Stephenson County, Illinois.* Chicago: S.J. Clarke, 1910.

Ladd, Dudley, III (1789–1875)
Ladd, Charlotte Eastman (ca. 1790–1826)
Ladd, Amanda Palmer (1809–ca. 1850s)

Tinsmith and hardware dealer Dudley Ladd III and his wife, Charlotte Eastman Ladd, rescued slaves passing through Franklin, in Merrimack County, New Hampshire. In accordance with the family's Congregational beliefs, Dudley Ladd established a two-story frame waystation on Webster Street, a house he occupied from 1823 to 1858 with his first and second wives, Charlotte Eastman Ladd and Amanda Palmer Ladd. Dudley's brother relayed passengers from Concord up the Merrimack River. Runaways hid in an attic space warmed by the kitchen chimney. For conveyance to Canada, Dudley may have chosen the Northern Railroad, which passed by his property, or he may have directed the runaways to walk along the tracks to freedom. Additional stops in Potter Place, New Hampshire, and White River Junction, Vermont, provided security from slave catchers. Dudley was arrested once for harboring fugitives, but a judge dropped the case for lack of evidence.

Source

Helm, Kathie, "Dudley Ladd Home a Haven for Slaves," *Concord (NH) Monitor,* January 18, 1999.

Lambdin, William H. (1814–1881)

One of a brotherhood of seamen rescuers, Captain William H. Lambdin (or Lambden) transported slaves from southern Atlantic ports to the waystation of Underground Railroad strategist Thomas Garrett in Wilmington, Delaware. Aboard the schooner *Mary Ann Elizabeth,* in November 1855, Lambdin left the James River east of Petersburg, Virginia, and boarded five fugitive slaves in Norfolk. Bound for Delaware during a storm, the ship ran aground on Virginia Beach, in Princess Anne County. Authorities arrested Lambdin on his arrival in Wilmington and seized the runaways.

On November 11, 1856, Garrett wrote to secret network supervisors James Miller McKim and William Still requesting books on abolitionism to help Lambdin defend himself in court. Garrett mentioned the writings of the Reverend William Goodell as valuable sources. Lambdin served a sentence in the Virginia penitentiary in Richmond. The captain and his fellow seagoing conductors of the Atlantic network earned Thomas Garrett's respect for their assistance to fugitive slaves.

See also: abolitionism.

Source

Grover, Kathryn. *The Fugitive's Gibraltar: Escaping Slaves and Abolitionism in New Bedford, Massachusetts.* Amherst: University of Massachusetts Press, 2001.

Lambert, William (ca. 1817–1890)

A follower of John Brown's Underground Railroad campaign, philanthropist William Lambert of Detroit, Michigan, reputedly saved 30,000 slaves from 1829 to 1862. Born in Trenton, New Jersey, to a free mother and slave father, Lambert studied at a Quaker school. On his own at age 12, he took a steamer from Buffalo, New York, to Detroit, which in 1848 became his home. He settled at 497 Larned Street East, opened a tailor shop and safehouse at 273 Jefferson Avenue, and became a warden of St. Matthew's Church, which he co-founded.

Lambert's Detroit headquarters was well connected with the hierarchy of the secret network, including Frederick Douglass, the Reverend Henry Highland Garnet, William Lloyd Garrison, Wendell Addison Phillips, and Gerrit Smith. Lambert's territory along the Michigan–Ontario route received refugees from Ann Arbor and Wayne, Michigan. Relays required ongoing collaboration with the Reverend William C.

The leader of Detroit's Underground Railroad, William Lambert created signals and passwords to conceal the movement of tens of thousands of passengers crossing the river to Windsor, Ontario. *(©Private Collection/Peter Newark American Pictures/The Bridgeman Art Library)*

Monroe, pastor of the Second Baptist Church, a depot at Beaubien and Monroe streets. With agent George DeBaptiste, Lambert founded The African-American Mysteries: The Order of the Men of Oppression, a refugee aid society. The secret fellowship used signals, passwords, and handshakes to identify Underground Railroad transporters. DeBaptiste and Seymour Finney aided Lambert on a significant slave rescue in February 1840 involving Robert Cromwell of Arkansas. The political repercussions influenced passage of the Fugitive Slave Law of 1850.

Because of the notoriety of the Detroit River crossing, from 1829 to 1862, much of Lambert's work was dangerous. At night, he brought passengers from as far south as Florida and Louisiana one by one to the wharf area. He placed them in boats hidden under piers for transport to Windsor, Ontario. In 1886, Lambert agreed to an interview with a journalist from the *Detroit Tribune.* The lengthy conversation preserved information about the Underground Railroad in Detroit and the dedication of insurrectionist John Brown to abolitionism. Lambert also denounced a con artist named Lovett, who conspired with blacks to travel south with him and be sold; they would then flee north and split the profits with Lovett. According to Lambert, these frauds were not welcome Underground Railroad passengers.

See also: Chatham Convention; Fugitive Slave Law of 1850.

Sources

Burton, Clarence Monroe. *The City of Detroit, Michigan, 1701–1922.* Detroit, MI: S.J. Clarke, 1922.

"Fifty Years a Detroiter," *Detroit Free Press,* January 5, 1890.

Lumpkin, Katherine DuPre. "The General Plan Was Freedom: A Negro Secret Order on the Underground Railroad." *Phylon* 28:1 (1967): 63–77.

Lane, Hester (fl. 1820s–1840s)

Hester Lane, a successful interior decorator in New York City, opened her home to refugees and spent her own money to rescue blacks from bondage. Her residence was a waystation of the Underground Railroad. She also journeyed to public auctions in Maryland and bought young, elderly, and frail slaves, whom she liberated. She bought an 11-year-old girl for $100 and a 14-year-old boy for twice that. A 30-year-old male cost $280. One ailing family of four was only $140. Money that Lane received as repayment enabled her to buy more human chattel.

Sources

Adams, H.G., ed. *God's Image in Ebony.* London: Partridge & Oakey, 1854.

Child, Lydia Maria. *A Lydia Maria Child Reader,* ed. Carolyn L. Karcher. Durham, NC: Duke University Press, 1997.

Lane, James Henry (1814–1866)

A pioneer and militant abolitionist in Kansas Territory, attorney James Henry Lane of Lawrenceburg, Indiana, promoted violent methods of ending slavery. A rash, compelling orator, he settled in Kansas in

> Among those agents who admired Hester Lane's diligence was editor Lydia Maria Francis Child. Child described Lane's labors at laundry, from which she earned small amounts of cash to lend the runaway. Child concluded, "The heart of a king may dwell in a pedlar's breast and right regal may be the soul of a washerwoman."

1855 and led the Jay Hawkers, the slang name for Kansas abolitionists. In summer 1856, he initiated the Lane Trail, a 140-mile route from Topeka, Kansas, to Nebraska City, Nebraska, and into Iowa by which slaves could avoid Missouri slave catchers. The trail enabled insurrectionist John Brown to escort passengers of the Underground Railroad unchallenged across the Midwest to Canada. After Lane's election to the U.S. Senate, in fall 1861, he gained a reputation for leading raids in slave territory to the east that left Osceola, Missouri, looted and burned. In August 1862, he began recruiting men for the First Kansas Colored Infantry.

Source

Fisher, H.D. *The Gun and the Gospel: Early Kansas and Chaplain Fisher.* Chicago: Medical Century, 1897.

Lane, Lunsford (1803–1863)

A slave for 32 years, Lunsford Lane left bondage and supported the Underground Railroad. A native of Raleigh, in Wake County, North Carolina, he was born on the plantation of Sherwood Haywood. Lane married Martha Curtis in 1828 and served in the governor's mansion during two administrations as messenger and waiter. Through skillful tobacco merchandising, he saved a tidy sum. After purchasing his liberation papers on May 17, 1841, he traveled through Philadelphia, where operatives provided the funds for travel to New York. Lane and his family located in Boston, Massachusetts. A protégé of William Lloyd Garrison, editor of the anti-slavery weekly *The Liberator,* Lane became a platform orator and recruiter of agents of the secret network. In 1842, he published *The Narrative of Lunsford Lane, Formerly of Raleigh, North Carolina.*

See also: agents, Underground Railroad; *Liberator, The.*

Sources

Andrews, William L., with David A. Davis, Tampathia Evans, Ian Frederick Finseth, and Andreá N. Williams. *North Carolina Slave Narratives: The Lives of Moses Roper, Lunsford Lane, Moses Grandy, and Thomas H. Jones.* Chapel Hill: University of North Carolina Press, 2003.

Lane, Lunsford. *The Narrative of Lunsford Lane, Formerly of Raleigh, North Carolina.* Boston: J.G. Torrey, 1842.

Langdon, Jervis (1809–1870)

A member of an anti-slavery confederacy in Elmira, New York, Jervis Langdon was a quick-thinking rescuer of fugitives. A storekeeper from age 18, he invested in the coal and iron trade at his building on Fifth and Hatch streets and generously applied his earnings to the rescue of slaves. For backup, he relied on the Reverend Thomas Kennicut Beecher, James M. Robinson, and William P. Yates. Conductor Riggs Watrous provided a haven in the upper story of his house on Lake Street. The area was so hospitable to runaways that some chose to settle in Elmira.

In 1844, Langdon and Edward Messer received passengers who responded to a whistle across a swamp. The two conductors directed 39 refugees from Elmira by night and supplied them with a carriage filled with provisions and with cash donated by local supporters. Before the party's departure to dangerous territory in Oswego, Langdon prayed for their safety. The refugees continued by schooner from agent Gerrit Smith's cove to Canada. The next summer, Langdon's daughter, Susan Langdon Crane, observed her father's hurried ride through the country to warn former slaves of the arrival of bounty hunters. In July 1851, Langdon alerted conductors John W. Jones and Sylvester G. Andrus to the peril of 12 slaves working farmland in Big Flats. The manhunters arrived in the rural area too late to seize their quarry.

Sources

Mutunhu, Tendal. "John W. Jones: Underground Railroad Stationmaster." *Negro History Bulletin* 41 (March 1978): 814–18.

Ramsdell, Barrbara S. "A History of John W. Jones." *Crooked Lake Review* (Winter 2003).

Langley, Louden Shubael (1838–1881)
Langley, Jane Maria (1842–ca. 1900)

A free mulatto farmer from Rutland, Vermont, Louden (or Loudon) Shubael Langley and his wife, Jane Maria Langley of Burlington, Vermont, aided desperate slaves in flight from bondage. Louden Langley was the grandson of Shubael Clark and a slave named Violet Clark. After settling in Hinesburg, in Chittendon County, Vermont, he served his community as county tax auditor. The Langleys contributed their safehouse to the rescue operation that followed passage of the Fugitive Slave Law of 1850. Through his letter to the Montpelier abolitionist paper *Green Mountain Freeman* in April 1854, Louden enlisted other volunteers to the Underground Railroad.

After the national emancipation of slaves on January 1, 1863, Langley joined the Fifty-fourth Massachusetts Volunteer Infantry and served the Thirty-third U.S.

Colored Infantry as a sergeant-major for the remainder of the Civil War. On March 9, 1864, Louden wrote the *Burlington (VT) Free Press* to commend the valor of black soldiers. During Reconstruction, the Langleys relocated to Beaufort, South Carolina, next door to Robert Smalls, another supporter of the secret network.

See also: black soldiers; Fugitive Slave Law of 1850.

Sources

Guyette, Elise A. "My Search for Louden Langley (1838–1881)." *The Flow of History* (Winter 2006): 3–5.

Zirblis, P.Z. *Friends of Freedom: The Vermont Underground Railroad Survey Report.* Montpelier: Vermont Division for Historic Preservation, 1996.

Langston, Charles Henry (1817–1892)

Abolitionist and educator Charles Henry Langston aided blacks seeking freedom. A native of Louisa County, Virginia, he was the son of a former slave, Lucy Jane Langston, and her owner, Captain Ralph Quarles. At age 20, Charles Langston gained liberation from Quarles and reunited with his siblings in Chillicothe, Ohio. The next year, he and his brother Gideon studied at Oberlin College. In 1836, Charles opened a school for former slaves in Chillicothe and Columbus, Ohio, and joined the Ohio Anti-Slavery Society. In 1842, he and David Jenkins edited the *Palladium of Liberty* in Columbus.

Charles Langston became more active in the secret network in his thirties. His efforts were supported by his brothers, Gideon Langston and John Mercer Langston. In 1848, while accompanying Martin Robinson Delany, a recruiter for the secret network, on a speaking tour, a lynch mob threatened the two men in Marseilles, Ohio. For conveying the runaway John Price to a safehouse during the Oberlin-Wellington rescue of September 13, 1858, a court found Langston guilty of violating the Fugitive Slave Law of 1850. In spring 1859, he paid a fine and began a 20-day prison term. The outcome of the rescue and legal retribution increased fervor for civil disobedience on behalf of slaves.

Langston's opinions took a radical turn. In a letter to the *Cleveland Plain Dealer* on November 18, 1859, he defended insurrectionist John Brown's raid on the federal arsenal in Harpers Ferry, Virginia, on October 16, 1859, an attack intended to supply blacks with arms for a war to end slavery. On the afternoon of Brown's hanging in the Jefferson County courthouse on December 2, 1859, Langston delivered a speech to 2,000 mourners in Cleveland. During the Civil War, he enlisted Kansas and Ohio volunteers for the Union army. After the Emancipation Proclamation of January 1, 1863, Langston continued organizing schools for freed slaves.

See also: civil disobedience; Fugitive Slave Law of 1850; Oberlin College.

Source

Delany, Martin Robinson. *Martin R. Delany: A Documentary Reader.* Ed. Robert S. Levine. Chapel Hill: University of North Carolina Press, 2003.

Langston, George R. (fl. 1840s)

An English immigrant, George R. Langston risked imprisonment to rescue a slave. In 1847, he was found guilty in Howard County, Missouri, of violating federal law. Leaving behind a wife and child, he faced a two-year sentence in the Missouri state penitentiary in Jefferson City. In midsummer 1848, a petition with 100 signatures influenced Governor John Cummins Edwards to pardon Langston. The prisoner exited his cell on July 24, 1848.

Source

Frazier, Harriet C. *Runaway and Freed Missouri Slaves and Those Who Helped Them, 1763–1865.* Jefferson, NC: McFarland, 2004.

Langston, John Mercer (1829–1897) Langston, Caroline Matilda Wall (1833–1915)

Attorney and politician John Mercer Langston and his wife, Caroline Matilda Wall "Carrie" Langston, joined the Ohio–Canada line as Underground Railroad conductors. Born in Louisa County, Virginia, to Afro-Indian freedwoman Lucy Jane Langston and a white planter, Captain Ralph Quarles, at age five Langston inherited one-third of his father's fortune, which he shared with two brothers, Charles Henry and Gideon. John Langston grew up in Cincinnati, obtained a degree from Oberlin College, and settled in Oberlin, Ohio. On September 3, 1841, he witnessed a riot in Cincinnati between pro-slavery forces and abolitionists over runaway slaves residing illegally in the city.

Influenced by orator Frederick Douglass, at age 19, Langston began enlisting support for the secret network and aiding runaways. With his marriage to activist Caroline Matilda Wall in 1854, he became the brother-in-law of agents Amanda A. Thomas Wall and Orindatus Simon Bolivar Wall. Langston continued his aid to desperate slaves from the family's two-story home at 207 East College Street, where he and his wife raised livestock and tended their orchards and pastures. Because of racial prejudice at law schools, Langston studied privately in Elyria, Ohio, with Philemon Bliss and became Ohio's first black attorney.

At the urging of Joshua Reed Giddings, on May 24, 1859, Langston joined secret network recruiter Salmon Portland Chase in informing an audience in Cleveland, Ohio, of President James Buchanan's favoritism toward the slave-holding South. Langston plotted anarchy with insurrectionist John Brown but chose not to join the raid on the federal arsenal at Harpers Ferry, Virginia, which took place on October 16, 1859. When the Civil War began, Langston solicited black volunteers for the Fifty-fourth Massachusetts Regiment, the nation's first all-black infantry, and for Ohio's 127th Colored Regiment. Carrie Langston supported black troops with fund-raising and the purchase of banners. In January 1863, Langston read aloud to the Oberlin College student body the Emancipation Proclamation. The Langstons' former residence is a National Historic Landmark.

See also: Oberlin College.

Sources

Griffler, Keith P. *Front Line of Freedom: African Americans and the Forging of the Underground Railroad in the Ohio Valley.* Lexington: University Press of Kentucky, 2004.

Sheridan, Richard B. "Charles Henry Langston and the African American Struggle in Kansas." *Kansas History* 22 (Winter 1999–2000): 268–83.

Lanphear, Ethan (1818–1903)

Amid the heavy traffic of fugitive slaves traveling along the eastern seaboard to Canada, Ethan Lanphear operated a memorable service. A native of Westerly, Rhode Island, he settled in Nile, in Allegany County, New York, among Seventh-Day Baptists. At a time and place where abolitionism was a minority opinion, he managed an Underground Railroad stop that harbored passengers received from John King in Ceres and passed them on to the residence of conductors Jeremiah Hatch, Jr., and Lucy Rigdon Hatch in Friendship. Lanphear claimed to have aided Frederick Douglass, George Harris, and the Reverend Jermaine Wesley Loguen, who settled in Syracuse. Lanphear maintained that obedience to divine will outweighed the wrong of civil disobedience. He later fought with the Union army during the Civil War and retired to Plainfield, New Jersey.

See also: abolitionism; civil disobedience.

Source

Minard, John S. *History of Allegany County, New York.* Alfred, NY: W.A. Fergusson, 1896.

Lansing, Wendell (1807–1887)
Lansing, Eliza Harrington Allen (1809–1858)

The owner and editor of the weekly *Essex County (NY) Republican* and the commander of the local militia, Wendell Lansing and his wife, Eliza Harrington Allen Lansing, conducted slaves along the New York–Quebec route of the Underground Railroad. Wendell Lansing was a trustee of the Wesleyan Methodist Church and a co-founder of the Washington County Anti-Slavery Society. As runaways passed through the Adirondack Mountains, they depended on the safehouse of Catherine R. Keese and Samuel Keese and their son, John Keese, in Peru. From there, the passengers arrived at the Lansing farm in Union Village, in Clinton County, New York. Lansing also aided the Reverend Jermaine Wesley Loguen and Uriah Dimond Mihills in counseling new arrivals to Canada on the purchase of land. During the Civil War, Lansing served as quartermaster of the Seventy-seventh New York Volunteers.

Source

Sylvester, Nathaniel Bartlett. *History of Saratoga County, New York.* Chicago: Gresham, 1893.

Latimer, George W. (1820–1896)
Latimer, Rebecca (ca. 1822–?)

The quandary of runaway mulatto George W. Latimer and his wife, Rebecca Latimer, helped to set the tone of eastern abolitionism. The son of a stonemason, Mitchell Latimer, and a slave, Margaret Olmstead, George was trained as a drayman and domestic and worked as a store clerk. Traveling in the ballast hold of a sloop out of Frenchtown, the Latimers fled merchant James B. Gray in Norfolk, Virginia, on October 4, 1842, and arrived in Boston, via Baltimore and Philadelphia, on October 7. When George Latimer was arrested and incarcerated at the Leverett Street jail on an unsubstantiated charge of stealing from Gray's store, Rebecca sheltered at a safehouse on High Street. She remained free and gave birth to a child at another waystation on Newhall Street in Lynn, Massachusetts.

The Boston Freedom Association failed to rescue George Latimer. Although sympathetic to runaways, Chief Justice Lemuel B. Shaw refused to intervene in a federal issue of slave recapture. Latimer remained in his cell while his owner sought proof of ownership. Defending Latimer at Faneuil Hall was a star abolitionist orator of his day, attorney Wendell Addison Phillips, along with journalist William Lloyd Garrison, agent John J. Fatal, and Dr. Henry Ingersoll Bowditch. Samuel Edmund Sewall coached Latimer on how to respond to jailing and how to summon help from the local Underground Railroad.

On November 11, 1842, George Latimer's owner won his case. There was a groundswell of protest, beginning with a short-lived daily newsletter, the *Latimer Journal and North Star,* established by supporters Dr. Henry Bowditch, Frederick Cabot, and William Francis Channing. In a few months, the paper attained a circulation of 20,000. While accusing authorities of abetting kidnap, volunteers raised $400 to buy Latimer from Gray. Condemning the purchase were William Lloyd Garrison and Maria Weston Chapman, who opposed the reimbursement of slave owners. The Latimers' notoriety prevented them from enjoying liberty while hiding at numerous waystations.

In defense of the Latimers, Garrison published the outrage of Frederick Douglass in *The Liberator.* Public anger resulted in 65,000 signers pressing a petition on the Massachusetts legislature, which, on March 24, 1843, passed the Personal Liberty Act. Under its statutes, state authorities could not aid federal agents during seizure of runaways or use local jails for slave incarceration. John Quincy Adams delivered to Congress another petition, containing 43,000 signatures, urging an end to the pursuit of slaves in free territory. George Latimer worked in Lynn as a paperhanger and developed a friendship with two Underground Railroad agents, Mary Saltmarsh Farnham "Polly" Jenkins and her husband, William Jenkins, of Andover, Massachusetts. On May 1, 1851, Latimer completed a six-day surveillance of a bounty hunter. During the Civil War, the Latimers' son, George, served the Connecticut Black Regiment.

See also: abolitionism; kidnap; *Liberator, The.*

Sources

Latimer, George. "The Two Autobiographical Fragments of George W. Latimer." *Journal of Afro-American Historical and Genealogical Society* 1 (Summer 1980).

Laurie, Bruce. *Beyond Garrison: Antislavery and Social Reform.* New York: Cambridge University Press, 2005.

Proceedings of the Citizens of the Borough of Norfolk, on the Boston Outrage, in the Case of the Runaway Slave George Latimer. Norfolk, VA: Broughton & Son, 1843.

Laughead, David (1813–1895)
Laughead, Rebecca A. (?–1861)
Laughead, David Mitchell (1789–1870)
Laughead, Elizabeth Kyle (1791–1861)

Rescuers of fugitive slaves, farmer David Laughead and his wife, Rebecca A. Laughead, excavated a hideaway in which to conceal refugees. David Laughead, the son and namesake of David Mitchell Laughead, a pioneer of Lancaster County, Pennsylvania, followed the principles of his abolitionist father and mother, Elizabeth Kyle Laughead. In 1988, the discovery of the trapdoor in the stone cellar of the family farmhouse on Clark's Run in Xenia, in Greene County, Ohio, revealed the elder Laughead's clever handiwork of 1810. Until the sale of the property in 1839, the younger David Laughead and his family received passengers by night at their two-story residence.

Source

Ellis, Franklin, and Samuel Evans. *History of Lancaster County, Pennsylvania.* Philadelphia: Everts & Peck, 1882.

Lay, Benjamin (1682–1759)

A rescuer of the destitute, Benjamin Lay introduced the tenets of civil disobedience into Quaker communities before the American Revolution. Lay lacked the physique of the stereotypical hero. He stood only 4 feet 6 inches in height, and his misshapen torso and hunched back earned his neighbors' pity. After his flight to the West Indies in 1730, he was scorned for involving himself in anti-slavery activism. The following year, he lived in a cave in Abington, Pennsylvania, outside Philadelphia, and set an example by boycotting slave-made, slave-harvested goods, including cotton, indigo, molasses, rice, rum, sugar, and tobacco. He regularly nettled Quakers who owned slaves. To illustrate the terrors of child auctions, he kidnapped the six-year-old son of a prominent white family. He chastised the parents for having no compassion for slave mothers and fathers. His melodramatic speeches won Quakers to the cause of aiding fugitives.

See also: American Revolution; kidnap; Quakers.

Source

Okur, Nilgun Anadolu. "Underground Railroad in Philadelphia, 1830–1860." *Journal of Black Studies* 25:5 (1995): 537–57.

Leary, Lewis Sheridan (1835–1859)

Lewis Sheridan Leary, a saddle and harness maker, was deeply involved in the Underground Railroad in Oberlin, Ohio. Of African, Croatan, and Irish lineage, he was born in Fayetteville, North Carolina. Leary was brother-in-law to two operatives of the secret network, Wilson Bruce Evans and his brother, Henry Evans, a mortician, who married Lewis Leary's sisters, Sarah Jane Leary and Henrietta R. Leary, respectively. The two couples lived in Ohio near the Evans brothers' sister, Delilah Evans Copeland, mother of John Anthony Copeland, Jr., who superintended refugee assistance in Lorain County, Ohio. Leary aided passengers in reaching Wilson and Sarah Evans's waystation at 33 East Vine Street in Oberlin. On September 13, 1858, Leary participated in what came to be called the Oberlin-Wellington rescue of escaped slave John Price, but Leary was not charged with liberating or harboring a fugitive.

Along with his nephew, John Copeland, Jr., Leary joined insurrectionist John Brown's abolitionist militia in an attack on the federal arsenal in Harpers Ferry, Virginia, on October 16, 1858. Leary left behind a wife, Mary S. Patterson Leary, and a six-month-old son. The failed raid was intended to launch a slave war for liberty. Wounded by military gunfire at the rifle works, Leary died eight hours later. Wendell Addison Phillips, an operative of the secret network, shared with James Redpath the costs of Leary's son's education.

Source

Hinton, Richard Josiah. *John Brown and His Men: With Some Account of the Roads They Travelled to Reach Harpers Ferry.* New York: Funk & Wagnalls, ca. 1894.

Leavitt, Chloe Maxwell (1772–1851)
Leavitt, Roger (1771–1840)

The parents of agent Joshua Leavitt, Chloe Maxwell Leavitt and Roger Leavitt assisted refugees fleeing to New England via the Underground Railroad. They married in June 1793 and opened a waystation in Charlemont, Massachusetts. Among the passengers they aided were Basil and Louisa Dorsey, who worked at the Leavitts' farm for five years and then settled in Florence, Massachusetts, at 191 Nonotuck Street.

Source

Blue, Frederick J. *No Taint of Compromise: Crusaders in Antislavery Politics.* Baton Rouge: Louisiana State University Press, 2005.

Leavitt, Joshua (1794–1873)

The Reverend Joshua Leavitt, the eldest son of agents Chloe Maxwell Leavitt and Roger Leavitt, contributed words and action to the cause of the Underground Railroad. Educated at Yale, he practiced law in Putney, Vermont, until his return to Yale to study for the ministry. He pastored a Congregational church in Stratford, Connecticut. In 1833, he co-formed the New York Anti-Slavery Society and suffered threats and mob violence for his aid to runaway slaves. In 1846, he edited the *Emancipator* in Boston, where his office sheltered fugitives. Among the refugees that Leavitt assisted were Basil and Louisa Dorsey, whom Leavitt helped to settle in Florence, Massachusetts.

Source

Blue, Frederick J. *No Taint of Compromise: Crusaders in Antislavery Politics.* Baton Rouge: Louisiana State University Press, 2005.

Lee, Amanda Jane Barker (fl. 1860s–1870s)

Amanda Jane Barker Lee, a Missouri quadroon, was both a passenger and an agent of the Underground Railroad. In 1861, she eluded her owner and hid at a Union army camp until she could gain passage along the secret network to Wisconsin. Led by an army surgeon, she traveled by train to Madison, where she settled and volunteered with the Relief Corps. In addition to nursing, she conducted runaways for the secret network. On New Year's Eve 1876, she married a barber, Arthur Lee, a widower from Charleston, South Carolina, with a young son. Her husband was a veteran of the first all-black Union army regiment, the Fifty-fourth Massachusetts Volunteer Infantry.

See also: black soldiers; Civil War.

Source

Clark, James I. *Wisconsin Defies the Fugitive Slave Law: The Case of Sherman M. Booth.* Madison: State Historical Society of Wisconsin, 1955.

Lee, Archy (1840–1873)

The emancipation of Archy Lee attests to an Underground Railroad in California. A native of Pike County, Mississippi, Lee was the chattel of John Stovall. In summer 1857, the owner's son, Charles V. Stovall, took 18-year-old Lee to Missouri and then to Sacramento, California. In January 1858, Lee fled to a safehouse, a black-owned hotel. On January 6, Coons, the city marshal, arrested Lee. After a lengthy court battle involving state law and the Fugitive Slave Law of 1850, Lee was returned to Stovall on February 11.

The owner concealed Lee from abolitionists and headed back to Mississippi by the steamer *Orizaba.* Police seized Stovall and Lee in San Francisco Bay and renewed litigation against Stovall on March 8 for kidnapping a black from the free state of California. David Ruggles, an agent of the American Anti-Slavery Society, raised funds to pay Lee's legal fees. Lee gained his freedom but was arrested by a U.S. commissioner. On April 14, 1858, the California Supreme Court freed Lee. After hiding in the residence of Mary Ellen Pleasant, he left the country and joined a gold rush outside Victoria, British Columbia. In response to Archy Lee's experience in California, attorney Mifflin Wistar Gibbs organized an abolitionist effort there.

See also: American Anti-Slavery Society; kidnap.

Source

Hudson, Lynne M. *The Making of Mammy Pleasant: A Black Entrepreneur in Nineteenth-Century San Francisco.* Champaign: University of Illinois Press, 2003.

Lee, Ishmael (1815–1879)
Lee, Sallie East (1814–1840)
Lee, Miriam Marmon (1817–1903)

Ishmael Lee, a cobbler from Blount County, Tennessee, joined a network of Quaker Underground Railroad agents in Cass County, Michigan, where he managed a safehouse a mile south of Cassopolis. He married Sallie East of Wayne County, Indiana, settled in Williamsville, Michigan, and rescued slaves. After his wife died, he continued his volunteerism and married Miriam Marmon of Ohio. On August 1, 1847, Sylvanus Erastus Hussey alerted Stephen A. Bogue, Josiah Osborn, and Zachariah Shugart to the arrival of a posse of 13 raiders from Bourbon County, Kentucky. The band stopped first at Bogue's safehouse at Cassopolis and seized a family of five refugees. Bogue, Shugart, and Osborn confronted the slave nabbers, who sought court action. Wright Modlin, a Quaker conductor at Williamsville, Michigan, obtained a writ demanding that the insurgents free their captives, who now numbered nine.

During arraignment and litigation, Shugart piloted the runaways to the Lee waystation. When the party grew to 50 runaways, Shugart continued the relay to Canada. When another slave disappeared from jail in February 1848, the Kentuckians sued the secret network agents Lee, Bogue, Osborn, Shugart, William Jones, Ebenezer McIlvain, and D.T. Nicholson. Because of the contentious nature of the trial, the matter remained unresolved until January 1851, when D.T. Nicholson paid $1,000 to rid himself and Lee of the Kentuckians and their lawsuits.

In September 1850, passage of the Fugitive Slave Law made recovery of escaping slaves easier for their owners. During the Civil War, Ishmael and Miriam Lee lost a son, Peter, in combat in Memphis, Tennessee, only days before the conflict ended.

See also: Fugitive Slave Law of 1850.

Sources

Glover, Lowell H. *A Twentieth Century History of Cass County, Michigan.* Chicago: Lewis, 1906.
Mathews, Alfred. *History of Cass County, Michigan.* Chicago: Waterman, Watkins, 1882.

Lee, Luther (1800–1889)

An evangelist, editor, and abolitionist orator, the Reverend Luther Lee served the Underground Railroad as a recruiter of agents and a conductor of runaways. A native of Schoharie, New York, and a son of Wesleyan Methodist pioneers, he worked at a gristmill and a tannery while learning to read and write. In 1825, he married Mary Miller, a teacher, and settled in Plymouth, New York. At age 37, he became an abolitionist. In partnership with a circuit-riding minister, Cyrus Prindle, Lee canvassed the area on behalf of the New York State Anti-Slavery Society.

In the July 19, 1845, issue of the *True Wesleyan*, the Reverend Luther Lee commented on the passage of runaways through the Wesleyan Church in Syracuse, New York: "We are to hold a public meeting this evening, and I hope to be able to introduce [the passengers] appropriately to the community; and, before the sun sets to-morrow evening, we design having these 'human cattle' introduced to Queen Victoria's pasture."

During their tour, Lee heaped scorn upon Christian churches for their lackluster record on denouncing slavery. His meticulous arguments earned him the nickname "Logical Luther."

As editor of the *True Wesleyan* from 1844 to 1852, Lee remained steadfast in the cause of liberty. He vowed never to obey fugitive slave laws, even if it meant going to prison. His newspaper reported slave relays, including a party of nine who advanced from Syracuse through a Methodist church in Fulton, New York.

In spring 1852, traffic through Lee's safehouse at 39 Onondaga Street across from his church averaged one fugitive per day. Most were exhausted from the long trek north. From Syracuse, passengers traveled to brothers Charles Merrick and Montgomery Merrick in Erie, New York, or by railroad car to Ontario. Lee made arrangements for the free passage through connections with railroad employees. While teaching theology at Leoni Institute and Adrian College in Adrian, Michigan, in the 1850s, Lee joined conductor Ovid Miner in directing slaves over the Michigan–Canada route. In December 1859, Lee eulogized insurrectionist John Brown at his grave site in Lake Placid, New York. In Lee's autobiography, which he wrote at age 82, he justified civil disobedience as a moral duty to defy an immoral law.

See also: civil disobedience.

Sources

Lee, Luther. *Autobiography of the Rev. Luther Lee.* New York: Phillips & Hunt, 1882.

———, "Fugitive Slaves," *True Wesleyan*, July 19, 1845.

Leggett, Joseph (1788–1871) Leggett, Fanny B. (1794–1883)

A Quaker libertarian from New York, Joseph Leggett pitied the desperate slave. He was born in Saratoga County of pioneer stock. He and his wife, Fanny B. Leggett, a native of Connecticut, served the Underground Railroad network in Warren County in cooperation with Abel Brown and Mary Ann Brown in Albany and with Caroline Mattocks Moore and Noadiah Moore in Clinton County, New York. The Leggetts received slaves at their safehouse south of Chestertown. Eyewitness reports of rescues survive from the couple's son, Benjamin Leggett.

Source

Brown, William H., ed. *History of Warren County, New York.* Saratoga, NY: Board of Supervisors, 1963.

LeMoyne, Francis Julius (1798–1879) LeMoyne, Madeleine Romaine Bureau (ca. 1799–1873)

A physician, an abolitionist, and a conductor of fugitives, Dr. Francis Julius LeMoyne and his wife, Madeleine Romaine Bureau LeMoyne, operated a two-story stone safehouse in Washington, in southwestern Pennsylvania. The son of a French physician, John Julius LeMoyne, who escaped the chaos of the French Revolution, Julius studied at Washington College and followed his father's profession. From the 1830s until the Emancipation Proclamation of January 1, 1863, the LeMoyne home, with the aid and cooperation of the eight LeMoyne children, was a major depot of the secret railway.

After establishing their family and a medical practice in the residence at 49 East Maiden Street in 1823, the LeMoynes concealed slaves, up to 25 at one time, in the cellar, in a third-floor bedroom, and in an attic, which they equipped with thick walls and narrow "eyebrow" windows. Passengers arrived along a rural route from Greene County, Pennsylvania. On the next leg of their journey, they passed through the care of Joseph Gray in Graysville, of Jane Campbell McKeever and Matthew McKeever in Middletown, or of Isaac Teagarden and Sarah Ann Parker Teagarden in Wheeling Creek before reaching Kenneth McCoy's rural stop in West Alexander.

In a predominantly anti-abolition neighborhood, the LeMoynes actively opposed human bondage. To protect residents and guests from pro-slavery mobs, the family hired night watchmen and armed them with stout sticks. In 1834, Julius LeMoyne founded the Washington (Pennsylvania) Anti-Slavery Society and served as its president as well as editor of the

Anti-Slavery Report. He also donated funds to the American and Foreign Anti-Slavery Society. His collaboration with James Gillespie Birney, an attorney in Cincinnati, Ohio, and John Baton Vashon, a barber in Pittsburgh, and his correspondence with agent Nelson T. Gant in Zanesville, Ohio, illustrates the doctor's interest in securing an exit route for fugitives. The LeMoyne house was Pennsylvania's first safehouse listed as a National Historic Landmark of the Underground Railroad.

Sources

McCulloch, Margaret Callender. *Fearless Advocate of the Right: The Life of Francis Julius LeMoyne, M.D., 1798–1879.* Boston: Christopher, 1941.

Rew, Kay Jenkins. "The Le Moyne House: An Inspiring Tale of Washington County's Secret Underground Railroad." *Pennsylvania Turnpike* (Fall 1998): 12.

Leonard, Jane (1806–1873)
Leonard, Thomas (1789–1877)

Two rescuers in Syracuse, New York, Jane Leonard and Thomas Leonard joined other black workers in helping slaves find freedom in Canada. After their arrival in Onondaga County from slavery in Virginia or Maryland in 1830, they settled on the Erie Canal and opened a waystation. Jane cooked at the Exchange Hotel. Thomas worked as a carter, boatman, day laborer, and waiter at Syracuse House, a downtown hotel. On October 7, 1839, he helped a Mississippi-born domestic, Harriet Powell, escape servitude and follow the Underground Railroad to Kingston, Ontario. Powell's owner, John Davenport, pressed a frivolous lawsuit against Thomas Leonard for allegedly stealing Powell's clothes. During the Civil War, Leonard served in the Fifty-fourth Massachusetts Regiment, the nation's first all-black infantry.

Source

"Slave Story of September 1839, Which Awakened Many Abolition Feelings," *Syracuse (NY) Sunday Times,* June 10, 1877.

Lewelling, Henderson W. (1809–1883)
Lewelling, Jane Elizabeth Presnall (1815–?)

An Iowa pioneer and influential Underground Railroad stationmaster, Henderson W. Lewelling (also Luelling), a Quaker merchant and tree grafter, was a source of rescue on the Iowa–Canada route. Born in Randolph County, North Carolina, to Jane Brookshire Lewelling and Dr. Meshack Lewelling, Henderson and his younger brother, Seth Lewelling, left their family home in Henry County, Indiana, in 1837. In Salem, Iowa, they opened a dry goods store and started a wholesale fruit tree nursery that propagated the Royal Anne bing cherry.

In 1840, at 401 South Main Street, about 25 miles from the slave state of Missouri, Henderson and his wife, Jane Elizabeth Presnall Lewelling, erected a two-story residence called the Old Stone House. The floor plan featured hidden doors in the kitchen, a closet, and a side room. The family removed rag rugs to reveal steps leading down to tunnels in the crawl space for concealing fugitives. Assisting Lewelling with the legalities of rescue was Nelson Gibbs, a justice of the peace, who held court in the front room of the Lewellings' home. For the family's abolitionist activism, they were ousted from the Salem Monthly Meeting of Friends. After the Lewellings organized a wagon train to the Willamette River valley in Oregon in 1847, Henderson Lewelling became known as the father of the Pacific Coast fruit industry.

Source

Richter, Shawna, "History Lies Underground," *Burlington (IA) Hawk Eye,* June 13, 2005.

Lewey, Henry (fl. 1850s)

A manager of the Underground Railroad, Henry "Blue Beard" Lewey chose oceangoing vessels as the safest conveyance for fugitive slaves. He advanced passengers from Norfolk, Virginia, by sea to Philadelphia, Pennsylvania. For the flight of his wife, Rebecca, he depended on a seasoned transporter, William "Captain B" Baylis of Wilmington, Delaware. Lewey continued aiding separated families by conveying letters and belongings to and from Canada. In 1856, local investigations of the secret network forced Lewey to flee to Ontario. His courage and ingenuity earned the admiration of William Still, author of *The Underground Railroad* (1872).

Source

Parramore, Thomas C. *Norfolk: The First Four Centuries.* Charlottesville: University of Virginia Press, 1994.

Lewis, Elijah (1751–1834)
Lewis, Martha (1753–1823)

Farmer Elijah Lewis, a captain during the American Revolution, and his wife, Martha Lewis, joined the

Underground Railroad effort in Farmington, in Hartford County, Connecticut. The Lewises welcomed fugitives at their three-story clapboard home at 738 Farmington Avenue. In times of danger, slaves could hurry to the basement and squeeze into a fireplace niche, which the couple capped with a stone.

See also: American Revolution.

Source

Chadwick, Bruce. *Traveling the Underground Railroad: A Visitor's Guide to More Than 300 Sites.* Secaucus, NJ: Citadel, 1999.

Lewis, Enoch (1776–1856)

Quaker rescuer Enoch Lewis was a great-hearted friend of refugees. In an active life in New Garden, Pennsylvania, he was a mathematics teacher at the Westtown Boarding School, a surveyor, an essayist, and an editor of the monthly journal *African Observer* (1827–1828) and the *Friends' Review* (1847–1856). He occupied a station that had formerly been managed by Isaac Jackson. Local abolitionists informed Lewis of spies in the area. On constant alert, he kept a horse and carriage ready for the next rescue. Some of the hastier passages involved slaves arriving from the station of his brother, Evan Lewis (1782–1834), in Wilmington, Delaware. In one instance, Enoch Lewis packed a woman and child in a load of wool and dispatched them to Nixon's mill in Pickering Creek. Joseph J. Lewis (1801–?), Enoch's oldest child, drove the cart to Emmor Kimber and Susannah Jackson Kimber's safehouse in Kimberton.

In addition to welcoming escapees to his home, Lewis promoted countermeasures to bondage, including collaboration with Thomas M'Clintock and Israel Johnson of Germantown on the establishment of the Free Produce Society, which offered groceries not made by slave labor. In defiance of fugitive slave laws, Lewis issued articles on the violation of the Bill of Rights. He fought in court for the release of free blacks seized by kidnappers for sale in the South. In one instance, he paid $300 and raised $100 more to pay for the freedom of a man whose wife begged for assistance. In another instance, Lewis helped conductor Israel Johnson retrieve a man unjustly imprisoned in Baltimore, Maryland, as a runaway. The Lewis family also reared the nephew of a preacher who escaped from the Deep South. The boy received 13 years of education before locating work on an ocean liner serving New York City and Liverpool, England.

See also: bloodhounds; free labor store; kidnap; spies.

Source

Smedley, Robert C. *History of the Underground Railroad in Chester and the Neighboring Counties of Pennsylvania.* Lancaster, PA: Office of *The Journal,* 1883.

Lewis (Esther Fussell and John, Jr.) Family

The Lewis family is a model of the family tradition of hosting refugees. A nurse, teacher, and conductor of the north–south line through Pennsylvania, Esther Fussell Lewis (1782–1848) aspired to be a doctor but lacked the opportunity in an era that denied women professional education. She was the daughter of Rebecca Bond and the Reverend Bartholomew Fussell, a Quaker minister, and the sister of Solomon Fussell and Dr. Bartholomew Fussell, an Underground Railroad agent and the founder of the Women's Medical College of Pennsylvania. After Esther's marriage to John Lewis, Jr. (1781–1824), the couple reared a family of activists who assisted runaway slaves. Among their precautions was the burning of coarse slave shifts, a crude, one-piece tow-cloth or burlap garment peculiar to the southern plantation system. John Lewis died of typhus after tending a black couple infected with the disease.

Living at Sunnyside Home, the family farm outside Kimberton, after her husband's death in 1824, Esther Lewis depended on her brother, Solomon Fussell, to help manage the property. She and her daughters—Elizabeth R. (1824–1863), Graceanna (1821–1912), and Mariann (1819–1866) Lewis and Rebecca Lewis Fussell (1820–1893)—operated a rehabilitation center for fugitives, which aided a man who injured his leg by leaping from a train. The family operation received assistance from Cyrus Moses Burleigh and Margaret Jones Burleigh in Erie County; Esther Logue Hayes and Mordecai Hayes and their son, Jacob Hayes, in Newlin; and Jonathan Paxson Magill and his sons, Edward Hicks Magill and Watson Magill, in Bucks County, Pennsylvania. The Lewises depended on William Still for information about incoming passengers from the stations of Ann Vickers Painter and Samuel M. Painter in West Chester and from Abigail Paxson Vickers and John Vickers in Lancaster County.

The Lewis women intervened in cases of contagious or chronic illness, pregnancy, infirmity, severe whipping, and exhaustion until slaves could recover.

Those ready for travel followed transporter Norris Maris to the stations of Lewis Peart in Lampeter, to Elijah Funk Pennypacker in Chester County, to Richard Moore and Sarah Foulke Moore in Quakertown, or to sympathetic ticket agents at depots of the Reading Railroad that served Toronto. Rebecca Lewis Fussell, wife of her cousin, Dr. Edwin Fussell, an agent in Media, collected respectable travel clothing to conceal slave identities. Contributing to her stock were her uncle, William Fussell, his sons, Joseph and Milton, and the Reverend John Price of Lawrenceville.

Continuing their mother's work after her death in 1848, Esther's four daughters received refugees from the stop managed by Benjamin and Jane Price in East Bradford. The Lewis women managed to house and feed 40 fugitives in a single week. One female slave, who died in childbirth in Canada, requested that her two children be fostered by the Lewises. Graceanna Lewis, an ornithologist and social reformer, recalled an ex-slave in Philadelphia who thanked her and her sisters for their tender care of an infant that died in Graceanna's arms. After the Christiana Riot of September 11, 1851, Bartholomew Fussell ferried three outlaws, William Parker and his accomplices, Abraham Johnson and Alexander Pinkney, from the Kennett Square station of Dinah Hannum Mendenhall and Isaac Mendenhall to Graceanna Lewis's care. At midnight, she admitted the trio and secured them on the third floor of the residence. To keep house servants from becoming suspicious, she sought food from a neighbor rather than feed the escapees from her own larder. The men traveled on to a station near Phoenixville the next day.

In her memoirs, Graceanna recorded episodes of concealing fugitives under her bed and of defying deputies who insisted on ransacking the women's quarters. On October 27, 1855, 11 escapees from a Maryland plantation passed through several stations to the Vickerses' depot and on to Sunnyside Home. The Confederate army marked the Lewis home for destruction but was unable to invade the North and carry out the plot. Elizabeth R. Lewis contracted a lethal fever from a soldier returning from the war and died in 1863. Her sudden death ended the Lewis sisters' humanitarian work.

See also: Christiana Riot.

Source

Smedley, Robert C. *History of the Underground Railroad in Chester and the Neighboring Counties of Pennsylvania.* Lancaster, PA: Office of *The Journal,* 1883.

Lewis, James (1802–1876)

James Lewis operated a tannery in Marple, in Delaware County, Pennsylvania, while rescuing slaves from bondage. He entered the secret web at the request of Nathan Evans of Willistown and connected with other rural stations or directly to Philadelphia. With James T. Dannaker of Chester, Pennsylvania, Lewis promoted home meetings with other abolitionists. The duo received slaves from Evans in Willistown and passed some to Hester Reckless in Philadelphia. One armed pair, the custodian of Reverdy Johnson's law office in Baltimore, Maryland, and a coachman named Charles from Mississippi, skirted surly proslavers in Wrightsville and halted at Lewis's waystation before continuing to Canada. The total travel time was two weeks.

The Dannaker-Lewis partnership altered in 1843, when Dannaker married and moved to Philadelphia to open his own depot. The effort proved problematic because of Lewis's notoriety. At one point, Lewis led 16 fugitives to the Dannaker house. Lewis walked ahead of the wagons and signaled with his handkerchief the safest route. On one of his rescues, he delivered two men to two sister conductors. The women revealed the arrival of a slave who recognized her husband as one of the newcomers. The chance nature of the meeting astounded Dannaker, who learned that the couple had separated four years earlier when the husband had been sold in the South.

Source

Smedley, Robert C. *History of the Underground Railroad in Chester and the Neighboring Counties of Pennsylvania.* Lancaster, PA: Office of *The Journal,* 1883.

Lewis, Pompey (fl. 1830s–1850s)

Pompey Lewis served an Underground Railroad route that carried the passengers of Harriet Tubman. He and Jubilee Sharper aided rescue operations at the Mount Zion African Methodist Episcopal Church, incorporated in 1832 at 172 Garwin Road in Small Gloucester (now called Woolwich), in Gloucester County, New Jersey. The church served as a depot and a rehabilitation station for weary fugitives, who received food, clothing, directions, and protection. Slaves hid in the sanctuary under a trapdoor in the foyer. The property is listed as an endangered historic site.

See also: African Methodist Episcopal Church.

Source

"*Steal Away, Steal Away . . .* " (pamphlet). Trenton: New Jersey Historical Commission, 2002.

Lewis, Thomas (fl. 1840s)

Quaker agent Thomas Lewis networked with conductors of the Pennsylvania–Canada route of the Underground Railroad. In Robinson (or Robeson), a safe haven for slaves in Berks County, he maintained White Bear, a depot hosting runaways traversing Quaker Valley. After receiving passengers from Arminda Taylor Haines and Joseph Haines's station in Bedford, in Coshocton County, Ohio, Lewis housed and fed the fugitives and offered them work. When slave catchers ventured too near, Lewis and his collaborators concealed runaways at the huts of charcoal burners in the woods.

Source

Smedley, Robert C. *History of the Underground Railroad in Chester and the Neighboring Counties of Pennsylvania.* Lancaster, PA: Office of *The Journal,* 1883.

Liberator, The

One of the print beacons of hope to slaves and their rescuers, the radical weekly newspaper *The Liberator* promoted Underground Railroad work. Published by William Lloyd Garrison from January 1, 1831, to 1865, it was the first nationally circulated abolitionist paper. Initially, *The Liberator* had no subscribers or financial backing, but Garrison felt called to a sacred duty to oppose the flesh trade and to liberate 3 million slaves. He began publication in Boston, with the assistance of one African American boy, William Cooper Nell. In one room, Garrison and Nell cooked, slept on the floor, and operated the press until the hiring of Oliver Johnson as printmaster.

The impact was immediate. *The Liberator* gained 25 subscribers and a donation of $50 with the first issue. From Portland, Maine, came funding from Quaker stationmasters Comfort Hussey Winslow and Nathan Winslow. Attorney Ellis Gray Loring of Brookline, Massachusetts, covered financial shortfalls. Author John Greenleaf Whittier of Amesbury, Massachusetts, and the brothers Arthur and Lewis Tappan of Northampton, Massachusetts, lent moral support and promoted readership. In Pittsburgh, Pennsylvania, abolitionist John Baton Vashon, a barber, collected donations. Even more encouraging was a reward of $1,500 that the Vigilance Association of South Carolina posted in October 1831 for the capture and prosecution of distributors or circulators of *The Liberator.*

Within a year, U.S. Postmaster William T. Barry suppressed Garrison's radical views by outlawing the mailing of issues. In southern states, slave dealers and plantation owners concentrated their hatred on Garrison, whose name epitomized abolitionist intrusion on the southern plantation system and its genteel lifestyle for aristocratic whites. To end an insidious plutocracy that extracted wealth from human torment, the publisher continued pelting slave owners with the views of editor Maria Weston Chapman, poet Frances Ellen Watkins Harper, former slave James Curry, and writer Lydia Maria Francis Child, lecturer Lucretia Coffin Mott, attorney Wendell Addison Phillips, and philanthropist Gerrit Smith, all agents of the Underground Railroad.

After passage of the Fugitive Slave Law of 1850, *The Liberator* excoriated legislators but advocated passive resistance and nonviolence rather than open insurrection. Articles championed civil disobedience to an unjust federal law and opposed a requirement that people in free states assist U.S. marshals in the recapture of runaways. Garrison denounced federal intervention in refugee rescues and cited as examples the escape of Ellen Smith Craft and William Craft and the return to bondage of Henry Long and Thomas M. Sims. On March 9, 1855, Garrison reported chaos in Boston over the jailbreak of Anthony Burns, a fugitive from bondage in Richmond, Virginia. To stimulate philanthropy and consumer activism, Garrison advertised abolitionist fairs, including the ones organized by his wife, Helen Eliza Benson Garrison. He also promoted the free labor markets that rejected goods grown, harvested, or manufactured by slave labor.

> The first issue of *The Liberator*, dated January 1, 1831, set the tone for all future issues with its uncompromising demand for the abolition of slavery. The journal's founder, William Lloyd Garrison, wrote, "I am in earnest—I will not equivocate—I will not excuse—I will not retreat a single inch—AND I WILL BE HEARD."

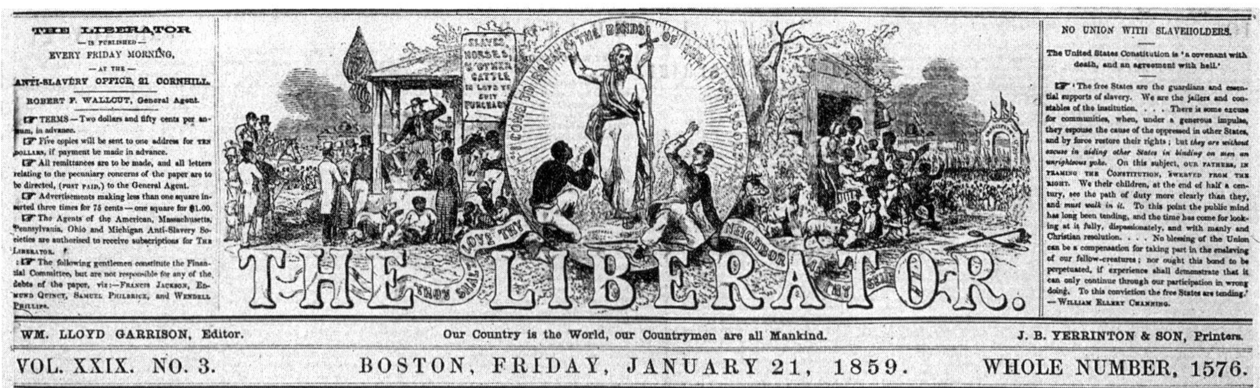
THE LIBERATOR

NO UNION WITH SLAVEHOLDERS.

WM. LLOYD GARRISON, Editor. Our Country is the World, our Countrymen are all Mankind. J. B. YERRINTON & SON, Printers.

VOL. XXIX. NO. 3. BOSTON, FRIDAY, JANUARY 21, 1859. WHOLE NUMBER, 1576.

An abolitionist weekly published in Boston by William Lloyd Garrison from 1831 to 1865, *The Liberator* stoked anti-slavery partisanship and cultivated unity among Underground Railroad operatives and other volunteers. *(MPI/Stringer/Hulton Archive/Getty Images)*

The quality and integrity of *The Liberator* fostered support initially from fellow publisher Frederick Douglass and from the clergy of all sorts of denominations. Articles championed the volunteerism of a number of secret network operatives, including George Fayerweather III, Sarah Ann Harris Fayreweather, and the Reverend Jehiel C. Beman in Connecticut, Edmund Carleton and Mary Kilburn Coffin Carleton in New Hampshire, Elizabeth Buffum Chace in Rhode Island, Josephine Sophie White Griffing in Ohio, the Jonathan Paxson Magill family in Pennsylvania, and Austin Bearse, who ferried slaves by sea from southern ports to New Bedford, Massachusetts. Farther afield was the expansion of the secret network to the frontier, growth encouraged by George Enoch Webber and Jane Ann Woodruff Webber in Ohio and Mary Ann Shadd Cary in Windsor, Ontario.

In its history of 1,820 issues, *The Liberator* developed a sense of unity among disparate segments of the Underground Railroad. Weekly issues fostered a two-way reportage between Garrison and agents in the field. One of his readers, Mordecai McKinney of Harrisburg, Pennsylvania, read of kidnap victim Jim Phillips and intervened in his plight. After making a cash offer, McKinney redeemed Phillips and his wife and children and saved them from bondage in Virginia. Garrison printed letters by lecturer Anna Elizabeth Dickinson of Philadelphia and by orator Abigail "Abby" Kelley Foster of Pelham, Massachusetts. A write-in from novelist Harriet Beecher Stowe, author of *Uncle Tom's Cabin* (1852), attempted to patch up the differences between Garrison and Frederick Douglass, whom Garrison lambasted as an extremist. Orator Sallie Holley quoted Garrison as an unimpeachable source of abolition data. Mary "Polly" Saltmarsh Farnham Jenkins and William Jenkins operated their waystation in Andover, Massachusetts, according to Garrisonian principles. Sally Morton Stephens acted on Garrison's editorials by founding an anti-slavery society in Plymouth, New York.

See also: abolitionist newspapers; agents, Underground Railroad; anti-slavery fairs; civil disobedience; free labor store; Fugitive Slave Law of 1850; philanthropists; *Uncle Tom's Cabin; or, Life Among the Lowly* (1852).

Sources

Diaz, Abby Morton. "Antislavery Times in Plymouth." *New England* 20:2 (April 1899): 216–25.

Garrison, William Lloyd. "To the Public." *The Liberator* 1:1 (January 1, 1831): 1.

Hume, John F. *The Abolitionists: Together with Personal Memories of the Struggle for Human Rights, 1830–1864.* New York: Putnam, 1905. Reprint New York: AMS, 1973.

Liberty League

A consortium of Underground Railroad organizers, the Liberty League got its start in 1847. It was born out of the disillusion of activists who had failed to achieve nationwide abolition of slavery. In a drive to end human bondage, the league coordinated the efforts of radicals George W. Brown and Glover Harrison of Toronto; roving agent John Brown; George J. Reynolds of Hamilton, Ontario; Dr. Alexander Milton Ross of Belleville, Ontario; William Goodell of Utica, New York; the Reverend Beriah Green of

Whitesboro, New York; and Gerrit Smith and Lewis Tappan of New York City. Ross described the league as "Liberators, as they were called—from Erie to Sandusky and Cleveland." According to the June 23, 1848, issue of William Lloyd Garrison's weekly newspaper, *The Liberator,* the idealism of Liberty Leaguers led them to denigrate the U.S. Constitution as a pro-slavery document and to demand immediate abolition of the flesh trade.

See also: *Liberator, The.*

Source

Hinton, Richard Josiah. *John Brown and His Men: With Some Account of the Roads They Travelled to Reach Harpers Ferry.* New York: Funk & Wagnalls, ca. 1894.

Liberty Tree

A huge sycamore on High Street in Brockton, Massachusetts, served passengers of the Underground Railroad as a route marker. Early planners of routes and depots met in secret under the Liberty Tree. Abolitionists Frederick Douglass, William Lloyd Garrison, and Wendell Addison Phillips gave speeches in the sycamore's shade to win converts to the anti-slavery cause and to enlist new conductors. In December 2004, storm damage and rot caused city officials to give up efforts to save the Liberty Tree and to cut it down. Supporters of the historic site sold branches and planted clones of the tree at the Brockton Historical Society.

See also: agents, Underground Railroad; routes, Underground Railroad.

Source

Trench, Megan, "A Witness to Freedom Takes a Fall," *Boston Globe,* December 14, 2004.

Lincoln, Abraham (1809–1865)

Before his election as the sixteenth U.S. president, Illinois attorney and politician Abraham Lincoln made no clear move toward abolitionism and left unclear the extent of his support for federal law. On the one hand, he befriended stationkeepers of the Underground Railroad, including John Albert Jones of Tremont, Illinois. In addition, at the funeral of secret network agent Elijah Parish Lovejoy on November 7, 1837, in Alton, Illinois, he delivered a stirring eulogy, "Let Every Man Remember." On the other hand, in October 1847, Lincoln represented a slave owner, Robert Matson, in a lawsuit against Hiram Rutherford for $2,500 for sheltering Anthony Bryant, Jane Bryant, and their four children at the hotel of Gideon Matthew Ashmore in Independence, Illinois. Lincoln lost the Matson case.

In 1849, Joshua Reed Giddings, an agent of the Underground Railroad, mapped strategy with Lincoln, then a U.S. congressman, and with attorney Salmon Portland Chase for the abolition of slavery in the District of Columbia. On October 16, 1854, in Peoria, Illinois, Lincoln delivered a speech entitled "Against the Extension of Slavery," a response to U.S. Senator Stephen Arnold Douglas, who tried to force Lincoln into taking sides on the slavery issue. Lincoln acknowledged the bold, dedicated activists of the Underground Railroad, who risked arrest, fining, and imprisonment for disobeying the Fugitive Slave Law of 1850. He warned that the ongoing battle between slave owners and abolitionists threatened the Union. Supporting his election in 1860 was Frederick Douglass, the first black adviser to gain the ear of a U.S. president.

In March 1861, Lincoln advanced to the presidency, replacing James Buchanan, a pro-South, pro-slavery disappointment to abolitionists. For secretary of state, Lincoln chose William Henry Seward, an operative of the Underground Railroad. Challenging the new president's thinking on slave rescue was attorney Salmon P. Chase, who urged Lincoln to defy slave owners and to end the Civil War by enlisting blacks in the Union army. Additional pressure on behalf of the secret network came from abolitionist orator Anna Elizabeth Dickinson, William Barnard, Thomas Garrett, Alice Eliza Betts Hambleton, Dinah Hannum Mendenhall, and Oliver Johnson, a representative of the American Anti-Slavery Society. In summer 1862, Ellen Davis Dana Conway and Moncure Conway petitioned Lincoln unsuccessfully to guarantee the safety of the Conway family's 31 slaves as they made their way from war-ravaged Virginia by train to Yellow Springs, Ohio. The president's refusal indicated that he opposed both slavery and abolitionism.

During the Civil War, Lincoln became more vocal on issues that threatened the Union. On August 22, 1862, he wrote a letter to the *New York Tribune*'s editor, Horace Greeley, who had written an editorial concerning what Greeley saw as Lincoln's unwillingness to abolish slavery. To Greeley's call for immediate and complete abolition, Lincoln stated that, as president, he owed allegiance to the whole nation. He indicated

Abraham Lincoln and abolitionist preacher Sojourner Truth met only once, at the White House in 1864. To commemorate the Emancipation Proclamation, the black community of Baltimore presented Lincoln with a painting of them examining the Bible. *(MPI/Stringer/Hulton Archive/Getty Images)*

that he would emancipate slaves if their liberty were in the best interest of national unity but that he would not jeopardize the country by freeing slaves. (Lincoln's reply to Greeley appeared in the *Washington Star.*) Greeley was unaware that Lincoln had drafted the Emancipation Proclamation, which was issued on September 22, 1862, and took effect on January 1, 1863. During this tense period, secret network operative Allan Pinkerton served as Lincoln's scout and bodyguard. After Lincoln's assassination on April 14, 1865, the Reverend Henry Highland Garnet, another agent of the Underground Railroad, led a drive for a national monument to honor the author of the Emancipation Proclamation.

See also: American Anti-Slavery Society; black soldiers; Civil War.

Sources

Burlingame, Michael. *The Inner World of Abraham Lincoln.* Champaign: University of Illinois Press, 1997.

Lincoln, Abraham. "Against the Extension of Slavery." In *Complete Works of Abraham Lincoln,* ed. John G. Nicolay and John Hay. New York: Lamb, 1905.

Lind, Sylvester (1808–1892)

A Scots immigrant, carpenter, and lumberman, Sylvester Lind managed a smuggling operation that delivered runaway slaves to Canada. While living at 255 Randolph Street in Lake Forest, Illinois, he established Lind and Dunlap, the headquarters of lumber mills on Washington Island, in Door County,Wisconsin, and in Cedar River, Michigan. He used his shipping business as a cover for transporting slaves over the Great Lakes. On stops between plants, he directed boat captains to off-load slaves onto steamers bound for Detroit, Michigan. The steamers halted long enough at the St. Clair River for runaways to escape to Ontario. Lind remained active in public service as mayor of Lake Forest and as a founder of Lake Forest University.

Source

Taylor, Glennette Tilley. *The Underground Railroad in Illinois.* Glen Ellyn, IL: Newman Educational, 2001.

Lindley, Jacob (1744–1814)
Lindley, Hannah Miller (ca. 1753–1789)

A Quaker precursor of the Underground Railroad conductor, the Reverend Jacob Lindley and his wife, Hannah Miller Lindley, ferried escapees across his 600 acres in New Garden, in Chester County, Pennsylvania. In 1801, the couple began receiving slaves from rescuer Elisha Tyson in Baltimore, Maryland. Jacob Lindley guided his passengers to Pughtown and Valley Forge and forwarded some to the safehouse of Benjamin Price and Jane Paxson Price in East Bradford, Pennsylvania. Lindley remained in service to liberty until his fall from a carriage at age 70.

Source

Smedley, Robert C. *History of the Underground Railroad in Chester and the Neighboring Counties of Pennsylvania.* Lancaster, PA: Office of *The Journal,* 1883.

Little, Sophia Louisa Robbins (1799–1893)

An abolitionist author and reformer, Sophia Louisa Robbins Little assisted runaway slaves on the way to liberty. A native of Newport, Rhode Island, at age 25

Sophia Robbins married William Little, Jr., of Boston. After he died, in the mid-1830s, she defied local sentiment and the opinions of her brother and her father, Senator Asher Robbins, by supporting the Underground Railroad. She gave speeches and published anti-slavery gift books as testimonials to her Episcopalianism. She supported humanitarian efforts through donations to abolitionist causes, including the Boston Anti-Slavery Fair. Her abolitionist letters appeared in William Lloyd Garrison's weekly *The Liberator.* She protested the imprisonment of the Reverend Charles Turner Torrey for harboring fugitives, the passage of the Fugitive Slave Law of 1850, and the branding of Jonathan Walker's right palm with the letters *SS*, for "slave stealer."

See also: anti-slavery fairs; Fugitive Slave Law of 1850; *Liberator, The.*

Source

Van Broekhoven, Deborah Bingham. *The Devotion of These Women: Rhode Island in the Antislavery Network.* Amherst: University of Massachusetts Press, 2002.

Littlefield, Hamilton B. (?–1894) Littlefield, Rhoda (1807–1888)

New York politician, real estate agent, and lumber dealer Hamilton B. Littlefield and his wife, Rhoda Littlefield of Champlain, New York, hosted fugitive slaves passing through New York's Fulton Valley. In 1836, Hamilton Littlefield was a founding member of the New York State Anti-Slavery Society; six years later, he was elected an officer of the Oswego County Anti-Slavery Society. The Littlefields concealed in their kitchen ceiling a wealth of abolitionist literature. The Littlefields established a waystation at 44 East Oneida Street in Oswego, New York. Hamilton scoured local woods by lantern light and received fugitives in a cellar room. From there, passengers boarded his boats and crossed Lake Ontario to freedom. Supporting the Littlefields' efforts were neighbors John B. Edwards, Lydia M. Hall Edwards, and Gerrit Smith, an organizer of the secret network. The Littlefield house is listed on the National Register of Historic Places.

Source

Mohr, Fred A, "Ex-Slaves Founded Oswego Businesses," *Syracuse Post-Standard,* February 25, 2005.

Livermore, Mary Ashton Rice (1820–1905)

One of the unusual reports of Underground Railroad activity came from Mary Ashton Rice Livermore, a Universalist laywoman and a Union army nurse during the Civil War. She stated in her memoir, *My Story of the War* (1888), that blacks stowed away in Union camps while awaiting transfer. At the St. Louis depot, she harbored a small boy named Ben Morris, a runaway from Louisiana passed to her by Hezekiah Ford Douglas. She smuggled Ben onto a Chicago-bound train, where a sleeping-car porter named Henry hid the child under Livermore's berth. The risk to Henry was considerable—black laws in Illinois punished those guilty of transporting slaves illegally with a year's imprisonment and a $1,000 fine. Although the child snored, Livermore and Morris remained undetected all the way to Centralia. When Livermore fell ill with swamp fever, the train conductor, an old hand at Underground Railroad relays, calmed her fears. In Chicago, Livermore personally delivered Ben to his mother, Sarah Morris.

While heading the Sanitary Commission in the Midwest in 1862, Livermore involved herself in hands-on rescues, including the conveyance of an abused child in a suitcase. She also attended to Lizzie and Johnny, siblings from Virginia on the way to a reunion with their father, a Union soldier. When she learned that the father had died in Libby Prison, Chaplain McCabe placed Johnny and Lizzie in a foster home. Johnny chose to enlist in the army as his father had done and died of pneumonia without serving in combat. Lizzie worked as a lady's companion. Livermore lauded long-termed agents, particularly Dinah Hannum Mendenhall and Isaac Mendenhall of Kennett Square, Pennsylvania.

See also: black soldiers; Civil War.

Source

Livermore, Mary A. *My Story of the War: A Woman's Narrative of Four Years Personal Experience.* Hartford, CT: A.D. Worthington, 1888.

Lockhart, Jesse (1793–?)

A colleague of abolitionists Dr. Alexander Campbell and Jean Lowry Rankin and John Rankin, the Reverend Jesse Lockhart became an abolitionist during his college years. He was a native of eastern Tennessee and an agent of the Ripley line, which ran from Kentucky across the Ohio River, through southern Ohio, and then north toward Canada. While preaching at the Presbyterian church in Decatur, Ohio, in the 1820s, he aided distressed runaways in the parsonage and the sanctuary. In the 1830s, he was settled in

Russellville, Ohio, and well connected to other networkers, including Isaac M. Beck in Sardinia, the Reverend James Gilliland in Red Oak, John Bennington Mahan in White Oak Creek, Martha West Lucas and William McCoy in Russellville, Thomas McCague and John P. Parker in Ripley, and the Pettijohn clan of Huntington, Ohio, headed by brothers Abraham and Amos. In 1912, Lockhart was an honoree of Ripley's Liberty Monument.

Source

History of Brown County, Ohio. Chicago: W.H. Beers, 1883.
Woodson, Carter G. "Freedom and Slavery in Appalachian America." *Journal of Negro History* 1:2 (April 1916).

Logan, John Wesley (1810–1872)

A former slave, Bishop John Wesley Logan joined a team of Underground Railroad agents to free runaways. In 1830, Logan fled North Carolina and settled in Canada. He relocated to Syracuse, New York, and conspired with supervisors Lewis Tappan and Gerrit Smith to extend routes of the secret network. In 1847, he pastored Zion Methodist Episcopal Church in Syracuse. During the Civil War, he joined the Twenty-ninth U.S. Colored Infantry.

See also: routes, Underground Railroad.

Source

Miller, Edward A. *The Black Civil War Soldiers of Illinois: The Story of the Twenty-ninth U.S. Colored Infantry.* Columbia: University of South Carolina Press, 1998.

Loguen, Jermaine Wesley (1814–1872) Loguen, Caroline E. Storum (1817–1867)

An abolitionist orator, a teacher, and a preacher at the African Methodist Church in Syracuse, New York, the Reverend Jermaine (also Jarm or Germain) Wesley Loguen was a model citizen, a bishop of his church, and a conductor of the Underground Railroad. Born in slavery near Manscoe's Creek in Davidson County outside Nashville, Tennessee, he was the son of Jane "Cherry" Logue, who had been kidnapped in early childhood from Ohio and sold to three brothers, Carnes, David, and Manasseth Loguen, in Davidson County to tend their house, field, and distillery. Jermaine, whose father was David Logue, was sold to Manasseth Logue on the Tombigbee River in southern Tennessee.

Jermaine witnessed the flogging of his mother and the sale of his siblings, Charley and Fanny Logue.

According to Samuel Joseph May's memoir *Some Recollections of Our Antislavery Conflict* (1869), the Loguen waystation was in constant use by runaway slaves: "Scarcely a week passed without some one, in his flight from slavedom to Canada, enjoyed shelter and repose at Elder Loguen's."

Their owner worked so diligently at shoving a wood block into Loguen's mouth that he suffered a permanent speech impairment. After being beaten nearly to death with a hominy pestle, he saw his mother and sister shackled and sold. On December 24, 1834, he stole Logue's swiftest horse, Old Rock, and fled. With fellow slave John Farney, Loguen set out for Canada by way of Nashville, Tennessee, during the early stirrings of an underground route through Brandenburg, Kentucky, and Corydon, Ohio, to the Detroit River, crossing in Detroit, Michigan. Along the way, Quakers offered the two slaves provisions and board. When their mounts and money were stolen, Farney separated from Jermaine, who never heard from his companion again. By spring 1837, Jermaine was sharecropping near Hamilton, Ontario, where he took the name Jermaine Wesley Loguen.

With money from his work in St. Catharines, Ontario, Loguen relocated to Rochester, New York, as porter and servant at Rochester House, an upscale hotel. The black clergyman Elymas P. Rogers urged him to attend Beriah Green's abolitionist school, Oneida Institute, in Whitesboro, New York. Loguen enrolled there in 1839 despite his lack of funds and formal education. By 1841, he was an elementary school teacher in Utica and a pastor in Syracuse, where he built a school near a candle factory. He canvassed liberal households to enlist others as Underground Railroad stationmasters. Among those who joined the secret network was Matilda Joslyn Gage of Fayetteville, New York.

With the aid of Dr. James Canning Fuller, Jr., Samuel Joseph May, and others at the Syracuse depot, Loguen joined in the freeing of William "Jerry" McHenry, a hero of the abolitionist era. In flight from U.S. marshals, Loguen sheltered in Waterloo, New York, with Quaker stationmasters Mary Ann Wilson M'Clintock and Thomas M'Clintock. Loguen married Caroline E. Storum, daughter of Sarah and William Storum, conductors in Busti, New York. In 1841, the Loguens fitted their home at 293 East Genesee Street in Syracuse with an apartment for runaways, some of whom came from the waystation of Eber M. Pettit in Versailles, New York.

Loguen received refugee Jack Watson, who was wanted for murder, after Watson passed from the hands of conductor John Young in Mercer County, Pennsylvania, to the Wesleyville Methodist Church garret under the care of Thomas Elliott of Harborcreek. The Loguens defrayed much of the cost of keeping the waystation, which was in constant demand.

Jermaine Loguen denounced the Fugitive Slave Law of 1850 for coercing citizens into aiding slave catchers. Within days of its passage, he, Patrick H. Agan, John Thomas, and 10 others pledged their protection of runaway slaves passing through Syracuse. When the Loguen family made a dash from slave catchers for safety in St. Catharines, Ontario, in 1851, they left their horse and carriage with the respected English Quaker philanthropists and conductors James Canning Fuller and Lydia Charleton Fuller and their son, Dr. James Canning Fuller, Jr., at their safehouse on West Genesee Street in Skaneateles, New York.

Upon the Loguens' return to Syracuse the next year, they required the aid of abolitionists, who rang the church bell at the Congregational church to alert agents. Shortly afterward, the Loguens arrived safely at the Fuller home in time for dinner. On December 24, 1855, the Reverend Loguen conducted the wedding of runaway slave Emily Foster of Oak Hill, Virginia, and transporter Frank Wanzer. Loguen joined the Union army during the Civil War and lost his left arm in a skirmish. The Loguens' daughter, Amelia Loguen, married Lewis Douglass, son of agent Anna Murray Douglass and orator Frederick Douglass.

See also: African Methodist Episcopal Church; Fugitive Slave Law of 1850; Quakers.

Sources

Loguen, Jermain Wesley. *The Rev. J.W. Loguen, as a Slave and as a Freeman: A Narrative of Real Life.* Syracuse, NY: J.C.K. Truair, 1859.

May, Samuel Joseph. *Some Recollections of Our Antislavery Conflict.* Boston: Fields, Osgood, 1869.

Severance, Frank H. *Old Trails on the Niagara Frontier.* Buffalo, NY: n.p., 1899.

Loney, Cordelia (ca. 1802–?)

Cordelia Loney, a mulatto chambermaid and field hand, freed herself from bondage with aid from the Philadelphia Vigilance Committee. On March 30, 1859, Loney was residing at a boardinghouse on Chestnut Street in Philadelphia with her mistress, Mrs. Joseph Cahell of Fredericksburg, Virginia. At the committee's suggestion, Loney slipped away to the committee headquarters, where she recounted the story of the sale of her two sons and two daughters since 1856. The *New York Evening Post* reported that Loney found freedom in Canada.

Source

Drew, Benjamin. *The Refugee: The Narratives of Fugitive Slaves in Canada.* Boston: John P. Jewett, 1856.

Long, Henry (fl. 1850s)

Henry Long was one of the early test cases of the Fugitive Slave Law of 1850. He was waiting tables at the Pacific Hotel in New York when U.S. marshals seized and arrested him at the insistence of slave owner John T. Smith of Richmond, Virginia. The confrontation aroused a crowd of protesters, including fugitive James Williams, author of *Life and Adventures of James Williams, a Fugitive Slave* (1873), who faced Smith's six-shooter and backed down. To spare Long a return to bondage, editor Horace Greeley and the American Anti-Slavery Society intervened.

Despite legal representation by abolitionist attorney John Jay, Jr., a federal court found in favor of Smith on January 8, 1851. The judgment earned a rebuke from William Lloyd Garrison's paper, *The Liberator,* on January 17. A slave buyer, David Clapton, purchased Long from the auction block on January 18 for $750 to labor on a Georgia cotton plantation. On April 9, 1851, Long's plight found its way into the anti-slavery speeches of conductor William Wells Brown, into Harriet Beecher Stowe's *A Key to Uncle Tom's Cabin* (1853), and, on October 30, 1851, into an editorial in the *National Anti-Slavery Standard* by agent William Peter Powell.

See also: American Anti-Slavery Society; Fugitive Slave Law of 1850; *Key to Uncle Tom's Cabin, A* (1853); *Liberator, The.*

Sources

Link, William A. *Roots of Secession: Slavery and Politics in Antebellum Virginia.* Chapel Hill: University of North Carolina Press, 2003.

Williams, James. *Life and Adventures of James Williams, a Fugitive Slave.* San Francisco: Women's Union Print, 1873.

Loring, Ellis Gray (1803–1858)
Loring, Louisa Gilman (1797–1868)

Attorney, abolitionist orator, and philanthropist Ellis Gray Loring and his wife, Louisa Gilman Loring, took part in stirring rescues by the Underground Railroad. Harvard educated, the Bostonian lawyer claimed friendships with agents Maria Weston Chapman, Frederick Douglass, the Reverend Theodore Parker, and Charles Sumner. After the Reverend Samuel Joseph May and his cousin, attorney Samuel Edmund Sewall, discovered the young orator William Lloyd Garrison, Loring helped to finance Garrison's weekly newspaper *The Liberator.* Following their wedding in 1827, the Lorings welcomed fugitive slaves to their home in Brookline, Massachusetts. The couple also harbored 13-year-old Robert Morris of Salem, Massachusetts, and tutored him in law. Morris passed the Massachusetts bar exam and opened his own practice; he was the nation's second black attorney.

In addition to serving the American Anti-Slavery Society as a manager, Ellis Loring was an officer of the Massachusetts Anti-Slavery Society and became a volunteer attorney for its legal cases. From 1830 to 1858, he defended slaves from recapture once they reached free territory, including the surviving 43 African mutineers of the slave ship *Amistad.* One of his landmark cases involved Med Slater, a six-year-old girl who traveled to the free state of Massachusetts in May 1836. Hired by the Boston Female Anti-Slavery Society, Loring protested the owner's plan to sell Med in New Orleans. Lemuel Shaw, chief justice of the Massachusetts Supreme Court, set the child free.

One of Loring's famous cases involved fellow attorney Richard Henry Dana, Jr., in the defense of three secret network operatives, Lewis Hayden, John J. Smith, and Robert Morris, for rescuing Fredric "Shadrach" Minkins from the Boston courthouse on February 15, 1851. Loring maintained his dedication in early January 1859, during the passage of Ellen Smith Craft and William Craft through Massachusetts further into New England. William Ingersoll Bowditch conveyed Ellen from his Brookline waystation to the Lorings. In the family's absence, Mary R. Courzon received the passenger. William Craft reunited with his wife in Loring's quarters. During the Civil War, the Lorings' daughter, Anna Loring, served as vice president of the Boston Sanitary Commission.

See also: American Anti-Slavery Society; *Amistad*; female anti-slavery societies; *Liberator, The.*

Source

Hansen, Debra Gold. *Strained Sisterhood: Gender and Class in the Boston Female Anti-Slavery Society.* Boston: University of Massachusetts Press, 1993.

Lott (Hendrick I. and Mary Brownjohn) Family

According to late twentieth-century archaeology, the Dutch-American Lott family of the Brooklyn flatlands, in Kings County, New York, harbored desperate runaway slaves. After emigration from a French Huguenot enclave in Drenton, Holland, in 1801, Hendrick I. Lott (1760–1840) and his wife, Mary Brownjohn Lott (1770–1853), freed their chattel. The Lotts grew wheat, potatoes, and cabbage at their farm and maintained a depot of the Underground Railroad at 1940 East Thirty-sixth Street in Marine Park. They paid destitute runaways to work as domestics.

In service to the secret network, in the 1840s, three generations of Lotts—the widow Mary Lott, her son Johannes H. Lott (1793–1874) and his wife, Gashe Bergen Lott (1797–1883), and their son, Henry DeWitt Lott (1821–1889)—received refugees arriving by the Staten Island route. The family hid the passengers behind a trapdoor that led to a small, windowless room above a lean-to. Slaves who wanted to avoid surveillance in Manhattan chose the easterly Brooklyn route. Transporters completed the relay through Queens, the Bronx, Westchester, and Albany, New York, to Ontario. In 1997, archaeologists from Brooklyn College located candles, corncobs, a hemp-tied cloth pouch, and an oyster shell, all evidence of fugitive residents. The Lott estate is currently part of a restoration project supervised by the Historic House Trust.

Source

Bankoff, H. Arthur, Christopher Ricciardi, and Alyssa Loorya. "Remembering Africa under the Eaves." *Archaeology* 54:3 (May–June 2001).

Lovejoy, Elijah Parish (1802–1837)

The Reverend Elijah Parish Lovejoy, a Presbyterian minister and publisher from Albion, Maine, supported the Underground Railroad and lost his life in the cause of abolition. Beginning in 1833, he preached at the Old Des Peres Meeting House on Geyer Road in St. Louis, Missouri. In 1836, he lived at the Hunterstown waystation of Charles Hunter. With the aid of his father, John Lovejoy, and a younger brother, Owen Glendower Lovejoy, Elijah Lovejoy edited the *St. Louis (MO) Observer,* a religious newspaper that

A monument in Alton, Illinois, commemorates local newspaper publisher Elijah Lovejoy, who became a martyr to abolitionism after his murder by a pro-slavery mob in 1837. Lovejoy was also active in the Underground Railroad. *(Schomburg Center for Research in Black Culture/General Research and Reference Division/New York Public Library)*

promoted national emancipation of slaves. In private, he conducted refugees west across the Missouri River from St. Louis, Missouri, to the Rock House at Clawson and College streets, his safehouse in Alton, Illinois.

After moving his newspaper to free territory across the Mississippi River to Alton, Lovejoy riled proslavery factions by protesting the decapitation and burning at the stake of fugitive Francis J. McIntosh, a steamboat cook who was accused of killing a deputy sheriff on April 28, 1836. In addition to pastoring the College Avenue Presbyterian Church, Lovejoy formed the Illinois Anti-Slavery Society, a cause of pro-slavery enmity. In the last year of his life, rowdies destroyed his pressroom four times and tossed equipment into the Mississippi River. On November 7, 1837, while he transferred a new press from the Godfrey & Gilman warehouse, a mob stoned and torched the property. A shotgun blast killed Lovejoy as he was extinguishing flames on the roof.

Lovejoy's murder was a moving experience to abolitionists. To protect the corpse from desecration, a free black stonecutter, William "Scotch" Johnston, buried Lovejoy in an unmarked plot. Aiding Johnston was Isaac Kelley, a free operative of the secret network on George and Sixth streets. Abraham Lincoln delivered a eulogy, "Let Every Man Remember." The backlash refueled the abolitionism of Underground Railroad operatives William Ellery Channing and Wendell Addison Phillips. In a letter to the *Cincinnati Journal,* the anti-slavery society in Ripley, Ohio, described the martyrdom as an outrage and a national disgrace. Members pledged financial support to Lovejoy's family. The next year, Lovejoy's brother, the Reverend Owen Glendower Lovejoy, and his wife, Eunice Storrs Lovejoy, kept up the family tradition of humanitarianism by opening an Underground Railroad depot in Princeton, Illinois.

See also: abolitionism; American Anti-Slavery Society; anti-slavery fairs.

Source

Blight, David W., ed. *Passages to Freedom.* Washington, DC: Smithsonian Books, 2004.

Lovejoy, Owen Glendower (1811–1864) Lovejoy, Eunice Storrs (1809–1899)

The Reverend Owen Glendower Lovejoy, like his older brother, journalist Elijah Parish Lovejoy, died a martyr to abolitionism. On November 7, 1837, Owen Lovejoy witnessed the murder of his brother from mob gunfire in Alton, Illinois, and dedicated the Lovejoy family to rescuing black fugitives. From 1838, Lovejoy preached at the Hampshire Colony Congregationalist Church, a refuge for runaways, and conspired with conductors Jane Bestor Eells and Dr. Richard Eells in Quincy, with David West in Sycamore, in De Kalb County, and with Almira Cady Willard, Julius Alphonso Willard, and Samuel Guild Willard in Jacksonville, Illinois. Lovejoy and his wife,

Eunice Storrs Lovejoy, operated the "Lovejoy line," which directed runaways from the "Brown line" in Kansas and Iowa toward freedom in Canada. Some passengers, concealed in Lovejoy's hay wagon, traveled all the way to Chicago to the safehouse of Zebina Eastman.

Eunice Lovejoy's white clapboard residence, Lovejoy Homestead, which she inherited from her first husband, Butler Denham, became a busy depot on Sixth Street in Princeton, Illinois. The first to arrive was a lone man, who requested shelter in 1837. The Lovejoy family concealed refugees behind a dresser, in the cellar, over a staircase, in the barn, and in cornfields. In October 1843, Owen Lovejoy successfully argued before a grand jury his innocence of a charge of harboring runaways named Agnes and Nancy in his residence. He continued his benevolent work and, in 1849, received John Bowen, a mulatto from Missouri whose owner had tied him to a tree. The Lovejoys sent a decoy on horseback to throw a posse off the trail. Meanwhile, Bowen, wearing a lady's sunbonnet, departed by carriage to freedom.

At age 43, Lovejoy was elected to the U.S. Congress, where he denounced slavery as barbaric. He proudly compared his slave interventions to the snatching of a babe from a wolf's jaws or an eagle's talons. After serving as a colonel in the Union infantry during the Civil War, on March 25, 1864, he died of Bright's disease under the care of Henry Ward Beecher, a fellow operative of the secret network. Lovejoy Homestead, which opened as a museum in 1972, is a National Historic Landmark.

See also: abolitionism.

Source

Blue, Frederick J. *No Taint of Compromise: Crusaders in Antislavery Politics.* Baton Rouge: Louisiana State University Press, 2005.

Lucas, Charles Peyton (1816–?)

Charles Peyton Lucas of Kentucky achieved liberty with the help of Pennsylvania Dutch Underground Railroad agents. Trained in blacksmithing in Leesburg, Virginia, Lucas was a valuable slave who suffered kicks and beatings on the head by his mistress, the wife of a Baptist minister. In 1841, when Lucas learned from his sister that his owner had sold him for $1,500, he fled. After swimming across the Potomac River, Lucas and two companions ran without directions, snatching milk and corn when they could steal them. An operative of the secret network directed them through the woods into free territory. Lucas was working in Pennsylvania when a pharmacist warned him that a handbill was circulating offering a $500 reward for his capture. He quickly relocated to Geneva, New York. With passage of the Fugitive Slave Law of 1850, he moved on to Toronto, Ontario, changed his name to Charles Bentley, and opened a shop on Centre Street that remained in business some 15 years.

See also: Fugitive Slave Law of 1850.

Source

Johnson, Walter. *Soul by Soul: Life inside the Antebellum Slave Market.* Cambridge, MA: Harvard University Press, 1999.

Lucas, George W.C. (fl. 1850s)

A mulatto operative in Salem, Ohio, George W.C. Lucas transported slaves to liberty. In the 1850s, he served as wagoneer for the Underground Railroad in Salem, Ohio, and concealed his refugees in a secret compartment of his vehicle. His relays covered round trips of 120 miles, passing through Cadiz, Wellsville, Cleveland, Sandusky, and Toledo and across Lake Erie to Canada.

Source

Shaffer, Dale. *Salem: A Quaker City History.* Charleston, SC: Arcadia, 2002.

Lucas, Marcus F. (ca. 1820–1901)

A former slave and superintendent of the Underground Railroad, Marcus F. Lucas aided refugees traveling through Bath, New York. After setting up a barbershop in 1840, he mapped escape routes to the west and over Lake Erie to Ontario. In September 1852, he executed a bold plan with a colleague, tobacco farmer Daniel Deming, to relay a three-generation party of 15 refugees through Dunkirk and by lake steamer to Fort Malden across the border from Detroit, Michigan. Lucas also conspired with Daniel Hughes in Horseheads, Judge Lyman Balcom in Painted Post, Fred Rogers in Hornby, and John W. Jones, Rachel Swailes Jones, and Hiram K. Wilson in Elmira. Lucas sped passengers from Corning west along the secret line to connect with the station of a family of conductors—Mowry, Otis, and T. Scott Thacher—in Hornellsville, New York. Some slave parties moved north to the Haskins depot in Cohocton and up the "Canada road" to St. Catharines, Ontario.

See also: routes, Underground Railroad.

Source

Phelan, Helene C. *And Why Not Every Man?* Almond, NY: privately published, 1987.

Lucas, Martha West (fl. 1830s)

A resident of Russellville, in Brown County, Ohio, rescuer Martha West Lucas was a clever stationmaster of the Underground Railroad. She lived due north of Ripley, the busy crossing point of the Ohio River northwest of Maysville, Kentucky. She hid slaves in an attic of her residence at North Columbus Street. Passengers arrived via the Ripley line from Jesse Lockhart, a Presbyterian minister. Because her rowhouse connected to that of a next-door neighbor, she could pass slaves directly across to foil posses.

Source

Hagedorn, Ann. *Beyond the River: The Untold Story of the Heroes of the Underground Railroad.* New York: Simon & Schuster, 2002.

Lundy, Benjamin (1789–1839)

Quaker diarist and pioneer abolitionist Benjamin Lundy penned an overview of the growing Canadian terminus of the Underground Railroad. A native of Hardwick, in Sussex County, New Jersey, he grew up in an abolitionist, nonviolent family. After studying saddlery in Wheeling, West Virginia, he founded the Union Humane Society in 1815 and, three years later, began writing columns for Charles W. Osborn's newspaper the *Philanthropist.* In 1819, Lundy settled his family in Mount Pleasant, Ohio, at Third and Union streets, where they operated a waystation. Despite the disapproval of others, Lundy considered his work a sacred cause. He journeyed south and witnessed bondage in Tennessee. On his return, he endured bullying, assault, and the threats of armed attackers.

In June 1821, Lundy began issuing an anti-slavery gazette, the *Genius of Universal Emancipation,* one of the nation's first abolitionist newspapers, which circulated for 16 years. In addition to applying pressure to end the flesh trade, the paper reported the terrors of slave flight. He reported the story of William Hunter, a runaway who was captured in fall 1823 by bounty hunters in Cincinnati, Ohio. News of this type informed readers across the country of Underground Railroad work and the punishments awaiting those runaways who returned to bondage.

Lundy established the Maryland Anti-Slavery Society in 1824 and began lecturing on the immorality of human bondage. More important to the abolitionist movement was Lundy's recruitment of editor Zebina Eastman in Chicago, Illinois; Joseph Fulton and Mary Ann Fulton in Sadsbury, Pennsylvania; and William Lloyd Garrison in Newburyport, Massachusetts, to join the underground network team. Lundy's dedication to abolition earned the regard of Horace Greeley, editor of the *New York Tribune.*

See also: abolitionist newspapers; free labor store; punishments.

Sources

Coffin, Addison. *Life and Travels of Addison Coffin.* Cleveland, OH: W.G. Hubbard, 1897.
Dillion, Merton L. *Benjamin Lundy and the Struggle for Negro Freedom.* Bloomington: University of Illinois Press, 1966.

Benjamin Lundy, an Ohio Quaker, supported the early abolitionist movement after witnessing the sufferings of Tennessee slaves. A newspaper editor, lecturer, organizer, and station operator, he regarded the cause as sacred. *(Stock Montage/Hulton Archive/Getty Images)*

Luse, A.B. (1809–?)

A Cincinnati physician, Dr. A.B. Luse, aided refugees in flight from bondage. Born in Butler County, Ohio, at age 21, he settled in Mount Healthy, Ohio. In 1831, he opened a practice in Hamilton to combat a two-year cholera epidemic. He also donated his time and medical skills to the Underground Railroad effort.

Source

Smiddy, Betty Ann. *A Little Piece of Paradise . . . College Hill, Ohio.* Cincinnati, OH: College Hill Historical Society, 1999.

Lyons, Albro (1814–1896)
Lyons, Mary Marshall (1814–1894)
Lyons, Maritcha Remond (1848–1929)

Underground Railroad agents Albro Lyons and Mary Marshall Lyons concealed runaway slaves arriving up the Atlantic coast by ship to New York harbor. The couple and their daughter, Maritcha Remond Lyons, were members of an activist congregation at St. Philipa's Episcopal Church. The Lyons family took over the management of the Colored Sailors' Home, which they moved to 20 Vandewater Street, near the docks on New York City's Lower East Side. After the departure of the original owners, Mercy O. Haskins Powell and William Peter Powell, to Liverpool, England, the Lyons family received sailors, disguised escaping slaves, and disseminated information arriving by grapevine telegraphy from the plantation South. During the draft riots of July 1863, the family defended the boardinghouse for one day but fled to Williamsburg in Brooklyn when looting and arson endangered their lives. Maritcha Lyons preserved the family's ordeal for history.

See also: disguise; grapevine telegraphy.

Sources

Harris, Leslie M. *In the Shadow of Slavery: African Americans in New York City, 1626–1863.* Chicago: University of Chicago Press, 2003.

Sachs, Charles L. "A Good and Convenient House: The Colored Sailors' Home Aided Over 17,000 Seamen in Its 33 Years." *Seaport* (Fall–Winter 1995): 24–29.

Mabbett, Anna Griffin (1813–?)
Mabbett, Lorenzo (1811–1859)

Two Quaker conductors of the Underground Railroad, Anna Griffin Mabbett (or Mabbet) and her husband, Lorenzo Mabbett, eased the way for runaways. After their marriage in 1831, the Mabbetts maintained a safehouse at their farm in Collins Center, in Erie County, New York. Lorenzo Mabbett corresponded with Frederick Douglass. On January 23, 1851, Douglass published in his paper, the *North Star,* an article about Anna Mabbett. In 1849, she helped two fugitives elude slave catchers by skillfully disguising the couple in women's farm clothes before transporting them to another stop. In 1850, the local literary society made a formal gesture of sympathy for the Mabbetts' labors for the secret network.

See also: disguise; *North Star.*

Source

"Rescue," *North Star,* January 23, 1851.

MacMillan, Joel (1822–1877)
MacMillan, Sarah M. Norris (1810–?)

A Quaker concealer of fugitive slaves, Joel MacMillan (or McMillan) of Mt. Pleasant, Ohio, operated a safehouse in Salem, in Columbiana County, Ohio. He wed Sarah M. Norris in 1848 and operated a bookstore at 1111 Southeast Boulevard. In the kitchen basement of their home, runaways hid in niches in a storage closet, reached by passing through the fireplace. One of the rescued slaves, a nursemaid, took the name Abby Kelly Salem, after the town and the abolitionist orator Abby Kelley Foster. Salem remained as a family employee of the MacMillans.

Source

Shaffer, Dale. *Salem: A Quaker City History.* Charleston, SC: Arcadia, 2002.

Magill, Jonathan Paxson (1798–1868)
Magill, Edward Hicks (1825–1907)
Magill, Watson P. (1827–1895)

A Quaker teacher and conductor on the Pennsylvania Underground Railroad, Jonathan Paxson Magill concealed from his neighbors his relays of slaves to freedom. In Solebury, in Bucks County, Pennsylvania, a less-traveled conduit than others through the state, Magill activated his idealism by serving as manager for the American Anti-Slavery Society. He and his sons, Edward Hicks Magill and Watson P. Magill, joined the secret network under the influence of William Lloyd Garrison's abolitionist newspaper *The Liberator,* John Greenleaf Whittier's *Pennsylvania Freeman,* and David Child and Lydia Maria Francis Child's *National Anti-Slavery Standard.* Aided by a black handyman, the Magills received passengers from Caroline Shoemaker Paxson and Dr. Jacob Longstreth Paxson in Norristown and passed them on to William Henry Johnson in Philadelphia or to Richard Moore and Sarah Foulke Moore's depot in Quakertown. One complicated rescue involved passage of Rachel Moore and her six children, refugees from Elkton, Maryland, who passed through Esther Lewis's safehouse, Sunnyside Home, outside Kimberton, Pennsylvania, and arrived in Bucks County cold and wet, wearing tow-cloth garments shredded to rags. The Magills kept Rachel and two of her children for several years.

In 1845, Edward Magill, a teacher in Langhorne, Pennsylvania, maintained the family tradition of harboring refugees. He accepted six Maryland runaways, who fled up the Delaware River to freedom. Posing as a farmer hauling produce to Trenton, New Jersey, he covered the refugee family with a tarp, boarded a ferry, and completed the 30-mile relay. Before the slaves could be hidden in the barn of the next depot, the presence of slave catchers made Magill concerned for their safety, and so he continued another 15 miles to Princeton. From there, the passengers journeyed undetected to Canada.

See also: abolitionist newspapers; American Anti-Slavery Society; *Liberator, The.*

Sources

Davis, William Watts Hart. *History of Bucks County, Pennsylvania.* New York: Lewis, 1905.

Magill, Edward H. "The Underground Railroad in Bucks County, Pennsylvania." *Friends Intelligencer* 55 (1898): 124–25, 142–44, 159–61, 276–77.

Magoffin, James, Jr. (1798–1879) Magoffin, Grace Elizabeth Mitcheltree (1806–1873)

Dr. James Magoffin, Jr., combined humanitarianism toward slaves with his medical practice. Born in Newry, Ireland, he completed his degree at the University of Glasgow. He left Ireland on May 4, 1821, at the outbreak of the Irish Rebellion and traveled across the Atlantic as ship's doctor. He arrived in Pennsylvania on July 19, 1821, and married Grace Elizabeth Mitcheltree of Dublin, Ireland. He opened a medical office and composed a memoir, *The Travel Diary of Dr. James Magoffin, Jr.* In observance of their Presbyterian faith, the Magoffins managed an Underground Railroad depot in their home at 119 South Pitt Street in Mercerville, Pennsylvania, where they hid slaves in the outbuildings. In 1951, their granddaughter deeded the residence to the Mercer County Historical Society.

Source

History of Mercer County. Chicago: Brown, Runk, 1888.

Mahan, John Bennington (1801–1844) Mahan, William Jacob (1803–1883)

Kentucky-born abolitionists, the Reverend John Bennington Mahan and his younger brother, William Jacob Mahan, transported slaves for the Underground Railroad along the Ripley, Ohio, route. In the 1820s, the Mahan brothers wed sisters, Cassandra Curtiss and Mary "Polly" Curtiss, and jointly farmed Bell's Run, a 160-acre parcel at Sardinia. The two men established a regular service to desperate slaves. William earned his living farming and constructing coffins. Despite his ouster from the Pleasant Hill Methodist Episcopal Church for abolitionist agitation around 1844, he refused to give up his campaign against slavery.

By the 1830s, John Mahan had set up his own home in White Oak Creek, in Brown County, Ohio, where he taught school, co-founded the Ohio Anti-Slavery Society, and oversaw the county poorhouse; he also established a Presbyterian congregation in Sardinia. In addition to attending the anti-slavery convention in Putnam on April 23–24, 1835, he maintained wider connections with the secret network through Catherine White Coffin and Levi Coffin in Cincinnati, John D. Hudson in Sardinia, Moses Cumberland in the Gist settlement, Alexander McCoy and his sons James and William in Eagle Creek, Joseph Pettijohn, Isaac Holmes Brown in Bethel, and Jean Lowry Rankin and John Rankin and their sons at their home, Liberty Hill, in Ripley. John Mahan concealed escaped slaves at his investment properties—a gristmill, a sawmill, and a temperance tavern at Main and Winchester streets. In early 1838, he conducted 15 Kentucky refugees to Ontario. For his boldness, he bore a price on his head—a cash bounty for his kidnap or murder, posted by southern slave owners.

Pro-slavery factions set a trap for John in early September 1838. Slave owner William Greathouse enlisted the aid of Ohio Governor Joseph Vance to have John and Joseph Pettijohn arrested, transported to Kentucky, and tried in Maysville for aiding slaves John and Nelson in fleeing bondage. The prosecution during the six-day trial attempted to elicit locations of the stops on the Ripley–Canada line. Through the intervention of Quaker defense attorney John Joliffe, Mahan was found not guilty. Nonetheless, Mahan spent 10 weeks in fetters in a windowless cell and had to pay $1,600 in a civil action brought by Greathouse. The outrage in the Kentucky legislature led to the passage of an Ohio fugitive slave act protecting runaways from extradition to slave states. Mahan published a monograph, *Trial of Rev. John B. Mahan, for Felony* (1838).

John Mahan, along with Amos and Joseph Pettijohn, was again the subject of litigation in 1839, when the trio was arrested for inciting a riot and for interfering in the duties of a Georgetown constable. Because they helped a slave escape, Mahan and Pettijohn faced fines of $50 each and sentences of 10 days in the dungeon of the Brown County jail on bread and water.

Although the state supreme court overturned the judgment, the sentence proved prophetic of the circumstances of Mahan's demise. In 1844, he died in prison of tuberculosis while serving a sentence of 10 days on bread and water for assisting in a slave rescue. His tombstone bears a sobering epitaph: "A victim to the slave power."

See also: Gist Settlement.

Sources

Galbreath, C.B. *History of Ohio.* Chicago: American Historical Society, 1925.
History of Brown County, Ohio. Chicago: W.H. Beers, 1883.
Richards, Leonard L. *Gentlemen of Property and Standing: Anti-Abolition Mobs in Jacksonian America.* Oxford: Oxford University Press, 1970.
Vaughan, John C. *Argument of John C. Vaughan, Esq., at the Trial of Rev. John B. Mahan for Felony.* Cincinnati, OH: Samuel A. Alley, 1838.

Mahoney, Charles (ca. 1823–?) Mahoney, Mary Jane Steward (fl. 1840s–1850s)

A black agent of the Underground Railroad, Charles Mahoney aided refugees on their way through Boston, Massachusetts. He married Mary Jane Steward in 1844. The couple migrated from North Carolina and settled at 31 Westminster Street in Roxbury, a Boston suburb in Suffolk County. As a member of the Boston Vigilance Committee, on February 26, 1851, Charles supplied travel money to escapee Cornelius Sparrow. Mahoney's daughter, Mary Eliza Mahoney, grew up among slave harboring and became the first black registered nurse.

Source

Ripley, C. Peter, et al., eds. *The Black Abolitionist Papers.* Chapel Hill: University of North Carolina Press, 1992.

Mahoney, Matilda (1833–?)

A bold mulatto abolitionist, Matilda Mahoney of Baltimore, Maryland, undertook dangerous spy missions into slave territory. The bondswoman of William Rigard of Frederick, Maryland, she was hired out to a family named Reese in Baltimore as a housekeeper and nurse. At age 21, she lived in fear that her owner would die and leave her to his son, a slave speculator in New Orleans. With the aid of James Jefferson, an Underground Railroad agent from Providence, Rhode Island, she escaped enslavement in 1854 and relocated to Philadelphia. As a volunteer slave rescuer there, she was able to apply a survivor's knowledge of the South and its protection of the flesh trade.

See also: spies.

Source

Still, William. *The Underground Railroad.* Philadelphia: Porter & Coates, 1872.

Malcolm, Howard (1799–1879) Malcolm, Ruth Dyer (fl. 1830s–1850s)

Dr. Howard Malcolm, the first president of Bucknell University, and his wife, Ruth Dyer Malcolm, served the Underground Railroad. A native of Philadelphia, Howard Malcolm studied at Dickinson College and Princeton and was ordained into the ministry in 1818. Following service in the mission fields of India, Malaya, Burma, and Siam, he married Ruth Dyer in 1838. In 1851, he began a six-year presidency of Bucknell, in Lewisburg, Pennsylvania. The Malcolms collaborated with fellow professors George Ripley Bliss and Thomas F. Curtis in the transportation of runaways. Passengers hid in the Malcolm barn until they could safely move north toward Canada.

Source

Snyder, Charles McCool. *Union County, Pennsylvania: A Celebration of History.* Montoursville: Penn State University Press, 2000.

Mallory, Maria (fl. 1990s)

Maria Mallory, a freelance writer in Atlanta, Georgia, set out on a 650-mile mid-Atlantic trek to retrace Harriet Tubman's steps along the Underground Railroad route. Traveling by car, she chose as her map historian Charles L. Blockson's *Hippocrene Guide to the Underground Railroad* (1994). From Cambridge, Maryland, Mallory surveyed Tubman's birthplace in Bucktown and moved on to Chester County, Pennsylvania, to view abolitionists' grave sites in Longwood Cemetery. Mallory visited waystations in Germantown and the Liberty Bell shrine in Philadelphia, the site of a slave auction block. She stopped at the corner of Sixth and Lombard streets to see Mother Bethel African Methodist Episcopal Church, a distribution center of food and clothing for refugees.

Mallory's odyssey intensified along the New York–Ontario route. Up the Hudson River to Albany, Troy, Syracuse, and the Finger Lakes of New

York, Mallory pushed on over known routes. She located Tubman's white clapboard house and the African Methodist Episcopal Zion Church museum in Auburn. Pressing on to Buffalo, New York, Mallory began the final leg to Niagara Falls and Whirlpool Bridge, the crossing into Ontario. Over the last 25 miles to St. Catharines, Ontario, Mallory located Tubman's final waystation and the 142-year-old Salem Chapel.

See also: African Methodist Episcopal Church.

Source

Mallory, Maria. "Bound for Freedom: Retracing the Footsteps of Runaway Slaves." *U.S. News & World Report* 122:14 (April 14, 1997): 78–81.

Maltby, Roger (1838–?)

Just out of his teens, Roger Maltby faced prison time for slave stealing. In 1858, he entered the Missouri penitentiary at Jefferson City to serve a three-year sentence. He gained his release in 1861.

Source

Frazier, Harriet C. *Runaway and Freed Missouri Slaves and Those Who Helped Them, 1763–1865.* Jefferson, NC: McFarland, 2004.

Malvin, John (1795–1880)
Malvin, Harriet Dorsey (ca. 1803–ca. 1870s)

An Underground Railroad conductor, the Reverend John Malvin fought the slavery he witnessed in boyhood. A native of Dumfries, in Prince William County, Virginia, John was born to a free mother, Dalcus Malvin, and an enslaved carpenter. He apprenticed as a domestic and woodworker; an old man taught Malvin to read the Bible. At age 32, Malvin migrated to Cincinnati, Ohio, where he joined the American Anti-Slavery Society and protested the so-called Black Laws against nonwhite immigrants. Through his work as a boatman, he aided refugees along the secret network and across Lake Erie to freedom. For his dedication, he was known as Father John.

In 1831, authorities in Louisville, Kentucky, seized Malvin as a suspected runaway. The experience encouraged him and his wife, Harriet Dorsey Malvin of Kentucky, to think about resettling in Canada, but they chose instead to live at 29 York Street in Cleveland, Ohio. As supporters of the Cleveland Anti-Slavery Society, they continued aiding fugitive slaves. Malvin prospered in lumber and limestone, canal barge transportation, and catering. In 1833, the Malvins founded Cleveland's First Baptist Church. Four years later, John chaired a community meeting to study the possibility of hiring a black agent to canvass the state and determine methods of helping blacks acclimate to free territory. In April 1861, he enlisted volunteers for the Fifty-fourth Massachusetts Regiment. Shortly before his death, he published *North into Freedom: The Autobiography of John Malvin, Free Negro, 1795–1880.*

See also: American Anti-Slavery Society.

Sources

Bordewich, Fergus M. *Bound for Canaan: The Underground Railroad and the War for the Soul of America.* New York: Amistad, 2005.
Malvin, John. *North into Freedom: The Autobiography of John Malvin, Free Negro, 1795–1880.* Cleveland, OH: Leader Printing, 1879.

Mann, John S. (1816–1879)
Mann, Mary Williams King (1820–1899)
Mann, Joseph (1810–1884)
Mann, Eloisa Adaline Dutton (1817–1881)

A respected attorney and publisher of the *Potter County (PA) Journal,* Quaker agent John S. Mann of London Grove, Pennsylvania, operated a slave refuge on the Pennsylvania–Canada line. Beginning in July 1857, he and his English wife, Mary Williams King Mann of Dover, rescued runaways fleeing Hagerstown, Maryland, along the Susquehanna River to their station at Main and Third streets in Coudersport, in Potter County, Pennsylvania. In a secret room at the two-story shop at Third and West streets, John also hid passengers of the Underground Railroad under the second-floor printing press. Mary once disguised a female in her own clothes and passed her by buggy to a neighbor woman, who completed the 100-mile transfer to Buffalo, New York.

Receiving passengers from the towns of Angelica and Ceres, the Mann family relied on assistance from Ephraim Bishop, Francis King, Rodney L. Nichols, and Hannah Tallcot Howland and Slocum Howland in Sherwood, New York. Family connections included John Mann's older brother, Joseph Mann, a land surveyor, lumber dealer, and merchant, who sheltered fugitives behind a fireplace niche at his store–post office in Millport. Aiding Joseph was his wife, Eloisa Adaline Dutton Mann, a non-Quaker, whom he marred in 1841. On March 14, 1859, John wrote a personal letter to agent Sala Stevens in Clara, New York, identifying a runaway in need of assistance. For slaves dodging pursuers, Mann depended on an Irish neighbor named Pat, who hid refugees in a chamber under the kitchen floor. Passengers continued in relative safety along the line to Nelson Clark's farm in Niles Hill two miles north of Coudersport, John Nichols in Millport, and John Mann's in-laws, Hannah Clendenon King and John King, English immigrants from Somersetshire living in Ceres, Pennsylvania. King welcomed runaways to a school in his kitchen, where he taught literacy. During the Civil War, John Mann rose to the rank of second lieutenant in the Seventy-second New York Volunteer Infantry.

See also: disguise.

Source

Switala, William J. *Underground Railroad in Pennsylvania.* Mechanicsburg, PA: Stackpole, 2001.

Manoka, Charles (1811–ca. 1880s)

Charles Manoka of Cambridge, Maryland, went to prison for operating a safehouse. On June 16, 1857, the Baltimore, Maryland, police arrested Manoka for rescuing a slave woman belonging to H.S. Sankford of Dorchester or Somerset County. At the completion of a six-year sentence in the state penitentiary, on June 16, 1863, Manoka returned to his wife, Ellen Manoka, at 190 South Durham Street and to his job as a day laborer.

Source

Prison records, Maryland State Archives.

Margru (1831–?)

A member of the *Amistad* mutineers, Margru (or Marghru) profited from her experience with members of the Underground Railroad. Margru, which means "black snake" in the Mandingo language, was born in Ben-dem-bu, 100 miles southeast of Freetown, in Sierra Leone. At age six, she was seized by Spanish slavers and shuttled to the barracoons on the Bight of Benin in West Africa. From there, captors forced her and three other children—Kagne, Kali, and Tehme—into the hold of the slave ship *Tecora* for transfer to Havana, Cuba, where Portuguese slave dealers loaded her aboard the clipper ship *Amistad.* On July 2, 1839, four days out of the harbor, Joseph Cinqué led a mutiny that placed the ship under African control.

After the *Amistad* sailed up the Atlantic coast, Margru and the others were seized by the crew of the the U.S. *Washington,* a coast guard surveying brig, and, on August 26, landed in New London, Connecticut. During years of litigation fostered by abolitionists, Margru lived with Congregationalists. In Farmington at 66 Main Street, Catherine Matilda Lewis Deming, Samuel Deming, and their teenage son, John Deming, provided a school for the Africans until their departure in 1841. Margru boarded at an Underground Railroad safehouse at 116 Main Street with the Reverend Noah Porter and Mehitable Meigs Porter. Aided by the Reverend James William Charles Pennington, philanthropist Lewis Tappan funded Margru's education in Christianity and the English language.

In November 1841, Margru and other surviving mutineers sailed home for West Africa aboard the *Gentleman.* In summer 1846, Margru became the first of the *Amistad* captives to return to the United States. Under the Christian name Sarah Kinson, she entered Oberlin College, an active stop of the Underground Railroad. Three years later, she settled among the Mende people to teach school.

See also: Amistad; Oberlin College.

Sources

Osagie, Iyunolu Folayan. *The* Amistad *Revolt: Memory, Slavery, and the Politics of Identity in the United States and Sierra Leone.* Athens: University of Georgia Press, 2000.
Owens, William A. *Black Mutiny: The Revolt on the Schooner* Amistad. New York: Plume, 1997.

Maris, Norris (1803–1893)
Maris, Ann Davis (fl. 1820s–1850s)

A Quaker employee of the Lewis family, Norris Maris aided five prominent secret Underground Railroad agents—Esther Fussell Lewis and her four daughters, Elizabeth R. Lewis, Graceanna Lewis, Mariann Lewis, and Rebecca Lewis Fussell. At Sunnyside Home, the Lewis family farm outside Kimberton, Pennsylvania, Maris served the secret network by conducting slaves to the next station. In 1854, he bought land in Kimberton, Pennsylvania, and established his own safehouse with the aid of his wife, Ann Davis Maris of Chester County, whom he married in 1827. Refugees from Maryland and Virginia passed from Abigail Paxson Vickers and John Vickers to the Maris waystation.

The couple employed a youth, John A. Groff, to relay passengers to the stations of Lewis Peart in Lamberton and Elijah Funk Pennypacker in Chester County, Pennsylvania. At other times, Maris's young children, Elizabeth Jones Maris (1833–1895) and George Lewis Maris (1842–1890), helped to feed fugitives. George Maris drew maps to show runaways the way north.

Source

Smedley, Robert C. *History of the Underground Railroad in Chester and the Neighboring Counties of Pennsylvania.* Lancaster, PA: Office of *The Journal,* 1883.

Markey, Joseph (fl. 1840s–1850s)
Markey, Jonas (fl. 1840s–1850s)

An agent of the Underground Railroad in the Salt Fork section of Ohio, the Reverend Joseph Markey teamed with his son during rescue operations. The Markey family operated a depot in Stafford Station in Monroe County near the Washington County line. During the 1840s and 1850s, they concealed fugitives in the cellar of their one-story frame house or in the hayloft of their barn. Markey's son, Jonas, relayed Virginia-born slaves Howard Neale and Rose Neale and their days-old infant six miles from the Philip Severance safehouse in Middleburg, Ohio.

Source

Burke, Henry Robert, and Charles Hart Fogle. *Washington County Underground Railroad.* Charleston, SC: Arcadia, 2004.

Marks, William (1814–1879)
Marks, Emily Catherine Holcomb (1838–1903)

Clever secret railway conductor in Naples, New York, William "Uncle Billy" Marks transported slaves in fake funeral processions. At his birthplace in Burlington, Connecticut, he required rehabilitation for a birth defect that crippled him. On September 1, 1834, he arrived in Naples; he peddled fabric and household implements, which he bore on a yoke over his shoulders as he journeyed over Ontario, Seneca, Wayne, and Yates counties. After four years on the road, he settled in a two-story frame dwelling at One Mechanic Street in Naples and donated funds to the Methodist Church. He opened a clothing, furniture, and notions business and married Emily Catherine Holcomb, who assisted him in Underground Railroad relays of passengers arriving from Naples Creek or by train from Elmira, New York.

Marks established a funeral business and built caskets that his wife lined and trimmed. In the late 1840s, his use of an outbuilding, coffins, and a hearse as hiding places for refugees furthered safe harboring. Business associate John Whiting helped the Marks family to convey passengers to Gideon Pitts and Jane Wells Pitts's station in Honeoye or to Cobblestone Farm, Dolly Root Parrish and Isaac Parrish's depot on West Lake Road in Canandaigua. Before departing, William directed passengers over planks from his porch to his horse-drawn van and then carried the planks along to conceal the human scent from the sheriff's bloodhounds. He added a trapdoor to his wagon so that he could carry two passengers in one trip. His outreach intensified after the passage of the Fugitive Slave Law of 1850 and continued into the Civil War years and the Reconstruction period. Three rescued slaves, Addie and Ed Graham and their daughter Rose, remained with the Marks family as domestics.

See also: bloodhounds; Fugitive Slave Law of 1850.

Sources

Flory, Beth B. "William Marks of Naples." *Crooked Lake Review* (Summer 2003).
Pettit, Eber M. *Sketches in the History of the Underground Railroad.* Fredonia, NY: W. McKinstry & Son, 1879.

maroon settlements

Some blacks on the run from slavery sheltered in maroon communities, free societies whose members protected their liberty by guerrilla warfare. The name *maroons* derives from the Spanish *Cimarrónes,* "wild savages" or "black rebels," perhaps a reflection of their notoriety as black Robin Hoods. These communities harbored fugitives without questioning a person's name or place of servitude. Maroon settlements ranged over Tuscarora territory in the wetlands of Virginia and the Carolinas, Cherokee enclaves in the southern Appalachian Mountains, the isolated forests and black Seminole villages of Spanish Florida, shore scavenger communities on Cape Florida in Key Biscayne and Tavernier, the bayous of Louisiana from New Orleans to Lake Borgne, Indian settlements of Alabama and Mississippi, the wilderness of Kentucky and Tennessee, the sea islands off Georgia, and into the tropical backcountry of Jamaica, Cuba, and Brazil.

Documented Maroon Communities	Date	Leader
Accomac County, VA	1781	
Bladen County, NC	1821; 1830	Isam
	1856	
Bovina, MS	1857	
Cabarrus County, NC	1811	
Cypress Swamp, LA	1836–1837	
Dismal Swamp, VA	1709; 1728	Captain Peter
Duplin County, NC	1830	
Edisto, SC	1686	
Elizabeth City, NC	1802–1803	Tom Copper
	1822	Manuel
Gastons Island, NC	1830	
Gates County, NC	1820	
Georgetown, SC	1821	
Gracia Real de Santa Teresa de Mose, FL	1728–1763	Francisco Menendez
Hanesville, MS	1844	
Jacksonborough, SC	1822	Denmark Vesey
Jones County, NC	1830; 1857	William Kinnegay
Middlesex County, VA	1691	Mingoe
Mobile County, AL	1827; 1841	
Nash County, NC	1859	
Natchez, MS	1731	Bambara
Negro Fort, FL	1816	
New Bern, NC	1857	
New Hanover County, NC	1830	
Norfolk, VA	1822–1823	Captain Mingo
Port Royal, SC	1686	
Princess Anne County, VA	1818	
Robeson County, NC	1856	
Sampson County, NC	1830	
Savannah River, GA	1786–1789	Cudjoe; Captain Lewis
St. Bernard Parish, LA	1783–1784	Juan San Malo
St. Charles and St. John, LA	1811	Charles Deslondes
St. John's Parish, SC	1819	
St. John's River, FL	1836–1837	John Horse; Abraham
St. Landry Parish, LA	1846	
Talladega County, AL	1860	
Terrebonne Parish, LA	1841	
Upson County, GA	1844	
Wake County, NC	1818	
Williamsburg County, SC	1819	
Wilmington, NC	1841	

In 1715, the first refugee settlement in North America developed in the Great Dismal Swamp of the eastern Carolinas and Virginia, the maroon community with the most documented history. The first permanent enclave, Gracia Real de Santa Teresa de Mose, emerged outside St. Augustine, Florida, established by slaves in 1739. Nearly half a century later, black refugees Cudjoe and Captain Lewis formed a village of 21 huts and rice paddies on the Savannah River until, in 1787, pursuers burned their holdings and hanged Lewis. As a warning to rescuers of slaves, authorities decapitated Lewis and fixed his head on a pike.

Underground Railroad conductor Lewis W. Paine noted in his memoir, *Six Years in a Georgia Prison* (1851), the importance of survivalism to marronage. Before a slave named Samson fled bondage in 1844, he and others chose "large tracts of land, covered with heavy timber, containing not only deep and almost impenetrable swamps, but caves, holes, shelving rocks, and banks. In these they secrete themselves during the day-time, venturing abroad only by night, in pursuit of food, and such articles as they may need, or to see those of their brother slaves whom they can trust. If they intend to 'stay out' long, they prepare some way to cook, and by taking fowls, and once in a while a pig, they make out very well; for they can get as many potatoes, and as much corn, as they wish. But if they are not going to tarry long, they depend on such things as they can get, or others may give them. Still, they suffer much at times through fear of being caught; for when there seems to be much danger they will keep close and go without eating for several days."

The fate of Captain Lewis echoed a similar execution of a maroon leader that occurred in the Land of Gaillarde, in St. Bernard Parish, Louisiana. In 1783, Juan San Malo (or St. Malo) and his confederates—Batista, Cecilia Canoy, Joly Coeur, and Henry—led runaways to freedom for a year on the fringes of New Orleans. Residents slid silently through swampland by pirogue (a kind of boat made from a hollowed-out log) and thrived at smuggling and trading. Planters, who were outnumbered by blacks, complained of their losses and feared an uprising. They mustered the *Maréchausée,* a rural French police force made up of whites and free blacks and led by Lieutenant Colonel Francisco Bouligny. The provincial governor, Esteban Miró, negotiated with the Biloxi, Pascagoula, and Yowani Indians to provide trackers; a turncoat black named Bastien earned 1,000 pesos for spying on the maroons. In 1784, San Malo was captured and hanged in Jackson Square in New Orleans and his corpse left for crows to pick.

Among Native Americans, blacks got their first taste of equality and acceptance in the New World and their first opportunities to establish homes. According to freedman Israel Massie of Greenville County, Virginia, fugitives dug underground cubbies to conceal themselves from posses or from raids organized by constables or plantation overseers. The more determined refugees constructed crude palisades as bulwarks against slave hunters, bloodhounds, kidnappers, and vigilantes out on a "marooning party." Dr. Henry Ravenel of St. John's Parish in eastern South Carolina recorded in his diary that a raid in 1819 on local swampland along the Santee River netted several captures at the cost of one white wounded and two runaways shot and killed, a loss calculated in dollars rather than in human lives. The valuation of maroons as a capital loss recurs in *The Colored Patriots of the American Revolution* (1855), in which black historian William Cooper Nell states that one Norfolk merchant estimated the collective worth of the area's runaway maroons at $1.5 million.

The white world had little knowledge of "outlyer" hideouts, where deer trails were the only access routes. Residents were mostly male. One fugitive, who lurked in the swamps of Suffolk, Virginia, lived 19 years without seeing a woman. Male maroons earned their living by hunting, fishing, and crafts. Enterprising runaways engaged in the cypress shingle trade, hawked mullet and shad for use as bait, salted herring by the barrel for sale, or sold fresh deer, rabbit, bass, and catfish to poor white squatters and flatboat traders. With the proceeds, fugitives bought lead shot and powder, essentials to the outlaw way of life. The most famous fen, the Great Dismal Swamp, drew local attention for bandit-style night raids on corncribs and livestock pens and for acts of vengeance against cruel overseers and owners.

A few maroons, such as Juan San Malo and Batista, made their way by name into history. According to an article in the *Norfolk Herald,* one successful recluse, escapee Tom Copper, nested in the fens near Elizabeth City, North Carolina, in summer 1802. He survived by networking with renegades and fugitive bands up and down the inland waterway. In 1833, a bandit named Manuel provided shelter and forged travel papers for two women escaping John Wood's plantation to a maroon hideaway on the Pasquotank River near Elizabeth City. In 1857, William Kinnegay fled bondage in Jones County, North Carolina, and retreated to the New Bern swamps, where he earned a living slaughtering livestock and swapping sides of pork or beef for ammunition and provisions.

Information on maroons was slow in reaching the outside world. In September 1858, *Harper's* published a pen-and-ink sketch by David Hunter Strother

(1816–1888) of Martinsburg, West Virginia, who worked under the pseudonym Porte Crayon. The drawing depicts a log road alongside an open-sided roofed ramada, cobbled together out of scrap lumber and limbs by black shingle cutters in the Dismal Swamp. Another of Strother's sketches pictures a grizzled armed man cautiously making his way through a tangle of vines. These hermits of the backcountry made contact with plantation slaves and established a communication grapevine that eased the way for others to escape bondage. An illustration in *Harper's* in 1860 characterized the close contact of lumber camp slaves with remote sluices overhung with Spanish moss and vines, the natural curtains that cloaked maroon settlements in mystery.

See also: American Revolution; bloodhounds; Dismal Swamp; grapevine telegraphy; kidnap; Seminoles; spies.

Sources

Bell, Caryn Cossé. *Revolution, Romanticism, and the Afro-Creole Protest Tradition in Louisiana, 1718–1868.* Baton Rouge: Louisiana State University Press, 2004.
Cecelski, David S. *The Waterman's Song: Slavery and Freedom in Maritime North Carolina.* Chapel Hill: University of North Carolina Press, 2001.
Cuthbert, John A., and Jessie Poesch. *David Hunter Strother: One of the Best Draughtsmen the Country Possesses.* Morgantown: West Virginia University Press, 1997.
Griffin, William A. *Ante-Bellum Elizabeth City: The History of a Canal Town.* Elizabeth City, NC: Roanoke, 1970.
Lause, Mark A. "Borderland Visions: Maroons and Outlyers in Early American History." *Monthly Review* 54:4 (September 2002): 38–44.
Leaming, Hugo Prosper. *Hidden Americans: Maroons of Virginia and the Carolinas.* New York: Garland, 1995.
Nell, William Cooper. *The Colored Patriots of the American Revolution.* Boston: Robert F. Wallcut, 1855.
Phillips, Ulrich Bonnell. *American Negro Slavery.* Baton Rouge: Louisiana State University Press, 1966.
Robinson, Cedric J. *Black Movements in America.* New York: Routledge, 1991.

Marriott, Charles (1782–1843)
Marriott, Sarah White (fl. 1830s–1840s)

English-born Quaker Charles Marriott and his wife, Sarah White Marriott, were cautious agents of the New York–Canada line of the Underground Railroad. While maintaining safehouses in the village of Hudson, in the Hudson Valley, and in New York City, from 1840 to 1842, Charles Marriott served the executive committee of the American Anti-Slavery Society. One well-documented rescue, that of John and Martha Williams, which took place around 1844, required passage from the Marriott safehouse on the

> In response to the backlash against slave rescue, Charles Marriott wrote, "For my share I hope it will never subside until slavery is abolished. There is tenfold more to be dreaded from our own relapsing into our former sleep of death."

Hudson River in New York to Rokeby Farm, the sanctuary of Quaker agents Rachel Gilpin Robinson and Rowland Thomas Robinson in Ferrisburg, Vermont. Charles Marriott chose the distant setting because of its relative safety from kidnappers and slave catchers. For their outspoken opposition to slavery, in 1841, Marriott and his colleagues James Sloan Gibbons and Isaac Tatem Hopper were expelled from the Society of Friends on a motion by Marriott's brother-in-law, George Fox White.

See also: American Anti-Slavery Society; kidnap; *Prigg v. Pennsylvania* (1842).

Sources

Bordewich, Fergus M. *Bound for Canaan: The Underground Railroad and the War for the Soul of America.* New York: Amistad, 2005.
Moger, Elizabeth H. "Quakers as Abolitionists: The Robinsons of Rokeby and Charles Marriott." *Quaker History* 92 (Fall 2003): 52–59.

Mars, John N. (1806–?)

A minister and abolitionist from Massachusetts, the Reverend John N. Mars aided runaways who were starting new lives in Canada. He joined the Reverend James William Charles Pennington and Henry Foster in reporting on the National Convention of Colored People in Maryland 1840. While selling subscriptions to the *Colored American,* an abolitionist newspaper published by the Reverend Charles Bennett Ray in New York City, Mars pastored the African Methodist Episcopal Zion Church of Poughkeepsie, New York, until 1845. During his tenure, on May 5, 1841, he addressed a public meeting in Hartford, Connecticut, concerning the welfare of the African mutineers seized from the *Amistad.* On a mission for the Wesleyan Methodists, in 1846, he aided the settlement of newcomers at the Ontario terminus of the Underground Railroad. During the Civil War, while serving the Union army as a chaplain, Mars entered a North Carolina hospital for treatment of arthritis. He settled in Portsmouth, Virginia, to aid freed slaves.

See also: African Methodist Episcopal Church; *Amistad.*

Sources

Levine, Robert S. *Martin Delany, Frederick Douglass, and the Politics of Representative Identity.* Chapel Hill: University of North Carolina Press, 1997.

Reid, Richard. "Raising the African Brigade: Early Black Recruitment in Civil War North Carolina." *North Carolina Historical Review* 70 (1993): 266–301.

Marsh, Gravner (1777–1848)
Marsh, Hannah (1789–1864)
Marsh, Sarah (1819–1887)

Abolitionists Gravner and Hannah Marsh and their daughter, Sarah, earned respect for their safehouse, Fallowfield, in Caln, west of Downington in Chester County, Pennsylvania. To end slavery, Gravner Marsh supported the Free-Soil Party; Hannah Marsh promoted anti-slavery strategies. The couple received refugees from Thomas Bonsall and Susan P. Johnson Bonsall in Lampeter, Deborah T. Simmons Coates and Lindley Coates in Sadsbury, James Fulton, Jr., in Ercildoun, Daniel Gibbons and Hannah Wierman Gibbons in Bird-in-Hand, Arminda Taylor Haines and Joseph Haines in Bedford, Esther Logue Hayes and Mordecai Hayes and their son Jacob Hayes and Isaac and Thamosin (or Thamazine) Pennock Meredith at Newlin. Runaways recognized the Marsh station by its stone buildings and whitewashed walls. Hannah provided meals and dressed the females in Quaker attire, which included bonnets and veils. Gravner concealed males under the haymow and females in the residence. One hired man, Richard Gibbs, had to drop his pitchfork and flee from the Marshes' fields to escape his former master. The Marsh family provided enough money for Gibbs and his wife to move away, assume aliases, and begin their lives anew.

In 1848, Hannah Marsh, in widowhood, continued the family work with the aid of her daughter Sarah. Depending on circumstances, Sarah was out in all weather, night and day, in service to refugees. She led parties by enclosed buggy in daylight to Dr. J.K. Eshleman, Graceanna Lewis, Micajah Speakman, John Vickers, or Allen Wills. One party of nine required her to send the men through the fields to avoid the tollgate. Overcrowding in the wagon posed no problem. The sight of Sarah riding on the front board with her feet on the shafts was common on market days, when she carried goods to Philadelphia. After passage of the Fugitive Slave Law of 1850, she curtailed daytime deliveries and traveled only by night. Her enthusiastic work continued after she became the second wife of the Reverend Eusebius Barnard of Pocopsin.

See also: Fugitive Slave Law of 1850.

Source

Smedley, Robert C. *History of the Underground Railroad in Chester and the Neighboring Counties of Pennsylvania.* Lancaster, PA: Office of *The Journal,* 1883.

Marshall, Harriet McClintock (1840–1923)
Marshall, Elijah (1838–1903)

Members of a close network of agents in Harrisburg, Pennsylvania, Harriet McClintock Marshall and her husband, Elijah Marshall, a fugitive slave, tended and transported refugees traveling via the Underground Railroad. They married in 1864. At their safehouse at Calder and Front streets, they received runaways and relayed them to Wesley Union African Methodist Episcopal Church, a log waystation of the secret network at Third and Mulberry streets. The Marshalls collaborated with fellow church members Dr. William M. "Pap" Jones and his wife, Mary Jones, in Tanner's Alley.

See also: African Methodist Episcopal Church.

Source

Scott, John Welden. *African Americans of Harrisburg.* Charleston, SC: Arcadia, 2005.

Marshall, Samuel (1800–1880)
Marshall, Mary Gilliland (fl. 1820s–1840s)

An Irish immigrant and influential abolitionist, Judge Samuel Marshall and his wife, Mary Gilliland Marshall of Connoquenessing, Pennsylvania, joined a smoothly run secret network aiding refugees near Pittsburgh. After making his home in Adams Township on Hespenheide Road in Butler County, Samuel Marshall became a conveyer for the Underground Railroad some 15 miles from the safehouse of Thomas McKeever and his sons, Thomas and William, in Middletown, Pennsylvania, and from John Baton Vashon and his son, George Boyer Vashon, in Pittsburgh. When the Marshalls opened a waystation, the family kept passengers safe from slave catchers. In 1843, one wanderer, Charles A. "Charley" Garlick of Shinntown, Virginia, passed on to Samuel Marshall's kinsman John Rainbow, an operative of the secret network in New Castle, and to Adam Chew in Brookfield, Pennsylvania.

Sources

Garlick, Charles A. *Life, Including His Escape and Struggle for Liberty, of Charles A. Garlick, Born a Slave in Old Virginia, Who Secured His Freedom by Running Away from His Master's Farm in 1843.* Jefferson, OH: Joseph Howells, 1902.

Guzzo, Maria, "Underground Railroad Stops Recall Region's Role in Anti-Slavery Movement," *Pittsburgh (PA), Tribune-Review,* February 18, 1996, 1, 5.

Mason, Amos (?–1842)
Mason, Hannah Seward (fl. 1830s–1840s)

Two members of the racially integrated Bristol Hill Congregational Church in Volney, in Oswego County, New York, grain miller and farmer Amos Mason and Hannah (or Hanna) Seward Mason supported the work of the Underground Railroad. They married in 1825. In collaboration with Hiram Gilbert and Lucy Harrington Gilbert in Fulton, New York, the Masons received runaways at their home at 541 Gilbert Mills Road. In December 1839, kidnappers abducted Hannah Mason's son, 27-year-old James Watkins Seward, whom New Orleans authorities jailed and put on a road gang. Because of the intervention by agents Starr Clark, Charlotte Clarke and Edwin E. Clarke, secret network coordinator Gerrit Smith, and New York Governor William Henry Seward, James Seward gained his freedom the next spring. He was hanged for robbing and murdering a store clerk on July 9, 1841.

See also: kidnap.

Sources

Henderson, Madison. *Trials and Confessions of Madison Henderson.* St. Louis: Chambers & Knapp, 1841.

McAndrew, Mike, "When Being Black Was Called a Crime," *Syracuse Post-Standard,* February 14, 2005.

Mason, Isaac (1822–1898)

A fugitive from Georgetown, in Kent County, Maryland, Isaac Mason welcomed the help of Underground Railroad agents in freeing him. The son of a domestic, Sophia Thompson, and freedman Zekiel Thompson, Mason was houseboy to Hannah Woodland. At her death in 1837, his parents fled to Baltimore; he passed to Dr. Hyde. After dodging the gunshots of a farmer named Mansfield and facing the possibility of being sold to a New Orleans slave dealer, in 1847, Mason escaped bondage and fled to Delaware. Two years later, he arrived in Philadelphia. His contentment ended after the passage of the Fugitive Slave Law of 1850. He describes in his autobiography, *Life of Isaac Mason as a Slave* (1893), the dilemma of carrying a hod of bricks up a ladder in Philadelphia and looking down at his owner's son.

In terror of recapture and return to Maryland, Mason sought legal counsel before journeying farther north to Massachusetts. By the arrangements of agent Gibbs in New York City, Mason and his wife boarded a vessel for New York, where a hack driver beat Gibbs severely for dissuading Mason from hiring his cab. The Masons rested for several weeks at the safehouse of Harriet Bell Hayden and Lewis Hayden in Boston and with Ebenezer Hemenway in Worcester, Massachusetts. Passage of the Fugitive Slave Law of 1850 forced the Masons farther north. On April 15, 1851, the Masons arrived in Montreal but found Canadian weather too brutal for their liking. With six dollars borrowed from Joshua Spooner, they returned to Worcester. Mason joined James Redpath's emigrant party in 1859 to survey the possibility of settling in Haiti. He determined that Worcester suited him better than the Caribbean isles.

See also: Fugitive Slave Law of 1850; safehouses.

Source

Mason, Isaac. *Life of Isaac Mason as a Slave.* Worcester, MA: privately published, 1893.

Mason, John (ca. 1820–?)

One of a long list of Underground Railroad conductors educated at Oberlin College, John Mason profited from liberty and an opportunity to learn. Born around 1820 in Kentucky, he escaped slavery at age 12. In his early twenties, he settled in Hamilton, Ohio, and became a secret operative on the Ohio Valley–Canada route. Mason completed close to 1,400 rescues. He conducted some refugees from Kentucky plantations over dangerous, closely watched territory. At the Ohio River crossing, he collaborated with Jean Lowry Rankin and John Rankin at Liberty Hill, in Ripley, Ohio. After Mason's recapture, his owner sold him to a New Orleans slave dealer for auction at a public market. Mason escaped his second owner and, accompanied by another refugee, traveled by steamer up the Mississippi River to Cincinnati, Ohio.

See also: Oberlin College.

Source

Griffler, Keith P. *Front Line of Freedom: African Americans and the Forging of the Underground Railroad in the Ohio Valley.* Lexington: University Press of Kentucky, 2004.

Mathews, Edward (fl. 1840s)
Mathews, Annie (fl. 1840s)

Freedman Edward Mathews and his wife, Annie Mathews, assisted runaways fleeing through Adams County, Pennsylvania. After their move to Yellow Hill, 10 miles north of Gettysburg, in 1842, the couple joined the secret network that passed through Quaker Valley and partnered with farrier Basil Biggs and Mary Jackson Biggs, who operated a waystation at their tenant farm south of town. During the Civil War, their son, William H. Mathews, who grew up at their safehouse, suffered permanent crippling from a bullet to the knee and pulmonary disease brought on by exposure to cold.

Source

Creighton, Margaret. *The Colors of Courage: Unheard Voices from the Battle of Gettysburg.* New York: Basic Books, 2005.

Mathews, Peter (1802–?)

A Virginia slave, Peter Mathews lived for 35 years under the whip of a cruel master, William S. Mathews of Oak Hill in Temperanceville. On October 1, 1833, Peter Mathews discovered an ox in the vegetable patch and forced it out. The master considered the slave's action impudent. William Mathews held Peter at gunpoint and stabbed him in the neck. The slave fled north by following the polestar. When he reached the Underground Railroad committee in Philadelphia, he surrendered his pistol and adopted an alias, Samuel Sparrow. Agents provided him with clean traveling clothes and letters of introduction and paid for his ticket to Canada.

See also: North Star.

Source

Williams, James. *Life and Adventures of James Williams, a Fugitive Slave.* San Francisco: Women's Union Print, 1873.

Matthews, Josiah (1802–1867)

One of the first Underground Railroad operatives in Elm Grove, in Tazewell County, Illinois, Josiah Matthews (or Mathews) adopted clever ruses to conceal his activities. He constructed a covered wagon that enabled him to transport slaves undetected across Lake Michigan into Canada. During one relay, to confuse spies, he whitened refugees' faces with flour and pretended to send the men with his son on a coon hunt. On another occasion Matthews dismantled a freight box and wiped the sweat from his horses to conceal from a posse a recent delivery of passengers to the next waystation. Assisting in local operations of the secret network were farmer Uriah Crosby in Morton and attorney John Albert Jones in Tremont.

See also: spies.

Source

History of Tazewell County, Illinois. Chicago: Charles C. Chapman, 1879.

Maudlin, Wright (1797–ca. 1866)
Maudlin, Mary Wickersham (1785–ca. 1838)

A Quaker spy, conductor, and transporter for the Underground Railroad in Kentucky, Wright Maudlin (or Modlin) undertook a dangerous job of rescuing slaves and transporting them north. He was born in Back Creek, in Randolph County, North Carolina. In 1817, he married Mary Wickersham and established a farm and safehouse in Williamsville, in Cass County, Michigan. With the aid of William "Bill" Jones, Maudlin made forays into Bourbon County, Kentucky, to direct runaways into free territory.

In September 1849, Maudlin pursued John Norris, a slave owner from Boone County, Kentucky, and his armed accomplices to stop them from retrieving Norris's chattel, David Powell, his wife Lucy, and their four sons, George, James, Lewis, and Samuel, who had escaped on October 9, 1847. In South Bend, Indiana, Maudlin engaged attorney Edwin B. Cocker and secured the Powells' freedom. At the pronouncement of the verdict, Norris held the captives at gunpoint until he and his confederates were subdued. Supporters from the black community in Cassopolis, Michigan, offered a wagon and departed with the Powells. The group sang freedom songs on their way out of town.

Maudlin rescued a mulatto from possible concubinage to her white half brother. He sped the girl north to the safehouse of Sarah E. Bowen Hussey and Sylvanus Erastus Fuller Hussey in Battle Creek, Michigan. With four mounted slave hunters in pursuit, Maudlin disguised the girl with a sunbonnet and drove her away in a buggy toward Canada. He knew the route and stopped only at familiar waystations. As they neared Detroit, he promised that he would slay the girl with his knife rather than send her back to sexual bondage in Kentucky. When the stalkers surrounded the buggy, Maudlin resorted to rural dialect: "Me an' the old woman is out land-lookin'" (Gardner, 1913, 92). At Woodward Avenue, he spied a fellow operative, who signaled by raising his hat and wiping his forehead with a white handkerchief. Maudlin completed the relay at a boathouse on the shore of the Detroit River, where rowers received the girl in their skiff and hurried her across to Windsor, Ontario.

On August 1, 1847, Sylvanus Erastus Hussey alerted neighboring conductors of a posse of 13 kidnappers from Bourbon County intent on recovering their chattel. Zachariah Shugart, Stephan A. Bogue, and Josiah Osborn confronted the thieves and followed them to court in Cassopolis. Maudlin obtained a writ requiring the freeing of the captives. During the proceedings, Shugart led nine of the runaways north to Canada. Another slave disappeared from jail. In February 1848, the owners sued eight secret operatives, including Bogue and Shugart. Claims and counterclaims pushed the litigation into January 1851 and concluded without a clear victory for the Kentuckians. In September 1850, passage of the Fugitive Slave Law made recovery of escaping slaves easier for their owners.

See also: disguise; Fugitive Slave Law of 1850; kidnap; slave recovery; spies.

Sources

Gardner, Washington, ed. *History of Calhoun County, Michigan.* Chicago: Lewis, 1913.
Glover, Lowell H. *A Twentieth Century History of Cass County, Michigan.* Chicago: Lewis Publishing, 1906.
Mathews, Alfred. *History of Cass County, Michigan.* Chicago: Waterman, Watkins & Co., 1882.

Maulsby, Samuel (1768–1838)
Maulsby, Susan Thomas (1779–1818)

Two Quaker conductors, Samuel Maulsby and Susan Thomas Maulsby of Plymouth Meeting, in Montgomery County, Pennsylvania, instilled humanitarianism in their daughter, Martha Maulsby Corson. The Maulsby family began sheltering slaves at their stone residence in 1820. They passed runaways to Philadelphia.

Source

Contosta, David R., and Gail C. Momjian. *Plymouth and Whitemarsh Townships, Pennsylvania.* Charleston, SC: Arcadia, 2003.

Maxson, Darwin Eldridge (1822–1895)

An altruist and teacher at Alfred Academy in Alfred, New York, the Reverend Darwin Eldridge Maxson, a Seventh-Day Baptist preacher, managed a safehouse on the secret network. Like fellow operatives Bayless S. Bassett and Esther Eliza Crandall Bassett at 29 North Main, Maxson took compassion on fugitives. His residence, built in 1840, contained a trapdoor in the parlor that opened on a crawl space leading to small subterranean rooms and a tunnel that ended at the creek. For six months during the Civil War, Maxson was a chaplain in the Eighty-fifth regiment of the Union army; malaria forced his retirement in 1862.

Source

Minard, John S. *Allegany County and Its People: A Centennial Memorial History of Allegany County, New York.* Alfred, NY: W.A. Fergusson, 1896.

Maxson, Delilah Bowland (1806–1850)
Maxson, William (1806–1877)
Maxson, Hannah Keislar (1827–?)

Stationmasters in Cedar County, Iowa, Delilah Bowland (or Bolon) Maxson of Virginia and William Maxson (also Maxon) of Fayette, Pennsylvania, promoted the Underground Railroad. In 1839, seven years after their marriage, the couple and their first three children—Jonathan, Helan Kirts, and Thaddeus Warsaw Maxson—migrated west by steamer up the Mississippi and Ohio rivers to Iowa. They built an oak and black walnut safehouse on 320 acres along the Cedar River in North Liberty, northeast of Springdale. They were known for their clever concealment of passengers in fruit barrels, baskets, and potato sacks in their full cellar.

After his first wife's death William Maxson married Hannah Keislar of Ohio and grew bolder in his activism. He was privy to the strategies of insurrectionist John Brown. In late December 1857, Brown and 10 of his confederates stopped at the Maxsons' rural waystation for the winter. While resting with the Maxson family and at the safehouse of John H. Painter, Brown and his staff recruited volunteers. The men drilled on the Maxson lawn with swords and pikes in preparation for a raid on the federal arsenal in Harpers Ferry, Virginia. Local Quakers disapproved of the show of arms but sided with Brown's radical abolitionism.

See also: abolitionism; Quakers.

Sources

Faux, Steven F., "Iowa's Underground Railroad Heroes," *Des Moines Register,* February 21, 1999.

Lord, Jeannette Mather. "John Brown: They Had a Concern." *West Virginia History* 20:3 (April 1959): 163–83.

Maxwell, Susannah Augusta Stokes (1805–1923)

Freeborn launderer Susannah Augusta Maxwell Stokes of Lancaster County, Pennsylvania, and later Ontario, Canada, lived to the age of 117, making her Canada's oldest citizen. Susannah's parents died during her childhood, and she grew up working as an indentured domestic. During the Christiana Riot of September 11, 1851, farmer Edward Gorsuch attempted to recapture four young runaways—Noah Baley, Nelson Ford, George Hammond, and Joshua Hammond—who fled Retreat Farm in Baltimore County, Maryland, in 1849. In the aftermath, bounty hunters flooded the area. Stokes fled the state via the Underground Railroad and lived in New York. In 1858, she moved to Toronto, Ontario. After her marriage to Henry Maxwell, she established a laundry business in Richmond Hill, Ontario.

See also: bounty hunters; Christiana Riot.

Source

Campbell, S.W. *The Slave Catchers: Enforcement of the Fugitive Slave Law, 1850–1860.* Chapel Hill: University of North Carolina Press, 1970.

May, Samuel Joseph (1797–1871)

A Unitarian abolitionist from Syracuse, New York, the Reverend Samuel Joseph May lectured on the evils of slavery. The uncle of agent Louisa May Alcott, May co-founded the American Anti-Slavery Society, and for a quarter century, served as its manager and vice president. In 1830, he and his cousin attorney Samuel Edmund Sewall discovered a young abolitionist orator, William Lloyd Garrison. With the assistance of another cousin, Amos Bronson Alcott, May and Sewall helped to boost Garrison to the lead in ending the flesh trade.

As an officer of the Massachusetts Anti-Slavery Society, May recruited such valuable Underground Railroad operatives as the Reverend Thomas Wentworth Higginson of Boston and Mary J. Mingo Durfree Johnson and Nathan Johnson in New Bedford, Massachusetts. While May resided in Brooklyn, Connecticut, he conducted refugees to the next waystation, usually after 11 P.M. and extending until 2 A.M. His contact in Uxbridge was Effingham L. Capron, an agent who guarded escapees at resting places. According to Thomas James Mumford, editor of *Memoir of Samuel Joseph May* (1873), May successfully conveyed hundreds of men, women, and children to Canada.

May's blatant denunciation of slave sellers and slave owners created enmity. When he spoke at the Old Brick Church in Montpelier, Vermont, in October 1835, his oration sparked a riot. Protecting him was another operative, Colonel Jonathan Peckham Miller. May's valor impressed journalist Joseph Poland of the *Vermont Watchman and Journal,* who devoted himself to the work of the Underground Railroad and to the founding of an abolitionist newspaper, the *Green Mountain Freeman.* To be nearer a nexus of the Underground Railroad, May moved to Syracuse, New York, in April 1845 and helped in the expansion of routes to the west. On May 26, 1851, he paid passage for Priscilla Hatton to Canada; in February 1852, he offered $35.75 to Sarah Ringola and a fellow passenger. On July 8, 1852, he paid Elizabeth Howard's passage to Canada. He extended his generosity in 1852 to Mrs. Howard and her daughters, in 1853

> In Syracuse, New York, the Reverend Samuel Joseph May openly defied the Fugitive Slave Law of 1850 from the pulpit by collecting donations to help refugees reach Canada. He declared, "I only insisted that all good and true men ought to withstand the execution of that infamous law, in the way and by the means that they each one of them conscientiously believed to be right. . . . I did enjoin it upon them, if it should seem necessary, to fight for the rescue of any black man from the horrors of a return into slavery." The backlash from his message was so intense that a crowd gathered outside the church and hurled a stone through the window, striking a female congregant.

A vocal abolitionist and charter member of the American Anti-Slavery Society, the Unitarian minister Samuel Joseph May put himself in peril by ushering slaves north through Connecticut and, later, western New York. *(Library of Congress)*

to Mrs. Brown and Mary L. Johnson and her child, and in June 1854 to William Johnson and William Patterson.

May not only rescued slaves, he also followed them to black settlements across the border—Buxton, Chatham, Sandwich, and Windsor, Ontario—to determine how well served they were by emancipation. He took a special interest in Buxton, which bore the name of Fowell Buxton, an English philanthropist. Under the leadership of the Reverend William King, a Scots Presbyterian, some 90 families settled the area between 1848 and 1852. They bought plots of land from King, who purchased 9,000 acres of woods for the purpose of beginning a community of escapees from slavery. He remarked on how families thrived in freedom and how much they appreciated Underground Railroad conductors.

At a crucial point in Underground Railroad history, May involved himself in a chancy rescue. At the dinner hour on October 1, 1851, May discovered that authorities had arrested William "Jerry" McHenry, a mulatto cooper, on the word of James Lear, agent of a Missouri slave owner named Reynolds. May and others were appalled that McHenry could not plead his own case nor refute charges against him. He escaped from custody and suffered bruises and a broken rib before being returned to the commissioner's office.

At the request of the police chief, May met privately with the prisoner and assured him that conductors planned to help him on his way to freedom. With the aid of some 30 men, including agents Gerrit Smith, Jermaine Wesley Loguen, and Charles A. Wheaton, May engineered the liberation. Amid gunfire and turmoil, McHenry escaped by buggy and lodged with Mr. and Mrs. Caleb Davis at the corner of Genesee and Orange streets. Agents sawed off McHenry's shackles and called a doctor to treat his wounds. After five days of rest, James Davis and Jason S. Hoyt dispatched McHenry to the next station, 3339 Main Street in Mexico, New York, the home of Amy Perkins Ames and Orson Ames. The second night, McHenry moved on to a barn at the rural depot of Asa Beebe and Mary Whipple Beebe. The journey continued to Charlotte Ambler Clarke and Edwin W. Clarke's depot in Oswego. A night transfer from a skiff to a steamer completed McHenry's transport to Kingston, Canada.

During an investigation into the jailbreak, 100 citizens of Onondaga County, both male and female, assembled in Auburn on October 5 to support the rescue party. Politician William Henry Seward posted bond, which several respected Syracusans pledged, and hosted the rescue party at his house. May stood out from the 18 culprits as a respected agent of the Underground Railroad who admitted complicity and vowed to stand trial. The prosecution chose to try three whites—J.B. Brigham, Ira H. Cobb, and W.L. Salmon—and a black man, Enoch Reed, for whom May testified. Brigham and Salmon were acquitted; Cobb died before he could appeal the verdict. The case against Reed passed to a U.S. district court in fall 1852. Congressman Gerrit Smith mounted a wagon at Canandaigua, New York, to harangue an abolitionist audience. The community outrage against slave capture was so widespread that no one remained to form juries to try all defendents. Jubilant citizens rejoiced at the rotunda of the New York Central Railroad, a symbolic location reflecting the efficacy of the Underground Railroad. For years, Syracusans celebrated October 1 as the anniversary of Jerry McHenry's rescue, which May dubbed "the greatest event in the history of Syracuse."

May refused to cancel the Anti-Slavery Convention in Syracuse on January 29–30, 1861, at the demand of a pro-slavery faction. He met with rowdies who threatened him bodily. Because police refused to intervene, a mob seized the hall, paraded through the streets to a marching band, and flaunted anti-abolition banners. They sported an effigy of May and burned it in Hanover Square, the city center.

May remained a supporter of liberty and peace throughout the Civil War. On August 10, 1990, residents of Syracuse unveiled a dramatic monument picturing McHenry in the company of rescuers Loguen and May.

See also: abolitionist newspapers; American Anti-Slavery Society; Anti-Slavery Society of Canada; routes, Underground Railroad; *Some Recollections of Our Antislavery Conflict* (1869).

Sources

Loguen, Jermain Wesley. *The Rev. J.W. Loguen, as a Slave and as a Freeman: A Narrative of Real Life.* Syracuse, NY: J.C.K. Truair, 1859.

May, Samuel Joseph. *Some Recollections of Our Antislavery Conflict.* Boston: Fields, Osgood, 1869.

Mumford, Thomas James, ed. *Memoir of Samuel Joseph May.* Boston: Roberts Brothers, 1873.

Mayhew, Allen B. (1826–1862)
Mayhew, Barbara A. Kagi (1833–1882)

Abolitionist Allen B. Mayhew, a farmer and follower of radical abolitionist John Brown, owned a famous stop on the Underground Railroad. In 1857, he and his father-in-law, Abraham Neff Kagi, built a one-room cabin and sleeping loft that became a waystation of the secret network in Nebraska City, Nebraska. During the occupancy of John Henry Kagi, the brother of Mayhew's wife, Barbara A. Kagi Mayhew, the stop earned notoriety as "John Brown's cabin." Large parties of refugees from John B. Boulware's ferry on Commercial Street in Fort Kearney, on the Missouri River, used the residence as a place to rest during long journeys to stops in Knox and Tabor, Iowa. Extending the capacity of the cabin was a tunnel to the so-called Black Den, a series of high-ceilinged chambers that could hold up to 15 runaways; on one occasion broom maker Henry Daniel Smith of Maryland was one of its occupants. Slaves remember Barbara Mayhew for distributing cornbread to departing fugitives. Corroborating information about the family waystation came from their eldest child, Edward F. Mayhew (1850–?).

Source

Potter, James E. "Fact and Folklore in the Story of 'John Brown's Cave' and the Underground Railroad in Nebraska." *Nebraska History* 83:2 (Summer 2002): 73–78.

Mayo, Ephraim (1789–1857)
Mayo, Sally Laughton (1793–1880)

A stout patriot, Captain Ephraim Mayo, and his wife, Sally Laughton Mayo, received slaves in their home in Kennebec County, Maine. Ephraim Mayo was a captain of the local light infantry during the War of 1812. The Mayos married in 1815. In service to the Underground Railroad from 1814, the couple became rescuers of fugitives arriving along the Kennebec River in Hallowell, Maine.

Source

Nason, Emma Huntington. *Old Hallowell on the Kennebec.* Augusta, ME: Burleigh & Flynt, 1909.

McAndrew, Helen Walker (1826–1906)
McAndrew, William (1824–1895)

A frontier physician in Ypsilanti in Washtenaw County, Michigan, Dr. Helen Walker McAndrew treated the sick while rescuing slaves. Helen and her husband, carpenter William McAndrew, emigrated from Scotland in 1850. William built their home at 1105 South Huron Street. Helen opened the state's first female-owned practice in 1854 and treated the poor and oppressed. The couple partnered on work for temperance, the Salvation Army, women's rights, higher education for women, and the Underground Railroad. They concealed passengers in their barns. In 1994, Dr. McAndrew was inducted into the Michigan Hall of Fame.

Source

Mann, James Thomas. *Ypsilanti: A History in Pictures.* Ypsilanti, MI: Arcadia, 2002.

McCague, Catherine Platter (1792–1879)
McCague, Thomas (1793–1864)

A prosperous, upstanding couple in Ripley, in Brown County, Ohio, Catherine "Kitty" Platter McCague and Thomas McCague were devoted agents of the

Underground Railroad. Proceeds from the McCague pork-packing factory paid for a house at 212 Front Street, known to conductors and passengers as the North Star Station. In February 1838, the McCagues aided Jean Lowry Rankin, John Rankin, and Thomas W. Collins in the rescue of Eliza Harris, a fugitive slave, who served as inspiration for a main character in Harriet Beecher Stowe's *Uncle Tom's Cabin* (1852). After Eliza crossed the Ohio River in Collins's skiff, she followed Chance Shaw to a safehouse and resided in the third story of the McCague residence. Kitty outfitted Eliza and her two-year-old son, Harry, and cooked their meals. In October 1861, the McCagues agreed to help President Abraham Lincoln by funding the equipment and pay of 100,000 Ohio volunteer soldiers. The Liberty Monument, erected on Main Street in 1912, features Thomas McCague along with fellow agents John P. Parker and the Reverend John Rankin.

See also: Uncle Tom's Cabin; or, Life Among the Lowly (1862).

Source

Parker, John P. *John P. Parker, His Promised Land: The Autobiography of John P. Parker, Former Slave and Conductor on the Underground Railroad.* New York: W.W. Norton, 1996.

McClain, Mary Miller (1819–1858)
McClain, William Wylie (1815–1855)

The daughter of Underground Railroad agent Cynthia Catlin Miller and Richard Bishop Miller in Sugar Grove, Pennsylvania, Mary Miller McClain, along with her husband, the Reverend William Wylie McClain, liberated black refugees. The McClains passed arrivals through their hotel, Monongahela House, at One Smithfield Street in Pittsburgh. A refined five-story establishment, it thrived as a safehouse near the black community in Hayti and near waystations in Arthursville, Pennsylvania. The establishment employed 300 free blacks, who gathered information during their service to stage celebrities, southern travelers, businessmen, and other river traffic. One slave woman, wearing men's attire supplied by the Pittsburgh Vigilance Committee, passed her owner in the dining room without stirring suspicion.

Source

Griffler, Keith P. *Front Line of Freedom: African Americans and the Forging of the Underground Railroad in the Ohio Valley.* Lexington: University Press of Kentucky, 2004.

McClew, Charles (?–1898)
McClew, Anna Maria (1827–?)

At Murphy Orchard, a 65-acre berry and fruit farm at 2402 McClew Road in Burt, New York, Charles McClew and his wife, Anna Maria "Libby" McClew, received runaways fleeing bondage. From 1850 to 1861, their farm, north of Lockport in Niagara County, harbored slaves and provided an escape route up Hopkins Creek three miles to Lake Ontario and from there across the international border to Canada. The McClews concealed Underground Railroad passengers in a tidy chamber under the barn vented by pipes to the outside. Arrivals entered through a trapdoor and climbed 14 feet down to a dirt floor. The McClews may have conveyed slaves west in produce wagons. The farm was the first property in the state to be listed on the National Underground Railroad Network to Freedom.

Source

Sylvester, Nathaniel Bartlett. *History of Saratoga County, New York.* Chicago: Gresham, 1893.

McCluer, Samuel (1765–1833)
McCluer, Sarah Allen (1766–1817)
McCluer, Nancy Rutan (fl. 1820s)

Samuel McCluer (or McClure) of Rockbridge, Virginia, and his first wife, Sarah Allen McCluer, were pioneers to Richland County, Ohio, and supporters of the Underground Railroad route from Kentucky to Ontario. Following settler James McCluer, Samuel's uncle, Samuel and Sarah McCluer, and their 16-year-old daughter, Elizabeth, arrived on the frontier in 1809. In 1815, Samuel built a home in Lexington, in Troy Township, where he received slaves and passed them by farm wagon to the next stop. After Sarah's death, in 1822, Samuel married Nancy Rutan. Elizabeth McCluer wed Benjamin Gass, an operative of the secret network who collaborated with agents John Finney and Joseph Roe. The McCluer safehouse was later covered over by the Clear Fork Reservoir.

Source

Graham, A.A., comp. *History of Richland County, Ohio: Its Past and Present.* Mansfield, OH: self-published, 1880.

McCoy, Alexander (1812–?)
McCoy, James (fl. 1840s–1850s)
McCoy, William (fl. 1840s–1850s)

Staunch Presbyterian abolitionists, Alexander McCoy of Pennsylvania and his sons, James and William, operated an Underground Railroad depot in Eagle Creek, in Portage County, Ohio. Alexander worked as a tanner. He shared rescues with agents Jane Campbell McKeever and Matthew McKeever, who operated a station in Middletown with the aid of their sons, Thomas Campbell and William. McCoy and his sons received passengers from Jean Lowry Rankin and John Rankin, stationkeepers some seven miles away at Liberty Hill, which overlooked a busy slave crossing of the Ohio River. The McCoys transported runaways to Bell's Run, the Reverend John Bennington Mahan's residence in White Oak Creek, in Brown County, Ohio.

Source

Hagedorn, Ann. *Beyond the River: The Untold Story of the Heroes of the Underground Railroad.* New York: Simon & Schuster, 2002.

McCoy, Jane Brownlee (1793–1869)
McCoy, Kenneth (1791–1873)

Members of a team of conductors along the Pennsylvania line of the Underground Railroad, Jane Brownlee McCoy and her husband, Kenneth McCoy, piloted desperate slaves. Kenneth McCoy was a first-generation Scots American reared in the Presbyterian faith. In 1817, he married Jane Brownlee, who helped him establish the Free Presbyterian Church. Passengers traveling a route from Greene County, Pennsylvania, encountered Isaac Teagarden and Sarah Ann Parker Teagarden's station on Wheeling Creek and Joseph Gray's farm in Graysville before reaching the McCoys' rural stop in West Finley, in Washington County.

At one time, the couple sheltered 10 passengers in their barn. From there, fugitives passed to the safehouse of Dr. Francis Julius LeMoyne and his wife, Madeleine Romaine Bureau LeMoyne, in Washington Township or to Jane Campbell McKeever and Matthew McKeever and their sons, Thomas Campbell and William, in Middleton. In 1844, Kenneth McCoy joined John Henderson, John McCoy, James Sprowls, Alexander Sprowls, Robert Sutherland, and Isaac Sutherland in forming an anti-slavery society, which headquartered at the McCoys' safehouse.

Source

Commemorative Biographical Record of Washington County, Pennsylvania. Chicago: J.H. Beers, 1893.

McCoy, John (1793–1854)
McCoy, Sabra Clark (1799–1884)

John McCoy and Sabra Clark McCoy of Wells, Vermont, dedicated themselves to Methodism and human liberty. A Scots American whose father was a veteran of the Revolutionary War, John McCoy was born in New Hampshire. After the McCoys married in 1817, they settled briefly in Maine and Vermont before pressing on to the Illinois frontier. Pioneers of Thornton traveling by ox-cart, in 1833, the couple built a cabin near Thorn Creek on the Sauk Trail west of Chicago, in Cook County, not far from Western Avenue. They established a reputation for fairness to the Potawatomi. In 1833, the McCoys extended their altruism by harboring runaway slaves. In league with Joseph Batcheldor and Louisa Ann Batcheldor's station in Chicago, the McCoy rescue operation thrived.

Source

Candeloro, Dominic, and Barbara Paul. *Chicago Heights at the Crossroads of the Nation.* Charleston, SC: Arcadia, 2005.

McCoy, Robert (ca. 1826–?)
McCoy, Eliza (fl. 1850s)

Robert McCoy was one of many slaves who fled the South and sought liberty in the North. After 28 years in bondage as valet to a man named Hall, in Norfolk, Virginia, McCoy suffered from arthritis and tuberculosis. He slipped away and hid for five months and then, accompanied by fugitive Ellen Saunders, fled up the Atlantic coast by sea to Pennsylvania, leaving behind his wife, Eliza McCoy. On October 7, 1854, he arrived at the office of William Still, a manager of the Philadelphia Vigilance Committee.

McCoy continued northeast with Saunders to New Bedford, Massachusetts. On November 1, 1854, Eliza McCoy, the personal slave of Andrew Sigany, followed her husband's Atlantic coast route to Still's office. She required rest before she could join Robert McCoy in Massachusetts. In 1855, the McCoys, under the names William and Mary Doner (or Donar), settled in New Bedford at 232 Middle Street, the home of seaman Henry Kent and his wife, Harriet.

Source

Grover, Kathryn. *The Fugitive's Gibraltar: Escaping Slaves and Abolitionism in New Bedford, Massachusetts.* Amherst: University of Massachusetts Press, 2001.

McCrummell, James (?–ca. 1867) McCrummell, Sarah (ca. 1830s)

A prominent mulatto grocer, dentist, and orator, James McCrummell (or McCrummel) of Virginia and his wife, Sarah McCrummell, aided in rescue operations for slaves passing through Pennsylvania. James McCrummell co-founded the Philadelphia Vigilance Committee, which he chaired. In addition to leading black refugees to freedom, on December 4, 1833, he joined James Barbados, James Forten, Jr., William Lloyd Garrison, Robert Purvis, and the Reverend Theodore Dwight Weld in establishing the American Anti-Slavery Society, which McCrummell managed for the next four years. In 1837, McCrummell collaborated with Forten, Purvis, and the Reverend Stephen Smith in founding the Pennsylvania Anti-Slavery Society. As McCrummell was skilled at parliamentary procedure, Lucretia Coffin Mott took Sarah McCrummell's advice and conferred with him on the chairing of the Philadelphia Female Anti-Slavery Society. At the beginning of the Civil War, James McCrummell encouraged volunteers to join the colored regiments. On June 26, 1863, he was among the original enlistees of Philadelphia's first black regiment.

See also: American Anti-Slavery Society; black soldiers; female anti-slavery societies; Pennsylvania Anti-Slavery Society; vigilance committees.

Source

Commemorative Biographical Record of Washington County, Pennsylvania. Chicago: J.H. Beers, 1893.

McDonald, Seth (fl. 1850s)

Seth McDonald (or McDaniels) conveyed slaves along the New York–Canada route of the Underground Railroad. He shared route responsibilities with Julia Catlin Pratt and Linus Humphrey Pratt, who hid passengers in their residence on East Mill Street in Sugar Grove, in Warren County, Pennsylvania. From there, runaways proceeded to the McDonald waystation in Lanning Hill, in Farmington Township. McDonald kept slaves in his barn until it was safe to advance them to the next safehouse. In October 1851, the Pratts and McDonald teamed with William Gray in Beaver Dam, in Wayne Township, who completed a relay to a steamer on Lake Erie.

Source

Schenck, J.S., ed. *History of Warren County.* Syracuse, NY: D. Mason, 1887.

McHenry, William "Jerry" (1812–1853)

After passage of the Fugitive Slave Law of 1850, William "Jerry" McHenry (or Henry), a mulatto cooper in Syracuse, New York, was the focus of one of the daring rescues orchestrated by the Underground Railroad to protest an unjust law. Defending McHenry in court was Leonard Gibbs, an anti-slavery advocate. On October 1, 1851, John Thomas, an editor of the *Liberty Party Paper* in Syracuse, New York, chaired the committee that plotted to free the runaway, whom James Lear, agent of a Mr. Reynolds of Missouri, had apprehended. A theft charge masked Lear's intent to return McHenry to bondage.

Church bells summoned rescuers while U.S. marshals from Auburn, Canandaigua, Rochester, and Syracuse, New York, held McHenry in shackles at the Clinton Square jail in Syracuse until U.S. Commissioner Joseph Sabine could hear the case. The Reverend Samuel Joseph May paid calls at the cell to calm and reassure Jerry. Meanwhile, Dr. James Canning Fuller, Jr., Dr. Hiram Hoyt, the Reverend Jermaine Wesley Loguen, Montgomery Merrick, Gerrit Smith, George Boyer Vashon, and Samuel Ringgold Ward planned strategy. While thousands assembled outside and hurled rocks at the jail, agent William Lyman "Old Oswego" Salmon of Granby, New York, used a battering ram to break down the cell door. Former slave Jo Norton of Washington, D.C., broke the arm of an officer who leaped out a window to escape the crowd. In May 1852, slavery apologist Daniel Webster stood on the square and denounced the jailbreak as treason. Of the eight rescuers charged with civil disobedience, only whaler Enoch Reed was found guilty. He died before he was sentenced.

After McHenry's freeing, he traveled to the residence of 16-year-old Susan Watkins, where the Reverend Samuel Ringgold Ward filed off McHenry's manacles. The runaway remained under the guardianship of Caleb Davis before the relay by cart to Orson Ames's waystation in Mexico, New York, and on to the safehouse of Asa and Mary Beebe outside of town. From the Oswego County safehouse, Dr. Fuller helped McHenry board a canal boat that crossed Lake Erie to Kingston, Ontario. Gerrit Smith initiated annual commemorations of the liberation as occasions for pro–Underground Railroad orations, given by himself, Frederick Douglass, and the Reverend Thomas Wentworth Higginson. A period bas-relief designed by Sharon BuMann and erected in 1990 features the likeness of McHenry, Loguen, and May at the assembly point of supporters in Clinton Square.

See also: Fugitive Slave Law of 1850; slave recovery.

Sources

McAndrew, Mike, "Bold Raid Freed a Man," *Syracuse Post-Standard,* February 14, 2005.

Ward, Samuel R. *Autobiography of a Fugitive Negro: His Anti-Slavery Labours in the United States, Canada, and England.* London: John Snow, 1855.

McIntosh, Henson (fl. 1850s–1860s)

A black activist promoting freedom, Henson McIntosh scoured the plantation South in search of potential runaways. A Maryland native and resident of New Albany, in Floyd County, Indiana, he married Elizabeth Meekes in 1843 in Clark County, Indiana. In New Albany, the couple lived on Main Street. Henson McIntosh worked as a day laborer and rope maker for the shipbuilding industry. On a benevolent mission in 1859, he crossed the Ohio River to survey Kentucky. During his rovings, he used the names Henry McIntosh and Henson Fremont and carried fake freedom papers, cash, and tickets for the Portland, Ohio, ferry and for Indiana railroads.

According to items in the *Louisville Daily Courier, Louisville Daily Democrat,* and *New Albany Daily Ledger,* Louisville policeman R.M. Moore halted McIntosh's liberation of two of Samuel K. Richardson's slaves, Betty and Frank Richardson, on July 3, 1859, aboard a train from Salem, Indiana, bound for Cincinnati, Ohio. The *Louisville Daily Journal* reported that, on February 12, 1861, Officer Moore arrested McIntosh on charges of illegal entry into Kentucky and slave abduction. McIntosh netted a five-year sentence in the Kentucky state penitentiary in Frankfort but escaped on April 15, 1862. He was recaptured and returned to prison, where he remained confined until May 20, 1868, five years after the Emancipation Proclamation had freed slaves.

Source

Peters, Pamela R. *The Underground Railroad in Floyd County, Indiana.* Jefferson, NC: McFarland, 2001.

McKay, Jean Gray (1811–1862)
McKay, Robert (1813–1896)

After emigrating from Great Britain, Jean Gray McKay of Ayrshire, Scotland, and her husband, investor Robert McKay, fought human bondage. On arrival from Johnston, in Renfrewshire near Glasgow, Scotland, Robert McKay apprenticed in marketing and publishing at age 17. While living in Baltimore, Maryland, and Nashville, Tennessee, he observed southern slavery at its worst in the auctioning of individuals and the separation of families. In 1841, he traveled through the Erie Canal and Lake Erie to Macomb County, Michigan, to farm 610 acres. After marrying that same year, he and his wife championed Presbyterianism and the abolition of slavery. While raising 600 sheep and growing wheat, the couple operated an Underground Railroad station.

Source

Eldredge, Robert F. *Past and Present of Macomb County, Michigan.* Chicago: S.J. Clarke, 1905.

McKeever Family

A prominent three-generation family of committed Underground Railroad conductors, Mary McFadden McKeever (1768–1840) and hatter William McKeever (1758–1838), Irish immigrants living in West Middletown, Pennsylvania, and their sons, Matthew (1797–1884) and Thomas (1791–1866), supported a route crossing Pennsylvania. The McKeevers received passengers from Elizabeth Snodgrass Holmes and George Young Holmes, Sr., in Claysville, New York. At the McKeever home in Middletown, in Greene County, Pennsylvania, the family collaborated with Isaac Teagarden and Sarah Ann Parker Teagarden on Wheeling Creek, Joseph Gray in Graysville, Jane Brownlee McCoy and Kenneth McCoy at their rural waystation in West Alexander, and Dr. Francis Julius LeMoyne and his wife, Madelaine Romaine Bureau LeMoyne, who maintained an armed security force at their depot in Washington, Pennsylvania. In 1819, Matthew McKeever married Jane Campbell (1800–1871) of Ahorey, Ireland, a teacher, whose older brother, Dr. Alexander Campbell, operated a rescue service for slaves at his medical practice in Ripley, Ohio.

The second generation of McKeevers enhanced the family tradition for altruism. Jane and Matthew McKeever collaborated with a black laborer, John Jordan of West Middletown, in piloting runaways to safety. The McKeever property was amply prepared to stow runaways in a Presbyterian church and in the attic, the barn, and a concealed basement chamber accessed through a trapdoor in the family's kitchen floor. Jordan hid a large group of escapees in Matthew's sheep loft and tended to them for a month, until they could be conveyed up the line toward Canada. When insurrectionist John Brown visited Middletown, Pennsylvania, in the 1840s, he stayed west of town at Jane and Matthew's home.

Thomas McKeever, who served the secret network for 40 years, was elected a justice of the peace in 1824. One black defendant who claimed to be a freeman from Somerset County, Pennsylvania, received Thomas's support. Another wanderer during the decade, Charles A. "Charley" Garlick of Shinntown, Virginia (now West Virginia), composed a slave narrative, in which he commented on Thomas McKeever's partnership with agent John Baton Vashon, a barber in Pittsburgh.

In the third generation of family agents, both the younger Matthew McKeever (1842–?) and his brother, the Reverend Thomas Campbell McKeever (1828–?), a minister of the Disciples of Christ, continued housing and feeding refugees and defending them in court against slave catchers.

Source

McCulloch, Margaret Callender. *Fearless Advocate of the Right: The Life of Francis Julius LeMoyne, M.D., 1798–1879.* Boston: Christopher, 1941.

McKenzie, Harriet (fl. 1840s–1850s)
McKenzie, John (fl. 1840s–1850s)

Two former slaves, Harriet McKenzie and her husband, John McKenzie, a carter, aided fugitives passing through Oswego, New York. Born into bondage in South Carolina, the couple operated a small one-story safehouse at 96 West Eighth Street from 1848 to 1857. Next door in a two-story home at 98 West Eighth Street lived Clarissa Green and her husband, Nathan Green, a runaway from Virginia in 1836 who purchased land from Underground Railroad organizer Gerrit Smith. To protect himself from recapture, Nathan Green lied to census officials when he claimed Pennsylvania as his birthplace. He worked on Lake Ontario as a steamboat cook, a position that enabled him to direct refugees to Canada. The McKenzie and Green residences are listed on the National Register of Historic Places.

See also: Fugitive Slave Law of 1850.

Source

"Nathan Green House in Oswego Listed as Historic Place," *Fulton (NY) Valley News,* July 20, 2002.

McKim, James Miller (1810–1874)
McKim, Sarah Allibone Speakman (1813–1891)

The Reverend James Miller McKim of Carlisle, Pennsylvania, zealously advocated the rights of slaves. He completed degrees from Dickinson College and Princeton and entered the Presbyterian ministry at age 25 in Womelsdorf, Pennsylvania. Influencing his abolitionism was William Lloyd Garrison's *Thoughts on Colonization* (1832). In 1833, McKim co-founded the American Anti-Slavery Society, which he served as manager for 10 years. He maintained a station of the Underground Railroad that received fugitives from Dinah Hannum Mendenhall and Isaac Mendenhall's sanctuary in Kennett Square, Pennsylvania, and passed them to Sarah Corson Read and Thomas Read near Norristown on the Schuylkill River and to the depot of Abigail and Elizabeth Goodwin in Salem, New Jersey. In October 1836, McKim resigned his ministry to lecture on the evils of bondage. A virulent attack by anti-abolitionists in Salem on June 21, 1847, forced McKim to shelter in the home of the Goodwin sisters.

While living in Philadelphia, at age 30, McKim converted to Quakerism after he married a Quaker, Sarah Allibone Speakman, daughter of agents Micajah Speakman and Phebe Smith Speakman and sister of agent William Allibone Speakman. McKim served the Pennsylvania Anti-Slavery Society as publisher, president, secretary, and general manager. He sold abolitionist tracts at the bookshop of conductor Samuel M. Painter in West Chester, Pennsylvania. In addition to writing for the *Anti-Slavery Standard,* McKim advised slaves and Underground Railroad conductors on court cases arising from the enactment of the Fugitive Slave Law of 1850. The McKims' daughter, Lucy (1842–1877), married Wendell Phillips Garrison, the son of William Lloyd Garrison. Lucy became the first collector and publisher of slave sorrow songs and spirituals.

An antislavery activist of wide-ranging service, J. Miller McKim piloted parties of slaves in both the western and eastern parts of Pennsylvania. He was on hand in Philadelphia to receive the crate containing Henry "Box" Brown in March 1849. *(Schomburg Center for Research in Black Culture/Manuscripts, Archives and Rare Books Division/New York Public Library)*

McKim's service to the abolition movement varied with the needs of the moment, which included piloting parties of slaves as large as 20. In 1855, he joined Quaker conductor Lucretia Coffin Mott in escorting Jane Johnson to a federal courtroom in Philadelphia to testify that attorney Passmore Williamson did not abduct Johnson and her sons from slavery. On a similar mission, on April 6, 1859, McKim and Mott urged the U.S. commissioner in Philadelphia to show mercy to Daniel Dangerfield, a freedman falsely accused of robbery at a public market in Harrisburg, Pennsylvania. Before the hanging of agent and revolutionary John Brown on December 2, 1859, for his raid on the federal arsenal in Harpers Ferry, Virginia, McKim accompanied Brown's wife, Mary Ann Day Brown, for a final prison visit. James and Sarah McKim attended the execution and with Brown's wife returned Brown's body to North Elba for interment in Lake Placid, New York, where Boston orator Wendell Addison Phillips addressed other sympathizers.

During the Civil War, McKim found new ways of channeling his activism. In winter 1862, he convened Philadelphians to survey the needs of 10,000 freedmen and to found the Port Royal Relief Committee. He canvassed black men for enlistment in 11 black regiments. After national emancipation on January 1, 1863, he set up freedmen's schools in the South. In the years preceding his death on June 13, 1874, in West Orange, New Jersey, he co-founded the *Nation*, edited by his son-in-law, Wendell Phillips Garrison.

See also: abolitionism; American Anti-Slavery Society; black soldiers; Civil War; Fugitive Slave Law of 1850; Quakers; Pennsylvania Anti-Slavery Society; spirituals.

Sources

Garrison, Wendell Phillips. *William Lloyd Garrison, 1805–1879: The Story of His Life Told by His Children.* Vol. 1. New York: Century, 1885.

Wilson, James Grant, and John Fiske, eds. *Appleton's Cyclopaedia of American Biography.* New York: D. Appleton, 1888.

McKinney, Mordecai (1796–1867)
McKinney, Rachel Graydon (1798–1856)

An attorney in service to runaway slaves, Judge Mordecai McKinney supported the work of the Underground Railroad in Harrisburg, Pennsylvania. A native of Carlisle, Pennsylvania, he grew up in a slave-holding household. He was educated at Dickinson College and, at age 21, began practicing law in Dauphin County. After marrying abolitionist Rachel Graydon of Cumberland, Pennsylvania, in October 1828, McKinney and his wife sheltered Jane Marie Morris, a fugitive from Maryland. Morris wed George Chester and became an activist of the secret network. She operated from their restaurant on Market Street.

In August 1850, agent William M. "Pap" Jones summoned Mordecai McKinney to aid George Brock, Sam William, and Billy, whom William Taylor sought to return to bondage in Clarke County, Virginia. McKinney teamed with Charles Coatesworth Rawn to defend the blacks from fabricated charges of horse thievery. In 1852, McKinney aided Jim Phillips, a kidnap victim whose plight appeared in William Lloyd Garrison's weekly, *The Liberator.* McKinney joined Dr. William Wilson Rutherford in collecting $900 to rescue Phillips. At an auction block in Virginia, McKinney and Rutherford purchased Phillips's freedom and that of his wife and children.

See also: kidnap; *Liberator, The.*

Sources
Rutherford, S.S. "The Underground Railroad." *Publications of the Historical Society of Dauphin County* (1928): 3–6.
Scott, John Welden. *African Americans of Harrisburg.* Charleston, SC: Arcadia, 2005.

McLean, Alexander (1844–1916) McLean, Catherine Boyd (1804–?) McLean, John (1794–?)

Journalist and historian Alexander McLean witnessed the workings of a major Jersey City depot of the Underground Railroad. He was born in Belleville, New Jersey, to Catherine Boyd McLean and John McLean, a cloth importer in Philadelphia, where Alexander attended school. While writing for the *Evening Journal,* Alexander reminisced that his father swore the household to secrecy about the horse blankets that were used to cover as many as 30 runaways at a time in the hayloft. From there, passengers could observe the comings and goings on the road. In times of danger, they descended a ladder at the back of the barn and hid in the woods. To avoid slave catchers at the Hackensack and Passaic rivers, the runaways fled by ferry to Belleville or Newark, New Jersey, and on to Albany or Syracuse, New York, by night train. They continued along the Hudson River by coal barge. Contributing to the success of the McLeans' Jersey City depot was the assistance of Quaker operative John Everett and Peter Phillips, who piloted runaways to Bergen, Passaic, and Rockland counties. At age 17, against his parents' wishes, Alexander MacLean attempted several times to enlist in New Jersey regiments. On the fourth attempt he succeeded in joining the Eighty-ninth Indiana Regiment, in which he gained the rank of first lieutenant in the signal corps. In 1895, McLean compiled a local chronicle, *History of Jersey City, New Jersey.*

Sources
Bogert, Fred W., "Tracking an Invisible Railroad," *Record Magazine,* March 6, 1965.
McLean, Alexander. *History of Jersey City, New Jersey.* Jersey City, NJ: Jersey City Printing, 1895.

M'Clintock, Mary Ann Wilson (1800–1884) M'Clintock, Thomas (1792–1876)

Quaker promoters of the Underground Railroad, orator Mary Ann Wilson M'Clintock and her scholarly husband, chemist Thomas M'Clintock, dedicated family activities to humanitarianism. The couple married in 1820. In collaboration with Enoch Lewis and Israel Johnson, in 1827, Thomas M'Clintock promoted the Free Produce Society, which offered groceries and pharmaceuticals free of the taint of slave labor. In 1836, the M'Clintocks relocated their family from Philadelphia to Waterloo, New York, where they moved into a two-story brick house at 14 East Williams Street. After they joined the Western New York Anti-Slavery Society, their residence became a gathering place for abolitionists and a stop on the secret network. Mary Ann M'Clintock raised funds for runaways and networked with agents Frederick Douglass, Abby Kelley Foster, William Lloyd Garrison, Lucretia Coffin Mott, and William Cooper Nell. Thomas M'Clintock and his daughter, Elizabeth (1821–1896), operated a pharmacy. In 1843, Thomas began a five-year stint as manager of the American Anti-Slavery Society.

Liberal Christianity separated the M'Clintocks from mainstream Quakerism by stressing the individual conscience in determining the morality of civil disobedience and feminism. In 1848, they formed a new assembly, the Congregational Friends of Waterloo, which welcomed Underground Railroad agents Amy Kirby Post and Isaac Post of Rochester. In 1850, the M'Clintocks offered a room to two former slaves on a permanent basis. After the rescue of William "Jerry" McHenry on October 1, 1851, the M'Clintock safehouse received the Reverend Jermaine Wesley Loguen, an Underground Railroad agent pursued by U.S. marshals. Now an historic site registered with the National Park Service, the M'Clintock house underwent renovation in 2004.

See also: American Anti-Slavery Society; civil disobedience.

Sources
Hewitt, Nancy A. *Women's Activism and Social Change: Rochester, New York, 1822–1872.* Ithaca, NY: Cornell University Press, 1984.
Wellman, Judith. *The Road to Seneca Falls: Elizabeth Cady Stanton and the First Woman's Rights Convention.* Champaign: University of Illinois Press, 2004.

McMahon, Sarah (fl. 1859)

Sarah McMahon was arraigned for violating the Fugitive Slave Law of 1850. She was arrested on December 28, 1859, in St. Mary's County, Maryland, for liberating and harboring 13-year-old Rose Crain, the chattel of Judge Peter W. Crain of Charles County. The trial reached the circuit court in November 1860; Judge Robert Ford sentenced McMahon to six years and six months in the Maryland state penitentiary in

Baltimore. Within weeks, Governor Thomas Holliday Hicks released her.

See also: Fugitive Slave Law of 1850.

Source

"Trustees Sale," *St. Mary's (MD) Beacon,* March 27, 1862, 3.

McNeely, Cyrus (1809–1890) McNeely, Jane Donaldson (1807–1887)

An abolitionist, pacifist, and Underground Railroad conductor, the Reverend Cyrus McNeely put his Presbyterian beliefs into daily practice. The native of Cadiz, Ohio, came under the influence of abolitionist Dr. Alexander Campbell, a physician and depot manager in Ripley, Ohio. Joining McNeely in slave rescues was his wife, educator Jane Donaldson McNeely of Cincinnati, Ohio, whom he married in 1837. McNeely expressed his principles in a sermon—"Address to Disciples: The Sin of Slavery" (1841). In 1850, the McNeelys launched a women's academy in Hopedale, Ohio, a town they established in 1849. The couple opened a normal school and remained committed to the secret network until the national emancipation of slaves on January 1, 1863.

Source

Dunnavant, Anthony L., et al., eds. *The Encyclopedia of the Stone-Campbell Movement: Christian Church.* Grand Rapids, MI: William B. Eerdmans, 2004.

McQuerry, George Washington (1825–?)

One of the test cases of the Fugitive Slave Law of 1850, the recapture of George Washington McQuerry demanded action by lawyers of the Underground Railroad. In 1849, McQuerry escaped his owner Henry Miller of Covington, in Washington County, Kentucky. After crossing the Ohio River, he settled in Miami County, Ohio, where he started a family. When Miller learned of McQuerry's whereabouts, in August 1853, he had U.S. marshals arrest the runaway, who crewed a canal boat outside of Troy, Ohio. Authorities subdued a mob outside McQuerry's cell in Cincinnati. Peter Clark, a black teacher, demanded McQuerry's release. Attorneys James Gillespie Birney and John Joliffe defended the fugitive on the grounds that the Fugitive Slave Law was unconstitutional. Judge John McLean disagreed and returned McQuerry to bondage. The judgment was a setback for abolitionists.

See also: Fugitive Slave Law of 1850.

Source

Campbell, Stanley W. *The Slave Catchers: Enforcement of the Fugitive Slave Law, 1850–1860.* Chapel Hill: University of North Carolina Press, 1970.

McWhorter (Francis and Lucy) Family

A conductor of slaves to freedom, Francis "Free Frank" McWhorter (1777–1854), was the first black to incorporate a community in the United States. He was born into slavery in Union County, South Carolina, near the Pacolet River and passed to owner George McWhorter, a Kentucky entrepreneur in Pulaski County, in 1795. In 1819, having sold saltpeter for explosives during the War of 1812, Frank McWhorter was able to buy liberation for himself and his wife, Lucy Denham McWhorter (1771–1870), for a total of $1,600. In September 1830, the McWhorters and their freeborn children—Commodore (1823–1855), Frank, Jr. (1804–1851), Lucy Ann (1825–1902), and Squire (1817–1855)—set out for Illinois, where Frank developed an all-black settlement. His town of New Philadelphia, near Barry in Pike County, Illinois, was chartered in 1836. With $10,000 from his investments, he bought the freedom of 15 additional family members, including his children, Juda (1800–1906), Sally (1811–1891), and Solomon (1815–1855), and their mates and families.

The McWhorter sons aided their father in work for the Underground Railroad, which they conducted out of the basement of their farm cabin. One of the walls had a stone door opening on a dugout chamber where slaves could hide. Lucy Ann disarmed posses by inviting them to stay for dinner. The stone walls concealed the human scent from bloodhounds. In more desperate circumstances, the family ferried some groups to Hadley Creek and offered directions through the network to Canada. When footwear was required, the family provided it or had the slaves' worn shoes repaired. For some parties, McWhorter sons Commodore, Frank, Jr., Solomon, and Squire provided personal escorts to the border. For McWhorter's generosity to runaways, he earned the nickname Free Frank. Although the family cabin burned in 1925, the slave hiding place in the cellar survived.

Sources

Turner, Glennette Tilley. "The Underground Railroad in Illinois." *American Visions* 13:2 (April–May 1998): 33–35.
Walker, Juliet E.K. *Free Frank: A Black Pioneer on the Antebellum Frontier.* Lexington: University Press of Kentucky, 1983.

Meachum, Mary (fl. 1850s)
Meachum, John Berry (1789–1854)

A famed hero of the Underground Railroad, former Kentucky slave Mary Meachum risked a prison sentence by guiding nine slaves toward freedom. Mary was the widow of a fugitive slave from Virginia, the Reverend John Berry Meachum, an abolitionist who founded the First African Baptist Church in St. Louis, Missouri. The Meachums owned two Mississippi steamers and employed runaways in their barrel factory. They raised funds to buy blacks from their owners and to educate ex-slaves, who attended classes on their floating school on the Mississippi River. After John's sudden collapse and death, Mary conducted their campaign alone from their safehouse on Fourth Street and signed legal papers with an X.

Near sunup on May 21, 1855, Mary Meachum and a freedman named Isaac loaded her passengers in a small boat tied on the west side of the Mississippi River. Among the escapees were slaves of the St. Louis sheriff and also a black family, Esther Shaw and her two children, the chattel of Henry Shaw. When the vessel reached the Illinois shore, slave owners and police opened fire on Freeman, a conductor who intended to ferry the passengers to Alton in wagons. The recapture resulted in Henry Shaw's vindictive sale of Esther Shaw to dealer Bernard M. Lynch, who netted a reward of $161.62 for the seizure. He negotiated her purchase for $350 and her transfer to Vicksburg, Mississippi. The transaction apparently condemned Esther to a life of hard labor and permanent separation from her children.

For violating the Fugitive Slave Law of 1850, Mary Meachum and Isaac went to jail. On May 24, a criminal court charged the pair with slave theft but dropped the case against Isaac. The *Weekly Saint Louis Pilot* revealed the use of the Meachum home as a safehouse, but further information about the widow is lacking. On November 1, 2001, the National Park Service honored the Mary Meachum Freedom Crossing site, the first in the state of Missouri.

See also: Fugitive Slave Law of 1850.

Sources

Frazier, Harriet C. *Runaway and Freed Missouri Slaves and Those Who Helped Them, 1763–1865.* Jefferson, NC: McFarland, 2004.

Wright, John. *African Americans in Downtown St. Louis.* Chicago: Arcadia, 2003.

Mendenhall, Dinah Hannum (1807–1889)
Mendenhall, Isaac (1806–1882)

Dinah Hannum Mendenhall and her husband, Isaac Mendenhall, established a secret station at their Oakdale farm in Kennett Square, Pennsylvania, only 10 miles from Wilmington, Delaware. Both husband and wife abhorred the Fugitive Slave Law of 1850 and vowed to help runaways, even at the cost of expulsion from the Society of Friends. Over 34 years of service, they received several hundred escapees from Rachel Mendenhall Garrett and Thomas Garrett in Wilmington, Delaware, and from James N. Taylor's waystation in West Marlborough, in Chester County, Pennsylvania. Garrett identified his passengers as "bales of black wool."

Teamwork was vital to successful rescues. The Mendenhalls hid women and children in the springhouse and placed men in the barn. Agents Isaac and Josiah Wilson made the next connection by ferrying escapees to John Jackson in Darby, to the Reverend Eusebius Barnard and Sarah Painter Barnard in Pocopsin, or to Benjamin Price and Jane Paxson Price in East Bradford, in Chester County, Pennsylvania. Others passed to Sarah Darlington Barnard and Simon Barnard in Newlin, to James Miller McKim and Sarah Allibone Speakman McKim or William Still in Philadelphia, or to Abigail Paxson Vickers and John Vickers in Lionville, in Lancaster County, Pennsylvania.

Among those the Mendenhalls rescued were William Parker and his accomplices, Abraham Johnson and Alexander Pinkney, participants in the Christiana Riot of September 11, 1851. In daylight, the trio husked field corn like farm employees. On the recommendation of Dr. Bartholomew Fussell, Isaac surrendered the next stage of the journey to Fussell, who had less to lose by being arrested, imprisoned, and fined for treason.

See also: Christiana Riot.

Source

Smedley, Robert C. *History of the Underground Railroad in Chester and the Neighboring Counties of Pennsylvania.* Lancaster, PA: Office of *The Journal,* 1883.

Mendenhall, George C. (1800–1860)
Mendenhall, Richard (1778–1851)

Brothers George C. Mendenhall and Richard Mendenhall, North Carolina Quakers, aided the local branch of the Underground Railroad in the early years of its formation. Surrounded by slave owners, the Mendenhalls lived in Jamestown near the waystation of Alethea Flukes Coffin and Vestal M. Coffin, founders of the state's secret network near Guilford College, outside Greensboro in Guilford County, North Carolina. In 1825, Richard, a tanner and leather dealer, presided over the North Carolina Manumission Society. He appears to have used his residence as a depot.

Richard's younger brother, George, an attorney and state legislator, created a manumission and tutorial system. First he bought large numbers of slaves and then trained them in trades before relaying them to freedom in Logan County, Ohio. On June 28, 1855, he freed 28 graduates of his vocational academy and sent them north to earn their living. At his death from drowning a few months before the outbreak of the Civil War, his will manumitted all slaves remaining in his custody.

George Mendenhall performed other services on behalf of liberty. In May 1850, he defended Adam Crooks and Jesse McBride, a Wesleyan missionary team arrested for distributing a pamphlet entitled *The Ten Commandments,* which outlined the methods of the Underground Railroad. The defense was successful for Crooks; McBride was sentenced to an hour in the pillory, 20 lashes on his bare back, and one year's confinment in the Guilford County jail. Mendenhall also represented agent David Beard, an elderly hat seller charged with harboring runaways at his store. Mendenhall's second wife, Delphina Mendenhall (1811–1882) of Randolph County, North Carolina, plotted with Beard on fugitive concealment.

See also: abolitionism; Quakers.

Sources

Beal, Gertrude. "The Underground Railroad in Guilford County." *Southern Friend: Journal of the North Carolina Friends Historical Society* (Spring 1980): 18–28.

Johnson, Guion Griffis. *Ante-Bellum North Carolina: A Social History.* Chapel Hill: University of North Carolina Press, 1937.

Sherrill, P.M. "The Quakers and the North Carolina Manumission Society." In *Historical Papers Published by the Trinity College Historical Society.* Durham, NC: Trinity College Historical Society, 1914.

Meredith, Isaac (1801–1874)
Meredith, Thamosin Pennock (1812–1894)

In Newlin, in Chester County, Pennsylvania, Quakers Isaac Meredith and Thamosin (or Thamazine) Pennock Meredith operated a waystation that cost them expulsion from the Society of Friends. Traffic was busiest in winter. Aided by pilot Lewis Marshall, the Merediths received runaways from Simon and William Barnard in Newlin, John Cox and J. William "Will" Cox in Longwood, Dr. Bartholomew Fussell in Chester County, Pennsylvania, and from Rachel Mendenhall Garrett and Thomas Garrett in Wilmington, Delaware. Additional passengers arrived from Thamosin Meredith's parents and brother, Moses Pennock, Mary Jones Lamborn Pennock, and Samuel Pennock in Kennett Square. The Merediths conveyed passengers to Dr. Jacob K. Eshleman in Lancaster County, Nathan Evans and Zillah Maule Evans in Willistown, Joseph Hawley in Wilmington, Gravener and Hannah Marsh and their daughter Sarah in Caln, Benjamin Price and Jane Paxson Price in East Bradford, Margaretta A. O'Daniel Woodward and Maris D. Woodward in Marshalltown, and Abigail Paxson Vickers and John Vickers in Lancaster County.

Among the Merediths' passengers were six men who arrived from Maryland with bullet holes in their coats from a posse's gunfire. When transporter Will Cox showed up at midnight in November, his party's haste allowed them only a change of horses. Thomasin and her daughter, Mary E. Meredith (1840–1899), supplied the 15 fugitives with the family's entire stock of fresh-baked bread. Isaac and his son, James L. Meredith (1838–1867), separated the group for flight to Dowingtown agents.

See also: Quakers.

Sources

McGowan, James A. *Station Master on the Underground Railroad: The Life and Letters of Thomas Garrett.* Jefferson, NC: McFarland, 2005.

Smedley, Robert C. *History of the Underground Railroad in Chester and the Neighboring Counties of Pennsylvania.* Lancaster, PA: Office of *The Journal,* 1883.

Merriam, Francis Jackson (1837–1865)

Francis Jackson Merriam grew up among abolitionists and remained dedicated to their beliefs. Born in Framingham, Massachusetts, he was the grandson of historian Francis Jackson, the treasurer of the Boston Vigilance Committee. Unlike his serious forebears, Francis Merriam was a flighty dreamer. He involved himself financially and personally with insurrectionist John Brown's raid on the federal arsenal in Harpers Ferry, Virginia. After Brown contacted Lewis Hayden, the central conductor of Framingham's Underground Railroad, Hayden petitioned Merriam for $500 to finance a plot that would provide arms for a slave rebellion. Merriam advanced his inheritance—$600 in gold—and delivered it the next day, only nine days before the foiled raid. Brown assigned him to remain at the farmhouse in the hills above Harpers Ferry to organize and arm runaway slaves.

After federal forces restored order to the area on October 16, 1859, Merriam fled to the Underground Railroad depot of siblings Frank B. Sanborn and Sarah Sanborn in Boston, Massachusetts. Fellow abolitionists urged Merriam to continue north to Canada to avoid bounty hunters seeking the $2,000 price on his head. Under the alias of Lockwood, Merriam traveled in a covered wagon driven by secret network operative Henry David Thoreau to the South Acton, Massachusetts, train station. Merriam arrived undetected in Montreal the next day. He enlisted in the Union army as a captain of the Third South Carolina Colored Infantry and died suddenly of complications from a leg wound.

See also: black soldiers.

Sources

Boteler, Alexander. "Recollections of the John Brown Raid by a Virginian Who Witnessed the Fight." *Century* 26 (July 1883): 399–411.

Robboy, Stanley J., and Anita W. Robboy. "Lewis Hayden: From Fugitive Slave to Statesman." *New England Quarterly* 46 (December 1973): 591–613.

Sanborn, Frank B. "Thoreau." *Harvard Register* 3 (April 1881): 215–16.

Merrick, Charles (1812–?)
Merrick, Montgomery (1815–?)
Merrick, Sylvanus (1786–1884)
Merrick, Chloe (1832–1897)

The Merrick brothers, Charles and Montgomery, sons of Sylvanus Merrick and siblings of Florida educator and social worker Chloe Merrick, grew up along the Erie Canal in Syracuse, in Onondaga County, New York. After establishing trade in brick making and masonry, in 1843, they convinced the local Wesleyan Methodist church to promote abolitionism. Charles, Montgomery, and Sylvanus Merrick established a secret depot and enlisted transporters of runaway slaves. Supporting their efforts were speeches by Frederick Douglass, William Lloyd Garrison, Horace Mann, and Gerrit Smith. In one four-month period, the brothers hosted 44 passengers forwarded by the Reverend Luther Lee from Plymouth, New York.

For financial help, the Merrick brothers depended on free train passes supplied by Horace White, an executive of the Syracuse and Utica Railroad. On October 1, 1851, in defiance of the Fugitive Slave Law of 1850, the Merrick brothers, their father, and possibly Chloe Merrick aided William "Jerry" McHenry to escape the Syracuse jail by joining a mob that forced entry into his cell. Contributing to the plot were John Thomas, the Reverend Samuel Joseph May, Dr. James Canning Fuller, Jr., Dr. Hiram Hoyt, the Reverend Jermaine Wesley Loguen, Gerrit Smith, George Boyer Vashon, and Samuel Ringgold Ward. In the legal furor that resulted, Sylvanus fled to Illinois.

At the beginning of the Civil War, Chloe Merrick founded a reception center for runaway slaves in Florida. In 1863, the Syracuse native moved to 102 South Tenth Street in Fernandina, Florida, on the Georgia border, where she established an outreach to former slaves who fled to Amelia Island. She also opened an orphanage and a freedmen's school. She continued influencing social programs after marrying Harrison M. Reed, Florida's governor.

See also: abolitionism; Civil War; Fugitive Slave Law of 1850.

Sources

Foster, Sarah Whitmer, and John T. Foster. "Chloe Merrick Reed: Freedom's First Lady." *Florida Historical Quarterly* 71:3 (January 1993): 279–99.

Loguen, Jermain Wesley. *The Rev. J.W. Loguen, as a Slave and as a Freeman: A Narrative of Real Life.* Syracuse, NY: J.C.K. Truair, 1859.

Merritt, William Hamilton (1793–1862)

An abolitionist and confederate of the Reverend Jermaine Wesley Loguen and Harriet Tubman, agent William Hamilton Merritt of Bedford, New York, received refugees at the terminus of the Underground Railroad in St. Catharines, Ontario. He knew the misery of persecution from his family's history as Loyalists to England during the American Revolutioin. He had a varied career as soldier, miller at Twelve Mile Creek, grocer, trader, designer of the Welland Canal around Niagara Falls, and mayor of St. Catharines. At his safehouse on Oak Hill at 12 Yates Street, he excavated tunnels to the carriage house for quick exits.

Merritt grew more militant toward the flesh trade after passage of the Fugitive Slave Law of 1850.

He supported the Refugee Slaves' Friends Society, a philanthropic project promoted by two fellow conductors of the secret network, Elias Smith Adams and Susan Merritt Adams, Hamilton Merritt's brother-in-law and sister. Merritt and fellow agent Oliver Phelps sold land for a pittance to the black community at Geneva and North streets for the building of Salem Chapel, a National Historic Site and part of the Niagara Freedom Trail.

See also: Fugitive Slave Law of 1850; philanthropists.

Source

Winks, Robin W. *The Blacks in Canada.* Montreal: McGill-Queen's University Press, 2005.

Middleton, Enoch (1798–1882)
Middleton, Hannah (1799–1879)

Quaker produce merchant, cobbler, brick mason, and townsman Enoch Middleton of Philadelphia served the Underground Railroad as an agent and recorded his work in a memoir. Along with food and clothing, he and his wife, Hannah, offered rest and protection at their safehouse on Old York Road in Hamilton, in Burlington County, New Jersey. From 1844 to 1848, the two-story summerhouse was the family waystation. After Enoch resettled at North Crosswicks, his home in Allentown, in Mercer County, New Jersey, his family received refugees and conveyed them by wagon to depots in Allentown, Cranbury, and New Brunswick. One documented passenger was Little Sittles, who arrived in the late 1840s. Sittles moved on to Canada and then returned to reside across the creek from his liberator. When a sheriff and bounty hunters menaced Sittles, the Middletons harbored the runaway a second time and returned him to Canada via the secret network.

See also: bounty hunters.

Source

Beck, Henry Charlton. *The Jersey Midlands.* New Brunswick, NJ: Rutgers University Press 1962.

Mifflin, Samuel Wright (1805–1885)
Mifflin, Elizabeth Brown Martin (1807–1858)
Mifflin, Hannah Wright (1817–1901)

A noted abolitionist from Wrightsville, Pennsylvania, Samuel Wright Mifflin derived from a long line of Quaker warriors against slavery. The nephew of Underground Railroad agents Phebe Wierman Wright and William Wright, Samuel grew up among agents. He became a civil engineer for the Pennsylvania Railroad and, at age 38, married a Quaker, Elizabeth Brown Martin. After his father's death in 1840, Samuel and his wife operated a waystation at their farm until 1847.

Samuel Mifflin maintained a working relationship with the Philadelphia Vigilance Committee and with conductor Charles Turner Torrey, who died in service to the clandestine network. When 13 escapees arrived during heavy rains, the Mifflins kept them for two days to protect them from an imminent flood of the Susquehanna River before passing them on to ferryman Robert Loney, a freedman who rowed them by skiff to Columbia, Pennsylvania. After Elizabeth's death in 1858, Samuel married his cousin, Hannah Wright, daughter of abolitionists Phebe and William Wright. Hannah Mifflin aided her husband in his slave rescues from 1861 until the abolition of slavery.

Source

Smedley, Robert C. *History of the Underground Railroad in Chester and the Neighboring Counties of Pennsylvania.* Lancaster, PA: Office of *The Journal,* 1883.

Mihills, Uriah Dimond (1818–1898)
Mihills, Caroline Partridge (1817–1891)

A middleman for land transfers between whites and runaways to Canada, Uriah Dimond Mihills aided in the settlement of fugitive slaves. A native of Stukely, Quebec, Mihills resided in the Adirondack Mountains in Keene, in Essex County, New York, where he served as a town supervisor. He married Caroline Partridge in 1839. The couple supported the Underground Railroad route to Canada. Mihills joined Wendell Lansing of Union Village, New York, and the Reverend Jermaine Wesley Loguen, of Rochester, New York, in helping newcomers buy homes. After passage of the Fugitive Slave Law of 1850, Mihills joined Lansing, James Kimball, and Roswell Thompson in determining a course of action calling for civil disobedience to federal law.

See also: civil disobedience; Fugitive Slave Law of 1850.

Source

Smith, H.P., ed. *History of Keene, N.Y.* Syracuse, NY: D. Mason, 1885.

Miller, Cynthia Catlin (1791–1883)

A wealthy idealist and abolitionist, Cynthia Catlin Miller, widow of Richard Bishop Miller, aided fugitive slaves by forming the Female Assisting Society and the Ladies Fugitive Aid Society to sew clothing for passengers of the Underground Railroad. She set up benevolent projects at the family mansion on Big Tree Road in Sugar Grove, in Warren County, Pennsylvania, on the southwestern border of New York State, where she reared eight children. Her son, Franklin Richard Miller, Jr., described her efforts in his journals, including her entertainment of Frederick Douglass at the Miller safehouse. Slaves who passed through the activist area found work in the black community of Africa Hill to earn cash for their journey to Ontario.

Miller networked with other female agents, including Julia Catlin Pratt, a fellow member of the Ladies Fugitive Aid Society. Among Miller's colleagues was a Quaker seamstress, Bebe Bullock Blodget Van Deusen, who lived on West Main Street. Another was Miller's sister-in-law, Dr. Martha Van Rensselaer Catlin, who treated a runaway for burns and frostbite. Miller's daughters Jane Miller Payne and Mary Miller McClain, the wife of the Reverend William Wylie McClain, continued the tradition of charity. In Pittsburgh, the McClains were known to pass refugees through their hotel, Monongahela House. The clan recorder, Caroline Miller (1825–1907), kept notes on the Millers' anti-slavery activities. In 2005, Sugar Grove citizens reenacted the Millers' contributions to the secret network.

Source

Switala, William J. *Underground Railroad in Pennsylvania.* Mechanicsburg, PA: Stackpole, 2001.

Miller, Hiram Barlow (1807–1888)
Miller, Mariah Deming (1808–1876)

After the opening of an Underground Railroad route in Ohio in the late 1820s, for three decades, farmer Hiram Barlow Miller and his wife, Mariah Deming Miller, operated a waystation in Strongsville, in Medina County. The Millers married in 1829. In 1833, Hiram, Mariah, and Hiram's father, Lyman Miller, moved from Henrietta, in Monroe County, New York, traveling via the Erie Canal and Lake Erie. The family resided on 650 acres near Brunswick Township, Ohio. Influenced by Amos Woodruff, a local shoemaker and father of agent Jane Ann Woodruff Webber, Miller preached abolitionism. In an area beset by racist violence, he introduced anti-slavery sentiments among his neighbors Ahijah Haynes, Elijah Lyman, and Philander Pope, all three operatives of the secret network. Providing a hideaway for hundreds of escaped slaves until they could journey by backroads to Cleveland or Oberlin, Ohio, the Millers' log farmhouse and barn at West 130th Street in Hinckley Township became an historic landmark to Ohio citizens.

Known throughout the South as a benevolent friend, Hiram Miller was nicknamed Nigger Miller by his enemies, who egged him, bashed him in the head, threw him out of church, and rode him on a rail. He treated blacks as equals and took some of them to worship services to tell their stories to the congregation. On lecture tours, he shared a dais with Joe Mason, a black orator. Such bold actions placed Miller in danger of arrest by U.S. marshals, whom he managed to dodge. For relays to Abraham "Abram" Conyne and Matilda Parker Conyne's shelter and beyond, Miller shipped runaways in dry goods boxes. He dispatched passengers five at a time from Dover Bay over Lake Erie on a boat funded by an abolition society. From Ohio, refugees, often hand-delivered by Miller to a freighter on Lake Erie, proceeded to Ontario. In 1931, the Hiram B. Miller Association erected a tablet crediting Miller with hundreds of interventions.

See also: abolitionism.

Sources

Dalakas, Amber. *Brunswick, Ohio.* Charleston, SC: Arcadia, 2005.
Holzworth, W.F. *Men of Grit and Greatness: A Historical Account of Middleburg Township, Berea, Brook Park, and Middleburg Heights.* Cuyahoga, OH: self-published, 1970.

Miller, John (1809–?)

A silversmith, John (or Johan) Miller conducted fugitives over the Underground Railroad routes. He was born in Cecil County, Maryland, to German Lutheran pioneers who moved to Washington County, Pennsylvania, when he was a year old. At age 13, he settled in Lisbon, Ohio, to study watchmaking. At age 25, he opened a jewelry store and served as mayor and city councilman. His membership in the Disciple Church prompted him to volunteer for the secret network.

Source

History of Logan County and Ohio. Chicago: O.L. Baskin, 1880.

Miller, Jonathan Peckham (1797–1847)
Miller, Sarah Arms (ca. 1801–?)

As an agent and financial backer of the Underground Railroad, Colonel Jonathan Peckham Miller joined his wife, Sarah Arms Miller, in harboring runaway slaves. Jonathan was born in Randolph, Vermont, and apprenticed as a tanner before fighting in the War of 1812. After graduation from the University of Vermont, he practiced law and supported the abolition of slavery in the District of Columbia. The Millers, who wed in June 1828, sheltered fugitives at their house in Montpelier, Vermont. Their daughter, Sarah Miller Keith, described the use of stagecoaches as relays for fugitive slaves. When proponents of slavery threatened the Reverend Samuel Joseph May at the Old Brick Church in Montpelier, on October 1835, Jonathan Miller interceded and shielded May. In 1840, Miller defended the election of women to membership in the American Anti-Slavery Society.

See also: American Anti-Slavery Society.

Source

Duffy, John J., Samuel B. Hand, and Ralph H. Orth, eds. *The Vermont Encyclopedia.* Lebanon, NH: University Press of New England, 2003.

Miller, Josiah (1828–1870)

The treasurer of the Topeka Underground Railroad and a probate judge in rural Douglas County, Kansas, Josiah Miller was a first-generation Irish American pioneer and an abolitionist orator and newspaperman. Born in Chester, South Carolina, Miller reached Kansas Territory in 1854 and cleared farmland in Wyandotte County. With Robert G. Elliot, he published an anti-slavery newspaper, the *Kansas Free State.* Miller owned a tinsmithing shop and operated a safehouse at 1111 East Nineteenth Street in Lawrence, where he hid runaways in the smokehouse. On May 16, 1856, Miller was arrested for treason by Major Jefferson Buford, leader of insurgent South Carolina troops, but he was acquitted by a military tribunal. Five days later, border ruffians destroyed Miller's printing operation as a territorial nuisance.

Source

Connelley, William E., comp. *A Standard History of Kansas and Kansans.* Chicago: Lewis, 1918.

Miller, Samuel (?–1895)
Miller, Sarah Orwig (1814–1899)

Samuel Miller and his wife, Sarah Orwig Miller, supported the Pennsylvania–Canada route of the Underground Railroad. After their marriage in 1832, they resided in Bellevue, in Union County, Pennsylvania. In addition to supporting the Methodist Episcopal Church, they operated a waystation.

Source

Snyder, Charles McCool. *Union County Pennsylvania: A Celebration of History.* Montoursville: Penn State University Press, 2000.

Miner, Ovid (1803–?)

An Underground Railroad agent and journalist, the Reverend Ovid (or Obed) Miner used a range of talents in fighting slavery. He was born in Middletown, Vermont, and trained in journalism while reporting for the *Northern Spectator* in East Poultney. At age 21, he founded the *Vermont Statesman* in Castleton. After abandoning journalism for the Congregational pulpit, at age 31, he settled in Peru, New York. From 1828 to 1835, he published the *Vermont American.* In 1835, he married Eliza M. Moore (1805–?) of Champlain, New York.

Miner's contributions to the secret network placed him in active settings. He assisted Nathaniel Colver in the founding of the Ticonderoga (New York) Anti-Slavery Society. From 1837 to 1841, he preached at the First Presbyterian Church in Penn Yan, New York. Because of his support of civil disobedience, he and 100 followers withdrew from conservative members and established the Union Free Congregational Church of Penn Yan at Chapel and Maine streets. During Miner's residence in Penn Yan and Syracuse, New York, and on lecture tours to Rochester and Lyons, New York, he partnered with the Reverend Luther Lee in slave rescues.

Source

Calarco, Tom. *The Underground Railroad in the Adirondack Region.* Jefferson, NC: McFarland, 2004.

Minkins, Fredric "Shadrach" (ca. 1814–1875)

A refugee to Boston, Fredric "Shadrach" (or Sherwood) Minkins set off a public outcry when he fled enslavement in Norfolk, Virginia. The son of David Minkins and an unidentified slave woman, Fredric Minkins had been sold several times in 1849, to tavernkeeper Thomas Glenn, grocer Martha Hutchings, and slave owner John Higgins, before passing to U.S. Navy purser John de Bree (or de Bere) of Norfolk. On May 3, 1850, Minkins fled bondage after de Bree advertised his chattel for sale at public auction. Minkins took the standard Norfolk sea route by ship to Boston, Massachusetts, where he worked as a waiter.

At 11:30 A.M. on February 15, 1851, deputy U.S. Marshal Patrick Riley and slave hunter John Caphart arrested Minkins in Taft's Cornhill Coffeehouse, where Minkins was serving breakfast. They remanded their quarry to the federal courthouse in Boston. Because the Massachusetts Personal Liberty Act of 1843 forbade the jailing of federal prisoners in state facilities, authorities searched for another stronghold. Within hours, news spread to the Boston Vigilance Committee, which convened at Faneuil Hall. Members dispatched prominent Underground Railroad defense attorneys—Charles D. Davies, Richard Henry Dana, Jr., Ellis Gray Loring, Robert Morris, and Samuel Edmund Sewall—to intervene. The committee posted large handbills alerting abolitionists to the presence of slave catchers in the city.

The press of 200 protesters to free Minkins found no favor with Lemuel B. Shaw, chief justice of the Massachusetts Supreme Court. At noon on February 15, 1851, Lewis Hayden and barber John J. Smith coordinated the inrush of 20 black agents, including the Massasoit Guards mustered by John P. Coburn and by other supporters of the Underground Railroad. The daring courthouse rescue of Minkins resulted in his extraction from the chaos in a state of stupefaction with his clothes half torn away. The rescuers rode Minkins on their shoulders to a getaway wagon. The swift retreat earned headlines across the nation as a model of bold civil disobedience to an inhumane federal law.

Lodged at a Beacon Hill house adjacent to that of Harriet Bell Hayden and Lewis Hayden, Minkins remained in the attic until nightfall, when he fled in John Smith's carriage to Cambridge. At 3 A.M., the conveyance arrived at the waystation of Ann H. Bigelow and Francis Edwin Bigelow in Concord. With a hat donated by a neighbor, Nathan Brooks, agent Francis Bigelow disguised Minkins for a transfer to the home of Frances Hills Wilder Drake and Jonathan Drake at 21 Franklin Street in Leominster, Massachusetts. In preparation for the relay to agents Benjamin Snow, Jr., and Mary Baldwin Boutolle Snow's depot in Fitchburg and then to La Prairie, in Quebec Province, Massachusetts abolitionists collected a small purse to defray the slave's expenses. The passage stalled in North Ashburnham, where agent Wood tended Minkins until the runaway's health improved for the border crossing.

The flouting of the Fugitive Slave Law of 1850 led to the arrest of Underground Railroad agents Lewis Hayden and Robert Morris, whom Richard Henry Dana, Jr., defended in court. The brazen slave rescue earned a rebuke from pro-slavery senators Daniel Webster and Henry Clay and from President Millard Fillmore, who launched an investigation and ordered the arrest of nine participants under a charge of treason. Minkins found a home in Montreal, worked as a barber, and established a restaurant. The Reverend Theodore Parker, a Unitarian abolitionist, championed Minkins's jailbreak as a libertarian gesture equal in significance to the Boston Tea Party of 1773. In later years, Benjamin Snow visited Minkins in Quebec, where Minkins owned a restaurant.

See also: civil disobedience; disguise; vigilance committees.

Sources

"Cheerful Yesterdays V. The Fugitive Slave Period." *Atlantic Monthly* 79 (1897): 345–46.

Collison, Gary. *Shadrach Minkins: From Fugitive Slave to Citizen.* Cambridge, MA: Harvard University Press, 1997.

Missouri Compromise of 1820

In 1820, the United States Congress, led by House Speaker Henry Clay of Kentucky and Senator Jesse B. Thomas of Illinois, mediated an accord between pro-slavery and abolitionist states that allowed admission of Maine to the Union as the twenty-third state and Missouri as the twenty-fourth state. By agreement Maine entered as the twelfth free state and Missouri as the twelfth slave state. The act outlawed slavery in the remaining part of the Louisiana Purchase. The compromise established a temporary political balance but worsened the sufferings of blacks in Missouri. Known as Little Dixie, Missouri was the major slave-breeding ground of farmers from Calloway to Clay counties. Farmers earned more from human chattel than from growing hemp and tobacco. In his history *Martyrdom in Missouri* (1870),

The Missouri Compromise of 1820 earned the scorn of Secretary of State John Quincy Adams, an egalitarian who anticipated the Civil War. In his diary, Adams prophetically called the Missouri Compromise "a mere preamble—a title page of a great, tragic volume."

the Reverend William M. Leftwich acknowledged that Missourians anticipated the collapse of the slave system. Nonetheless, they resented the invasion of northern agitators, abolitionists, and Underground Railroad agents with their devious methods of liberating slaves.

Because of the increase in slave stalking, the Ohio legislature made it a crime for bounty hunters to invade Ohio to pursue and apprehend runaways. Kentuckians riposted by demanding the rights of slave owners to reclaim fugitives harbored by abolitionists in free states. One agent, the Reverend John Rankin, denounced the fervor of slave owners as a violation of divine law. He settled his family at Liberty Hill, an historic crossing point in Ripley, Ohio, where he received desperate slaves as they crossed the Ohio River. Publishing his outrage was a bold abolitionist newspaper, the *Abolition Intelligencer and Missionary Magazine,* which John Finley Crow issued from 1822 to 1823 in Shelbyville, Kentucky.

The Missouri Compromise remained in effect until 1854, when the Kansas-Nebraska Act negated it. Orator and publisher Frederick Douglass charged that blacks had no rights in a white-controlled government. His efforts helped to repeal the 34-year-old accord. Upon the shift in the balance of free and slave states, the confrontation between Missourians and Kansans generated border vigilantism and endangered the homes and lives of Underground Railroad agents, who took risks by conveying runaway slaves to freedom. On October 16, 1859, insurrectionist John Brown carried the slavery issue to radical extremes by raiding the federal arsenal in Harpers Ferry, Virginia.

See also: abolitionist newspapers; bounty hunters; Kansas-Nebraska Act of 1854.

Sources

Leftwich, William M. *Martyrdom in Missouri.* St. Louis: Southwestern Book & Publishing, 1870.

Weeks, William Earl. *John Quincy Adams and American Global Empire.* Lexington: University Press of Kentucky, 1992.

Mitchell, Jane Clark (1805–1890)
Mitchell, Robert (1786–1863)

Abolitionists Jane Clark Mitchell of Ireland and her husband, Dr. Robert Mitchell of Indiana in Indiana County, Pennsylvania, defied federal law by harboring fugitive slaves. In 1845, they received at their safehouse three passengers from Hardy County, Virginia (now West Virginia)—12-year-old Anthony B. Hollingsworth, Charles Brown, and Jared (also Jerry or Garrett) Harris. The refugees lived in a cabin on Two Lick Creek and worked as spare labor during the harvest season. In June, when their master, Garrett Van Metre (or Van Meter), returned for his slaves, Hollingsworth hid on the roof. Van Metre's confederates recaptured the trio and locked them in the Indiana House Hotel.

After a mob threatened to free the runaways and burn the hotel, the Mitchells sought a writ of habeas corpus. Judge Thomas White, who was also an operative of the secret network, freed the runaways from unlawful seizure. Two years later, in fall 1847, while Hollingsworth worked on the Mitchell farm, Brown slipped back to the South to visit his wife, Dinah. Van Metre trailed Brown on his return north to the Mitchell waystation. The subsequent seizure of Brown and Harris forced Hollingsworth to flee to Windsor, Ontario. He found work as a beautician in Stratford, Ontario. On October 18, 1862, he wrote to Mitchell from Canada.

In eight years of litigation, the Mitchells suffered the consequences of liberating Anthony Hollingsworth. In November 1847, Van Metre sued Robert Mitchell for harboring a slave. In a Pittsburgh court, judges R.C. Grier and Thomas Irwin fined Mitchell $500 plus costs and lost labor. The total was $10,000 for violating the Fugitive Slave Law of 1793. To pay the debt, the Mitchells had to sell their residence and much of their property. Journalist Jane Grey Cannon Swisshelm reported the details in her memoir, *Half a Century* (1880), and added that the Mitchells did not fear the loss of their last dollar to aid runaway slaves. Agent James Levi Thompson helped the Mitchells keep their property.

The Mitchells' daughter, Jennie, preserved clippings of the legal entanglements in her scrapbook along with items on her heroes—John Brown, Levi Coffin, Frederick Douglass, Abraham Lincoln, and Harriet Beecher Stowe, author of *Uncle Tom's Cabin* (1852).

See also: Uncle Tom's Cabin; or, Life Among the Lowly (1852).

Sources

Egle, William Henry. *An Illustrated History of the Commonwealth of Pennsylvania: History of Indiana County, Pennsylvania.* Harrisburg, PA: W.C. Goodrich, 1876.

Sajna, Mike, "Underground Railroad Leaves Tracks in Southwestern Pa.," *Pittsburgh (PA) Tribune-Review,* February 25, 1990, 6, 10.

Swisshelm, Jane Grey. *Half a Century.* Chicago: Jansen, McClurg, 1880.

Mitchell, William (1825–1903)
Mitchell, Mary A. (1837–1915)

Captain William Mitchell bolstered the secret route through Kansas by operating a waystation of the Underground Railroad. A native of Kilmarock, Scotland, he grew up in Middletown, Connecticut, where he met his future wife, educator Mary A. Mitchell. After his travels to California and Australia, in 1855, he settled in Wamego, in Potawatomi County, Kansas. Members of the Beecher Bible and Rifle Company helped build a log cabin at the frontier settlement of Wabaunsee for the Mitchells. When slaves from Arkansas, Missouri, and Texas passed through the Mitchell safehouse, they climbed the china cabinet like a ladder to a garret hideaway. The repeal of the Missouri Compromise of 1820 raised turmoil near the Mitchells' home. Over six weeks in 1856, Captain Mitchell led the Prairie Guard in local skirmishes against border vigilantes. On one occasion, he eluded a pro-slavery faction that tried to lynch him. At his funeral, eulogists extolled him for sheltering slaves and for conducting them by night to liberty.

See also: Missouri Compromise of 1820.

Source

Cutler, William G. *History of the State of Kansas.* Chicago: A.T. Andreas, 1883.

Mitchell, William H. (fl. 1840s–1850s)

A generous host, the Reverend William H. Mitchell welcomed hundreds of runaways to his home. For 12 years, his Ross, Ohio, safehouse was a flurry of slave arrivals and departures. In 1855, he ceased operations and ministered to ex-slaves in Toronto, Ontario, for the American Baptist Free Mission Society.

Source

Quarles, Benjamin. *Black Abolitionists.* New York: Oxford University Press, 1969.

Monroe, David (1783–1848)
Monroe, Barbara (1782–?)

Two Underground Railroad agents in Xenia, in Greene County, Ohio, David Monroe and his wife, Barbara Monroe, ignored the price on David's head for aiding runaways. David Monroe emigrated from Scotland in 1818 and settled the frontier town of Chillicothe, three miles from Xenia, Ohio. In addition to his support of Presbyterianism, he served the town of Xenia as treasurer and combined his building and transportation trade with humanitarian work. In 1838, Monroe was a school board member; in 1842, he was appointed as overseer of the poor.

The Monroes collaborated with their neighbor, the Reverend Samuel Wilson of the United Presbyterian Church, to rescue fugitives. In the role of a carriage and cabinet maker and member of the anti-slavery society, David Monroe made regular trips to North Carolina and stowed runaway slaves in his freight wagon. According to the diary of a townswoman, Rebecca Thompson Galloway, which she kept from 1840 to 1842, the Monroes concealed runaways in the underfloor of their carriage house at their home at 246 East Market Street. Their sons, George (1810–1879) and William (1814–1836), aided the effort by receiving slaves at their leather shop and hiding them in the basement.

See also: Fugitive Slave Law of 1850.

Source

Dills, R.S. *History of Greene County Together with Historic Notes on the Northwest and the State of Ohio.* Dayton, OH: Odell & Mayer, 1881.

Monroe, James (1821–1898)
Monroe, Elizabeth Maxwell (1825–1862)

An abolitionist college professor, the Reverend James Monroe operated an Underground Railroad waystation in Oberlin, Ohio. The son of Quakers in Plainfield, Connecticut, he grew up among reformers and joined the state anti-slavery society. Because he differed with the Quaker stance on civil disobedience, he allied with the Congregationalists. Recruited by activists Charles Callistus Burleigh, Frederick Douglass, William Lloyd Garrison, Wendell Addison Phillips, and Alvan Stewart, Monroe served the American Anti-Slavery Society as a touring lecturer on the frontier. At the conclusion of his studies at Oberlin College in 1846, he championed the work of the Underground Railroad in a speech entitled "Moral Heroism."

Monroe accepted a post at Oberlin College teaching literature and rhetoric. At his two-story brick residence at 73 South Professor Street, he and first wife, Elizabeth Maxwell Monroe, received refugees from around 1850. In league with Henry Everard Peck, a bold operative, Monroe rejected the usual discretionary procedures and declared himself a rescuer of slaves, in violation of the Fugitive Slave Law of 1850. After Elizabeth Monroe's death in the first months of the Civil War, James Monroe established a political career.

See also: American Anti-Slavery Society; Fugitive Slave Law of 1850; Oberlin College; Quakers.

Source

Rokicky, Catherine M. *James Monroe: Oberlin's Christian Statesman & Reformer, 1821–1898.* Kent, OH: Kent State University Press, 2002.

Monroe, Robert (1828–1882)

A runaway slave on the frontier, Robert Monroe received help from the Underground Railroad. Monroe fled Parkville, Missouri, to Sortor's Hollow, a rural settlement near Quindaro, Kansas, named for agents Effie Ann Sortor and Elisha Sortor and their family, who provided food and a sleeping place. To complete the journey, Monroe crossed a frozen Missiouri River by skiff and hid in corn shocks. In free territory, he settled among fugitive families named Banks, Creek, and Grisby. Corroborating oral tradition was Monroe's grandson, Jesse Hope, who reported that slave posses surveyed territory around Quindaro and kidnapped Monroe's daughter.

See also: kidnap.

Source

Eklund, Mark. "Quindaro Area Was Haven for Slaves." *Heritage* (February 1976).

Monroe, William Charles (?–ca. 1860)

The Reverend William Charles Monroe served a Baptist congregation and the Underground Railroad. An activist and organizer from Indiana, he was an emissary from the American Baptist Foreign Mission Society to Port-au-Prince, Haiti. At the height of slave traffic through Michigan, he was the first pastor of the Second Baptist Church, a waystation in Detroit. The congregation consisted of 13 former slaves who left the First Baptist Church to form an all-black assembly. Monroe led the group and, from 1836 to 1846, sheltered slaves until they could cross the Detroit River into Windsor, Ontario. In his honor, the street where the congregation built a church home was named Monroe Street.

Monroe extended outreach to destitute runaways by joining George DeBaptiste and William Lambert in forming the Detroit Vigilance Committee. In 1840, Monroe successfully foiled the plot of John Dunn, an Arkansas slave owner who attempted to return Robert Cromwell south to bondage. In the early 1840s, one escapee, Henry Walton Bibb, credited Monroe with teaching him to read and write. Monroe also supported the plotting of insurrectionist John Brown, who led an unsuccessful raid on the federal arsenal in Harpers Ferry, Virginia, on October 16, 1859. Later that year, Monroe joined a mission to Liberia.

Sources

Cooper, Afua. "The Fluid Frontier: Blacks and the Detroit River Region: A Focus on Henry Bibb." *Canadian Review of American Studies* 30:2 (2000): 129–49.

Leach, Nathaniel. *The Second Baptist Connection: Reaching Out to Freedom—History of the Second Baptist Church.* Detroit, MI: self-published, 1988.

Montague, Henry (1815–1889)
Montague, Mary Elizabeth Sinclair (1818–1888)

Henry Montague and his wife were the first Underground Railroad agents to convey runaways through Kalamazoo County, Michigan. A native of Saco, Maine, Henry Montague became an abolitionist in his teens and pledged himself to civil disobedience on behalf of the oppressed. He married Mary Elizabeth Sinclair of London, Ontario. The Montagues moved to Michigan in 1836 and built a waystation in Oshtemo, in Washtenaw County, where Henry delivered mail. By spring 1837, the Montagues received their first passengers, a young couple from Virginia and a single male from Alabama. Henry relayed them to Galesburg, in Kalamazoo County, Michigan, to the waystation of Hugh M. Shafter. The Montagues continued receiving fugitive slaves and transporting them to Battle Creek or Galesburg until national emancipation on January 1, 1863.

See also: civil disobedience.

Source

Fisher, David. *Compendium of History and Biography of Kalamazoo County, Michigan.* Chicago: A.W. Bowen, 1906.

Monteith, John (1788–1868)
Monteith, Abigail Harris (1801–?)

A conductor from Gettysburg, Pennsylvania, the Reverend John Monteith supervised relays over the southern shore of Lake Erie. A first-generation Scots

American, he graduated from Princeton Theological Seminary. He and his wife, Abigail "Abby" Harris Monteith, served Presbyterian churches in Detroit, Monroe, and Blissfield, Michigan, and in Elyria, Ohio. On April 23–24, 1835, he was elected a delegate to the first Pennsylvania Anti-Slavery Society Convention, held in Putnam, Ohio.

At the family's three-story wood frame residence, Monteith Hall, at 218 East Avenue in Elyria, Ohio, John Monteith superintended a girl's academy by day and operated an Underground Railroad depot by night. Passengers arriving by wagon could hide in the cellar or in niches in the walls. Historians corroborated the use of a 50-yard tunnel that led from Black River to the Monteith family cellar. Slaves could hide from pursuers before rowing skiffs downriver and boarding schooners, such as the one provided by agent Aaron Root, captain of the lake steamer *Amaranth,* for the crossing of Lake Erie to Ontario. Since 1995, the Elyria Woman's Club has offered tours of the Monteith house and tunnel.

See also: Pennsylvania Anti-Slavery Society.

Source

Thomas, James B. *Down Through the Years in Elyria.* Oberlin, OH: Oberlin Printing, 1967.

Montgomery, James (1814–1871)

An abolitionist colleague of editor Horace Greeley and John E. Stewart, James Montgomery of Ashtabula, Ohio, involved himself in conspiracies to liberate Missouri slaves. After attempts at teaching and preaching, he superintended Underground Railroad activities from his farm near Mound City, in Linn County, Kansas Territory. To ward off Missouri ruffians and compromise the Missouri slave economy, in 1857, he mustered a volunteer militia, which gained a reputation for horse thievery, arson, and general outlawry in Bourbon and Linn counties. In summer 1858, at the log cabin of his mother-in-law on Little Sugar Creek, Montgomery supported the plotting of John Brown, John Henry Kagi, and a dozen other insurrectionists to end slavery by armed violence.

Montgomery took part in peace initiatives, but expressed his true intent on December 16, 1858, when he aided in the attempted jailbreak of free-state advocate Benjamin Rice, who was lodged in the Fort Scott Hotel. Montgomery warned of an explosive buildup of tensions on November 27, 1860, when the new arrival of fugitive slaves and the proposed dispatch of federal troops threatened a fragile peace. In 1862 during the Civil War, Montgomery served with the Tenth Kansas Volunteers.

Source

Sheridan, Richard B., ed. and comp. *Freedom's Crucible: The Underground Railroad in Lawrence and Douglas County, Kansas, 1854–1865.* Lawrence: University of Kansas, 1998.

Moore, Caroline Mattocks (1792–1878)
Moore, Noadiah (1788–1859)

Underground Railroad confederates in Clinton County, New York, Caroline Mattocks Moore of Champlain and her husband, Noadiah Moore of Kinderhook, aided runaways on the last leg of their flight through the Adirondack Mountains to Quebec. Noadiah supported other farmers forming the Clinton Agricultural Society. After their marriage in 1814, the Moores received passengers relayed through the Champlain Valley from the waystation of Catherine R. Keese and Samuel Keese and their son John in Peru, New York, and from Fanny B. Leggett and Joseph Leggett in Chestertown, New York. Noadiah went the extra mile by ferrying runaways personally to settlements in Canada and by helping them find work.

See also: Canada.

Source

Calarco, Tom. *The Underground Railroad in the Adirondack Region.* Jefferson, NC: McFarland, 2004.

Moore, Jeremiah (1803–1887)
Moore, Elizabeth W. Ely (1802–1874)

A farmer and mortician in southern Pennsylvania, Jeremiah Moore of Half Moon Valley and his wife, Elizabeth W. Moore of Christiana, in Lancaster County, operated Station 6 of the Pilgrim's Pathway, a 17-stage network of the Underground Railroad. Receiving escapees from Daniel Gibbons and Hannah Wierman Gibbons's station in Bird-in-Hand, near Wrightsville, Pennsylvania, the Moores hid runaways in an upstairs room behind bolted doors. The family provided medical care and clothing donated by neighbors. The Moores completed the passage by concealing slaves in a furniture delivery wagon for a trusted black employee to transport from Christiana to the next stop, the home of James Fulton, Jr., in

Ercildoun. One family, that of Abraham Johnson from Cecil County, Maryland, arrived in the mid-1840s and remained as hired help for over five years. At the time of the Christiana Riot on September 11, 1851, the Johnsons moved on to Canada.

See also: Christiana Riot; Pilgrim's Pathway.

Source

Smedley, Robert C. *History of the Underground Railroad in Chester and the Neighboring Counties of Pennsylvania.* Lancaster, PA: Office of *The Journal,* 1883.

Moore, Joseph (fl. 1840s–1850s)

Quaker abolitionist Joseph Moore was a member of a wily team of slave conveyors through Sadsbury, in Chester County, Pennsylvania. He operated a waystation in Little Britain and passed runaways to a stop in Selma, Ohio. To confuse posses, Moore sent passengers to safer housing with Dr. Augustus W. Cain or Joseph Fulton and Mary Ann Fulton in West Sadsbury, Joseph Brinton in Salisbury, Jeremiah Moore in Christiana, Seymour C. Williamson in Caln, William Trimble in West Whiteland, Charles Moore in Lionville, Mary Charles Thorne and William J. Thorne in Clark County, and J. Williams Thorne or James "Abolition Jim" Williams, a freedman conductor in Sadsbury. In 1857, Moore served the American Anti-Slavery Society as vice president, a post he held until 1864.

See also: American Anti-Slavery Society.

Source

Smedley, Robert C. *History of the Underground Railroad in Chester and the Neighboring Counties of Pennsylvania.* Lancaster, PA: Office of *The Journal,* 1883.

Moore, Richard (1794–1875)
Moore, Sarah Foulke (1797–1852)

An Underground Railroad agent, Richard Moore and his wife, Sarah Foulke Moore, both devout Quakers, maintained an outreach to the desperate. In Quakertown, in Bucks County, Pennsylvania, they owned a pottery business and managed a respected stone waystation at 401 South Main Street and Edgemont Road. They received passengers from Jonathan Paxson Magill and his sons, Edward Hicks Magill and Watson Magill, in Solebury and from Sunnyside Home, the safehouse of Esther Fussell Lewis and her daughters, Elizabeth R. Lewis, Graceanna Lewis, Mariann Lewis, and Rebecca Lewis Fussell. Slaves hid in the barn in straw. After passage of the Fugitive Slave Law of 1850, the Moores received Bill Budd, the slave of Abraham Shriner of Pipe Creek, Maryland. Budd changed his name to Henry Franklin and served Moore as a coal carter until he earned enough to pay his way to Canada. On missions from Lehigh Valley to Quakertown, Franklin carried runaways one way and returned with coal.

See also: Fugitive Slave Law of 1850.

Sources

Davis, William Watts Hart. *History of Bucks County, Pennsylvania.* New York: Lewis, 1905.

Magill, Edward H. "The Underground Railroad in Bucks County, Pennsylvania." *Friends Intelligencer* 55 (1898): 124–25, 142–44, 159–61, 276–77.

Moore, Samuel Asbury (1816–1902)

A generous abolitionist, financier, and landowner, Colonel Samuel Asbury Moore of Circleville, Ohio, provided advice, board, and cash to runaways. Born on November 1, 1816, he lived his entire 86 years at 306 Court and Mound streets. In 1843, he married Harriet Maria Doane. While pursuing business and serving Pickaway County as clerk of court, he earned a reputation for probity and for supporting the Underground Railroad.

Source

Van Cleaf, Aaron R. *History of Pickaway County, Ohio and Representative Citizens.* Chicago: Biographical, 1906.

Morehead, Henry (fl. 1850s)
Morehead, Malinda (fl. 1850s)

A former slave, Henry Morehead called on agents of the Underground Railroad to rescue his wife, Malinda Morehead, and their three children. He educated himself in night school. In winter 1854, the Moreheads left Louisville, Kentucky, before Malinda, their infant, and a two-year-old and four-year-old could be sold south. One hundred miles from the departure point, they observed wanted posters offering $500 for their recapture. Slowing their advance was miserable cold, which threatened their extremities with frostbite on the long route to Canada.

Source

Drew, Benjamin. *The Refugee: The Narratives of Fugitive Slaves in Canada.* Boston: John P. Jewett, 1856.

Morris, Abel H. (1818–1886)
Morris, Martha R. (1827–1884)

Farmer, miller, and merchant Abel H. Morris and his wife, Martha R. Morris, maintained a frontier waystation of the Underground Railroad. Native to Wayne County, North Carolina, Abel lived in Park County, Indiana, from 1833. After marrying in 1841, the Morrises settled in a log cabin in Henry County, Iowa, where they welcomed runaway slaves en route to Canada.

Source

History of Hardin County, Iowa. Springfield, IL: Union, 1883.

Morris, Edward (fl. 1840s)

At a Quaker center of the Underground Railroad in Pennsdale, near Williamsport, Pennsylvania, Edward Morris operated a unique depot. The Bull's Tavern was a stagecoach stop in Lycoming County. Built into a hillside out of lime and fossil aggregate, it was known as the House of Many Stairs, for its numerous flights of steps. The unusual shelter served runaways, who could elude posses by fleeing down a distant flight of stairs or by hiding in paneled nooks under the steps.

Source

Van Auken, Robin, and Louis E. Hunsinger. *Williamsport: Boomtown on the Susquehanna.* Charleston, SC: Arcadia, 2003.

Morris, Jane Warrington (1810–1897)
Morris, Joseph (1806–1898)

Quaker conductors Jane Warrington Morris and Joseph Morris operated a segment of the Ohio–Canada route of the Underground Railroad. A native of Burlington County, New Jersey, Joseph Morris conducted missionary work among Indians and southern blacks. The Morrises married in 1828. They farmed 120 acres in Richland Township, in Marion County, Ohio, in 1837 and established an orchard and nursery business. In collusion with the Reverend Aaron Lancaster Benedict, they turned their two-story frame house into a depot for escapees, who hid in small rooms in the attic and cellar. In times of danger, refugees could escape through subterranean passages to a barn or corncrib. The text of *Reminiscences of Joseph Morris* (1881) mentions Joseph's association with secret network superintendent Levi Coffin.

Sources

Baxter, W.H. *History of Champaign County, Ohio.* Chicago: W.H. Beers, 1881.

Morris, Joseph. *Reminiscences of Joseph Morris.* Columbus, OH: Friends, 1881.

Morris, Robert (1823–1882)

Robert Morris's life intersected numerous times with the ideals and actions of the Underground Railroad. The grandson of an African slave, Morris was born in Salem, Massachusetts. At age 13, he was welcomed to the home of two Boston agents, attorney Ellis Gray Loring and Louisa Gilman Loring. With Ellis Loring's aid, Morris passed the bar exam and began practicing law. In Washington, D.C., Morris was part of a litigation team that included Salmon Portland Chase, Samuel Gridley Howe, Francis Jackson, Horace Mann, and Samuel Edmund Sewall. The attorneys defended Daniel Drayton, captain of the sloop *Pearl,* whom authorities arrested on February 18, 1848, for attempting one of the largest mass slave escapes in U.S. history. The defense team secured a reduction in prison time from 20 to four years. Because he was one of the abolitionists of the Boston Vigilance Committee who helped free Fredric "Shadrach" Minkins from the Boston courthouse on February 15, 1851, Morris later defended himself against a federal charge of treason. Representing Morris and Lewis Hayden in federal court was Richard Henry Dana, Jr., another defender of agents of the secret network.

See also: vigilance committees.

Source

McDougall, Marion G. *Fugitive Slaves (1619–1865).* Boston: n.p., 1891.

Morris, Shelton (1806–1889)
Morris, Horace (1832–1897)

An unusual rescuer of slaves, Shelton Morris and his son, Horace, engaged likely participants in a buy-back project. Shelton Morris's father and owner, Colonel Richard Morris of Louisa County, Virginia, freed Shelton, his mother, Fanny Morris, and five siblings in April 1820. In Louisville, Kentucky, Shelton operated a land speculation business, a bathhouse, and a barbershop in partnership with his brothers, Alexander and

John, both barbers. Shelton and Horace barbered on steamers on the Ohio and Mississippi rivers and channeled runaways from the South to freedom. Horace, a leader during Reconstruction, became a steward at the Marine Hospital and the first black teller at the Freeman's Savings and Trust Bank of Louisville, Kentucky. After the demise of Evelina Spradling Morris, Shelton's wife, he settled in Cincinnati with his sister, Elizabeth Morris, and then established a farm in Xenia, Ohio.

Source

Buchanan, Thomas C. *Black Life on the Mississippi: Slaves, Free Blacks, and the Western Steamboat World.* Chapel Hill: University of North Carolina Press, 2004.

Morrison, Hannah (1806–?) Richardson, Susan (ca. 1805–?)

Two successful passengers, Hannah Morrison and Susan "Sukey" Richardson, chose the Underground Railroad as a means of escaping onerous indenture in free territory. In bondage to Andrew Borders in Knox County, Illinois, they were two of 19 people abused and illegally held captive. Hannah Morrison, the Kentucky-born daughter of 40-year-old slave Sarah Morrison, entered service in 1825 to Andrew Borders, who forced her to serve more than a year beyond her agreed term. Another servant, Susan Richardson, arrived from Georgia to work her indenture, but she suspected that Borders would return her to a slave state before she could escape with her three children, Anderson, Harrison, and Jarrot Richardson.

Because Borders brutalized Sarah Morrison, local abolitionists formed the Friends of Rational Liberty and sued on her behalf in April 1842. Borders won the first round of litigation. While the case was awaiting a hearing before the Illinois Supreme Court, Hannah Morrison, Susan Richardson, and Susan's three children fled to Cairo, Illinois. Secret operatives forged liberty papers for them; agent William James Hayes, a neighboring farmer, conducted the party of five to Farmington, Illinois. On September 5, 1842, they passed to Eli Wilson in Harkness Grove and lodged in Elba, in Knox County, with the Reverend John Cross. After authorities found evidence of slave harboring, the case went to court. A judge fined members of the posse for their attack on an innocent man. Underground Railroad agents organized a defense team and collected funds to cover costs. As litigation dragged on, the sheriff put the slaves up for auction but got no serious offers. He let the inmates go free.

After Susan Richardson established a home for her family, she found work as a laundress at the Presbyterian manse in Knoxville, Tennessee. Borders tracked her and locked her three children in a log shed as a lure to the mother. Supporters disguised Susan in the veil and dress of the minister's wife and posted her by sleigh to the waystation of Charles Gilbert in Galesburg, Illinois. Agents had Borders charged with trespass and with the abduction and imprisonment of the three children. The sheriff sided with Borders and helped him return the children to slavery.

Outrage among slavery advocates received comment in the journal of Samuel Guild Wright, who noted the bolstering of anti-abolitionist spy networks to trail Underground Railroad agents. On February 10, 1843, agent Nehemiah West wrote stationkeeper William Hayes requesting a search of Randolph County records for information about Susan Richardson and her children. In May 1843, Borders pressed suit against Cross, West, and Gilbert for sheltering fugitives. To shift popular opinion toward abolitionism, Cross exploited the unwieldy litigation. Upon his jailing in a log cabin lockup at Elba, he issued press releases to the Chicago paper *Western Citizen* about the filth, indignity, and injustice of his incarceration. After two weeks, Cross passed to the custody of Galesburg abolitionists, who paid his bond. The courts dropped the case. Hannah Morrison sued unsuccessfully for back wages.

Susan Richardson's 12-year-old son died from an accident in Borders's horse-powered mill. She never reunited with her other two children. Following her marriage, at Knox College in Galesburg, Illinois, she operated a safehouse and received passengers whom conductor Jonathan Blanchard relayed to the next stop. Among her rescues was Bill Casey, who arrived shoeless and exhausted after fleeing an armed posse. On Casey's behalf, Susan petitioned confederates of the secret network, who outfitted him and sent him along the line in new shoes. Within a year, he returned to Knox College to work in the timber industry. When slave hunters approached, abolitionist Charlie Love pretended ignorance of Casey and then hurried to warn him of imminent danger.

See also: abolitionism; disguise; spies.

Sources

Muelder, Hermann R. *Fighters for Freedom: The History of Anti-Slavery Activities of Men and Women Associated with Knox College.* New York: Columbia University Press, 1959.

Pirtle, Carol. "A Flight to Freedom: A True Story of the Underground Railroad in Illinois." *Ohio Valley History* 3:1 (2003): 3–16.

Moseby, Solomon (fl. 1830s)

In spring 1837, a fugitive named Solomon Moseby escaped from a Kentucky plantation and rode boldly into Niagara, Ontario. Following his incarceration in the city jail, he stood trial for horse thievery after his master traced him to the Niagara area. Despite the owner's intent to make an example of Moseby by beating him to death, the provincial governor, Sir Francis Bond Head, found in favor of the owner. For a week, unarmed blacks and abolitionist whites camped outside the jail to protest the judgment. A mulatto schoolteacher named Holmes and a black speaker named Mrs. Carter aroused abolitionist protest while raising the money to repay the owner for his horse.

The imbroglio reached a peak in the transfer of Moseby from jail to a cart when the assembly attacked city constables. The governor ordered the militia to shoot into the mob. Moseby escaped, but two of his supporters died at the scene. One of the dead was Holmes. Several more sustained wounds.

Governor Head awaited clarification from the colonial secretary concerning extradition of runaway slaves from the United States. Head stated on October 8, 1837, that slave kidnap is comparable to horse theft. Nonethless, Moseby appears to have remained in St. Catharines, Ontario, for the rest of his life.

See also: kidnap.

> In the account of Anna Brownell Jameson, author of *Winter Studies and Summer Rambles in Canada* (1838), females took a prominent role in freeing Solomon Moseby. Black women "had been most active in the fray, throwing themselves fearlessly between the black men and the whites, who, of course, shrank from injuring them. One woman had seized the sheriff, and held him pinioned in her arms; another, on one of the artillery-men presenting his piece, and swearing that he would shoot her if she did not get out of his way, gave him only one glance of unutterable contempt, and with one hand knocking up his piece, and collaring him with the other, held him in such a manner as to prevent his firing."

Sources

Murray, David. "Hands Across the Border: The Abortive Extradition of Solomon Moseby." *Canadian Review of American Studies* 30:2 (2000).

Power, Michael, and Nancy Butler. *Slavery and Freedom in Niagara.* Niagara-on-the-Lake, Ontario: Niagara Historical Society, 1993.

Mosher, Lucinda Richardson (1812–?)
Mosher, Robert (1825–?)

Quaker conductors Lucinda "Lucy" Richardson Mosher, a teacher from Vermont, and Robert Mosher began receiving slaves early in Ohio's involvement in the Underground Railroad. Robert Mosher resided near relatives in his native Morrow County. After his marriage in 1849, he and his wife served the secret network at their 80-acre farm in Chester Township. One night, Robert took charge of half of a party of 24 and, within the hour, conveyed them toward freedom. When the railroad reached Morrow County, Mosher transported fugitives by rail to Sandusky or Port Huron, Ohio, where they boarded schooners to cross Lake Erie to Canada. In 1862, he joined the Thirty-second Wisconsin Volunteer Infantry.

Source

Baxter, W.H. *History of Champaign County, Ohio.* Chicago: W.H. Beers, 1881.

Mott, Abigail (1792–?)
Mott, Lydia (1793–1880)

While selling linens and clothing, Quaker sisters Abigail (also Abigale) Mott and Lydia Mott contributed to the slave rescue effort in Albany, New York. At 37 Maiden Lane, in the 1840s, the women operated a safehouse of the secret network. They corresponded on Underground Railroad matters with Amy Kirby Post and Isaac Post in Rochester and with Frederick Douglass, whom they hosted at their home. Lydia Mott served on the executive committee of the American Anti-Slavery Society from 1840 to 1841. In July 1847, she and Abigail summoned Captain Austin Bearse, a seaman from Barnstable, Massachusetts, who aided the Boston Vigilance Committee. The Motts sought his help in transporting a runaway, George Lewis, to Boston. The sisters relayed Lewis to the wharf by night for the voyage to Long Island and then to Boston.

Lydia Mott read Harriet Beecher Stowe's *Uncle Tom's Cabin* (1852) after abolitionist tailor William

H. Topp, a fellow operative in Albany, gave Mott an inscribed copy in 1853. In 1858, Lydia tutored Frederick Douglass's nine-year-old daughter, Annie. On April 30, 1861, Underground Railroad operative Lucretia Coffin Mott, wife of Abigail and Lydia's brother James, sent Lydia $20 from the Philadelphia Female Anti-Slavery Society to defray some of the costs of educating, feeding, healing, and outfitting runaways.

See also: American Anti-Slavery Society; female anti-slavery societies; *Uncle Tom's Cabin; or, Life Among the Lowly* (1852).

Sources

Bearse, Austin. *Reminiscences of Fugitive Slave Law Days in Boston.* Boston: 1880.

Mott, Abigail. *Narratives of Colored Americans.* New York: William Wood, 1875.

Mott, James (1742–1823)
Mott, Mary Underhill (1745–1776)

Quaker agents for good during the American Revolution, James Mott of Roslyn, and Mary Mott of Oyster Bay, both on New York's Long Island, received runaway slaves passing through Westchester County, New York. After their marriage in 1765, they settled at Premium Point, a waystation that predates the Underground Railroad. James Mott joined the New York City Manumission Society and worked toward the abolition of the flesh trade. Mary Mott continued the work of her parents, slave rescuers Ann Carpenter Underhill and Samuel Underhill of Mamaroneck, New York.

At a choice location overlooking a landing site in Hempstead Harbor, Long Island, the Mott home was ideally situated to receive fugitives arriving by sloop and to pass them on to safehouses in New Rochelle, New York. The family boycotted slave-made or slave-harvested goods, including coffee, cotton, indigo, molasses, pharmaceuticals, rice, rum, sugar, tea, and tobacco, by sweetening their food with maple sugar rather than cane sugar or molasses, by wearing undyed linen garments, and by avoiding alcohol, tobacco, tea, and coffee. The Mott tradition of humanitarianism continued in the work of their sons, Richard and Samuel, and their daughter, Mary Underhill Mott Hicks. The next generation claimed two famous Underground Railroad agents, the Motts' grandson, James Mott, Jr., and Lucretia Coffin Mott of Philadelphia, Pennsylvania.

See also: American Revolution.

Source

Driscoll, James, et al. *Angels of Deliverance: The Underground Railroad in Queens, Long Island, and Beyond.* Flushing, NY: Queens Historical Society, 1999.

Mott, Lucretia Coffin (1793–1880)
Mott, James, Jr. (1788–1868)

Known primarily as a suffragist orator and reformer, Quaker activist Lucretia Coffin Mott joined her extended family in funding and operating a depot of the Underground Railroad in Philadelphia, Pennsylvania. A native of Nantucket, Massachusetts, at age 18, Lucretia Coffin married James Mott, Jr., of Cowneck, New York. The grandson of slave rescuers James Mott and Mary Underhill Mott, James Mott, Jr., was a teacher at Nine Partners, the Quaker school Lucretia attended in Poughkeepsie, New York. Unlike modest abolitionist

Quaker orator Lucretia Coffin Mott—revered as America's first feminist—began her work as a social reformer in the thick of the abolitionist movement. She helped groom the next generation of Underground Railroad conductors. *(Hulton Archive/Stringer/Getty Images)*

Rachel Seaman Hicks in Westbury, New York, Lucretia became an outspoken opponent of the flesh trade. Under the influence of anti-slavery editor William Lloyd Garrison and of the tracts of Philadelphia abolitionist Angelina Emily Grimké, at age 40, Lucretia Mott co-founded the Philadelphia Female Anti-Slavery Society. For the fine points of parliamentary procedure, she conferred with James McCrummell, a black grocer and respected freedom fighter. The society profited from the membership of intellectual libertarian Lydia Maria Francis Child and Philadelphia depot manager Hester Reckless. Lucretia also befriended Philadelphia agents George Corson and Jacob C. White, Sr.; Sydney Howard Gay in New York City; and two New Jersey conductors, Abigail and Elizabeth Goodwin, who operated a safehouse in Salem.

The Motts supported the American Anti-Slavery Society and, in 1838, initiated a free produce society that boycotted cotton, indigo, molasses, pharmaceuticals, rice, rum, sugar, tea, tobacco, and other slave-made, slave-harvested goods. At their home at 338 Arch Street in Philadelphia, the couple coordinated conveyance of refugees with Hannah Cox in Kennett Square, Pennsylvania, and with Isaac Tatem Hopper and Sarah Tatum Hopper along the Delaware River at Dock Street in Philadelphia. In 1840, Lucretia Mott attended the World Anti-Slavery Convention in London even though the platform rules rejected women delegates. That same year, the election of Maria Weston Chapman, Lydia Maria Francis Child, and Lucretia Mott to the American Anti-Slavery Society offices precipitated the resignation of antifeminists James Gillespie Birney, Gerrit Smith, Arthur Tappan, and Lewis Tappan.

The Motts remained in the thick of secret network action. In 1842, a mob threatened James Mott, who joined Frederick Douglass in convening an anti-slavery assembly at the First Baptist Church in Norristown, Pennsylvania. Pro-slavery ruffians hurled stones at the sanctuary until abolitionists and freedmen drove them away. In 1849, the Motts sequestered Henry "Box" Brown after his arrival in Philadelphia in a wooden express crate sent from Richmond, Virginia. In November 1851, at Independence Hall in Philadelphia, Lucretia Mott displayed cool abolitionist sentiment by knitting during the trial of Castner Hanway for his role in the Christiana Riot the previous September. For her handiwork, she chose red, white, and blue yarn.

Lucretia and James Mott were skilled at weathering protest and dissent. On August 29, 1855, James Mott, aided by agents Corson and the Reverend James Miller McKim, escorted Jane Johnson to a Philadelphia federal courtroom to testify on behalf of Passmore Williamson, an attorney charged with abducting Johnson from her master, North Carolina planter John Hill Wheeler. After the arrest of runaway slave Daniel Dangerfield for robbery in Harrisburg, Pennsylvania, on April 2, 1859, Lucretia Mott hired legal counsel and joined Mary Grew and diarist Charlotte L. Forten Grimké in sitting through 14 hours of court proceedings. After Dangerfield cleared his name, Mott superintended his flight to Canada. Because of Dangerfield's exoneration of the charge, a street parade resulted in cheers for the slave and for Mott. In December 1859, Lucretia comforted Mary Ann Day Brown, insurrectionist John Brown's wife, in the days preceding his execution for engineering the raid on Harpers Ferry. Late in Lucretia Mott's activism, she encouraged the next generation of abolitionist speakers and secret railway agents, including Anna Elizabeth Dickinson, an orator and writer for William Lloyd Garrison's *The Liberator.* At the end of the Civil War, Lucretia Mott deeded acreage to black veterans near her home in Elkins Park, Pennsylvania.

> Concerning the death of Maryland slave owner Edward Gorsuch as a result of the Christiana Riot of September 11, 1851, Judge Robert C. Grier indirectly implicated James Mott, Jr., and defense attorney Thaddeus Stevens: "The guilt of this foul murder rests not alone on the deluded individuals who were its immediate perpetrators, but the blood taints with even deeper dye the skirts of those who promulgated doctrines subversive of all morality and all government."

See also: American Anti-Slavery Society; Christiana Riot; civil disobedience; female anti-slavery societies; free labor store.

Sources

Hensel, W.U. *The Christiana Riot and the Treason Trials of 1851.* Lancaster, PA: New Era, 1911.
Holley, Sallie. *A Life for Liberty.* New York: Knickerbocker, 1899.

Mott, Peter (1810–1881)
Mott, Elizabeth Ann Thomas (1808–?)

A farmer, trader, and preacher, the Reverend Peter Mott, a runaway slave from Delaware, and his Virginia-born wife, Elizabeth Ann Thomas Mott, served the

Underground Railroad by rescuing fugitive slaves. The couple married in 1833 and purchased land from Dr. Jacob C. White, Sr., a member of the Philadelphia Vigilance Committee. In the all-black community of Snow Hill (now Lawnside), in Camden County, New Jersey, they began boarding black refugees in 1844 after the construction of a two-story clapboard residence at Gloucester and Moore avenues. A basement chamber lay below a secret room concealed by double doors for the protection of runaways. Before passengers departed for Mount Holly and Mount Laurel, the Motts provided both meals and clothes.

Remaining as an operative of the secret network through the Civil War, Peter Mott also pastored the Mount Pisgah African Methodist Episcopal Church, a depot at Moudly and Warrick roads. It was the church of agent William Still, the chairman of the Philadelphia Vigilance Committee. Under the supervision of the Lawnside Historical Society and the National Register of Historic Places, the Mott station survives as a museum and monument to black history.

See also: African Methodist Episcopal Church; vigilance committees.

Source

Yamin, Rebecca. *Archeological Investigations at the Peter Mott House, Lawnside Borough, Camden County, New Jersey.* Philadelphia: John Milner, 1995.

Mott, Samuel (1773–1864) Mott, Richard (1767–1856)

A respected slave transporter, Samuel "Uncle Sammy" Mott conspired with his brother, the Reverend Richard Mott, a Quaker minister and Underground Railroad agent, and with Richard's partner and brother-in-law, trader Robert Hicks, to convey escapees. The two men were sons of James Mott and Mary Underhill Mott, members of the secret network at Premium Point on Oyster Bay, Long Island. Both Hicks and Richard Mott supported the work of the New York City Manumission Society, which abolitionists established in 1785 to liberate blacks. Runaways traveled by sloop from Front Street in New York City to Samuel Mott's waystation in Cowneck, New York. Because Samuel made his living as a shipper and operated the sloop *Harry Maybe,* he traveled frequently from Fulton Street across Long Island Sound to Motts Point or to the safehouse of Abigail Field Mott (1766–1851) and Richard Mott in Mamaroneck, New York. Others of the Mott clan in Rochester completed rescues by passing slaves over the Canadian border. Richard and Samuel Mott were uncles of agents Abigail Mott and Lydia Mott of Albany and of James Mott, Jr., a noted Philadelphia operative and husband of orator Lucretia Coffin Mott.

See also: slave tokens.

Sources

Cornell, Thomas C. *Adam and Anne Mott: Their Ancestors and Their Descendants.* Poughkeepsie, NY: privately printed, 1890.

Vahey, Mary Feeney. *A Hidden History: Slavery, Abolition, and the Underground Railroad in Cow Neck and on Long Island.* Port Washington, NY: Cow Neck Peninsula Historical Society, 1998.

Mowry, Angelina Gifford (1817–1856) Mowry, William H. (1811–1850)

Conductors of the Underground Railroad, Angelina Gifford Mowry and William H. Mowry aided passengers traveling through Washington County, in New York's Adirondack Mountains. William Mowry served the Eastern New York Anti-Slavery Society and, with the Reverend Nathaniel Colver, formed an anti-slavery church, the Congregational Free Church. The Mowrys harbored fugitives at their safehouse on Church Street and assisted Dr. Hiram Corliss and Leonard Gibbs, conductors in Union Village. William Mowry's sudden death left a vacancy among local abolitionists that Leonard Gibbs filled.

Source

Calarco, Tom. *The Underground Railroad in the Adirondack Region.* Jefferson, NC: McFarland, 2004.

Mudge, Benjamin Franklin (1817–1879) Mudge, Mary Eusebia Armstrong Beckford (1820–1904)

Geologist and attorney Benjamin Franklin Mudge aided the Underground Railroad on the frontier. A native of Orrinton, Maine, he was reared in Lynn, Massachusetts, and studied earth science and law at Wesleyan University. In 1846, he married Mary Eusebia Armstrong Beckford. In 1861, the couple moved to Quindaro, in Wyandotte County, Kansas, where Benjamin Mudge taught at the Kansas State Agricultural College. During an influx of Missouri slaves to Kansas, the Mudges established a waystation of the secret network, which they operated with the help of their two sons, Josiah Bowler Mudge (1849–1931) and Melville Rhodes Mudge (1847–1929). In one intervention, Benjamin Mudge armed himself with a shotgun to protect a woman and her three children from recapture. The passengers continued to stops in Franklin County and Leavenworth.

Source

Mudge, Melville R., ed. "Benjamin Franklin Mudge: A Letter from Quindaro." *Kansas History* 13 (Winter 1990–1991): 218–22.

Murray, Charles L. (fl. 1850s)

The home of Charles L. Murray, an abolitionist publisher, was a stopping place for slave transports through Elkhart County, Indiana. Five miles north of Goshen, Murray hosted fugitives that route superintendent Levi Coffin piloted from Fountain City, Indiana, to Cass County, Michigan. In 1854, a Kentucky slave owner's daughter took pity on the family slaves and hurried them to free territory. The party crossed the Ohio River and passed through the safehouse of Abner Blue before reaching the Murray home. The passengers arrived safely in Michigan.

Source

Bordewich, Fergus M. *Bound for Canaan: The Underground Railroad and the War for the Soul of America.* New York: Amistad, 2005.

Murray, Samuel (fl. 1830s–1850s)
Murray, Sarah (fl. 1830s–1850s)

A freeborn shoemaker from Reading, Pennsylvania, Samuel Murray used his hotel job as a means of aiding escaping slaves. In 1837, he helped to construct Reading's Bethel African Methodist Episcopal Church, a station of the Underground Railroad at 119 North Tenth Street. Samuel and his wife, Sarah Murray, settled in Buffalo, New York, in 1852, where Samuel worked at the three-story American Hotel. He aided refugees by sneaking food from the kitchen and by accompanying fugitives to the ferry in Niagara. He reported on a local black conductor who specialized in reuniting Canadian men with their wives enslaved in southern states.

Murray recalled a spy—a black turncoat from Detroit, Michigan—who spotted black runaways and informed their owners in exchange for a fee. Members of the secret network took the traitor to the woods for a severe cowhiding. Although the victim reported his assailants to the police, the sheriff jailed the men only briefly and then dropped all charges.

See also: African Methodist Episcopal Church; spies.

Sources

"Betrayal of a Fugitive," *Buffalo (NY) Courier,* March 5, 1857.
Severance, Frank H. *Old Trails on the Niagara Frontier.* Buffalo, NY: n.p., 1899.

Murrow, Andrew Caldwell (1820–1904)

A farmer and wagoneer, Andrew Caldwell Murrow operated a safehouse at the Centre community in rural Guilford County, North Carolina. He depended on the support of Underground Railroad progenitor Levi Coffin and on Murrow's foster father, Joshua Stanley, an outspoken abolitionist. In Murrow's barn, he concealed a chamber with feed sacks stacked around the entrance. Traveling with an outrider, he conveyed runaways by false-bottomed wagon from station to station along the route to Newport, Indiana. At night, he and his passengers stayed with known conductors. In daytime, Murrow sold cornmeal and pottery from his wagon as a cover for his courier service. He encountered U.S. marshals at the Ohio River but convinced them that he was traveling west on a commercial venture. One of Murrow's rescues was a freedman whose manumission papers were stolen. The fugitive was so thrilled to reach free territory that he collected Indiana soil in a fur pouch to pass down to his children as a legacy.

Source

Beal, Gertrude. "The Underground Railroad in Guilford County." *Southern Friend: Journal of the North Carolina Friends Historical Society* (Spring 1980): 18–28.

Myers, Elizabeth Parks (1794–1870)
Myers, Josiah (?–1879)

Pioneeers Elizabeth Parks Myers and Josiah Myers settled on the frontier and opened a depot of the Underground Railroad. After departing Hampshire County, West Virginia, in 1839, they traveled by covered wagon to Wood County, near Toledo, Ohio. In addition to farming and rearing eight children, they welcomed runaways on their way to Canada. The Myers' sons—John, Lambert, Samuel, and William—served in the Union army during the Civil War.

Source

Baxter, W.H. *History of Champaign County, Ohio.* Chicago: W.H. Beers, 1881.

Myers, Harriet (?–1865)
Myers, Stephen (1800–ca. 1870s)

Harriet and Stephen Myers, activists on behalf of the Albany Vigilance Committee, aided runaways passing through New York's Hudson Valley. A native of Hoosick Four Corners, in Rensselaer County, New York, Stephen Myers was manumitted in 1818. Working as a grocer and as cook and steward on the steamers *Armenia* and *Diamond,* he directed refugees on their way from Albany and eventually superintended the Philadelphia–Canada route. In 1831, Harriet Myers began soliciting cash from female supporters and offering welcome and food at their Underground Railroad waystation in a two-story brick rowhouse at 194 Lumber Street (now Livingstone Avenue). Strategy planners met in the family's parlor and at the African Baptist Church on Hamilton Street.

In his forties, Stephen Myers masterminded the Northern Star Association, a vigilance committee. With his wife's aid as proofreader, at 46 Green Street in Albany, he published the *Northern Star & Freemen's Advocate,* coedited by Charles Morton and John N. Stewart. Assisting the Myers in their rescue work were Abigail Mott and Lydia Mott, grocer Primus Robinson, tailor William H. Topp, and, after 1851, William Henry Johnson, a runaway from Alexandria, Virginia. Stephen Myers chaired the Albany Vigilance Committee from 1853 to 1856. From late summer 1855 to July 15, 1856, members aided 287 runaways. In his autobiography *My Bondage and My Freedom* (1857), Frederick Douglass saluted Stephen Myers for his aid to refugees. When the Civil War began, Myers recruited blacks for the Union army. The only documented safehouse in Albany, the Myers residence is listed on the State Register of Historic Places.

See also: black soldiers; vigilance committees.

Source

Ripley, C. Peter, et al., eds. *The Black Abolitionist Papers.* Vol. 3. Chapel Hill: University of North Carolina Press, 1992.

Myers, Michael (fl. 1850s)

An Underground Railroad agent east of Coatesville in Chester County, Pennsylvania, Michael Myers guided refugees and offered others work. Receiving passengers from James Williamson, Myers remained an active participant in relaying slaves to Canada. When kidnappers named Cooke and Windle seized Myers's employee Thomas Hall at dawn from a tenant house, gunshots alerted Myers. Within a half hour, 30 freedmen dashed to the scene brandishing clubs, hoes, and pitchforks. Agent Isaac Preston summoned the sheriff, who arrested the attackers. Meanwhile, Hall escaped from the scene. When the case came to trial, the judge disallowed as evidence the kidnappers' claim on Hall. Another of Myers's employees attended a political meeting in New Garden and vanished, presumably at the hands of slave catchers.

See also: kidnap.

Source

Smedley, Robert C. *History of the Underground Railroad in Chester and the Neighboring Counties of Pennsylvania.* Lancaster, PA: Office of *The Journal,* 1883.

Myers, Susanna (1833–1912)
Myers, Nancy Robinson (1809–1893)
Myers, Samuel (1807–1872)

An unusual operative, 10-year-old Susanna (or Susan A.) Myers, served the Underground Railroad at Salem, Ohio, as wagoneer. Her parents, Nancy Robinson Myers and Samuel Myers, married in 1831 and volunteered to pilot slaves for the secret network. Susanna undertook dangerous night relays to the rural station of Daniel Bonsall and Martha W. Sharp Bonsall outside Salem.

Source

Shaffer, Dale. *Salem: A Quaker City History.* Charleston, SC: Arcadia, 2002.